Hungary

Steve Fallon
Neal Bedford

LONELY PLANET PUBLICATIONS
Melbourne • Oakland • London • Paris

HUNGARY

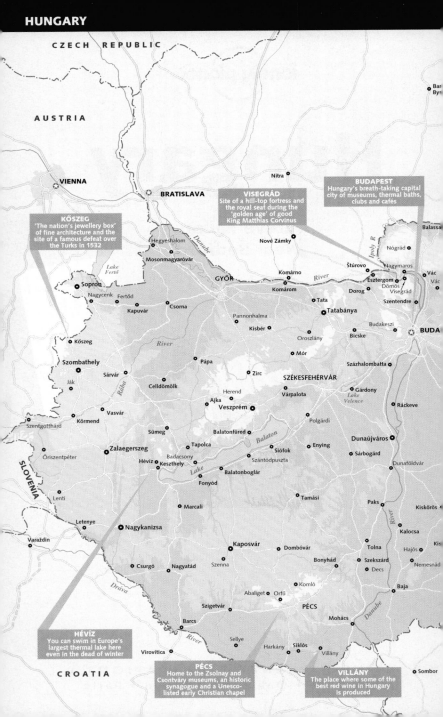

CZECH REPUBLIC

AUSTRIA

VIENNA

BRATISLAVA

Nitra

Nové Zámky

Hegyeshalom

Mosonmagyaróvár

Lake Fertő

Sopron

Nagycenk

Fertőd

Kapuvár

Csorna

GYŐR

Komárno

Komárom

River

Štúrovo

Dorog

Esztergom

Pannonhalma

Kisbér

Tata

Oroszlány

Tatabánya

Mór

Budakeszi

Bicske

Nógrád

Vác

Vác

Nagymaros

Dömös

Visegrád

Szentendre

Balassa

Ipoly R

BUDA

Köszeg

Szombathely

Ják

Sárvár

Celldömölk

Pápa

Zirc

Herend

SZÉKESFEHÉRVÁR

Várpalota

Százhalombatta

Gárdony

Lake Velence

Ráckeve

Rába River

Vasvár

Körmend

Szentgotthárd

Őriszentpéter

Sümeg

Ajka

Veszprém

Polgárdi

Tapolca

Balatonfüred

Balaton

Siófok

Enying

Dunaújváros

Sárbogárd

Dunaföldvár

Zalaegerszeg

Badacsony

Hévíz

Keszthely

Lake

Szántódpuszta

Balatonboglár

Fonyód

Lenti

Marcali

Tamási

Paks

Kiskőrös

Letenye

Nagykanizsa

Kalocsa

Varaždin

Kaposvár

Dombóvár

Tolna

Hajós

Kis

Csurgó

Nagyatád

Szenna

Bonyhád

Szekszárd

Decs

Nemesnád

Komló

Baja

SLOVENIA

Dráva

Szigetvár

Barcs

Abaliget

Orfű

PÉCS

Mohács

Danube

River

Sellye

Virovitica

Harkány

Siklós

Villány

Sombor

CROATIA

KŐSZEG
'The nation's jewellery box' of fine architecture and the site of a famous defeat over the Turks in 1532

VISEGRÁD
Site of a hill-top fortress and the royal seat during the 'golden age' of good King Matthias Corvinus

BUDAPEST
Hungary's breath-taking capital city of museums, thermal baths, clubs and cafés

HÉVÍZ
You can swim in Europe's largest thermal lake here even in the dead of winter

PÉCS
Home to the Zsolnay and Csontváry museums, an historic synagogue and a Unesco-listed early Christian chapel

VILLÁNY
The place where some of the best red wine in Hungary is produced

SLOVAKIA

UKRAINE

LILLAFÜRED
The 'green lung' of Miskolc and
where to ride the nation's
favourite forest train

TOKAJ
Where the sweet 'king of wines
and wine of kings' is made

HOLLÓKŐ
The last bastion of
traditional Palóc folk
culture in Hungary

Košice

Užgorod

Mukačevo

Aggtelek

Lučenec

Sátoraljaújhely

Encs   Boldogkőváralja
Edelény   Sárospatak

Dombrád

Kisvárda

Ózd   Kazincbarcika

Szerencs

River

Vásárosnamény

Szécsény

Somoskő
Salgótarján

Lillafüred

Tokaj

Mátészalka
Fehérgyarmat

Hollókő

Szilvásvárad

MISKOLC

Tiszavasvári

NYÍREGYHÁZA

Máriapócs

Parád

Tiszaújváros

Nyírbátor

Mátraháza

Eger

Tiszaújváros

Polgár

Hajdúnánás
Nagykálló

Gyöngyös

Mezőkövesd

Hatvan

Füzesabony

Tisza

Hajdúböszörmény

Heves

Lake
Tisza

Tiszafüred

Hortobágy

DEBRECEN

Jászberény

Jászapáti

Nagykáta

Nádudvar

Hajdúszoboszló

HORTOBÁGY
Birthplace of the Hungarian cowboy,
mirages and all the myths
and legends that go with both

Berekfürdő

Püspökladány

Karcag

Cegléd

Kisújszállás

Berettyóújfalu

Szolnok

Törökszentmiklós

GREAT   PLAIN

River

ORADEA

Mezőtúr

Szeghalom

KECSKEMÉT

Vésztő

Kunszentmárton

Szarvas

Kiskunfélegyháza

Mezőberény

Csongrád

Békés

Sarkad

NÁDUDVAR
The unique black pottery
thrown and fired here is famous
throughout Hungary

Bugac

Szentes

Békéscsaba

Gyula

Orosháza

ROMANIA

Kiskunmajsa

Kistelek   Ópusztaszer

Hódmezővásárhely

Tótkomlós

Mezőhegyes

SZEGED

Makó

Nagylak

ARAD

0   25   50km
0   15   30mi

SZEGED
An important university city
that has earned itself the nickname
'the cultural capital of the Great Plain'

Subotica

Tisza

ELEVATION

900m
600m
300m
200m
150m
0

YUGOSLAVIA

TIMIŞOARA

Hungary
4th edition – March 2003
First published – February 1994

Published by
Lonely Planet Publications Pty Ltd ABN 36 005 607 983
90 Maribyrnong St, Footscray, Victoria 3011, Australia

Lonely Planet Offices
Australia Locked Bag 1, Footscray, Victoria 3011
USA 150 Linden St, Oakland, CA 94607
UK 10a Spring Place, London NW5 3BH
France 1 rue du Dahomey, 75011 Paris

Photographs
Many of the images in this guide are available for licensing from
Lonely Planet Images.
w www.lonelyplanetimages.com

Front cover photograph
Hungarian folk dancers swing their striped skirts while performing the
Székelyföldi dance for the Tihany Wine Festival.
(APL/Corbis © Barry Lewis/CORBIS)

ISBN 174059 152 6

text & maps © Lonely Planet Publications Pty Ltd 2003
photos © photographers as indicated 2003

Printed by SNP Security Printing Pte Ltd, Singapore

Contents – Text

Contents – Maps

HUNGARY MAP INDEX

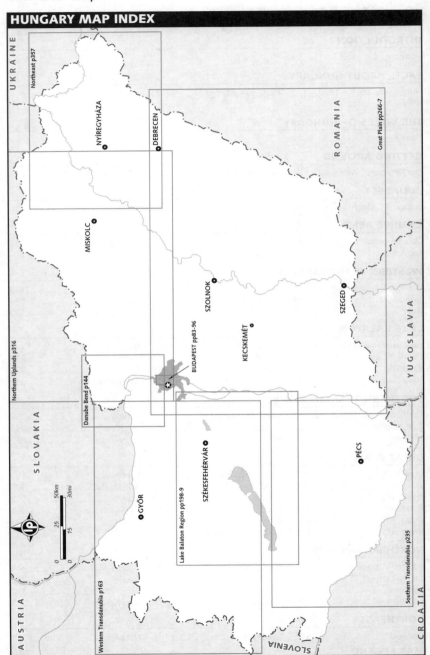

UKRAINE

SLOVAKIA

AUSTRIA

ROMANIA

YUGOSLAVIA

CROATIA

SLOVENIA

Northeast p357

Great Plain pp266-7

Northern Uplands p316

Danube Bend p144

BUDAPEST pp83-96

Western Transdanubia p163

Lake Balaton Region pp198-9

Southern Transdanubia p235

NYÍREGYHÁZA

DEBRECEN

MISKOLC

SZOLNOK

SZEGED

KECSKEMÉT

SZÉKESFEHÉRVÁR

GYŐR

PÉCS

0   25   50km
0   15   30mi

The Authors

Steve Fallon

A native of Boston, Massachusetts, Steve graduated from Georgetown University with a Bachelor of Science in modern languages and then taught English at the University of Silesia near Katowice in Poland. After working for several years for an American daily newspaper and earning a master's degree in journalism, his fascination with the 'new' Asia led him to Hong Kong. He stayed there for over a dozen years, working for a variety of media and running a travel bookshop.

Steve lived in Budapest for 2½ years before moving to London in 1994. He has written or contributed to more than two dozen Lonely Planet titles, including the Lonely Planet Journeys title *Home with Alice: A Journey in Gaelic Ireland*.

Neal Bedford

Born in Papakura, New Zealand, Neal gave up an exciting career in accounting after university to experience the mundane life of a traveller. With the urge to move, travel led him through a number of countries and jobs, ranging from an au pair in Vienna, lifeguard in the USA, fruit-picker in Israel and lettuce-washer at rock concerts. Deciding to give his life some direction, he well and truly got his foot stuck in the door by landing the lucrative job of packing books in Lonely Planet's London office. One thing led to another and he managed to cross over to the mystic world of authoring. He has worked on a number of books for Lonely Planet, including *Vienna, Texas* and *New Zealand*, his three favourite places in the world.

FROM THE AUTHORS

Steve Fallon

Special thanks to Bea Szirti and to Erzsébet Tiszai, who helped with the research of the Budapest and transport chapters. Péter Lengyel and Balázs Váradi showed me the correct wine roads to follow and Gerard Gorman where to find the birds; I am very grateful. Once again Dr Zsuzsa Medgyes of M&G Marketing in Budapest came forward with all those wonderful little details. Many thanks to *bon vivant* Dr Mihály Perec and his incomparable choice of restaurants. Tourinform remains the most authoritative and knowledgeable source of information on Hungary and things Hungarian; *köszönöm szépen* to Ágnes Padányi in Budapest and staff elsewhere in Magyarország. I am indebted to Michael Kovrig and to András Cseh for their hospitality in Budapest and Eger; Ildikó Nagy Moran was as welcoming and helpful as always in the capital. It was a pleasure working again with Neal Bedford, who cast a pair of fresh eyes on a country I sometimes feel I know too well.

Once again, this book is dedicated to Michael Rothschild, *sine quo non*, with love, gratitude and memory.

Neal Bedford

Longest and loudest thanks has to go to Steve Fallon, firstly for asking me to hop aboard the Hungary Express, secondly for putting me up in Budapest and London so often, thirdly for all his worldly advice, fourthly for the friendship and beer, and lastly for getting rid of that yellow shirt. Special thanks goes to Zsuzsa Gaspar, for the brief Hungarian lessons, the critical praise of any Hungarian wine I managed to smuggle back home, and for looking after my plants.

A heartfelt thanks to all the Tourinform staff who helped me in so many ways, and thankfully spoke English and/or German. Also a big *köszönöm szépen* to the Hungarian folk I met along the way – especially the people at the Király Pension in Sümeg who managed to turn around my disastrous start to the day with mountains of home-cooked goodies.

This Book

The previous three editions of *Hungary* were written and updated by Steve Fallon. Steve lived in Budapest for 2½ years (from where he wrote the first edition).

From the Publisher
Production of this edition was coordinated by Gina Tsarouhas and Suzannah Shwer (editorial) and Csanad Csutoros (mapping). Imogen Franks commissioned the book and it was project managed by Ray Thomson. Assisting with editing and proofing were Susannah Farfor, Liz Filleul, Lara Morecombe, Cherry Prior and Nick Tapp, and with mapping Tony Fankhauser, Louise Klep, Tessa Rottiers, Helen Rowley, Sarah Sloane, Andrew Smith, Chris Thomas and Chris Tsismetzis. Lisa Borg, Bruce Evans, Kate McDonald and Nina Rousseau helped with final layout and artwork checks and Sonya Brooke, Indra Kilfoyle and Tasmin Wilson worked on layout design.

Thanks to Quentin Frayne for the language chapter, Csanad for the colourwraps (and to Indra for assistance), Nick Stebbing for Quark support, Brendan Dempsey for the cover design, and to LPI for providing the images.

THANKS
Many thanks to the travellers who used the last edition and wrote to us with helpful hints, advice and interesting anecdotes. Your names appear in the back of this book.

Foreword

ABOUT LONELY PLANET GUIDEBOOKS

The story begins with a classic travel adventure: Tony and Maureen Wheeler's 1972 journey across Europe and Asia to Australia. There was no useful information about the overland trail then, so Tony and Maureen published the first Lonely Planet guidebook to meet a growing need.

From a kitchen table, Lonely Planet has grown to become the largest independent travel publisher in the world, with offices in Melbourne (Australia), Oakland (USA), London (UK) and Paris (France).

Today Lonely Planet guidebooks cover the globe. There is an ever-growing list of books and information in a variety of media. Some things haven't changed. The main aim is still to make it possible for adventurous travellers to get out there – to explore and better understand the world.

At Lonely Planet we believe travellers can make a positive contribution to the countries they visit – if they respect their host communities and spend their money wisely. Since 1986 a percentage of the income from each book has been donated to aid projects and human rights campaigns, and, more recently, to wildlife conservation.

Although inclusion in a guidebook usually implies a recommendation we cannot list every good place. Exclusion does not necessarily imply criticism. In fact there are a number of reasons why we might exclude a place – sometimes it is simply inappropriate to encourage an influx of travellers.

UPDATES & READER FEEDBACK

Things change – prices go up, schedules change, good places go bad and bad places go bankrupt. Nothing stays the same. So, if you find things better or worse, recently opened or long-since closed, please tell us and help make the next edition even more accurate and useful.

Lonely Planet thoroughly updates each guidebook as often as possible – usually every two years, although for some destinations the gap can be longer. Between editions, up-to-date information is available in our free, monthly email bulletin *Comet* (W www.lonelyplanet.com/newsletters). You can also check out the *Thorn Tree* bulletin board and *Postcards* section of our website, which carry unverified, but fascinating, reports from travellers.

Tell us about it! We genuinely value your feedback. A well-travelled team at Lonely Planet reads and acknowledges every email and letter we receive and ensures that every morsel of information finds its way to the relevant authors, editors and cartographers.

Everyone who writes to us will find their name listed in the next edition of the appropriate guidebook. The very best contributions will be rewarded with a free guidebook.

We may edit, reproduce and incorporate your comments in Lonely Planet products such as guidebooks, websites and digital products, so let us know if you don't want your comments reproduced or your name acknowledged.

How to contact Lonely Planet:
Online: e talk2us@lonelyplanet.com.au, W www.lonelyplanet.com
Australia: Locked Bag 1, Footscray, Victoria 3011
UK: 10a Spring Place, London NW5 3BH
USA: 150 Linden St, Oakland, CA 94607

Introduction

Hungary is *the* place to visit for those looking for the very heart and soul of Europe. The land of Franz Liszt and Béla Bartók, Gypsy music, the romantic Danube River and piquant paprika continues to entice and enchant visitors. What's more, here you will find much of the glamour and excitement of Western Europe at half the cost.

But there are a few things you need to know first. Hungary (Magyarország) is a kidney-shaped country in the centre of Europe whose impact on the continent's history has been far greater than its present size and population would suggest. Hungarians, who call themselves Magyars, speak a language and form a culture unlike any other in the region – a distinction that has been both a source of pride and an obstacle for more than 1100 years. Firmly entrenched in the Soviet Bloc until the late 1980s, Hungary is today an independent republic making its own decisions and policies.

The allure of Budapest, once an imperial city, is apparent on arrival, but other cities such as Pécs, the sunny heart of the south, Eger, the wine capital of the north, and Szeged, the buzzy university centre in the southwest, have much to offer travellers.

Certainly, these places should be visited, but don't ignore other towns and regions off the beaten track. You could include *a tanya világ*, 'the farm world' of the southern Plain; the ethnically rich Northeast; the Villány Hills in Southern Transdanubia, awash in vineyards and wine; and the traditional Őrség region of the far west of Transdanubia. This is not a case of 'authentic' versus 'touristy'; a supermarket check-out counter in a Budapest mall is as much a part of the real Hungary today as a village greengrocer's in the Zemplén Hills. But life in the provinces is more redolent of times past – simpler, slower, often more friendly – and the countryside offers endless opportunities for those with special interests – from horse riding and cycling to bird-watching and 'taking the waters' at the country's many thermal spas.

Most of the 1990s were not glory days for the reborn Republic of Hungary. Serious

economic problems affected all aspects of daily life, and the country's economy was very much in limbo. Gone were the days when job security, free medical insurance and sustainable pensions were a national assumption, and for the first time people had to work very hard for little return. A majority of Hungarians were extremely disappointed with what the change to a capitalist economy had brought them – and said so.

Thankfully, those days are over for most. Foreign investment has increased substantially, living standards have risen, many people have extra cash for a new VCR or a winter holiday in the Canary Islands and historical buildings have received long-overdue face-lifts. Many now view Hungary and its intelligent, hard-working population as the star performer of the new Europe, and the nation is on the fast track to membership of the European Union.

When the Renaissance man the Magyars call 'the greatest Hungarian' – a 19th-century reformer and patriot who did more for his nation than any other – wrote the following words, they were but a distant dream. The good count would be happy to learn that they've come a lot closer to reality.

Many people think that Hungary was;
I like to believe that she will be!

Count István Széchenyi (*Credit*, 1830)

Facts about Hungary

HISTORY
Early Inhabitants
The Carpathian Basin, in which Hungary lies, has been populated for hundreds of thousands of years. Bone fragments that were found and exhibited at Vértesszőlős, some 4.5km southeast of Tata, in Western Transdanubia in the 1960s are believed to be half a million years old. These findings suggest that Palaeolithic and later Neanderthal humans were attracted to the area by the warm-water springs and the abundance of reindeer, bears and mammoths. Stone Age pottery shards and bone-tipped arrowheads have been found at Istállóskő Cave near Szilvásvárad in the Northern Uplands.

During the Neolithic period (3500–2500 BC), changes in the climate forced much of the indigenous wildlife to migrate northward. The domestication of animals and the first forms of agriculture appeared, as indeed they did in much of Europe. Remnants of the Körös culture suggest that these goddess-worshipping people lived in the Szeged area at this time and herded sheep, fished and hunted.

Indo-European tribes from the Balkans stormed the Carpathian Basin from the south in horse-drawn carts in about 2000 BC, bringing with them copper tools and weapons. After the introduction of more durable bronze, forts were built and a military elite developed.

Over the next millennium, invaders from the west (Illyrians, Thracians) and east (Scythians) brought iron, but the metal was not in common use until the Celts arrived at the start of the 4th century BC. They introduced glass and crafted some of the fine gold jewellery that can still be seen in museums throughout Hungary.

Some three decades before the start of the Christian era the Romans conquered the area west and south of the Danube River and established the province of Pannonia – later divided into Upper (Superior) and Lower (Inferior) Pannonia. Subsequent victories over the Celts extended the Roman domination across the Tisza River as far as Dacia (now Romania). They brought writing, viticulture and stone architecture, and established garrison towns and other settlements, the remains of which can still be seen in Óbuda, which the Romans called Aquincum, Szombathely (Savaria), Pécs (Sophianae) and Sopron (Scarabantia). They also built baths near the region's thermal waters and their soldiers introduced a new cult: Christianity.

The Great Migrations
The first of the so-called Great Migrations of nomadic peoples from Asia reached the eastern outposts of the Roman Empire late in the 2nd century AD, and in 270 the Romans abandoned Dacia. Within less than two centuries they were also forced to flee Pannonia by the Huns, whose short-lived empire was established by Attila. He had previously conquered the Magyars near the lower Volga River, and for centuries the two groups were thought – erroneously – to share a common ancestry. Attila remains a very common given name for males in Hungary, however.

Such Germanic tribes as the Goths, Gepids and Longobards occupied the region for the next century and a half until the Avars, a powerful Turkic people, gained control of the Carpathian Basin in the late 6th century. They in turn were subdued by Charlemagne in 796 and converted to Christianity. By that time, the Carpathian Basin was virtually unpopulated except for groups of Turkic and Germanic tribes on the plains and Slavs in the northern hills.

The Magyars & the Conquest of the Carpathian Basin
The origin of the people called the Magyars is a complicated issue, not in the least helped by the similarity – in English at least – of the words 'Hun' and 'Hungary', which are *not* related. One thing is certain: Magyars are part of the Finno-Ugric group of peoples who inhabited the forests somewhere between the middle Volga River and the Ural Mountains in western Siberia as early as 4000 BC.

By about 2000 BC population growth had forced the Finnish-Estonian branch to move westward, ultimately reaching the Baltic Sea. The Ugrians moved from the southeastern slopes of the Urals into the valleys of the region and switched from hunting and fishing to primitive farming and raising livestock, especially horses. Their equestrian skills proved useful half a millennium later when climatic changes brought drought, forcing them to move northward onto the steppes.

Hungary's Dates with Destiny

ca. 895–6	Magyars enter and settle in the Carpathian Basin	1945	**(April)** Budapest liberated by the Soviet army
1000	Stephen (István) crowned king at Esztergom	1949	Hungary declared a People's Republic
1222	King Andrew II signs the Golden Bull	1956	**(October)** Hungary in revolution; János Kádár installed as leader
1241–2	Mongol invasion	1958	Imre Nagy executed by communist regime
1456	János Hunyadi defeats the Ottomans at Nándorfehérvár		
1458–90	Reign of Matthias Corvinus; medieval Hungary's golden age	1962	Amnesty for those involved in 1956 uprising
1514	Peasant uprising crushed; leader György Dózsa executed	1968	Plans for liberalised economy introduced and rejected
1526	Battle of Mohács	1988	**(May)** Kádár forced to retire
1541	Buda falls; Hungary divided into three parts	1989	**(February)** Communists agree to give up power monopoly
1686	Buda liberated		**(July)** Electrified fence separating Hungary and Austria demolished
1699	Turks driven from Hungarian soil		
1703–11	Ferenc Rákóczi II's War of Independence against Habsburgs		**(October)** Republic of Hungary declared
1848–9	Petőfi War of Independence	1990	**(April)** Centrist MDF becomes government in the first free elections in 43 years
1867	Act of Compromise creates Dual Monarchy		
1867–1918	Age of Dualism; Hungary's second golden age		**(August)** Árpád Göncz elected president; serves two five-year terms
1918	**(November)** Austria-Hungary loses WWI and the political system collapses	1991	**(June)** Last Soviet troops leave Hungary
1920	Treaty of Trianon reduces Hungary by two-thirds	1994	Socialists win national elections
		1998	Fidesz-MPP elected to government in national vote
1941	Hungary joins German led Axis in WWII	1999	Hungary joins NATO
		2000	Ferenc Mádl elected president
1944	Germany invades and occupies Hungary	2002	Socialists returned to power in national elections

On the grasslands, the Ugrians turned to nomadic herding. After 500 BC, by which time the use of iron had become common among the tribes, a group moved westward to the area of Bashkiria in central Asia. Here they lived among Persians and Bulgars and began referring to themselves as Magyars (from the Finno-Ugric words *mon*, 'to speak', and *er*, 'man').

After several centuries another group split away and moved south to the Don River under the control of the Turkic Khazars. Here they lived among different groups under a tribal alliance called *onogur* ('10 peoples'). This is the derivation of the word 'Hungary' in English and 'Ungarn' in German. Their last migration before the conquest of the Carpathian Basin brought them to what modern Hungarians call the Etelköz, the region between the Dnieper and lower Danube Rivers above the Black Sea.

Nomadic groups of Magyars probably reached the Carpathian Basin as early as the mid-9th century AD, acting as mercenaries for various armies. It is believed that while the men were away during one such campaign in about 889, a fierce people from the Asiatic steppe called the Pechenegs allied themselves with the Bulgars and then attacked the Etelköz settlements. When they were attacked again in about 895, seven tribes under the leadership of Árpád – the *gyula* (chief military commander) – struck out for the Carpathian Basin. They crossed the Verecke Pass in today's Ukraine some three years later.

The Magyars met almost no resistance and the tribes dispersed in three directions. The Bulgars were quickly dispatched eastward; the Germans had already taken care of the Slavs in the west; and Transylvania was wide open.

Known for their ability to ride and shoot – a common Christian prayer during the so-called Dark Ages was 'Save us, O Lord, from the arrows of the Hungarians' – and no longer content with being hired guns, the Magyars began plundering and pillaging on their own, taking slaves and amassing booty. Their raids took them as far as Spain, northern Germany and southern Italy, but in the early 10th century they began to suffer a string of defeats. In 955 they were stopped definitively by the German King Otto I at the battle of Augsburg.

This and subsequent defeats – raids on Byzantium ended in 970 – left the Magyar tribes in disarray. And, like the Bohemian, Polish and Russian princes of the time, they had to choose between their more powerful neighbours – Byzantium to the south and east or the Holy Roman Empire to the west – to form an alliance. Individual Magyar chieftains started acting independently. This began to change in 973 when Prince Géza, the great-grandson of Árpád, asked the Holy Roman emperor Otto II to send Catholic missionaries to Hungary. Géza was baptised, as was his son Vajk, who took the Christian name Stephen (István). When Géza died, Stephen ruled as prince. Three years later, on Christmas Day in the year 1000, he was crowned 'Christian King' Stephen I with a crown sent from Rome by Otto's erstwhile tutor, Pope Sylvester II. Hungary the kingdom – and the nation – was born.

King Stephen I & the Árpád Dynasty

Stephen ruthlessly set about consolidating royal authority by expropriating the land of the clan chieftains and establishing a system of counties (*megye*) protected by fortified castles (*vár*). The crown began minting coins and, shrewdly, Stephen transferred much land to loyal (mostly Germanic) knights. The king sought the support of the church throughout and, to hasten the conversion of the populace, ordered that one in every 10 villages build a church. He also established 10 episcopates, two of which – Kalocsa and Esztergom – were later made archbishoprics. Monasteries were set up around the country and staffed by foreign scholars. By the time Stephen died in 1038 (he was canonised in 1083), Hungary was a nascent Christian nation, increasingly westward-looking and multiethnic.

Despite this apparent consolidation, the next two and a half centuries until 1301 – the reign

of the House of Árpád – would test the kingdom to the limit. The period was one of relentless struggles between rival pretenders to the throne, which weakened the young nation's defences against its powerful neighbours. There was a brief hiatus under King Ladislas I (László; r. 1077–95), who fended off attacks from Byzantium, and under his successor Koloman the Bookish (Könyves Kálmán), who encouraged literature, art and the writing of chronicles until his death in 1116.

Tensions flared up again when the Byzantine emperor made a grab for Hungary's provinces in Dalmatia and Croatia, which it had acquired by the early 12th century. Béla III (r. 1172–96) successfully resisted the Emperor's invasion and had a permanent residence built at Esztergom (at the time an alternative royal seat to Székesfehérvár). Béla's son, Andrew II (András; r. 1205–35), however, weakened the crown when he gave in to local barons' demands for more land in order to fund his crusades. This led to the Golden Bull, a kind of Magna Carta signed at Székesfehérvár in 1222, which limited some of the king's powers in favour of the nobility.

When Béla IV (r. 1235–70) tried to regain the estates, the barons were able to oppose him on equal terms. Fearing Mongol expansion and realising he could not count on local help, Béla looked to the west and brought in German and Slovak settlers. He also gave asylum to Turkic Cuman (Kun) tribes displaced by the Mongols in the east. In 1241 the Mongols arrived in Hungary and charged through the country, virtually burning it to the ground and killing an estimated one-third of its two million people.

To rebuild the country as quickly as possible Béla again encouraged immigration, inviting Germans to settle in Transdanubia, Saxons in Transylvania and Cumans on the Great Plain. He also built a string of defensive hilltop castles (including the ones at Buda and Visegrád). But in a bid to appease the lesser nobility, he handed over large tracts of land to the barons. This strengthened their position and bids for more independence even further. At the time of Béla's death in the late 13th century, anarchy gripped Hungary. The rule of his reprobate son and heir Ladislas the Cuman (so-called because his mother was Cuman princess) was equally unsettled. The Árpád line died out in 1301 with the death of Andrew III, who left no heir.

Medieval Hungary

The struggle for the Hungarian throne after the death of Andrew III involved several European dynasties, but it was Charles Robert (Károly Róbert) of the French House of Anjou who, with the pope's blessing, finally won out in 1308 and ruled for the next 34 years. Charles Robert was an able administrator who managed to break the power of the provincial barons (though much of the land remained in private hands) and sought diplomatic links with his neighbours. In 1335 he met the Polish and Czech kings at the new royal palace in Visegrád to discuss territorial disputes and to forge an alliance that would smash Vienna's control of trade.

Under Charles Robert's son and successor, Louis the Great (Nagy Lajos; r. 1342–82), Hungary returned to a policy of conquest. A brilliant military strategist, Louis acquired territory in the Balkans as far as Dalmatia and Romania and as far north as Poland; he was crowned king of Poland in 1370. But his successes were short-lived and the menace of the Ottoman Turks had begun.

As Louis had sired no sons, one of his daughters Mary (r. 1382–87) succeeded him. This was deemed unacceptable by the barons, who rose up against the 'petticoat throne'. Within a short time Mary's husband, Sigismund (Zsigmond; r. 1387–1437) of Luxembourg, was crowned king. Sigismund's 50-year reign brought peace at home, and there was a great flowering of Gothic art and architecture in Hungary. But while he managed to procure the coveted crown of Bohemia and was made Holy Roman emperor in 1433, he was unable to stop the Ottoman march up through the Balkans.

A Transylvanian general born of a Wallachian (Romanian) father, János Hunyadi began his career at the court of Sigismund. When Vladislav I (Úlászló) of the Polish Jagiellon dynasty was killed fighting the Turks at Varna in 1444, Hunyadi was declared regent. His 1456 victory over the Turks at Belgrade (in Hungarian, Nándorfehérvár) checked the Ottoman advance into Hungary for 70 years and assured the coronation of his son Matthias (Mátyás), the greatest ruler of medieval Hungary.

Wisely, Matthias (r. 1458–90), nicknamed 'the Raven' (Corvinus) from his coat of arms, maintained a mercenary force of 8000 to 10,000 men through taxation of the nobility,

and this 'Black Army' conquered Moravia, Bohemia and even parts of lower Austria. Not only did Matthias Corvinus make Hungary one of central Europe's leading powers, but under his rule the nation enjoyed its first golden age. His second wife, the Neapolitan princess Beatrice, brought artisans from Italy who completely rebuilt and extended the Gothic palace at Visegrád; the beauty and sheer size of the Renaissance residence was beyond comparison in the Europe of the time. Matthias was celebrated for his fairness and justice, and Hungarian mythology and folk tales are full of stories illustrating 'Good King' Matthias' love of his subjects.

But while Matthias busied himself with centralising power for the crown, he ignored the growing Turkish threat. His successor Vladislav II (Úlászló; r. 1490–1516) was unable to maintain even royal authority, as the members of the diet (assembly), which met to approve royal decrees, squandered royal funds and expropriated land. In May 1514, what had begun as a crusade organised by the power-hungry archbishop of Esztergom, Tamás Bakócz, turned into a peasant uprising against landlords under the leadership of one György Dózsa.

The revolt was brutally repressed by noble leader John Szapolyai (Zápolyai János), some 70,000 peasants were tortured and executed, and Dózsa himself was fried alive on a red-hot iron throne. The retrograde Tripartitum Law that followed codified the rights and privileges of the barons and nobles, and reduced the peasants to perpetual serfdom. By the time Louis II (Lajos) took the throne in 1516 at the tender age of nine, he couldn't rely on either side.

The Battle of Mohács & Turkish Occupation

The defeat of Louis' ragtag army by the Ottoman I Turks at Mohács in 1526 is a watershed in Hungarian history. On the battlefield near this small town in Southern Transdanubia a relatively prosperous and independent medieval Hungary died, sending the nation into a tailspin of partition, foreign domination and despair that can be felt right up to our day.

It would not be fair to put all the blame on the weak and indecisive teenaged King Louis or on his commander-in-chief, Pál Tomori, the archbishop of Kalocsa. Bickering among the nobility and the brutal crackdown of the

peasant uprising a dozen years before had se-
verely weakened Hungary's military power
and there was virtually nothing left in the
royal coffers. By 1526 the Ottoman sultan
Suleiman the Magnificent had taken much of
the Balkans, including Belgrade, and was
poised to march on Buda and then Vienna
with a force of 100,000 men.

Unable – or, more likely, unwilling – to
wait for reinforcements from Transylvania
under the command of his rival John Szapolyai, Louis rushed south with a motley
army of 25,000 men to battle the Turks and
was soundly thrashed in less than two hours.
Along with bishops, nobles and an estimated
20,000 soldiers, the king himself was killed –
crushed by his horse while trying to retreat
across a stream. John Szapolyai, who had sat
out the battle in Tokaj, was crowned king six
weeks later but, despite grovelling before the
Turks, he was never able to exploit the power
he had sought so madly. In many ways, greed,
self-interest and ambition had led Hungary to
defeat itself.

After Buda Castle fell to the Turks in 1541,
Hungary was torn into three parts. The central section, including Buda, went to the
Turks, while parts of Transdanubia and what
is now Slovakia were governed by the Austrian House of Habsburg and assisted by the
Hungarian nobility based at Bratislava (in
Hungarian, Pozsony). The principality of
Transylvania, east of the Tisza River, prospered as a vassal state of the Ottoman Empire, initially under Szapolyai's son John
Sigismund (Zsigmond János). Though heroic
resistance continued against the Turks, most
notably at Kőszeg (1532), Eger (1552) and
Szigetvár (1566), this division would remain
in place for more than a century and a half.

The Turkish occupation was marked by
constant fighting among the three divisions;
Catholic 'Royal Hungary' was pitted against
not only the Turks but the Protestant Transylvanian princes as well. Gábor Bethlen, who
ruled Transylvania from 1613 to 1629, tried to
end the incessant warfare by conquering
Royal Hungary with a mercenary army of
Heyduck peasants and some Turkish assistance in 1620. But the Habsburgs and the
Hungarians themselves viewed the Ottomans
as the greatest threat to Europe since the Mongols and blocked the advance.

As Ottoman power began to wane in the
17th century, Hungarian resistance to the

Habsburgs, who had used Royal Hungary as a
buffer zone between Vienna and the Turks, increased. A plot inspired by the palatine Ferenc
Wesselényi was foiled in 1670, and a revolt by
Imre Thököly (1682) and his army of *kuruc*
(anti-Habsburg mercenaries) was put down.
But with the help of the Polish army, Austrian
and Hungarian forces liberated Buda in 1686.
An imperial army under Eugene of Savoy
wiped out the last Turkish army in Hungary at
the Battle of Zenta (now Senta in Yugoslavia)
11 years later. Peace was signed with the
Turks in 1699.

Habsburg Rule

The expulsion of the Turks did not result in a
free and independent Hungary, and the policies
of the Catholic Habsburgs' Counter-Reformation and heavy taxation further alienated the
nobility. In 1703 the Transylvanian prince Ferenc Rákóczi II assembled an army of *kuruc*
forces against the Austrians at Tiszahát in
northeast Hungary. The war dragged on for
eight years, and in 1706 the rebels 'dethroned'
the Habsburgs as the rulers of Hungary. Superior imperial forces and lack of funds, however,
forced the *kuruc* to negotiate a separate peace
with Vienna behind Rákóczi's back. The
1703–11 War of Independence had failed, but
Rákóczi was the first leader to unite Hungarians against the Habsburgs.

Though the armistice had brought the fighting to an end, Hungary was now a mere
province of the Habsburg Empire. Five years
after Maria Theresa ascended the throne in
1740, the Hungarian nobility pledged their
'lives and blood' to her at the diet in
Bratislava in exchange for tax exemptions on
their land. Thus began the period of 'enlightened absolutism' that would continue under
the rule of Maria Theresa's son Joseph II
(r. 1780–90), who was called the 'hatted king'
as Joseph was never actually crowned in the
country of Hungary.

Under both Maria Theresa and Joseph, the
Hungary took great steps forward economically and culturally. The depopulated areas in
the east and south were settled by Romanians
and Serbs, while German Swabians were sent
to Transdanubia. Joseph's attempts to mod-
ernise society by dissolving the all-powerful
(and corrupt) religious orders, by abolishing
serfdom and replacing 'neutral' Latin with
German as the official language of state administration (1781–85) were opposed by the

Kings, Saints, Strong Men & Premiers

The following is a list of the most important monarchs, rulers, dictators and leaders in Hungarian history. Names are given in English, with the Magyar equivalents in brackets. The dates refer to their reign or term of office.

Árpád Dynasty
Árpád 886–907
Géza 972–97
Stephen I (István) 1000–38
Ladislas I (László) 1077–95
Koloman the Bookish (Könyves Kálmán) 1095–1116
Béla III 1172–96
Andrew II (András) 1205–35
Béla IV 1235–70
Ladislas the Cuman (Kun László) 1272–1290
Andrew III (András) 1290–1301

Mixed Dynasties
Charles Robert (Károly Róbert) 1308–42
Louis I the Great (Nagy Lajos) 1342–82
Mary (Mária) 1382–87
Sigismund (Zsigmond) 1387–1437
János Hunyadi (regent) 1446–56
Matthias (Mátyás) Corvinus 1458–90
Vladislav II (Úlászló) 1490–1516
Louis II (Lajos) 1516–26
John Szapolyai (Zápolyai János) 1526–40

Habsburg Dynasty
Ferdinand I (Ferdinánd) 1526–64
Maximilian I (Miksa) 1564–76
Leopold I (Lipót) 1657–1705
Maria Theresa (Mária Terézia) 1740–80
Joseph II (József) 1780–90
Ferdinand V (Ferdinánd) 1835–48
Franz Joseph (Ferenc József) 1848–1916
  (of Hungary from 1867)
Charles IV (Károly) 1916–18

Political Leaders
Mihály Károlyi Jan–March 1919
Béla Kun March–Aug 1919
Miklós Horthy (regent) 1920–44
Ferenc Szálasi 1944–45
Mátyás Rákosi 1947–56
János Kádár 1956–88
Károly Grósz 1988–90
József Antall 1990–93
Péter Baross 1993–94
Gyula Horn 1994–98
Viktor Orbán 1998–2002
Péter Medgyessy 2002–

Hungarian nobility, and the king rescinded most of these orders on his deathbed.

Dissenting voices could still be heard, and the ideals of the French Revolution of 1789 began to take root in certain intellectual circles in Hungary. In 1795 Ignác Martonovics, a former Franciscan priest, and six other pro-republican Jacobites were beheaded at Vérmező (Blood Meadow) in Buda for plotting against the crown.

Liberalism and social reform found their greatest supporters among certain members of the aristocracy. Count György Festetics (1755–1819), for example, founded Europe's first agricultural college at Keszthely. Count István Széchenyi (1791–1860), a true Renaissance man and called 'the greatest Hungarian' by his contemporaries, advocated the abolition of serfdom and returned much of his own land to the peasantry. He also oversaw the regulation of the Tisza and Danube Rivers for commerce and irrigation, and cleverly promoted horse racing among the upper classes in order to improve breeding stock for use in agriculture.

The proponents of gradual reform were quickly superseded by a more radical faction demanding more immediate action. The group included Miklós Wesselényi, Ferenc Deák and Ferenc Kölcsey, but the predominant figure was Lajos Kossuth (1802–94). It was this dynamic lawyer and journalist who would lead Hungary to its greatest confrontation with the Habsburgs.

The 1848–49 War of Independence
Early in the 19th century the Habsburg Empire began to weaken as Hungarian nationalism increased. The Hungarians, suspicious of Napoleon's policies, ignored French appeals to revolt against Vienna, and certain reforms were introduced: the replacement of Latin, the official language of administration, with Magyar; a law allowing serfs alternative means of discharging their feudal obligations of service; and increased Hungarian representation in the Council of State.

The reforms carried out were too limited and far too late, however, and the diet became more defiant in its dealings with the crown. At the same time, the wave of revolution sweeping Europe spurred on the more radical faction. In 1848 the liberal count Lajos Batthyány was made prime minister of the new Hungarian

St Stephen's Crown, Parliament, Budapest

MARTIN MOOS

Bags of fiery paprika and souvenir spoons

JONATHAN SMITH

Outdoor chess at the Széchenyi baths, Budapest

MARTIN MOOS

Hungarian newspaper selection

JONATHAN SMITH

Groovy club atmosphere, Budapest

MARTIN MOOS

GUY MOBERLY

Souvenir bottles of Tokaj for sale, Budapest

JONATHAN SMITH

Guard of Honour in front of Parliament, Budapest

ministry, which counted Deák, Kossuth and Széchenyi as members. The Habsburgs also reluctantly agreed to abolish serfdom and proclaim equality under the law. On 15 March a group calling itself the Youth of March, led by the poet Sándor Petőfi, took to the streets to press for even more radical reforms and revolution. Habsburg patience was wearing thin.

In September of that year the Habsburg forces under the governor of Croatia, Josip Jelačić, launched an attack on Hungary and Batthyány's government was dissolved. The Hungarians hastily formed a national defence commission and moved the government seat to Debrecen, where Kossuth was elected governor-president. In April 1849 the parliament declared Hungary's full independence and the dethronement of the Habsburgs for the second time.

The new Habsburg emperor, Franz Joseph (r. 1848–1916), was nothing like his feeble-minded predecessor Ferdinand V (r. 1835–48) and quickly took action. He sought the assistance of Russian Tsar Nicholas I, who obliged with 200,000 troops. Support for the revolution was already crumbling, however, particularly in areas of mixed population where the

Magyars were seen as oppressors. Weak and vastly outnumbered, the rebel troops were defeated by August 1849.

A series of brutal reprisals ensued. In October Batthyány and 13 of his generals were executed (the so-called Martyrs of Arad) October, and Kossuth went into exile in Turkey. (Petőfi had been killed in battle in July.) Habsburg troops then went around the country systematically blowing up castles and fortifications lest they be used by resurgent rebels. What little of medieval Hungary that was left after the Turks and the 1703–11 War of Independence was now reduced to rubble.

The Dual Monarchy

Hungary was again merged into the Habsburg Empire as a conquered province and 'neo-absolutism' was the order of the day. Passive resistance among Hungarians and disastrous military defeats for the Habsburgs in 1859 and 1865, however, pushed Franz Joseph to the negotiating table with liberal Hungarians under Deák's leadership.

The result was the Compromise of 1867 (*Ausgleich* in German, which translates as 'balance' or 'reconciliation'), which created

the Dual Monarchy of Austria (the empire) and Hungary (the kingdom). It was a federated state of two parliaments and two capitals: Vienna and – when Buda, Pest and Óbuda were merged six years later – Budapest (Pest was the other capital until 1872). Only defence, foreign relations and customs were shared. Hungary was even allowed to raise a small army.

This 'Age of Dualism' would carry on until 1918 and would spark an economic, cultural and intellectual rebirth in Hungary. Agriculture developed, factories were established, and the composers Franz (Ferenc) Liszt and Ferenc Erkel made beautiful music. The middle class, dominated by Germans and Jews in Pest, burgeoned, and the capital entered into a frenzy of building. Much of what you see in Budapest today – from the grand boulevards and their Eclectic-style apartment blocks to the Parliament building and Matthias Church in the Castle district – was built at this time. The apex of this golden age was the six-month exhibition in 1896 celebrating the millennium of the Magyar conquest *(honfoglalás)* of the Carpathian Basin.

But all was not well in the kingdom. The city-based working class had almost no rights, and the situation in the countryside remained as dire as it had been in the Middle Ages. Minorities under Hungarian control – Czechs, Slovaks, Croatians and Romanians – were under increased pressure to 'Magyarise' and viewed their new rulers as oppressors. Increasingly they worked to dismember the empire.

WWI, the Republic of Councils & Trianon

On 28 July 1914, a month to the day after the assassination of Archduke Franz Ferdinand, the heir to the Habsburg throne, by a Bosnian Serb in Sarajevo, the Dual Monarchy declared war on Serbia and entered WWI allied with the German Empire. The result was disastrous, with heavy destruction and hundreds of thousands killed on the Russian and Italian fronts. At the armistice in 1918 the fate of the Dual Monarchy (and Hungary as a multinational kingdom) was sealed.

A republic under the leadership of Count Mihály Károlyi was declared five days after the armistice was signed, but the fledgling republic would not last long. Widespread destitution, the occupation of Hungary by the Allies and the success of the Bolshevik Revolution in Russia had radicalised much of the Budapest working class. In March 1919 a group of Hungarian communists under Béla Kun seized power. The so-called Republic of Councils *(Tanácsköztársaság)* set out to nationalise industry and private property and build a fairer society, but mass opposition to the regime led to a reign of 'red terror'. Kun and his comrades were overthrown in just five months by Romanian troops, who occupied the capital.

In June 1920 the Allies drew up a postwar settlement under the Treaty of Trianon that enlarged some countries, truncated others and created several 'successor states'. As one of the defeated enemy nations with large numbers of minorities demanding independence within its borders, Hungary stood to lose more than most, and it did. The nation was reduced to one-third its historical size and, while it was now largely a uniform, homogeneous nation-state, for millions of ethnic Hungarians in Romania, Yugoslavia and Czechoslovakia, the tables had turned: they were now in the minority.

'Trianon' became the singularly most hated word in Hungary, and the *diktátum* is often reviled today as if it were imposed on the nation just yesterday. Many of the problems it created remain, and it has coloured Hungary's relations with its neighbours for more than four score years.

The Horthy Years & WWII

In Hungary's first-ever election by secret ballot (March 1920), parliament chose a kingdom as the form of state and – lacking a king – elected as its regent Admiral Miklós Horthy, who would remain in the position until the latter days of WWII. The arrangement confused even US President Franklin D Roosevelt in the early days of the war. After being briefed by an aide on the government and leadership of Hungary, he reportedly said: 'Let me see if I understand you right: Hungary is a kingdom without a king run by a regent who's an admiral without a navy?'

Horthy embarked on a 'white terror' – every bit as brutal as the red one of Béla Kun – that attacked communists and Jews for their roles in supporting the Republic of Councils. As the regime was consolidated it showed itself to be extremely rightist and conservative, advocating the status quo and 'traditional values' – family, state, religion. Though the country had the remnants of a parliamentary system, Horthy was all-powerful, and very few reforms were enacted. On the contrary, the lot of the working class and the peasantry worsened.

One thing on which everyone agreed was that the return of the 'lost' territories was essential for Hungary's development. Early on Prime Minister István Bethlen was able to secure the return of Pécs, illegally occupied by Yugoslavia, and the citizens of Sopron voted in a plebiscite to return to Hungary from Austria, but that was not enough. Hungary obviously could not count on the victors – France, Britain and the USA – to help recoup its land; instead, it sought help from the fascist governments of Germany and Italy.

Hungary's move to the right intensified throughout the 1930s, though it remained silent when WWII broke out in September 1939. Horthy hoped an alliance would not actually mean having to enter the war, but after recovering northern Transylvania and part of Croatia with Germany's assistance, he was forced to join the German and Italian led Axis in June 1941. The war was as disastrous for Hungary as WWI had been and hundreds of thousands of Hungarian troops died while retreating from Stalingrad, where they'd been used as cannon fodder. Realising too late that his country was again on the losing side, Horthy began negotiating a separate peace with the Allies.

The result was the total occupation of Hungary by the German army in March 1944. Under pressure, Horthy installed Ferenc Szálasi, the deranged leader of the pro-Nazi Arrow Cross Party, as prime minister in October and the regent was deported to Germany. (Horthy would later find exile in Portugal, where he died in 1957. Despite some public outcry, his body was returned to Hungary in September 1993 and reburied in the family plot at Kenderes, east of Szolnok.)

The Arrow Cross moved quickly to quash any opposition, and thousands of liberal politicians and labour leaders were arrested. At the same time, its puppet government introduced anti-Jewish legislation similar to that in Germany, and Jews, relatively safe under Horthy, were rounded up into ghettos by Hungarian Nazis. In the summer of 1944, less than a year before the war's end, some 400,000 Jewish men, women and children were deported to Auschwitz and other labour camps, where they starved to death, succumbed to disease or were brutally murdered.

Hungary now became an international battleground for the first time since the Turkish occupation, and bombs began falling on Budapest. The resistance movement drew support from many sides, including the communists. Fierce fighting continued in the countryside, especially near Debrecen and Székesfehérvár, but by Christmas 1944 the Soviet army had encircled Budapest. When the Germans and Hungarian Nazis rejected a settlement, the siege of the capital began. By the time the German war machine had surrendered in April 1945, many of Budapest's homes, historical buildings and churches had been destroyed. The vindictive Germans even blew up every bridge spanning the Danube in the capital while retreating.

The People's Republic of Hungary

When free parliamentary elections were held in November 1945, the Independent Smallholders' Party received 57% (245 seats) of the vote. In response, Soviet political officers, backed by the occupying Soviet army, forced three other parties – the Communists, Social Democrats and National Peasants – into a coalition. Limited democracy prevailed, and land-reform laws, sponsored by the communist minister of agriculture, Imre Nagy were enacted, wiping away the prewar feudal structure.

Within a couple of years, the Communists were ready to take complete control. After a rigged election held under a complicated new electoral law in 1947, they declared their candidate, Mátyás Rákosi, victorious. The following year the Social Democrats merged with the Communists to form the Hungarian Workers' Party.

Rákosi, a big fan of Stalin, began a process of nationalisation and unfeasibly fast industrialisation at the expense of agriculture. Peasants were forced into collective farms, and all produce had to be delivered to state warehouses. A network of spies and informers exposed 'class enemies' (such as Cardinal József Mindszenty) to the secret police (the ÁVO or, after 1949, the ÁVH). The accused were then jailed for spying, sent into internal exile or condemned to labour camps, like the notorious one at Recsk in the Mátra Hills. It is estimated that during this period a quarter of the adult population faced police or judicial proceedings.

Bitter feuding within the party began, and purges and Stalinesque show trials became the norm. László Rajk, the Communist minister of the interior (which also controlled the ÁVH) was arrested and later executed for 'Titoism'; his successor János Kádár was tortured and jailed. In August 1949, the nation was proclaimed the 'People's Republic of Hungary'.

After the death of Stalin in March 1953 and Krushchev's denunciation of him three years later, Rákosi's tenure was up and the terror began to abate. Under pressure from within the party, Rákosi's successor, Ernő Gerő, rehabilitated Rajk posthumously and readmitted Nagy, who had been expelled from the party a year earlier for suggesting reforms. But Gerő was ultimately as much a hardliner as Rákosi had been, and by October 1956 during Rajk's reburial, murmured calls for a real reform of the system – 'Socialism with a human face' – could already be heard.

The 1956 Uprising

The nation's greatest tragedy – an event that shook the world, rocked communism and pitted Hungarian against Hungarian – began on 23 October when some 50,000 university students assembled at Bem tér in Buda, shouting anti-Soviet slogans and demanding that Nagy be named prime minister. That night a crowd pulled down the colossal statue of Stalin near Heroes' Square and shots were fired by ÁVH agents on another group gathering outside the headquarters of Hungarian Radio in Pest. In a flash, Hungary is in revolution.

The next day Nagy, the reform-minded minister of agriculture, formed a government while János Kádár was named president of the Hungarian Workers' Party Central Committee. For a short time it appeared that Nagy might be successful in transforming Hungary into a neutral, multiparty state. On 28 October the government offered an amnesty to all those involved in the violence and promised to abolish the ÁVH. On 31 October hundreds of political prisoners were released and widespread reprisals began against ÁVH agents. The next day Nagy announced that Hungary would leave the Warsaw Pact and become a neutral state.

At this, Soviet tanks and troops crossed into Hungary and within 72 hours began attacking Budapest and other centres. Kádár, who had slipped away from Budapest to join the Russian invaders, was installed as leader.

Fierce street fighting continued for several days – encouraged by Radio Free Europe broadcasts and disingenuous promises of support from the West, which was embroiled in the Suez Canal crisis at the time. When the fighting was over, 25,000 people were dead. Then the reprisals – the worst in Hungarian history and lasting several years – began. An estimated 20,000 people were arrested and 2000 – including Nagy and his associates – were executed. Another 250,000 refugees fled to Austria. The government lost what little credibility it had enjoyed and the nation some of its most competent and talented citizens. As for the physical scars, look closely at many of the older buildings in Pest: the bullet holes and shrapnel damage on the exterior walls still cry out in silent fury.

Hungary under Kádár

The transformation of János Kádár from traitor and most hated man in the land to respected reformer is one of the most astonishing *tours de force* of the 20th century. No doubt it will keep generations of historians busy well into the future.

After the revolt, the ruling party was reorganised as the Hungarian Socialist Workers' Party, and Kádár, now both party president and premier, launched a programme to liberalise the social and economic structure, basing his reforms on compromise. (His most quoted line was 'Whoever is not against us is with us' – a reversal of the Stalinist adage that 'Those not with us are against us'.) In 1968, he and the economist Rezső Nyers unveiled the New Economic Mechanism (NEM) to introduce elements of a market to the planned economy. But even this proved too daring for many party conservatives. Nyers was ousted and the NEM was whittled away.

Kádár managed to survive that power struggle and went on to introduce greater consumerism and market socialism. By the mid-1970s Hungary was light years ahead of any other Soviet bloc country in its standard of living, freedom of movement and opportunities to criticise the government. People may have had to wait seven years for a Lada car or 12 years for a telephone, but most Hungarians could at least enjoy access to a second house in the countryside through work or other affiliation and a decent material life. The 'Hungarian model' attracted much Western attention – and investment.

But things began to sour in the 1980s. The Kádár system of 'goulash socialism', which had seemed 'timeless and everlasting' (as one Hungarian writer has put it) was incapable of dealing with such 'unsocialist' problems as unemployment, soaring inflation and the largest per-capita foreign debt in Eastern and central Europe. Kádár and the 'old guard' refused to hear talk about party reforms. In June 1987 Károly Grósz took over as premier and in May 1988 Kádár was booted out of the party and forced to retire.

Renewal & Change

A group of reformers – among them Nyers, Imre Pozsgay, Miklós Németh and Gyula Horn – took charge. Party conservatives at first put a lid on real change by demanding a retreat from political liberalisation in exchange for their support of the new regime's economic policies. But the tide had already turned.

Throughout the summer and autumn of 1988 new political parties were formed and old ones revived. In January 1989 Pozsgay, seeing the handwriting on the wall as Mikhail Gorbachev kissed babies and launched his reforms in the Soviet Union, announced that the events of 1956 had been a 'popular insurrection' and not the 'counter-revolution' that the regime had always said it was. Four months later some 250,000 people attended the reburial of Imre Nagy, and other victims of 1956, in Budapest.

In July 1989, again at Pozsgay's instigation, Hungary began to demolish the electrified wire fence separating it from Austria. The move released a wave of East Germans holidaying in Hungary into the West and the opening (in the fence) attracted thousands more. The collapse of the communist regimes around the region had become unstoppable. What Hungarians now call *az átkos 40 év* ('the accursed 40 years') had come to a withering, almost feeble, end.

The Republic of Hungary Again

At their party congress in February 1989 the communists had agreed to give up their monopoly on power, paving the way for free elections in March/April 1990. On 23 October 1989, the 33rd anniversary of the 1956 Uprising, the nation once again became the Republic of Hungary. The party's name was changed from the Hungarian Socialist Workers' Party to the Hungarian Socialist Party (MSZP).

The MSZP's new programme advocated social democracy and a free-market economy,

but this was not enough to shake off the stigma of its four decades of autocratic rule. The 1990 vote was won by the centrist Hungarian Democratic Forum (MDF), which advocated a gradual transition to capitalism. The social-democratic Alliance of Free Democrats (SZDSZ), which had called for much faster change, came second and the Socialists trailed far behind. As Gorbachev looked on, Hungary changed political systems with scarcely a murmur and the last Soviet troops left Hungary in June 1991.

In coalition with two smaller parties – the Independent Smallholders (FKgP) and the Christian Democrats (KDNP) – the MDF provided Hungary with sound government during its painful transition to a full market economy. Those years saw Hungary's northern (Czechoslovakia) and southern (Yugoslavia) neighbours split along ethnic lines. Prime Minister József Antall did little to improve relations with Slovakia, Romania or Yugoslavia by claiming to be the 'emotional and spiritual' prime minister of the large Hungarian minorities in those countries. In mid-1993 the MDF was forced to expel István Csurka, a party vice president, after he made ultra-nationalistic and anti-Semitic statements that tarnished Hungary's image as a bastion of moderation and stability in a volatile region. Antall died after a long fight with cancer in December 1993 and was replaced by Interior Minister Péter Boross.

Despite initial successes in curbing inflation and lowering interest rates, a host of economic problems slowed the pace of development, and the government's laissez-faire policies did not help. Like most people in the region, Hungarians had unrealistically expected a much faster improvement in their living standards. Most of them – 76% according to a poll in mid-1993 – were 'very disappointed'.

In the May 1994 elections the Socialist Party, led by Gyula Horn, won an absolute majority in parliament. This in no way implied a return to the past, and Horn was quick to point out that it was in fact his party that had initiated the whole reform process in the first place. (As foreign minister in 1989 he had played a key role in opening the border with Austria.) Árpád Göncz of the SZDSZ was elected for a second five-year term as president of Hungary in 1995.

The Road to Europe

After its dire showing in the 1994 elections, the Federation of Young Democrats (Fidesz)

– which until 1993 limited membership to those aged under 35 in order to emphasise a past untainted by communism, privilege and corruption – moved to the right and added 'MPP' (Hungarian Civic Party) to its name to attract the support of the burgeoning middle class. In the elections of 1998, during which it campaigned for closer integration with Europe, Fidesz-MPP won government by forming a coalition with the MDF and the agrarian conservative Independent Smallholders' Party (FKgP). The party's youthful leader, Viktor Orbán, was named prime minister.

Despite the astonishing economic growth and other gains made by the coalition government, the electorate grew increasingly hostile to Fidesz-MPP's – and Orbán's – strongly nationalistic rhetoric and perceived arrogance. In April 2002 the largest turnout of voters in Hungarian history unseated the government and returned the MSZP, allied with the Alliance of Free Democrats (SZDSZ), to power under Prime Minister Péter Medgyessy, a free-market advocate who had served as finance minister in the Horn government.

Hungary became a fully fledged member of NATO in 1999 and hopes to join the European Union (EU) by 2004. In June 2000 parliament elected Ferenc Mádl as president of the republic to succeed Göncz.

GEOGRAPHY

Hungary occupies the Carpathian Basin in the very centre of Eastern Europe. It covers just over 93,000 sq km – about the size of Portugal – and shares borders with seven countries: Austria, Slovakia, Ukraine, Romania, Yugoslavia, Croatia and Slovenia.

There are three basic topographies: the low-lying regions of the Great Plain (Nagyalföld) in the east, centre and southeast, and of the Little Plain (Kisalföld) in the northwest, which together account for two-thirds of Hungary's territory; the northern mountain ranges; and the hilly regions of Transdanubia in the west and southwest. The longest rivers are the Tisza (597km in Hungary) and the Danube (417km), which divide the country into three parts. Next longest are the Rába (192km) in the west and the Dráva (143km), which forms the southwestern border with Croatia. The country has well over 1000 lakes, of which the largest by far is Lake Balaton at 596 sq km followed by Lake Tisza) at 127 sq km, and is riddled with thermal springs.

Main Regions

Hungary's topographical divisions do not accurately reflect the country's cultural and subtler geographical differences, nor do the 19 administrative *megye* (counties) help travellers much. Instead, Hungary can be divided into eight main regions: Budapest and its environs; the Danube Bend; Western Transdanubia; the Lake Balaton region; Southern Transdanubia; the Great Plain; the Northern Uplands; and the Northeast.

Greater Budapest, by far Hungary's largest city, with just under two million people, has for its borders Csepel Island in the Danube River to the south, the start of the Great Plain to the east, the Buda Hills to the west and the Danube Bend in the north. The Danube bisects the city, with flat Pest on the east side (or the left bank as you follow the flow of the river) and hilly Buda to the west.

The Danube Bend is the point at which the river, flowing eastward across Europe, is forced southward by two small ranges of hills. It is an area of great beauty and historical significance; its main city is Esztergom.

Transdanubia – the area 'across the Danube' to the west has great variety. Western Transdanubia is both hilly and flat (the Little Plain is to the north), and its chief centres are Győr, Sopron and Szombathely. Central Transdanubia is dominated by Balaton, the largest lake in Europe outside Scandinavia; Székesfehérvár is the largest city in the region. Southern Transdanubia, with Pécs as its 'capital', is less hilly but richer in minerals. Wine is produced throughout Transdanubia.

The Great Plain, often referred to as the *puszta*, is a prairie scarcely 200m above sea level that stretches for hundreds of kilometres east of the Danube. The central part, the most industrialised area of the Plain, has Szolnok as its major town. The Eastern Plain is largely saline grassland and given over to the breeding of livestock; Debrecen is the main seat. The Southern Plain is agriculturally rich, with cereal crops and fruit in abundance and the occasional farmstead breaking the scenic monotony. Kecskemét and Szeged are market towns that have grown into cities on the Southern Plain.

The Northern Uplands is Hungary's 'mountainous' region and has a number of peaks averaging between 400m and 800m, the highest of which is Kékes in the Mátra Hills (1014m). Abutting the forested hills and

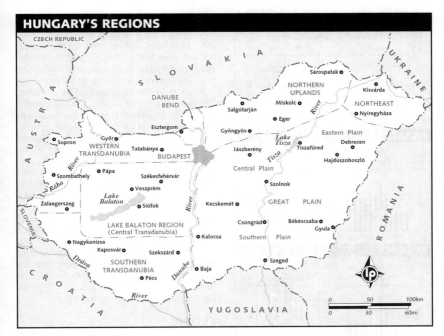

HUNGARY'S REGIONS

valleys of the Northern Uplands are lush vineyards and sprawling factories, many now in decline. Miskolc and Eger are the region's main cities.

Northeast Hungary is much lower than the Northern Uplands but not quite as flat as the Great Plain. It is a fruit-growing region and ethnically quite heterogeneous, with the bulk of the nation's Roma population living here. Nyíregyháza is the main centre.

CLIMATE

Hungary has a temperate climate with three climatic zones: Mediterranean in the south, Continental in the east and Atlantic in the west.

In general winters are cold, cloudy and damp or windy, and summers are warm – sometimes very hot. March, April and November are the wettest months. The number of hours of sunshine averages 2209 a year – among the highest in Europe. From late April to the end of September, you can expect the sun to shine for about 10 hours a day. August is the hottest month (average temperature 21°C) and January the coldest (-2°C).

In Southern Transdanubia, spring arrives early and its famous Indian summers can stretch into early November. Winters are mild and wet.

The Great Plain has the most extreme seasonal differences, with very cold, windy winters and hot, usually dry, summers (though sudden storms are a common occurrence on the Plain at this time). The climate of the Northern Uplands is also Continental, but it gets more sun in autumn and winter than any other part of Hungary.

Spring arrives in early April in Budapest and Western Transdanubia and usually ends in showers. Summers can be very hot and humid (especially in the capital). It rains most of November and doesn't usually get cold until mid-December, with an average temperature of 3°C. Winters are relatively short, often cloudy and damp but sometimes brilliantly sunny. What little snow this area gets tends to disappear after a few days.

The climate charts overleaf show you what to expect and when to expect it. For more detailed information on specific weather conditions nationwide, you can telephone the national weather forecast service on ☎ 06-90 304 621 or ☎ 06-90 304 611, or visit the website Ⓦ www.met.hu.

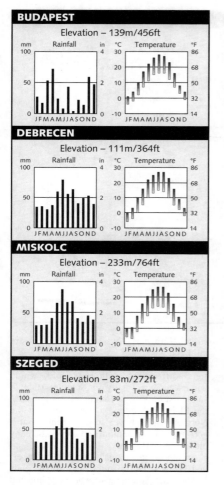

ECOLOGY & ENVIRONMENT

Pollution is a large and costly problem. Low-grade coal that fuels some industry and heats some homes creates sulphur dioxide and acid rain. Nitrogen oxide emitted by cars on highways and in city centres causes severe air pollution. Over-use of nitrate fertilisers in agriculture has caused groundwater beneath the plains to become contaminated with phosphates, which even threatened to affect Lake Balaton.

There has, however, been a marked improvement in air and water quality in recent years as Hungary attempts to conform to EU environmental standards. Between 1990 and 1997, for example, sulphur dioxide emissions fell by one-third and are expected to decrease further; from 2004, when EU energy regulations come into force, Hungary will be down to two coal-fired power stations. At the same time nitrogen oxide levels decreased by one-fifth. The Soviet-designed nuclear power generator at Paks in Southern Transdanubia produces about one-third of the nation's electricity.

The most serious environmental disaster in recent years occurred in January 2000, when cyanide from a gold mine being exploited in Baia Mare in Romania emptied into the Tisza River. It poisoned the water, killing fish, other animals and plant life for hundreds of kilometres downstream. Environmentalists suspect that the heavy metal contamination will affect the food chain for years, and the regeneration of the flora and fauna of the Tisza could take decades. The Szentendre-based Regional Environmental Center for central and Eastern Europe is now developing a common ecosystem strategy for the five nations who share the Tisza.

FLORA

Hungary is home to more than 2000 flowering plant species, many of which are not normally found at this latitude. Much of the flora in the Villány Hills of Southern Transdanubia, for example, is usually seen only around the Mediterranean, and the salty Hortobágy region on the Eastern Plain hosts many plants normally found by the seashore. The Gemenc Forest on the Danube near Szekszárd, the Little Balaton in the centre of Transdanubia and the Tisza River backwater east of Kecskemét, are all important wetlands. Most of the trees in the nation's forested areas are beech, oak and birch; only a small percentage are fir.

FAUNA

There are a lot of common European animals in Hungary (for example, deer, wild hare, boar, otter, wolves) as well as some rare species (wild cat, lake bat, Pannonian lizard). But three-quarters of the country's 450 vertebrates are birds, especially waterfowl, which are attracted by the rivers, lakes and wetlands. Parts of the Great Plain and the Northern Uplands are important nesting or migratory areas for hundreds of bird species; for details see 'The Birds of Hungary' boxed text, later in this chapter.

NATIONAL PARKS

There are 10 national parks in Hungary. The three on the Great Plain – Hortobágy (also a Unesco World Heritage site), Kiskunság and Körös-Maros – protect the wildlife, fragile wetlands, marsh and saline grasslands of the *puszta* (great plain). There are two in the Northern Uplands: the almost completely wooded Bükk Hills and the Aggtelek region, with its extensive system of karst caves and streams hewn into the limestone. Other national parks include Danube-Dráva National Park, which incorporates the Gemenc Forest and a recently allocated area in the Őrség region of Southern Transdanubia; the hilly areas north of Lake Balaton; Danube-Ipoly National Park on the Danube Bend; and Fertő-Hanság at Lake Fertő, which Hungarians share with Austrians (who call it Neusiedlersee). Fertő-Hanság National Park was declared a Unesco biosphere reserve in 1979.

GOVERNMENT & POLITICS

Hungary's 1989 constitution provides for a parliamentary system of government. The unicameral assembly consists of 386 members (32 women at present) chosen for four years in a complex, two-round system that balances direct ('first past the post') and proportional representation. The youngest MP is currently 25, the oldest 92. The head of state, the president, is elected by the house for a five-year term. The prime minister is head of government.

The main political parties, four of which are represented in parliament, are the rightist Federation of Young Democrats–Hungarian Civic Party (Fidesz-MPP); the conservative Hungarian Democratic Forum (MDF); the agrarian conservative Independent Smallholders' Party (FKgP); the socialist Hungarian Socialist Party (MSZP); the liberal Alliance of Free Democrats (SZDSZ); and the xenophobic and ultra-nationalist Hungarian Justice and Life Party (MIÉP). See History earlier in this chapter for more details.

ECONOMY

Hungary can now boast the strongest economy in Eastern Europe, and its painful restructuring appears to be over. The spiralling inflation of the early to mid-1990s has finally settled, with the figure – just under 10% – now approaching those of Western Europe. As long as economic targets are met and administrative reform continues, Hungary should be one of the first countries admitted to the EU when it expands its membership, possibly as soon as 2004.

Behind the economic surge are European, Asian and North American companies that have invested more than US$20 billion over the past decade, mainly because wages and operational costs are relatively low. Hungary's workforce is also considered flexible, skilled and highly educated. The unemployment rate nationwide is currently just under 6% but that is deceptive. While it's only about 5% in Budapest, the figure reaches as high as 20% in the Northeast. Wage growth lags behind inflation, and the country's poorer areas are yet to feel the boom that has buoyed Budapest and the western counties.

POPULATION & PEOPLE

When the Italian-American Nobel Prize-winning physicist Enrico Fermi (1901–54) was asked whether he believed that extraterrestrial beings existed, he replied in the affirmative. 'Of course they do and they are already here among us,' he said. 'They are called Hungarians.' Dr Fermi was, of course, referring to the Magyars, an Asiatic people of obscure origins who do not speak an Indo-European language (Hungarians like to boast that their language ranks with Japanese and Arabic as among the world's most difficult) and make up the vast majority of Hungary's 10.2 million people.

There are 3200 settlements in Hungary; the population density is 110 people per sq km. Almost five million Magyars (or descendants of ethnic Hungarians) live outside the national borders, mostly as a result of the Trianon Treaty, WWII and the 1956 Uprising. The estimated 1.65 million Hungarians in Transylvania (now Romania) constitute the largest ethnic minority in Europe, and there are another 600,000 Magyars in Slovakia, 350,000 in Yugoslavia, 180,000 in Ukraine and 35,000 in Austria. Hungarian immigrants to the USA, Canada, Australia and Israel add up to more than half a million.

Ethnic Magyars make up some 97.7% of Hungary's population. Minorities include Germans (0.3%), Slovaks (0.1%), Croatians (0.1%) and Romanians (0.1%). The number of Roma is officially put at 1.4% of the population (or 132,600 people), though in some sources the figure is twice as high.

Life expectancy in Hungary is very low by European standards: about 67 years for men

The Birds of Hungary

It may come as a surprise, but Hungary has some of the best bird-watching sites in Europe. Indeed, some 380 of the continent's 400-odd species have been sighted here, and a full 250 are resident or regular visitors. The country's indigenous populations of great white egrets (over 2000 pairs), spoonbills (up to 100 pairs) and red-footed falcons (2000 pairs) as well as endangered eastern imperial eagles (70 pairs), white-tailed eagles (70 pairs), aquatic warblers (600 singing males), saker falcons (150 pairs) and great bustards (1200 birds) are among the most important in Europe. The arrival of the storks onto the Great Plain, the Northern Uplands and the Northeast in spring is a wonderful sight to behold.

There are some 30 distinct sites for bird-watching in Hungary but the best ones overall are the Hortobágy region, the Kiskunság, Lake Fertő, Aggtelek, the Little Balaton (Kis-Balaton) and Lake Tisza. The Pilis, Vertés and Buda Hills and even small lakes like the ones at Tata and Feher-tó north of Szeged attract a wide variety of bird life. Spring and autumn are always good seasons for sightings, but the best month in general is May, when breeding is in full swing.

First of all you could get one of Gerard Gorman's books on the birds of Hungary or at least Eastern Europe (see Specialised Guidebooks under Books in the Facts for the Visitor chapter). His company **Birding Hungary** (☎ 06-70 214 0261; W www.birdinghungary.com) runs between one and four organised birding tours a month from spring to late autumn that last between four and eight days. Tailor-made tours and daily guiding are also available for around €100 a day.

A Debrecen-based company called **Aquila Nature Tours** (☎/fax 36-52 456 744; W www.hungary bird.hu; 2nd floor, Péterfia utca 46) offers both specialised bird-watching and nature tours in the Hortobágy and Zemplén Hills. The price is about €60 a day and accommodation less than €25. Another group – though not as serious – with tours of between six and eight hours (average 8000Ft to 9500Ft per person plus 70Ft to 100Ft per driven kilometre) in and around the Hortobágy is **Hortobágy Bird-watching** (☎ 36-30 490 9303; W www.birdwatching.hu). Tours of between three and nine hours in the Hortobágy, Bükk Hills and at Lake Tisza can be organised by the **Great Bustard Protection Centre** (☎/fax 36-441 020; e fater.imre@axelero.hu) at the Fauna Hotel in Besenyőtelek, some 30km northwest of Tiszafüred.

The **Hungarian Ornithological & Nature Conservation Society** (MME; ☎ 1-275 6247; W www .mme.hu; XII Költő utca 21) in Budapest can help with general information, too.

Hortobágy This area of grassy, saline steppe, large fish ponds and marshes on the Great Plain is one of the best bird areas of Europe, with more than 300 species sighted, including great bustards, red-footed

and just over 76 for women. The nation also has one of Europe's lowest rates of natural population increase – 9.32 per 1000 population, with a population growth of -0.32%.

EDUCATION

Hungary is a well educated society with a literacy rate of about 98%. School is compulsory until the age of 16 – about 63% of the population have secondary-school degrees.

The education system generally follows the German model. From ages three to six children attend nursery school (óvoda), followed by primary or elementary school (általános iskola) to age 14. Secondary education lasts four years and can be either in grammar (gimnázium) or vocational (trade) schools (szakközépiskola or szakiskola). College and university entrance is very competitive and decided by matriculation exams (érettségi vizsgák) at the age of 18. About 10% of the population hold university degrees, a quarter of which are in engineering and economics.

Hungary has an international reputation in certain areas of specialised education. A unique method of music education devised by the composer Zoltán Kodály (1882–1967) is widespread. The Pető Institute in Budapest has a very high success rate in teaching children with cerebral palsy to walk.

SCIENCE

Hungary's contributions to the sciences and related fields have been far greater than its present size and population would suggest. Albert Szent-Györgyi (1893–1986) won the Nobel Prize for Medicine or Physiology in 1937 for his discovery of vitamin C; Georg von Békésy

The Birds of Hungary

falcons and aquatic warblers. Almost any time of year is good for saker falcons, long-legged buzzards and white-tailed eagles; September/October is when geese and up to 60,000 cranes pass through. The Hortobágy fishponds are home to four species of grebes and eight species of herons as well as several varieties of terns. In winter they host white-tailed eagles.

Lake Fertő Some 210 nesting and migrant species have been registered at Fertő-Hanság National Park, which includes the southern end of shallow, saline Lake Fertő, near the Austrian border in Western Transdanubia. April to June sees the most activity in the lake's reedbeds, August sees the arrival of white storks, and autumn is the best time to sight white-fronted and bean geese.

Aggtelek The hilly karst region of Aggtelek is a breeding ground for the strictly protected hazel grouse and black storks, as well as corncrakes, Ural owls, rock buntings, honey buzzards and various woodpeckers. The best time to visit is April to September.

Little Balaton The Kis Balaton, a vast wetland made up of impenetrable reed-choked ponds and a reservoir created in 1984, is home to about 100 breeding species. The best place to view little egrets, spoonbills, terns and warblers is from Kányavári-sziget, a tiny island with two observation towers. The optimum season is April to August. In autumn tens of thousands of birds stop here on passage.

Lake Tisza The northern third of this vast manmade lake, the area just east of Poroszló, is a bird reserve under the jurisdiction of Hortobágy National Park. The reedbeds and forests along the Tisza River attract large numbers of purple herons, little bitterns, great white egrets, cormorants and black kites. Any time is good for birding at Lake Tisza, but May and June are best for breeding birds and August and September for passage storks and raptors.

Vertés Hills This low range of wooded limestone hills west of Budapest, which make up the Vertés Landscape Protection Reserve, supports a good variety of woodpeckers and flycatchers from May to July, and in winter hosts imperial eagles, hen harriers and great grey shrikes.

Tata As odd as it may seem with a main highway only 100m away, Öreg-tó (Old Lake), a nature conservation area at Tata in Western Transdanubia, attracts a considerable number and variety of waterfowl from October to February; between 20,000 and 40,000 bean and white-fronted geese can pass through in February alone. The best viewing spot is the southern end of the lake, where a thermal spring prevents that part of the lake from freezing over. The adjoining park and woodland attracts waxwings, hawfinches, bramblings and various woodpeckers in winter.

(1899–1972) won the same prize in 1961 for his research on the inner ear; and Eugene Paul Wigner (1902–95) received a Nobel Prize in 1963 for his research in nuclear physics. Both Edward Teller (1908–) and Leo Szilárd (1898–1964) worked on the so-called Manhattan Project, (which led to the development of the atomic bomb) under Enrico Fermi, who may have drawn his conclusions about the origins of the Magyars from them (see Population & People earlier).

ARTS

Hungarian art has been both stunted and spurred on by the pivotal events in the nation's history. King Stephen's conversion to Catholicism brought Romanesque and Gothic art and architecture to Hungary, while the Turkishoccupation nipped most of Hungary's

Renaissance in the bud. The Habsburgs opened the doors to baroque influences. The arts thrived under the Dual Monarchy, through truncation and even under fascism. The early days of communism brought socialist-realist art celebrating wheat sheaves and musclebound steelworkers to a less-than-impressed populace, but much money was spent on music and 'correct art' such as classical theatre. All in all it's not surprising that the works of Hungarian writers and artists have tended to reflect the struggle against oppression.

Music & Dance

Hungary has made many contributions to the music world, but one person stands head and shoulders above everyone else: Franz – or Ferenc – Liszt (1811–86). Liszt established the Academy of Music in Budapest, and liked

Rubik Cubes, Biros, Vitamin C & Zsa Zsa

'It is not enough to be Hungarian – one must also have talent.'
Slogan spotted in a Toronto employment office in the early 1960s

The contributions made by Hungarians in any number of fields – from films and toys to science and fine art – both at home and abroad have been enormous, especially when you consider the nation's size and relatively small population. The following is a list of people whom you may not have known were Hungarian or of Hungarian ancestry:

Biro, Leslie (László Bíró; 1899–1985) Inventor of the ballpoint pen in 1938.

Brassaï (Halász Gyula; 1899–1984) French poet, draftsman, sculptor and photographer, known for his dramatic photographs of Paris by night.

Capa, Robert (Friedmann Endre; 1913–54) One of the greatest war photographers and photojournalists of the 20th century.

Cukor, George (Cukor György; 1899–1983) Legendary American film producer/director (*The Philadelphia Story*, 1940)

Curtis, Tony (Bernard Schwartz; 1925–) Evergreen American actor (*Spartacus*, 1960).

Eszterhas, Joe (1944–) American scriptwriter (*Basic Instinct*, *Showgirls*).

Gabor, Eva (1921–95) American actress chiefly remembered for her starring role as a New York city socialite making her comical life on a farm in the 1960s TV series *Green Acres*; younger sister of Zsa Zsa.

Gabor, Zsa Zsa (?–) Ageless-ish American starlet of grade BBB films and older sister of Eva.

Houdini, Harry (Weisz Erich; 1874–1926) American magician and celebrated escape artist.

Howard, Leslie (Steiner László; 1893–1943) Quintessential English actor most famous for his role in *Gone with the Wind* (1939).

Lauder, Estée (1910?–) American fragrance and cosmetics baroness.

Liszt, Franz (Liszt Ferenc; 1811–86) Piano virtuoso and composer.

Lugosi, Béla (Blasko Béla; 1884–1956) The film world's only real Dracula – and Minister of Culture under the Béla Kun regime (see the History section earlier in this chapter).

Rubik, Ernő (1944–) Inventor of the hottest toy of the 1980 Christmas season – an infuriating plastic cube with 54 small squares that when twisted out of its original arrangement has 43 quintillion variations.

Soros, George (Soros György; 1930–) Billionaire financier and philanthropist.

Szent-Györgyi, Dr Albert (1893–1986) Nobel Prize-winning biochemist who discovered vitamin C.

Vasarely, Victor (Vásárhelyi Győző; 1908–97) French painter of geometric abstractions and the 'father of Op Art'.

Wilder, Billy (Wilder Samuel; 1906–2002) American film director and producer (*Some Like It Hot*, 1959).

---

to describe himself as 'part Gypsy'. Some of his works, notably the 20 *Hungarian Rhapsodies*, echo traditional Roma music.

Ferenc Erkel (1810–93) is the father of Hungarian opera, and two of his works – the stirringly nationalistic *Bánk Bán*, based on József Katona's play of that name, and *László Hunyadi* – are standards at the State Opera House in Budapest. Erkel also composed the music for the Hungarian national anthem.

Imre Kálmán (1882–1953) was Hungary's most celebrated composer of operettas. *The Queen of the Csárdás* and *Countess Marica* are two of his popular works.

Béla Bartók (1881–1945) and Zoltán Kodály (1882–1967) made the first systematic study of Hungarian folk music together, travelling and recording throughout the Magyar linguistic region in 1906. Both integrated some of their findings into their own compositions – Bartók in *Bluebeard's Castle*, for example, and Kodály in his *Peacock Variations*.

Away from classical music, it is important to distinguish between 'Gypsy music' and real Hungarian folk music. Gypsy music as it is known and heard in Hungarian restaurants from Budapest to Boston is urban schmaltz and based on recruiting tunes called *verbunkos* played during the Rákóczi independence wars. At least two fiddles, a bass and a cymbalom (a curious stringed instrument played with sticks) are *de rigueur*. If you want to hear this saccharine *csárdás* music, almost any fancy hotel restaurant in the land can oblige, or you can buy a tape or CD by Sándor Lakatos or his son Déki.

Hungarian folk musicians play violins, zithers, hurdy-gurdies, bagpipes and lutes on a five-tone diatonic scale. There are lots of different performers, but watch out especially for Muzsikás and the incomparable Marta Sebestyén. Any group (eg, Ghymes) playing the doleful and haunting music of the Csángó, (groups of Hungarians living in eastern Transylvania and Moldavia) is a good bet. The **Csángó Festival** of folk dancing and music in Jászberény in late July attracts aficionados from all over.

To confuse matters even further, real Roma music does not use instruments but is sung as a cappella (though sometimes it is backed with percussion and even guitar). A very good tape of Hungarian Roma folk songs is *Magyarországi Cigány Népdalok*, produced by Hungaroton. The best modern Roma group is Kalyi Jag (Black Fire) from northeastern Hungary and led by Gusztav Várga.

Attending a *táncház* (dance house; see Folk & Traditional Music under Entertainment in the Budapest chapter) is an excellent way to hear Hungarian folk music and even to learn to dance. It's all good fun and they're easy to find in Budapest, where the dance house revival began.

Traditional Yiddish music is not as well known as Gypsy and Roma music but is of similar origin, having once been closely associated with central European folk music. Until WWI so-called *klezmer* dance bands were led by the violin and cymbalom, but the influence of Yiddish theatre and the first wax recordings inspired a switch to the clarinet, which is the predominant instrument in this type of music today. *Klezmer* music is currently going through a great renaissance both in Budapest and abroad; the best local group is the Budapest Klezmer Band.

Hungary has ballet companies based in Budapest, Pécs and Szeged but the best by far is the Győr Ballet. Groups like the State Folk Ensemble perform dances essentially for tourists throughout the year; visit a *táncház* if you prefer authentic folk dance and not touristy two-stepping.

There are many symphony orchestras both in the capital and provincial cities. Among the best are the Budapest Festival Orchestra and the Hungarian Radio & Television Orchestra.

Literature

The poet Gyula Illyés (1902–83) wrote, 'The Hungarian language is at one and the same time our softest cradle and our most solid coffin.' No one could have put it better.

The difficulty and subtlety of the Magyar tongue has excluded most outsiders from Hungarian literature and, though it would be wonderful to be able to read the swashbuckling odes and love poems of Bálint Balassi (1554–94) or Miklós Zrínyi's *Peril of Sziget* (1651) in the original, most people will have to make do with their works in English translation (see Bookshops under Information in the Budapest chapter).

Sándor Petőfi (1823–49) is Hungary's most celebrated and accessible poet, and a line from his work *National Song* became the rallying cry for the 1848–49 War of Independence, in which Petőfi fought and died. A deeply philosophical play called *The Tragedy of Man* by Imre Madách (1823–64), published a decade after Hungary's defeat in the War of Independence, is still considered to be the country's greatest classical drama.

The defeat in 1849 led many writers to look to Romanticism for inspiration and solace: winners, heroes, and knights in shining armour became popular subjects. Petőfi's comrade-in-arms, János Arany (1817–82), whose name is synonymous with impeccable Hungarian, wrote epic poetry (including *Toldi Trilogy*) and ballads.

Another friend of Petőfi, the prolific novelist and playwright Mór Jókai (1825–1904), gave expression to heroism and honesty in such wonderful works as *The Man with the Golden Touch* and *Black Diamonds*. This 'Hungarian Dickens' still enjoys widespread popularity. Another perennial favourite, Kálmán Mikszáth (1847–1910), wrote satirical tales such as *The Good Palóc People* and *St Peter's Umbrella* in which he poked fun at the declining gentry. Apparently the former US president Theodore Roosevelt (1858–1919) enjoyed the latter work so much that he insisted on visiting the ageing novelist during a European tour in 1910.

Zsigmond Móricz (1879–1942) was a very different type of writer. His works, in the tradition of the French naturalist Émile Zola (1840–1902), examined the harsh reality of peasant life in Hungary during the late 19th century. His contemporary Mihály Babits (1883–1941), poet and the editor of the influential literary magazine *Nyugat* (West), made the rejuvenation of Hungarian literature his lifelong work.

Two 20th-century poets are unsurpassed in Hungarian letters. Endre Ady (1877–1919), who is sometimes described as a successor to Petőfi, was a reformer who ruthlessly attacked the complacency and materialism of Hungary at that time, provoking a storm of protest from right-wing nationalists. The work of socialist poet Attila József (1905–37) expressed the alienation felt by individuals in the modern age; *By the Danube* is brilliant even in English translation. József fell afoul of both the underground communist movement and the Horthy regime. Tragically, he threw himself under a train near Lake Balaton at the age of 32.

Among Hungary's most important contemporary writers are György Konrád (1933–), Péter Nádas (1942–), Péter Esterházy (1950–) and Imre Kertész (1929–). Konrád's *A Feast in the Garden* (1985) is an almost autobiographical account of the fate of the Jewish community in a small eastern Hungarian town. *A Book of Memoirs* by Nádas concerns the decline of communism in the style of Thomas Mann and has been made into a film. In his *The End of a Family Story*, he uses a child narrator as a filter for the adult experience of 1950s communist Hungary. Esterházy's *Harmonia Cælestis* (2000) is a partly autobiographical novel that paints a favourable portrait of the protagonist's father. His recent *Revised Edition* (2002) is based on documents revealing his father to have been a government informer during the communist regime.

In 2002 novelist and Auschwitz survivor Kertész was awarded the Nobel Prize for Literature, the first time Hungary has gained that distinction. Of his seven novels, only two – *Fateless* (1975) and *Kaddish for a Child Not Born* (1990) – have been translated into English in the past 10 years, though that will almost certainly change soon.

The following key Hungarian literary works are available in English translation at the Írók Boltja (Writers' Bookshop) or at the CEU Bookshop in Budapest (see Bookshops under Information in the Budapest chapter). If you are interested in contemporary short stories, pick up a copy of either *Thy Kingdom Come* or *Give or Take a Day*. For poetry try *The Lost Rider: A Bilingual Anthology* or the hefty, 1200-page *In Quest of the Miracle Stag: The Poetry of Hungary*, edited by Adam Makkai, which traces the genre from the 13th century to the present day.

Other works available in English translation include: Géza Gárdonyi's *Eclipse of the Crescent Moon* and *Slave of the Huns*; Dezső Kosztolányi's *Skylark* and *Anna Édes*; Gyula Krúdy's *The Adventures of Sindbadb* and *Sunflower*; Sándor Márai's *Embers*; Zsigmond Móricz's *Be Faithful unto Death* and *Relations;* Péter Nádas' *A Lovely Tale of Photography;* Sándor Petőfi's *János Vitez/ John the Valiant* (bilingual edition); and Miklós Radnóti's *Foamy Sky* and the collection *Major Poems by Miklós Radnóti*.

Architecture & Painting

The abbey churches at Ják and Lébény are fine examples of Romanesque architecture, and there are important Gothic churches in Nyírbátor and Sopron. For Gothic paintings, have a look at the 15th-century altarpieces done by various masters at the Christian Museum in Esztergom. The Corpus Christi Chapel in the cathedral at Pécs, the Bakócz Chapel in Esztergom Basilica and the Royal Palace at Visegrád contain exceptional examples of Renaissance stonework.

Baroque abounds in Hungary; you'll see architectural examples in virtually every town in the country. For something on a grand scale, visit the Esterházy Palace at Fertőd or the Minorite Church in Eger. The ornately carved altars in the Minorite church at Nyírbátor and the Abbey Church in Tihany are baroque masterpieces. The greatest painters of this style were the 18th-century artists Anton Maulbertsch (you can see examples of his frescoes in the Ascension Church at Sümeg) and István Dorffmeister (check out the Bishop's Palace, Szombathely).

Distinctly Hungarian art and architecture didn't come into its own until the mid-19th century when Mihály Pollack, József Hild and Miklós Ybl were changing the face of Budapest or racing around the country building mansions and cathedrals. The Romantic Nationalist school of heroic paintings, best exemplified by Bertalan Székely (1835–1910) and Gyula Benczúr (1844–1920), fortunately gave way to the realism of Mihály Munkácsy (1844–1900), the 'painter of the *puszta*'. The greatest painters from this period were Tivadar Kosztka Csontváry (1853–1919), who has been compared with Van Gogh, and József Rippl-Rónai (1861–1927), the key exponent of Secessionist art in Hungary. There are museums dedicated to their best work in

Pécs and Kaposvár, respectively. Favourite artists of the 20th century include Victor Vasarely (1908–97), the so-called father of Op Art who began life as Győző Vásárhelyi but changed his name to Victor Vasarely when he emigrated to Paris in 1930, and the sculptor Amerigo Tot (1909–84).

The Romantic Eclectic style of Ödön Lechner (Budapest Museum of Applied Art) and Hungarian Secessionist or Art Nouveau (Reök Palace in Szeged) brought unique architecture to Hungary at the end of the 19th century and the start of the 20th. Fans of Art Nouveau will find in Hungary some of the best examples of that style outside Brussels, Nancy and Vienna.

Postwar architecture in Hungary is almost completely forgettable. One exception is the work of Imre Makovecz, who has developed his own 'organic' style (not always popular locally) using unusual materials like tree trunks and turf. His work is everywhere, but among the best (or strangest) examples are the cultural centres at Sárospatak and Szigetvár and the Lutheran church in Siófok.

Folk Art

Hungary has one of the richest folk traditions in Europe and, quite apart from its music, this is where the country often has come to the fore in art. Many urban Hungarians probably wouldn't want to hear that, considering folk art a bit *déclassé* and its elevation the work of the communist regime, but it's true.

From the start of the 18th century, as segments of the Hungarian peasantry became more prosperous, ordinary people tried to make their world more attractive by painting and decorating objects and clothing. It's important to remember two things when looking at folk art. First, with very few exceptions (such as the 'primitive' paintings in Kecskemét's Museum of Naive Artists), only practical objects used daily were decorated. Second, this is not 'court art' or the work of artisans making Chinese cloisonné or Fabergé eggs. It is the work of ordinary people trying to express the simple world around them in a new and different way.

Outside museums most folk art in Hungary is all but dead (though the ethnic Hungarian regions of Transylvania in Romania are a different story). Through isolation or a refusal to let go for economic or aesthetic reasons, however, pockets remain throughout the country. Ignore the central *népművészeti bolt* (folk-art

shops) you'll find in most towns: they're mostly full of mass-produced kitsch.

The main centre of cottage weaving has always been the Sárköz region near Szekszárd in Southern Transdanubia – its distinctive black and red fabric is copied everywhere. Simpler homespun material can be found in the Northeast, especially around the Tiszahát. Because of the abundance of reeds in these once marshy areas, the people here became skilled at cane weaving as well.

Three groups stand out for their embroidery, the acme of Hungarian folk art: the Palóc people of the Northern Uplands, especially around the village of Hollókő; the Mátyó folk from Mezőkövesd; and the women of Kalocsa. The various differences and distinctions are discussed in the appropriate chapters, but to our minds no one works a needle like a Mátyó seamstress. Also impressive are the heavy woollen waterproof coats called *szűr,* once worn by herders on the Great Plain, which were masterfully embroidered by men using thick, 'furry' yarn.

Folk pottery is world-class here, and no Hungarian kitchen is complete without a couple of pairs of matched plates or shallow bowls hanging on the walls. The centre of this industry is the Great Plain – Hódmezővásárhely, Karcag and Tiszafüred, in particular – though fine examples also come from Transdanubia, especially from the Őrség region. There are jugs, pitchers, plates, bowls and cups, but the rarest and most attractive are the inscribed pots *(írókázás fazékok)* usually celebrating a wedding day or in the form of animals or people such as the Miska jugs *(Miskai kancsó)* from the Tisza River region. Nádudvar near Hajdúszoboszló on the Great Plain specialises in black pottery – striking items and far superior to the greyish stuff produced in Mohács in Southern Transdanubia.

Objects carved from wood or bone – mangling boards, honey-cake moulds, mirror cases, tobacco holders, saltcellars – were usually the work of herders or farmers idle in winter. The shepherds and swineherds of Somogy County south of Lake Balaton and the cowherds of the Hortobágy excelled at this work, and their illustrations of celebrations and local 'Robin Hood' outlaws like Horseshoe Steve are always fun to look at.

Most people made and decorated their own furniture in the old days, especially cupboards for the *tiszta szoba* (parlour) and *tulipán láda* (trousseau chests with tulips painted on them). Among the finest traditional furniture in Hungary are the tables and chairs made of golden spotted poplar from the Gemenc Forest near Tolna. The oaken chests decorated with geometrical shapes from the Ormánság region of Southern Transdanubia are superior to the run-of-the-mill tulip chests.

One art form that ventures into the realm of fine art is ceiling and wall folk painting. Among the best examples of the former can be found in churches, especially in the Northeast (eg, Tákos), the Northern Uplands (Füzér) and the Ormánság (Drávaiványi). The women of Kalocsa also specialise in wall painting, but some of their work is so colourfully overwrought that it borders on the garish.

Cinema

The scarcity of government grants has limited the production of quality Hungarian films in recent years, but a handful of good (and even great) ones still get produced every year. For classics, look out for anything by the Oscar-winning István Szabó *(Sweet Emma, Dear Böbe, The Taste of Sunshine)*, Miklós Jancsó *(Outlaws)* and Péter Bacsó *(The Witness, Live Show)*.

Other favourites are *Simon Mágus*, the epic tale of two magicians and a young woman in Paris directed by Ildikó Enyedi, and many of the films of comic director Péter Timár. Timár's *Csinibaba* is a satirical look at life – and film production quality – during the communist regime. *Zimmer Feri*, set on Lake Balaton, pits a young practical joker against a bunch of loud German tourists; the typo in the title is deliberate. Timár's *6:3* takes viewers back to 1953 to that glorious moment when Hungary defeated England in football (see Spectator Sports in the Facts for the Visitor chapter). Ga'bor Herendi's *Valami Ameikai* (Something America) is the comic tale of a filmmaking team trying to profit from an expatriate Hungarian who pretends to be a rich producer.

SOCIETY & CONDUCT
Traditional Culture

Apart from the Busójárás festival in Mohács, Farsang and other pre-Lenten carnivals are now celebrated at balls and private parties, to which some people go in costume. The sprinkling of water or perfume on young girls on Easter Monday is now rare (except in Hollókő), though the Christmas tradition of *Betlehemzés*, where young men and boys carry model churches containing a manger from door to door, can still be seen in some parts of the countryside. A popular event for city folk with tenuous ties to the countryside is the *disznótor*, the slaughtering of a pig followed by an orgy of feasting and drinking. (The butchering, thankfully, is done somewhere out the back by an able-bodied peasant.) Wine harvest festivals, now commercial events with rock bands and a late-night outdoor disco, occur throughout the wine-growing regions in September and October.

Social Life

In general Hungarians are not uninhibited like the extroverted Romanians or sentimental Slavs who will laugh or cry at the drop of a hat (or drink). They are reserved, somewhat formal people. Forget about the impassioned, devil-may-care Gypsy-fiddling stereotype – it doesn't exist and probably never did. The national anthem calls Hungarians 'a people torn by fate' and the overall mood is one of *honfibú* (literally 'patriotic sorrow', but really a penchant for the blues with a sufficient amount of hope to keep most people going).

This mood certainly predates communism. To illustrate what she called the 'dark streak in the Hungarian temperament', the late US foreign correspondent Flora Lewis recounted a story in *Europe: A Tapestry of Nations* that was the talk of Europe in the early 1930s. 'It was said,' she wrote, 'that a song called *Gloomy Sunday* so deeply moved otherwise normal people (in Budapest) that whenever it was played, they would rush to commit suicide by jumping off a Danube bridge.' The song has been covered in English by several artists, including Billie Holiday and Sinéad O'Connor. Boy, is it a downer...

Hungarians are almost always extremely polite in social interaction, and the language can be very courtly – even when doing business with the butcher or having your hair cut. The standard greeting for a man to a woman (or youngsters to their elders, regardless of sex) is *Csókolom* ('I kiss it' – 'it' being the hand, of course). People of all ages – even close friends – shake hands profusely when meeting.

Perhaps as an extension of this desire to keep everything running as smoothly as possible, Hungarians are always extremely helpful in an emergency – be it an accident, a pick-pocketing or simply helping someone who's lost their way. But while all this gentility certainly oils the wheels that turn a sometimes difficult society, it can be used to keep 'outsiders' (foreigners and other Hungarians) at a distance.

Like Spaniards, Poles and many others with a Catholic background, Hungarians celebrate name days rather than birthdays. Name days are usually the Catholic feast day of their patron saint, but less holy names have a date too. Most calendars in Hungary list them.

Drinking is an important part of social life in a country that has produced wine and fruit brandies for thousands of years. Consumption is high; only France and Germany drink more alcohol per capita. Alcoholism in Hungary is not as visible to the outsider as it is, say, in Poland, but it's there nonetheless; official figures suggest that as many as 900,000 people – almost 9% of the population – are fully fledged alcoholics, and some experts say that between 40% and 50% of all males

Last Name First

Following a practice unknown outside Asia, Hungarians reverse their names in all uses, and their 'last' name (or surname) *always* comes first. For example, John Smith is never János Kovács to Hungarians but Kovács János, while Elizabeth Taylor is Szabó Erzsébet and Francis Flour is Liszt Ferenc.

Most titles also follow the structure: Mr John Smith is Kovács János úr. Many women follow the practice of taking their husband's full name. If Elizabeth were married to John, she might be Kovács Jánosné (Mrs John Smith) or, increasingly popular among professional women, Kovácsné Szabó Erzsébet.

To avoid confusion, all Hungarian names in this guide are written in the usual Western manner – Christian name first – including the names of museums, theatres etc if they are translated into English. Budapest's Arany János színház is the János Arany Theatre in English. Addresses are always written in Hungarian as they appear on street signs: Kossuth Lajos utca, Rákóczi Ferenc tér etc.

drink 'problematically'. Cirrhosis of the liver is the third most common cause of death here.

Hungarians let their hair – and most of their clothes – down in summer at lake and riverside resorts; going topless is almost the norm for women. In warm weather you'll see more public displays of affection on the streets than perhaps any place else in the world. It's all very romantic, but beware: in remote corners of city parks you may stumble upon more passionate displays (which always seems to embarrass the stumbler more than the active participants).

RELIGION

Throughout history, religion in Hungary has often been a question of expediency. Under King Stephen, Catholicism won the battle for dominance over Orthodoxy and, while the majority of Hungarians were quite happily Protestants by the end of the 16th century, many donned a new mantle during the Counter-Reformation under the Habsburgs. During the Turkish occupation, thousands of Hungarians converted to Islam – though not always willingly.

As a result, Hungarians tend to have a more pragmatic approach to religion than most of their neighbours, and almost none of the bigotry. It has even been suggested that this generally sceptical view of matters of faith has led to Hungarians' high rate of success in science and mathematics. Except in villages and on the most important holy days (Easter, the Assumption of Mary, Christmas), churches are never full. The Jewish community in Budapest, though, has seen a great revitalisation in recent years.

Of those Hungarians declaring religious affiliation, about 68% say they are Roman Catholic, 21% Reformed (Calvinist) Protestant and nearly 6% Evangelical (Lutheran) Protestant. There are also small Greek Catholic and Orthodox congregations. Hungary's Jews number about 100,000, down from a prewar population of nearly 10 times that amount, with almost 90% living in Budapest. Some 400,000 died during deportation under the fascist Arrow Cross in 1944 or were murdered in Nazi concentration camps. Many others emigrated after 1956. The HNTO (Hungarian National Tourism Office) publishes a fully illustrated free brochure called *Shalom: Jewish Relics in Hungary*.

Facts for the Visitor

HIGHLIGHTS
Historic Towns
Many of Hungary's historic towns, including Eger, Győr, Székesfehérvár and Veszprém, were rebuilt in the baroque style during the 18th century after being destroyed by the Turks. Sopron and Kőszeg are among the few Hungarian towns with a strong medieval flavour. The greatest monuments of the Turkish period are in Pécs. Kecskemét and Budapest have wonderful examples of Art Nouveau and Secessionist architecture.

Castles, Palaces & Manors
Hungary's most celebrated castles are those that resisted the Turkish onslaught in Eger, Kőszeg and Szigetvár. Though in ruins, the citadel at Visegrád evokes the power of medieval Hungary. The fortresses at Siklós, Sümeg, Hollókő and Boldogkőváralja have dramatic locations.

Among Hungary's finest palaces and manor houses are Esterházy Palace at Fertőd; Festetics Palace at Keszthely; Széchenyi Manor at Nagycenk; and the Royal Palace at Gödöllő.

Museums & Galleries
Hungary is loaded with museums, galleries and other priceless collections, and many stand out not just for the treasures they contain, but also for the way they present them. Balassagyarmat's Palóc Museum is unsurpassed for folklore and other items related to the Palóc people (see the boxed text 'The Good Palóc People' in the Northern Uplands chapter) while Budapest's Ethnography Museum casts a wider net. Also in the capital the Applied Arts Museum has the nation's largest and finest collection of furniture and decorative items. If sacred art is your thing, Esztergom's Christian Museum has a superb collection of Gothic paintings. For Romanesque and Gothic furnishings head for the Storno Collection in Sopron.

It's admittedly not Hungarian, but the Asian and African art exhibited at the Imre Patkó Collection in Győr is an outstanding assortment for a provincial city. Two of Hungary's foremost artists, Tivadar Kosztka Csontváry and Victor Vasarely, have their own dedicated museums in Pécs; the Zsolnay

Museum in that city, especially, is a treasure trove of Art Nouveau and Secessionist porcelain art.

Churches & Synagogues
Among Hungary's most beautiful houses of worship are:

- baroque Minorite church in Eger
- baroque cathedral at Kalocsa
- Gothic Calvinist church in Nyírbátor
- Minorite church in Nyírbátor (for its carved wooden altars)
- Romanesque church at Őriszentpéter
- Pécs Synagogue
- Gothic Old Synagogue in Sopron
- Church of the Ascension in Sümeg (for its frescoes)
- Art Nouveau synagogue in Szeged
- Romantic Nationalist synagogue in Szolnok (now the Szolnok Gallery)
- Abbey Church in Tihany

Outdoor Activities
Among the top outdoor activities in Hungary are the following.

- caving in Aggtelek
- cycling in the Danube Bend area
- bird-watching in the Hortobágy region
- riding the narrow-gauge railway from Miskolc into the Bükk Hills
- horse-riding around Szilvásvárad in the Northern Uplands
- canoeing or kayaking on the Tisza River
- hiking in the Zemplén Hills

SUGGESTED ITINERARIES
Hungary is compact enough that all of the regions mentioned in this book could be visited in one month. If you don't have that long, you could always try any one of the following tours.

Two days
Visit Budapest
One week
Visit Budapest, the Danube Bend and one or two of the following places: Eger, Kecskemét, Pécs, Sopron and Szeged
Two weeks
Visit Budapest, the Danube Bend, the northern shore of Lake Balaton, Kőszeg, and two or three of the following: Eger, Kecskemét, Pécs, Sopron and Szeged

PLANNING
When to Go
Every season has its attractions in Hungary, but do yourself a favour and drop the romantic notion of a winter on the *puszta* (Great Plain). Aside from being cold and often bleak, winter sees museums and other tourist sights closed or their hours sharply curtailed.

Though it can be pretty wet in April and May, spring is excellent as the weather is usually mild and the crowds of tourists have not yet arrived. The Hungarian summer is warm, sunny and unusually long, but the resorts at Lake Balaton and the Mátra Hills get very crowded in late July and August.

As elsewhere in Europe, Budapest and other Hungarian cities come to a grinding halt in August, which Hungarians traditionally call 'the cucumber-growing season' (because that's about the only thing happening). There are lots more festivals now scheduled for August, however.

Autumn is beautiful, particularly in the hills around Budapest and in the Northern Uplands. In Transdanubia and on the Great Plain it's harvest and vintage time. November is one of the rainiest months of the year.

For more information on Hungary's weather, see Climate in the Facts about Hungary chapter.

Maps
In this small country you could easily get by with the *Road Map Hungary*, free from branches of the Hungarian National Tourist Office (HNTO) abroad and from Tourinform offices in Hungary, though motorists will want something a bit more detailed.

Cartographia (W *www.cartographia.hu*), Hungary's largest map-making company, publishes a useful 1:450,000-scale sheet map (800Ft) and its Magyarország autóatlasza (Road Atlas of Hungary) is indispensable if you plan to do a lot of travelling in the countryside by car. It comes in two sizes and scales – 1:360,000 (1600Ft) and 1:250,000 (2000Ft). The smaller-scale atlas has thumbnail plans of virtually every community in the land while the larger one has 23 city maps. Bookshops in Hungary generally stock a wide variety of maps or you could go directly to the Cartographia outlet (☎ 1-312 6001; VI Bajcsy-Zsilinszky út 37; open 9am-5pm Mon-Wed, 9am-6.30pm Thur, 9am-3.30pm Fri) in Budapest.

Cartographia also produces national, regional and hiking maps (average scales 1:40,000 or 1:60,000) as well as city plans, though smaller companies such as Magyar Térképház (MT) and Nyír-Karta also publish excellent city and specialised maps.

What to Bring
There are no particular items of clothing to remember – an umbrella in spring and autumn, perhaps, and a warm hat in winter – unless you plan to do some serious hiking or other sport. A swimsuit for use in the mixed-sex thermal spas and pools is a good idea, as are plastic sandals or thongs (flip-flops). If you plan to stay in hostels, pack a towel and a plastic soap container. Bedclothes are usually provided, though you might want to bring your own sheet bag as well as a padlock for storage cupboards.

In general, Hungarian dress is very casual – daringly brief, even by European standards in summer – and many people attend even the opera in denim. Men needn't bother bringing a tie; it will *never* be used.

Other items you might need include a torch (flashlight), an adaptor plug for electrical appliances (such as a small electric kettle or coil immersion heater to make your own tea or instant coffee), a universal bath/sink plug (a plastic film canister sometimes works), sunglasses, a few clothes pegs and premoistened towelettes or a large cotton handkerchief that you can soak in fountains and use to cool off while touring cities and towns in the warmer months.

TOURIST OFFICES
Local Tourist Offices & Travel Agencies
The Hungarian National Tourist Office (HNTO) has a chain of 120 tourist information bureaus called Tourinform across the country. These are the best places to ask general questions and pick up brochures – and can sometimes provide more comprehensive assistance. The main **Tourinform office** (☎ 1-438 8080, fax 318 9059; e *hungary@tourinform.hu*; W *www.hungarytourism.hu*; V Vigadó utca 6; open 24hr) is in Budapest.

If your query is about private accommodation, flights or international train travel or you need to change money, you could turn to a commercial travel agency, such as: Ibusz, arguably the best for private accommodation; Cooptourist; or Express, which issues student,

youth, teacher and hostel cards and sells discounted Billet International de Jeunesse (BIJ)
train tickets and cheap airfares. See individual
chapters for details.

Tourist Offices & Travel Agencies Abroad

The HNTO has offices in some 19 countries,
including the following.

Austria (☎ 01-585 20 1213, fax 585 20 1214,
  e htvienna@hungarytourism.hu)
  Opernring 5/2, A-1010 Vienna
Czech Republic (☎ 02-2109 0135, fax 2109
  0139, e htpragaue@hungarytourism.hu)
  Rumunská 22, 22537 Prague 2
France (☎ 01 53 70 67 17, fax 01 47 04 83 57,
  e htparis@hungarytourism.hu)
  140 ave Victor Hugo, 75116 Paris
Germany (☎ 030-243 1460, fax 243 146 13,
  e htberlin@hungarytourism.hu)
  Karl Liebknecht Strasse 34, D-10178 Berlin
Netherlands (☎ 070-320 9092, fax 327 2833,
  e htdenhaga@hungarytourism.hu) Laan van
  Nieuw Oost Indie 271, 2593 BS The Hague
UK (☎/fax 020-7823 1032, fax 7823 1459,
  e htlondon@hungarytourism.hu)
  46 Eaton Place, London SW1X 8AL
USA (☎ 212-355 0240, fax 207 4103,
  e htnewyork@hungarytourism.hu)
  33rd floor, 150 East 58th St, New York, NY
  10155-3398

VISAS & DOCUMENTS
Passport

Everyone needs a valid passport or, for citizens
of 11 European countries (Austria, Belgium,
Croatia, France, Germany, Italy, Liechten-
stein, Luxembourg, Slovenia, Spain and
Switzerland), a national identification card,
to enter Hungary. It's a good idea (though not
a requirement) to carry your passport or other
identification at all times.

Visas

Citizens of virtually all European countries, the
USA, Canada, Israel, Japan and New Zealand
do not require visas to visit Hungary for stays
of up to 90 days. UK citizens do not need a visa
for a stay of up to six months. Nationals of
Australia and now South Africa (among others)
still require visas. Check current visa requirements at a consulate, any HNTO or Malév
Hungarian Airlines office or on the website of
the **Foreign Ministry** (w *www.kum.hu*) as
requirements often change without notice.

Visas are issued at Hungarian consulates or
missions, most international highway border

crossings (see the boxed text 'Major Border
Crossings' in the Getting There & Away
chapter), Ferihegy airport and the Inter
national Ferry Pier in Budapest. They are
rarely issued on international buses and *never*
on trains. Be sure to retain the separate entry
and exit forms issued with the visa that is
stamped in your passport.

Single-entry tourist visas are issued at Hungarian consulates or missions in applicants'
country of residence upon receipt of US$40
and three photos (US$65 at a mission outside
the country of residence or at the border). A
double-entry tourist visa costs US$75/100,
and you must have five photos. A multiple-
entry visa is US$180/200. Express service (on
the spot as opposed to overnight) costs US$15
extra. Single and double-entry visas are valid
for six months prior to use. Multiple-entry
ones are good for a year.

Be sure to get a tourist rather than a transit visa; the latter – available for single
(US$38/50), double (US$65/90) and multiple
(US$150/180) entries – is only good for a
stay of 48 hours, you must enter and leave
through different border crossings and already hold a visa (if required) for the next
country you visit.

Tourist visas are only extended in emer-
gencies (eg, medical ones; 3000Ft) and this
must be done at the central police station
(*rendőrkapitányság*) of any city or town 15
days before the original one expires. It's no
longer an option to go to a neighbouring
country, such as Austria or Slovakia, and then
re-enter; as of January 2002, tourist visas
allow visitors to stay for 90 days within a six-
month period only.

You are supposed to register with the local
police if staying in one place for more than 30
days, and your hotel, hostel, camp site or
private room booked through an agency will
do this for you. In other situations – if you're
staying with friends or relatives, for example –
you or the head of household has to take care
of this yourself within 72 hours. Don't worry
if you haven't got round to it; it's a hangover
from the old regime, and enforcement is
pretty lax. Address registration forms for foreigners (*lakcímbejelentő lap külföldiek részére*)
are available at main post offices.

Travel Insurance

A travel insurance policy to cover theft, loss
and medical problems is a good idea. Some

policies offer lower and higher medical-expense options; the higher ones are chiefly for countries such as the USA, which have very high medical costs. There is a wide variety of policies available, so check the small print.

Some policies specifically exclude 'dangerous' activities, which can include motorcycling and even trekking. A locally acquired motorcycle licence is not valid under some insurance policies.

You may prefer a policy which pays doctors or hospitals directly rather than you having to pay on the spot and claim later. If you have to claim later make sure you keep all documentation. Some policies ask you to call back (reverse charges) to a centre in your home country where an immediate assessment of your problem is made.

Be sure to check that the policy covers ambulances or an emergency flight home.

Driving Licence & Permits
If you don't hold a European driving licence and plan to drive in Hungary, obtain an International Driving Permit (IDP) from your local automobile association before you leave – you'll need a passport photo and a valid local licence. It is usually inexpensive and valid for one year only. Remember: An IDP is not valid unless accompanied by your original driver's licence.

Hostel Cards
A hostel card is not particularly useful in Hungary as no hostels here require you to hold one and most of the properties associated with Hostelling International are fairly remote. Having said that, an HI (or associated hostel association) card will sometimes get you a 10% discount on quoted rates. Express charges less if you have a card. Express issues Hungarian Youth Hostel Association cards to Hungarian citizens and residents for 1600Ft, which includes a 400Ft Matáv Barangoló phonecard.

Student, Youth & Teacher Cards
The International Student Identity Card (ISIC; ⓦ www.isic.org), a plastic ID-style card with your photograph, provides bona fide student discounts on some forms of transport and cheap admission to museums and other sights. If you're aged under 26 but not a student, you can apply for an International Youth Travel Card (IYTC) issued by the Federation of

International Youth Travel Organisations (FIYTO), which gives the same discounts as the ISIC. Teachers can apply for the International Teacher Identity Card (ITIC). Express sells all these cards for 1100Ft each.

Seniors' Cards
Many attractions offer reduced-price admission for people over 60 or 65 (sometimes as low as 55 for women) but this is usually just for Hungarian *nyugdíjasok* (pensioners) holding national ID cards. Indeed, Hungarian citizens over 65 travel for free on MÁV trains.

Discount Cards
Those planning on travelling extensively in the country might consider buying the **Hungary Card** (☎ 1-266 3741; ⓦ www.hungarycard.hu), which gives free admission to many museums nationwide, 50% discounts on all railway fares and some bus and boat travel as well as other museums and attractions, up to 25% off selected accommodation and 20% off the price of the Budapest Card (see Discount Cards under Information in the Budapest chapter). The card, available at Tourinform and Volánbusz offices, most larger train stations, some newsagents and petrol stations throughout Hungary, costs 6888Ft and is valid for 13 months.

Copies
All important documents (passport data and visa pages, credit cards, travel insurance policy, transport tickets, driving licence etc) should be photocopied *before* you leave home. Leave one copy behind with someone and keep another with you, separate from the originals.

EMBASSIES & CONSULATES
Hungarian Embassies & Consulates
Hungarian embassies (and consulates as indicated) around the world include the following.

Australia (☎ 02-6282 2555) 17 Beale Crescent, Deakin, ACT 2600
  Consulate: (☎ 02-9328 7859) Suite 405, Edgecliff Centre, 203–233 New South Head Rd, Edgecliff, NSW 2027
Austria (☎ 01-537 80300) 1 Bankgasse 4–6, 1010 Vienna
Canada (☎ 613-230 9614) 299 Waverley St, Ottawa, ON K2P 0V9
  Consulate: (☎ 416-923 8981) Suite 1115, 121 Bloor St East, Toronto, ON M4W 3M5

Croatia (☎ 01-489 0900) Krlezin gvozd 11/a, 10000 Zagreb
Germany (☎ 030-203 100) Unter den Linden 76, 10117 Berlin
  Consulate: (☎ 089-911 032) Vollmannstrasse 2, 81927 Munich
Ireland (☎ 01-661 2902) 2 Fitzwilliam Place, Dublin 2
Romania (☎ 01-311 0062) Strada Jean-Louis Calderon 63–65, Bucharest 70202
Slovakia (☎ 02-544 30541) ul Sedlárska 3, 81425 Bratislava
Slovenia (☎ 01-512 1882) Konrada Babnika ulica 5, 1210 Ljubljana-Sentvid
South Africa (☎ 012-430 3030) 959 Arcadia St, Hatfield, 0083 Pretoria
UK (☎ 020-7235 5218) 35 Eaton Place, London SW1X 8BY
  Consulate: (☎ 020-7235 2664) 35/b Eaton Place, London SW1X 8BY
Ukraine (☎ 044-212 4134) ul Rejtarskaja 33, Kyiv 01034
USA (☎ 202-362 6730) 3910 Shoemaker St NW, Washington, DC 20008
  Consulate: (☎ 212-752 0661) 223 East 52nd St, New York, NY 10022
  Consulate: (☎ 310-473 9344) Suite 410, 11766 Wilshire Blvd, Los Angeles, CA 90025
Yugoslavia (☎ 011-444 0472) ul Ivana Milutinovica 74, Belgrade 11000

Embassies & Consulates in Hungary

Selected countries with representation in Budapest (where the telephone code is ☎ 1) are listed here. The opening hours indicate when consular or chancellery services are available. The Roman numerals preceding the street name indicate the *kerület*, or district, in the capital.

Australia (☎ 457 9777) XII Királyhágó tér 8–9. Open 9am to noon Monday to Friday
Austria (☎ 352 9613) VI Benczúr utca 16. Open 9am to 11am Monday to Friday
Canada (☎ 392 3360) XII Budakeszi út 32. Open 8.30am to 11am and 2pm to 3.30pm Monday to Thursday
Croatia (☎ 354 1315) VI Munkácsy Mihály utca 15. Open 1pm to 3pm Monday, Tuesday, Thursday and Friday
Germany (☎ 488 3500) I Úri utca 64–66. Open 9am to noon Monday to Friday
Ireland (☎ 302 9600) V Szabadság tér 7–9. Open 9.30am to 12.30pm and 2.30pm to 4.30pm Monday to Friday
Romania (☎ 352 0271) XIV Thököly út 72. Open 8.30am to noon Monday to Friday
Slovakia (☎ 460 9010) XIV Stefánia út 22–24. Open 8am to noon Monday to Friday

Slovenia (☎ 438 5600) II Cseppkő utca 68. Open 9am to noon Monday to Friday
South Africa (☎ 392 0999) II Gárdonyi Géza út 17. Open 9am to 12.30pm Monday to Friday
UK (☎ 266 2888) V Harmincad utca 6. Open 9.30am to 12.30pm and 2.30pm to 4.30pm Monday to Friday
Ukraine (☎ 355 2443) XII Nógrádi utca 8. Open 9am to noon Monday to Wednesday and Friday by appointment only
USA (☎ 475 4400) V Szabadság tér 12. Open 8.15am to 5pm Monday to Friday
Yugoslavia (☎ 322 9838) VI Dózsa György út 92/b. Open 9am to 1pm Monday to Friday

CUSTOMS

You can bring the usual personal effects, 200 cigarettes, 1L of wine or champagne and 1L of spirits. When leaving the country, you are not supposed to take out valuable antiques without a 'museum certificate', which should be available from the place of purchase. You must declare the import/export of any amount of cash exceeding the sum of 1,000,000Ft.

MONEY
Currency

The Hungarian forint (Ft) was once divided into 100 fillér, worthless little aluminium coins that have now been withdrawn from circulation (*filléres* actually means 'cheap' or 'inexpensive' in Hungarian). There are coins of 1Ft, 2Ft, 5Ft, 10Ft, 20Ft, 50Ft and 100Ft. Notes come in seven denominations: 200Ft, 500Ft, 1000Ft, 2000Ft, 5000Ft, 10,000Ft and 20,000Ft.

The green 200Ft note features the 14th-century King Charles Robert and his castle at Diósgyőr near Miskolc. The hero of the independence wars, Ferenc Rákóczi II, and Sárospatak Castle are on the burgundy-coloured 500Ft note.

The 1000Ft note is blue and bears a portrait of King Matthias Corvinus, with Hercules Well at Visegrád Castle on the verso. The 17th-century prince of Transylvania, Gábor Bethlen, is on his own on one side of

Euro vs Forint

Because of the changing value of the forint, many hotels quote their rates in euros, as does the national rail company. In such cases, we have followed suit.

the 2000Ft bill and meeting with advisers on the other.

The 'greatest Hungarian', Count István Széchenyi, and his family home at Nagycenk are on the purple 5000Ft note. The 10,000Ft bears a likeness of King Stephen, with a scene in Esztergom appearing on the other side. The 20,000Ft note, currently the highest denomination, has Ferenc Deák, the architect of the 1867 Compromise, on the recto and the erstwhile House of Commons in Pest (now the Italian Institute of Culture on VIII Bródy Sándor utca) on the verso.

Exchange Rates

Exchange rates at the time this book goes to press are as follows:

country	unit		forint
Australia	A$1	=	139Ft
Canada	C$1	=	163Ft
euro zone	€1	=	245Ft
Japan	¥100	=	206Ft
New Zealand	NZ$1	=	120Ft
UK	UK£1	=	378Ft
USA	US$1	=	247Ft

Exchanging Money

Cash & Travellers Cheques Nothing beats cash for convenience – or risk. It's always prudent to carry a little foreign cash, though, preferably euros or US dollars, in case you can't find an automated teller machine (ATM) nearby or there's no bank or travel office open to cash your travellers cheques. You can always change cash at a hotel.

You can exchange cash and travellers cheques – American Express, Visa and Thomas Cook are the most recognisable brands – at most banks and post offices. Banks and *bureaux de change* generally don't take a commission, but exchange rates can vary; private agencies are always the most expensive. The national savings bank, Országos Takarékpénztár (OTP), has branches everywhere and offers among the best rates; Ibusz is also a good bet. Travel agents usually take a commission of 1% to 2%. Shops never accept travellers cheques in Hungary.

Though the forint is now a totally convertible currency, you should avoid changing too much as it will be difficult exchanging forint beyond the borders of Hungary and its immediate neighbours.

ATMs & Credit Cards The hassle of trying to change travellers cheques at the weekend, rip-off *bureaux de change* and the allure of the black market have all gone the way of the dodo in Hungary, with the arrival of ATMs that accept most credit and cash cards in even the tiniest of villages. All the banks listed in the Information sections in this guide have ATMs unless noted otherwise. The best ATMs to use are the Euronet ones as they dispense sums in units of 5000Ft. OTP ATMs give out 20,000Ft notes, which are tough to break.

The use of credit cards is gaining ground in Hungary, especially Visa, MasterCard and American Express (AmEx). You'll be able to use them at upmarket restaurants, shops, hotels, car-rental firms, travel agencies and petrol stations but not museums, supermarkets or train and bus stations.

Many banks, including K&H and Postabank (at post offices nationwide) give cash advances on most major credit cards.

International Transfers Having money wired to Hungary through **Western Union Money Transfer** (☎ *1-266 4995; open 7am-midnight daily*) or **American Express** is fast and fairly straightforward; for AmEx (see Money under Information in the Budapest chapter) you don't need to be a card holder but the sender does. The procedure takes less than 30 minutes. You should know the sender's full name, the exact amount and the reference number when you're picking up the cash. You'll be given the amount in US-dollar travellers cheques or forint. The sender pays the service fee (about US$40 for US$500 sent, US$60 for US$1000).

Black Market It's senseless to make use of the black market to change money. The advantage – 5% on the outside – is not worth the bother. In any case, it's illegal and you are almost certain to be ripped off.

Costs

Hungary remains a bargain destination for foreign travellers for food, lodging and transport. If you stay in private rooms, eat at medium-priced restaurants and travel on public transport, you should get by on US$30 a day without scrimping. Those staying at hostels, dormitories or camp sites and eating at food stalls or self-catering will cut costs substantially.

Tipping & Bargaining

Hungary is a very tip-conscious society and virtually everyone routinely tips waiters, hairdressers and taxi drivers. Doctors and dentists accept 'gratitude money' (see Health later in this chapter), and even petrol station and thermal spa attendants expect something. If you were less than impressed with the service at the restaurant, the joyride in the taxi or the way someone cut your hair, leave next to nothing or nothing at all. He or she will get the message loud and clear.

The way you tip in restaurants is unusual. You never leave the money on the table – this is considered both rude and stupid in Hungary – but tell the waiter how much you're paying in total. If the bill is 1540Ft, you're paying with a 2000Ft note and you think the waiter deserves the extra 10%, first ask if service is included (some restaurants in Budapest and other big cities add it to the bill automatically, which makes tipping unnecessary). If it isn't, say you're paying 1700Ft or that you want 300Ft back.

Though you'll never be able to bargain in shops, you may haggle at flea markets or with individuals selling folk crafts. But even this is not as commonplace as it is in other parts of Eastern Europe.

Taxes & Refunds

ÁFA, a value-added tax of between just under 11% and 25%, covers the purchase of all new goods in Hungary. It's usually included in the quoted price but not always, so it pays to check. Visitors are not exempt, but they can claim refunds for total purchases of more than 50,000Ft on one receipt as long as they take the goods out of the country within 90 days. The ÁFA receipts (available from the shops where you made the purchases) should be stamped by customs at the border, and the claim has to be made within 183 days of exporting the goods.

Budapest-based **Global Refund Hungary** (☎/fax 1-468 2965, fax 468 2966; W www .globalrefund.com; XIV Zászlós utca 54) can help you with refunds for a fee.

Most municipalities in Hungary levy a local tourist tax on accommodation (see Accommodation later in this chapter).

POST & COMMUNICATIONS

The Hungarian Postal Service (Magyar Posta) has improved in recent years; perhaps its jaunty logo of a stylised St Stephen's Crown has helped kick-start it into the 21st century. But post offices are usually still crowded, service is slow and staff remain Magyar monoglots.

Postal Rates

A letter sent within any Hungarian city or town costs 33Ft, while for the rest of Hungary and neighbouring countries it's 38Ft (add 96/200Ft if you want to send the letter registered/express).

Postcards within Hungary and to neighbouring countries cost 30Ft to send. Airmail letters up to 20/50g cost 150/240Ft within Europe and 160/260Ft for the rest of the world. Postcards cost 100Ft and 110Ft, respectively.

Sending & Receiving Mail

To beat the crowds at the post office, ask at kiosks, newsagents or stationery shops if they sell stamps (bélyeg). If you must deal with the post office, you'll be relieved to learn that most people are there to pay electricity, gas and telephone bills or parking fines. To get in and out with a minimum of fuss, look for the window marked with the symbol of an envelope. Make sure the destination of your letter is written clearly, and simply hand it over to the clerk, who will apply the stamps for you, postmark it and send it on its way.

To send a parcel, look for the sign 'Csomagfeladás' or 'Csomagfelvétel'. Packages sent within Hungary generally cost 360/400/480Ft for up to 2/5/10kg. Packages going abroad must not weigh more than 2kg or you'll face a Kafkaesque nightmare of permits and queues; try to send small ones. You can send up to 2kg in one box for 2840Ft to Europe and 3150Ft to the rest of the world. If you want to send books or other printed matter abroad, up to 5kg can be sent to the same destinations for 4250Ft (Europe) and 6000Ft (rest of world).

Hungarian addresses start with the name of the recipient, followed on the next line by the postal code and city or town and then the street name and number. The postal code consists of four digits. The first one indicates the city, town or region (eg, '1' is Budapest, '6' is Szeged), the second and third is the district and the last is the neighbourhood.

Mail addressed to poste restante in any town or city will go to the main post office (főposta), which is listed under Information in the relevant section. When collecting poste restante mail, look for the sign *postán maradó küldemények* and make sure you have identification. Since the family name always comes first in Hungarian usage, have the sender underline your last name, as letters are often misfiled under foreigners' first names.

If you hold an American Express credit card or are carrying its travellers cheques, you can have your mail sent to **American Express** *(Deák Ferenc utca 10, 1052 Budapest)*, where it will be held for one month.

Telephone

You can make domestic and international calls from public telephones, which are usually in good working order. They work with both coins and phonecards, though the latter are now far more common. Phonecards (which come in message units of 50/120 and cost 800/1800Ft) are available from post offices, newsagents, hotels and petrol stations. Telephone boxes with a black and white arrow and red target on the door and the word '*Visszahívható*' display a telephone number, so you can be phoned back.

All localities in Hungary have a two-digit telephone area code, except for Budapest, which has just a '1'. Local codes appear in small point type under the name of each city and town in this book.

To make a local call, pick up the receiver and listen for the neutral and continuous dial tone, then dial the phone number (seven digits in Budapest, six elsewhere). For an intercity call within Hungary, dial ☎ 06 and wait for the second, more musical, tone. Then dial the area code and phone number. You must *always* dial ☎ 06 when ringing mobile telephones, which have area codes ☎ 06-20 (Pannon), ☎ 06-30 and ☎ 06-60 (Westel) and ☎ 06-70 (Vodafone). Cheaper or toll-free blue and green numbers start with ☎ 06-40 and ☎ 06-80, respectively.

The procedure for making an international call is the same except that you dial ☎ 00, wait for the second dial tone, then dial the country code, the area code and then the number. International phone charges from a public/private phone are: 131/90Ft per minute to neighbouring countries and 136/94Ft to Europe, North America, Australia, New Zealand and East Asia. Other rates include 447/307Ft to Southeast Asia, the Middle East and South America; 524/360Ft to Africa, South Asia and the Caribbean; 633/435Ft to the Pacific and

parts of Asia and Africa. The country code for Hungary is ☎ 36.

Lonely Planet's ekno global communication service provides low-cost international calls – for local calls you're usually better off with a local phonecard, though. ekno also offers free messaging services, email, travel information and an online travel vault, where you can securely store all your important documents. You can join online at ⓦ www.ekno.lonelyplanet.com, where you'll find the local-access numbers for the 24-hour customer-service centre. Once you've joined, always check the ekno website for the latest access numbers for each country and updates on new features.

You can get straight through to an operator in your home country by dialling the appropriate Country Direct number from a public phone, but you need a coin or phonecard for the initial connection. Some of the services listed below are very expensive, although they will still be cheaper than a normal call from a phone in a hotel room.

country	number	provider
Australia	☎ 06-800 11573	
	☎ 06-800 11720	
	☎ 06-800 06111	(Telstra)
UK	☎ 06-800 04411	
	☎ 06-800 04413	(BT)
Canada	☎ 06-800 01211	
	☎ 06-800 01212	
New Zealand	☎ 06-800 06411	
South Africa	☎ 06-800 02711	
USA	☎ 06-800 01111	(AT&T)
	☎ 06-800 01411	(MCI)
	☎ 06-800 01877	(Sprint)

A much better deal is the Barangoló card (3000Ft) from **Matáv** *(☎ 06-80 495 949, 06-80 424 424;* ⓦ *www.matav.hu)*, which will bring the per-minute costs to certain countries down substantially: 70Ft to Austria, Germany, the USA and Canada and 75Ft to Italy, France and the UK.

Telephone numbers you may find useful include:

domestic operator (English spoken)	☎ 198
international operator (English spoken)	☎ 199
time/speaking clock (in Hungarian)	☎ 180
wake-up service (in Hungarian)	☎ 193

Fax

You can send faxes from most main post offices and Internet cafés for 150/500Ft per page within/outside Hungary.

Email & Internet Access

Internet cafés have sprouted in Budapest (see Information in that chapter) like mushrooms after rain and all of the capital's year-round hostels offer access. Public Internet connections in the provinces are harder to find, though most major towns now have a Matáv Pont outlet, which usually has at least a couple of terminals available for 300/500Ft for 30/60 minutes or 4000Ft for 10 hours).

DIGITAL RESOURCES

The World Wide Web is a rich resource for travellers. You can research your trip, hunt down bargain air fares, book hotels, check on weather conditions or chat with locals and other travellers about the best places to visit – or avoid.

There's no better place to start your Web explorations than the Lonely Planet website (W www.lonelyplanet.com). Here you'll find succinct summaries on travelling to most places on earth, postcards from other travellers and the Thorn Tree bulletin board, where you can ask questions before you go or dispense advice when you get back. You can also find travel news and updates to many of our most popular guidebooks, and the subwwway section links you to the most useful travel resources elsewhere on the Web.

Tourinform's informative website (W www .hungarytourism.hu) should be your first portal of call. For information on hotels, try any of the following.

W www.hotelshungary.com
W www.hotelsinfo.hu
W www.holidayhungary.com
W www.szallasinfo.hu

A good website for short-term flat rentals is W www.alfaapartments.com. Check out W www.youthhostels.hu for hostel accommodation and W www.camping.hu for camping sites in Hungary.

For national news and myriad excellent links on everything from business to culture, visit W www.insidehungary.com or subscribe to *Hungary Around the Clock* (☎ 01-351 7142; e info@hatc.hu). The weekly news magazine

HVG (see Newspapers & Magazines) gives summaries of its lead stories in English on its website (W www.hvg.hu).

Virtually every town and city in Hungary has its own Web page – usually (though not always) in Hungarian only – and these are provided in the relative sections. As expected, they range from the sublime to the ridiculous.

The Yellow Pages telephone directory is found at W www.aranyoldalak.hu.

BOOKS

There's no shortage of books on Hungary and things Hungarian – from travel guides and histories to accounts of personal journeys and cookery books. Once regarded as one of Hungary's biggest bargains, books have become more expensive, though they haven't reached Western prices yet.

Lonely Planet

Lonely Planet's *Eastern Europe*, *Central Europe* and *Europe on a shoestring* all contain chapters on Hungary. The *Budapest* city guide takes an in-depth look at the capital. LP's *Eastern Europe phrasebook* contains sections of useful words and expressions in Hungarian.

Specialised Guidebooks

Where to Watch Birds in Eastern Europe by Gerard Gorman is the bible for assistance in spotting the best of Hungary's (and Eastern Europe's, for that matter) feathered friends. It contains a 40-page chapter on Hungary. Gorman's *The Birds of Hungary* is indispensable but becoming hard to find; you may pick up a copy in second-hand bookshops or on Web bookseller sites.

Jewish Heritage Travel: A Guide to East-Central Europe by Ruth Gruber is a reissue of a classic and contains a comprehensive chapter on Hungary.

The Wines & Vines of Hungary by Stephen Kirkland is hard to find but is the best guide to Hungarian wine in English, leaving no leaf, grape or bottle unturned.

Travel

Travellers writing diary accounts usually treat Hungary rather cursorily as they make tracks for 'more exotic' Romania or points beyond.

However, *Between the Woods and the Water* by Patrick Leigh Fermor, describing the author's 1933 walk through Hungary en route to Constantinople, is the classic account of Hungary.

In *Stealing from a Deep Place* by Brian Hall, sensitive but never cloying, the author describes his tempered love affair with the still communist Budapest of the 1980s.

The City of the Magyar by Miss Julia Pardoe, published in 1840, is one of the best sources for contemporary views of early 19th-century Hungary. You'll only find this three-volume set in a library or antiquarian bookshop, though.

History & Politics

The Lawful Revolution: Kossuth Lajos and the Hungarians, 1848–1849 by István Deák takes a close look at the pivotal role played by Kossuth in Hungary's first major war against foreign aggression.

We the People by Timothy Garton Ash and *The Rebirth of History: Eastern Europe in the Age of Democracy* by Misha Glenny are still classic and insightful interpretations of what led to the collapse of communism in 1989.

A History of Modern Hungary by Jörg K Hoensch covers the period from 1867 to 1994 in a balanced, not overly academic, fashion.

Government & Politics in Hungary by András Körösényi is a very scholarly work that covers the period up to 1999.

The Magyars: Their Life & Civilisation by Gyula László is a dense anthology of the beliefs, traditions and culture of the Hungarians at the time of the conquest.

Hungary: A Brief History is a light, almost silly, history by geologist-cum-journalist István Lázár. His *An Illustrated History of Hungary* is an easy introduction to the nation's past, profusely illustrated and in large format.

A History of Hungary, edited by Peter F Sugar is arguably the best single-volume history of Hungary in English, written by 20 scholars (14 of them Hungarians) and edited by one of the most incisive historians of Central and Eastern Europe.

A Concise History of Hungary by Miklós Molnár is the book to read if you find Sugar's tome too daunting.

Hungary's Negotiated Revolution by Rudolf L Tőkés, subtitled 'Economic Reform, Social Change and Political Succession, 1957–1990', is based on interviews with former top communist leaders and transcripts of the Hungarian Socialist Workers Party Central Committee.

A Cultural History of Hungary: From the Beginnings to the 18th Century and *A Cultural History of Hungary: in the 19th & 20th Centuries* by László Kósa offer an easy (and illustrated) introduction from earliest times to the end of the last century.

General

Hungarian Ethnography and Folklore by Iván Balassa & Gyula Ortutay is a real gem – an 800-page opus weighing in at 3kg and leaving no question on traditional Hungarian culture unanswered. It's out of print but can still be found in Budapest and some provincial bookshops and on the Web. Highly recommended.

Hungary & the Hungarians: The Keywords by István Bart, subtitled 'A Concise Dictionary of Facts, Beliefs, Customs, Usage & Myths', will guide you from ABC (a kind of greengrocers under the old regime) to Zsolnay.

Under the Frog by Tibor Fischer is an amusing account of a basketball team's antics in the Hungary of the early 1950s.

Hungarian Folk Art by Tamás Hofer & Edit Fél is an oversized picture book that offers a good introduction to the subject.

Culinaria Hungary by Aniko Gegely et al is a lavish, 320-page tome on all things involving Hungarian food, from soup to nuts and more.

In *George Lang's Cuisine of Hungary*, celebrated restaurateur Lang offers a comprehensive history of Magyar cooking and examination of its regional differences.

Memoir of Hungary: 1944–1948 by Sándor Márai contains the remembrances of the celebrated author of *Embers* and playwright who fled Hungary in 1948 to escape communist persecution.

Homage to the Eighth District by Giorgio & Nicola Pressburger is a poignant account of life in what was a Jewish working-class section of Budapest during and after WWII by twin brothers who emigrated to Italy in 1956.

The Architecture of Historic Hungary by Dora Wiebenson & József Sisa takes a very serious look at important buildings and their place in history throughout the country, with lavish photos and schematic drawings.

NEWSPAPERS & MAGAZINES

English-language Western newspapers available on the day of publication at many large kiosks, newsagents and hotels in Budapest and certain other large cities in western Hungary include the *International Herald Tribune*, the

European edition of the *Wall Street Journal*, the *Financial Times* and the weekly *Guardian International*.

As in most European countries, printed news has strong political affiliations in Hungary. The two main exceptions are the highly respected news magazine *Heti Világgazdaság* (World Economy Weekly), better known as *HVG*, and the former Communist Party mouthpiece *Népszabadság* (People's Freedom), which is now completely independent (though socialist-oriented) and has the highest paid circulation of any newspaper. (The daily commuter freebie *Metro* counts more readers, however.)

Budapest has two English-language weeklies: the fluffy tabloid *Budapest Sun* (298Ft), with a useful *Style* arts and entertainment supplement, and the archival *Budapest Business Journal* (550Ft). The *Hungarian Spectator* (100Ft), which tries (unsuccessfully) to do the job of both those papers, appears twice a month.

Other English-language periodicals include the erudite *Hungarian Quarterly* (950Ft), which examines a wide variety of issues in great depth and is a valuable source of current Hungarian thinking in translation; the feature-oriented *Business Hungary* (900Ft), published by the American Chamber of Commerce; the *Central European Business Weekly* (Ⓦ www.ceebiz.com); *Business & Economy Invest in Hungary* (600Ft); and the bilingual (English and German) *Home in Hungary* (230Ft), which is a rather sketchy 'lifestyle magazine for expatriots [*sic*]'.

RADIO & TV

With the sale of the state-owned TV2, Magyar Televízió (MTV) controls only one channel (M1) though there are public channels (M2 and Duna TV) and a host of cable and satellite ones (eg, RTL Klub and Magyar ATV) broadcasting everything from game and talk shows to Pokémon, all in – or dubbed into – Hungarian. Most larger hotels and pensions have satellite TV, mainly German, but sometimes Sky News, CNN, Eurosport and BBC News.

Hungarian Radio has three stations, named after Lajos Kossuth (jazz and news; 98.6 AM), Sándor Petőfi (1960s to 1980s music and news; 94.8 FM) and Béla Bartók (classical music and news; 105.3 FM). Est.fm (98.6 FM) is a popular alternative music station while Rádió © (88.8 FM) is excellent for Roma music, as well

as jazz, Latino and North African sounds. Budapest Rádió is on 88.1 FM and 91.9 FM.

VIDEO SYSTEMS

If you want to record or buy video tapes to play back home, you won't get the picture if the image registration systems are different. Like most of Europe and Australia, Hungary uses PAL, which is incompatible with the North American and Japanese NTSC system or the SECAM system used in France.

PHOTOGRAPHY & VIDEO

Major brands of film are readily available and one-hour processing places are common in Budapest and larger Hungarian cities and towns.

Film prices vary but generally 24 exposures of 100 ISO Kodacolor II, Agfa or Fujifilm costs 999Ft, and 36 exposures is 1290Ft. Ektachrome 100 costs 1790Ft for 36 exposures. Developing print film is 1099Ft a roll; for the prints themselves, you choose the size and pay accordingly (eg, 10cm x 15cm prints cost 89Ft each). Developing a 40-exposure roll of Kodak 400 APS film costs from 2800Ft; slide film costs only 1099Ft to process. Video tape such as TDK EHG 30/45 minutes costs 990/1310Ft.

TIME

Hungary lies in the Central European Time Zone. Winter time is GMT/UTC plus one hour and in summer it's GMT/UTC plus two hours. Clocks are advanced at 2am on the last Sunday in March and set back at the same time on the last Sunday in October.

Without taking daylight-saving times into account, when it's noon in Budapest, it's:

11pm in Auckland
1pm in Bucharest
11am in London
2pm in Moscow
6am in New York
noon in Paris
3am in San Francisco
9pm in Sydney
8pm in Tokyo

An important note on the complicated way Hungarians tell time: 7.30 is 'half eight' (*fél nyolc óra*) and the 24-hour system is often used in giving the times of movies, concerts etc.

So a film at 7.30pm could appear on a listing as 'f8', 'f20', '½8' or '½20'. A quarter to the hour has a ¾ in front (thus '¾8' means 7.45) while quarter past is ¼ of the next hour (eg, '¼9' means 8.15).

ELECTRICITY

The electric current in Hungary is 220V, 50Hz AC. Plugs are the European type with two round pins.

WEIGHTS & MEASURES

Hungary uses the metric system (see the conversion table on the inside back cover of this book). In supermarkets and outdoor markets, fresh food is sold by weight or by piece *(darab)*. When ordering by weight, you specify by kilos or *deka* (decagrams – 50dg is equal to 0.5kg or a little more than 1lb).

Beer at a *söröző* (pub) is served in a *pohár* (0.3L) or a *korsó* (0.4L or 0.5L). Wine in an old-fashioned *borozó* (wine bar) is ladled out by the *deci* (decilitre, 0.1L), but in more modern places it comes by the undefined *pohár* (glass).

LAUNDRY

Most hostels and camp sites have some sort of laundry facilities; expect to pay from 500Ft to 1000Ft per load.

Commercial laundries *(patyolat)* are fairly common in Hungary, especially in Budapest, though they're almost never self-service. You can elect to have your laundry done in six hours or one, two or three days – and pay accordingly (from 1500Ft). Dry-cleaning is of a low standard except at big international hotels.

TOILETS

Public toilets in Hungary are invariably staffed by an old *néné* (auntie), who mops the floor continuously, hands out sheets of grade AAA sandpaper as toilet tissue and has seen it all before. The usual charge is 50Ft a go, and even restaurants and cafés sometimes charge their patrons.

HEALTH

Mosquitoes are a real scourge around lakes and rivers in summer, so be armed with insect repellent *(rovarírtó)*. One insect that can bring on more than just an itch, though, is the forest tick *(kullancs)*, which burrows under the skin causing inflammation and even encephalitis. It has become a common problem in parts of Central and Eastern Europe, especially eastern Austria, Germany, Hungary and the Czech Republic. You might consider getting an FSME (meningo-encephalitis) vaccination if you plan to do extensive hiking and camping in Transdanubia or the Northern Uplands between May and September.

The numbers of registered AIDS cases in Hungary and those who are HIV-positive are relatively low (below 800) though the Hungarian epidemiologists estimate the actual number of those infected with HIV to be 3500 to 4000 or more. That number could multiply substantially as Budapest claims its less-than-distinctive title of 'sex industry capital of Eastern and Central Europe'. Two AIDS lines operate in Budapest: a 24-hour **AIDS information line** (☎ *1-338 4555*) and a **help line** (☎ *1-338 2419; open 8am-3pm Mon-Thur, 8am-1pm Fri*), with some English spoken.

Foreigners are entitled to first-aid and ambulance services only when they have suffered an accident and require immediate medical attention; follow-up treatment and medicine must be paid for. Treatment at a public outpatient clinic *(rendelő intézet)* costs little, but doctors working privately will charge much more. Very roughly, a consultation in a Hungarian doctor's surgery *(orvosi rendelő)* costs from 5000Ft while a home visit is 10,000Ft. Consultations and treatment are much more expensive in the Western-style clinics in Budapest (see Medical Services under Information in that chapter).

Dental work is usually of a high standard and cheap by Western standards (at least the Austrians seem to think so, judging from the numbers who regularly cross the border to have their teeth cleaned or fixed). Some dentists advertise in the English-language press in Budapest.

Most large towns and all of Budapest's 23 districts have a rotating all-night pharmacy open every day; a sign on the door of any pharmacy will help you locate the closest 24-hour one.

SOCIAL GRACES

If you're invited to a Hungarian home, bring a bunch of flowers (available in profusion all year and very inexpensive) or a bottle of good local wine. You can talk about anything, but money is a touchy subject. Traditionally, the discussion of wealth – or wearing flashy jewellery, for example – was considered gauche in Hungary (as it was throughout Eastern Europe). Nowadays no one thinks they have enough money, and those still in the low-paying public sector are often jealous of people who have made the leap to better jobs in the private sector. Your salary – piddling as you may think it is back home – will astonish many Hungarians.

Though it's almost impossible to calculate (the 'black economy' being so widespread and important), the average monthly salary in Hungary at the time of writing was 120,000Ft (about 72,500Ft net); the new minimum wage is set at 50,000Ft (35,000Ft to 40,000Ft net).

Magyar, the Hungarian language, is extraordinarily difficult. Don't let this put you off attempting a few words and phrases, though. Partly as a reaction to the compulsory study of Russian in all schools until the late 1980s, Hungarians prefer to speak only Hungarian – attempt a few words in Magyar and they'll be impressed, take it as a compliment and will be extremely encouraging.

The second most useful language for getting around in Hungary is German. Historical ties, geographical proximity and the fact that it was the preferred language of the literati up until the turn of the 20th-century have given it almost semi-official status. Still, outside Budapest and Transdanubia, the frequency and quality of spoken German is low.

While English is becoming more common, it's rarely heard outside the capital. If you're desperate, look for someone young, preferably under the age of 25. Familiarity with Italian is increasing due to tourism, but French and Spanish will be of little use.

For more on what to say and how to say it Magyarul (literally 'Hungarian-ly'), see the Language chapter at the back of this book.

WOMEN TRAVELLERS
Hungarian men can be sexist in their thinking, but women do not suffer any particular form of harassment (though domestic violence and rape get little media coverage). Most men – even drunks – are effusively polite with women. Women may not be made to feel especially welcome when eating or drinking alone; it's really no different from many other countries in Europe.

For assistance and/or information ring the **Women's Line** (*Nővonal;* ☎ 06-80 505 101) or **Women for Women Against Violence**

(*NANE;* ☎ 1-267 4900), which operates from 6pm to 10pm daily.

GAY & LESBIAN TRAVELLERS
There's not much gay life beyond Budapest (see Gay & Lesbian Venues under Entertainment in that chapter for listings in the capital) unless you take it with you, but the Budapest-biased freebie pamphlet *Na végre!* (At last!) lists some venues in the *vidék* (countryside). Pick it up at a gay venue in Budapest or contact them directly via email (e navegre@hotmail.com). Useful websites include w www.gayguide.net/europe/hungary/budapest and w http://masprogram.freeweb.hu.

For one-to-one contact, ring either **Gay Switchboard** (☎ 06-30 932 3334, 1-351 2015; *open 4pm-8pm Mon-Fri)* or **Háttér Gay & Lesbian Association** (☎ 1-329 3380; *open 6pm-11pm daily).*

The age of consent for gays and lesbians is 18 years, as against 14 years of age for heterosexual couples.

DISABLED TRAVELLERS
Most of Hungary has a long way to go before it becomes accessible to the disabled. Wheelchair ramps, toilets fitted for the disabled and inward opening doors are virtually nonexistent, though audible traffic signals for the blind are becoming increasingly commonplace and the higher-denominated forint notes have markings in Braille.

For more information, contact the **Hungarian Disabled Association** (*MEOSZ;* ☎ 1-388 5529, 388 2387; e *meosz@matavnet.hu; San Marco utca 76, Budapest 1035)* from 8am to 4pm Monday to Friday.

SENIOR TRAVELLERS
Seniors are sometimes entitled to discounts in Hungary on things like public transport and museum admission fees, provided they show proof of their age. See Seniors' Cards under Visas & Documents earlier in this chapter for more information.

TRAVEL WITH CHILDREN
Successful travel with young children requires planning and effort. Don't try to overdo things; packing too much into the time available can cause problems. Make sure the activities include the kids as well – balance that morning at Budapest's Museum of Fine Arts with an afternoon at the nearby Municipal

Great Circus or a performance at the Budapest Puppet Theatre. Include children in the trip planning; if they've helped to work out where you will be going, they'll be much more interested when they get there. Lonely Planet's *Travel with Children* is a good resource.

Most car-rental firms in Hungary have children's safety seats for hire at a nominal cost (€2), but it is essential that you book them in advance. The same goes for highchairs and cots (cribs); they're standard in many restaurants and hotels but numbers are limited.

DANGERS & ANNOYANCES

Hungary is not a violent or dangerous society, but crime (mostly theft) has increased fourfold from a communist-era base of virtually nil over the past 15 years. Racially motivated attacks against Roma, Africans and Arabs are not unknown, but violence is seldom directed against travellers.

As a traveller, you are most vulnerable to pickpockets, taxi louts, car thieves and the scams of the capital's *konzumlányok*, attractive young women in collusion with rip-off bars and clubs who will see you relieved of a serious chunk of money. These scams have become as common as the stars judging from the number of readers' letters and complaints filed with foreign embassies in Budapest. To learn how to keep out of the clutches of these 'consume girls', see Dangers & Annoyances under Information in the Budapest chapter.

Pickpocketing is most common at popular tourist sights, in flea markets and on certain forms of transport in Budapest (see Dangers & Annoyances in that chapter). Always put your wallet in your front pocket, hold your purse close to your body and keep your backpack or baggage in sight. And watch out for tricks. The usual method on the street is for someone to distract you by running into you and then apologising profusely – as an accomplice takes off with the goods.

Taking a taxi in the provinces is seldom a problem. For information about arriving at your destination in a Budapest taxi without tears (or bruises), see Getting Around in the Budapest chapter.

Most Hungarian car thieves are not after fancy Western models because of the difficulty in getting rid of them. But Volkswagens, Audis and the like are very popular, and are easy to dismantle and ship abroad; one of us had all the hubcaps of a rental car nicked while jaunting

Emergency Numbers

central emergency number (English spoken)	☎ 112
police	☎ 107
English-language crime hotline	☎ 1-438 8000
fire	☎ 105
ambulance	☎ 104 (24-hour)
car assistance	☎ 188

around the countryside. Don't leave anything of value inside the car, even if hidden.

We have received numerous reports of unscrupulous waiters, shop assistants and even an immigration officer at Ferihegy making high-tech duplicates of credit- or debit-card information with a machine. If your card leaves your possession for a considerable length of time, consider having it cancelled.

The boxed text here contains the most important numbers to know in an emergency anywhere in Hungary.

BUSINESS HOURS

With rare exceptions, the opening hours *(nyitvatartás)* of any concern are posted on the front door; *nyitva* means 'open' and *zárva* is 'closed'.

Grocery stores and supermarkets open from about 7am to 6pm or 7pm on weekdays, and department stores generally from 10am to 6pm. Most shops stay open until 8pm on Thursday, but on Saturday they usually close at 1pm. Many private retail shops close early on Friday and throughout most of August.

Restaurants in Budapest can stay open till midnight or even later, but don't arrive at one in the provinces after 9pm or 9.30pm and expect to get much to eat.

Banking hours vary but are usually 8am to about 4pm Monday to Thursday and to 1pm on Friday. The main post office in any town or city opens from 8am to 6pm weekdays, and to noon or 1pm Saturday. Branch offices close much earlier – usually at 4pm – and are never open at the weekend.

With few exceptions, museums are open from 10am to 6pm Tuesday to Sunday from April to October and to 4pm on the same days the rest of the year.

Most places have a 'nonstop' – a convenience store, open very late or round-the-clock and selling basic food items, bottled drinks and cigarettes. Many of the hyper-supermarkets outside the big cities open on Sunday.

PUBLIC HOLIDAYS & SPECIAL EVENTS

Hungary celebrates 10 public holidays *(ünnep)* each year:

New Year's Day 1 January
1848 Revolution/National Day 15 March
Easter Monday March/April
International Labour Day 1 May
Whit Monday May/June
St Stephen's/Constitution Day 20 August
1956 Remembrance/Republic Day 23 October
All Saints' Day 1 November
Christmas holidays 25–26 December

Hungary's most outstanding annual events include:

February/March
Busójárás Pre-Lenten carnival held in Mohács on the weekend before Ash Wednesday

March
Budapest Spring Festival Hungary's largest cultural festival

May
Balaton Festival Music and street theatre to welcome in summer at Keszthely

June
Budapesti Búcsú Citywide 'Budapest Farewell' festival marking the departure of Soviet troops from Hungarian soil in 1991
Savaria International Dance Competition Ballroom dancing at its tackiest best in Szombathely
Sopron Festival Weeks Theatre, quiet music, folk dancing
Hungarian Dance Festival The nation's most prestigious dance festival, held in Győr
Debrecen Jazz Days Oldest jazz festival in the country

July
Hortobágy International Equestrian Days The largest horse and pony show around, held at Hortobágy-Máta
Winged Dragon International Street Theatre Festival Held in Nyírbátor
Kaláka Folk Festival Music, táncház and concerts at Miskolc and Diósgyőr
Danube Banks Folklore Festival Very authentic folk music and dance in Kalocsa, Baja and Szekszárd
Szeged Open-Air Festival The most celebrated theatre festival in Hungary
Haydn Festival A week of classical music performance at the Esterházy Castle in Fertőd

Martonvásár Days Held in the Martonvásár mansion where Ludwig van Beethoven once slept

August
Jászberény Summer/Csángó Festival A festival of folk dancing and music held in Jászberény
Pepsi Sziget Music Festival One of the biggest and best popular music festivals in Europe, held on Hajógyár Island in Budapest
Hungarian Formula One Grand Prix Held in Magyoród, 24km northeast of Budapest
St Stephen's/Constitution Day Marked nationwide with sporting events, parades and fireworks
Floral Carnival Held in Debrecen
Zemplén Arts Days Held in venues around the region but based in Sárospatak

September
Vintage and grape harvest festivals Held in wine-growing areas throughout Hungary

October/November
Budapest Marathon Race held along the Danube and across its bridges
Budapest Autumn Festival Held in venues throughout the capital from mid-October to early November

For more detailed coverage, pick up a copy of the HNTO's annual *Events in Hungary from January to December*.

ACTIVITIES

While Hungary is more of an educational and cultural experience than an active one when compared with, say, Australia, there's still plenty to do here. You could forsake many of the country's sights and spend your entire time boating, bird-watching or folk dancing.

Hungarians love a day out in the country to escape their relatively cramped living quarters and the pollution of the towns and cities, and nothing is more sacred than the *kirándulás* (outing), which can be a day of hiking, cycling, horse riding or just a picnic of *gulyás* cooked in a *bogrács* (kettle suspended over a fire with a tripod) in the open air by a river or lake.

Cycling

Hungary now counts 2500km of dedicated bicycle lanes, with more on the way. In addition, there are thousands of kilometres of roads with light traffic and dikes suitable for cycling. Among the areas to explore on two wheels are the Danube Bend, the Kál Basin southeast of Tapolca, the Hortobágy, the Őrség, Sopron and the Zemplén range.

[Continued on page 54]

The Wines of Hungary

ŐRNYEI BÉLA HALMAI JÁNOS ŐHEGYI JÁNOS MART

GÜNZER ZOLTÁN SÉLLYEI ANDRÁS

FEKETE KÁROLY ALBE

PELTZ ÁDÁM VÍGH JÓZSEf

MÜLLER JÁNOS

Previous page: Family-owned vineyard, Tokaj (Photo by David Greedy)

Top: Ponzichter Wine Cellar, Kőszeg

Bottom: Bottles of Villány wine stored in a 200-year-old cellar

THE WINES OF HUNGARY

Wine has been produced in Hungary for thousands of years, and it remains very important both economically and socially. You'll find it available by the glass or bottle everywhere in Budapest – at *borozók* (wine bars, but very basic affairs, almost like 'wine pubs'), food stalls, restaurants, supermarkets and 24-hour grocery stores – at reasonable prices. If you're seriously into wine, visit the speciality wine shops listed under Shopping in the Budapest chapter.

Before WWII Hungarian wine was much in demand throughout Europe, but with the advent of socialism and mass production, quality went down the drain. Most of what wasn't consumed at home went to the Soviet Union where, frankly, they were prepared to drink anything. Political and economic circumstances provided little incentive to upgrade antiquated standards of wine-making and to apply modern methods to traditional grape varieties.

All of that has changed over the past decade or so. Small- to medium-sized family-owned wineries such as Tiffán, Bock, Szeremley, Thummerer Szepsy and Demeter are now producing very fine wines indeed. Joint ventures with foreign vintners (for example, GIA in Eger partnered with Italians and the Hungarian-Austrian Gere-Weninger winery in Villány and Disznókő joined with French vintners in Tokaj) are helping to restructure the industry. All in all, wine production is arguably the most exciting business in Hungary right now.

When choosing a Hungarian wine, look for the words *minőségi bor* (quality wine) or *különleges minőségű bor* (premium quality wine), Hungary's version of the French quality regulation *appellation controlée*. Generally speaking, vintage *(évjárat)* has become important only recently; see the boxed text 'The Best Years of Their Lives' later in this special section.

WINE REGIONS

The quality of a label on a Hungarian wine can vary widely from bottle to bottle; a cheesy-looking label can sometimes announce a great wine. The first word of the name indicates where the wine comes from while the second word is the grape variety (eg, Villányi Kékfrankos) or the type or brand of wine (eg, Tokaji Aszú, Szekszárdi Bikavér). Other important words on a Hungarian wine label include: édes (sweet), fehér (white), féledes (semisweet), félszáraz (semidry or medium), pezsgő (sparkling), száraz (dry) and vörös (red).

With the inclusion in 1998 of two new wine regions (Balaton-melléke and Tolna, both producing mostly whites), Hungary now counts 22 distinct areas in Transdanubia, the Balaton region, the Northern Uplands and on the Great Plain. They range in size from tiny Somló (essentially just one hill) in Western Transdanubia, to the vast vineyards of the Kunság on the Southern Plain, with its sandy soil nurturing more than a third of all the grapevines growing in the country.

Of course it's all a matter of taste, but the most distinctive red wines come from Villány and Szekszárd in Southern Transdanubia and the best whites are produced around Lake Balaton and in Somló. The reds from Eger and sweet whites from Tokaj are much better known abroad, however, and these two regions are the most dynamic when it comes to wine production.

If you want to try the whites from Hungary's two 'new' regions, go for Lászlo Bussay's Csörnyeföldi Szürkebarat (Pinot Gris) from Balaton-melléke and Eurobor's Möcsényi Sauvignon Blanc from Tolna.

Tokaj

The volcanic soil, sunny climate and protective mountain barrier of the Tokaj-Hegyalja region in the Northern Uplands make it ideal for growing grapes and making wine. Tokaj wines were exported to Poland and Russia in the Middle Ages and reached the peak of their popularity in Europe in the 17th and 18th centuries, gaining some illustrious fans along the way. King Louis XIV famously called Tokaj 'the wine of kings and the king of wines', while Voltaire wrote that 'this wine could only be given by the boundlessly good God'.

Tokaj dessert wines are rated according to the number – from three to six – of *puttony* (butts, or baskets for picking) of sweet Aszú grapes added to the base wines. These are grapes infected with 'noble rot', a mould called *botrytis cinera* that almost turns them into raisins on the vine. Aszú Eszencia, an essence even sweeter than six-*puttony* wine, is added – very judiciously – to improve the wine.

Tokaj also produces less-sweet wines, including dry Szamorodni (an excellent aperitif) and sweet Szamorodni, which is not unlike an Italian *vin santo*. Of the four grape varieties gown here, Furmint and Hárslevelű (Linden Leaf) are the driest. Some Hungarian wine connoisseurs believe Furmint, with a flavour recalling apples, has the potential to become the best white wine in the country.

For Tokaji Aszú *the* name to look out for is István Szepsy, one of Hungary's most innovative winemakers, who concentrates on the upscale six-*puttony* variety as well as the Aszú *eszencia* itself. His 1998 six-*puttony* Aszú currently retails for a cool 13,750Ft a bottle (where available) and his Szepsy Cuvée 2000 for 10,900Ft. The Cuvée, aged in stainless steel barrels for a year or two (against the usual five for Tokaji Aszú) was first bottled in 1999 and is a complex, elegant blend comparable to Sauternes. Château Pajzos has produced an *eszencia* with such a high concentration of honey-sweet free-run juice that it is almost a syrup – a bottle of 1993 Pajzos Eszencia will set you back 65,300Ft. Disznókő produces a six-*puttony* Aszú (9000Ft) reminiscent of apricots, and a fine, sweet Szamorodni (2500Ft). Other names to watch out for in quality Tokaj wines are Oremus, Hétszőlő, Demeter and Degenfeld.

Vintage has always played a more important role in Tokaj than elsewhere in Hungary, and it is said that there is only one truly excellent year each decade. The wines produced in 1972, 1988, 1999 and 2000 were superb, though 1993 was almost as good.

Eger

Flanked by two of the Northern Uplands' most beautiful ranges of hills Eger is the home of the celebrated Egri Bikavér (Eger Bull's Blood). By law, Hungarian winemakers must spell out the blend on the label; the sole exception is Bikavér, though it's usually Kékfrankos (Blaufränkisch) mixed with other reds, sometimes including Kadarka. One of the few winemakers whose blend of Bikavér is known for sure is Tibor Gál. His blend is 50% Kékfrankos and 50% Cabernet and it is excellent. Other producers of Bikavér to watch out for include István Toth and Pók-Polonyi.

Eger produces Pinot Noir and some think Vilmos Thummerer's 1999 vintage (3400Ft) is on par with the *premiers crus* from Burgundy. Thummerer's 1999 Vili Papa Cuvée (Grandad Bill's Cuvée), a blend of Cabernet Franc, Cabernet Sauvignon and Merlot, is a monumental wine aged in new wood with fleshy fruit flavours, priced at 8000Ft. You'll also find several decent whites in Eger, including Leányka (Little Girl), Olaszrizling (Italian Riesling) and Hárslevelű from Debrő.

Villány

Villány-Siklós, in Hungary's southernmost and warmest region, is one of Hungary's principal producers of wine, noted especially for its red Kékoportó (Blauer Portugieser), Cabernet Franc, Cabernet Sauvignon and Merlot wines. They are almost always big-bodied Bordeaux-style wines and are high in tannin. Many are *barrique* wines – those aged in new oak barrels that are then discarded or passed on to other wineries – and remain a favourite of Hungarian yuppies, who like the 'big', recognisable flavours.

Among the best vintners in Villány is József Bock, whose Cuvée Barrique (4950Ft) is a smoky, earthy special blend of Kékfrankos (Blaufränkisch), Cabernet Franc and Merlot. Other wines to try include Attila Gere's elegant and complex Cabernet Sauvignon (3290Ft); Kopár, a blend of Cabernet Sauvignon, Cabernet Franc and Merlot; and Ede Tiffán's austere, tannic Kékoportó and Cabernet Franc. Among those to watch out for in the second generation are Márton Mayer and Alajos Wunderlich, especially his Cabernet Sauvignon (2700Ft).

The Best Years of Their Lives

1997 Excellent year for reds across the board, especially in Eger and Szekszárd

1998 Very mediocre year, except for producers of the very best reds (such as those from Villány)

1999 Superb year; biggest vintage for both whites and reds ever

2000 Very hot summer raised alcohol levels in whites, impairing acids and lowering quality; excellent year for reds in Eger, Sopron, Szekszárd and Villány

2001 Decent year for whites in general; very good for some top-end reds (such as those from Eger and Villány)

2002 Promises to be an extremely mixed year, estate by estate, and is dependent on how judiciously vintners chose the date of harvest in a difficult year. Expect some great wines, though.

Because of their international exposure, Villány wines tend to be overpriced. At present there is not much competition as the government slaps a duty of 70% on all imported wine. But once Hungary joins the European Union and the barriers come down, Villány wine, especially low- to medium-priced table wine, will suffer.

Szekszárd

Mild winters and warm, dry summers combined with favourable loess soil help Szekszárd in Southern Transdanubia to produce some of the best red wines in Hungary. They are not like the big-bodied reds of Villány, but softer and less complex, with a distinctive paprika flavour, and are easy to drink. In general they are much better value, with an excellent, premium-quality Szekszárd retailing from 2000Ft.

The premier grape here is Kadarka, a late-ripening and vulnerable variety which is produced in limited quantities. The best Kadarka is made by Ferenc Takler. Kadarka originated in the Balkans – the Bulgarian Gamza grape is a variety of it – and is a traditional ingredient in making Szekszárd Bikavér, a wine usually associated with Eger. In fact, many wine aficionados in Hungary prefer the Szekszárd variety of 'Bull's Blood'; try the Heimann 1999 label. The best Merlot and Kékfrankos from Szekszárd is produced by Ferenc Vesztergombi, who also makes an excellent Bikavér. Tamás Dúzsi is acknowledged to be the finest producer of Hungarian rosés; try his very dry 1999 Zweigelt.

Badacsony

The Badacsony region is named after the 400m-high basalt massif that rises like a bread loaf from the Tapolca Basin along the northwestern shore of Lake Balaton. Wine has been produced here for centuries, and the region's Olaszrizling, especially that produced by Huba Szeremley's Szent Orbán Winery (1500Ft), is arguably the best dry white wine for everyday drinking to be had in Hungary. Olaszrizling, a straw-blond Welschriesling high in acid that is related to the famous Rhine vintages in name only and is actually French in origin, is drunk young – in fact, the younger it is, the better. Szeremley's 2000 late harvest Olaszrizling (5500Ft) is sweeter.

The area's volcanic soil gives the unique Kéknyelű (Blue Stalk) wine its distinctive mineral taste; it is a blunt, complex and age-worthy tipple wine of very low yield. Szeremley's 2000 Kéknyelű (1970Ft) is the only reliably authentic example.

Somló

The entire region of Somló is a single volcanic dome, and the soil (basalt talus and volcanic tuff) helps to produce wine that is mineral-tasting, almost flinty. The region can boast two great and indigenous varieties: Hárslevelű and Juhfark (Sheep's Tail); the latter takes its name from the shape of its grape cluster. Firm acids give 'spine' to this wine, and it is best when five years old.

Foremost among the producers of Somló Hárslevelű and Juhfark (under 1000Ft) is Béla Fekete. Another big name in these parts is Imre Györgykovács, whose Olaszrizling (1500Ft) is a big wine with a taste vaguely reminiscent of burnt almonds. His 2000 Hárslevelű (3280Ft) is a brilliant golden wine, with a tart, mineral flavour.

Wine & Food

The pairing of food with wine is as great an obsession in Hungary as it is elsewhere. Everyone agrees that sweets like strudel *(rétes)* go very well indeed with a Tokaji Aszú, but what is less appreciated is the wonderful synergy that this wine enjoys with savoury foods like *foie gras* and such cheeses as Roquefort, Stilton and Gorgonzola. A bone-dry Olaszrizling from Badacsony is a superb accompaniment to any fish dish, but especially the *fogas* (pike-perch) indigenous to nearby Lake Balaton. Villány Sauvignon Blanc is an excellent accompaniment to goat's cheese.

It would be a shame to 'waste' a big wine like a Vili Papa Cuvée on traditional but simple Hungarian dishes like *gulyás* or *pörkölt*; save it for a more complex or sophisticated meat dish. Try Kékfrankos or Szekszárd Kadarka with the simpler dishes. Cream-based dishes stand up well to late-harvest Furmint, and pork dishes are nice with new Furmint or Kékfrankos. Try Hárslevelű with poultry.

For those who would like to learn more about Hungarian wines, the best source of information is the *Borkalauz* (Wine Guide) by István Mészáros and Gábor Rohály, published annually by the Borkollégium (Wine College) in Budapest. It is now available in English as *Rohály's Wine Guide Hungary* from Akó Publishing, III Retek utca 33 in Budapest. *The Wines and Vines of Hungary* by Stephen Kirkland is an introduction to Hungarian wines, but is fast going out of date. A specialised title is *Tokaj: The Wine of Freedom* by László Alkonyi.

Borbarát (or Friends of Wine) is a bilingual, fully illustrated quarterly magazine available at wine shops and some newsstands for 1120Ft, or 3600Ft for an annual subscription. Check out its English-language newsletter on the website at Ⓦ www.friendsofwine.com.

[Continued from page 48]

The HNTO produces the useful *Cycling in Hungary* brochure, with 12 recommended routes with maps, as well as a 60-page insert crammed with practical information. Cartographia publishes a series of regional 1:100,000 Tourist Maps (*Turistatérkép*; 650Ft), with bicycling routes marked and explanatory notes in English. Another option is the 1:250,000-scale *Cycling around Hungary* (*Kerékpártúrák Magyarországon*; 2600Ft) from Frigoria, with 100 tours outlined and places of interest and service centres listed in several languages, including English.

For information and advice on cycling contact the helpful **Hungarian Bicycle Touring Association** (*MKTSZ;* ☎ *1-311 2467;* e *mktsz@dpg.hu; VI Bajcsy-Zsilinszky út 31)* in Budapest. Also in the capital, the enthusiastic **Friends of Nature Bike Touring Association** (*TTE;* ☎ *1-316 5867; II Bem rakpart 51)* can answer questions, help organise bike tours (5000Ft) and supply guides (2500Ft plus board and lodging).

Balázs and Friends Bike Club (*BBBSE;* ☎/*fax 1-227 6236; XXII Háros utca 47-49)* in Budapest has one- or two-day cycle trips (2000Ft to 9000Ft, including transport and accommodation) throughout the year. Also in the capital, **Velo-Touring** (☎ *1-319 0571;* w *www.velo-touring.hu; XI Előpatak utca 1)* is a large cycling travel agency that sponsors an eight-day spa tour (five thermal spas Budapest to Hajdúszoboszló; €645), an 11-day Danube Bend to Balaton tour (€717) and an 11-day tour of the *puszta* (€706). Prices include bike, accommodation and two meals a day; groups can range from eight to 20 cyclists.

Hiking

Though Hungary does not have high mountains, you can enjoy good hiking in the forests around Visegrád, Esztergom, Badacsony, Kőszeg and Budapest. North of Eger are the Bükk Hills, and south of Kecskemét is the Bugac Puszta; both areas contain national parks (Bükk and Kiskunság, respectively) with marked hiking trails.

Cartographia publishes three dozen hiking maps (average scales 1:40,000 and 1:50,000; 650/1600Ft folded/spiral-bound) to the hills, forests, rivers and lakes of Hungary. Most are available from its outlet in Budapest (see

Maps under Planning earlier, or under Orientation in the Budapest chapter). On hiking maps, paths usually appear as a red line and with a letter, or an abbreviation in Hungarian, indicating the colour-coding of the trail. Colours are painted on trees and markers and are 'K' for *kék* (blue), 'P' for *piros* (red), 'S' for *sárga* (yellow) and 'Z' for *zöld* (green).

Contact the nonprofit **Hungarian Friends of Nature Federation** (*MTSZ;* ☎ *1-311 2467, 332 7177;* w *www.fsz.bme.hu/mtsz; VI Bajcsy-Zsilinszky út 31)* in Budapest for information and advice. The HNTO produces the free *The Beauty of Nature: 11,000 kms of Marked Rambling Paths*, with ideas for treks and walks around the country and an insert with practical information and tips.

Swimming

Swimming is extremely popular in Hungary, and most towns have both a covered and an outdoor pool, allowing enthusiasts to get into the water all year. The entry fee is low (from 500Ft), and you can often rent swimming costumes and bathing caps (the latter are mandatory in some pools for both sexes) for about the same price. All pools have a locker system. Find one, get changed in it (or beside it) and call over the attendant. He or she will lock the door with your clothes inside and hand you a numbered tag to tie on your costume. Note: In order to prevent theft lest you lose or misplace the tag, the number is not the same as the one on the locker, so commit the *locker* number to memory. Lakes and rivers of any size have a grassy *strand* (beach), usually with showers and changing facilities.

Thermal Baths

Since Roman times settlers have been enjoying Hungary's ample thermal waters, and today there are no fewer than 100 spas open to the public throughout the country. Many spas, such as those at Hajdúszoboszló, Sárvár, Gyula and Balatonfüred, are very serious affairs indeed, and people come to 'take the waters' for specific maladies, be they respiratory, muscular, cardiac or gynaecological. Many spa hotels at such places offer cure packages (including accommodation, board, use of the spa and other facilities, medical examination etc) that last a week or longer. **Danubius Travel** (☎ *1-317 3562;* w *www.danubiusgroup.com; V Szervita tér 8)* in Budapest is the expert in this field and books packages.

The procedure for getting into the warm water is similar to the one for swimming pools, though in Budapest's baths you will sometimes be given a number and will have to wait until it is called or appears on the electronic board. Though some of the local spas and baths look a little rough around the edges, they are clean and the water is changed regularly. You might consider taking along a pair of plastic sandals or thongs, however.

Windsurfing

Wherever there's water, a bit of wind and a camp site, you'll find sailboards for rent (eg, on Lake Tisza at Abádszalók, Lake Pécs at Orfű, Lake Velence at Gárdony and Velence town and Lake Fertőd near Fertőrákos. The main place for the sport, however, is Lake Balaton, especially at Keszthely, Balatonszabadi, Balatonvilágos and Balatonaliga. The best time for the sport is early and late summer, as the wind tends to die down in July and August.

The **Hungarian Surfers Association** (MSZSZ; ☎ 1-319 9304; e husurf@freemail .hu; XII Jagelló utca 26) in Budapest can answer any questions you may have about the sport.

Boating & Kayaking

Qualified sailors can rent boats at locations around Lake Balaton, including Balatonfüred, Siófok, Balatonaliga, Balatonalmádi and Balatonkenese. Only sailing boats and those with electric motors are allowed on the lake. For information check out w www .yacht.hu. Expect to pay from 200,000Ft to 400,000Ft per week for a yacht holding six to eight people.

As Hungary is in a basin, it has many rivers of varying sizes; there are some 4000km of passable waterways and up to 40,000km are navigable by canoe or kayak at some point during the year. Boat rental, food and camping along the rivers and lakes is cheap; in fact an *evezőstúra* (rowing outing) is considered the 'poor man's holiday' in Hungary and is popular with students and intellectuals.

There are many canoe and kayak trips available. Following the Danube from Rajka to Mohács (386km) or the Tisza River from Tiszabecs to Szeged (570km) are popular runs, but there are less congested waterways and shorter trips such as the 210km stretch of the Körös and Tisza Rivers from Békés to Szeged or the Rába River from Szentgotthárd to Győr (205km).

The HNTO publishes a brochure titled *Water Tourism: 3500km of waterways*, which introduces what's available on Hungary's rivers, streams and canals and offers practical information. Magyar Térképház and Cartographia publish several water-sport maps (Vízitúrázók Térképei; 400Ft to 1000Ft) to the rivers and lakes of Hungary (eg, the 1:50,000 *Sajó* and the 1:20,000 *Duna*).

The water tours section of the **Hungarian Friends of Nature Federation** (☎ 1-311 9289; w www.fsz.bme.hu/mtsz; VI Bajcsy-Zsilinszky út 31) in Budapest will be of assistance. You can find all the kayak and canoe clubs in Hungary listed on the website of the **Hungarian Kayak-Canoe Association** (MKKSZ; w www.mkksz.hu), and many of them can provide information or help you plan a route in their area.

Vizitura (☎ 1-280 8182, 06-20 939 0786; w www.vizitura.hu; IX Pöttyös utca 3) in Budapest organises tours on all Hungary's rivers. A four-seat canoe rents for 1000Ft to 1500Ft a day and a guide is 8000Ft (in Hungarian) and 16,000Ft (in English) a day.

Bird-watching

For details on the excellent possibilities for bird-watching in Hungary and a list of the best sites, see the boxed text 'The Birds of Hungary' in the Facts about Hungary chapter.

Fishing

You'll see people fishing in waterways everywhere. The water surface area of Hungary measures 130,000 hectares, and anglers make use of almost half of it.

In order to fish, you need a national fishing licence valid for a year as well as a local one issued by the day, week, month or year for the area that interests you. You can usually buy them at the same place – anglers' clubs and associations, tackle shops or even ticket booths by the water at the more popular venues.

The best source of information is the **National Federation of Hungarian Anglers** (MOHOSZ; ☎ 1-319 9790, fax 319 9792; w www.mohosz.hu; XII Korompai utca 17) in Budapest.

Horse Riding

There's a Hungarian saying that the Magyars were 'created by God to sit on horseback'.

Judging from the number of stables, riding schools and courses around the country, that is still true today. The HNTO produces a useful 64-page brochure called *Riding in Hungary* with both general and very detailed information.

A lot of the horse riding in Hungary is the follow-the-leader variety up to a castle or through open fields, but larger schools have horses for more advanced equestrians that can be taken into the hills or across the *puszta*. These schools also offer lessons. Not surprisingly, the best centres are on the Great Plain – at Máta near Hortobágy, Lajosmizse and Bugacpuszta near Kecskemét, and Solt, north of Kalocsa. In Transdanubia you'll find good schools at Nagycenk and Szombathely while around Lake Balaton they're at Szántódpuszta and Keszthely. Gizellatelep near Visegrád has some of the best horse flesh in the country, but nothing beats mounting a Lipizzaner at the stud farm at Szilvásvárad in the Northern Uplands.

It's risky – particularly in the high season – to show up at a riding centre without a booking. The non-profit **Hungarian Equestrian Tourism Association** *(MLTSZ; ☎ 1-456 0444;* w *www.equi.hu; IX Ráday utca 8)* in Budapest can provide you with a list of recommended riding schools. Also in the capital, **Pegazus Tours** *(☎ 1-317 1644, fax 266 2827;* e *oryc silla@pegazus.hu; V Ferenciek tere 5)* organises riding tours of between three days and a week (€290 to €850) in Transdanubia, the Great Plain and around Lake Balaton.

The **Somogy Provincial Association for Nature Conservation** *(STVSZ; ☎ 06-30 226 9553;* w *www.stvsz.hu; Kossuth Lajos utca 62)* in Somogyfajsz northwest of Kaposvár is a conservation NGO that organises excellent six-day riding tours in open countryside from Lake Balaton to the Dráva River. Prices are €100 per day (€60 if you opt to ride in the carriage) with everything included, and children go half-price.

Hunting

Whether you like it or not, hunting is big business in Hungary, and roe and red deer, mouflon, wild pig, hare, pheasant and duck abound in wooded areas such as the Gemenc Forest in Southern Transdanubia and wild boar in the Zemplén. Of the latter we are certain; one of us struck a three-year-old *vaddisznó* while cruising along highway No 37 from

Sárospatak to Tokaj in broad daylight! Strict rules apply, and you must do your hunting through one of the large hunting agencies such as Budapest-based **Pannonvad** *(☎ 1-375 4089; I Várfok utca 15/b)* or **Mavad** *(☎ 1-201 6445, fax 201 6371; I Úri utca 39)*.

LANGUAGE COURSES

Schools teaching Hungarian to foreigners have proliferated – at least in Budapest – over the past five years. For more information and a list of reliable Hungarian-language schools in the capital see Language Courses in the Budapest chapter.

The granddaddy of all Hungarian language schools is the **Debrecen Summer University** *(Debreceni Nyári Egyetem; ☎/fax 52-489 117;* w *www.nyariegyetem.hu; Egyetem tér 1)* in Debrecen. It organises intensive two- and four-week courses in July and August and 80-hour, two-week advanced courses in winter. The emphasis is not just on language but the whole Magyar picture: art, history, culture, literature. The two-week/four-week (60-hour/120-hour) summer courses cost €350/640; board and lodging in a triple room costs €200/390 (singles and doubles are available at extra cost). There's also now a Budapest branch *(☎/fax 1-320 5751; Jászai Mari tér 6)* with regular and intensive courses lasting three/six weeks (60/120 hours) for €240/470.

WORK

Travellers on tourist visas in Hungary are not supposed to accept employment, but many end up teaching, doing a little writing for the English-language press or even working for foreign firms without permits. Check the English-language telephone book or advertisements for English-language schools in the *Budapest Sun*, which also has job listings though pay is generally pretty low. You can do much better teaching privately (2000Ft to 4000Ft per 45-minute 'hour', depending on your experience).

Obtaining a work permit *(munkavállalási engedély)* involves a Byzantine paper chase. You'll need a letter of support from your prospective employer, copies of your birth certificate, your academic record officially translated into Hungarian (about 3000Ft per page) and results of a recent medical examination (including a test for exposure to HIV; 4000Ft). The employer then submits these to the local labour centre *(munkaügyi központ)*, and you *must* return to your country of residence and apply for the work permit (about US$40 or equivalent) at the Hungarian embassy or consulate there.

When you return to Hungary, you have 15 days to gather all the documents required to apply for a one-year renewable residence permit (*tartózkodási engedély*; 8000Ft) through the main police station (*főkapitányság*) in your district or city.

ACCOMMODATION

Except during the peak summer season (ie, July and August) in Budapest, most of Lake Balaton, the Danube Bend and the Mátra Hills, you should have no problem finding accommodation to fit your budget in Hungary. Camp sites are plentiful, university and college dormitories open their doors to guests during summer and other holiday periods, former trade-union holiday homes have been converted into hostels and hotels and family-run pensions have sprung up everywhere. It's unusual for even a small town not to have a hotel, and paying-guest services (see Private Rooms later) are available everywhere.

The price quoted should be the price you pay, but it's not as cut-and-dried. There's a 10% turnover tax on all hotels, though this should definitely be included in the price you've been told. In the past, all hotels and pensions included breakfast in their rates, but this is changing – now quite a few don't. Certain places insist on a 'mandatory breakfast' and charge you from 500Ft even if you don't want it.

Tourist offices and bureaus charge you a small fee for booking a private room or other accommodation, and there's usually a surcharge if you stay for less than three nights. Most cities and towns now levy a local tourist tax of 150Ft to 250Ft per person per night (more in Budapest), though sometimes only after the first 48 hours. People under 18 years of age or staying at camp sites may be exempt.

It is sometimes difficult to get a single room. Outside expensive hotels, a room is designated a single, double or triple according to how many beds it has and not by the number of occupants. If you are travelling solo and the owners try to charge you for a double, insist – pleasantly – that you are alone. You should be able to negotiate the price down depending on the location, season and staff.

Inflation is running at just under 10%, so prices will almost certainly be higher than those quoted in this book, although they shouldn't change much when quoted in euros, and the relative differences between various establishments in forint should stay the same. The room rate usually increases in April for the summer season – sometimes by as much as 30%. Where possible, we've indicated seasonal price differences in this book (eg, 'doubles 8000Ft to 11,500Ft').

Camping

Hungary has more than 400 camp sites, and these are the cheapest places to stay. Small, private camp sites accommodating as few as six tents are usually preferable to the large, noisy, 'official' sites. Prices for two adults plus tent vary from as low as 1500Ft off the beaten track in the Northern Uplands, to 10 times that amount on Lake Balaton in summer.

Most camp sites open from April or May to September or October and also rent small bungalows (*üdölőházak* or *faházak*) from around 4000Ft to those without tents. In midsummer the bungalows may all be booked, so it pays to check with the local Tourinform office before making the trip. A Camping Card International will sometimes get you a discount of 5% or 10%. Camping 'wild' is prohibited in Hungary. Tourinform's *Camping Hungary* map lists every site in the land.

For more information, contact the **Hungarian Camping and Caravaning Club** (MCCC; ☎ 1-317 3703; VIII Üllői út 6) in Budapest.

Hostels & University Accommodation

Despite all the places listed in the handbook of the Budapest-based **Hungarian Youth Hostel Association** (MISZSZ; ☎ 1-413 2065, fax 321 4851; Ⓦ www.youthhostels.hu; 3rd floor, VII Baross tér 15), an HI card doesn't get you very far in Hungary. With the exception of those in Budapest, most of the youth hostels (*ifjúsági szállók*) are in places well off the beaten track. Generally, the only year-round hostels are in Budapest.

Hostel beds cost from 1700Ft to 3300Ft, depending on room size, and doubles 2800Ft to 4700Ft in Budapest; the prices drop considerably in the countryside. An HI card is not required, although you will occasionally get 10% off the price or not be required to pay the tourist tax if you have one. There's no age limit at hostels, which remain open all day and are often good places to meet other travellers. The hostels almost always have cooking facilities and most now have Internet access and laundry facilities.

From 1 July to 20 August and sometimes during Eastern holidays, Hungary's cheapest rooms are available at vacant student dormitories, known as a *kollégium* or *diákszálló*, where beds in double, triple and quadruple rooms begin at around 800Ft per person. There's no need to show a student or hostel card, and it usually won't get you any discount anyway.

Private Rooms

Hungary's 'paying-guest service' *(fizetővendég szolgálat)* is a great deal and still relatively cheap though perhaps not as widespread as it once was. Expect to pay from 2000Ft (from 3600Ft in Budapest) per person, depending on the class and location of the room. Private rooms at Lake Balaton are always more expensive, even in the shoulder seasons. Single rooms are often hard to come by, and you'll usually have to pay a 30% supplement if you stay less than three nights.

Private rooms are usually assigned by travel agencies, which give you a voucher bearing the address and sometimes even the key to the house or flat. If the first room you're offered seems too expensive, ask if there's something cheaper. There are usually several agencies offering rooms, so ask around if the price seems higher than usual or the location inconvenient.

If you decide to take a private room, you'll share a house or flat with a Hungarian widow, couple or family. The toilet facilities are usually communal, but otherwise you can close your door and enjoy as much privacy as you please. All 1st- and some 2nd- and 3rd-class rooms have shared kitchen facilities. In Budapest you may have to take a room far from the centre of town, but public transport is good and inexpensive. Some agencies also have entire flats or holiday homes for rent without the owner in residence. These can be a good deal if there are four or more of you travelling together and you want to stay put for a while.

Individuals at train stations and travel agencies in Budapest and around Lake Balaton may offer you an unofficial private room. The prices these people ask are often higher than those at the agencies, and you will have no one to complain to in case of problems. They vary considerably and cases of travellers being promised an idyllic room in the centre of town, only to be taken to a dreary, cramped flat in some distant suburb, are not unknown. On the other hand, we've received dozens of letters extolling the virtues of the landlords whom readers have dealt with directly in this way. You really have to use your own judgement here. In resort areas look for houses with signs reading '*szoba kiadó*' or '*Zimmer frei*', advertising private rooms in Hungarian or German.

Farmhouses

'Village tourism', which means staying at a farmhouse, can be even cheaper than a private room in a town or city but most of the places are truly remote, and you'll usually need your own transport. Contact Tourinform or the **National Association of Village & Agrotourism** *(FAOSZ; ☎/fax 1-268 0592; VII Király utca 93)* in Budapest for information.

Pensions

Privately run pensions *(panziók)*, which have formed the biggest growth area in the Hungarian hospitality trade over the past decade, are really just little hotels of up to a dozen or so rooms charging from 8500Ft for a double with shower. They are usually new and very clean and usually have an attached restaurant.

Most pensions in Budapest (where there are as many pensions as there are hotel rooms) are up in the Buda Hills, while in the provinces they're usually a couple of kilometres on the road out of town. Thus they're best for people travelling under their own steam, and visitors from Austria and Germany seem to favour them. But that's changing too, and you'll sometimes find them downtown in cities like Budapest, Győr, Sopron and Pécs, along the Danube Bend and on Lake Balaton. Always ask to see a room first as they can vary. Those under the roof – so-called 'mansard rooms' – are cramped but a lot cheaper. You are sometimes allowed to use the kitchen at a pension.

Hotels

Hotels, called *szállók* or *szállodák*, run the gamut from luxurious five-star palaces to the run-down old communist-era hovels that still survive in some towns.

A cheap hotel will be more expensive than a private room, but it may be the answer if you're only staying one night or if you arrive too late to get a private room through an agency. Two-star hotels usually have rooms with a private bathroom; it's always down the hall in a one-star place. Three- and four-star hotels – many of which are brand-new or newly renovated old villas – can be excellent value compared with those in other European countries.

Breakfast – a meal at which the Hungarians decidedly do not excel – is usually (but not always) included in the room price. Expect ersatz coffee, weak tea, unsweetened lemon 'juice', tiny triangles of processed 'cheese' and stale bread.

For the big splurge, if you're romantically inclined, or if you're travelling with a rich uncle or aunt, check Hungary's network of castle or mansion hotels (*kastély szállók* or *kúria szállók*). These need not break the bank: the one at Esterházy Palace in Fertőd, for example, charges 4200/5800/6600Ft for doubles/triples/quads with shared bathroom, and the stunning Kastély hotel at the Zichy family's country manor house at Seregélyes near Székesfehérvár costs €78 for a double. But most of the fancy castle hotels have at least three stars and charge accordingly. The HNTO brochure *Historic Mansions, Castles and Palaces* lists more than two dozen of the nation's finest residences, including those that accept guests.

FOOD

Much has been written about Hungarian food – some of it silly, much of it downright false. It's true that Hungarian cuisine has had many outside influences and that it makes great use of paprika. But that spice is pretty mild stuff; a taco with salsa or a chicken vindaloo from the corner takeaway will taste a lot more 'fiery' to you. It's also true that Hungarians eat an astonishing amount of meat.

Hungary's reputation as a food centre dates partly from the last century and partly from the chilly days of communism. In the heady days following the advent of the Dual Monarchy and right up to WWII, food became a passion among well-to-do city folk, and writers and poets sang its praises. This was the 'gilded age' of the famous chef Károly Gundel, the confectioner József Dobos and the Gypsy violinists Jancsi Rigo and Gyula Benczi, an age when nothing was too extravagant. The world took note and Hungarian restaurants sprouted up in cities around the world – including a 'Cafe Budapest' in Boston, Massachusetts – complete with imported Gypsy bands and waiters who sounded like Bela Lugosi and Zsa Zsa Gabor.

After the war, Hungary's gastronomic reputation lived on – most notably because everything else in the region was so very bad. Hungarian food was, as one observer noted, 'a bright spot in a culinary black hole'. But most of the best chefs, including Gundel himself, had voted with their feet and left the country in the 1950s, and restaurants were put under state control. The reputation and the reality of food in Hungary had diverged.

Although inexpensive by Western standards and served in huge portions, Hungarian food today remains heavy and, frankly, can be unhealthy. Meat, sour cream and fat abound and, except in season, *saláta* means a plate of pickled beets, cabbage and peppers. There are some bright spots, though – especially in Budapest. A fair few vegetarian restaurants (or ones at least halfway there) have opened up, and ethnic food – from Middle Eastern and Italian to fast-food Thai and Chinese – is very popular. And even Hungarian food itself is undergoing a long-awaited transformation at many middle-level and upmarket restaurants. Many Magyars have tried 'New Hungarian' cuisine and seem to like it – to judge from the bookings at the establishments serving it.

On the whole, Hungarians are not big breakfast eaters at home, preferring a cup of tea or coffee with an unadorned bread roll at the kitchen table or on the way to work. (It is said that Hungarians will 'eat bread with bread'.) Lunch, eaten at 1pm, is traditionally the main meal in the countryside and can consist of two or three courses, but this is no longer the case for working people in the cities and towns. Dinner – supper, really – is less substantial when eaten at home, often just sliced meats, cheese and some pickled vegetables.

Dishes & Cooking Methods

The most famous traditional meal is *gulyás* (or *gulyásleves*), a thick beef soup cooked with onions and potatoes and usually eaten as a main course. *Pörkölt* (stew) is closer to what we call 'goulash' abroad; the addition of sour cream and paprika makes the dish, whatever it may contain, *paprikás*.

Many dishes are seasoned with paprika, which appears on restaurant tables as a condiment beside the salt and pepper shakers. It's quite a mild spice and is used predominantly with sour cream or in *rántás*, a heavy roux of pork lard and flour added to cooked vegetables.

Things stuffed *(töltött)* with meat and rice, such as cabbage or peppers, are cooked in *rántás*, tomato sauce or sour cream. *Lecsó* is a tasty stewed sauce of peppers, tomatoes and onions served with meat.

Another Hungarian favourite is fisherman's soup *(halászlé)*, a rich mixture of several kinds of poached freshwater fish, tomatoes, green peppers and paprika. It's a meal in itself.

Pork, beef, turkey and chicken are the most common meats and can be breaded and fried or baked. Chicken and goose legs and turkey breasts – though not much else of the birds – make it on to most menus, as does beef. Freshwater fish from Lake Balaton, such as the indigenous *fogas* (pike-perch), is plentiful, but quite expensive and often overcooked. Lamb and mutton are rarely eaten in Hungary.

A main course usually comes with some sort of starch and a little garnish of pickles. Vegetables and salads must be ordered separately. A typical menu will have up to 10 pork and beef dishes, a couple of fish ones and usually only one poultry dish.

Vegetarian Food

In restaurants, vegetarians can usually order fried mushroom caps *(gombafejek rántva)*, pasta dishes with cheese such as *túrós csusza* and *sztrapacska*, or plain little dumplings *(galuszka)*. Salad as it's usually known around the world is called *vitamin saláta* here and is usually available when in season; everything else is *savanyúság* (literally 'sourness') or pickled things. Boiled vegetables *(zöldség)* are 'English-style' or *angolos zöldség*. The traditional way of preparing vegetables is in *főzelék*, where they're fried or boiled and then mixed into a roux with cream.

Other vegetarian dishes include *rántott sajt* (fried cheese), *gomba leves* (mushroom soup), *gyümölcs leves* (fruit soup) and *sajtos kenyér* (sliced bread with soft cheese). *Bableves* (bean soup) usually contains meat. Pancakes *(palacsinta)* may be savoury and made with cheese *(sajt)* or mushrooms *(gomba)* or sweet and prepared with nuts *(dió)* or poppy seeds *(mák)*.

Lángos, a deep-fried dough with various toppings, is a cheap meatless snack sold on streets throughout the land.

Restaurants

It's useful to know the names of the types of Hungarian eateries though distinctions are sometimes blurred.

An *étterem* is a restaurant with a large selection, including international dishes. A *vendéglő* or *kisvendéglő* is smaller and is supposed to serve inexpensive regional dishes or 'home cooking', but the name is now 'cute' enough for a lot of large places to use it. An *étkezde* is something like a *vendéglő* but cheaper, smaller and often with counter seating. The overused term *csárda* originally signified a country inn with a rustic atmosphere, Gypsy music and hearty local dishes. Now any place that strings dry paprikas on the wall is a *csárda*. Most restaurants offer a good-value set menu *(menü)* of two or three courses at lunch. A *bisztró* is a much cheaper sit-down place that is usually *önkiszolgáló* (self-service). A *büfé* is cheaper still with a very limited menu. Here you eat while standing at counters.

Many butcher shops *(hentesáru bolt)* have a *büfé* selling boiled or fried *kolbász* (sausage), *wirsli* (frankfurters), roast chicken, bread and pickles. Point to what you want; the staff will weigh it all and hand you a slip of paper with the price. You usually pay at the *pénztar* (cashier) and hand the stamped receipt back to the staff for your food. Food stalls, known as *Laci konyha* (Larry's kitchen) or *pecsenyesütő* (roast oven), sell the same sorts of things, as well as fish when located beside lakes or rivers. At these last few places you pay for everything, including a dollop of mustard for your *kolbász*, and eat with your hands.

An *eszpresszó* is essentially a coffee house, but usually also sells alcoholic drinks and light snacks. A *cukrászda* serves cakes, pastries and ice cream.

Restaurant menus are often translated into German and sometimes into English, with mixed degrees of success. The main categories on a menu are *előételek* (appetisers), *levesek* (soups), *saláták* (salads), *készételek* (ready-made dishes that are just heated up), *frissensültek* (dishes made to order), *halételek* or *halak* (fish dishes), *szárnyasok* (poultry dishes), *köretek* (side dishes), *édességek* or *tészták* (desserts) and *sajtok* (cheese).

It is not unknown for waiters to try to rip you off once they see you are a foreigner. They may try to bring you an unordered dish or make a 'mistake' when tallying the bill. If you think there's a discrepancy, ask for the menu and check the bill carefully. The most common ruse is to bring you the most expensive beer or wine when you order a draught or a glass. Ask the price before you order.

If you've been taken for more than 15% or 20% of the bill, call for the manager. Otherwise just don't leave a tip (see Tipping & Bargaining earlier in this chapter).

DRINKS
Nonalcoholic Drinks

Most international soft drink brands are available in Hungary, but mineral water seems to be the most popular libation for teetotallers in pubs and bars. Fruit juice is usually canned or boxed fruit 'drink' with lots of sugar added.

Hungarians drink a tremendous amount of coffee *(kávé)* – as a single black *(fekete)*, a double *(dupla)* or with milk *(tejes kávé)*. Most better cafés now serve some variation of cappuccino. Decaffeinated coffee is *koffeinmentes kávé'*.

Black tea *(tea;* **tay**-ah) is not popular in Hungary (though teahouses have become the bee's knees in the trendier neighbourhoods of Budapest in recent years). In fact, it can often be difficult to find 'English' tea in small grocery stores, though you'll always be able to choose from a wide range of herbal teas and fruit tisanes. When Hungarians do drink tea they never add milk, preferring lemon or honey.

Alcoholic Drinks

Places in which to sample the local vintage or brew include: a *borozó*, an establishment (usually a dive) serving wine; a *pince*, which can be a beer or wine cellar; and a *söröző*, a pub with draught beer *(csapolt sör)* on tap.

Wine Wine has been produced in Hungary for thousands of years and you'll find it available by the glass or bottle everywhere. See the special section 'The Wines of Hungary'.

Brandy & Liqueur An alcoholic drink that is as Hungarian as wine is *pálinka*, a strong brandy distilled from a variety of fruits but most commonly from plums or apricots. There are many different types and qualities but the best is Óbarack, the double-distilled 'Old Apricot', and the Gundel label.

Hungarian liqueurs are usually unbearably sweet and taste artificial, though the Zwack brand is reliable. Zwack also produces Unicum, a bitter aperitif that has been around since 1790. The Austrian emperor Joseph II christened the liqueur when he tasted it and supposedly exclaimed *'Das ist ein Unikum!'*

(This is a unique drink!). It remains an acquired taste for most non-Magyars.

Beer Hungary produces a number of its own beers for national distribution (eg, Dreher and Kőbanyai). Some, though, are usually found only near where they are brewed – such as Kanizsai in Nagykanizsa and Szalon in Pécs. Bottled Austrian, German and Czech beers are readily available. Locally brewed and imported beer in Hungary is almost always lager, though occasionally you'll come across Dreher stout.

ENTERTAINMENT

Hungary is a *very* cultured society, and the arts – particularly music – are dear to the hearts (and ears) of most people. Many cities and even some large towns have a symphony or chamber orchestra, a theatre where plays and musicals are staged, and a cultural centre where other events take place. Outside Budapest, cultural life is especially active in Debrecen, Eger, Győr, Kecskemét, Pécs, Sopron, Szeged, Szombathely and Veszprém. Festivals in spring, summer and autumn are scheduled in cities throughout the country (see Public Holidays & Special Events earlier in this chapter), and some of them (eg, the Budapest Spring Festival) attract both talent and spectators from abroad. Some useful words to remember are *színház* (theatre), *pénztár* (box office), *jegy* (ticket) and *elkelt* (sold out).

In the first few years after the fall of communism, the loss of state subsidies forced many smaller festivals and groups to cut back their events and performances. Theatre troupes, which now had to rely on box-office receipts, abandoned classical and avant-garde drama in favour of imported musical productions such as *Macskák* (Cats), *Sakk* (Chess) or *Funny Girl*. But things seem to have gone full circle and along with popular musicals and classic and modern Hungarian plays by Mihály Babits and István Örkény, theatregoers can choose anything and everything from Joe Orton's *Amit a Lakáj Látott* (What the Butler Saw) and Shakespeare's *A Vihar* (The Tempest) to Martin McDonagh's *A Kripli* (The Cripple of Inishmaan) and Marie Jones' *Kövek a Zsebben* (Stones in His Pockets).

Your best single source of information for performances nationwide is the bilingual monthly *Programme in Ungarn/in Hungary*. Complete listings of plays, concerts, exhibitions and films for the capital can be found in the weekly *Pesti Műsor* and the freebie *Pesti Est*, available in Hungarian only (see Entertainment in the Budapest chapter for details). The latter publishes editions to almost 18 other cities and regions – from *Békés Est* to *Zalai Est*. You can pick these up for free in tourist offices.

Tickets, for as little as 600Ft to the opera in Budapest, can be purchased at the venue. It's always safer to get tickets in advance, though, particularly in smaller towns where the production may be the big event of the month and the place 'to be seen'. You'll find the addresses of ticket offices and information sources under individual cities and towns.

Of course, it's not all Beethoven and Brecht here. Hungary is now on the circuit for big international pop and rock bands, and the Pepsi Sziget Music Festival in Budapest in August (see Public Holidays & Special Events earlier) is now Europe's largest outdoor music festival.

The *táncház* (literally 'dance house'), an evening of Hungarian folk music and some traditional dance, is great entertainment and an excellent way to meet Hungarians. You'll find few *táncház* venues outside the capital, though.

Be aware that many foreign films are dubbed into Hungarian, so try asking the ticket seller if the film retains the original soundtrack and has Hungarian subtitles (*feliratos*) – all films listed under their English titles are in this category – or is dubbed (*szinkronizált* or *magyarul beszélő*, often abbreviated as 'mb' in listings).

Seats are assigned in most cinemas, and admission costs between 350Ft and 950Ft, depending on the time and day of the week. In theatres, there are *bal* (left) and *jobb* (right) seats with the same numbers so make sure you know which one you are. To make sure you arrive at the correct time, see Time earlier in this chapter.

Discos and clubs – which range from Budapest's rollicking rave houses to unpretentious get-togethers in provincial sport halls – are the most popular form of entertainment for young people and are usually always good fun. Striptease and sex shows attract foreigners and the well-heeled Hungarian *új gazdag* (nouveau riche).

SPECTATOR SPORTS

Swimming is extremely popular as is water polo, a sport at which Hungary excels. For its size, Hungary has done extremely well in the Olympics. At the 2000 Olympic Games in Sydney, for example, they finished 10th overall, with 17 medals (including eight gold, six silver and three bronze). At the 1996 games in Atlanta, they placed 12th with 21 medals and at Barcelona in 1992 they ranked eighth with 30 medals. Chess is also hugely popular – even as a spectator sport!

Football is far and away the nation's favourite sport, and people still talk about the 'match of the century' at Wembley in 1953 when the Magic Magyars beat England 6-3 (the first time England lost a home match). The Hungarian Formula One Grand Prix in August is the sporting event of the year for those in and around the capital.

For more details on Hungarian sports and where and when to watch them see the Spectator Sports section in the Budapest chapter.

SHOPPING

Hungarian shops are well stocked with generally high-quality products. Books and folk-music tapes and CDs are affordable, and there is an excellent selection. Traditional products include folk-art embroidery and ceramics, wall hangings, painted wooden toys and boxes, dolls, all forms of basketry and porcelain (especially Herend, Zsolnay or the cheaper Kalocsa). Feather or goose-down pillows and duvets (comforters) are of exceptionally high quality.

Foodstuffs that are expensive or difficult to buy elsewhere – goose liver (both fresh and potted), caviar and some prepared meats such as Pick salami – make nice gifts (if you are allowed to take them home), as do the many varieties of paprika.

Some of Hungary's 'boutique' wines – especially those with imaginative labels – make good, inexpensive gifts. A bottle of dessert Tokaj always goes down well.

Getting There & Away

AIR
Airports

Malév Hungarian Airlines *(MA;* w *www .malev.hu)*, the national carrier, flies nonstop to Budapest's **Ferihegy International Airport** (☎ *1-296 9696)* from North America, the Middle East and almost three dozen cities in Continental Europe and the British Isles. It links up with flights from Asia and Australasia at some of its European gateways (eg, through Paris, Frankfurt or Helsinki for Hong Kong; London, Frankfurt or Rome for Sydney).

Malév flights and those of its 10 code-share partners arrive and depart from Ferihegy's **Terminal 2A** *(departures information* ☎ *1-296 7000, arrivals information* ☎ *1-296 8000)*. All other international airlines use **Terminal 2B** *(departures information* ☎ *1-296 5882, arrivals information* ☎ *1-296 5052)*. The terminals are beside one another and within walking distance. The old Terminal 1, about 5km to the west, is now used only for cargo and by air-taxi companies.

Malév has a ticketing desk at **Terminal 2A** (☎ *1-296 7211)* and another desk at **Terminal 2B** *(☎ 1-296 5767)*.

Departure Tax

An air passenger duty *(illeték)* of between 8000Ft and 10,000Ft is levied on all air tickets written in Hungary. The one exception is JFK International Airport in New York, which attracts a tax of 20,000Ft. This duty is almost always incorporated in the quoted fare. There are no other departure or port taxes.

Continental Europe & the UK

Malév flies nonstop to Budapest from Amsterdam, Athens, Berlin, Brussels, Bucharest, Copenhagen, Dublin, Düsseldorf, Frankfurt, Hamburg, Helsinki, Istanbul, Kyiv, Larnaca, London, Madrid, Milan, Moscow, Munich, Paris, Prague, Rome, Sarajevo, Skopje, Sofia, Stockholm, Stuttgart, Thessaloniki, Tirana, Vienna, Warsaw, Zagreb and Zürich.

Other airlines serving Budapest from European gateways include:

Aeroflot (SU)	Moscow
Aerosvit Airlines (VV)	Kyiv
Air France (AF)	Paris
Air Malta (KM)	Malta

Air Ukraine (6U)	Kyiv
Alitalia (AZ)	Rome, Milan
British Airways (BA)	London
CarpatAir (V3)	Cluj-Napoca
Crossair (LX)	Zürich
Czech Airlines (OK)	Prague
EgyptAir (MS)	Cairo
Finnair (AY)	Helsinki
KLM-Royal Dutch Airlines (KL)	Amsterdam
LOT (LO)	Warsaw
Pulkovo Aviation (Z8)	St Petersburg
Tarom (RO)	Bucharest
Turkish Airlines (TK)	Istanbul

At the time of writing, **British Airways** (☎ *0845 773 3377;* w *www.britishairways.co .uk)* was offering basic return excursion tickets with fixed dates (and heavy penalties if you changed them) from London to Budapest for UK£239 and £279, depending on whether travel was on a weekend or midweek; the fares were £10 less if booked online. You can always fly to Prague on the budget airline, **Go** (☎ *0845 605 4321;* w *www.go-fly .com)* for around UK£100 and then cover the last leg by bus or train.

From Budapest, most destinations in Europe on Malév cost from 63,000Ft to 80,000Ft return, including Warsaw and Prague (63,000Ft each) and Moscow and London (75,000Ft).

You may find cheaper tickets through discount travel agencies. At the time of writing Budapest-based **Ázsia Travel** (☎ *1-318 0505, fax 1-317 6013; V Városház utca 16)* had a return fare to London for 57,000Ft and one to Paris for just under 40,000Ft.

The USA & Canada

Malév runs a daily nonstop flight to/from New York (JFK International Airport), or you can fly with KLM or Northwest Airlines and Malév via Amsterdam. Malév also has a nonstop to/from Toronto four times a week. For Montreal fly Air Canada and Malév via Paris (CDG). From New York with Malév the standard return fare hovers around US$850, though a discount one with the usual restrictions costs about US$515.

From Budapest, travelling with Malév, a return fare to New York starts at about 129,000Ft but can go as low as 85,000Ft.

Australia & New Zealand

Although there are no direct flights to Budapest there are a number of options from Australia. Qantas have flights from Sydney or Melbourne direct to London's Heathrow airport, connecting with a Malév or British Airways flight to Budapest. Another option is to fly from Sydney to Frankfurt or another European capital and then with Malév to Budapest. Return low season fares from Sydney are from A$1865 to A$2300. As with travel from Australia, there are a number of flights from New Zealand to European cities with connecting flights to Budapest. Air New Zealand flies daily from Auckland to Heathrow and connects with a nonstop Malév flight to Budapest. Return fares in the low season are from NZ$2299 to NZ$2599. A standard return flight to Sydney or Melbourne from Budapest costs 336,000Ft, but official discounts and special deals are available direct from the airline from time to time.

Africa & the Middle East

Malév flies nonstop six times a week (daily in summer) to/from Tel Aviv while El Al has a service three or four times a week, depending on the season. Return flights start from around US$400. Malév serves Cairo three times a week (four daily departures in summer) while EgyptAir has two weekly nonstop flights. Return fares start from US$310. Malév also flies nonstop twice a week to both Beirut ($350 return) and Tripoli (US$345 return). Tunis Air flies nonstop charter once a week to Budapest and Lufthansa has regular flights starting from US$530 return.

Asia

Return flights from Hong Kong (with Cathay Pacific via Frankfurt or Paris, or with Finnair via Helsinki) start from US$1240, from Taipei (with Cathay Pacific via Paris or Frankfurt) fares start at US$1250 and from Bangkok (with Air France via Paris) for US$890.

A return Budapest–Bangkok ticket should cost from 157,000Ft to 163,000Ft, though you might find a discounted one far as low as 149,000Ft. Expect to pay 240,000Ft from Budapest to Bangkok via London on British Airways and from 210,000Ft to Hong Kong.

LAND

Budapest is very well connected with all seven of its neighbours by road, rail and even river ferries, though most transport begins or ends its journey in Budapest.

As elsewhere in Europe, timetables for both domestic and international trains and buses use the 24-hour system. Remember that 0.05 means five minutes past midnight (or 12.05am) while 12.05 indicates five minutes after noon (12.05pm).

On many bus and train timetables, Hungarian names are used for cities and towns in neighbouring countries. See the Alternative Place Names appendix at the back of this book.

Border Crossings

Bus There are bus services to all neighbouring countries from Budapest, as well as from certain cities and towns closer to the borders. This is often the cheapest – if not the easiest – way to enter a neighbouring country if you are away from the capital.

For example, from Pécs in Southern Transdanubia you can catch one of three daily buses to Osijek in Croatia, and there are three or four departures from Barcs, 32km southwest of Szigetvár, to Zagreb. From Lenti, buses cross the border into Slovenia and carry on to Ljubljana. From Győr and Sopron in Western Transdanubia, between one and three buses go to Vienna each day.

From Szeged, buses cross the Romanian border for Arad up to 10 times a week and leave for Timişoara three times weekly. There are also buses from Szeged to Novi Sad (daily) and Subotica (three daily) in Yugoslavia.

Nyíregyháza is a springboard for Užgorod in Ukraine, (buses leave twice daily), and for Satu Mare in Romania (twice a week).

Train The main entry points for international trains to Hungary include the following (clockwise from Austria): Szentgotthárd and Szombathely (from Graz); Sopron and Hegyeshalom (from Vienna and much of Western Europe); Komárom and Szob (from Berlin and Prague); Miskolc (from Warsaw, Kraków, and Košice in Slovakia); Nyíregyháza (from St Petersburg, Moscow and Lvov); Békéscsaba (from Bucharest, Timişoara and Arad); Szeged (from Subotica); Kelebia and Kiskunhalas (from Belgrade); Pécs (from Sarajevo and Osijek); and Nagykanizsa (from Ljubljana and Zagreb). See the map 'Hungary's Rail Network' in the Getting Around chapter for stations in Hungary.

Car & Motorcycle Of the 60-odd border road crossings Hungary maintains with its neighbours, about a third (mostly in the north and northeast) are restricted to local citizens on both sides of the border (or, in the case of Austria, Hungarian and EU citizens).

See the boxed text 'Major Border Crossings' later for a list of crossings that are open to all motorists round the clock. Check out Tourinform's website (W www.hungarytourism.hu) for any changes.

Bicycle Cyclists may have problems crossing Hungarian border stations connected to main roads since bicycles are banned on motorways and national highways with single-digit route numbers.

Walking & Hitching To save the cost of an international ticket, or just for fun, consider walking across the frontier into or out of Hungary. But many border guards frown on this practice, particularly in Romania, Yugoslavia and Ukraine; try hitching a ride instead.

If you're heading north, there are three crossings to Slovakia where you shouldn't have any problems. Bridges link Esztergom with Štúrovo and Komárom with Komárno. At Sátoraljaújhely, northeast of Miskolc, there's a highway border crossing over the Ronyva River which links the centre of town with Slovenské Nové Mesto.

For Romania, the easiest place to cross on foot is Nagylak/Nădlac between Szeged and Arad (border open 7am to 7pm daily). There are six local trains daily from the train station at Újszeged, across the Tisza River from Szeged proper, to Nagylak (1¼ hours, 47km) near the border. After crossing into Romania you must walk, cycle or hitch for 3km to Nădlac, where you can connect with a local train to Arad (1½ hours, 52km).

If you're bound for Slovenia, take one of up to 11 daily trains from Zalaegerszeg to Rédics (1½ hours, 49km), which is only 2km from the main highway border crossing from Hungary into Slovenia. From the border it's a 5km walk south to the Lendava bus station, where you can catch a bus to Maribor (1¾ hours, 92km) or to Ljubljana (four hours, 212km).

Bus

Most international buses are run by **Eurolines** (☎ 1-219 8080/00; W www.eurolines.com) or its Hungarian associate, **Volánbusz** (☎ 1-485 2162/00; W www.volanbusz.hu). In Budapest, all international buses now arrive at and depart from the new **Népliget bus station** (☎ 1-264 3939; IX Üllői út 131; metro Népliget; ticket office open 6am-6pm Mon-Fri, 6am-4pm Sat & Sun) in Pest. The ticket office is upstairs.

Bus Passes Eurolines has passes valid for 15/30/60 days that allow unlimited travel between 32 European cities, including Budapest. You are not allowed to travel on the same routing more than twice. Adults pay €189/269/339 in the low season (mid-September to May) and €249/369/429 in the high season. Passes for those aged under 26 cost €159/219/269, for those aged over 60 they cost €209/299/329.

Western Europe From Népliget bus station there's a bus on Monday, Wednesday, Friday and Saturday throughout the year to Amsterdam (19 hours, 1435km) via Frankfurt and Düsseldorf and carrying on to Rotterdam (21½ hours, 1510km). Tickets cost 24,900/37,900Ft one way/return, with a 10% discount for those under 26 or over 60. From early June to late September the Amsterdam bus runs on Thursday and Sunday too and in July and early August it goes daily at slightly higher rates: 25,900/39,900Ft. In summer this bus fills up quickly, so try to book ahead.

The Budapest–Amsterdam bus goes through Austria, precluding the need for a Czech or

Major Border Crossings

The following is a list of border crossings between Hungary and its neighbouring countries (beginning in Austria and moving clockwise) that are open to all motorists 24 hours a day, all year. The left column shows the check point in Hungary, the right column shows the check point over the border.

Hungary	Austria
Rábafüzes (5km north of Szentgotthárd)	Heiligenkreuz
Bucsu (13km west of Szombathely)	Schachendorf
Kőszeg	Rattersdorf
Kópháza (11km southeast of Sopron)	Deutschkreutz
Sopron (7km northwest of the city)	Klingenbach
Hegyeshalom (51km northwest of Győr)	Nickelsdorf

Hungary	Slovakia
Rajka (18km northwest of Mosonmagyaróvár)	Rusovce
Vámosszabadi (13km north of Győr)	Medvedov
Komárom	Komárno
Esztergom	Štúrovo
Hont (40km north of Vác)	Šahy
Balassagyarma	Slovenské Darmoty
Somoskőújfalu (8km north of Salgótarján)	Šiatorska Vukovina (nearest town, Filakovo)
Bánréve (43km northwest of Miskolc)	Král
Tornyosnémeti (60km northeast of Miskolc)	Milhost
Sátoraljaújhely	Slovenské Nové Mesto

Hungary	Ukraine
Záhony (23km north of Kisvárda)	Čop (23km south of Užgorod)
Beregsurány (21km northeast of Vásárosnamény)	Berehove
Tiszabecs (27km northeast of Fehérgyarmat)	Vilok

Hungary	Romania
Csengersima (40km southeast of Mátészalka)	Petea (11km northwest of Satu Mare)
Nyírábrány (30km east of Debrecen)	Valea lui Mihai
Ártánd (25km southeast of Berettyóújfalu)	Borş (14km northwest of Oradea)
Méhkerék (24km north of Gyula)	Salonta
Gyula	Varşand (66km north of Arad)
Battonya (45km southeast of Orosháza)	Turnu
Nagylak (52km west of Szeged)	Nădlac (54km west of Arad)

Hungary	Yugoslavia
Rözske (16km southwest of Szeged)	Horgos (30km northeast of Subotica)
Tompa (30km south of Kiskunhalas)	Kelebija (11km northwest of Subotica)
Hercegszántó (32km south of Baja)	Baèki Breg (28km northwest of Sombor)

Hungary	Croatia
Udvar (12km south of Mohács)	Kneľvevo
Drávaszabolcs (9km south of Harkány)	Donji Miholjac (49km northwest of Osijek)
Barcs (32km southwest of Szigetvár)	Terezino Polje
Berzence (24km west of Nagyatád)	Gola
Letenye (26km west of Nagykanizsa)	Gorican

Hungary	Slovenia
Rédics (9km southwest of Lenti)	Dolga Vas
Bajánsenye (60km west of Zalaegerszeg)	Hodos

Slovakian visa. In Amsterdam tickets are sold by **Eurolines Nederland** (☎ 020-560 87 88; *Rokin 10)*, and at **Amstel bus station** (☎ 020-560 87 88; *Julianaplein 5).* In Budapest you can buy them at the Népliget bus station.

Buses to London (26 hours, 1755km) via Brussels and Lille depart on Monday, Wednesday, Thursday and Sunday (32,900/47,900Ft one way/return). From May to late October the bus also runs on Friday, from late June to September on Saturday and from July to mid-October on Tuesday. In London check with **Eurolines** (☎ 0870 514 3219; 52 Grosvenor Gardens SW1).

Other Eurolines services between Budapest and Western European cities, with high-season (mid-June to mid-September) one-way/return fares quoted, include the following:

Athens (via Thessaloniki, 19,000/32,000Ft, 16 hours, 1560km, three a week) If you only go as far as Thessaloniki the ticket price is the same.
Berlin (via Prague, 19,900/33,900Ft, 15 hours, 915km) If you continue on to Hamburg the cost goes up to 22,900/37,900Ft. Buses depart three days a week year-round, five times weekly from early June to late September.
Paris (via Strasbourg and Reims, 27,900/42,900Ft, 22 hours, 1525km) Buses run two to three days a week from April to late October. As far as Strasbourg only the price is 25,900/40,900Ft.
Rome (23,500/37,900Ft, 15 hours, 1330km) Goes via Bologna (16,900/27,500Ft), and Florence (18,900/30,500Ft), continuing on to Naples (25,500/39,500Ft). Buses run four days a week year-round, five to six days from early April to late October to Rome; two days a week year-round to Naples.
Venice (13,500/22,500Ft, 13½ hours, 770km) Goes via Graz (8400/13,500Ft). Buses run three times a week year-round, five to six times from mid-May to early October.
Vienna (6390/9390Ft, 3½ hours, 254km) Goes via Győr (4400/6400Ft). There are three buses daily, four on Saturday.

Czech Republic, Slovakia & Poland
From Népliget station there are buses to Bratislava (in Hungarian, Pozsony; 3100/4900Ft one way/return, four hours, 213km) daily and to Prague (8900/14,500Ft, 10½ hours, 640km) three times weekly year-round. Extra overnight buses to Prague run on Sunday and Monday from July to mid-September, leaving Budapest at 7pm and arriving at 5.30am. Buses also leave on Saturday year-round for Kråkow (6900/10,900Ft, 11 hours, 491km) via Zakopane (5600/8900Ft).

Romania There are buses scheduled regularly on Saturday year-round to Arad (4000/5700Ft one way/return, seven hours, 282km) and Timişoara (Temesvár; 4900/6900Ft, eight hours, 334km).

Croatia & Yugoslavia From late June to early September a bus leaves Népliget for Pula (9900/15,800Ft one way/return, 14½ hours, 775km) every Friday travelling through Rijeka (7900/12,600Ft) and Porec (9300/14,900Ft). There's a daily service year-round to Belgrade (4100/6800Ft, nine hours, 422km) and another bus to Subotica (Szabatka; 3300/5300Ft, 4½ hours, 224km).

Train
Magyar Államvasutak (W *www.mav.hu)*, which translates as Hungarian State Railways and is known as MÁV, links up with the European rail network in all directions, running trains as far as London (via Cologne and Brussels), Paris (via Frankfurt), Stockholm (via Hamburg and Copenhagen), Moscow, Rome, and Istanbul (via Belgrade).

The international trains listed here are expresses, and many – if not all – require seat reservations. On long hauls, sleepers are almost always available in both 1st and 2nd class, and couchettes are available in 2nd class. Not all express trains have dining or even buffet cars; make sure you bring along some snacks and drinks as vendors can be few and far between. Most Hungarian trains are hardly what you would call luxurious but they are generally clean and always punctual.

In Budapest, most international trains arrive and depart from **Keleti station** *(Eastern;* ☎ 1-313 6835; *VIII Kerepesi út 2-6)*; trains to certain destinations in Romania and Germany leave from **Nyugati station** *(Western;* ☎ 1-349 0115; *VI Nyugati tér)*, while **Déli station** *(Southern;* ☎ 1-355 8657; *I Krisztina körút 37/a)* handles trains to/from Zagreb and Rijeka in Croatia. These are not hard-and-fast rules, so always make sure you check which station the train leaves from when you buy a ticket. For 24-hour information on international train services call ☎ 1-461 5500 in Budapest.

To reduce confusion, specify your train by the name listed in the following sections or on the posted schedule when requesting information or buying a ticket. You can buy tickets at the three international train stations in Budapest, but it's easier at the **MÁV central**

ticket office (☎ 1-461 5500/400; ⓦwww
.mav.hu; VI Andrássy út 35; open 9am-6pm
Mon-Fri Apr-Sept; 9am-5pm Mon-Fri Oct-
Mar). It accepts credit cards.

If you just want to get across the border,
local trains are cheaper than international expresses, especially if you're on a one-way
trip. Concession fares between cities of the
former socialist countries are only available
on return tickets.

Tickets & Fares There are big discounts on
return fares from Hungary to most of the for-
mer socialist countries: 30% to Bulgaria, the
Czech Republic and Poland; 40% to Yugo-
slavia and the Baltic countries; 50% to Belarus,
Russia and Ukraine; up to 65% to Slovakia and
Slovenia, and up to 75% to Romania. Also,
there's a 40% concession on return fares from
Budapest to six selected cities: Prague and
Brno in the Czech Republic, and Warsaw,
Kraków, Katowice and Gdynia in Poland.
Some 2nd-class return fares are: Prague €56;
Moscow €103; Warsaw €71.

For tickets to Western Europe you'll pay the
same as everywhere else unless you're under
26 and qualify for the 30% to 50% BIJ discount. For that, ask at MÁV, Express or
Wasteels (☎ 1-210 2802; open 8am-7pm
Mon-Fri, 8am-1pm Sat) in Keleti train station.

The following are sample return 2nd-class
fares from Budapest: Amsterdam €212,
Berlin €126 (via Prague) and €198 (via
Vienna), London €352, Munich €91, Rome
(via Ljubljana) €172 and Vienna €41. There's
a 30% discounted return fare to Vienna of
7150Ft if you come back to Budapest within
four days. Three daily EuroCity (EC) trains
to Vienna and points beyond charge a supplement (650Ft to 1500Ft). The 1st-class
seats are around 50% more expensive than
2nd class, but it depends on the destination.

International seat reservation costs vary
according to the destination (eg, €6.60 to
Prague, €10.60 to Warsaw). Fines are levied
on those without tickets (400Ft plus full single
fare) or seat reservations (1000Ft plus reservation fee) on trains where they are mandatory.

Costs for sleepers depend on the destination, but a two-berth 2nd-class sleeper to
Berlin/Prague/Venice/Moscow costs 5350/
5250/8000/7000Ft per person per night; a
sleeper to yourself always costs at least
double the price. A 2nd-class couchette in a
compartment for six people costs between

1800Ft on the *Transbalkan* to Romania and
Greece and 5500Ft on the *Kálmán Imre* to
Munich. Tickets are valid for 60 days from
purchase and stopovers are permitted.

Budapest is no longer the bargain basement
that it once was for tickets on the Trans-
Siberian or the Trans-Mongolian railways. In
fact, MÁV will only write you a ticket to
Moscow; you have to buy the onward ticket
from there. Of course, if you are coming back
to Budapest from Moscow you get a 50% discount on the Moscow–Budapest ticket.

When pricing train tickets from Western
Europe remember that airfares (especially
those out of London) usually beat surface al-
ternatives (especially trains) hands down. For
example, a return airfare from London to
Budapest is available through discount travel
agencies low season for about or under
UK£200. By comparison, a two-month return
ticket by rail to Budapest available from **Rail
Europe** (☎ 0870 584 8848; ⓦ www.euro
starplus.com, ⓦ www.raileurope.com) costs
UK£397 per adult, though the fare drops to
UK£356 if the ticket is purchased a month prior.

Rail Passes Covering from one to eight
'zones', passes from **Inter Rail** (ⓦ www.inter
railnet.com) can be purchased by nationals of
European countries (or residents of at least six
months) from MÁV. There are three price
groups for Inter Rail passes: adult, ages 12 to
26 (referred to here as 'youth') and child (four
to 12). The price for any one zone is €248/
169/124 for adult/youth/child for 12 days and
€300/206/150 for 22 days. Hungary is in Zone
D along with the Czech Republic, Slovakia,
Poland and Croatia. Multizone passes are
better value and are valid for one month: two
zones cost €386/274/193 and three zones
€440/309/220. A Global pass (all eight zones)
costs €518/365/259. It's almost impossible for
a standard **Eurail pass** (ⓦ www.eurailnet.com)
to pay for itself in Hungary, though you may
consider a Europe East pass (available to non-
European residents only). This allows five days
of unlimited travel over a one-month period on
the rail networks of Hungary as well as those
in Austria, the Czech Republic, Poland and
Slovakia. It also offers discounts on some river
and lake steamers and bicycle rentals. Adult
1st-class/2nd-class passes cost US$220/154;
children aged four to 12 pay US$110/77. Ad-
ditional days (maximum five) cost US$25. Buy
the pass before you leave home.

For information on Eurail's Hungarian Flexipass, see Train Passes under Train in the Getting Around chapter.

Western Europe Seven trains daily link Vienna with Budapest (three hours, 273km) via Hegyeshalom and Győr. Most depart from Vienna's Westbahnhof, including the *Arrabona* and the EuroCity *Bartók Béla*. The EuroNight *Kálmán Imre* from Munich (7½ hours, 742km) via Salzburg (six hours, 589km) also goes through Westbahnhof, as do the EC *Liszt Ferenc* from Cologne (11 hours, 1247km) via Frankfurt (10 hours, 1026km), the *Dacia Express* to Bucharest (15½ hours, 874km), and the InterCity *Avala* to Belgrade (10 hours, 647km). The early morning EC *Lehár* departs from Vienna's Südbahnhof. None requires a seat reservation, though they're highly recommended in summer.

Up to nine trains leave Vienna's Südbahnhof every day for Sopron (75 minutes, 76km) via Ebenfurth. As many as 10 a day also serve Sopron from Wiener Neustadt (easily accessible from Vienna). Five milk trains daily make the four-hour, 136km-long trip from Graz to Szombathely.

The EC *Hungária* travels from Berlin (Zoo and Ostbahnhof stations) to Budapest (12½ hours, 1002km) via Dresden, Prague and Bratislava. The express *Spree-Donau Kurier* arrives from Berlin via Nuremberg.

Czech Republic, Slovakia & Poland In addition to the EC *Hungária*, Budapest can be reached from Prague (seven hours, 611km) on the EC *Comenius*, the IC *Csárdás*, the *Slovan* and the *Pannónia Express*, which then carries on to Bucharest. The *Amicus* runs directly from Bratislava (three hours, 215km) every day.

The EC *Polonia* and the *Báthory* leave Warsaw daily for Budapest (12 hours, 802km) passing through Bratislava or Štúrovo and Katowice. The *Cracovia* runs from Kraków to Budapest (10½ hours, 598km) via Košice. From Miskolc in northern Hungary, you can pick up the *Karpaty* to Warsaw via Kraków and Košice.

Another train, the *Rákóczi*, links Budapest with Košice and Bratislava. The *Bem* connects Budapest with Szczecin (17 hours, 1019km) in northwestern Poland via Wrocław and Poznań.

Three local trains daily cover the 90km from Košice to Miskolc (two hours). The 2km hop from Sátoraljaújhely to Slovenské

Nové Mesto is only a four-minute ride on the train, which runs twice daily.

Ukraine & Russia From Moscow to Budapest (42 hours, 2106km) there's only the *Tisza Express*, which travels via Kyiv and Lvov in Ukraine. The *Partium* crosses the Ukranian border to Csop. Most nationalities require a transit visa to travel through Ukraine.

Romania From Bucharest to Budapest (14 hours, 874km) you can choose from six trains: the EC *Traianus*, the *Dacia Express*, the *Ovidius*, the EN *Ister*, the *Muntenia* and the *Pannonia*. All go via Arad (5½ hours, 253km) and some require seat reservations. The *Karpaty* links Miskolc and Bucharest.

There are two daily connections from Cluj-Napoca to Budapest (eight hours, 402km) via Oradea: the *Ady Endre* and the *Corona*. The *Partium* links Budapest with Oradea only. All three trains require a seat reservation.

Two local trains daily connect Baia Mare in northern Romania with Bucharest (8¾ hours, 285km) via Satu Mare and Debrecen.

Bulgaria & Yugoslavia The *Transbalkan*, which originates in Thessaloniki, Greece and travels through Bucharest, links Sofia with Budapest (25 hours, 1366km). Trains between Budapest and Belgrade (seven hours, 374km) via Subotica include the *Beograd*, the *Ivo Andrić* and the IC *Avala*. You must reserve your seats on some of these trains. Two local trains make the 1¾-hour, 45km-long journey daily between Subotica and Szeged.

Croatia, Slovenia & Bosnia-Hercegovina You can get to Budapest from Zagreb (seven hours, 386km) on two trains that pass through Siófok on Lake Balaton's southern shore: the *Maestral*, which originates in Split, and the *Venezia Express*, which goes to Budapest from Venice via Ljubljana (10 hours, 504km). Two other trains from Ljubljana are the IC *Citadella* and the IC *Dráva*, which also comes from Venice. The IC *Kvarner* links Budapest with Rijeka (nine hours, 591km) via Siófok on Lake Balaton, and Zagreb. The nameless train linking Sarajevo with Budapest (616km) takes 14 hours and goes via Pécs.

RIVER

A hydrofoil service on the Danube between Budapest and Vienna (5½ hours, 282km) has the option of disembarking at Bratislava (on request). It operates daily from April to early November, with an extra daily sailing in August. Adult one-way/return fares for Vienna are €65/89 and for Bratislava €59/83. Students with ISIC cards pay €51/75, and children under six go free. Taking along a bicycle costs €16 each way.

In Budapest, ferries arrive and depart from the International Ferry Pier (Nemzetközi hajóállomás) on V Belgrád rakpart, between Erzsébet and Szabadság Bridges on the Pest side. In Vienna, the boat docks at the Reichsbrücke pier near Mexikoplatz.

In April and from September to early November there is a daily sailing at 9am from Budapest and from Vienna. From May to August the boats leave both of these cities at 8am. In August an additional boat departs from both cities at 1pm daily.

To find out more details on these ferries, information on tickets, and for bookings you could contact **Mahart PassNave** (☎ *1-484 4010, 318 1704;* Ⓦ *www.maharttours.com; V Belgrád rakpart; 8am-4pm Mon-Fri)* in Budapest; and **Mahart PassNave Wien** (☎ *01-72 92 161/2; Handelskai 265/3/517),* its branch in Vienna.

Getting Around

Hungary's domestic transport system is efficient, comprehensive and inexpensive. In general, almost everything runs to schedule, and the majority of Hungary's towns and cities are easily negotiated on foot.

AIR

There are no scheduled flights within Hungary. The cost of domestic air taxis is prohibitive (eg, from 140,000Ft for up to three people from Budapest to Szeged and back), and the trips can take almost as long as the train when you add the time required to get to and from the airports. Several better-known firms with offices in Budapest are: **Indicator Aviation** (☎ 1-202 6284; Ⓦ www.indicator.hu; XII Városmajor utca 30); **FarnAir Hungary** (☎ 1-347 6040; Ⓦ www.farnair.com; XIX Üllői út); and **Avia Express** (☎ 1-296 7092, 296 7791; fax 296 7891; Ferihegy Terminal 1).

BUS

Hungary's **Volánbusz** (Ⓦ www.volanbusz .hu) network is a good – and sometimes necessary – alternative to the trains. In Southern Transdanubia and many parts of the Great Plain, buses are essential unless you are prepared to make several time-consuming changes on the train. For short trips around the Danube Bend or Lake Balaton areas, buses are preferable to trains.

In most cities and large towns it is usually possible to catch at least one direct bus a day to fairly far-flung areas of the country (Pécs to Sopron, for example, or Eger to Szeged).

Of course, not everyone likes travelling by bus, but in Hungary it's a better way to see the deep countryside than the train – those areas 'somewhere behind the back of God', as the Magyars call them. Seats on Volánbusz are spaced far enough apart for you to be able to fit your pack between your knees. A few large bus stations have luggage rooms, but they generally close early (around 6pm). Check your bag at the train station, which is almost always nearby; the left-luggage offices there keep much longer hours.

National buses arrive and depart from Budapest's long-distance bus stations (távolságiautóbusz pályaudvar), not the local stations, which are called helyiautóbusz pályaudvar. In the countryside these are often found side by side or share the same space. Arrive early to confirm the correct departure bay or stand (kocsiállás), and be sure to check the individual schedule posted at the stop itself; the times shown can be different from those shown on the main board (tábla).

Tickets are usually purchased directly from the driver, who gives change and will hand you a receipt as a ticket. There are sometimes queues for intercity buses (especially on Friday afternoon) so it's wise to arrive early. Smoking is not allowed on buses in Hungary, though a 10- or 20-minute rest stop is made about every two or three hours.

Posted bus timetables can be horribly confusing if you don't speak Hungarian. The basics to remember when reading a timetable are that *indulás* means 'departures' and *érkezés* means 'arrivals'. Some timetable symbols are shown in the box.

Numbers one to seven in a circle refer to the days of the week, beginning with Monday. Written footnotes you might see include *naponta* (daily), *hétköznap* (weekdays), *munkanap* (workdays), *szabadnap* (Saturday), *szabad és munkaszünetes nap* (Saturday and holidays), *munkaszünetes nap* (holidays), *iskolai nap* (school days), *szabadnap kivételével naponta* (daily except Saturday) and *munkaszünetes nap kivételével naponta* (daily except holidays).

With the recent closure of the Erzsébet tér bus station on Deák tér in Budapest, things were in a state of flux at the time of writing. But in general for bus services to inland destinations south and west of Budapest, go to the new **Népliget bus station** (☎ 1-264 3939; IX Üllői út 131; metro Népliget; ticket office open 6am-6pm Mon-Fri, 6am-4pm Sat & Sun). Generally the **Népstadion bus station** (☎ 1-252 4498, 251 0125; XIV Hungária körút 48-52; metro Népstadion; ticket office open 6am-6pm Mon-Fri, 6am-noon Sat & Sun) serves cities and towns to the east of the capital. The **Árpád Bridge bus station** (☎ 1-329 1450; XIII Róbert Károly körút; metro Árpád híd; ticket office open 7am-4pm Mon-Fri) on the Pest side of Árpád Bridge is the place to catch buses for the Danube Bend and parts of the Northern Uplands (eg, Balassagyarmat, Szécsény and Salgótarján). The small **Széna tér bus station** (☎ 1-201 3688; I Széna tér 1/a;

Bus Timetable Symbols

✕	Monday to Saturday (except public holidays)
⊗	Monday to Friday (except public holidays)
☒	Monday to Thursday (except public holidays)
☐	first working day of the week (usually Monday)
⊤	last working day of the week (usually Friday)
⊙	Saturday & public holiday
⊕	Saturday, Sunday and public holidays
✛	Sunday and public holidays
⊞	day before the first working day of the week (usually Sunday but Monday when a public holiday)
▼	school days
▽	on working days during school holidays (mid-June to August; Christmas and New Year; two weeks in April)

metro Moszkva tér) in Buda handles some traffic to and from the Pilis Hills and towns northwest of the capital, with a half-dozen departures to Esztergom as an alternative to the Árpád Bridge bus station.

Costs

Bus fares are slightly more expensive than comparable 2nd-class train fares. At present Volánbusz charges:

fare	distance
80Ft	for up to 5km
108Ft	for 10km
150Ft	for 15km
994Ft	for 100km
1992Ft	for 200km
2974Ft	for 300km

TRAIN

MÁV (W www.mav.hu) operates reliable and relatively comfortable train services on just under 8000km of track, about a third of which is electrified. All the main railway lines converge on Budapest, though many secondary lines link provincial cities and towns. There are three main stations in Budapest. In general, Keleti station serves destinations in the Northern Uplands and the Northeast, Nyugati station those in the Great Plain and the Danube Bend and trains from Déli station head for Transdanubia and Lake Balaton. But these are not hard-and-fast rules; confirm the departure station when you buy your ticket. The 24-hour number for domestic train information is ☎ 1-461 5400.

Tickets for one-way *(egy útra)* and return *(oda-vissza* or *menettérti jegy)* journeys in 1st and 2nd class are available at stations, the **MÁV central ticket office** *(☎ 1-461 5500, 322 8082; W www.mav.hu; VI Andrássy út 35; open 9am-6pm Mon-Fri Apr-Sept, 9am-5pm Mon-Fri Oct-Mar)* and certain travel agencies.

There are several types of train. The Inter-City Express (ICE) and InterCityRapid (ICR) trains levy a supplement, which includes a seat. ICE trains stop at main centres only while ICR usually just head for their destination. They are the fastest and most comfortable trains in Hungary. *Gyorsvonat* (fast trains) and *sebesvonat* (swift trains), indicated on the timetable by boldface type, a thicker route line and/or an 'S', often require a seat reservation. *Személyvonat* (passenger trains) are the real milk runs and stop at every city, town, village and hamlet along the way.

Depending on the station, departures and arrivals are announced by loudspeaker/ Tannoy or on an electronic board and are always on a printed timetable – yellow for departures *(indul)* and white for arrivals *(érkezik)*. On these, fast trains are marked in red, local trains in black. The number (or sometimes letter) next to the word *vágány* indicates the 'platform' from which the train departs or arrives; for symbols and abbreviations used, see Bus earlier.

If you plan to do a lot of travelling by train, get yourself a copy of MÁV's official timetable (Menetrend; 650/1350Ft in small/large format), which is available at most large stations, the MÁV office on Andrássy út or at **U-Tours** *(☎ 1-303 9818, 343 0273; VIII Kerepesi út 2-6)* in Keleti station. It also has explanatory notes in a half-dozen languages, including English and – wait for it – Esperanto.

All train stations have left-luggage offices, some of which stay open 24 hours a day. You sometimes have to pay the fee (150Ft to 200Ft per item per day) at another office or window nearby, which is usually marked *pénztár* (cashier).

HUNGARY'S RAIL NETWORK

Schematic Map of
Railway Connections

Some trains have a dedicated carriage for bicycles; on other trains, bicycles must be placed in the first or last cars. You are able to freight a bicycle for 25% of a full 2nd-class fare (ie, 193/389/542/622/702Ft for 100/200/300/400/500km).

The Road Distances chart on page 76 shows distances and approximate times to provincial cities from Budapest via express trains (on which you might expect to cover from 65km/h to 70km/h) or slow passenger trains, which take longer.

Train Passes

Euro Domino Hungary is a pass that allows residents of Europe to travel on the entire rail network for between three and eight days of travel over a one-month period for free or with a big discount. A three-day pass costs per adult €72/48 in 1st/2nd class and €37 for those aged 12 to 25. Eight-day passes cost €167/113/82.

Eurail's Hungarian Flexipass, available to non-European residents only, costs US$67 for five days' 1st-class travel in a 15-day period or US$84 for 10 days' travel within a month. Children five to 14 pay half-price.

Reservations

On Hungarian domestic trains, seat reservations may be compulsory (indicated on the timetable by an 'R' in a box), mandatory only on trains departing from Budapest (an 'R' in a circle) or simply available (just a plain 'R').

Express trains usually require a seat reservation costing 110Ft while the intercity ones levy a surcharge of between 250Ft and 500Ft, which includes the seat reservation.

Costs

Domestic 2nd-class train fares are 770/1556/2166/2486/2806Ft for 100/200/300/400/500km. To travel 1st class costs 50% more: 1155/2334/3249/3729/4209Ft.

Passengers holding a ticket of insufficient value must pay the difference plus a fine of 200Ft. If you buy your ticket on the train rather than at the station, there's a 400Ft surcharge. You can be fined 1000Ft for travelling on a train without a seat reservation when it is compulsory.

Special Trains

A dozen narrow-gauge trains *(keskenyny-omközű vonat)* run by Állami Erdei Vasutak

Trains Within Hungary

from Budapest to	distance	duration (hrs) slow	express
Danube Bend			
Esztergom	53km	1¾	1½
Szentendre	20km	40 min (on HÉV)	
Vác	49km	1¾	1½
Transdanubia			
Győr	131km	1½	–
Sopron	216km	3	–
Szombathely	236km	3½	2¾
Pécs	228km	–	2½
Lake Balaton Area			
Siófok	115km	2½	1½
Balatonfüred	132km	–	2½
Veszprém	112km	2½	1¾
Székesfehérvár	67km	1½	50 min
Great Plain			
Szolnok	100km	2½	1¼
Kecskemét	106km	–	1½
Debrecen	221km	4½	3
Békéscsaba	196km	3½	2½
Szeged	191km	3½	2½
Northern Hungary			
Nyíregyháza	270km	4½	3
Eger	143km	3	2
Miskolc	183km	2¾	2
Sátoraljaújhely	267km	4½	3½

(ÁEV; United Forest Railways) can be found in many wooded and hilly areas of the country. They are usually taken as a return excursion by holiday-makers, but in some cases can be useful for getting from A to B, eg, Miskolc to Lillafüred and the Bükk.

An independent branch of MÁV runs vintage steam trains *(nosztalgiavonat)* in summer, generally along the northern shore of Lake Balaton (eg, from Keszthely to Talpoca via Badacsonytomaj) and along the Danube Bend from Budapest to Szob or even Esztergom. For information contact **MÁV Nostalgia** (☎ 1-428 0180, 269 5242; fax 302 0069; ⓦ www .mavnosztalgia.hu) in Keleti train station.

The only private train line in Hungary is called GySEV and links Győr and Sopron with Ebenfurth in Austria.

CAR & MOTORCYCLE

Roads in Hungary are generally good – in some cases excellent nowadays – and there are several basic types. Motorways, preceded by an 'M' (including the curiously named M0 half-ring road around Budapest), will eventually total seven. At present they link the capital with Vienna via Győr (M1) and with Lake Balaton almost to Siófok (M7). They also run along the eastern bank of the Danube Bend (M2) and part of the way to Miskolc (M3) and Szeged (M5). National highways (dual carriageways) are designated with a single digit without prefix and fan out mostly from Budapest. Secondary and tertiary roads have two or three digits.

You must obtain a motorway pass to access the M1 and M3 (1500Ft for nine days). Passes are available at petrol stations, post offices and some motorway entrances and border crossings. The M5 is a toll road costing from 400Ft to 1820Ft for a passenger car.

Petrol *(benzin)* of 91 and unleaded *(ólommentes)* 95 and 98 octane is available everywhere and costs 219/222/231Ft per litre respectively. Most stations also have diesel fuel *(gázolaj)* costing 203Ft. Payment by credit card is now standard at Hungarian petrol stations.

Foreign driving licences are valid for one year after entering Hungary. Third-party liability insurance is compulsory. If your car is registered in the EU, it is assumed you have it. Other motorists must show a Green Card or they will have to buy insurance at the border.

The so-called **Yellow Angels** (*Sárga Angyal; nationwide 24hr ☎ 188, in Budapest ☎ 1-345 1744)* of the **Hungarian Automobile Club** *(Magyar Autóklub; ☎ 1-212 2821; II Rómer Flóris 4/a)* do basic car repairs free of charge in the event of a breakdown if you belong to an affiliated organisation such as AAA in the USA or AA in the UK. Towing, however, is still very expensive even with these reciprocal memberships.

For information on traffic and public road conditions nationwide, contact **Útinform** *(☎ 1-322 2238, 322 7643; ⓦ www.kozut.hu)*. In the capital ring **Főinform** *(☎ 1-317 1173)*.

Road Rules

You must drive on the right. Speed limits for cars and motorbikes are consistent throughout the country and strictly enforced: 50km/h in built-up areas (from the town sign as you enter to the same sign with a red line through it as you leave); 80km/h on secondary and tertiary roads; 100km/h on most highways/dual carriageways; and 120km/h on motorways. Exceeding the limit will earn you a fine of between 5000Ft and 30,000Ft, which must be paid by postal cheque or at any post office.

The use of seat belts in the front (and in the back – if fitted – outside built-up areas) is compulsory in Hungary, but this rule is often ignored. Motorcyclists must wear helmets, a law strictly enforced. Another law taken very seriously indeed is the one requiring *all* drivers to use their headlights throughout the day outside built-up areas. Motorcycles must illuminate headlights at all times everywhere. Using a mobile phone while driving is prohibited in Hungary.

There is virtually a 100% ban on alcohol when you are driving, and this rule is *very* strictly enforced. Do not think you will get away with even a few glasses of wine at lunch; if found to have even 0.001% of alcohol in the blood, you will be fined up to 30,000Ft. If the level is high, you will be arrested and your licence almost certainly taken away. In the event of an accident, the drinking party is automatically regarded as guilty.

Mind you, when driving in Hungary you'll want to keep your wits about you; Hungary can be quite a trying place for motorists. It's not that drivers don't know the road rules; everyone has to attend a driver's education course and pass an examination. (A 'T' on the roof or back of a vehicle indicates *tanuló vezető* or 'learner driver', by the way – not 'taxi'.) But overtaking on blind curves, making turns from the outside lane, running stop signs and lights, and jumping lanes in roundabouts are everyday occurrences.

All accidents should be reported to the police (☎ 107) immediately. Several insurance companies handle auto liability, and minor claims can be settled without complications. Any claim on insurance policies bought in Hungary can also be made to **Hungária Biztosító** *(☎ 1-301 6565; I Dísz tér 4-5)* in Budapest. It is one of the largest insurance companies in Hungary and deals with foreigners all the time.

Though many cities and towns have a confusing system of one-way streets, pedestrian zones and bicycle lanes, parking is not a big problem in the provinces. Most centres now require that you 'pay and display' when parking your vehicle – parking disks, coupons or

Road Distances (km)

	Békéscsaba	Budapest	Debrecen	Dunaújváros	Eger	Győr	Kaposvár	Kecskemét	Miskolc	Nyíregyháza	Pécs	Sopron	Szeged	Székesfehérvár	Szolnok	Szombathely	Veszprém	Zalaegerszeg
Békéscsaba	---																	
Budapest	203	---																
Debrecen	130	226	---															
Dunaújváros	210	67	277	---														
Eger	220	128	130	194	---													
Győr	327	123	350	142	251	---												
Kaposvár	314	189	381	146	317	201	---											
Kecskemét	124	85	191	86	158	208	190	---										
Miskolc	228	179	98	246	61	303	368	199	---									
Nyíregyháza	179	245	49	311	145	368	434	240	93	---								
Pécs	283	198	367	131	326	241	67	176	377	416	---							
Sopron	414	217	436	229	338	87	220	295	390	455	287	---						
Szeged	94	171	224	158	245	294	251	86	286	273	189	381	---					
Székesfehérvár	258	66	292	55	194	87	126	134	245	310	153	174	206	---				
Szolnok	107	97	129	148	121	220	252	62	162	179	238	307	130	163	---			
Szombathely	404	222	448	211	350	105	178	280	402	467	245	70	352	156	319	---		
Veszprém	292	110	336	99	238	77	127	168	289	355	166	143	240	44	207	111	---	
Zalaegerszeg	392	224	450	216	352	154	124	268	403	468	190	124	342	161	321	54	119	---

stickers are available at newsstands, petrol stations or, increasingly, automated ticket machines. In smaller towns and cities a warden (usually a friendly pensioner) will approach you as soon as you emerge from the car and collect from 80Ft for each hour you plan to park. In Budapest parking on the street now costs between 80Ft and 180Ft per hour.

Rental

In general, you must be at least 21 years old and have had your licence for a year or longer to rent a car. Drivers under 25 sometimes have to pay a surcharge. All the big international firms have offices in Budapest, and there are scores of local companies throughout the country, but don't expect many bargains. For more details, see Car & Motorcycle under Getting There & Away in the Budapest chapter.

BICYCLE

Hungary offers endless opportunities to cyclists. The slopes of northern Hungary can be challenging, while the terrain of Transdanubia is much gentler; the Great Plain is flat though windy (and hot in summer). The problem is bicycle rentals, which can be very hard to

come by in Hungary. Your best bets are camp sites, resort hotels and – very occasionally – bicycle repair shops. See Things to See & Do or Activities under the various cities and towns later in this book for guidance.

Remember when planning your itinerary that bicycles are banned from all motorways and national highways with a single digit, and bikes must be equipped with lights and reflectors. Bicycles can be taken on many trains but not on buses.

For more information, see Cycling under Activities in the Facts for the Visitor chapter.

HITCHING

Hitching is never entirely safe in any country in the world, and we don't recommend it. Travellers who decide to hitch should understand that they are taking a small but potentially serious risk. However, many people do choose to hitch, and the advice that follows should help to make their journeys as fast and safe as possible.

Hitchhiking is legal everywhere in Hungary except on motorways. Though this form of transport is not as popular as it once was (and can be very difficult here, according to readers), the road to Lake Balaton is always jammed with hitchhikers in the holiday season. There is a service in the capital called Kenguru that matches drivers and passengers for a fee. For details, see Hitching under Getting There & Away in the Budapest chapter.

BOAT

From April to October or early November the Budapest-based shipping company Mahart PassNave runs hydrofoils on the Danube from Budapest to Szentendre, Vác, Visegrád and Esztergom. Mahart services on certain sections of the Tisza River – Sárospatak to Tokaj (2¼ hours, 36km), for example, and Szeged to Csongrád (4¼ hours, 72km) – are available only to groups of at least 40 people between April and mid-October and cost 32,000Ft an hour for up to 80 passengers. The Budapest transport company BKV runs passenger ferries on the Danube within the capital in summer. Passenger ferries on Lake Balaton are the responsibility of a firm called the Balaton Shipping Co (Balatoni Hajózás Rt). Full details on these are given in the relevant chapters.

LOCAL TRANSPORT
Public Transport
Urban transport is well developed in Hungary, with efficient buses and, in many cities and towns, trolleybus services. Budapest, Szeged, Miskolc and Debrecen also have trams, and there's an extensive metro (underground or subway) system and a suburban railway known as the HÉV in the capital.

You'll probably make extensive use of public transport in Budapest but little (if any) in provincial towns and cities: with very few exceptions, most places are quite manageable on foot, and bus services are not all that frequent except in the largest settlements. Generally, city buses meet incoming long-distance trains; hop onto anything standing outside when you arrive, and you'll get close to the city centre.

You must purchase transport tickets (generally from 100Ft) at newsstands or ticket windows beforehand and validate them once aboard. Travelling without a ticket ('riding black', as the Hungarians say) is an offence; you'll be put off and fined on the spot. Don't try to argue; the inspector has heard it all before.

Taxi
Taxis are plentiful on the streets of most Hungarian cities and, if you are charged the correct fare, very reasonably priced. Flag fall varies, but a fair price is 150Ft to 200Ft, with the charge per kilometre about the same, depending on whether you booked it by telephone (cheaper) or hailed it on the street. The best places to find taxis are in ranks at bus and train stations, near markets and around main squares. But you can flag down cruising taxis anywhere at any time. At night, vacant taxis have an illuminated sign on the roof.

To minimise the chances of being ripped off, try to book a cab with a reliable company by telephone; numbers are listed under Getting Around for many towns and cities. You don't have to call from a private phone; Hungarian taxi companies use a 'reverse' telephone directory, with cabs dispatched to the address of where the phone is listed – including phone boxes, which post numbers either above the handset or on the door outside.

While taking a taxi is almost always without incident in the provinces, it is not uncommon in Budapest and some touristy places outside the capital for taxi drivers to try to rip foreigners off. See Getting Around in the Budapest chapter for advice on how to avoid this.

A Street by Any Other Name

After WWII, most streets, squares and parks were renamed after people, dates or political groups that have since become anathema to an independent and democratic Hungary. From April 1989, names were changed at a frantic pace and with a determination that some people felt was almost obsessive; Cartographia's *Budapest Atlas* lists almost 400 street name changes in the capital alone. Sometimes it was just a case of returning a street or square to its original (perhaps medieval) name – from Lenin útja, say, to Szent korona útja (Street of the Holy Crown). Other times the name is new.

The new (or original) names are now in place after more than a decade, the old street signs with a red 'X' drawn across them have all but disappeared and virtually no one refers to Ferenciek tere (Square of the Franciscans) in Budapest, for example, as Felszabadulás tér (Liberation Square), which honoured the Soviet Army's role in liberating Budapest in WWII.

ORGANISED TOURS

A number of travel agencies, including Vista, Ibusz, Cityrama and Hungary Program Centrum (see Travel Agencies under Information, and also Organised Tours, in the Budapest chapter) offer excursions and special-interest guided tours (horse riding, cycling, bird-watching, Jewish culture etc) to every corner of Hungary.

A 4½-hour tour by boat and bus to Szentendre or to Gödölö by bus with Cityrama costs 10,000Ft (children under 12 half-price) while a 10-hour tour of the Danube Bend by coach and boat with stops at Szentendre, Visegrád and Esztergom costs 16,000Ft. Cityrama also offers day trips to Lake Balaton (Balatonfüred, Tihany and the southern shore) and Herend (nine hours) as well as to Lajosmizse on the Southern Plain (eight hours) for 17,000Ft each.

Hungary Program Centrum offers similar tours at almost the same prices as well as an eight-hour trip to Bugac in Kiskunság National Park and a nine-hour tour of the Eger wine region (19,000Ft each). Vista tours of the countryside start at 9750Ft.

If you're interested in touring the Northeast (a difficult area to appreciate without your own wheels), contact Nyíregyháza-based **Air Mediterran** (☎/fax 42-314 303; **W** www .airmed.hu); no one knows that part of the country better than it does. All-inclusive programmes include an week-long tour along the Tisza River to Tokaj on horseback (€450) and an eight-day bicycle tour of the Northeast (€375). It also does shorter wine-tasting tours in and around Tokaj for between €10 and €45.

Budapest

☎ 1 • pop 1,886,000

There is no other city in Hungary like Budapest. With just under two million inhabitants, the metropolis is home to almost a fifth of the national population. As Hungary's capital *(főváros)*, Budapest is the administrative, business and the cultural centre of the country; virtually everything in this amazing country starts, finishes or is taking place in Budapest.

But it is the beauty and the location of Budapest that really set it apart. Straddling a gentle curve in the Danube River, the city is flanked by the Buda Hills on the western bank and what is essentially the start of the Great Plain region to the east. Architecturally, it is a gem. What the city may lack in medieval buildings (thank the Turks and the Habsburgs for that) Budapest more than makes up for with baroque, neoclassical, Eclectic and Art Nouveau (or Secessionist) architecture.

Overall, however, Budapest has a *fin-de-siècle* feel to it, for it was then – during the industrial boom and the capital's 'golden age' in the late 19th century – that most of today's city was built. In some places, particularly along the two ring roads and up Andrássy út to the City Park, Budapest's nickname – 'the Paris of Central Europe' – is well deserved. Nearly every building in this district has some interesting or unusual detail – from Art Nouveau glazed tiles and neoclassical reliefs to bullet holes left over from WWII or the 1956 Uprising (see that section under History in the Facts about Hungary chapter for details).

In fact, Budapest's scars are not well hidden. Industrial and automobile pollution have exacerbated the decay, but in recent years the rebuilding and renovations have been nothing short of astonishing.

Budapest is at its best in the spring and summer months, or just after dark when Castle Hill is bathed in a warm yellow light. You could stroll along the Danube River embankment (Duna korzó) on the Pest side or across any of the bridges, past young couples embracing passionately – and it is then that you will feel the romance of a city that, despite all attempts both from within and outside it to destroy it, has never died.

Highlights

- The view from Fishermen's Bastion on Castle Hill
- A night at the Hungarian State Opera House
- A soak at any of the following thermal baths: Gellért, Rudas, Király or Széchenyi
- The two icons of Hungarian nationhood: the Crown of St Stephen in the Parliament building and the saint-king's mortal remains in the Basilica of St Stephen
- The period furniture and bric-a-brac inside the Applied Arts Museum and the external Secessionist features

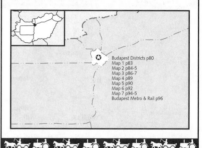

Budapest Districts p80
Map 1 p83
Map 2 p84-5
Map 3 p86-7
Map 4 p89
Map 5 p90
Map 6 p92
Map 7 p94-5
Budapest Metro & Rail p96

HISTORY

Strictly speaking, the story of Budapest begins only in 1873 when hilly, residential Buda and historic Óbuda on the western bank of the Danube merged with flat, industrial Pest on the eastern side to form what was at first called Pest-Buda. But like so much in Hungary it's not that simple.

The Romans had an important colony here called Aquincum until the 5th century, when they were forced to flee the settlement by the Huns. The Magyars arrived nearly half a millennium later, but Buda and Pest were no more than villages until the 12th century, when foreign merchants and tradespeople settled here. In the late 13th century King Béla IV built a fortress in Buda, but it was King Charles Robert (Károly Róbert) who moved the court from Visegrád to Buda 50 years later. His son Louis the Great (Nagy Lajos) began the construction of a royal palace.

The Mongols had burned Buda and Pest to the ground in 1241–42, and thus began a pattern of destruction and rebuilding that would last until the 20th century. Under the Turks, the two towns lost most of their populations, and when the Turks were defeated by the Habsburgs in the late 17th century Buda Castle was in ruins. The 1848 Revolution, WWII and the 1956 Uprising all took their toll.

Budapest is on the mend in a big way, with new buildings erected, old ones refaced and streets pedestrianised. Before long it will again rank as one of Europe's most elegant cities.

ORIENTATION

Budapest lies in the northcentral part of Hungary, some 250km southeast of Vienna. The Danube River (Duna), the city's traditional artery, is spanned by nine bridges that link hilly, historic Buda with bustling, commercial and very flat Pest.

It's a large, sprawling city measuring 525 sq km but, with few exceptions (the Buda Hills, City Park and some excursions), the areas beyond the Nagykörút (literally the 'big ring road') in Pest and west of Moszkva tér in Buda are residential or industrial and of little interest to visitors. It is a well laid-out city, so much so that it is almost difficult to get lost here.

If you look at a map of the city you'll see that two ring roads – Nagykörút (the big one) and the semicircular Kiskörút (the 'little ring road') – link three of the bridges across the Danube and essentially define central Pest. The Nagykörút consists of Szent István körút, Teréz körút, Erzsébet körút, József körút and

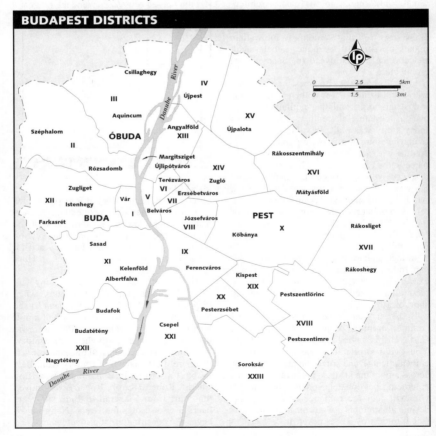

BUDAPEST DISTRICTS

Ferenc körút (all contiguous). The Kiskörút comprises Károly körút, Múzeum körút and Vámház körút. Important boulevards like Bajcsy-Zsilinszky út, leafy Andrássy út, Rákóczi út and Üllői út fan out from the ring roads, creating large squares and circles.

Buda is dominated by Castle and Gellért Hills; the main square is Moszkva tér. Important roads on this side are Margit körút (the only part of either ring road to cross the river), Fő utca and Attila út on either side of Castle Hill, and Hegyalja út and Bartók Béla út running westerly and southwesterly.

Budapest is divided into 23 kerület (districts), which usually also have traditional names like Lipótváros (Leopold Town) in the district XIII or Víziváros (Watertown) in district I. The Roman numeral appearing before each street address signifies the district.

Maps

Lonely Planet's *Budapest City Map* covers the more popular parts of town in detail.

The best folding maps of the city are Cartographia's 1:20,000 (550Ft) and 1:28,000 (450Ft) for *Budapest*. If you plan to explore the city thoroughly, the *Budapest Atlas*, also from Cartographia, is indispensable. It comes in two scales: 1:25,000 (1900Ft) and the larger format 1:20,000 (2900Ft) one. There is also a 1:25,000 pocket atlas of just the Inner Town available for 900Ft.

Many bookshops, including Libri Könyvpalota (see Bookshops later), stock a wide variety of maps. **Cartographia** *(Map 5; ☎ 312 6001; VI Bajcsy-Zsilinszky út 37; metro M3 Arany János utca; open 9am-5pm Mon-Wed, 9am-6.30pm Thur, 9am-3.30pm Fri)* has its own outlet in Budapest, but it's not self-service, which can be annoying. A better bet (if you're looking for maps) is the small **Páriszi Udvari Könyvesbolt** *(Páriszi Udvar Bookshop; Map 6; ☎ 235 0379; V Petőfi Sándor utca 2; metro M3 Ferenciek tere; open 9am-7pm Mon-Fri, 10am-2pm Sat)* in the Páriszi Udvar, or the larger **Térképkirály** *(Map King; Map 6; ☎ 266 0561; V Sas utca 1; metro M1/2/3 Deák tér; open 10am-5pm Mon-Fri)*.

INFORMATION
Tourist Offices

The best single source of information about Budapest is **Tourinform** *(Map 6; ☎ 438 8080, fax 356 1964; e hungary@tourinform.hu; w www.hungarytourism.hu; V Vigadó utca 6;*

metro M1 Vörösmarty tér; open 24hr). It has a nearby branch *(Map 6; ☎ 438 8080, fax 356 1964; V Sütő utca 2; metro M1/2/3 Deák Ferenc tér; open 8am-8pm daily)* and a **24-hour information hotline** *(☎ 06-80 66 0044)*.

Another option for tourist information is the **Budapest Tourist Office** *(BTO; fax 266 7477; e info@budapestinfo.hu; w www.buda pestinfo.hu)*, with a Castle Hill branch *(Map 4; ☎ 488 0453, fax 488 0474; I Szentháromság tér; bus No 16 or Várbusz; open 8am-8pm daily Apr-Oct; 9am-6pm daily Nov-Mar)* in a kiosk opposite Saint Matthias Church; a Pest branch *(Map 5; ☎ 322 4098, fax 342 9390; VI Liszt Ferenc tér 11; metro M1 Oktogon; open 8am-8pm daily Apr-Oct; 9am-6pm daily Nov-Mar)* and a Nyugati train station branch *(Map 5; ☎/fax 302 8580; Nyugati pályaudvar, track No 10; metro M3 Nyugati pályaudvar; open 8am-8pm daily Apr-Oct; 9am-6pm daily Nov-Mar)*.

For details on commercial outfits that can book accommodation and transport and change money, see Travel Agencies later.

Money

OTP bank *(Map 6; V Nádor utca 6; metro M1 Vörösmarty tér, bus No 15; open 7.45am-5pm Mon, 7.45am-4pm Tues-Fri)* offers among the best exchange rates for cash and travellers cheques, but get there at least an hour before closing to ensure the *bureau de change* counter is still open. **K&H** *(Map 6; V Váci utca 40; metro M3 Ferenciek tere; open 8am-5pm Mon, 8am-4pm Tues-Thur, 8am-3pm Fri)* often offers good rates, too. There are automated teller machines (ATMs) all around the city, including in the train and bus stations, and quite a few foreign-currency exchange machines, including one at V Károly körút 20.

Though credit cards are widely accepted nowadays in Budapest – even at some youth hostels – it is always more prudent to consider plastic an option rather than the rule. The **Tribus Nonstop Hotel Service** *(Map 6; ☎ 318 3925, 318 4848; w www.tribus.hu; V Apáczai Csere János utca 1; metro M3 Ferenciek tere)*, near the Budapest Marriott Hotel, is a 24-hour facility with exchange.

American Express *(Map 6; ☎ 235 4330; V Deák Ferenc utca 10; metro M1/2/3 Deák tér; open 9am-5.30pm Mon-Fri, 9am-2pm Sat)* changes its own travellers cheques without commission, but its rates are poor. Its commission on converting US-dollar travellers cheques into cash dollars is 7%. Citibank cardholders should go to **Citibank** *(Map 6; ☎ 458 2351, 266 9895; V Vörösmarty tér 4; open 8am-5pm Mon-Fri)*.

Whatever you do, avoid the big commercial *bureaux de change*, such as Interchange in Vörösmarty tér or on Castle Hill. Some deduct exorbitant 10% commissions while others have huge signs reading 'no commission' and advertise a rate – forgetting to mention you have to change the equivalent of US$1000 or more to get it or receive 10% below the bank rate. Moneychangers on the street come with the usual risks.

Post

The **main post office** *(Map 6; V Petőfi Sándor utca 13-15 or V Városház utca 18; metro 1/2/3 Deák tér; open 8am-8pm Mon-Fri, 8am-2pm Sat)* is a few minutes' walk from Deák tér and the Tourinform branch office. This is where you buy stamps, mail letters, send packages and faxes and pick up poste restante. There are also branches at the Nyugati train station *(Map 5; VI Teréz körút 51-53; metro M3 Nyugati pályaudvar; open 7am-9pm Mon-Sat, 8am-8pm Sun)* and at the Keleti train station *(Map 3; VIII Kerepesi út 2-6; metro M2 Keleti pályaudvar; open 7am-9pm Mon-Sat)*.

Telephone

The best place to make international telephone calls in Budapest is from a phone box with a phonecard. The phone boxes just inside the front door of the main post office (see Post earlier) are relatively quiet.

You can send faxes from the main post office as well as from Internet cafés for 150/500Ft per page within/outside Hungary. it is also possible to make calls and send or receive faxes at hotel business centres like the one at the **Kempinski Hotel Corvinus** *(Map 6; ☎ 429 3777; V Erzsébet tér 7-8; metro M1/2/3 Deák tér)*.

Budapest's telephone code is ☎ 1.

Email & Internet Access

Many of the year-round hostels and almost all hotels (see Places to Stay later) in Budapest now offer Internet access. If the place you're staying at doesn't have it or you just feel like checking your mail on the trot, the following are among the more central Internet cafés.

Ami Internet Coffee (Map 6; ☎ 267 1644, ⓦ www .amicoffee.hu) V Váci utca 40 (metro M3 Ferenciek tere) Open 9am to 2am daily. This very central place has 50 terminals and charges 200/400/700 for up to 15/30/60 minutes. Five/10 hours cost 3250/6400Ft. The website is in Hungarian only.

Budapest Net Internet Café (Map 6; ☎ 328 0292, ⓦ www.budapestnet.hu) V Kecskeméti utca 5 (metro M3 Kálvin tér) Open 10am to 10pm daily. With more than 50 terminals, this place attracts students from nearby ELTE university. It charges 150/350/700Ft for up to 10/30/60 minutes (2400/4600Ft for five/10 hours). The website is in Hungarian only.

Matáv Telepont Internet Café (Map 6; ☎ 485 6612) V Petőfi Sándor utca 17–19 (metro M1/2/3 Deák tér) Open 9am to 8pm Monday to Friday, 10pm to 3pm Saturday. This smallish café (eight terminals) is run by the national telecommunications company and charges 300/500Ft for 30/60 minutes. A 10-hour pass costs 4000Ft.

Vista Internet Café (Map 6; ☎ 429 9952, 269 6032, fax 429 9951, ⓔ icafe@vista.hu) VI Paulay Ede utca 7 (metro M1/2/3 Deák tér) Open 10am to 10pm Monday to Friday, 10am to 8pm Saturday. This café at the Vista Visitor Center (see Travel Agencies later) charges 11/660Ft per minute/hour.

Internet Resources

The best overall site for Budapest is ⓦ www.budapestinfo.hu. Budapest Week Online, with events, music and movie listings nationwide, is at ⓦ www.budapestweek.com. Budapest Sun Online (ⓦ www.budapestsun.com) is similar, but also has local news, interviews and features.

For Hungarian websites with Budapest links, see Digital Resources in the Facts for the Visitor chapter.

Travel Agencies

Many of the offices listed here and those listed under Private Rooms in the Places to Stay section later also provide information and often brochures and maps.

The main office of **Ibusz** *(Map 6; ☎ 485 2723, 485 2767; ⓦ www.ibusz.hu; V Ferenciek tere 10; metro M3 Ferenciek tere; open 8.15am-5.30pm Mon-Fri, 9am-1pm Sat in summer; 8.15am-4.30pm Mon-Fri in winter)* supplies travel brochures, changes money, books all types of accommodation and accepts credit-card payments. The website is in Hungarian only. The nearby branch *(Map 6; ☎ 322 7214; VII Dob utca 1; metro M2 Astoria)* is good for booking train tickets.

[Continued on page 97]

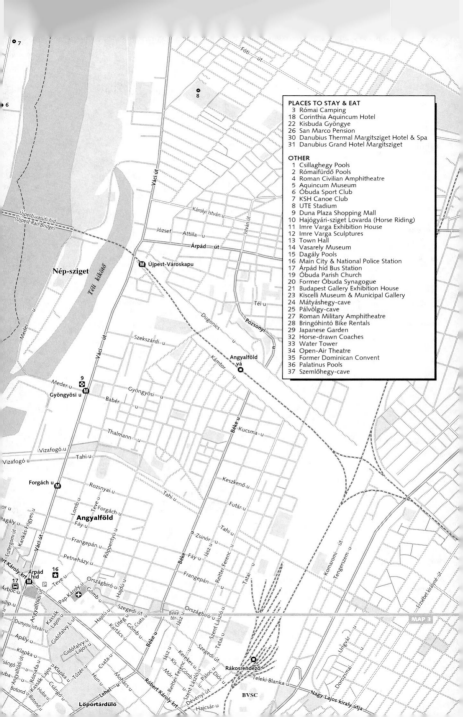

PLACES TO STAY & EAT
3 Római Camping
18 Corinthia Aquincum Hotel
22 Kisbuda Gyöngye
26 San Marco Pension
30 Danubius Thermal Margitsziget Hotel & Spa
31 Danubius Grand Hotel Margitsziget

OTHER
1 Csillaghegy Pools
2 Rómaifürdő Pools
4 Roman Civilian Amphitheatre
5 Aquincum Museum
6 Óbuda Sport Club
7 KSH Canoe Club
8 UTE Stadium
9 Duna Plaza Shopping Mall
10 Hajógyári-sziget Lovarda (Horse Riding)
11 Imre Varga Exhibition House
12 Imre Varga Sculptures
13 Town Hall
14 Vasarely Museum
15 Dagály Pools
16 Main City & National Police Station
17 Árpád híd Bus Station
19 Óbuda Parish Church
20 Former Óbuda Synagogue
21 Budapest Gallery Exhibition House
23 Kiscelli Museum & Municipal Gallery
24 Mátyáshegy-cave
25 Pálvölgy-cave
27 Roman Military Amphitheatre
28 Bringóhintó Bike Rentals
29 Japanese Garden
32 Horse-drawn Coaches
33 Water Tower
34 Open-Air Theatre
35 Former Dominican Convent
36 Palatinus Pools
37 Szemlőhegy-cave

MAP 3

MAP 3

PLACES TO STAY
3 Hotel Margitsziget
12 Papillon Pension
22 Büro Panzió
36 Diáksport Hostel
37 Hotel Góliát
50 Hotel Délibáb
52 Andrássy Hotel
55 Hotel Pedagógus
56 Radio Inn
71 Dominik Panzió
73 Station Guesthouse
75 Hotel Baross Panzió
76 Aquarium Youth Hostel
81 Danubius Gellért Hotel & Baths

PLACES TO EAT
15 Marxim Pizzeria
20 Íz-É Faloda
21 Fény utca Market
27 Kacsa
31 Móri Borozó
33 Firkász Restaurant
34 Lehel Csarnok
41 Bagolyvár
58 Angelika Café
60 Nagyi Palacsintázója Branch
62 Nagyi Palacsintázója
65 Il Treno Pizzeria
66 Mongolian Barbecue
67 Nonstop Food Shop
83 Coquan's Café
91 Nonstop Food Shop

MUSEUMS
42 Museum of Fine Arts
44 Transport Museum

47 Hungarian Agricultural Museum & Vajdahunyad Castle
48 Palace of Art (Műcsarnok)
53 Ferenc Hopp Museum of East Asia Art
57 György Ráth Museum
86 Museum of Applied Arts

OTHER
1 Danubius Helia Hotel Spa & Pools
2 Franciscan Church & Monastery Ruins
4 Újlak Synagogue
5 Alfréd Hajós National Sports Pool
6 Centennial Monument
7 Sétacikli Bike Rental & Stadium
8 Béla Komjádi Swimming Pool
9 Lukács Bath
10 Tomb of Gül Baba's
11 Magyar Autóklub
13 Marczibányi tér Cultural Centre
14 Millennium Exhibition Hall
16 International House Language School
17 Millennium Park
18 Mammut II Shopping Mall
19 Mammut I Shopping Mall
23 Széna tér Bus Station
24 BÁV Store
25 St Florian Chapel
26 Király Baths
28 Military Court of Justice & Fő utca Prison
29 Herend Village Pottery

30 Raoul Wallenberg Memorial
32 Pendragon Bookshop
35 Lehel Church
38 BVSC Swimming Pool
39 Municipal Great Circus
40 City Zoo & Botanical Garden
43 Széchenyi Bath
45 Petőfi Csarnok
46 Petőfi Csarnok Flea Market
49 Millenary Monument
51 Hungarian Language School
54 British Council
59 St Anne's Church
61 American Clinics
63 Oscar's American Bar
64 Budapest Wine Society Shop
68 Almássy tér Recreation Centre
69 Angel Club
70 Central Europe Dance Theatre
72 Kisstadion
74 Népstadion Bus Station
77 Budapest Congress Centre
78 Citadella; Citadella Hostel & Hotel
79 Independence Monument
80 Cave Chapel
82 Budapest Economics University
84 Paris, Texas
85 Monarchia Wine Shop
87 Corvin Film Palace
88 Trafó House of Contemporary Arts
89 Rákóczi tér Market
90 Erkel Theatre
92 Hungária Stadium

MARTIN MOOS

Interesting restaurant shutters in central Pest

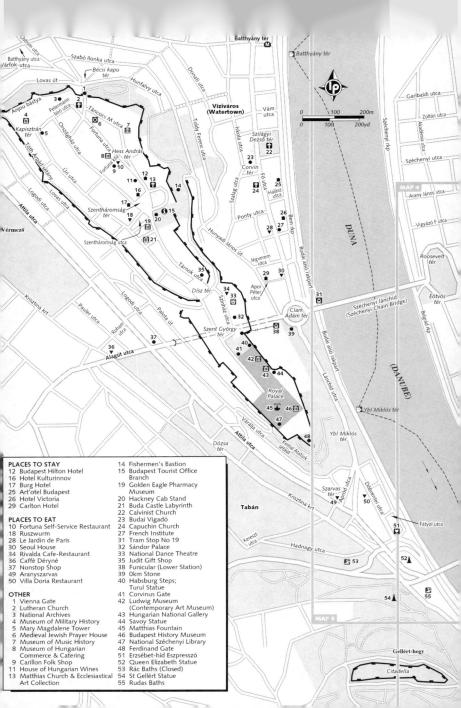

PLACES TO STAY
12 Budapest Hilton Hotel
16 Hotel Kulturinnov
17 Burg Hotel
25 Art'otel Budapest
26 Hotel Victoria
29 Carlton Hotel

PLACES TO EAT
10 Fortuna Self-Service Restaurant
18 Ruszwurm
28 Le Jardin de Paris
30 Seoul House
34 Rivalda Cafe-Restaurant
37 Nonstop Shop
49 Aranyszarvas
50 Villa Doria Restaurant

OTHER
1 Vienna Gate
2 Lutheran Church
3 National Archives
4 Museum of Military History
5 Mary Magdalene Tower
6 Medieval Jewish Prayer House
7 Museum of Music History
8 Museum of Hungarian
  Commerce & Catering
9 Carillon Folk Shop
11 House of Hungarian Wines
13 Matthias Church & Ecclesiastical
  Art Collection

14 Fishermen's Bastion
15 Budapest Tourist Office
  Branch
19 Golden Eagle Pharmacy
  Museum
20 Hackney Cab Stand
21 Buda Castle Labyrinth
22 Calvinist Church
23 Budai Vigadó
24 Capuchin Church
27 French Institute
31 Tram Stop No 19
32 Sándor Palace
33 National Dance Theatre
35 Judit Gift Shop
36 Funicular (Lower Station)
39 0km Stone
40 Habsburg Steps;
  Turul Statue
41 Corvinus Gate
42 Ludwig Museum
  (Contemporary Art Museum)
43 Hungarian National Gallery
44 Savoy Statue
45 Matthias Fountain
46 Budapest History Museum
47 National Széchényi Library
48 Ferdinand Gate
51 Erzsébet-híd Eszpresszó
52 Queen Elizabeth Statue
53 Rác Baths (Closed)
54 St Gellért Statue
55 Rudas Baths

MAP 5

PLACES TO STAY
18 Yellow Submarine Youth Hostel
19 Best Hostel
39 Hotel Medosz
45 Garibaldi Guesthouse & Apartments
60 Caterina Hostel
77 Hostel Marco Polo
80 Mercure Nemzeti Hotel
85 Museum Castle Youth Guest House

PLACES TO EAT
1 Mézes Kuckó
2 Rothschild Supermarket
5 Szeráj
7 Művész Bohém
9 Okay Italia
10 Három Testvér Branch
11 Wabisabi
12 Don Pepe Pizzeria
13 Okay Italia Branch
14 Kaiser's Supermarket
20 Lukács Café
31 Marquis de Salade
34 Három Testvér Branch
35 Arigato
36 McDonald's (24 Hours)
37 Butterfly Ice Cream Shop
38 Teaház a Vörös Oroszlánhoz
42 Hold utca Food Market
44 Pick Ház
47 Iguana
56 Művész Café
58 Bombay Palace

62 La Tasca
64 Café Vian
68 Incognito Café
69 Frici Papa Kifőzdéje
72 Kádár Canteen
73 Három Testvér
78 Match Supermarket

PUBS, BARS & CLUBS
8 Trocadero Club
16 Bank Music Club
25 Becketts Irish Pub
32 New Orleans Music Club
40 Piaf
59 Cactus Juice
70 Szimpla
75 Old Man's Music Pub

TOURIST OFFICES, ACCOMMODATION SERVICES & BOOKING AGENCIES
27 Cooptourist
46 Express Branch
61 Budapest Tourist Office Branch
67 MÁV Central Ticket Office

MUSEUMS
22 Franz Liszt Memorial Museum
23 House of Terror
29 Ethnography Museum

SHOPPING
3 Szőnyi Antiquarian Bookshop
4 BÁV Store

15 West End City Centre Shopping Mall
52 Haas & Czjzek Porcelain
55 BÁV Store
65 Writers' Bookshop
66 Liszt Music Shop
81 Libri Könyvpalota Bookshop

OTHER
6 Comedy Theatre
17 Post Office
21 Budapest Puppet Theatre
24 Teréz Patika (Pharmacy)
26 Inner Town Police Station
28 Parliament
30 Cityrama Bus Tours
33 Művész Cinema
41 Cartographia Map Shop
43 Imre Nagy Monument
48 Soviet Army Memorial
49 US Embassy
50 National Bank of Hungary
51 Top Clean Laundry
53 Hungarian State Opera House
54 Goethe Institute
57 Budapest Operetta Theatre
63 Liszt Academy of Music
71 Örökmozgó Film Museum
74 New York Palace
76 BKV Lost & Found Office
79 Csillag Gyógyszertár (Pharmacy)
82 Uránia National Cinema
83 Kenguru Ride Service
84 Former Hungarian Radio Headquarters

One of Budapest's fashionable shopping arcades

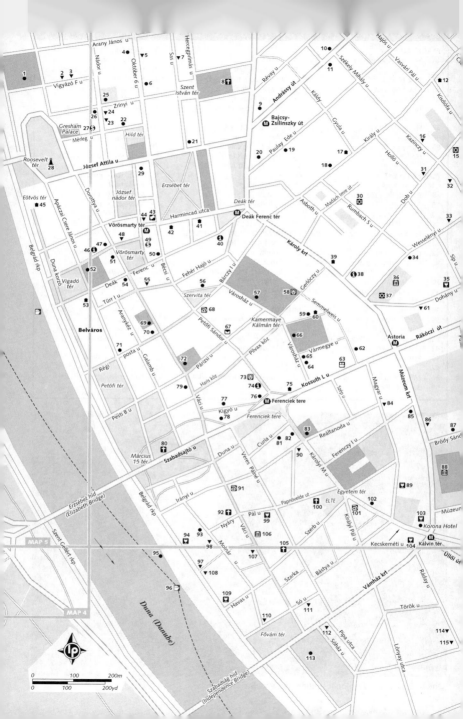

MAP 6

PLACES TO STAY
12 Club Hotel Ambra
17 Hotel Fiesta
39 Carmen Mini Hotel
41 Le Meridien Budapest
42 Kempinski Hotel Corvinus
45 Budapest Inter-Continental
   Hotel (big landmark)
53 Budapest Marriott Hotel
60 Red Bus Hostel &
   Second-hand Bookstore
75 Leó Panzió

PLACES TO EAT
2 Gandhi
3 Lou Lou
5 Kisharang
7 Café Kör
14 Zazie
16 Kővári Kosher Delicatessen
23 Xi Hu
24 Coquan's Cafe
31 Fröhlich Cake Shop
32 Kosher Bakery
33 Kinor David
44 Sushi An
48 Gerbeaud
55 Cosmo
61 Fausto's
84 Baraka Restaurant
86 Múzeum Café-Restaurant
90 Centrál Kávéház
97 Taverna Dionysos
98 Sole d'Italia
107 1000 Tea
108 Trattoria Toscana
110 Rembetiko Pireus
111 Bangkok House Restaurant
112 Nagycsarnok (Great Market)
114 Teaház a Vörös Oroszlánhoz
115 Soul Café

PUBS, BARS & CLUBS
35 Champs Sport Pub
89 Action
94 Capella Café
99 Fat Mo's Music Club
103 Irish Cat Pub

104 Cha Cha Cha Café-Bar
109 Limo Café

**TOURIST OFFICES,
ACCOMMODATION SERVICES &
BOOKING AGENCIES**
4 To-Ma Travel Agency
9 Budatours
10 Ticket Express
11 Central Ticket Office
19 Vista Visitor Center; Vista
   Internet Café
20 Vista Travel Center
22 Philharmonic Ticket Office
38 Ibusz Branch
40 Tourinform Branch
46 Tourinform (Main Branch)
47 Malév Ticket Office
51 Vigadó Ticket Office
62 Express
71 Tribus Nonstop Hotel Service
74 Ibusz (Main Office)
78 Starting Point Tourist Service
82 Pegazus Tours
102 Music Mix Ticket Office

MUSEUMS
36 Jewish Museum
88 Hungarian National Museum

SHOPPING
6 Bestsellers Bookshop
13 Kosher Wine Shop
29 Herend
59 Holló Atelier
69 Philanthia Flower Shop
70 Polgár Gallery; Thonet House
72 Libri Studium Bookshop
77 Zsolnay
85 Központi Antikvárium
106 Folkart Centrum

OTHER
1 Hungarian Academy of
   Sciences
8 St Stephen's Basilica
15 Orthodox Synagogue; Hanna
   Restaurant

18 S.O.S. Dental Service
21 Térképkirály Map Shop
25 Central European University;
   Bookshop; Cafeteria
26 Duna Palota
27 OTP Bank
28 Deák Statue
30 Rumbach Sebestyén utca
   Synagogue
34 Holocaust Memorial
37 Great Synagogue
43 UK Embassy
49 Citibank
50 American Express; American
   Chamber of Commerce
52 Pesti Vigadó
54 Bank Palace
56 Avis
57 City Hall
58 Merlin Theatre
63 Puskin Cinema
64 World Press House
65 Irisz Szalon
66 Pest County Hall
67 Main Post Office
68 Matáv Telepont Internet Café
73 József Katona Theatre;
   Kamra
76 Párizsi Udvar
79 Rent-A-Bike
80 Inner Town Parish Church
81 Friends of the City Cycling
   Group
83 University Library
87 Italian Institute of Culture
91 Ami Internet Coffee; K&H
   Bank
92 St Michael's Church
93 Aranytíz Youth Centre
   (Kalamajka Táncház)
95 Mahart PassNave Ticket
   Office
96 International Ferry pier
100 University Church
101 Budapest Net Internet Café
105 Serbian Orthodox Church
113 Budapest Economics
   University; Közgáz Pince Klub

Budapest's Castle Hill displays its stunning architecture

MARTIN MOOS

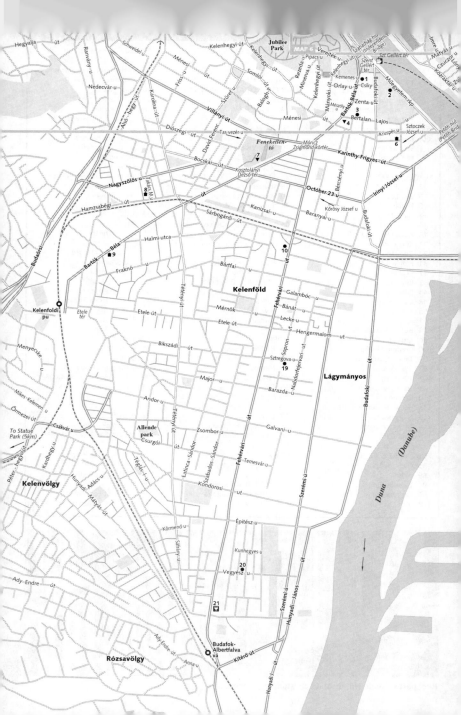

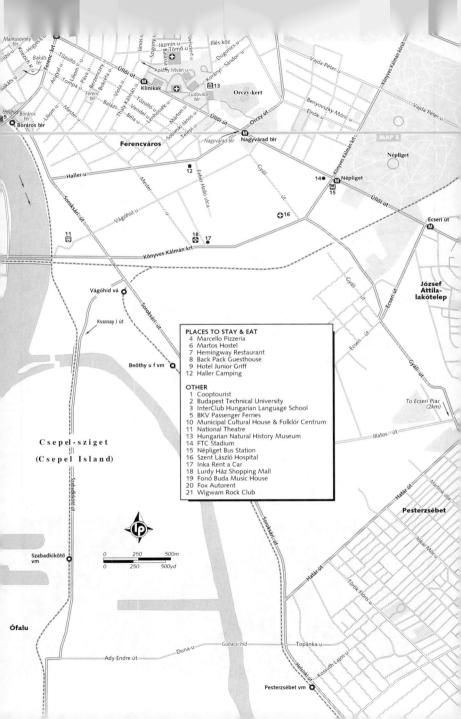

PLACES TO STAY & EAT
4 Marcello Pizzeria
6 Martos Hostel
7 Hemingway Restaurant
8 Back Pack Guesthouse
9 Hotel Junior Griff
12 Haller Camping

OTHER
1 Cooptourist
2 Budapest Technical University
3 InterClub Hungarian Language School
5 BKV Passenger Ferries
10 Municipal Cultural House & Folklór Centrum
11 National Theatre
13 Hungarian Natural History Museum
14 FTC Stadium
15 Népliget Bus Station
16 Szent László Hospital
17 Inka Rent a Car
18 Lurdy Ház Shopping Mall
19 Fonó Buda Music House
20 Fox Autorent
21 Wigwam Rock Club

BUDAPEST METRO & RAIL

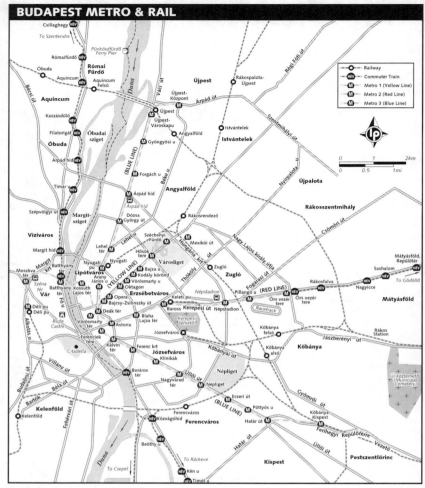

Legend:
- Railway
- HÉV Commuter Train
- M Metro 1 (Yellow Line)
- M Metro 2 (Red Line)
- M Metro 3 (Blue Line)

0   1   2km
0   0.5   1mi

Csillaghegy HÉV
To Szentendre
Pünkösdfürdő Ferry Pier
Rómaifürdő HÉV
Óbuda
Aquincum
Aquincum Felső
Bécsi út
Római Fürdő
Újpest
Rákospalota-Újpest
Régi Fóti út
Váci út
Aquincum
Kaszásdűlő
Újpest-Központ
Árpád út
Szentmihályi út
Óbuda
Filatorigát HÉV
Óbudai sziget
Újpest-Városkapu
Angyalföld
Istvántelek
Istvántelek
Gyöngyösi u
Újpalota
Árpád híd HÉV
Forgách u
Béke út
Angyalföld
Nyírpalota u
Rákosszentmihály
Tímár u HÉV
Árpád híd
Szépvölgyi út HÉV
Margit-sziget
Dózsa György út
Rákosrendező
Csömöri út
Vízíváros
Margit hid
Margit krt
Lehel tér
Lehel u
Széchenyi Fürdő
Mexikói út
Nagy Lajos király útja
Mátyásföld, Repülőtér
Moszkva tér
Batthyány tér
Nyugati pu
Nyugati
Hősök tere
Hungária krt
Zugló
Sashalom
Szép utca
Lipótváros
Arany János u
Bajza u
Kodály körönd
Városliget
Zugló
Fogarasi út
Rákosfalva
Nagyicce
To Gödöllő
Vár
Batthyány tér
Kossuth Lajos tér
Vörösmarty u
Oktogon
Thököly
Pillangó u
Örs vezér tere
Örs vezér tere
Mátyásföld
Déli pu
Déli pu
Opera
Bajcsy-Zsilinszky út
Keleti pu
Népstadion
Buda Castle
Deák tér
Kerepesi út
Népstadion
Vörösmarty tér
Astoria
Blaha Lujza tér
Baross
Racetrack
Rákos Station
Allatlás u
Ferenciek tere
Kálvin tér
Kerepesi temető
Józsefváros
Kőbánya felső
Kőbánya
Jászberényi út
Citadella
Ferenc krt
Klinikák
Kőbánya alsó
Budaörsi út
Villányi út
Boráros tér
Józsefváros
Üllői út
Béla út
Bartók
Nagyvárad tér
Népliget
Gyömrői út
Új köztemető (Municipal Cemetery)
Fehérvári út
Ecseri út
Pöttyös u
Kőbánya-Kispest
Kelenföld
Kelenföld
Ferencváros
Határ út
Ferihegyi Repülőtérie
Vezető út
Közvágóhíd
Ferencváros
Határ út
Üllői út
Pestszentlőrinc
Duna
Beöthy u
To Ráckeve
Kispest
To Csepel
Kén u HÉV
Tímót u HÉV

One of Budapest's efficient trains leaves the Vorosmarty utca station

MARTIN MOOS

[Continued from page 82]

The main office of **Express** (Map 6; ☎ 317 8600; ⓦ www.express-travel.hu; V Semmelweiss utca 1-3; metro M2 Astoria; open 8am-6pm Mon-Fri, 9am-1pm Sat) can book accommodation in Budapest, particularly hostels and colleges, while the branch (Map 5; ☎ 311 6418; V Zoltán utca 10; metro M2 Kossuth Lajos tér; open 8.30am-4.30pm Mon-Thur, 8.30am-4pm Fri) books international and domestic trains, Eurolines buses, and sells cheap airline tickets.

An excellent one-stop shop for all your outbound needs (air tickets, package tours etc) is the massive **Vista Travel Center** (Map 6; ☎ 429 9999, 429 9760; ⓦ www.vista.hu; VI Andrássy út 1; metro M1/2/3 Deák tér; open 9am-6.30pm Mon-Fri, 9am-2.30pm Sat). Its website is in Hungarian only. The **Vista Visitor Center** (Map 6; ☎ 429 9950; VI Paulay Ede utca; metro M3 Deák tér; open 9am-8pm Mon-Fri, 10am-6pm Sat) handles all the incoming stuff – tourist information, study and ecological tours in Hungary, room bookings, organised tours etc. There's a popular café and Internet centre here, too (see its entry under Email & Internet Access earlier).

The **Wasteels agency** (Map 3; ☎ 210 2802, 343 3492; VIII Kerepesi út 2-6; metro M2 Keleti pályaudvar; open 8am-7pm Mon-Fri, 8am-1pm Sat) at the top of platform No 9 at Keleti train station sells BIJ tickets. You must have an ISIC or IYTC card (see Student, Youth & Teacher Cards under Visas & Documents in the Facts for the Visitor chapter) in order to get the discounted fare, available at Express or Vista for 1100Ft.

Another helpful agency is **Cooptourist** (Map 5; ☎ 312 1017, 332 6387; Kossuth Lajos tér 13-15; metro M2 Kossuth Lajos tér; open 8am-4pm Mon & Tues, Thur & Fri, 8am-5pm Wed). It also has a branch (Map 7; ☎ 466 5349, 209 6667; XI Bartók Béla út 4; tram No 47 or 49; open 9am-5pm Mon-Sat) at Buda.

Bookshops

Top of the pops for English-language bookshops in Budapest is the recently expanded **Bestsellers** (Map 6; ☎ 312 1295; V Október 6 utca 11; metro M1/2/3 Deák tér; open 9am-6.30pm Mon-Fri, 10am-5pm Sat, 10am-4pm Sun), which has novels, travel guides, Hungarica, magazines and newspapers. Under the same management is the nearby **CEU Bookshop** (Map 6; ☎ 327 3096; V Nádor utca 9; open 9am-6pm Mon-Fri, 10am-4pm Sat), at the Central European University, which has an excellent selection of academic and business titles with a regional focus.

The huge **Libri Könyvpalota** (Map 5; ☎ 267 4844; VII Rákóczi út 12; metro M2 Astoria; open 10am-7.30pm Mon-Fri, 10am-3pm Sat) really is a 'book palace'. Spread over two floors it has a huge selection of English-language novels, art books, guidebooks and maps and a café on the 1st floor. Try the more central **Libri Studium** (Map 6; ☎ 318 5881; V Váci utca 22; metro M3 Ferenciek tere; open 10am-7pm Mon-Fri, 10am-3pm Sat & Sun) for books in English on Hungarian subjects.

Pendragon (Map 3; ☎ 340 4426; XIII Pozsonyi út 21-23; tram No 4 or 6; open 10am-6pm Mon-Fri, 10am-2pm Sat) has an excellent selection of English books and guides (including Lonely Planet titles) as does the small Páriszi Udvari Könyvesbolt (see Maps earlier in this chapter), and the Bamako bookshop at the Vista Travel Center (see Travel Agencies earlier for details) stocks guides as well as maps.

For Hungarian authors in translation, **Writers' Bookshop** (Írók Boltja; Map 5; ☎ 322 1645; VI Andrássy út 45; metro M1 Oktogon, tram No 4 or 6; open 10am-6pm Mon-Fri, 10am-1pm Sat) is the place to go.

For antique and second-hand books in Hungarian, German and English try **Központi Antikvárium** (Map 6; ☎ 317 3514; V Múzeum körút 13-15; metro M3 Kálvin tér; open 10am-6.30pm Mon-Fri, 10am-2pm Sat), which was established in 1881 and is the largest antiquarian bookshop in Budapest. Another good *antikvárium* is **Szőnyi** (Map 5; ☎ 311 6431; V Szent István körút 3; tram No 4 or 6; open 10am-6pm Mon-Fri, 9am-1pm Sat), with an excellent selection of antique prints and maps as well as books.

The **Red Bus Second-hand Bookstore** (Map 6; ☎ 337 7453; V Semmelweiss utca 14; metro M2 Astoria; open 10am-7pm Mon-Fri, 10am-2pm Sat), below the popular hostel of that name (see Hostels under Places to Stay – Budget, later), is the only shop in town selling used English-language books.

The best place in town for foreign-language newspapers and magazines is **World Press House** (Világsajtó Háza; Map 6; V Városház utca 3-5; metro M3 Ferenciek tere; open 7am-7pm Mon-Fri, 7am-6pm Sat, 8am-4pm Sun).

Cultural Centres

In Budapest you'll find the following centres. Hours vary according to the department (library, media centre, gallery etc) and what's on.

British Council (Map 3; ☎ 478 4741, 478 4779, W www.britishcouncil.hu) VI Benczúr utca 26 (metro M1 Bajza utca) Open 11am to 7pm Monday to Friday
French Institute (Map 4; ☎ 489 4200, W www .inst-france.hu) I Fő utca 17 (bus No 86, tram No 19) Open 8am to 9pm Monday to Friday, 8.30am to 1.30pm Saturday
Goethe Institute (Map 5; ☎ 374 4070, W www .goethe.de) VI Andrássy út 24 (metro M1 Opera) Open 9am to 7pm Monday to Friday
Italian Institute of Culture (Map 6; ☎ 483 2040, W www.datanet.hu/iic) VIII Bródy Sándor utca 8 (metro M3 Kálvin tér, tram No 47 or 49) Open 10am to 1pm and 4pm to 6pm Monday to Thursday, 10am to1pm Friday

Laundry

If your hostel or hotel does not have laundry facilities (see Laundry in the Facts for the Visitor chapter), about the only self-service laundrette is **Irisz Szalon** (Map 6; ☎ 317 2092; V Városház utca 3-5; metro M3 Ferenciek tere; open 7am-7pm Mon-Fri, 7am-1pm Sat).

The **Top Clean chain** (☎ 227 1500) does a fairly reliable and affordable job on both laundry and dry cleaning and has some 30 locations around Budapest, including a branch in district V (Map 5; ☎ 312 5418; V Arany János utca 34; metro Arany János utca; open 7am-6.30pm Mon-Fri, 8am-1pm Sat) and a West End City Centre branch (Map 5; ☎ 238 0388; VI Váci út 3; metro Nyugati pályaudvar; open 7am-6.30pm Mon-Fri, 8am-1pm Sat).

Left Luggage

Budapest's three major train stations, two bus stations and Ferihegy Airport all have left-luggage offices or lockers. For more information see the Bus and Train sections under Getting There & Away later, and To/From the Airport under Getting Around later.

Medical & Dental Services

The **American Clinics** (Map 3; ☎ 224 9090; W www.americanclinics.com; I Hattyú utca 14, 5th floor; metro M2 Moszkva tér; open 8.30am-7pm Mon-Thur, 8.30am-6pm Fri, 8.30am-noon Sat, 10am-2pm Sun) is a flash private medical clinic and can help you in an emergency (24-hour service), but it's not cheap: a basic consultation costs 28,600Ft.

S.O.S Dental Services (Map 6; ☎ 267 9602, 269 6010; VI Király utca 14; metro M1/2/3 Deák tér; open 24hr) charges 2000Ft for a consultation, 5000Ft to 6000Ft for extractions and from 6000Ft to 10,000Ft for fillings.

All of Budapest's 23 districts have a rotating all-night pharmacy; a sign on the door of any pharmacy will help you locate the nearest 24-hour place. Pharmacies with extended hours include the **Teréz Patika** (Map 5; ☎ 311 4439; VI Teréz körút 41; metro Nyugati pályaudvar; open 8am-8pm Mon-Fri, 8am-5pm Sat, 8am-1pm Sun) and the **Csillag Gyógyszertár** (Map 5; ☎ 314 3695; VIII Rákóczi út 39; metro Blaha Lujza tér; open 7.30am-9pm Mon-Fri, 7.30am-2pm Sat).

Emergency

If you need to report a crime or a lost or stolen passport or credit card, first call the central (☎ 112) or police (☎ 107) emergency help numbers or the English-language crime hotline (☎ 438 8000). Any crime must then be reported at the police station of the district you're in. In central Pest that would be the **District V Police Station** (☎ 302 5935; V Szalay utca 11-13). If possible, bring along a Hungarian speaker. In the high season, police officers pair up with university students (who act as translators) and patrol the busiest areas.

Dangers & Annoyances

No parts of Budapest are 'off-limits' to visitors, although some locals now avoid Margaret Island after dark and both residents and visitors give the dodgier parts of the 8th and 9th districts (areas of prostitution) a wide berth.

As in the rest of Hungary, you are most vulnerable to pickpockets, taxi louts, car thieves and the scammers. To avoid having your car ripped off, follow the usual security procedures: don't park it in a darkened street, make sure the burglar alarm is armed, have a steering-wheel lock in place and leave nothing of value inside.

Pickpocketing is most common in markets, the Castle District, Váci utca and Hősök tere, and on certain popular buses (eg, No 7) and trams (Nos 2, 4, 6, 47 and 49).

Scams involving attractive young women, gullible guys, expensive drinks in nightclubs and a frog-marching to the nearest ATM by gorillas-in-residence are all the rage in Budapest for several years now, and we get stacks of letters all the time from male readers complaining they've been ripped off. Guys, please: if it seems too good to be true, it is. Trust us and the mirror; such vanity has cost some hapless victims hundreds and even thousands of dollars.

Taking a taxi in Budapest can be an expensive and even unpleasant experience. Never hail a cab on the street; call one from a phone – private, mobile or public – and give the number (almost always posted somewhere in the phone box) to the dispatcher. For more information see Taxi under Getting Around later in this chapter.

If you've left something on any form of public transport in Budapest contact the **BKV lost & found office** *(Map 5; ☎ 267 5299; VII Akácfa utca 18; metro M2 Blaha Lujza tér; open 7am-3pm Mon-Thur, 7am-2pm Fri).*

Discount Cards

The **Budapest Card** *(☎ 266 0479; W www .budapestinfo.hu)* offers free admission to most museums and galleries in town and unlimited travel on all forms of public transport. It also gives discounts on organised tours, at thermal baths and at selected shops and restaurants. A card valid for 48/72 hours costs 3700/4500Ft. The card is sold at Tourinform offices and travel agencies, hotels and train, bus and main metro stations.

Also worth considering is the Hungary Card (see Discount Cards under Visas & Documents in the Facts for the Visitor chapter).

BUDA

Leafy and unpolluted, Buda as seen from Pest is not just a pretty face. The city's more majestic western side contains some of its most important and historical landmarks (eg, Castle Hill, the Citadella) and museums (National Gallery, Budapest History Museum) as well as the original Roman settlement at Aquincum.

Castle Hill (Map 4)

Castle Hill (Várhegy), a 1km-long limestone plateau towering 170m above the Danube, contains Budapest's most important medieval monuments and museums and is a Unesco World Heritage Site. Below it is a 28km-long network of caves formed by thermal springs that were supposedly used by the Turks for military purposes, as air-raid shelters during WWII, and as a secret military installation during the Cold War.

The walled Castle area consists of two distinct parts: the Old Town, where commoners lived in the Middle Ages (the current owners of the coveted burgher houses here are no longer so 'common') and the Royal Palace, the original site of the castle built in the 13th century.

The easiest way to get to Castle Hill from Pest is to take bus No 16 from Deák tér to Dísz tér, midway between the Old Town and the Royal Palace. Much more fun, though, is to stroll across Chain Bridge and board the **Sikló** *(uphill/downhill ticket 450/250Ft adult, 350/250Ft child aged 2-10; open 7.30am-10pm daily)*, a funicular railway built in 1870 that ascends from Clark Ádám tér to Szent György tér near the Royal Palace. The funicular does not run on the first and third Monday of each month.

Alternatively, you can walk up the Király lépcső, the 'Royal Steps' that lead from I Hunyadi János út northwest of Clark Ádám tér, or the wide staircase that goes to the southern end of the Royal Palace from I Szarvas tér.

Another option is to take metro M2 to Moszkva tér, cross the footbridge above the square and walk up Várfok utca to Vienna Gate. A minibus with a logo of a castle and labelled 'Várbusz' or 'Dísz tér' follows the same route from the start of I Várfok utca.

Vienna Gate Vienna Gate (Bécsi kapu), the medieval entrance to the Old Town, was rebuilt in 1936 to mark the 250th anniversary of the retaking of the castle from the Turks. You can climb to the top at any time; it's always open.

Medieval Jewish Prayer House The Medieval Jewish Prayer House *(középkori zsidó imaház; ☎ 225 7815; I Táncsics Mihály utca 26; adult/student or child 300/100Ft; open 10am-6pm Tues-Sun May-Oct)*, parts of which date from the 14th century, contains documents and items linked to the Jewish community of Buda as well as Gothic stone carvings and tomb stones from the Great Synagogue in Pest.

Museum of Music History The Museum of Music History *(Zenetörténeti Múzeum; ☎ 214 6770; I Táncsics Mihály utca 7; adult/child 400/200Ft; open 10am-6pm Tues-Sun Mar–mid-Nov)*, housed in an 18th-century palace with a lovely courtyard, traces the development of music and musical instruments in Hungary from the 18th century till today. The violin maker's workbench and the unusual 18th-century sextet table are particularly interesting. The paintings on loan from the Museum of Fine Arts all have musical themes. A special room upstairs is devoted to the work of Béla Bartók, with lots of scores.

Museum of Hungarian Commerce & Catering The catering section of the Museum of Hungarian Commerce & Catering *(Kereskedelmi és Vendéglátóipari Múzeum; ☎ 375 6249; I Fortuna utca 4; adult/student or child 100/50Ft; open 10am-5pm Wed-Fri, 10am-6pm Sat & Sun)*, to the left as you enter the archway, contains an entire 19th-century cake shop in one of its three rooms, complete with a pastry kitchen. There are moulds for every occasion, a marble-lined icebox and an antique ice-cream maker. Much is made of those great confectioners Emil Gerbeaud of *cukrászda* (cake shop) fame and József Dobos, who gave his name to Dobos torta, a layered chocolate and cream cake topped with caramelised brown sugar.

The commerce collection, to the right as you enter the archway, traces retail trade in the capital. Along with electric toys and advertisements that still work, there's an exhibit on the hyperinflation that Hungary suffered after WWII when a basket of money would buy no more than four eggs. Before you leave, check the great old pub sign of a satyr and foaming mug in the courtyard out the back.

Museum of Military History The Museum of Military History *(Hadtörténeti Múzeum; ☎ 356 9522; I Tóth Árpád sétány 40; adult/student or child 250/80Ft; open 10am-6pm Tues-Sun Apr-Sept; 10am-4pm Oct-Mar)*, loaded with weaponry dating from before the Turkish conquest, also does a pretty good job with uniforms, medals, flags and battle-themed fine art. Exhibits focus on the 15th-century fall of Buda Castle, the 1848–49 War of Independence, the Hungarian Royal Army under Admiral Miklós Horthy and the 1956 Uprising.

Mary Magdalene Tower The Mary Magdalene Tower *(Magdolna-torony; I Kapisztrán tér)*, visible for kilometres to the west of Castle Hill, is the reconstructed spire of an 18th-century church destroyed during WWII. The church, once reserved for Hungarian-speakers in this district (German-speakers worshipped at

Matthias Church), was used as a mosque during the Turkish occupation and was destroyed in an air raid in 1944. Normally visitors not worried about claustrophobia or nose bleeds are allowed to climb the 163 steps for a great view of Castle Hill and beyond, but the tower was under renovation at the time of writing.

Buda Castle Labyrinth The Buda Castle Labyrinth *(Budavári Labirintus; ☎ 212 0207; I Úri utca 9; adult/student or child 1000/800Ft; open 9.30am-7.30pm daily)*, a 1200m-long cave system some 16m under the Castle District, looks at how the caves have been used – from prehistoric times to the 20th century. The admission fee is extortionate by Hungarian standards, but it's all good fun and a relief from the heat and the crowds above on a hot summer's day.

House of Hungarian Wines The House of Hungarian Wines *(Magyar Borok Háza; ☎ 212 1030; ⓦ www.kertnet.hu/mbh; I Szentháromság tér 6; sampling 3500Ft; open noon-8pm daily)* offers the chance of a crash course in Hungarian viticulture in the heart of the Castle District. But with over 700 wines on display from Hungary's 22 wine regions and up to 70 to sample, 'crash' may soon become the operative word.

Matthias Church Parts of Matthias Church *(Mátyás templom; ☎ 489 0717; ⓦ www.matyas-templom.hu; I Szentháromság tér 2; adult/student or child 300/150Ft, with guide 600/300Ft; open 9am-5pm Mon-Fri, 9am-1pm Sat, 1pm-5pm Sun)* date back some 500 years, notably the carvings above the southern entrance. But basically the church (so named because the 15th-century Renaissance king Matthias Corvinus married Beatrix here in 1474) is a neo-Gothic creation designed by the architect Frigyes Schulek in 1896. The church has a colourful tiled roof and a lovely tower; the interior is remarkable for its stained-glass windows, frescoes and wall decorations by the Romantic painters Károly Lotz and Bertalan Székely. There are organ concerts in the church on certain evenings, continuing a tradition that began in 1867 when Franz Liszt's *Hungarian Coronation Mass* was first played here for the coronation of Franz Joseph and Elizabeth as king and queen of Hungary.

Steps to the right of the main altar lead to the crypt. The **Matthias Church Collection**

of Ecclesiastical Art *(Mátyás Templom Egy-házművészeti Gyűjteménye;* ☎ *355 5657; admission 300Ft)* contains ornate monstrances, reliquaries, chalices and other church plates, as well as a copy of the Coronation Jewels. You'll get some interesting views of the chancel from high up in the Royal Oratory.

Fishermen's Bastion Fishermen's Bastion *(Halászbástya; admission 250/120Ft; open 8.30am-11pm daily)* is another neo-Gothic masquerade that most visitors (and Hungarians) believe to be much older. But who cares? It looks medieval and still offers among the best views in Budapest. Built as a viewing platform in 1905 by Schulek, the bastion's name was taken from the guild of fishermen responsible for defending this stretch of the wall in the Middle Ages. The seven gleaming white turrets represent the Magyar tribes who entered the Carpathian Basin in the late 9th century. In front of the bastion is a fine equestrian **statue of St Stephen**; the ornate detailing reflects sculptor Alajos Stróbl's deep leap into 11th-century art history.

Golden Eagle Pharmacy Museum The Golden Eagle Pharmacy Museum *(Arany Sas Patikamúzeum;* ☎ *375 9772; I Tárnok utca 18; adult/student or child 100/50Ft; open 10.30am-6pm Tues-Sun Mar-Oct; 10.30am-3.30pm Tues-Sun Nov-Feb)*, just north of Dísz tér on the site of Budapest's first pharmacy (1681), contains an unusual mixture of displays.

Royal Palace The former Royal Palace (Budavári Palota) has had a turbulent – burned, bombed, razed, rebuilt and redesigned at least a half-dozen times over the past seven centuries – though somewhat under-utilised past. Béla IV established a royal residence here in the mid-13th century and subsequent kings either rebuilt their own residences or added on to them. The palace was destroyed in the battle to rout the Turks in 1686; the Habsburgs rebuilt it but spent very little time here. Today the Royal Palace contains not royal residences but museums – three of them – and the **National Széchenyi Library**.

There are two entrances to the Royal Palace. The first is via the **Habsburg Steps**, southeast of Szent György tér and through an ornamental gateway dating from 1903. The other way in is via **Corvinus Gate**, with its

big black raven symbolising King Matthias Corvinus, southwest of the square.

Ludwig Museum The Ludwig Museum, also known as the Museum of Contemporary Art *(Kortárs Művészeti Múzeum;* ☎ *375 9175; Royal Palace, Wing A; adult/student or child 400/300Ft; open 10am-6pm Tues-Sun)* surveys American Pop art as well as works by Russian, German and French contemporary artists over the past 50 years. There are also Hungarian contemporary works from the 1990s. The temporary exhibits are often better than the permanent collection.

Hungarian National Gallery The Hungarian National Gallery *(Magyar Nemzeti Galéria;* ☎ *375 7533, 375 8584; Royal Palace, Wings B, C & D; adult/student or child 600/300Ft; open 10am-6pm Tues-Sun Mar-Nov; Tues-Sun 10am-4pm Dec-Feb)* is an overwhelmingly large collection that traces the development of Hungarian art from the 10th century to the present day. The largest collections include medieval and Renaissance stonework, Gothic wooden sculptures and panel paintings, late-Gothic winged altars, and late Renaissance and baroque art.

The museum also has an important collection of Hungarian paintings and sculpture from the 19th and 20th centuries. You won't recognise many names, but keep an eye open for the harrowing depictions of war and the dispossessed by László Mednyánszky, the unique portraits by József Rippl-Rónai, the mammoth canvases by Tivadar Csontváry and the paintings of carnivals by the modern artist Vilmos Aba-Novák.

Budapest History Museum The Budapest History Museum *(Budapesti Történeti Múzeum;* ☎ *225 7815, 375 7533; Royal Palace, Wing E; adult/student or child/family 600/300/1000Ft ; open 10am-6pm daily mid-May–mid-Sept; 10am-6pm Wed-Mon Mar–mid-May & mid-Sept–Oct; 10am-4pm Wed-Mon Nov-Feb)*, also known as the Castle Museum (Vár Múzeum), traces the 2000 years of the city on three floors of jumbled exhibits. Restored palace rooms dating from the 15th century can be entered from the basement, which contains an exhibit on the Royal Palace in medieval Buda.

Three vaulted halls, one with a magnificent door frame in red marble bearing the seal of

Queen Beatrice and tiles with a raven and a ring (the seal of her husband King Matthias Corvinus), lead to the **Gothic Hall**, the **Royal Cellar** and the 14th-century **Tower Chapel**.

On the ground floor is an exhibit entitled 'Budapest in the Middle Ages' as well as Gothic statues discovered during excavations in 1974. The exhibit on the 1st floor – **Budapest in Modern Times** – traces the history of the city from the expulsion of the Turks in 1686 to the collapse of communism.

Statues & Monuments Flanking the Habsburg Steps to the northeast of the palace is an enormous **statue of the turul** (1905), an eagle-like totem of the ancient Magyars (see the boxed text 'Blame it on the Bird' in the Western Transdanubia chapter) honoured as an ancestor of the Magyars.

Due south in front of Wing C stands a **statue of Eugene of Savoy** (1663–1736), who wiped out the last Turkish army in Hungary at the Battle of Zenta in 1697. Designed by József Róna 200 years later, it is considered to be the finest equestrian statue in the capital.

To the west and facing the palace's large northwestern courtyard is the Romantic-style **Matthias Fountain** (Mátyás kút), which portrays the young King Matthias Corvinus in hunting garb. To the right below is Szép Ilonka (Beautiful Helen), a protagonist of a Romantic ballad by Mihály Vörösmarty. Apparently the poor girl fell in love with the dashing 'hunter' and, upon learning his true identity and feeling unworthy, she died of a broken heart.

Gellért Hill & the Tabán (Maps 3 & 4)

Gellért hegy, a 235m-high rocky hill southeast of the Castle, is crowned with a fortress of sorts and the Independence Monument, Budapest's unofficial symbol. From Gellért Hill, you can't beat the views of the Royal Palace and the Danube. The Tabán, the leafy area between Gellért and Castle Hills, is associated with the Serbs, who settled here after fleeing from the Turks in the early 18th century. Later it became known for its restaurants and wine gardens – a kind of Montmartre for Budapest. Most of them burned to the ground at the turn of the 20th century.

Today Gellért Hill and the Tabán are given over to private homes, parks and three thermal spas that make good use of the hot springs gushing from deep below Gellért Hill. The **Rudas Baths** and the **Gellért Baths** are open to the public (see the boxed text 'Taking the Waters in Budapest' under Activities later in this chapter); the **Rác Baths** was under renovation at the time of writing and its future was unclear.

Szent Gellért tér Szent Gellért tér faces **Independence Bridge** (Szabadság-híd; Maps 3 & 4) and is dominated by the **Gellért Hotel**, an Art Nouveau pile (1918) and the city's favourite old-world hotel and spa.

Cave Chapel (Sziklakápolna; Map 3; ☎ 385 1529; open 9am-9pm), on a small hill directly north of the hotel, was built into a cave in 1926. It was the seat of the Pauline order until 1951, when the priests were arrested and imprisoned by the communists and the cave sealed off. It was reopened in 1992 and reconsecrated. The chapel is closed to the public during Mass services.

Gellért tér can be reached from Pest on bus No 7 or tram No 47 or 49 and from the Buda side on bus No 86 and tram Nos 18 and 19.

Citadella The Citadella (Map 3; admission 300Ft; open 8am-10pm daily) is a fortress that never did battle. Built by the Habsburgs after the 1848–49 War of Independence to 'defend' the city from further insurrection, by the time it was ready (1851) the political climate had changed and the Citadella had become obsolete. It was given to the city in the 1890s and parts of it were symbolically blown to pieces. There's not much inside the Citadella today except for some big guns and dusty displays in the central courtyard, a hotel/hostel (see Places to Stay), a casino, a restaurant and a pleasant outdoor café.

To get here from Pest cross Erzsébet Bridge and take the stairs leading up behind the waterfall and statue of St Gellért, or cross Independence Bridge and follow the path through the park starting at the Cave Chapel. Bus No 27 runs almost to the top of the hill from Móricz Zsigmond körtér, southwest of the Gellért Hotel (and accessible on tram Nos 18, 19, 47 and 49).

Independence Monument Independence Monument (Szabadság szobor; Map 3), the lovely lady with the palm frond proclaiming freedom throughout the city and the land, is to the east of the Citadella. Some 14m high, it was erected in 1947 in tribute to the Soviet soldiers who died liberating Budapest in 1945, but the victims' names in Cyrillic letters on the plinth and the statues of the Soviet soldiers were removed in the early 1990s. If you walk westwards for a few minutes along Citadella sétány north of the fortress, you'll come to what is the best vantage point in Budapest.

Statues & Bridges The **Elizabeth Bridge** *(Erzsébet-híd; Maps 3 & 4)* is the gleaming white (though rather generic) suspension bridge northeast of Gellért Hill. It enjoys a special place in the hearts of Budapesters as it was the first newly designed bridge to re-open after the war (1964).

Looking down on Elizabeth Bridge from Gellért Hill is the **statue of St Gellért** (Map 4), an Italian missionary invited to Hungary by King Stephen. The monument marks the spot where the bishop was hurled to his death in a spiked barrel in 1046 by pagan Hungarians resisting conversion.

To the north of the bridge and through the underpass is a **statue of Elizabeth** (Map 4), the Habsburg empress and Hungarian queen and the consort of Franz Joseph much beloved by Hungarians because, among other things, she learned to speak Hungarian. Sissi, as she was affectionately known, was assassinated by an Italian anarchist in Geneva in 1898.

Víziváros (Maps 3 & 4)

Víziváros (Watertown) is the narrow area between the Danube and Castle Hill that widens as it approaches Óbuda to the north and Rózsadomb (Rose Hill) to the northwest, spreading as far west as Moszkva tér (one of Buda's main transport hubs). In the Middle Ages, those involved in trades, crafts and fishing lived here. Under the Turks many of the district's churches were used as mosques, and baths were built, one of which is still functioning. Today Víziváros is the heart of urban Buda.

You can reach Víziváros on foot from the metro M2 Batthyány tér stop by walking south along the river or via tram No 19, which links it with Szent Gellért tér. Bus No 16 from Deák tér stops here on its way to/from Castle Hill.

Clark Ádám tér Clark Ádám tér (Map 4) is named after the Scottish engineer who supervised the building of the **Széchenyi Chain Bridge** *(Széchenyi lánchíd; Map 4)*,

leading from the square, and who designed the **tunnel** *(alagút; Map 4)* under Castle Hill, which took eight months to carve out of the limestone. (The bridge was actually the idea of Count István Széchenyi – see the boxed text 'The Greatest Hungarian' in the Western Transdanubia chapter – and when it opened in 1849 it was unique for two reasons: it was the first link between Buda and Pest, and the nobility, previously exempt from all taxation, had to pay the toll like everybody else.) The curious sculpture, which looks like a elongated doughnut, hidden in the bushes to the south is the **0km stone**; all Hungarian roads to and from the capital are measured from this point.

Fő utca Fő utca is the 'Main Street' running through Víziváros and dates from Roman times. At the former **Capuchin church** *(Map 4; I Fő utca 30-32)*, used as a mosque during the Turkish occupation, you can see the remains of Islamic-style ogee-arched doors and windows on the southern side. Around the corner there's the seal of King Matthias Corvinus – a raven and a ring – and the little square under renovation and expansion is called **Corvin tér**. The Eclectic building on the north side is the **Budai Vigadó** *(Buda Concert Hall; Map 4; Corvin tér 8)*, much less grand than its counterpart in Pest.

Batthyány tér, a short distance to the northwest, is the centre of Víziváros and the best place to snap a picture of the Parliament building across the river. In the centre of this rather shabby space is the entrance to both metro M2 and the HÉV suburban line to Szentendre. On the southern side is **St Anne's Church** *(Szent Ana templom; Map 3; II Batthyány tér 7)*, with one of the loveliest baroque interiors of any church in Budapest.

A couple of streets north is **Nagy Imre tér**, with the enormous **Military Court of Justice** *(Map 3; II Fő utca 70-78)* on the northern side. Here Imre Nagy and others were tried and sentenced to death in 1958 (see The 1956 Uprising under History in the Facts about Hungary chapter). It was also the site of the notorious Fő utca prison where many lesser mortals (but victims nonetheless) were incarcerated and tortured.

The **Király Baths** *(Király Gyógyfürdő; Map 3; II Fő utca 82-86)*, parts of which date from 1580, is one block north (see the boxed text 'Taking the Waters in Budapest' under

Activities). Next to it, across pedestrianised Ganz utca, is the Greek Catholic **St Florian Chapel** *(Szent Flórián kápolna; Map 3; II Fő utca 88-90)*, built in 1760 and dedicated to the patron saint of firefighters.

Fő utca ends at **Bem József tér**, named after the Polish general Josef Bem (1794–1850) who fought on the Hungarian side in the 1848–49 War of Independence. In 1956 students from the Technical University rallied in front of the statue here at the start of the Uprising.

Millennium Park Millennium Park *(Millenáris Park; Map 3; ☎ 438 5300; II Kis Rókus utca; metro M2 Moszkva tér, tram No 4 or 6)*, one of the more successful urban redevelopment projects on either side of the Danube in recent years, is a large landscaped complex behind the Mammut shopping mall comprising fountains, ponds, little bridges a theatre, and the **Millenium Exhibition Hall** *(Millenáris Kiállítócsarnok; ☎ 438 5335; II Kis Rókus utca; adult/student or child 1000/500Ft)*, which hosts some unusual cultural exhibits.

Frankel Leó út At Bem tér, Fő utca turns into Frankel Leó út, a tree-lined street of pricey antique shops. At its northern end is the **Lukács Bath** *(Lukács Gyógyfürdő; Map 3; II Frankel Leó út 25-29; tram No 17, bus No 60 or 86)*, which caters to an older crowd (see the boxed text 'Taking the Waters in Budapest' under Activities). A short distance north and tucked away in an apartment block is the **Újlak Synagogue** *(Újlaki zsinagóga; II Frankel Leó út 49)*, built in 1888 on the site of an older prayer house. It is the only functioning synagogue left on the Buda side.

Tomb of Gül Baba The reconstructed Tomb of Gül Baba *(Gül Baba türbéje; ☎ 355 8764; Map 3; II Mecset utca 14; HÉV station Margit-híd, tram No 4, 6 or 17; adult/student or child 300/150Ft; open 10am-6pm daily May-Sept; 10am-4pm Tues-Sun Oct)* contains the remains of Gül Baba, an Ottoman Dervish who took part in the capture of Buda in 1541, and is known in Hungary as the 'Father of Roses'. To reach it from Török utca, which runs parallel to Frankel Leó út, walk west along steep Gül Baba utca to the set of steps just past No 16; this will lead you to a small octagonal building and a lookout tower. You can also reach here along Mecset utca, which runs north from Margit utca. The

tomb is a pilgrimage place for Muslims, and you must remove your shoes.

Óbuda (Map 2)

Ó means 'ancient' in Hungarian; as its name suggests, Óbuda is the oldest part of Buda. The Romans settled at Aquincum north of here (see History in the Facts about Hungary chapter) and when the Magyars arrived, they named it Buda, which became Óbuda when the Royal Palace was built on Castle Hill.

You can reach the heart of Óbuda on the HÉV commuter train (Árpád-híd stop) from Batthyány tér, which is on the M2 metro line, or bus No 86 from along the Danube on the Buda side. If you're up near City Park (Városliget) in Pest, walk southeast to the intersection of Hungária körút and Thököly út and catch the No 1 tram, which avoids Buda and crosses Árpád Bridge into Óbuda.

Around Flórián tér This square, split in two by the Árpád Bridge flyover and ringed with prefabricated housing blocks, is not the best introduction to Óbuda, but it remains the district's historic centre.

The yellow baroque **Óbuda Parish Church** *(Óbudai plébániatemplom; III 168 Lajos utca)*, built in 1749, dominates the easternmost side of Flórián tér. There's a massive rococo pulpit inside. To the south, the large neoclassical building beside the Corinthia Aquincum Hotel is the **former Óbuda Synagogue** *(Óbudai zsinagóga; III Lajos utca 163)*, dating from 1821. It now houses the sound studios of Hungarian Television (MTV).

Directly opposite, the **Budapest Gallery Exhibition House** *(Budapest Galéria Kiállítóháza; ☎ 388 6771; III Lajos utca 158; adult/child 150/50Ft; open 10am-5.30pm Tues-Sun)* hosts some of the most interesting avant-garde exhibitions in town. It also has a standing exhibit of works by Pál Pátzay, whose sculptures can be seen throughout the city (eg, the fountain on Tárnok utca in the Castle District and the *Serpent Slayer* in honour of Raoul Wallenberg in Szent István Park).

Roman Military Amphitheatre To explore the Roman Military Amphitheatre (Római katonai amfiteátrum), built in the 2nd century for the garrisons, archaeology buffs taking the No 86 bus to Flórián tér should descend at Nagyszombat utca (for HÉV passengers, it's the Tímár utca stop), about 800m south of

Flórián tér on Pacsirtamező utca. It could accommodate up to 15,000 spectators and was larger than the Colosseum in Rome. The rest of the military camp extended north to Flórián tér.

Kiscelli Museum & Municipal Gallery
Housed in an 18th-century monastery, later a barracks that was badly damaged in WWII and again in 1956, to the west of Flórián tér, the exhibits at the Kiscelli Museum *(☎ 388 8560; III Kiscelli utca 108; tram No 17, bus No 60; adult/child 400/200Ft; open 10am-6pm Tues-Sun Apr-Oct; 10am-3.30pm Nov-Mar)* attempt to tell the story (from the human side) of Budapest since liberation from the Turks. The museum counts among its best exhibits a complete 19th-century apothecary moved here from Kálvin tér and rooms furnished in Empire, Biedermeier and Art Nouveau furniture and bric-a-brac. The Municipal Gallery (Fővárosi Képtár) upstairs, with its impressive art collection (József Rippl-Rónai, Lajos Tihanyi, István Csók, Béla Czóbel etc) is also here. The erstwhile **monastery church** attached to the museum is used for temporary exhibits.

Szentlélek tér & Fő tér Two squares northeast of Flórián tér – Holy Spirit Square (Szentlélek tér), a transport hub, and Main Square (Fő tér), a quiet square of baroque houses, public buildings and restaurants – contain Óbuda's most important museums.

Vasarely Museum The Vasarely Museum *(☎ 250 1540; III Szentlélek tér 6; adult/child 200/50Ft; open 10am-5.30pm Tues-Sun)*, housed in the crumbling Zichy Mansion, is devoted to the works of Victor Vasarely (or Vásárhelyi Győző before he emigrated to Paris in 1930), the 'Father of Op Art'. The works, especially ones like *Dirac* and *Tlinko-F*, are excellent and fun to watch as they swell and move around the canvas. On the 1st floor are some of the unusual advertisements Vasarely did for French firms before the war.

Imre Varga Exhibition House The Imre Varga Exhibition House *(Varga Imre kiállítóháza; ☎ 250 0274; III Laktanya utca 7; adult/child 250/100Ft; open 10am-6pm Tues-Sun)*, part of the Budapest Gallery, includes sculptures, statues, medals and drawings by Hungary's foremost sculptors, who seems to have sat on both sides of the fence

politically for decades – sculpting Béla Kun and Lenin as easily as he did St Stephen and St Elizabeth. En route to the museum from Fő tér, you'll pass some of Varga's work: a group of odd metal **sculptures** of rather worried-looking women in the middle of the road.

Aquincum (Map 2)
Aquincum, the most complete Roman civilian town in Hungary and now an indoor and outdoor museum, had paved streets and fairly sumptuous single-storey houses with courtyards, fountains and mosaic floors, as well as sophisticated drainage and heating systems. Not all that is easily apparent today as you walk among the ruins, but you can see its outlines as well as those of the big public baths, market, an early-Christian church and a temple dedicated to the god Mithra. Across Szentendrei út to the northwest is the **Roman Civilian Amphitheatre** (Római polgári amfiteátrum), about half the size of the one reserved for the garrison.

You can reach Aquincum on the HÉV (Aquincum stop) or on bus No 34 or 43 from Szentlélek tér.

Aquincum Museum The Aquincum Museum *(Aquincumi Múzeum; ☎ 368 4260, 250 1650; III Szentendrei út 139; grounds adult/student or child 400/150Ft, grounds & museum adult/student or child 700/300Ft, family 1200Ft; grounds/museum open 9am/10am-6pm Tues-Sun May-Sept; 9am/10am-5pm Tues-Sun 15-30 Apr & Oct)*, in the centre of what remains of this Roman civilian settlement, tries to put the ruins in perspective, with some success. Most of the big sculptures and stone sarcophagi are outside to the left of the museum or behind it along a covered walkway. A new exhibition space focuses on Roman weaving, dyeing and dress and there's now a mock-up of a Roman bath. English-language tours (3000Ft) are available by arrangement.

Buda Hills (Map 1)
With 'peaks' reaching over 500m, a comprehensive system of trails and no lack of unusual transport, the Buda Hills are the city's true playground and a welcome respite from hot, dusty Pest in summer. If you're walking, take along a copy of Cartographia's 1:30,000 *A Budai hegység* map (No 6; 650Ft). Aside from the Béla Bartók Memorial House (see its entry later), there are few sights, though

you might want to poke your head in one of the Buda Hills' pair of caves (see Caving under Activities, later in this chapter).

With all the unusual transport options, heading for the hills is more than half the fun. From the Moszkva tér metro station on the M2 line in Buda, walk westward along Szilágyi Erzsébet fasor for 10 minutes (or take tram No 18 or bus No 56 for two stops) to the circular high-rise Hotel Budapest at No 47. Directly opposite is the terminus of the **Cog Railway** (Fogaskerekű; ☎ 355 4167; admission one BKV ticket; open 5am-11pm daily). Built in 1874, the cog climbs for 3.5km to **Széchenyi-hegy** (427m), one of the prettiest residential areas in the city.

At Széchenyi-hegy, you can stop for a picnic in the pretty park south of the station or board the narrow-gauge **Children's Railway** (Gyermekvasút; ☎ 395 5429, 397 5394; adult/child 150/50Ft; open 10am-5pm Mon-Fri, 9.45am-5.30pm Sat & Sun mid-Mar–late Oct; 10am-4pm Tues-Fri, 10am-5pm Sat & Sun late Oct–mid-Mar), two minutes to the south on Hegyhát út. The railway was built in 1951 by Pioneers (socialist Scouts) and is staffed entirely by schoolchildren aged 10 to 14 – the engineer excepted. The little train chugs along for 12km, terminating at **Hűvös-völgy** (Chilly Valley). There are walks fanning out from any of the stops along the way, or you can return to Moszkva tér on tram No 56 from Hűvös-völgy. The train operates about once an hour.

A more interesting way down from the hills, though, is to get off at **János-hegy**, the fourth stop on the Children's Railway and the highest point (527m) in the hills. The **Elizabeth Lookout** (Erzsébet-kilátó), a tower built on the summit in 1910, has excellent views of the city, and there are some good walks. About 700m due east of the station is the **chair lift** (libegő; ☎ 394 3764; adult/child 300/150Ft; open 9.30am-6pm daily mid-May–mid-Sept; 9.30am-4pm mid-Sept–mid-May), which will take you down to Zugligeti út. (Note the chair lift is closed on the Monday of every even-numbered week.) From here bus No 158 returns to Moszkva tér.

Béla Bartók Memorial House (Map 1)

The Béla Bartók Memorial House (Bartók Béla Emlékház; ☎ 394 2100; II Csalán út 29; bus No 29; adult/child 300/150Ft; open 10am-5pm Tues-Sun), north of Szilágyi Erzsébet fasor but still very much in the Buda Hills, is where the great composer resided from 1932 until 1940, when he emigrated to the USA. Among other things on display is the old Edison recorder (complete with wax cylinders) he used to record Hungarian folk music in Transylvania, as well as furniture and other objects he collected. Concerts are held in the music hall most Friday evenings at 6pm and occasionally outside in the garden in summer.

MARGARET ISLAND (MAPS 2 & 3)

Neither Buda nor Pest, 2.5km-long Margaret Island (Margit-sziget) in the middle of the Danube River was always the domain of one religious order or another until the Turks came and turned what was then called the Island of Rabbits into – appropriately enough – a harem, from which all 'infidels' were barred. It's been a public park open to everyone since the mid-19th century.

Cross over to Margaret Island from Pest or Buda via tram No 4 or 6. Bus No 26 covers the length of the island as it makes the run between Nyugati train station and Árpád Bridge. Cars are allowed on Margaret Island from Árpád Bridge only as far as the two big hotels at the northeastern end; the rest is reserved for pedestrians, cyclists and horse-drawn carriages.

Medieval Ruins

The ruins of the **Franciscan church and monastery** (Ferences templom és kolostor; Map 3) – no more than a tower and a wall dating from the late 13th century – are almost in the exact geographical centre of the island. The Habsburg archduke Joseph built a summer residence here when he inherited the island in 1867. It was later converted into a hotel that operated until 1949.

The former **Dominican convent** (Domonkos kolostor; Map 2) lies to the northeast of the Franciscan church and monastery. It was built by Béla IV whose scribes played an important role in the continuation of Hungarian scholarship. Its most famous resident was Béla's daughter, St Margaret (1242–71). As the story goes, the king promised to commit his daughter to a life of devotion in a nunnery if the Mongols were driven from the land. They were and she was – at nine years of age. Still, she seemed to enjoy it – if we're to believe the Lives of the Saints – especially the mortification-of-the-flesh parts and never bathing above the ankles. St Margaret, only canonised in 1943, commands something of a cult following in Hungary. A red marble sepulchre cover surrounded by a wrought-iron grille marks her original resting place, and there's a much visited shrine with votives nearby.

Water Tower & Open-Air Theatre
The octagonal **water tower** (*víztorony; Map 2*), erected in 1911 in the north-central part of the island, rises 66m above the **open-air theatre** (*szabadtéri színpad;* ☎ 239 0920), which is used for opera, plays and concerts in summer. The tower now houses the **Lookout Gallery** (*Kilátó Galéria;* ☎ 340 4520; adult/ child 350/200Ft; open 11am-7pm daily May-Oct), which exhibits some interesting folkcraft and contemporary art on the ground floor. But the main reason for entering is to climb the 153 steps for a stunning 360-degree view of the island, Buda and Pest from the cupola terrace.

Activities
If you follow the shoreline of Margaret Island in winter, you'll see thermal water gushing from beneath the island into the river.

The Romans used the springs both as drinking water and therapy, and so do modern Magyars. Margitszigeti Krisztályvíz, one of the more popular brands of mineral water in Hungary, is sourced and bottled here, and the **thermal spa** (Map 2) at the Danubias Grand Hotel Margitsziget (see the boxed text 'Taking the Waters in Budapest' under Activities later), to the northeast, is one of the cleanest, most modern spas in Budapest.

Margaret Island boasts two popular swimming pools on its western side. The first is the indoor/outdoor **National Sports Pool** (*Nemzeti Sportuszoda; Map 3*), officially named after the Olympic swimming champion Alfréd Hajós, who won the 100m and 1200m races at the first modern Olympiad in 1896, and who actually built the place. Farther north is the recently renovated **Palatinus** (Map 2), which is a large complex of outdoor pools, huge water slides and strands, and is a madhouse on a hot summer afternoon. For details on both swimming complexes see the boxed text 'Taking the Waters in Budapest'.

You can hire a **bicycle** from one of several stands, including **Sétacikli** (*Map 3;* ☎ 06-30

966 6453; open 10am-dusk Mar-Oct), which is on the western side just before the athletic stadium as you walk from Margaret Bridge. It charges 400/600/1200Ft per 30 minutes/hour/ day for a three-speed bicycle, and for a pedal coach 1800/2800Ft per hour for three/five people. **Bringóhintó** (*Map 2;* ☎ 329 2073, 329 2746; open 8am-dusk year-round), at the refreshment stand near the Japanese Garden in the north of the island, charges 560/920Ft per 30 minutes/hour for mountain-bike hire, a pedal coach for four persons costs 1380/ 2180Ft, and inline skates cost 820/1380Ft.

A twirl around the island in one of the **horse-drawn coaches** (Map 2), stationed just south of the Bringóhintó bike-rental stand, costs 1000Ft per person.

PEST (MAP 6)
While Buda can often feel like a garden, Pest is an urban jungle, with a wealth of architecture, museums, historic buildings and broad boulevards unmatched on the other side. And there's no shortage of open, green spaces – City Park at the end of Andrássy út is the largest park in the city.

Inner Town
The Inner Town (Belváros) is the heart of Pest and contains the most valuable commercial real estate in the city, but it retains something of a split personality. North of Ferenciek tere is the 'have' side with the flashiest boutiques, the biggest hotels, some expensive restaurants and the lion's share of tourists. You'll often hear more German, Italian and English spoken here than Hungarian. Until recently the south was the 'have not' side – studenty, quieter and much more local. Now it too has been reserved for pedestrians and is full of trendy clubs, cafés and restaurants.

Busy Ferenciek tere, which divides the Inner Town at Szabadsajtó út (Free Press Avenue), is on the M3 metro line and can be reached by bus No 7 from Buda or points east in Pest.

Around Egyetem tér The centre of the Inner Town south of Szabadsajtó út is Egyetem tér (University Square), a five-minute walk south along Károly Mihály utca from Ferenciek tere. The square's name refers to the branch of the prestigious **Loránd Eötvös Science University** (*ELTE; V Egyetem tér 1-3*). Next to the university building to the west is the **University Church**, a lovely baroque structure built in 1748. Over the altar inside is a copy of the **Black Madonna of Czecstochowa** so revered in Poland.

Leafy Kecskeméti utca runs southeast from the square to **Kálvin tér**. At the end of it, near the Korona Hotel, there's a plaque marking the location of the **Kecskemét Gate** (Kecskeméti-kapu), part of the medieval city wall that was pulled down in the 1700s. **Ráday utca**, which leads south from Kálvin tér and is full of cafés, clubs and restaurants, is where university students entertain themselves these days.

Along Váci utca The best way to see the posher side of the Inner Town is to walk up pedestrian Váci utca, the capital's premier – and most expensive – shopping street, with designer clothes, antique jewellery shops, pubs and some bookshops for browsing. This was the total length of Pest in the Middle Ages. To gain access from Ferenciek tere, walk through **Páriszi Udvar** (Parisian Court; V Ferenciek tere 5), a gem of a Parisian-style arcade built in 1909, out onto tiny Kigyó utca. Váci utca is immediately to the west.

Many of the buildings on Váci utca are worth a closer look, but as it's a narrow street you'll have to crane your neck or walk into one of the side lanes for a better view. **Thonet House** at No 11/a is another masterpiece built by Ödön Lechner (1890), and the **Philanthia** flower shop at No 9 has an original Art Nouveau interior. The **Polgár Gallery** at No 11/b, in a building dating from 1912, has undergone a spectacular renovation and contains a stained-glass domed ceiling.

Around Vörösmarty tér Váci utca ends at Vörösmarty tér, a large square of smart shops, galleries, airline offices, cafés and an outdoor market with stalls selling tourist schlock, and artists who will draw your portrait or caricature. Suitable for framing – just maybe.

In the centre is a statue of the 19th-century poet after whom Vörösmarty tér was named. The statue is made of Italian marble and is protected in winter by a bizarre plastic 'iceberg' that kids love sliding on. The first – or last – stop of the little yellow (or Millenium) metro line is also in the square, and at the northern end is **Gerbeaud**, Budapest's most famous café and cake shop (for details see Pest's Cafés & Teahouses under Places to Eat later).

The despised modern building on the western side of Vörösmarty tér (No 1) contains a music shop and ticket office for concerts in the city. South of it is the sumptuous **Bank Palace** (Bank Palota; Deák utca 5) built in 1915 and now housing the Budapest Stock Exchange.

The **Pesti Vigadó**, the Romantic-style concert hall built in 1865, but badly damaged during the war, faces the river at Vigadó tér 1, to the west of Vörösmarty tér.

Duna korzó An easy way to cool down on a warm afternoon (and enjoy the best views of Buda Hill in Pest) is to stroll along the Duna korzó, the riverside 'Danube Promenade' between Chain Bridge and Elizabeth Bridge and above Belgrád rakpart. It's full of cafés, musicians and handicraft stalls by day, and hookers and hustlers by night. The promenade leads into **Petőfi tér**, named after the poet of the 1848–49 War of Independence and the scene of political rallies (both legal and illegal) over subsequent years. **Március 15 tér**, which marks the date of the outbreak of the revolution, abuts it to the south.

On the eastern side of Március 15 tér, sitting uncomfortably close to the Elizabeth Bridge flyover, is the **Inner Town parish church** (Belvárosi plébániatemplom; V Március 15 tér 2), where a Romanesque church was first built in the 12th century within a Roman fortress. You can see a few bits of the fort, **Contra Aquincum**, in the square to the north. The church was rebuilt in the 14th and 18th centuries, and you can easily spot Gothic, Renaissance, baroque, and even Turkish elements, both inside and out.

Northern Inner Town (Maps 5 & 6)

This district, also called Lipótváros (Leopold Town), is full of offices, government ministries, 19th-century apartment blocks and grand squares.

Roosevelt tér (Map 6) This large square, named in 1947 after the long-serving (1933–45) American president, is at the foot of Chain Bridge and offers among the best views of Castle Hill. Reach it on tram No 2 or 2/a.

On the southern end of the square is a **statue of Ferenc Deák**, the Hungarian minister largely responsible for the Compromise of 1867, which brought about the Dual Monarchy of Austria and Hungary. The statues on the western side are of an Austrian and a Hungarian child holding hands in peaceful bliss.

The Art Nouveau building with the gold tiles to the east is the **Gresham Palace** *(V Roosevelt tér 5-6)*, built by an English insurance company in 1907. It is under renovation and will soon reopen as a five-star hotel. The **Hungarian Academy of Sciences** *(Magyar Tudományos Akadémia; V Roosevelt tér 9)*, founded by Count István Széchenyi, is at the northern end of the square.

Szabadság tér (Map 5) 'Independence Square' *(bus No 15)*, one of the largest squares in the city, is a few minutes' walk northeast of Roosevelt tér. It has a **monument to the Soviet army**, one of the Budapest's few remaining, in the centre; in 2002 it was closed to traffic when the remains of 10 to 15 Soviet soldiers were discovered during excavations to build an underground car park.

On the eastern side of the square is the **US Embassy** *(V Szabadság tér 12)* where Cardinal József Mindszenty took refuge for 15 years until leaving for Vienna in 1971 (see the boxed text 'Cardinal Mindszenty' under Esztergom in the Danube Bend chapter).

South of the embassy is the former **Post Office Savings Bank** *(Szabadság tér 8)*, now part of the **National Bank of Hungary** (Magyar Nemzeti Bank; MNB) next door. The former, a Secessionist extravaganza of colourful tiles and folk motifs built by Ödön Lechner in 1901, is sensational; go around the corner for a better view from Hold utca.

Kossuth Lajos tér (Map 5) Northwest of Szabadság tér is Kossuth Lajos tér *(metro M2 Kossuth Lajos tér)*, the site of Budapest's most photographed building and the best museum in the country for traditional arts and crafts. Southeast of the square in Vértanúk tere is a **statue of Imre Nagy**, the reformist Communist prime minister executed in 1958 for his role in the Uprising two years before (see The 1956 Uprising under History in the Facts about Hungary chapter for more information). It was unveiled with great ceremony in the summer of 1996.

Parliament The Eclectic Parliament *(Országház; ☎ 441 4904; V Kossuth Lajos tér 1-3, Gate X; adult/student 1700/800Ft)*, designed by Imre Steindl and completed in 1902, has almost 700 sumptuously decorated rooms but you'll only get to see three in the North Wing: the main staircase and landing, where the Crown of St Stephen, the nation's most important national icon, is on display (see the boxed text 'The Crown of St Stephen'); the Loge Hall; and the Congress Hall, where the House of Lords of the one-time bicameral assembly sat until 1944. The building is a blend of many architectural styles neo-Gothic, neo-Romanesque, neobaroque) and in sum works very well. Members of Parliament sit in the National Assembly Hall in the South Wing from February to June and from September to December.

There are English language tours at 10am, 12pm and 2pm daily.

Ethnography Museum The Ethnography Museum *(Néprajzi Múzeum; ☎ 473 2400; Ⓦ www.hem.hu; V Kossuth Lajos tér 12; adult/child 500/200Ft; open 10am-6pm Tues-Sun Mar-Oct; 10am-5pm Nov-Feb)*, opposite

The Crown of St Stephen

Legend tells us that it was Asztrik, the first abbot of the Benedictine monastery at Pannonhalma in Western Transdanubia, who presented a crown to Stephen as a gift from Pope Sylvester II around the year 1000, thus legitimising the new king's rule and assuring his loyalty to Rome over Constantinople. It's a nice story but has nothing to do with the object on display in the Parliament building. That two-part crown with its characteristic bent cross, pendants hanging on either side, and enamelled plaques of the Apostles, dates from the 12th century. Regardless, the Crown of St Stephen has become the very symbol of the Hungarian nation.

The crown has disappeared several times over the centuries, only to reappear later. During the Mongol invasions of the 13th century, the crown was dropped while being transported to a safe house, giving it that slightly jaunty, skewed look. More recently, in 1945 Hungarian fascists fleeing the Soviet army took it to Austria. Eventually the crown fell into the hands of the US Army, which transferred it to Fort Knox in Kentucky. In January 1978 the crown was returned to Hungary with great ceremony – and relief. Because legal judgments had always been handed down 'in the name of St Stephen's Crown' it was considered a living symbol and had thus been 'kidnapped'.

the Parliament building, offers visitors an easy introduction to traditional Hungarian life with thousands of displays in a dozen rooms on the 1st floor. The mock-ups of peasant houses from the Őrség and Sárköz regions of Western and Southern Transdanubia (respectively) are well done, and there are some excellent rotating exhibits. On the 2nd floor, another permanent display deals with the other peoples of Europe and farther afield. The website is in Hungarian only.

Bajcsy-Zsilinszky út (Map 6)

Bajcsy-Zsilinszky út is the arrow-straight boulevard that stretches from central Deák tér, the only place in the city where all three metro lines converge, and Nyugati tér, where the Western Railway Station (Nyugati train station) is located.

Basilica of St Stephen The neoclassical Basilica of St Stephen *(Szent István Bazilika; ☎ 311 0839; V Szent István tér; metro M2 Arany János utca; open 9am-7pm Mon-Sat, 1pm-4.30pm Sun)*, built over the course of half a century, was not completed until 1905. Much of the interruption had to do with the fiasco in 1868 when the dome collapsed during a storm, and the structure had to be demolished and rebuilt. The basilica is rather dark and gloomy inside, but take a trip to the top of the **dome** *(☎ 403 5370; adult/student or child 500/400Ft; open 10am-5pm daily Apr, May, Sept & Oct; 10am-6pm daily June-Aug)*, which can be reached by lift or 370 steps and offers one of the best views in the city.

To the right as you enter the basilica is a small **treasury** *(kincstár; open 10am-5pm daily Apr-Sept, 10am-4pm daily Oct-Mar)* of ecclesiastical objects. Behind the main altar and to the left is the basilica's major drawing card: the **Holy Right Chapel** *(Szent Jobb Kápolna; open 9am-4.30pm Mon-Sat, 1am-4.30pm Sun May-Sept; 10am-4pm Mon-Sat, 1am-4.30pm Sun Oct-Apr)*. It contains the Holy Right (also known as the Holy Dexter), the mummified right hand of St Stephen and an object of great devotion. To view it, you have to put a 100Ft coin into a little machine in front of it; this lights up the glass casket containing the Holy Right.

Szent István körút (Maps 3 & 5)

Szent István körút, the northernmost stretch of the Big Ring Road (Körút) in Pest, runs in an easterly directon from Margaret Bridge and the Danube to Nyugati tér. It's an interesting street to stroll along, with many fine Eclectic-style buildings decorated with Atlases, reliefs and other details. Don't hesitate to explore the inner courtyards here and farther on.

You can reach Jászai Mari tér, the start of Szent István körút, on tram No 4 or 6 from either side of the river or via tram No 2 from the Inner Town in Pest – hop on the waterfront tram No 2 to the terminus.

Újlipótváros The area north of Szent István körút is known as Újlipótváros *(New Leopold Town; Maps 3 & 5)* to distinguish it from Lipótváros in the Northern Inner Town. (Archduke Leopold was the grandson of Habsburg Empress Maria Theresa.) The area was upper middle class and Jewish before the war, and many of the 'safe houses' organised by the Swedish diplomat Raoul Wallenberg during WWII were here (see the boxed text 'Raoul Wallenberg, Righteous Gentile' later). A street named after this great man, two blocks to the north, bears a commemorative plaque, and a **statue of Wallenberg** (Map 3) doing battle with a snake (evil), was erected in Szent István Park in 1999, replacing the one torn down in 1948.

Comedy Theatre The attractive little theatre roughly in the middle of this section of the Big Ring Road is the Comedy Theatre *(Vígszínház; Map 5; ☎ 329 2340; XIII Szent István körút 14)*, a popular venue for comedies and musicals. When it was built in 1896, the new theatre's location was criticised for being too far out of the city.

Western Railway Station The large iron and glass structure on Nyugati tér (once known as Marx tér) is the Western Railway Station *(Nyugati pályaudvar; Map 5)* built in 1877 by the Paris-based Eiffel Company. In the early 1970s a train actually crashed through the enormous glass screen on the main facade when its brakes failed, coming to rest at the tram line.

Erzsébetváros (Maps 5 & 6)

The Big Ring Road slices district VII (also called Erzsébetváros or Elizabeth Town) in half between two busy squares: Oktogon and Blaha Lujza tér. The eastern side is a rather poor area with little of interest to travellers

Raoul Wallenberg, Righteous Gentile

Of all the 'righteous gentiles' honoured by Jews around the world, one of the most revered is Raoul Wallenberg, the Swedish diplomat and businessman who rescued as many as 35,000 Hungarian Jews during WWII.

Wallenberg, who came from a long line of bankers and diplomats, began working in 1936 for a trading firm whose president was a Hungarian Jew. In July 1944 the Swedish Foreign Ministry, at the request of Jewish and refugee organisations in the USA, sent the 32-year-old Wallenberg on a rescue mission to Budapest as an attaché to the embassy there. By that time, almost half a million Jews in Hungary had been sent to Nazi death camps.

Wallenberg immediately began issuing Swedish safe-conduct passes (called 'Wallenberg passports') and set up a series of 'safe houses' flying the flag of Sweden and other neutral countries where Jews could seek asylum. He even followed German 'death marches' and deportation trains, distributing food and clothing and actually pulling some 500 people off the cars along the way.

When the Soviet army entered Budapest in January 1945, Wallenberg went to Debrecen to report to the authorities, but in the wartime confusion was arrested for espionage and sent to Moscow. In the early 1950s, responding to reports that Wallenberg had been seen alive in a labour camp, the Soviet Union announced that he had in fact died of a heart attack in 1947. Several reports over the next two decades suggested Wallenberg was still alive, but none was ever confirmed. Many believe Wallenberg was executed by the Soviets, who suspected him to be a spy for the USA.

except the Keleti train station on Baross tér. The western side, bounded by the Little Ring Road, has always been predominantly Jewish, and this was the ghetto where Jews were forced to live behind wooden fences when the Nazis occupied Hungary in 1944.

Oktogon is on the M1 metro line, Blaha Lujza tér on the M2. You can also reach this area via tram Nos 4 and 6 from both Buda and the rest of Pest.

Liszt Academy of Music The Liszt Academy of Music (Liszt Zeneakadémia; Map 5; ☎ 342 0179; VI Liszt Ferenc tér 8; metro M2 Oktogon), one block southeast of Oktogon, was built in 1907. It attracts students from all over the world and is one of the top venues for concerts in Budapest. The interior, with large and small concert halls richly embellished with Zsolnay porcelain and frescoes, is worth a look even if you're not attending a performance.

The Jewish Quarter (Map 6) The heart of the old Jewish quarter, Klauzál tér (Map 5), and its surrounding streets retain a feeling of prewar Budapest. Signs of a continued Jewish presence are still evident – in a kosher bakery at Kazinczy utca 28, the Kővári delicatessen at Kazinczy utca 41, the Frölich cake shop and café, which has old Jewish favourites, at Dob utca 22 and a kosher wine shop at Klauzál tér 16.

There are about half a dozen synagogues and prayer houses in the district, and these were reserved for different sects and ethnic groups: conservatives, the Orthodox, Poles, Sephardics etc. The **Orthodox Synagogue** (Ortodox zsinagóga; VII Kazinczy utca 29-31), which is also accessed from Dob utca 35, was built in 1913 for Budapest's Orthodox community, and the Moorish **Rumbach Sebestyén utca Synagogue** (Rumbach Sebestyén utcai zsinagóga; VII Rumbach Sebestyén utca 11) in 1872 by Austrian Secessionist architect Otto Wagner for the conservatives.

Great Synagogue & Jewish Museum The Great Synagogue (Nagy zsinagóga; VII Dohány utca 2-8) is the largest Jewish house of worship in the world outside New York and can seat 3000 of the faithful. Built in 1859 with Romantic and Moorish elements, the copper-domed synagogue was renovated with funds raised by the Hungarian government and a New York-based charity headed by the actor Tony Curtis, whose parents emigrated from Hungary in the 1920s. In an annexe of the synagogue is the Jewish Museum (Zsidó Múzeum; Map 6; ☎ 342 8949; VII Dohány utca 2; synagogue & museum adult/student or child 600/200Ft; open 10am-5pm Mon-Thur, 10am-3pm Fri, 10am-2pm Sun Apr-Oct; 10am-3pm Mon-Thur, 10am-2pm Fri, 10am-2pm Sun), which contains objects related to religious and everyday life, and an interesting hand-written book of the local Burial Society from the 18th century. The Holocaust Memorial Room – dark and sombre – relates the events of 1944–45, including the infamous mass murder of doctors and patients at a hospital on Maros utca.

The **Holocaust Memorial** on VII Wesselényi utca, on the northern side of the synagogue, stands over the mass graves of those murdered by the Nazis in 1944–45. On the leaves of the metal 'tree of life' are the family names of some of the 400,000 victims.

Blaha Lujza tér & Rákóczi út The subway beneath Blaha Lujza tér, named after a leading 19th-century stage actress, Lujza Blaha, is one of the liveliest in the city, with hustlers, beggars, peasants selling their wares, musicians and, of course, pickpockets. Just north of the square is the Art Nouveau **New York Palace** (Map 5; New York Palota; VII Erzsébet körút 9-11) erstwhile home of the celebrated **New York Kávéház**, scene of many a literary gathering over the years. It is currently being developed as a hotel.

Rákóczi út, a busy shopping street cuts across Blaha Lujza tér and ends at Baross tér and **Keleti pályaudvar** (Eastern Railway Station; Map 3). It was built in 1884 and renovated a century later.

Józsefváros & Ferencváros (Maps 3, 5 & 7)

From Blaha Lujza tér, the Big Ring Road runs through district VIII, also called Józsefváros (Joseph Town). The western side transforms itself from a neighbourhood of lovely 19th-century townhouses and villas around the Little Ring Road to a large student quarter. East of the boulevard is the rough-and-tumble district so poignantly described in the Pressburger brothers' *Homage to the Eighth District*. It is the area where much of the fighting in October 1956 took place.

The neighbourhood south of Üllői út is Ferencváros (Francis Town), home of the city's most popular football team, Ferencvárosi Torna Club (FTC), and many of its rougher, green-and-white-clad supporters. Most of the area was washed away in the Great Flood of 1838.

The Józsefváros and Ferencváros areas are best served by tram Nos 4 and 6.

Around Rákóczi tér Rákóczi tér (Map 5), the only real square right on the Big Ring Road, is as good a place as any to get a feel for this area. It is the site of a busy **market hall** (vásárcsarnok), erected in 1897 and renovated in the early 1990s after a bad fire.

Across the boulevard, Bródy Sándor utca runs west from Gutenberg tér (with a lovely Art Nouveau building at No 4) to the old headquarters of **Hungarian Radio** (Magyar Rádió; Map 5; VIII Bródy Sándor utca 5-7), where shots were first fired on 23 October 1956.

Hungarian National Museum The Hungarian National Museum (Magyar Nemzeti Múzeum; Map 6; ☎ 338 2122, 317 7806; VIII Múzeum körút 14-16; tram No 47 or 49; adult/student or child 600/300Ft; open 10am-6pm Tues-Sun mid-Apr–mid-Oct; 10am-5pm Tues-Sun mid-Oct–mid-Apr) contains the nation's most important collection of historical relics, in a large neoclassical building purpose-built in 1847. Exhibits trace the history of the Carpathian Basin from earliest times, of the Magyar people to 1849 and of Hungary in the 19th and 20th centuries in 16 comprehensive rooms. Look out for the enormous 3rd-century Roman mosaic from Balácapuszta, near Veszprém, at the foot of the central staircase, the crimson silk royal coronation robe stitched by nuns at Veszprém in 1031, the reconstructed 3rd-century Roman villa from Pannonia, the treasury room with pre-Conquest gold jewellery, a second treasury room with later gold objects (including the 11th-century Monomachus crown), the Turkish tent, the stunning baroque library, and Beethoven's Broadwood piano that toured world capitals in 1992.

Museum of Applied Arts The galleries of the Museum of Applied Arts (Iparművészeti Múzeum; Map 3; ☎ 456 5100; IX Üllői út 33-37; adult/child 500/250Ft; open 10am-6pm Tues-Sun mid-Mar–Oct; 10am-4pm Tues-Sun Nov–mid-Mar), which surround a central hall of white marble supposedly modelled on the Alhambra in southern Spain, contain a wonderful array of Hungarian furniture dating from the 18th and 19th centuries, Art Nouveau and Secessionist artefacts, and objects related to the history of trades and crafts (glass making, bookbinding, goldsmithing, leatherwork etc). The building, designed by Ödön Lechner and decorated with Zsolnay ceramic tiles, was completed for the Millenary

Exhibition (1896) but was badly damaged during WWII and again in 1956.

Hungarian Natural History Museum

The Hungarian Natural History Museum *(Magyar Természettudományi Múzeum; Map 7; ☎ 333 0655; w www.nhmus.hu; VIII Ludovika tér 6; metro M3 Klinikák; adult/ senior & child 400/200Ft; open 10am-6pm Wed-Mon Apr-Sept; 10am-5pm Wed-Mon Oct-May)*, one metro stop southeast of the Ferenc körút station, has lots of hands-on interactive displays. The geological park in front of the museum is well designed and there's an interesting exhibit focusing on both the natural resources of the Carpathian Basin and the flora and fauna of Hungarian legends and tales.

National Theatre

The long-awaited National Theatre *(Nemzeti Színház; Map 7; ☎ 476 6800; w www.nemzetiszinhaz.hu; IX Bajor Gizi park 1; tram No 2 or 2/a)* in southwestern Ferencváros and by the Danube, opened in March 2002 and its detractors have not ceased braying since. The design, by architect Mária Siklós, is supposedly 'Eclectic' to mirror other great Budapest buildings of that style (Gellért Hotel, Gresham Palace, Parliament). But in reality it is a pick-and-mix jumble sale of classical and folk motifs, porticoes, balconies and columns on the outside that just does not work. As one local wag put it: 'It looks like a cross between a five-star hotel and Ceauşescu's House of the People'.

Guided tours *(☎ 476 6866)* of the theatre lasting 30 minutes leave hourly from 11am to 3pm on Saturday and Sunday. The website is in Hungarian only.

Andrássy út (Maps 3 & 5)

Andrássy út starts a short distance north of Deák tér and stretches for 2.5km to the northeast, ending at Hősök tere and Városliget, Pest's sprawling 'City Park'. Andrássy út is such a pretty boulevard and there's so much to enjoy en route that the best way to see it is on foot, though the M1 metro runs beneath Andrássy út from Deák tér as far as the City Park.

Hungarian State Opera House

The neo-Renaissance Hungarian State Opera House *(Magyar Állami Operaház; Map 5; ☎ 332 8197; VI Andrássy út 22; metro M1 Opera; adult/student 1500/900Ft)* was designed by Miklós Ybl in 1884, and for many it is the city's most beautiful building. The interior is especially lovely and sparkles after a total overhaul in the 1980s. If you cannot attend a concert or an opera at least join one of the guided tours (conducted in English 3pm and 4pm daily), which includes a brief musical performance. Tickets are available from the office on the eastern side of the building facing Hajós utca.

House of Terror

Budapest's newest museum *(Terrorháza; Map 5; ☎ 374 2600; w www.terrorhaza.hu; Andrássy út 60; metro M1 Vörösmarty utca; adult/student or child 1000/500Ft; open 10am-6pm Tues-Sun)* is the House of Terror. In what was once the headquarters of the dreaded ÁVH secret police, it focuses on the crimes and atrocities committed by Hungary's fascist and Stalinist regimes. Although well received (expect a long wait to get in), it's a rather superficial look at totalitarian rule in Hungary and needs to be expanded. The tank in the central courtyard is a jarring introduction, however, and the wall displaying many of the victims' photos speaks volumes. The exhibit bears remarkable similarity to the Topographie des Terrors (Topography of Terror) in Berlin, which opened in the former headquarters of the SS and Gestapo in 1990. The website is in Hungarian only.

Franz Liszt Memorial Museum

The Franz Liszt Memorial Museum *(Liszt Ferenc Emlékmúzeum; Map 5; ☎ 322 9804; VI Vörösmarty utca 35; metro M1 Vörösmarty utca; adult/student or child 300/150Ft; open 10am-6pm Mon-Fri, 9am-5pm Sat)* is situated in the house where the great composer lived in an apartment on the 1st floor from 1881 until his death in 1886. The four rooms are filled with his pianos (including a tiny glass one), the composer's table, portraits and personal effects.

Asian Art Museums

This area has two fine museums devoted to Asian arts and crafts, within easy walking distance of one another.

The **Ferenc Hopp Museum of East Asian Art** *(Hopp Ferenc Kelet-ázsiai Művészeti Múzeum; Map 3; ☎ 322 8476; VI Andrássy út 103; metro M1 Bajza utca; adult/student or child 300/150Ft; open 10am-6pm Tues-Sun)* is in the former villa of its benefactor and namesake. Founded in 1919, the museum

BUDAPEST

has a good collection of Indonesian *wayang* puppets, Indian statuary and lamaist sculpture and scroll paintings from Tibet. There's an 18th-century Chinese moon gate in the back garden, but most of the Chinese and Japanese collection of ceramics and porcelain, textiles and sculpture is housed in the **György Ráth Museum** (*Ráth György Múzeum; Map 3; ☎ 342 3916; VI Városligeti fasor 12; metro M1 Bajza utca; adult/student or child 300/150Ft; open 10am-6pm Tues-Sun*), in a gorgeous Art Nouveau residence a few minutes southwards down Bajza utca.

Heroes' Square (Map 3)

Andrássy út ends at Heroes' Square (Hősök tere), which in effect forms the entrance to City Park and is on the M1 metro line (Hősök tere stop). The city's most flamboyant monument and two of its best exhibition spaces are here.

Millenary Monument A 36m-high pillar backed by colonnades to the right and left, the Millenary Monument (Ezeréves emlékmű) defines Heroes' Square. About to take off from the top of the pillar is the Angel Gabriel, who is holding the Hungarian crown and a cross. At the base are Árpád and the six other Magyar chieftains who occupied the Carpathian Basin in the late 9th century. Beneath the column and under a stone tile is the nation's most solemn memorial – an empty coffin representing one of the unknown insurgents from the 1956 Uprising.

The 14 statues in the colonnades behind are of rulers and statesmen – from King Stephen on the left to Lajos Kossuth on the right. The reliefs below show a significant scene in the honoured man's life. The four allegorical figures atop are (from left to right): Work & Prosperity, War, Peace and Knowledge & Glory.

Museum of Fine Arts The Museum of Fine Arts (*Szépművészeti Múzeum; ☎ 363 2675; XIV Hősök tere; 700/350Ft adult/student or child; open 10am-5.30pm Tues-Sun*), on the northern side of the square, houses the city's outstanding collection of foreign art works in a renovated building dating from 1906. The Old Masters collection is the most complete, with thousands of works from the Dutch and Flemish, Spanish, Italian, German, French and British schools between the 13th and 18th centuries, including seven paintings by El Greco. Other sections

include Egyptian and Greco-Roman artefacts and 19th- and 20th-century paintings, watercolours, graphics and sculpture, including some important impressionist works. Free tours of key galleries are available in English at 11am Tuesday to Friday.

Palace of Art The Palace of Art (*Műcsarnok; ☎ 460 7000, 363 2671; W www.mucsarnok .hu; XIV Dózsa György út 37; adult/student or child 600/300Ft; open 10am-6pm Tues-Sun*), the ornate gallery to the south of Heroes' Square, was built for the Millenary Exhibition of 1896. It is the city's largest exhibition hall and hosts temporary exhibits of works by Hungarian and foreign artists in fine and applied art, photography and design. Concerts are sometimes staged here as well.

City Park (Map 3)

City Park (Városliget) is Pest's green lung, an open space measuring almost a square kilometre that hosted most of the events during Hungary's 1000th anniversary celebrations in 1896. It's not so cut and dry, but in general museums lie to the south of XIV Kós Károly sétány, while activities of a less cerebral nature – including the Municipal Great Circus (see Circus under Entertainment later) and the Széchenyi Baths (see the boxed text 'Taking the Waters in Budapest' under Activities) – are to the north.

City Park is served by the M1 metro (Széchenyi fürdő stop) as well as trolleybus Nos 72, 75 and 79.

Hungarian Agricultural Museum The Hungarian Agricultural Museum (*Magyar Mezőgazdasági Múzeum; ☎ 363 1973, 363 1117; XIV Vajdahunyad sétány; adult/child 400/200Ft; open 10am-5pm Tues-Fri & Sun, 10am-6pm Sat mid-Feb–mid-Nov; 10am-4pm Tues-Fri, 10am-5pm Sat & Sun mid-Nov–mid-Feb*), in the stunning baroque wing of Vajdahunyad Castle, built for the 1896 millenary celebrations, is Europe's largest such collection. After a visit here there's not much you won't know about Hungarian fruit production, cereals, wool, poultry and pig slaughtering – if that's what you want.

Transport Museum The Transport Museum (*Közlekedési Múzeum; ☎ 363 2658; XIV Városligeti körút 11; adult/child 350/150Ft; open 10am-5pm Tues-Fri, 10am-6pm*

Sat & Sun May-Sept; 10am-4pm Tues-Fri, 10am-5pm Sat & Sun Oct-Apr) may not sound like a crowd-pleaser, but it is one of the most enjoyable in Budapest and great for children. In an old and a new wing there are scale models of ancient trains (some of which run), classic late-19th-century automobiles and lots of those old wooden bicycles called 'boneshakers'. There are a few hands-on exhibits and lots of show-and-tell from the attendants. Outside are pieces from the original Danube bridges that were retrieved after the bombings of WWII and a café in an old MÁV coach.

City Zoo & Botanical Garden The large City Zoo and Botanical Garden *(Városi Állatket és Növénykert; ☎ 363 3797, 364 0109; XIV Állatkerti út 6-12; adult/student/child/family 900/750/650/2800Ft; open 9am-7pm daily May-Aug; 9am-6pm daily Apr & Sept; 9am-5pm daily Mar & Oct; 9am-4pm daily Nov-Feb)* has a good collection of animals (big cats, rhinos, hippopotamuses), but some visitors come here just to look at the Secessionist animal houses built in the early part of the 20th century, such as the Elephant House with pachyderm heads in beetle-green Zsolnay ceramic and the Palm House erected by the Eiffel Company of Paris.

Funfair Park The Funfair Park *(Vidám Park; ☎ 363 2660, 343 9810; W www.vidampark.hu; XIV Állatkerti körút 14-16; admission 200Ft; rides 100-500Ft; open 10am-8pm Mon-Fri & Sun, 10am-10pm Sat July & Aug; 11am-7pm Mon-Fri, 10am-10pm Sat, 10am-8pm Sun May & June; noon-7pm Mon-Fri, 10am-7.30pm Sat & Sun Apr & Sept; noon-6pm Mon-Fri, 10am-7pm Sat & Sun Mar & Oct)* is a 150-year-old luna park on 2½ hectares next to the circus (see Entertainment later). There's a couple of dozen new rides, including the heart-stopping Ikarus Space Needle and the looping Star roller coaster, go-karts, dodgem cars and a carousel built in 1906, and protected as a monument.

ACTIVITIES
Cycling
Parts of Budapest, including City and Népliget Parks, Margaret, Óbudai and Csepel Islands and the Buda Hills, are excellent places for cycling. At present bike paths in the city total about 300km, including the path along Andrássy út, which has bicycle traffic signals.

There are places to rent bicycles on Margaret Island (see Activities under Margaret Island earlier for details) and in City Park.

Rent-a-Bike *(Map 6; ☎ 06-30 922 3113, 06-30 971 0941; open 9am-8pm daily)* has bikes available from several locations in Pest, including a stand opposite V Váci utca 30. It charges 2000/3000Ft for six/12 hours.

Yellow Zebra Bikes *(☎ 06-30 399 7093)* rents out bikes for 3000/5000Ft for one/two days; it's 2000Ft daily after that.

The agency **Starting Point** *(Map 6; ☎ 266 5563; e startingpont@mailbox.hu; V Szabadsajtó utca 6; metro M3 Ferenciek tere; open 9am-9pm daily July-Oct; 9am-7pm Nov-June)* rents bicycles out for 2400Ft per day.

The **Friends of the City Cycling Group** *(Map 6; VBB; ☎ 318 0933; W www.vbb.hu; V Curia utca 3)* has the useful four-sheet *Budapesti bringás térkép* (Budapest Map for Bikers; 980Ft). Frigoria publishes a number of useful guides and maps, including one called *Kerékparral Budapest környéken* (By Bike around Budapest; 1890Ft) that takes in the surrounding areas and describes 30 different routes. Both publications are available in most bookshops.

Bicycles can be transported on the HÉV, all Mahart boats and the Cog Railway but *not* on the metro, buses or trams.

Horse Riding
Recommended riding schools in Budapest include the **Hajógyári-sziget Lovarda** *(Map 2; ☎/fax 457 1025; III Obudai hajógyári-sziget; HÉV Árpád-híd)* where riding costs 1300/2000Ft for 25/45 minutes (no cross-country riding possible on the island) and the **Petneházy Lovascentrum** *(☎ 397 5048; W www.petnehazy-lovascentrum.com; II Feketefej utca 2-4; bus No 63; open 9am-8pm Fri-Sun)* at Adyliget near Hűvös-völgy. The latter offers beginner's lessons (2500Ft per 25 minutes), paddock practice (3000Ft per hour), trail riding (4500Ft per hour) and carriage rides (10,000Ft for 25 minutes for 10 people). If you want to ride at either place, make sure you book in advance before you set out to avoid disappointment.

The Hungarian Equestrian Tourism Association has a list of recommended riding schools in Hungary and Pegazus Tours can book riding programmes. See Horse Riding under Activities in the Facts for the Visitor chapter for details.

BUDAPEST

Taking the Waters in Budapest

Budapest lies on the geological fault separating the Buda Hills from the Great Plain; more than 30,000 cubic metres of warm to scalding (21°C to 76°C) mineral water gush forth daily from 118 thermal springs. As a result, the city is a major spa centre and 'taking the waters' at one of the many baths or spa-swimming pools is a real Budapest experience. Some baths date from Turkish times, others are Art Nouveau wonders, and others are spic-and-span modern establishments.

THERMAL BATHS

Generally, entry to the baths allows you to stay for two hours on weekdays and 1½ hours at weekends, though this rule is not always enforced. Most of the baths offer a full range of serious medical treatments plus services like massage (1100/2000Ft for 15/30 minutes) and pedicure (1200Ft). Specify what you want when buying your ticket. For the procedure for getting out of your street clothes and into the water see Thermal Baths under Activities in the Facts for the Visitor chapter. In order to prevent theft in case you lose or misplace your locker tag or disk, the number is not the same as the one on the locker, so commit the *locker* number to memory.

The baths may sometimes look a bit rough around the edges, but they are clean and the water is changed continuously. You may want to wear rubber sandals, though. Some bathhouses require you to wear a bathing suit while others do not; take one just in case. Most of them hire out bathing suits and towels (500Ft) if you don't have your own.

Please note: some of the baths become gay venues on male-only days – especially the Király and, to a lesser extent, the Gellért. Not much actually goes on except for some intensive cruising, but those not into it may feel uncomfortable.

Gellért Soaking in this Art Nouveau palace *(Map 3; ☎ 466 6166, XI Kelenhegyi út, admission 1600Ft, tram No 18, 19, 47 or 49, open 6am-7pm Mon-Fri, 6am-5pm Sat & Sun May-Sept; 6am-7pm Mon-Fri, 6am-2pm Sat & Sun Oct-April)*, open to both men and women in separate sections, has been likened to taking a bath in a cathedral. The pools maintain a constant temperature of 44°C and a large outdoor pool is open from April to September.

Király Baths The four pools here *(Map 3; ☎ 202 3688, 201 4392, II Fő utca 82-86, bus* No 60 or 86, admission 800Ft, open to men 9am-8pm Mon, Wed & Fri, to women 6.30am-6pm Tues & Thur, 6.30am-12.30pm Sat)* are genuine Turkish baths erected in 1570 and have a wonderful skylit central dome.

Lukács This sprawling 19th-century establishment *(Lukács Gyógyfürdő; Map 3; ☎ 326 1695, II Frankel Leó út 25-29, tram No 17 or bus No 60 or 86, admission 600/800Ft for 3/4 hrs, open 6am-7pm Mon-Fri, 6am-1pm Sat & Sun)*, popular with an older crowd, has everything from thermal and mud baths to a swimming pool. The thermal baths are open to both men and to women in separate sections; the mud and weight baths (1500Ft) are open to men on Tuesday, Thursday and Saturday and women on Monday, Wednesday and Friday.

Rudas This is the most Turkish of all the baths in Budapest *(Map 4; ☎ 356 1322, 356 1010, I Döbrentei tér 9, tram No 18 or 19, bus No 7 or 86, admission 1000Ft, open to men only 6am-8pm Mon-Fri, 6am-1pm Sat & Sun)*, built in 1566, with an octagonal pool, domed cupola with coloured glass and massive columns.

Széchenyi This bath in City Park *(Map 3; ☎ 363 3210, 321 0310, XIV Állatkerti út 11, metro M1 Széchenyi fürdő, admission deposit 1500/900Ft before/after 3pm, open 6am-7pm daily May-Sept; 6am-7pm Mon-Fri, 6am-5pm Sat & Sun Oct-Apr)* is unusual for three reasons: its immense size (nine indoor and outdoor pools); its bright, clean look; and its water temperatures, which really are what the wall plaques say they are. It is open to both men and women in separate sections, and the entrance fee is actually a kind of deposit; you get back 900/600/300Ft if you leave within two/three/four hours before 3pm and 600/300Ft if you exit within two/three hours after 3pm. Just make sure you hold on to your receipts.

Thermal This thermal bath *(Map 2; ☎ 452 6237, XIII Margit-sziget, bus No 26, admission 4000/5000Ft weekday/weekend, open 6.30am-9.30pm daily)*, in the Danubius Grand Hotel Margitsziget on leafy Margaret Island, is the most upmarket (and expensive) baths in town. It is open to men and women in separate sections.

SWIMMING POOLS

Every town of any size in Hungary has at least one indoor and outdoor swimming pool *(úszoda)*, and Budapest boasts dozens. They're always

Taking the Waters in Budapest

excellent places to get in a few laps (if indoor), cool off on a hot summer's day (if outdoor) or watch all the posers strut their stuff.

The system inside is similar to that at the baths except that rather than a cabin or cubicle, there are sometimes just lockers. Get changed and call the attendant, who will lock it, write the time on a chalkboard and hand you a key. Many pools require the use of a bathing cap, so bring your own or wear the plastic one provided or sold for a nominal fee. Most pools hire out bathing suits and towels (500Ft).

Following are the best outdoor and indoor pools in the city. The former are usually open from May to September unless otherwise specified.

Csillaghegy At this place (Map 2; ☎ 250 1533, III Pusztakúti út 3, HÉV: Csillaghegy, adult/child aged 2-12 1000/900Ft, outdoor pools open 7am-7pm daily May-Sept, indoor pools open 6am-7pm Mon-Fri, 6am-4pm Sat, 6am-1pm Sun Oct-Apr) there's a nudist section on the southern slope, popular in summer.

Dagály This huge complex (Map 2; ☎ 452 4500, 320 2203, XIII Népfürdő utca 36, metro M3 Árpád híd or tram No 1, admission 1100/1000Ft with/without cabin, outdoor pools open 6am-7pm daily May-Sept, indoor pools open 6am-7pm Mon-Fri, 6am-5pm Sat & Sun Oct-Apr) has a total of 12 pools, with plenty of grass and shade.

Gellért The indoor pools (Map 3; ☎ 466 6166, XI Kelenhegyi út, admission to swimming pool & thermal baths with locker/cabin 2000/2400Ft, 1700Ft after 5pm daily May-Sept, after 5pm Mon-Fri & after 2pm Sat & Sun Oct-Apr; open 6am-7pm daily May-Sept; 6am-7pm Mon-Fri, 6am-5pm Sat & Sun Oct-April) are the most beautiful in Budapest. The outdoor pools have a wave machine and nicely landscaped gardens.

Hajós Alfréd National Sports Pool The pools (Map 3; ☎ 340 4946, 349 2357, XIII Margit-sziget; tram No 4 or 6, bus No 26, admission 330/550Ft winter/summer, outdoor pools open 6am-7pm daily May-Sept, indoor pools 6am-7pm Mon-Fri, 6am-5pm Sat & Sun Oct-Apr), one indoor and two outdoor, form the National Sports Swimming Pool where Olympic teams train.

Helia This ultra-modern spa and swimming pool (Map 3; ☎ 452 5800, XIII Kárpát utca 62-64, metro Dózsa György út or trolleybus No 79,

admission 4200Ft, open 7am-10pm daily) in four-star Danubius Helia Hotel boasts three pools, sauna and steam room and a health-food bar.

Béla Komjádi This very serious pool (Map 3; ☎ 335 2097, II Árpád fejedelem útja 8, tram No 17 or bus No 60 or 86, admission 330/500Ft winter/summer, open 6am-9pm Mon-Sat, 6am-7pm Sun) has widely varying opening hours depending on the time of year and day of the week.

Lukács This sprawling 19th-century establishment (Lukács Gyógyfürdő; Map 3; ☎ 326 1695, II Frankel Leó út 25-29, tram No 17 or bus No 60 or 86, admission 600/800Ft for 3/4 hours, open 6am-7pm daily May-Sept, 6am-7pm Mon-Fri, 6am-5pm Sat & Sun Oct-Apr), popular with an older crowd, has a swimming pool. See also Thermal Baths earlier.

Palatinus The largest series of pools in the capital (Map 2; ☎ 340 4505, XIII Margit-sziget; bus No 26), with a total of seven plus a wave pool, was being extensively renovated at the time of research but promises to be better then ever. There are same-sex roof decks for nude sunbathing.

Rómaifürdő The outdoor pools here (Map 2; ☎ 388 9740, III Rozgonyi Piroska utca 2, HÉV Rómaifürdő or bus No 34, admission 1000/900Ft adult/child aged 2-12, 900Ft for all after 5pm Mon-Fri) are north of Óbuda.

Rudas These pools (Map 4; ☎ 356 1322, 356 1010, I Döbrentei tér 9, tram No 18 or 19, bus No 7 or 86, admission 700/600Ft adult/child aged 2-12, open 6am-6pm Mon-Fri, 6am-1pm Sat & Sun), close to the river, were built by the Turks in 1566 and retain a strong Turkish atmosphere.

Széchenyi The enormous and renovated pools of the Széchenyi baths (Map 3; ☎ 363 3210, 321 0310, XIV Állatkerti út 11, metro M1 Széchenyi fürdő, admission deposit 1500/900Ft before/after 3pm, open 6am-7pm daily May-Sept; 6am-7pm Mon-Fri, 6am-5pm Sat & Sun Oct-Apr), the largest medicinal bath extant in Europe, contain thermal water and are thus open year-round.

Thermal Admission to the Thermal bath (Map 2; ☎ 452 6237, XIII Margit-sziget, bus No 26, admission 4000/5000Ft weekday/weekend, open 6.30am-9.30pm daily) on Margaret Island includes the swimming pool.

Thermal Baths & Swimming

For information see the boxed text 'Taking the Waters in Budapest' earlier in this section.

Boating

The best place for canoeing and kayaking in Budapest is on the Danube at Romai-part; take the HÉV suburban line to Rómaifürdő and walk westwards toward the river. Two reliable places to rent kayaks (1000Ft per day) or canoes (1300Ft per day) are from **Óbuda Sport Club** (ÓSE; Map 2; ☎ 240 3353; III Rozgonyi Piroska utca 28; open 7am-7pm daily) and from **KSH** (Map 2; ☎ 368 8967; III Királyok útja 31; open 8am-6pm daily mid-Apr–mid-Oct). You'll probably find a boat available if just you go to either place but it's always safer to book ahead.

Caving

Budapest has a number of caves, two of which are open for walk-through guided tours in Hungarian. **Pálvölgy Cave** (Pálvölgyi-barlang; Map 2; ☎ 325 9505; II Szépvölgyi út 162; bus No 65 from Kolosy tér in Óbuda; adult/student or child 450/350Ft), the third-largest cave in Hungary, is noted for its stalactites and bats. Hourly tours are conducted from 10am to 4pm Tuesday to Sunday; be advised that the tour involves climbing some 400 steps and a ladder so it may not be suitable for children.

A more beautiful cave, with stalactites, stalagmites and weird grape-like formations, is **Szemlőhegy Cave** (Szemlőhegyi-barlang; Map 2; ☎ 325 6001; II Pusztaszeri út 35; bus No 29 from III Kolosy tér; open 10am-3pm Mon & Wed-Fri, 10am-4pm Sat & Sun), about 1km southeast of Pál-völgy. Admission costs 400/300Ft per adult/student or child.

You can book more adventurous caving possibilities through the adventure sports department of the Vista Visitor Center (see Travel Agencies in the Information section earlier), as well as through many of the hostels listed under Places to Stay (see later). Some offer 2½-hour excursions for 2800Ft to **Mátyáshegy Cave** (Mátyáshegyi-barlang; Map 2), a cave opposite the Pál-völgy, at 11am on Tuesday and Thursday and at 5pm on Monday, Wednesday and Friday.

LANGUAGE COURSES

In addition to the courses offered by the Budapest branch of the Debrecen Summer University (see Language Courses in the Facts for the Visitor chapter), the following Hungarian-language schools are recommended for either classroom study or one-to-one instruction.

Hungarian Language School
(Map 3; ☎ 351 1191, fax 351 1193; W www.hls.hu) VI Rippl-Rónai utca 4
InterClub Hungarian Language School
(Map 7; ☎ 279 0831, fax 365 2535; W www.interclub.hu) XI Bertalan Lajos utca 17
International House
(Map 3; ☎ 212 4010, fax 316 2491; W www.ih.hu) II Bimbó út 7

ORGANISED TOURS
Bus

Many travel agencies, including **Cityrama** (Map 5; ☎ 302 4382; W www.cityrama.hu; V Báthory utca 22) and **Program Centrum** (☎ 317 7767; W www.programcentrum.hu; V Erzsébet tér 9-10) at the Hotel Le Meridien, offer three-hour city tours with three stops from 6000/3000Ft per adult/child under 12. They also have excursions to the Danube Bend, Lake Balaton, the Southern Plain, the Eger wine region etc (see Organised Tours in the Getting Around chapter for details).

Budatours (Map 6; ☎ 353 0558, 374 7070; W www.budatours.hu; VI Andrássy út 2) runs eight bus tours daily in both open and covered coaches in July and August (between two and three the rest of the year) from V Andrássy út 3 across the street. It's a two-hour nonstop tour with taped commentary in 16 different languages and costs 5300/2700Ft per adult/child under 16.

Queenybus (☎ 247 7159, fax 309 0395) has buses departing three times daily (10am, 11am and 2.20pm) from in front of St Stephen's Basilica on V Bajcsy-Zsilinszky út (Map 6) for three-hour city tours; it charges 6000/4000/3000Ft per adult/student/child 10 to 16.

Boat

From late April to September **Mahart Pass-Nave** (Map 6; ☎ 484 4013, 318 1223; V Belgrád rakpart) has 1½-hour cruises on the Danube at noon and 7.30pm daily for 1200/600Ft per adult/child under 10. In April the noon cruise operates on Saturday and holidays only, and from mid-June to August the evening programme begins at 8.15pm and includes music and dance (1800/900Ft). There are other, more expensive, cruises that also operate on the river, including those offered by

Legenda (☎ 266 4190, fax 317 2203; W www
.legenda.hu), which runs tours by day (3400/
1600Ft) and night (4000Ft), with taped commentary in up to 30 languages.

Walking

Highly recommended is **Absolute Walking
Tours** (☎ 06-30 211 8861; W www.budapes
tours.com), a 3½-hour guided promenade
through City Park, central Pest and Castle
Hill. Tours (3500/3000Ft per adult/student or
under-26) depart at 9.30am and 1.30pm daily
from the steps of the yellow Lutheran church
on Deák tér (Map 6), and at 10am and 2pm
daily from the steps of the Műcsarnok art
gallery in Heroes' Square (Map 3) from mid-
May to September. During the rest of the year
tours leave from the Deák tér Lutheran church
at 10.30am and from the Műcsarnok at 11am
only, with tours curtailed over Christmas and
in January. It has some cracker specialist
tours, including the Hammer & Sickle Tour.

Castle Walks (☎ 488 0453), sponsored by
the Tourism Office of Budapest, will lead
you through the winding ways and tortuous
tales of the historic Castle District starting
from Matthias Church (Map 4) for 2400Ft.
Tours leave at 11am and 3.30pm daily from
late June to mid-September and on Saturday
and Sunday only from late April to late June
and late September to late October.

More personal are **Paul Street Tours** (☎ 06-
20 958 2545; e kfaurest@hotmail.com). It
covers the Castle District (1½ hours), less-
explored areas of Pest, such as the Jewish
Quarter and Andrássy út (two hours), the Little Ring Road, the parks and gardens of Budapest and shopping, with lots of anecdotal
information on architecture and social history,
especially life in and around the udvar (courtyards) of fin-de-siècle Pest. Tours are available
year-round in English or Hungarian and cost
around €25 per hour for up to 15 people.

Cycling

Yellow Zebra Bikes (☎ 06-30 399 7093), run
by the same people behind Absolute Walking
Tours (see Walking earlier), has cycling tours
of Budapest by day at 11.30am May to October and by night at 8pm on Sunday, Tuesday
and Thursday from June to September. Tours
cost 4000/3500Ft per adult/student and under
26, which include the bike and a drink, and
depart from the yellow Lutheran church on
Deák tér (Map 6).

SPECIAL EVENTS

Many festivals and events are held in and
around Budapest; look out for the tourist
board's annual *Events in Hungary from January to December* for a complete listing. Among
the most important annual events are:

January
New Year Opera Gala Held at the Pesti Vigadó on
1 January

February
Opera Ball Held at the Hungarian State Opera
House

March
Budapest Spring Festival Held at venues throughout the capital

April
World Dance Festival Held at venues throughout
the capital
Spring Running Carnival Marathon between
Budapest and Visegrád

May
Ancient Music Festival Held at the Liszt Music
Academy, and at -churches around Budapest

June
Danube Folklore Carnival Pan-Hungarian inter-
national carnival held in Vörösmarty tér and on
Margaret Island
Budapest Búcsú A festival of rock and pop music
that originally marked the departure of the last
Soviet soldier from Hungarian soil
Ferencváros Summer Festival Held in late June
and July

July
Pepsi Sziget Music Festival Europe's largest out-
door music festival, held on Óbuda Hajógyár
Island late July to early August

August
BudaFest Summer Opera & Ballet Festival Held
at the Hungarian State Opera House
Hungarian Formula One Grand Prix Held in the
Hungaroring at Mogyoród, 24km northeast of
the capital

September
International Wine & Champagne Festival Held
in the Castle District
European Heritage Days Doors are opened to
buildings and other sites around the city nor-
mally closed to the public
Budapest Marathon Race held up and down the
Danube and across its bridges

October
Budapest Autumn Festival Held at venues
throughout the city until early November

December
New Year's Gala & Ball Held at the Hungarian
State Opera House on 31 December

PLACES TO STAY – BUDGET
Camping

Buda Located in a leafy park north of the city, **Római Camping** *(Map 2; ☎ 388 7167, fax 250 0426; III Szentendrei út 189; camping per person/tent site/campervan/caravan 990/1990/2200/3300Ft, 2-bed cabins 3600-6000Ft; camping open year-round, cabins mid-Apr–mid-Oct)* is Budapest's largest site. To get there, take the HÉV suburban railway from the Batthyány tér metro station in Buda to the Rómaifürdő station, which is almost opposite the camp site. Use of the adjacent strand and swimming pool is included.

Niche Camping *(Map 1; ☎ 200 8346; XII Zugligeti út 101; bus No 158 from Moszkva tér; 2-person tent site 2900-3000Ft, caravan 3950-4400Ft, 2-person/4-person bungalow 4000/6000Ft, car 700Ft; open year-round)* is a small site in the Buda Hills at the bottom station of the chair lift.

Pest In the back garden of a cultural centre in urban Pest, **Haller Camping** *(Map 7; ☎ 215 5741, 215 4775, fax 218 7909; IX Haller utca 27; metro M3 Nagyvárad, tram No 24; camping per person/tent/car from 400/1800/300Ft; open June–mid-Sept)* is about the most central – but hardly attractive – site you'll find to pitch a tent.

Hostels

Though you can go directly to all the hostels mentioned here, **Travellers' Youth Hostels-Mellow Mood** *(☎ 413 2062, 215 0660; W www.hostels.hu, W www.backpackers.hu)*, which is affiliated with Hostelling International (HI), runs two year-round and six summer hostels. Staff at its three booths in Keleti train station *(☎ 343 0748; open 7.30am-11pm daily in summer; 7.30am-9pm daily rest of year)*, in the international ticket hall, at the Tourinform office and under the large clock near track No 9, make bookings and may arrange to transport you there. You can also go directly to either of their two year-round hostels – Marco Polo or Diáksport (see Pest under Hostels, in this section later).

Express is the best travel agency to approach for hostel information; for details see Travel Agencies under Information, earlier.

Hostel, student and youth cards are not required at any hostels in Budapest, but they'll often get you a discount of up to 10%; make sure to ask beforehand. Prices almost always include breakfast; otherwise it may cost you between 350Ft and 400Ft.

Hostels usually have laundry facilities (about 1000Ft per load), a fully equipped kitchen, storage lockers, TV lounge, no curfew and computers for accessing the Internet (usually from 20Ft per minute).

Buda A colourful place with 50 beds and a friendly, much-travelled manager is **Back Pack Guesthouse** *(Map 7; ☎ 385 8946; W www .backpackbudapest.hu; XI Takács Menyhért utca 33; black-numbered bus No 7 or 7/a from Keleti train station, tram No 49 from central Pest or tram No 19 from I Batthyány tér; dorm beds 1800-2300Ft, doubles 2800Ft per person)*. There are dormitories with between five and 11 beds and one small double, a lovely garden and very laid-back clientele. It's in south Buda and not central but transport is reliable.

Citadella Hotel *(Map 3; ☎ 466 5794; W www.citadella.hu; XI Citadella sétány; bus No 27 from XI Móricz Zsigmond körtér; dorm beds 2200Ft)* in the fortress atop Gellért Hill has a room with 14 beds as well as hotel rooms (see Hotels under this Buda section later). The dorms are usually booked by groups a week ahead – call for a reservation.

Martos Hostel *(Map 7; ☎ 209 4883, fax 463 3650; e reception@hotel.martos.bme.hu; XI Sztoczek Jozsef utca 5-7; tram No 4 or 6; singles 3500Ft, doubles/triples/quads 2200Ft per person)*, though primarily a summer hostel, has 20 beds available year-round. It's reasonably well located, near the Danube, and it's a few minutes' walk from Petőfi Bridge.

Pest With 22 beds, **Aquarium Youth Hostel** *(Map 3; ☎ 322 0502, 344 6143; e aquarium@budapesthostel.com; VII Alsóerdősor utca 12, 2/F; metro M2 Keleti pályaudvar; 4–8-bed dorms 2500Ft, doubles 8000Ft)* is 250m northwest of Keleti train station, but a second choice after most of the other hostels in this section.

Best Hostel *(Map 5; ☎ 332 4934; e best yh@mail.datanet.hu; VI Podmaniczky utca 27, 1/F; metro M3 Nyugati pályaudvar; dorm beds 2800Ft, doubles/quads 4000/3400Ft per person)*, with accommodation in rather rickety bunk beds, has big, airy and relatively quiet rooms. It can organise caving excursions in the Buda Hills (see Caving under Activities earlier).

Caterina Hostel *(Map 5; ☎ 342 0804, fax 352 6147; ℮ caterina@mail.inext.hu; VI Andrássy út 47, 3/F; metro M1 Oktogon; dorm beds/singles/doubles 2500/3500/7000Ft)*, run by an affable English-speaking woman, has 32 beds and is within spitting distance of all the pubs and bars on Liszt Ferenc tér.

Diáksport Hostel *(Map 3; ☎ 340 8585, 413 2062; W www.hostels.hu or W www .backpackers.hu; XIII Dózsa György út 152; metro M3 Dózsa György út; beds in 6-bed dorm 3300Ft, singles & doubles with bathroom 4600Ft per person, doubles/triples & quads with shared bathroom from 3600/ 3500Ft per person)* is the Travellers' Youth Hostels-Mellow Mood group's original flagship property with 131 beds. It is a bit far from the action but compensates by having its own 24-hour pub. This is definitely a party place so go elsewhere if you've come to Budapest to sleep. Breakfast is not included.

Hostel Marco Polo *(Map 5; ☎ 413 2555; W www.marcopolohostel.com; VII Nyár utca 6; metro M2 Blaha Lujza tér; dorm beds €17/46 low/high season, singles €19/51, doubles/triples/quads €31/26/22 per person low season, €34/29/24 high season)*, the same group's 47-room property, is more central, swish and expensive. In fact, it's almost like a mid-range hotel, with telephones in the rooms, a lovely courtyard and a great bar with cheap drinks and a restaurant (set meals 1000Ft; open 10am to 10pm). Even the five spotless 12-bed dorm rooms (one reserved for women only) are 'private', with beds separated by lockers and curtains. Breakfast is included.

Museum Castle Youth Guest House *(Map 5; ☎ 318 9508, 266 8879; ℮ museumgh@ freemail.C3.hu; VIII Mikszáth Kálmán tér 4, 1/F; metro M3 Kálvin tér; dorm beds 2500Ft)* is a poky but creatively decorated and friendly place, with six to nine dorm beds in three rooms. Its free Internet access, location on a lovely square, and proximity to the nightlife of VIII Krúdy utca and IX Ráday utca are all pluses.

Red Bus Hostel *(Map 6; ☎/fax 266 0136; ℮ redbusbudapest@hotmail.com; V Semmelweiss utca 14, 1/F; metro M2 Astoria; dorm beds 2700Ft, singles 6000/7000Ft winter/summer, doubles 7000Ft)*, a very central, well-managed and friendly place, has 28 beds in large, airy and spotlessly clean rooms cobbled from two flats and a modern kitchen. It's for those looking for peace and quiet – not a party.

Station Guesthouse *(Map 3; ☎ 221 8864; W www.stationguesthouse.hu; XIV Mexikói út 36/b; metro M1 Mexikói út, red-numbered bus No 7 from Keleti station; 14-bed/8-bed dorms 1700/2400Ft, doubles & triples/quads 3200/2700Ft per person)* is a tad off the beaten track but has a great atmosphere. It's a real party place with a 24-hour bar, pool table and occasional live entertainment. It has between 42 and 56 beds, depending on the season. HI card-holders get 200Ft off the above prices and rates drop by 100Ft per night from the second to sixth night of stay.

Yellow Submarine Youth Hostel *(Map 5; ☎/fax 331 9896; W www.yellowsubmarine hostel.com; VI Teréz körút 56, 3/F; metro M3 Nyugati pályaudvar; dorm beds/doubles/ quads 2500/3750/2800Ft per person)*, with 44 beds, has lots of facilities and high ceilings, but overlooks one of Pest's busiest boulevards and there's no lift.

Private Rooms

Private rooms in Budapest generally cost from 3600Ft to 5000Ft for a single, 5000Ft to 7000Ft for a double and 8000Ft to 15,000Ft for a small apartment, with a 30% supplement if you stay less than four nights. To get a room in the centre of town, you may have to try several offices. There are lots of rooms, and even in July and August you'll be able to find something. You'll probably need an indexed city map to find the block where your room is located, though (see Maps under Information, earlier, for more details).

Tourinform in Budapest does not arrange private accommodation, but will send you to a travel agency, such as the ones listed below.

Among the best places to try for private rooms are Ibusz and Vista (see Travel Agencies under Information earlier). Other good places are **To-Ma** *(Map 6; ☎ 353 0819; W www.tomatour.hu; V Október 6 utca 22; metro M1/2/3 Deák tér; open 9am-noon & 1pm-8pm Mon-Fri, 9am-5pm Sat-Sun)*, which offers these extended opening hours, **U Tours** *(Map 3; ☎ 303 9818; W www.utours.hu; VIII Kerepesi út 2-4; metro M3 Keleti pályaudvar; open 7am-7pm daily May-Sept; 9am-5pm Oct-Mar)*, at the end of platform No 6 in Keleti station; and **Starting Point** *(Map 6; ☎ 266 5563; ℮ startingpont@mailbox.hu; V Szabadsajtó utca 6; metro M3 Ferenciek tere;*

open 9am-9pm daily July-Oct, 9am-7pm Nov-June), which offers for rent private rooms, apartments and even bicycles (see also Cycling under Activities earlier for details).

After hours, try **Tribus Nonstop Hotel Service** (Map 6; ☎ 266 8942, 318 5776; w www.tribus.hu; V Apáczai Csere János utca 1; metro M1 Vörösmarty tér; open 24hr) near the Budapest Marriott Hotel.

Pensions & Guesthouses
Buda A pension just a block off the northern side of Moszkva tér, **Büro Panzió** (Map 3; ☎ 212 2929, fax 212 2928; e buro-panzio@ axelero.hu; II Dékán utca 3; metro M2 Moszkva tér; singles/doubles with shower 9000/ 13,500Ft) looks basic from the outside, but its 10 rooms are comfortable and have TVs and telephones.

Papillon (Map 3; ☎ 212 4750, fax 212 4003; e rozsahegy@axelero.hu; II Rózsahegy utca 3/b; singles 6000-8800Ft, doubles 8000-11,500Ft), one of Buda's best-kept accommodation secrets (quiet, off the beaten track and cheap), has 20 rooms with bathrooms; prices depend on the season.

San Marco Pension (Map 2; ☎/fax 388 9997; e saiban@elender.hu; III San Marco utca 6; tram No 17; singles/doubles 11,000/ 12,000Ft) is a small, family-run and very friendly place in Óbuda. It has five spic-and-span rooms on the 2nd floor (three with private bathroom), a pleasant courtyard out back and air conditioning.

Pest Just two stops northeast of Keleti train station by bus is **Dominik Panzió** (Map 3; ☎ 460 9428; fax 343 7655; e domini kpanzio@axelero.hu; XIV Cházár András utca 3; bus No 7; singles/doubles €26/31 Apr-Oct; €21/27 Nov-Mar), beside a large church just off Thököly út. The 36 rooms, which could use an upgrade, come with shared bathroom.

Garibaldi Guesthouse & Apartments (Map 5; ☎ 302 3457, fax 302 3456; e gari baldiguest@hotmail.com; V Garibaldi utca 5, 5/F; metro M2 Kossuth Lajos tér; singles/ doubles 5000/7000Ft), arguably the most welcoming guesthouse in Budapest, has five rooms with shared bathrooms and kitchen in a flat just around the corner from Parliament, and a number of other rooms and self-contained flats with all facilities in the same building costing from €20 to €45 per person.

Leó Panzió (Map 6; ☎ 266 9041, fax 266 9042; e panzioleo@mail.datanet.hu; V Kossuth Lajos utca 2/a, 2/F; metro M3 Ferenciek tere; singles €45-66, doubles €69-82, triples €88-108) offers excellent value for its location and immaculate 14 rooms, all of which have double-glazing, minibar and television.

Hotels
A room in a budget (ie, one- or two-star) hotel will cost more than a private room – roughly 7500Ft to 13,500Ft (€30 to €55) for a double – though the management won't mind if you stay only one night.

Buda There are 12 big, clean, dark-wood rooms at **Citadella Hotel** (Map 3; ☎ 466 5794; w www.citadella.hu; XI Citadella sétány; bus No 27 from XI Móricz Zsigmond körtér; doubles with/without bathroom from €55/50), though we've heard complaints about the noisy dance club below.

Hotel Junior Griff (Map 7; ☎ 203 2398, fax 203 1255; e reserve@hotelgriffjunior .hunguesthotels.hu; XI Bartók Béla út 152; tram No 19 or 49, red-numbered bus No 7; singles €35, doubles with wash basin €47-57, quads with wash basin €70, singles with shower €40, doubles with shower €53-66) has 71 basic rooms at rock-bottom prices in a low-rise office block.

Pest In Angyalföld northeast of the Inner Town and the Lehel market, **Hotel Góliát** (Map 3; ☎ 350 1456, fax 349 4985; e hotel golita@gerandhotels.hu; XIII Kerekes utca 12-20; bus No 4; singles/doubles/triples/quads 5200/6200/6700/7700Ft) has accommodation in 135 basic rooms, with between one and four beds per room.

Hotel Medosz (Map 5; ☎ 374 3000, fax 332 4316; VI Jókai tér 9; metro M1 Oktogon; singles/doubles/triples 10,000/13,000/ 15,000Ft), one of the most central cheap hotels in Pest, is the just opposite the restaurants and bars of Liszt Ferenc tér. The 70 rooms are well worn but have private bath and satellite TV; the best ones are in the main block, not in the labyrinthine wings.

Radio Inn (Map 3; ☎ 342 8347, fax 322 8284; e radioinn@elender.hu; VI Benczúr utca 19; metro M1 Bajza utca; singles €43-48, doubles €48-65), just off leafy Andrássy út, is a real find, with 33 large suites with bathroom, kitchen and bed (or beds).

Margaret Island In the middle of Margaret Island, **Hotel Margitsziget** *(Map 3; ☎ 329 2949, fax 340 4846;* e *hotelmargitsziget@ axelero.hu; XIII Margit-sziget; bus No 26; singles €43-48, doubles €43-56)* is good value and almost feels like a budget resort, with free use of tennis courts, swimming pool and sauna.

PLACES TO STAY – MID-RANGE
Budapest is not as well endowed with hotels in the middle price range as it is in budget and top-end places. Expect to pay 13,500Ft to 25,000Ft (€55 to €81) for a double, depending on the season.

Buda
Beatrix Panzió *(Map 1; ☎ 275 0550, fax 394 3730;* e *beatrix@pronet.hu; II Széher út 3; bus No 29; singles/doubles €55/60),* up in the Buda Hills but easily accessible by bus, is an attractive 15-room pension with a lovely garden in a leafy neighbourhood.

Hotel Kulturinnov *(Map 4; ☎ 355 0122, fax 375 1886;* e *mka3@axelero.hu; I Szentháromság tér 6; bus No 16 or Várbusz; singles €35-65, doubles €55-80, triples €70-110),* a 16-room hotel in the former Finance Ministry, can't be beat for location and price in the Castle District. The guestrooms, though clean and with private bathrooms, are not as nice as the opulent public areas.

Pest
Hotel Baross Panzió *(Map 3; ☎ 461 3010, fax 343 2770;* e *info@budapestpensions.hu; VII Baross tér 15, 5/F; metro M3 Keleti pályaudvar; singles/doubles/triples/quads €55/65/75/85 low season, €75/85/95/105 high season)* is yet to establish its true identity, but it is a comfortable, 29-room caravanserai owned by the Travellers' Youth Hostels-Mellow Mood group (see Hostels earlier), and is conveniently located across from Keleti train station.

Carmen Mini Hotel *(Map 6; ☎ 352 0798, fax 318 3865;* e *carmen@axelero.hu; Károly körút 5/b; 2/F; metro M1/2/3 Deák tér; singles/doubles €50/60),* very close to Deák tér, has nine large and spotless rooms all protected by double-glazing from the noise of the Little Ring Road.

Hotel Délibáb *(Map 3; ☎ 342 9301, fax 342 8153; VI Délibáb utca 35; metro M1 Hősök tere; singles €51-66, doubles €59-76),*

with 34 rooms, is housed in what was once a Jewish orphanage across from Heroes' Square and City Park.

Hotel Pedagógus *(Map 3; ☎ 322 0821, fax 322 9019;* e *pedhotel@axelero.hu; VI Benczúr utca 35; metro M1 Bajza utca; singles/doubles/triples/2-person suite €50/ 64/78/82 low season, €67/84/98/102 high season)* is a moderately priced, 62-room guesthouse in a block behind the more expensive Hotel Benczúr.

PLACES TO STAY – TOP END
Double room rates at top-end hotels range from 21,000Ft to 37,000Ft (€85 to €150).

Buda
Burg Hotel *(Map 4; ☎ 212 0269, fax 212 3970;* e *hotel.burg@mail.datanet.hu; I Szentháromság tér 7-8; bus No 16 or Várbusz; singles €73-97, doubles €85-109, 2-person suites €103-127)* is a new, 26-room hotel with all the mod cons in the Castle District, just opposite Matthias Church.

Carlton Hotel *(Map 4; ☎ 224 0999, fax 224 0990;* e *carltonhotel@axelero.hu; I Apor Péter utca 3; bus No 86; singles/doubles/ triples €75/85/100 low season, €90/105/ 126 summer),* the erstwhile Alba Hotel with a facelift and extra star, is a spotless 95-room hotel in a quiet cul-de-sac in the Víziváros area.

Hotel Victoria *(Map 4; ☎ 457 8080, fax 457 8088;* e *victoria@victoria.hu; I Bem rakpart 11; tram No 19, bus No 86; singles/ doubles/triples €74/79/109 low season, €97/102/143 summer)* has 27 rooms with larger-than-life views of Parliament and the Danube, and gets high marks for friendly service and facilities. It's very good value for a four-star hotel.

Pest
Andrássy Hotel *(Map 3; ☎ 462 2100;* w *www .andrassyhotel.com; VI Andrássy út 111; metro M1 Hősök tere; standard singles & doubles €100-145, deluxe €175-250, suites €210-400),* an ugly caterpillar formerly known as the Centrál Hotel, has metamorphosed into a stunning butterfly with 70 stunning rooms (most with balconies or terraces). Enter from VI Munkácsy Mihály utca 5–7.

Club Hotel Ambra *(Map 6; ☎ 321 1538; fax 321 1540;* e *ambrahotel@axelero.hu; VII Kisdiófa utca 13; metro M1 Opera; singles €65-75, doubles €85-95; triples & quads*

€105/115) doesn't look like much on the outside, but its 21 air-conditioned rooms and suites are spacious and nicely furnished in a modern, streamlined way. There's a sauna and Jacuzzi.

Hotel Fiesta (Map 6; ☎ 266 6021; W www .hotelfiesta.hu; VI Király utca 20; metro Deák tér; singles €74-93, doubles €93-119, triples/ quads €112-122), a positive stunner of a new boutique hotel, has 112 tastefully furnished rooms and a vaulted wine cellar restaurant minutes from Budapest's main square.

Mercure Nemzeti (Map 5; ☎ 477 2000, fax 477 2001; e h1686@accor-hotels.com; VIII József körút 4; metro M2 Blaha Lujza tér; singles €80-105, doubles €85-115), with 76 rooms, has a beautifully renovated Art Nouveau exterior and fabulous common areas, including a dining room with a skylight of stained glass. The neighbourhood is centrally located but noisy and less than salubrious.

PLACES TO STAY – LUXURY
A double room in a luxury hotel will cost a minimum of €150. From there the sky's the limit.

Buda
Art'otel Budapest (Map 4; ☎ 487 9487; W www.parkplazaww.com; I Bem rakpart 16- 19; tram No 19, bus No 86; singles/doubles from €198/218, suites from €298) is a new luxury hotel with 165 rooms along the Danube in Buda that would not look out of place in London or New York.

Danubius Gellért Hotel (Map 3; ☎ 385 2200; W www.danubiusgroup.com/gellert; XI Szent Gellért tér 1; tram No 18, 19, 47 or 49; singles €115-150, doubles €190-235, suites €270-300), Budapest's grande dame of hotels, is a 234-room, four-star hotel with loads more personality than most. The gorgeous thermal baths are free for guests, but with the exception of the terrace restaurant on the Kelenhegyi út side, its other facilities are forgettable. Prices depend on which way your room faces and what sort of bathroom it has.

Budapest Hilton (Map 4; ☎ 488 6600; W www.hilton.com; I Hess András tér 1; bus No 16 or Várbusz; singles/doubles from €210/240), perched above the Danube on Castle Hill, was built carefully in and around a 14th-century church and baroque college (though it still has its detractors). It has 321 rooms, great views and some good facilities.

Pest
Kempinski Hotel Corvinus (Map 6; ☎ 429 3777; W www.kempinski-budapest.com; V Erzsébet tér 7-8; metro M1/2/3 Deák tér; singles €300-410, doubles €340-450, suites from €500) is Budapest's (and Hungary's) most expensive hotel. Essentially for business travellers on hefty expense accounts, the hotel has European service, American efficiency and Hungarian charm.

Le Meridien Budapest (Map 6; ☎ 429 5500; W www.lemeridien-budapest.com; V Erzsébet tér 9-10; metro M1/2/3 Deák tér; singles €235-385, doubles €275-425, suites from €360), Budapest's newest luxury hotel, has 218 rooms and public areas furnished in over-the-top Louis XIV brocade and French polished furniture.

Margaret Island A posh and tranquil hotel, the **Danubius Grand Hotel Margit- sziget** (Map 2; ☎ 452 6200; W www.danu biusgroup.com/grand; XIII Margit-sziget; bus No 26; singles €136-176, doubles €168- 208, suites €254), built in 1873, is connected to the Thermal spa via an underground corridor (see Thermal Baths in the boxed text 'Taking the Waters', earlier, for details).

PLACES TO EAT
Very roughly, a two-course sit-down meal for one person with a glass of wine or beer for under 2000Ft in Budapest is 'cheap', while a 'moderate' meal will cost up to 4000Ft. There's a big jump to an 'expensive' meal (4000Ft to 7000Ft), and 'very expensive' is anything above that. Most restaurants are open till 11pm or midnight, but it's best to arrive by 9pm or 10pm. It is advisable to book tables at medium-priced to expensive restaurants.

Buda Restaurants
Hungarian Set in an old 18th-century inn at the foot of Castle Hill, **Aranyszarvas** (Golden Stag; Map 4; ☎ 375 6451; I Szarvas tér 1; mains 1500-2500Ft; open noon-11pm daily) serves – what else? – game dishes. The outside terrace is lovely in summer.

Kacsa (Map 3; ☎ 201 9992; II Fő utca 75; starters 1200-3300Ft, mains 2500-5400Ft; open noon-3pm & 6pm-1am Mon-Fri, 6pm- 1am Sat & Sun) is the place for duck (which is what its name means) but not exclusively so. It's a fairly elegant place, with piano music in the evening.

Kisbuda Gyöngye (Map 2; ☎ 368 6402; III Kenyeres utca 34; mains 1780-4980Ft; open noon-midnight Mon-Sat) is a favourite traditional but elegant Hungarian restaurant in Óbuda; the antique-strewn dining room and attentive service manage to create a *fin-de-siècle* atmosphere. Try the excellent goose liver dishes and more pedestrian things like *csirke paprikás* (chicken paprika).

Szép Ilona (Map 1; ☎ 275 1392; II Budakeszi út 1-3; about 2000Ft per person; open 11am-10pm daily), in the Buda Hills and opposite Remíz (see its entry under Continental, later in this section), is the place to come for heavy, indigenous Hungarian and other dishes at very modest prices.

Continental In a fabulous location in small park overlooking Feneketlen-tó (Bottomless Lake), **Hemingway** (Map 7; ☎ 381 0522; XI Kosztolányi Dezső tér 2; mains 1400-3800Ft; open noon-midnight daily) has a varied and ever-changing menu and a wonderful terrace.

Rivalda (Map 4; ☎ 489 0236; I Színház utca; mains 2900-5200Ft; open 11.30am-11.30pm daily) is an international café-restaurant in an old convent next to the Castle Theatre. With a thespian theme and garden courtyard, it is the place to choose if you are going to splash out in the touristy, expensive Castle District.

Remíz (Map 1; ☎ 275 1396; II Budakeszi út 5; about 3500Ft per person; open 9am-1am daily), next to an old tram depot (*remíz*) in the Buda Hills, remains excellent for its food (try the grilled dishes, especially the ribs), prices and verdant garden terrace.

French A regular haunt of staff from the French Institute across the road is **Le Jardin de Paris** (Map 4; ☎ 201 0047; II Fő utca 20; mains 1760-3500Ft; open noon-midnight daily) – and they should know their *cuisine française*. The back garden ablaze in fairy lights is a delight in summer.

Italian Popular with students from the nearby university, **Marcello** (Map 7; ☎ 466 6231; XI Bartók Béla út 40; pizza & pasta 720-850Ft; open noon-10pm Mon-Sat) offers reliable Italian fare at affordable prices. It's also non-smoking.

Villa Doria (Map 4; ☎ 225 3233; I Döbrentei utca 9; mains 2800-4100Ft; open noon-11pm Tues-Sun), a flash new restaurant

in a mid-18th century townhouse below Castle Hill, has everything from simple pasta to complex seafood, and veal dishes.

Asian Another one of those all-you-can-eat pseudo-Asian places that includes as much beer and wine as you can sink, too, is **Mongolian Barbecue** (Map 3; ☎ 353 6363; XII Márvány utca 19/a; buffet before/after 5pm 1990/3690Ft; open noon-5pm & 6pm-midnight daily).

Seoul House (Map 4; ☎ 201 9607; I Fő utca 8; mains 1700-2200Ft; open noon-3pm & 6pm-11pm Mon-Sat) serves excellent Korean food from *bulkoki* and *galbi* grills to *bibimbab* rice and kimchi.

Buda Cafés

For the past two centuries, Budapest has been as famous as Vienna for its cafés, cake shops and café life; at the start of the 20th century, the city counted more than 500 cafés but by the time of the change in 1989 (ie, the collapse of communism), there were scarcely a dozen left. The majority of the traditional ones are in Pest but Buda can still lay claim to several.

Ruszwurm (Map 4; ☎ 375 5284; I Szentháromság utca 7; open 10am-7pm daily) is the perfect place for coffee and cakes in the Castle District, though it can get pretty crowded.

Angelika (Map 3; ☎ 212 3784; I Batthyány tér 7; open 9am-midnight daily) is another charming café (this time attached to a church) with a lovely terrace overlooking the Danube.

Caffè Déryné (Map 4; ☎ 212 3864; I Krisztina tér 3; open 8am-10pm Mon-Fri, 8am-9pm Sat, 9am-9pm Sun) is as untourised a café as you'll find in Buda. It's famed for its cakes and ice cream.

Buda Fast Food

You'll find cheap and quick weekday lunches in the Castle District at **Fortuna Self-Service Restaurant** (Fortuna Önkiszolgáló; Map 4; ☎ 375 2401; I Hess András tér 4; about 600Ft per person; open 11.30am-2.30pm Mon-Fri), a self-service place above the Fortuna restaurant.

Íz-É Faloda (Map 3; ☎ 345 4130; II Lövőház utca 12; mains 320-590Ft; open 11am-6pm Mon-Fri, 11am-4pm Sat) is a clean, modern and very cheap self-service place in the Fény utca market next to the Mammut shopping mall. It has excellent *főzelék* (the traditional way of preparing vegetables, where they're fried or boiled and then mixed into a roux with cream) dishes (180Ft to 260Ft).

Nagyi Palacsintázója *(Granny's Palacsinta Place; Map 3; ☎ 201 8605, 212 4866; I Hattyú utca 16; menus 568-888Ft; open 24hr)* serves Hungarian pancakes – both savoury (148Ft to 248Ft) and sweet (80Ft to 250Ft) – throughout the day. There's another Buda branch *(Map 3; ☎ 212 4866; I Batthyány tér 5)* nearby.

Il Treno *(Map 3; ☎ 356 4251, XII Alkotás utca 15; set menu 690Ft; open 11am-midnight Sun-Thur, 11am-1am Fri & Sat)*, with pizzas and a cheap set menu, is a popular place near Déli train station.

Marxim *(Map 3; ☎ 316 0231; II Kisrókus utca 23; pizza 490-1130Ft; open noon-1am Mon-Thur, noon-2am Fri & Sat, 6pm-1am Sun)*, a short walk from the Mammut shopping mall on Széna tér, is a hang-out for teens who have added a layer of their own graffiti to the communist memorabilia. OK, we all know Stalin *szuksz*, but it's still a curiosity for those who appreciate the Gulag, Lenin and Red October pizzas, and the campy Stalinist decor.

Buda Self-Catering
Budapest counts some 20 markets, though the lion's share of them are in Pest.

The **Fény utcai market** *(Fény utca piac; Map 3; II Fény utca)*, one of the largest markets in Buda, is just next to the Mammut shopping mall.

There are 24-hour **nonstop shops** selling everything from cheese and cold cuts to cigarettes and beer all over Buda, including shops at I Attila utca 57 (Map 4) and I Alkotás utca 27 (Map 3).

Pest Restaurants
Hungarian With reworked classics that make it a winner, **Bagolyvár** *(Owl's Castle; Map 3; ☎ 343 0217; XIV Állatkerti út 2; mains 1180-2380Ft, set menu 3050Ft; open noon-11pm)* attracts the Budapest cognoscenti (who leave its sister restaurant, Gundel, to the expense-account brigade and who instead head next door to the 'Owl's Castle').

Firkász *(Scribbler; Map 3; ☎ 450 1118; Tátra utca 18; mains 950-2050Ft; open noon-midnight Sun-Thur, noon-2am Fri & Sat)*, popular with local hacks, is a new retro Hungarian restaurant with lovely decor, excellent home cooking and a great wine list. Would that they were all like this.

Móri Borozó *(Map 3; ☎ 349 8390; XIII Pozsonyi út 37; mains 500-750Ft; open 10am-8pm Mon-Thur, 10am-3pm Fri)* is a simple wine bar and restaurant, a short walk north of Szent István körút. It has some of the best home-cooked Hungarian food in Budapest.

Művész Bohém *(Map 5; ☎ 339 8008; XIII Vígszínház utca 5; mains 750-1700Ft; open 11am-11pm daily)*, with antique furniture, photos of Magyar stars of stage and screen bedecking the walls, and someone softly tickling the ivories in the background, is the perfect place for a romantic Hungarian meal. It's just behind the Comedy Theatre.

Múzeum *(Map 6; ☎ 338 4221, 267 0375; VIII Múzeum körút 12; starters 1200-3500Ft, mains 1700-4100Ft; open noon-midnight Mon-Sat)* is the place to come if you to dine in style. It's a café-restaurant that is still going strong after more than a century at the same location near the National Museum.

Continental Fusion food in modern, upbeat surrounds is the order of the day at **Baraka** *(Map 6; ☎ 483 1355; V Magyar utca 12-14; mains 1250-2290Ft; open noon-3pm & 6pm-11pm Mon-Fri, 6pm-11pm Sat)*.

Café Kör *(Map 6; ☎ 311 0053; V Sas utca 17; mains 1450-2980Ft; open 10am-10pm Mon-Sat)*, near St Stephen's Basilica in Pest, is a great place for a light meal at any time, including breakfast (550Ft). Salads, desserts and daily specials are very good, though you should book.

Cosmo *(Map 6; ☎ 266 4747, 266 6818; V Kristóf tér 7-8, 1st floor; mains 1990-3870Ft; open noon-3pm & 5pm-11pm Mon-Sat, 5pm-11pm Sun)*, a postmodern, minimalist restaurant in the Inner Town, is the place to hop to if you really want to be in the thick of things hip.

Marquis de Salade *(Map 5; ☎ 302 4086; VI Hajós utca 43; mains 1100-2800Ft; open 11am-1am daily)* is a serious hybrid, with dishes from as far apart as Russia and Japan, Greece and Azerbaijan. There are lots of quality vegetarian choices, too, in this attractively decorated place.

Soul Café *(Map 6; ☎ 217 6986; IX Ráday utca 11-13; mains 1200-2300Ft; open noon-1pm daily)*, one of the better choices along a street heaving with restaurants and cafés, has inventive Continental food and decor.

French One of the most popular places with expatriate *français* in Pest is **Lou Lou** *(Map 6;*

☎ 312 4505; V Vigyázó Ferenc utca 4; mains 1850-3600ft; open noon-3pm & 7pm-11pm Mon-Fri, 7pm-11pm Sun). It's a lovely bistro with excellent daily specials.

Zazie (Map 6; ☎ 321 2405; VII Klauzál tér 2; mains 1800-2500Ft, lunch menu 1700Ft; open noon-midnight daily), the new kid on the block in the Jewish quarter, serves earthy Provençal fare in a setting reminiscent of a rustic farmhouse.

Italian Still the most upmarket Italian restaurant in town with excellent (though pricey) pasta dishes, daily specials and desserts is **Fausto's** (Map 6; ☎ 269 6806; VIII Dohány utca 5; mains 2600-5400Ft; open noon-3pm, 7pm-11pm Mon-Sat). There are lots of choices for vegetarians.

Okay Italia (Map 5; ☎ 349 2991; XIII Szent István körút 20; pizza & pasta 1090-1640Ft, mains 1390-2480Ft; open 11am-11.30pm daily) is a perennially popular Italian-run place with a nearby branch (Map 5; ☎ 332 6960; V Nyugati tér 6), serving just pasta and pizza.

Sole d'Italia (Map 6; ☎ 337 9638; V Molnár utca 15; pasta & pizza 370-1150Ft, mains 990-1800Ft; open noon-midnight daily) has super-friendly service, good, inexpensive pizzas and pastas and – wait for it – some of the cleanest toilets in town.

Trattoria Toscana (Map 6; ☎ 327 0045; V Belgrád rakpart 13; mains 1090-2800Ft; open noon-midnight daily), hard by the Danube, serves as authentic Italian (rather than Tuscan) food as you are going to find in Hungary.

Greek Overlooking a leafy square and the Great Market Hall, **Rembetiko Pireus** (Map 6; ☎ 266 0292; V Fóvám tér 2-3; starters 450-1290, mains 990-22990Ft; open noon-midnight) serves reasonably priced and authentic Greek fare. There are regular live music performances, and Greek dancing on Friday.

Taverna Dionysos (Map 6; ☎ 318 1222; V Belgrád rakpart 16; mains 1290-2490Ft), all *faux* Greek columns and a blue and white colour scheme, packs in diners on its three floors.

Spanish & Mexican A bit off the beaten track is **La Tasca** (Map 5; ☎ 351 1289; VII Csengery utca 24; starters 530-1950Ft, mains 1290-2590Ft; open noon-11pm daily), but the paella (2440Ft) and flamenco music in this cellar restaurant is worth the trip.

Iguana (Map 5; ☎ 331 4352; Zoltán utca 16; starters 590-750Ft; mains 1080-1890Ft; open 11.30am-12.30am daily) serves decent-enough Mexican food (not a difficult task in these parts) but it's hard to say whether the pull is the chicken and prawn *fajitas*, the enchiladas and burritos or the frenetic, boozy 'we-party-every-night' atmosphere.

Kosher In an old school behind the Orthodox Synagogue, **Hanna** (Map 6; ☎ 342 1072; VII Dob utca 35; lunch about 2500Ft per person; open 11.30am-3pm Sun-Fri) serves very, very basic kosher fare at lunch only.

Kinor David (David's Harp; Map 6; ☎ 352 1341; VII Wesselényi utca 18; mains 2500-3500Ft; open 11am-11pm Mon-Fri & Sun, 11am-3pm Sat), Budapest's newest kosher restaurant, is no great shakes but at least serves dinner. You have to order and pay in advance for Friday dinner and Saturday lunch.

Chinese & Japanese There's an inexpensive sushi lunch menu and plenty of other choices at **Arigato** (Map 5; ☎ 353 3549; VI Teréz körút 23; mains 1180-2800Ft; open noon-11pm Mon-Sat), but eating alongside a car showroom – a Suzuki one at that – may not be everyone's idea of a Budapest experience.

Sushi An (Map 6; ☎ 317 4239; V Harmincad utca 4; sushi 600-1800Ft, sets 2700-3900Ft; open noon-3.30pm & 5pm-10pm daily), next door to the British embassy, is the best place in Pest for sushi and sashimi.

Xi Hu (West Lake; Map 6; ☎ 337 5697; Nádor utca 5; mains 950-3300Ft; open noon-11pm daily), a decent Chinese eatery in the centre, is popular with the staff of the nearby Central European University.

Thai There's kitsch, Asianesque decor, acceptable Thai and Laotian dishes, and Indonesian waiters at **Bangkok House** (Map 6; ☎ 266 0584; V Só utca 3; mains 1050-3350Ft; open noon-11pm daily). Didn't fool us.

Indian The best place for Indian food in Budapest is **Bombay Palace** (Map 5; ☎ 332 8363; VI Andrássy út 44; curries & tandoori dishes 1700-2850Ft; open noon-2.45pm & 6pm-11pm daily), a flashy place just opposite VI Liszt Ferenc tér.

Vegetarian As well as wholesome salads, soups and desserts, **Gandhi** (Map 6; ☎ 269

1625; V Vigyázó Ferenc utca 4; dishes 980-1690Ft; open noon-10pm Mon-Sat) serves up a daily Sun and Moon set menu plate. It's in a cellar near Chain Bridge.

Wabisabi *(Map 5; ☎ 412 0427; XIII Visegrádi utca 2; mains 1080-1480Ft; open 9am-11pm Mon-Sat)* has wonderful Asian-inspired vegan dishes in a clean and fresh environment.

Pest Cafés & Teahouses

Along with traditional cafés in Pest, a new breed of café has emerged on the scene – all polished chrome, halogen lighting and straight lines. Teahouses have made a big splash in recent years in Budapest, the capital of a country not usually associated with that beverage.

Traditional Cafés A recently reopened grande dame jostling to reclaim her title as *the* place to sit and look intellectual is **Centrál Kávéház** *(Map 6; ☎ 266 4572; V Károlyi Mihály utca 9; open 8am-1am Mon-Sat, 8am-midnight Sun)*. It serves meals (mains 1990Ft to 3590Ft) as well as fine coffee and cakes.

Gerbeaud *(Map 6; ☎ 429 9000; V Vörösmarty tér 7; open 9am-9pm daily)* is the most famous of the famous cafés in Budapest – bar none. Founded in 1858, it has been a fashionable meeting place for the city's elite, on the western side of Pest's busiest square since 1870. A visit is mandatory.

Lukács *(Map 5; ☎ 302 8747; VI Andrássy út 70; open 9am-8pm Mon-Fri, 10am-8pm Sat & Sun)* is once again dressed up in the finest of divine decadence – all mirrors and gold and soft piano music (with a nonsmoking section too) – after a major renovation.

Művész *(Map 5; ☎ 352 1337; VI Andrássy út 29; open 9am-11pm daily)*, almost opposite the State Opera House, is a more interesting place to people-watch than most, though its cakes are not what they used to be, with the exception of the *almás torta* (apple cake).

Modern Cafés Leafy VI Liszt Ferenc tér is surrounded by hip cafés. If they're not playing music on site, you can catch strains from musicians practising in the Liszt Music Academy at the southern end of the square.

Café Vian *(Map 5; ☎ 268 1154; VI Liszt Ferenc tér 9; open 9am-midnight daily)* remains the anchor tenant of 'the tér' and the court of Pest's arty set.

Incognito *(Map 5; ☎ 342 1471; VI Liszt Ferenc tér 3; open 10am-midnight Mon-Fri,*

noon-midnight Sat & Sun) was the first on the square and is still going strong.

The cafés along pedestrian IX Ráday utca offer less hip but better drip.

Coquan's *(Map 3; ☎ 215 2444; IX Ráday utca 15; open 7.30am-7pm Mon-Fri, 9am-5pm Sat & Sun)* has a long list of cakes and bagels, and the best brews in Budapest. Another branch *(Map 6; ☎ 266 9936; V Nádor utca 5; open 8am-7pm Mon-Fri, 9am-5pm Sat)* serves similar fare.

Teahouses Located in a small courtyard off lower Váci utca, **1000 Tea** *(Map 6; ☎ 337 8217; V Váci utca 65; noon-9pm Mon-Sat, 3pm-8pm Sun)* is the place to go if you want to sip a soothing blend, made by tea-serious staff, and lounge on pillows in a Japanese-style tearoom or on tea chests in the courtyard.

Teaház a Vörös Oroszlánhoz *(Teahouse at the Red Lion; Map 5; ☎ 269 0579; VI Jókai tér 8; open 11am-11pm Mon-Sat, 3pm-11pm Sun)* is a funky (and quite serious) teahouse north of Liszt Ferenc tér. It also has a second branch *(Map 6; ☎ 215 2101; IX Ráday 9; open 11am-11pm Mon-Sat, 3pm-11pm Sun)*.

Pest Fast Food

Fast-food places like McDonald's – the one at VI Teréz körút 19 near Oktogon (Map 5) is open almost 24 hours – Burger King, Pizza Hut, KFC, Wendy's and the local Paprika chain abound in Budapest (Oktogon is full of them) but old-style self-service restaurants, the mainstay of both white- and blue-collar workers in the old regime are disappearing fast.

Pick Ház *(Map 5; V Kossuth Lajos tér 9; open 6am-7pm Mon-Fri)*, next to the M2 metro, has a self-service eatery upstairs. The **Central European University cafeteria** *(Map 6; ☎ 327 3000; V Nádor utca 9; dishes 210-695Ft; open 11.30am-4pm Mon-Fri)* is good value.

Much more salubrious places and better value in the long run are the wonderful little restaurants called *étkezde* – canteens not unlike British 'cafs' that serve simple dishes that change every day. A meal should easily cost under 800Ft. Some of the best ones are:

Frici Papa Kifőzdéje (Papa Frank's Canteen; Map 5; ☎ 351 0197) VI Király utca 55 Mains 250Ft to 460Ft. Open 11am to 9pm Monday to Saturday.
Kádár (Map 5; ☎ 321 3622) X Klauzál tér 9 Mains 450Ft to 820Ft. Open 11.30am to 3.30pm Tuesday to Friday.

Kisharang (Map 6; ☎ 269 3861) V Október 6 utca 17 Mains 400Ft to 750Ft. Open 11am to 8pm Monday to Friday, 11.30am to 4.30pm Saturday and Sunday.

Middle Eastern A very inexpensive self-service place for Turkish kebabs, with some 10 on offer, is **Szeráj** (Map 5; ☎ 311 6690; XIII Szent István körút 13; mains 350-800Ft; open 9am-4am daily).

Három Testvér (Three Brothers; Map 5; ☎ 342 2377; VII Erzsébet körút 17; gyros & kebabs 390-700Ft; open 9am-3am daily) is great any time but especially for a late-night snack or post-club bit of blotter. It has a second branch (☎ 06-30 201 1661; XIII Szent István körút 22) and also a third branch (Map 5; ☎ 363 6646; VI Teréz körút 23) nearby.

Pizza Along with **Okay Italia** (see Italian under Pest Restaurants earlier) there are several pizzerias in Nyugati tér, including **Don Pepe** (Map 5; ☎ 332 2954; Nyugati tér 8; pizzas 380-980Ft; open noon-6am daily), which is open till the very wee hours.

Pest Self-Catering

Budapest counts some 20 large food markets, most of them in Pest. Markets are usually open from 6am or 6.30am to 6pm Monday to Friday, and till 2pm on Saturday. Monday is always very quiet (if the market isn't closed altogether).

Nagycsarnok (Great Market; Map 6; IX Fővám tér) is Budapest's biggest, though it has become a bit of a tourist trap since it was renovated for the millecentenary in 1996. Still, plenty of locals head there for fruit and vegetables, deli items, fish and meat. There are good food stalls on the upper level.

Lehel Csarnok (Map 3; XIII Lehel tér) is one of Pest's more interesting traditional markets, recently rehoused in a modern, boat-like structure that has to be seen to be believed. It was designed by László Rajk, son of the Communist Minister of the Interior executed for 'Titoism' in 1949. This is apparently his revenge.

Among other colourful **food markets** in Pest are the ones at VIII Rákóczi tér 34 (Map 3) and V Hold utca 11 near V Szabadság tér (Map 5).

Large supermarkets are everywhere in Pest, including **Match** (Map 5; VIII Rákóczi út; open 6am-9pm Mon-Fri, 7am-8pm Sat, 7am-4pm Sun) facing Blaha Lujza tér, and **Kaiser's** (Map 5; VI Nyugati tér 1-2; open 7am-8pm Mon-Sat, 7am-3pm Sun), opposite Nyugati train station.

Rothschild (Map 5; XIII Szent István körút 4; open 6am-8pm Mon-Fri, 7am-4pm Sat, 9am-5pm Sun) is part of another chain, with a good supply of kosher products.

Mézes Kuckó (Honey Nook; Map 5; XIII Jászai Mari tér 4/b; open 10am-6pm Mon-Fri, 9am-1pm Sat) is the place to go if you've got the urge for something sweet; its nut and honey cookies (100Ft per 10dg) are to die for.

Butterfly (Map 5; VI Teréz körút 20; 70Ft per scoop; open 10am-6pm Mon-Fri, 10am-3pm Sat) – and *not* the pastry shop next door called Vajassütemények boltja – is *the* place in Pest for ice cream.

There are **nonstop shops** open very late or even 24 hours in Pest, including the ones at the Nyugati train station (next to track No 13; Map 5) and at VIII Baross tér 3 near Keleti train station (Map 3).

ENTERTAINMENT

For a city of its size, Budapest has a huge choice of things to do and places to go after dark – from opera and folk dancing to jazz and meet-market clubs. It's almost never difficult getting tickets or getting in; the hard part is deciding what to do.

Listings

Your best sources of information for what's on in the city are the weekly freebie *PestiEst* (Ⓦ www.est.hu), published every Thursday (website in Hungarian only), available at bars, cinemas and fast-food joints and popular with party people, and the more thorough weekly – with everything from clubs and films to art exhibits and classical music – *Pesti Műsor* (Budapest Program; Ⓦ www.pestimusor.hu), also called *PM Program Magazin*, available at newsstands every Thursday for 99Ft (website in Hungarian only).

Other freebies include the vastly inferior (though English-language) *Look*, published on Thursday, and the bilingual publications *Programme in Ungarn/in Hungary* and its scaled-down monthly version for the capital, *Budapest Panorama*. The free *Koncert Kalendárium*, published monthly (bimonthly in summer), has more serious offerings: concerts, opera, dance etc. The bimonthly *Budapest in Your Pocket* (750Ft) also lists events and concerts.

Booking Agencies

Ticket Express (for information ☎ 312 0000, for bookings ☎ 06-30 303 0999; W www .ticketexpress.hu) is the largest ticket-office network in the city with half a dozen outlets, including a branch in district VI (Map 6; Andrássy út 18; metro M1 Opera; open 9.30am-6.30pm Mon-Fri, 9am-1pm Sat). The website is in Hungarian only.

Vigádó Ticket Office (Map 6; ☎ 327 4322; V Vörösmarty tér 1; metro M1 Vörösmarty tér; open 9am-7pm Mon-Fri, 10am-5pm Sat) is another office with tickets for all types of concerts, dance performances and theatre.

Central Ticket Office (Központi Jegyiroda; Map 6; ☎ 267 9737, 318 1920; VI Andrássy út 15; metro M1 Opera; open 10am-6pm Mon-Fri) is the busiest theatrical ticket agency, with tickets to plays and other events at theatres around Budapest. Go to the **Philharmonic Ticket Office** (Filharmónia Jegyiroda; Map 6; ☎ 318 0281; V Mérleg utca 10; metro M1/2/3 Deák tér, bus No 15; open 10am-5.30pm Mon-Thur, 10am-5pm Fri) for tickets to the philharmonic and other classical concerts.

Music Mix (Map 6; ☎ 266 7070, 317 7736; W www.musicmix.hu; V Kecskeméti utca 8; metro M3 Kálvin tér; open 10am-6pm Mon-Fri) has tickets to special events such as rock-music spectaculars and big-ticket concerts by foreign superstars. The website is in Hungarian only.

Pubs & Bars

Buda With film memorabilia on the wood-panelled walls and leather directors' chairs on the floor, **Oscar's American Bar** (Map 3; ☎ 212 8017; I Ostrom utca 14; metro M2 Moszkva tér; open 5pm-2am Sun-Thur, 5pm-4am Fri & Sat) serves powerful cocktails (some 150, in fact).

Erzsébet-híd Eszpresszó (Map 4; I Döbrentei tér 1; tram No 19; open 10am-10.30pm daily), if you're in the mood for something simpler, is a wonderful old dive with a large terrace under a big plane tree and views of Elizabeth Bridge.

Pest Inevitably the capital has a number of 'Irish' pubs on offer; if you're into these McDonald's of drinking venues head for **Becketts** (Map 5; ☎ 311 1035; V Bajcsy-Zsilinszky út 72; metro M3 Nyugati pályaudvar; open 10am-1am Sun-Thur, 10am-3am Fri & Sat), the best of the lot, or the **Irish Cat** (Map 6; ☎ 266 4085; V Múzeum körút 41; metro M3 Kálvin tér; 11am-2am Mon-Thur, 11am-4am Fri & Sat, 5pm-2am Sun), which has Guinness and Kilkenny on tap, tattooed and pierced waiters, and dancing in the narrow spaces between tables at the weekend.

Cactus Juice (Map 5; ☎ 302 2116; VI Jókai tér 5; metro M1 Oktogon; open noon-2am Mon-Thur, noon-4am Fri & Sat, 4pm-2am Sun) is supposed to be 'American rustic' but it's really Wild West out of Central Casting. The Juice is a good place to sip and sup with no distractions except at the weekend, when there's dancing.

Cha Cha Cha (Map 6; ☎ 215 0545; metro M3 Kálvin tér; open 8am-3am Mon-Thur, 10am-4am Fri & Sat), in the underpass/subway at the Kálvin tér metro, is a campy/groovy café-bar with zebra- and leopard-print armchairs, a very – and we're talking Star Wars here – mixed crowd, and bopping from the start of the 'artists weekend' (Thursday).

Champs Sport Pub (Map 6; ☎ 413 1655 VII Dohány utca 20; metro M2 Astoria; open noon-2am daily) is the place for sports fans and the vicarious, with two huge screens and 35 TVs.

Paris, Texas (Map 3; ☎ 218 0570; IX Ráday utca 22; metro M3 Kálvin tér; open 10am-2am Mon-Fri, 4pm-2am Sat & Sun), one of the original bars on the Ráday nightlife strip, has a coffee-house feel to it with old sepia-tinted photos on the walls and pool tables downstairs.

Szimpla (Map 5; ☎ 342 1034; VII Kertész utca 46; tram 4 or 6; open noon-2am Mon-Sat, 4pm-2am Sun), a distressed-looking, less flashy place (and the name says it all), is a hop, skip and a jump south of Liszt Ferenc tér.

Discos & Clubs

Bank Music Club (Map 5; ☎ 414 5025, 302 1142; VI Teréz körút 55; open 9pm-5am Thur-Sat), in the southern wing of Nyugati train station next to McDonald's, is a cavernous disco with funky, Latino, hip-hop and concerts on the 1st floor, and international hit music on the 2nd.

Piaf (Map 5; ☎ 312 3823; VI Nagymező utca 25; metro Arany János, trolleybus No 70 or 78; open 10pm-6am daily) is the place to go when everything else slows down. There's dancing and action well into the new day.

Közgáz Pince Klub (Map 6; ☎ 215 4359, 218 6855; IX Fővám tér 8; tram No 47 or 49; open 9pm-3am Mon, 9pm-5am Tues-Sat), with few frills and cheap covers at the Economics University, is the pick-up venue of choice for many a student.

Trocadero *(Map 5; ☎ 311 4691; VI Szent István körút 15; tram No 4 or 6; open 9pm-2am Tues-Thur, 9pm-5am Fri & Sat)* attracts one of the most diverse crowds in Budapest with its great canned Latin, salsa, reggae and soul nights.

Gay & Lesbian Venues

Angel *(Map 3; ☎ 351 6490; VII Szövetség utca 33; metro M2 Blaha Lujza tér, bus No 7 or 7/a; open 10pm-5am Fri-Sun)*, which is sometimes called by its Hungarian name, Angyal, is Budapest's flagship gay club. It welcomes girls on Friday and Sunday.

Capella Café *(Map 6; ☎ 318 6231; V Belgrád rakpart 23; tram No 2 or 2/a; open 10pm-5am Wed-Sat)* and its new extension, **Limo Café** *(Map 6; ☎ 266 5455; V Belgrád rakpart 9; open noon-5am Sun-Thur, noon-6am Fri & Sat)*, a few doors down, are twin clubs frequented by gays, lesbians and fellow travellers.

Action *(Map 6; ☎ 266 9148; V Magyar utca 42; open 9pm-4am daily)* is where to head if you want just that. Take the usual precautions and have a ball.

Rock & Pop Music

Kisstadion *(Little Stadium; Map 3; ☎ 251 1222; XIV Szabó József utca 1; bus No 7 or 67)* is where the likes of Jamiroquai and other big names warble.

Petőfi Csarnok *(Map 3; ☎ 251 7266, 363 3730; W www.petoficsarnok.hu; XIV Zichy Mihály út 14; metro M1 Széchenyi fürdő, trolleybus No 72 or 74)* in City Park is the place for smaller rock concerts.

Almássy tér Recreation Centre *(Almássy téri Szabadidő Központ; Map 3; ☎ 342 0387, 352 1572; W www.almassy.hu; VII Almássy tér 6; trolleybus 74)* is a venue for just about anything that's in and/or interesting, from rock and blues to folk music. The website is in Hungarian only.

Wigwam Rock Club *(Map 7; ☎ 208 5569; XI Fehérvári utca 202; tram No 41 or 47; open 8pm-5am daily)*, one of the best of its kind in Hungary, hosts some big-name Hungarian bands on Saturday.

You simply can't miss a **Cinetrip Vízi-Mozi** *(Cinetrip Water-Movie; ☎ 212 2297, 266 0314; W www.cinetrip.net; 3200-4000Ft)*

event at the Rudas bath (see Thermal Baths in the boxed text 'Taking the Waters in Budapest' under Activities, earlier) and other party venues if one is taking place during your visit. These events combine partying and dancing with music, film and bathing and are held monthly or bimonthly (usually from 9pm to 3.30am Saturday); schedules are available at tourist offices and other venues around town.

Jazz & Blues

New Orleans Music Club *(Map 5; ☎ 354 1130; VI Lovag utca 5; trolleybus 72 or 73, tram No 4 or 6; open 6pm-late)*, an upscale jazz supper club (starters 950Ft to 1500Ft, mains 1200Ft to 2650Ft) has live international jazz and blues bands at 9pm Tuesday to Saturday.

Old Man's Music Pub *(Map 5; ☎ 322 7645; VII Akácfa utca 13; metro M2 Blaha Lujza tér; open 3pm-4am daily)* pulls in some of the best live blues and jazz acts in town; shows are from 9pm to 11pm. A dinner reservation (soups 400Ft to 800Ft, mains 1800Ft to 2950Ft, pizza 1100Ft to 1900Ft) is usually required to score a table.

Fat Mo's Music Club *(Map 6; ☎ 267 3199; V Nyáry Pál utca 11; metro M3 Ferenciek tere, bus No 15; open noon-2am Mon & Tues, noon-3am Wed, noon-4am Thur & Fri, 6pm-4am Sat, 6pm-2am Sun)*, with a speak-easy Prohibition theme, has jazz and country from 9pm Sunday to Tuesday before the bar gets too packed for anything but schmoozin' and cruisin'.

Folk & Traditional Music

Authentic *táncház*, literally 'dance house' but really folk-music workshops, are held at various locations throughout the week but less frequently in summer. Times and venues change frequently; consult one of the publications under Listings earlier in this Entertainment section or check out the website of the Dance House Guild (W www.tanchaz.hu) or the Hungarian-only W www.folkinfo.net for updates.

Venues in Buda include **Fonó Buda Music House** *(Fonó Budai Zenehaz; Map 7; ☎ 206 5300; W www.fono.hu; XI Sztregova utca 3; tram No 41 or 47)*, with programmes at 8pm Wednesday and at 7pm on the first and second Friday of the month (the popular folk group Muzsikás also plays here every odd Tuesday) – note that the website is in Hungarian only.

The **Folklór Centrum** in the **Municipal Cultural House** (*Fővárosi Művelődési Háza; Map 7; ☎ 203 3868; XI Fehérvári út 47; tram No 41 or 47*), with music every Friday at 7.30pm or 8pm; and the **Marczibányi tér Cultural Centre** (*Marczibányi téri Művelődési Központ; Map 3; ☎ 212 2820; ⓦ www.marczi.hu; II Marczibányi tér 5/a; tram No 4, 6 or 49*), where Muzsikás jams at 8pm on each odd Thursday a month and where Ghymes, a group specialising in Csángó music, is also heard from time to time. The website is in Hungarian only.

In Pest there's the wonderful **Kalamajka Táncház** at the **Aranytíz Youth Centre** (*Aranytíz Ifjúsági Centrum; Map 6; ☎ 317 5928; V Molnár utca 9; tram No 2 or 2/a*), with programmes from 7pm on Monday and Wednesday and from 8.30pm on Saturday

Classical Music

The *Koncert Kalendárium* (see Listings earlier in this Entertainment section) highlights all concerts in Budapest each month. The main concert halls are the stunning **Liszt Academy of Music** (*Liszt Zeneakadémia; Map 5; ☎ 342 0179; VI Liszt Ferenc tér 8; metro M2 Oktogon; tickets 600-5000Ft*) in Pest and the modern **Budapest Congress Centre** (*Budapesti Kongresszusi Központ; Map 3; ☎ 372 5700, 372 5429; XII Jagelló út 1-3; bus No 8 or 112*) in Buda. The **Pesti Vigadó** (*Map 6; ☎ 318 9903; V Vigadó tér 2; metro M1 Vörösmarty tér; tram No 2 or 2/a*) and the **Duna Palota** (*Map 6; ☎ 317 2790; V Zrínyi utca 5; bus No 15*) have light classical music, and touristy musical revues in summer.

Opera

The **Hungarian State Opera House** (*Magyar Állami Operaház; Map 5; ☎ 332 7914, 331 2550; ⓦ www.opera.hu; VI Andrássy út 22; metro M1 Opera; tickets 300-6900Ft; ticket office open 11am-7pm Mon-Sat, 4pm-7pm Sun*) should be visited at least once – to admire the incredibly rich decoration inside as much as to view a performance. (See also its entry earlier in the Andrássy út section under Pest.)

Erkel Theatre (*Erkel Színház; Map 3; ☎ 333 0540; VIII Köztársaság tér 30; metro Keleti pályaudvar, bus No 7 or 7/a; tickets 500-4500Ft; ticket office open 11am-7pm Tues-Fri, 11am-3pm Sat, 10am-1pm & 4pm-7pm Sun*), Budapest's modern (and ugly) second opera house, is southwest of Keleti train station.

Budapest Operetta Theatre (*Budapesti Operettszínház; Map 5; ☎ 269 3870; ⓦ www .operettszinhaz.hu; VI Nagymező utca 17; metro M1 Opera*) presents operettas, which are always good, campy fun. The **box office** (*☎ 269 0118; VI Nagymező utca 19; open 10am-6pm Mon-Thur, 10am-5pm Fri*) is next door.

Dance

Budapest's two so-so ballet companies perform at the Opera House and the Erkel Theatre (for details see Opera earlier).

For modern dance fans, there are several good options. The best stage on which to see it is the **Trafó House of Contemporary Arts** (*Trafó Kortárs Művészetek Háza; Map 3; ☎ 456 2045, 215 1600; ⓦ www.trafo.hu; IX Liliom utca 41; metro M3 Ferenc körút*), which presents the cream of the crop, including a good pull of international acts. The website is in Hungarian only.

Trafó and **Kamra** (*Chamber; Map 6; ☎ 318 2487; V Ferenciek tere 4; metro M3 Ferenciek tere*), the studio theatre of the József Katona theatre, sometimes hosts Yvette Bozsik's contemporary dance ensemble.

Central Europe Dance Theatre (*Közép-Európa Táncszínház; Map 3; ☎ 342 7163; ⓦ www.cedt.hu; VII Bethlen Gábor tér 3; trolleybus No 74 or 78*) has some fine contemporary dance performances.

Folk Dancing From May to mid-October and on Saturday and/or Sunday only the rest of the year, the 30 dancers of the Hungarian State Folk Ensemble (Állami Népi Együttes) perform at the **Budai Vigadó** (*Map 4; I Corvin tér 8; bus no 86, tram No 19*) in Buda on Tuesday, Thursday and Sunday; the Rajkó Folk Ensemble (Rajkó Népi Együttes) stages folkdance performances at the **Budapest Puppet Theatre** (*Bábszínház; Map 5; VI Andrássy út 69; metro M1 Vörösmarty utca*) on Saturday; and the Duna Folk Ensemble (Duna Népi Együttes) dances at the **Duna Palota** just off Roosevelt tér in Pest on Monday and Wednesday. The 1½-hour programmes begin at 8pm, and tickets cost 5600/5100Ft per adult/student. Contact Hungaria Koncert (*☎ 317 2754, 201 5928; ⓦ www.ticket.info.hu*) for information and bookings.

The **National Dance Theatre** (*Nemzeti Táncszínház; Map 4; ☎ 201 4407; ⓦ www .nemzetitancszinhaz.hu; I Színház utca 1-3*)

usually hosts the Honvéd Ensemble, one of the city's best folk troupes and now experimenting with modern choreography as well.

Theatre

In Pest, the **Merlin Theatre** (Map 6; ☎ 318 9338, 266 4632; W merlin.szinhaz.hu/merlin; V Gerlóczy utca 4; metro M1/2/3 Deák tér, tram No 47 or 49; tickets 1000-1800Ft), stages numerous plays in English, often put on by the Merlin's Atlantis Company and the local Madhouse troupe.

The **International Buda Stage** (IBS; Map 1; ☎ 391 2525; II Tárogató út 2-4; tram No 56, bus No 29), a more recent arrival but further afield in Buda, is another theatre with performances in English.

The new **Nemzeti Színház** (National Theatre; Map 7; ☎ 476 6800; W www.nemzeti szinhaz.hu; IX Bajor Gizi park 1; tram No 2 or 2/a; tickets 1500-3500Ft; box office open 10am-5.30pm Mon-Fri, 2pm-5.30pm Sat & Sun) is the place to go if you want to brave a play in Hungarian or just check out the bizarre architecture (see Józsefváros & Ferencváros under Pest, earlier). The website is in Hungarian only.

The **Budapest Puppet Theatre** (Bábszínház; Map 5; ☎ 342 2702; W www.budapest-babszinhaz.hu; VI Andrássy út 69; metro M1 Vörösmarty utca; tickets 350-580Ft), which usually doesn't require fluency in Hungarian, presents shows designed for children during the day and programmes for adults occasionally in the evening. The website is in Hungarian only.

Cinema

A couple of dozen movie houses show English-language films with Hungarian subtitles. Consult the listings in the Budapest Sun newspaper, Pesti Est or Pesti Műsor (see Listings earlier). See also Entertainment in the Facts for the Visitor chapter for more details on cinemas and prices.

The **Corvin Film Palace** (Corvin Filmpalota; Map 3; ☎ 459 5050; VIII Corvin köz 1; metro M3 Ferenc körút), which saw a lot of action during the 1956 Uprising, has been fantastically renovated and is worth a visit.

The **Uránia National Cinema** (Uránia Nemzeti Filmszínház; Map 5; ☎ 486 3400; VIII Rákóczi út 21; bus No 7 or 7/a), all Art Deco/neo-Moorish extravaganza, is another newly tarted-up film palace.

The **Örökmozgó Film Museum** (Örökmozgó Filmmúzeum; Map 5; ☎ 342 2167; VII Erzsébet körút 39; tram No 4 or 6), part of the Hungarian Film Institute, shows an excellent assortment of foreign classic films in their original languages.

Művész (Map 5; ☎ 332 6726; VI Teréz körút 30; metro M1 Oktogon, tram No 4 or 6) shows artsy and cult films while **Puskin** (Map 6; ☎ 429 6080; V Kossuth Lajos utca 18; bus No 7 or 7/a) has a mix of art and popular releases.

Circus

The **Municipal Great Circus** (Fővárosi Nagycirkusz; Map 3; ☎ 343 8300, 343 6002; XIV Állatkerti körút 7; metro Széchenyi fürdő; adult 800-1200Ft, child 600-1000Ft) has performances at 3pm and 7pm on Wednesday and Friday, at 3pm on Thursday, at 10.30am, 3pm and 7pm on Saturday and at 10am and 3.30pm on Sunday from mid-April to August.

SPECTATOR SPORTS
Water Polo

Hungary has dominated the men's European (12 times champions) and Olympic (six times champions) water-polo championships for decades so it's worthwhile catching a professional or amateur match of this exciting seven-a-side sport. The Magyar Vízilabda Szövetség (MVLSZ; Hungarian Water Polo Association) is based at the **Alfréd Hajós National Sports Pool** (Hajós Alfréd Nemzeti Sportuszoda; Map 3; ☎ 349 2357; e mvlsz@euroweb.hu; XIII Margit-sziget; tram No 4 or 6, bus No 26) on Margaret Island and matches take place here and at two other pools – the **Béla Komjádi** (Map 3; ☎ 212 2750; II Árpád fejedelem útja 8; bus No 60 or 86, tram No 17) and the **BVSC** (Map 3; ☎ 251 3888; XIV Szőnyi út 2; trolleybus 74 or 74/a) – from September to May. If you want to see a match or watch the lads in training in summer, call or email the MVLSZ for times and dates or get someone to check schedules for you in the Nemzeti Sport (National Sport; 79Ft) daily newspaper.

Football

Hungary's descent from being on top of the heap of European football to a béka segge alatt – 'under the arse of the frog' as the Hungarians describe something really far down – remains one of life's great mysteries. Hungary's defeat of the England team both at

Wembley (6-3) in 1953 and at home (7-1) the following year, are still talked about as if the winning goals were scored yesterday.

There are four premier league football teams in Budapest out of a total 12 nationwide, including: Kispest-Honvéd, which plays at **Bozsik Stadium** *(Map 1; ☎ 282 9791; XIX Új temető út 1-3; bus No 36)*; MTK at **Hungária Stadium** *(Map 3; ☎ 333 6758; VIII Hungária körút 12-14; tram No 37 or 37/a)*; and UTE at **UTE Stadium** *(Map 2; ☎ 369 7333; IV Megyeri út 13; bus No 47 or 96)*. But no club dominates Hungarian football like Ferencváros (FTC), the country's loudest and brashest team, and its only hope. You either love the Fradi boys in green and white or you hate them. Watch them play at **FTC stadium** *(Map 7; ☎ 215 1013; IX Üllői út 129; metro M3 Népliget)*. *Nemzeti Sport* (see Water Polo earlier for details) has the game schedules.

Horse Racing

The descendants of the nomadic Magyars are keen on horse racing. The **Ügetőpálya** *(Map 3; ☎ 263 7817; X Albertirsai út 2; metro M2 Pillangó utca)* is the place to go for trotting. Seven or eight races are held on Saturday and Sunday from 3pm and on Wednesday from 5pm.

SHOPPING

Upstairs at the **Nagycsarnok** *(Map 6; IX Fővám tér)* there are dozens of stalls selling Hungarian folk costumes, dolls, painted eggs, embroidered tablecloths etc. If you prefer your prices clearly labelled, head for the **Folkart Centrum** *(Map 6; ☎ 318 4697; V Váci utca 58; open 10am-7pm daily)*, a large shop where everything Magyar-made is available. **Holló Atelier** *(Map 6; ☎ 317 8103; V Vitkovics Mihály utca 12; open 10am-6pm Mon-Fri, 10am-1pm Sat)*, off the northern end of Váci utca, has attractive folk art with a modern look, and remains a favourite place to shop for gifts.

Good bets in the Castle District for all your knick-knacks include **Judit** *(Map 4; ☎ 212 7050; I Tarnok utca 1; open 10am-6.30 daily)* for blue-dyed fabrics and crafts, and the nearby **Carillon Folk Shop** *(Map 4; ☎ 201 6692; Fortuna Passage off I Fortuna utca; open 10am-6pm Mon-Fri, 10am-1pm Sat)*.

If you don't have time to get to the Ecseri or Petőfi Csarnok markets or it's the wrong day of the week (see Flea Markets later for details), check any of the BÁV stores (open 10am to 6pm Monday to Friday, 9am to 1pm

Saturday), essentially a chain of pawn and second-hand shops with several branches around town. Try VI Andrássy út 27 (Map 5) for old jewellery and bric-a-brac; V Bécsi utca 1–3 (Map 5) for knick-knacks, porcelain and glassware; XIII Szent István körút 3 (Map 5) for chinaware and textiles; and II Frankel Leó út 13 (Map 3) for furniture and porcelain.

For both contemporary and traditional fine porcelain, check out **Zsolnay** *(Map 6; ☎ 318 3712; V Kigyó utca 4; open 10am-6pm Mon-Fri, 10am-1pm Sat)* and **Herend** *(Map 6; ☎ 317 2622, 318 9200; V József nádor tér 11; open 10am-6pm Mon-Fri, 9am-1pm Sat)*.

Haas & Czjzek *(Map 5; ☎ 311 4094; VI Bajcsy-Zsilinszky út 23; open 9am-6pm Mon-Fri, 10am-3pm Sat)*, just up from Deák tér, also sells more affordable Hungarian-made Hollóháza and Alföldi porcelain.

Herend Village Pottery *(Map 3; ☎ 356 7899; II Bem rakpart 37; open 9am-5pm Mon-Fri, 9am-noon Sat)* is an alternative to prissy, fragile Herend flatware. It stocks pottery and dishes decorated with bold fruit patterns.

The **Budapest Wine Society** *(Map 3; ☎ 212 2569; w www.bortarsasag.hu; I Batthyány utca 59; open 10am-8pm Mon-Fri, 10am-6pm Sat)* has a retail outlet with an exceptional selection of fine Hungarian wines. No one, but no one, knows Hungarian wines like these guys do, and there are free tastings on Saturday afternoon.

Monarchia Borászati Wine Shop *(Map 3; ☎ 456 9817; w www.magyarborok.hu; IX Kinizsi utca 30-36; metro M3 Ferenc kőrút; open 10am-6pm Mon-Fri, 10am-1pm Sat)*, opposite the Applied Arts Museum, has an extensive selection from both established and new Hungarian vintners but the best are those bottled under their own label. There's always a bottle open for tasting.

Flea Markets

Ecseri Piac *(Map 7; ☎ 282 9563, XIX Nagykőrösi út 156; open 8am-3.30pm Mon-Fri, 8am-2pm Sat)*, often just called the *piac* (market), is one of the biggest and best flea markets in Central Europe, selling everything from antique jewellery and Soviet army watches to old musical instruments and Fred Astaire-style top hats. Saturday is the best day to go. To get there, take bus No 54 from Boráros tér in Pest near the Petőfi Bridge or, better, the red express bus No 54 from the Határ utca stop on the M3 metro line and get off at the Fiume utca stop, and walk over the pedestrian bridge.

Petőfi Csarnok Flea Market *(Map 3; ☎ 251 7266, 343 4327; XIV Zichy Mihály utca; open 7am-2pm Sat & Sun)* is a huge outdoor flea market – a kind of Hungarian boot or garage sale – held next to the Petőfi Csarnok (Concert Hall) in City Park. The usual diamonds-to-rust stuff is on offer – from old records and draperies to candles, honey and herbs. Sunday is the better day.

GETTING THERE & AWAY
Air
The main **Malév ticket office** *(Map 6; ☎ 235 3534, 235 3417; w www.malev.hu; V Dorttya utca 2; open 8.30am-5.30pm Mon-Wed & Fri, 8.30am-6pm Thur)* is near Vörösmarty tér. (The website is in Hungarian only.) In addition Malév has ticket-issuing desks at Ferihegy Airport's **Terminal 2A** *(☎ 296 7211)* and at **Terminal 2B** *(☎ 296 5767)*. Other major carriers include the following.

Aeroflot *(☎ 318 5892)* V Váci utca 4
Air Canada *(☎ 317 9109)* V Ferenciek tere 10
Air France *(☎ 318 0441)* V Kristóf tér 6
Alitalia *(☎ 483 2170)* V Bajcsy-Zsilinszky út 12
Austrian Airlines *(☎ 327 9080)* V Régiposta utca 5
Balkan Airlines *(☎ 317 1818)* V Párizsi utca 7
British Airways *(☎ 411 5555)* VIII Rákóczi út 1–3 (East-West Business Centre)
CSA Czech Airlines *(☎ 318 3175)* V Vörösmarty tér 2
Finnair *(☎ 317 4022)* V Bajcsy-Zsilinszky út 12
KLM Royal Dutch Airlines *(☎ 373 7737)* VIII Rákóczi út 1–3 (East-West Business Centre)
LOT Polish Airlines *(☎ 317 2444)* V Vigadó tér 3
Lufthansa *(☎ 266 4511)* V Váci utca 19–21
SAS *(☎ 266 2633)* V Bajcsy-Zsilinszky út 12
Swiss *(☎ 328 5000)* V Kristóf tér 7–8
Tarom Romanina Airlines *(☎ 317 2307)* V Apáczai Csere János utca 4
Turkish Airlines *(☎266 4269)* V Apáczai Csere János utca 4

Bus
All international buses and some – but not all – domestic ones to/from southern and western Hungary now arrive at and depart from the new **Népliget bus station** *(Map 7; ☎ 264 3939; IX Üllői út 131; metro M3 Népliget)* in Pest. The **international ticket office** *(open 6am-6pm Mon-Fri, 6am-4pm Sat & Sun)* is upstairs. **Eurolines** *(☎ 219 8080, 219 8000; w www.eurolines.com)* is represented here as is its Hungarian associate **Volánbusz** *(☎ 485 2162, 485 2100; w www.volanbusz.hu)*. The

website is in Hungarian only. There's a **left-luggage office** *(open 6am-9pm daily)* downstairs that charges 150Ft per piece per day.

Népstadion bus station *(☎ 252 4498, 251 0125; XIV Hungária körút 48-52; metro M3 Népstadion)* serves cities and towns to the east of Budapest. Things were in state of flux at the time of research while the adjacent Budapest Sportscsarnok, destroyed by fire in 1999, was being rebuilt, but you should find the **ticket office** *(open 6am-6pm Mon-Fri, 6am-noon Sat & Sun)* as well as the **left-luggage office** *(open 6am-6pm daily)* here.

The **Árpád Bridge bus station** *(Map 2; ☎ 329 1450, XIII Róbert Károly körút; metro M3 Árpád híd; ticket office open 7am-4pm Mon-Fri)*,on the Pest side of Árpád Bridge, is the place to catch buses for the Danube Bend and parts of the Northern Uplands (eg, Balassagyarmat, Szécsény, Salgótarján etc). The small **Széna tér bus station** *(Map 3; ☎ 201 3688; I Széna tér 1/a; metro M3 Moszkva tér)* in Buda handles some traffic to and from the Pilis Hills and towns northwest of the capital, with a half-dozen departures to Esztergom as an alternative to the Árpád Bridge bus station.

For details of international bus services, see the Getting There & Away chapter.

Train
Budapest has three main train stations. Most international trains arrive and depart from **Keleti pályaudvar** *(Eastern Railway Station; ☎ 313 6835; VIII Kerepesi út 2-6; metro M3 Keleti pályaudvar)*; trains to certain destinations in Romania and Germany leave from **Nyugati pályaudvar** *(Western Railway Station; ☎ 349 0115; VI Teréz körút 55-57; metro M3 Nyugati pályaudvar)*, while **Déli pályaudvar** *(Southern Railway Station; ☎ 355 8657; I Krisztina körút 37; metro M2 Déli pályaudvar)* handles trains to/from Zagreb and Rijeka in Croatia. But these are not hard-and-fast rules, so always make sure you check which station the train leaves from when you buy a ticket. For 24-hour information on international train services call ☎ 461 5500 in Budapest.

The handful of secondary train stations are of little importance to long-distance travellers. Occasionally, though, a through train will stop at **Kelenföldi pályaudvar** *(Kelefold Railway Station; Map 7; ☎ 203 9609; XI Etele tér 5-7; tram No 19 or 49)* in Buda.

The stations are pretty dismal places, with unsavoury-looking characters hanging about day and night, but all have some amenities. Keleti station's left-luggage office *(open 24hr)* is next to platform No 6, at Nyugati station it's beside platform No 10 (open 5am-midnight) and at Déli station it's next to platform No 1 (open 3.30am to 11.30pm). They charge 200/400Ft for a normal/large piece. You'll also find post offices and grocery stores that are open late or even round the clock.

All the stations are on metro lines, and night buses serve them when the metro is closed. If you need to take a taxi, avoid the sharks hovering around the stations. At Déli, cross over to I Alkotás utca and hail one there. At Keleti station, get into one of the legal cabs at the rank on VIII Kerepesi út, just south of the terminal. Nyugati tér is a major intersection, so you'll have no problem finding a legitimate taxi.

You can buy tickets and reserve seats directly at all three stations, but the queues are often long, passengers are in a hurry, and sales staff at the stations are not the most patient in the city. Some of the travel agencies listed in the Information section earlier in this chapter will get you train tickets, and you can buy advance tickets for express trains at the **MÁV central ticket office** *(Map 5; ☎ 461 5500, 461 5400; W www.mav.hu; VI Andrássy út 35; open 9am-6pm Mon-Fri Apr-Sept; 9am-5pm Mon-Fri Oct-Mar)*. The website is in Hungarian only.

For more information about international train travel see the Getting There & Away chapter.

Car & Motorcycle

All the international car-rental firms have offices in Budapest but don't expect many bargains. An Opel Corsa from **Avis** *(Map 6; ☎ 318 4158, fax 318 4859; V Szervita tér 8)*, for example, costs €35/215 per day/week plus €0.35 per kilometre and €23 CDW and theft protection insurance. The same car with unlimited kilometres and insurance costs from €131 per day or €146 per weekend. The 25% ÁFA (value-added tax) doesn't apply to nonresidents paying with foreign currency or credit card.

One of the cheapest outfits for renting cars is **Inka Rent a Car** *(Map 7; ☎ 456 4666, fax 456 4699; e mail@inkarent.hu; IX Könyves Kálmán körút; open 8am-7pm Mon-Sat, 8am-2pm Sat)* near the Lurdy Ház shopping mall. Their Opel Corsas cost €20 per day

plus €0.20 per kilometre (or €250 per week with up to 800km a day included). Another good bet is **Fox Autorent** *(Map 7; ☎ 382 9004; W www.fox-autorent.com; XI Vegyész utca 24-28)*, which charges €30/166 per day/week for a Smart car, €46/230 for a Fiat Seicento, €59/359 for a Fiat Puntos and €69/420 for a Suzuki Swift, kilometres and insurance included.

Assistance and/or advice for motorists is available from the **Magyar Autóklub** *(Map 3; ☎ 345 1800, 212 2821; II Rómer Flóris utca 4/a; tram No 4 or 6)* off Margit körút near Margaret Bridge. Motorists anywhere in Hungary can call the automobile club on ☎ 188 for assistance.

For information on traffic and public road conditions in the capital ring Főinform on ☎ 317 1173.

Hitching

Kenguru *(Map 5; ☎ 266 5837, 483 0105; W www.kenguru.hu; VIII Kőfaragó utca 15; open 8am-6pm Mon-Fri, 10am-2pm Sat & Sun)* is a ride service that matches up drivers and riders for a fee – mostly to points abroad. Approximate one-way fares include Amsterdam 13,800Ft, London 15,200Ft, Munich 7300Ft, Paris 14,400Ft, Prague 5400Ft and Vienna 2800Ft.

Boat

Hydrofoils to Bratislava and Vienna run by Mahart PassNave *(Map 6; ☎ 484 4010, 318 1704; W www.maharttours.com; V Belgrád rakpart; 8am-4pm Mon-Fri)* arrive at and depart from the International Ferry Pier on V Belgrád rakpart. For more information see River in the Getting There & Away chapter.

From April to October or early November (seasonal shutdown) Mahart PassNave runs hydrofoils on the Danube from Budapest to Szentendre, Vác, Visegrád and Esztergom on the Danube Bend; see the Danube Bend chapter for details. In the capital the boats leave from the pier off V Vigadó tér (Map 6; ☎ 318 1223; metro M3 Ferenciek tere) on the Pest side. The first stop is usually I Batthyány tér on the Buda side, which is on the M2 metro line.

GETTING AROUND
To/From the Airport

Budapest's **Ferihegy International Airport** *(☎ 296 9696)*, 24km southeast of the city centre, has two modern terminals side by side and within easy walking distance of one another. For information on which airlines use which terminal see Airports & Airlines under Air in the Getting There & Away chapter. Terminal 2B has an OTP bank and an ATM, car rental and hotel booking desks, a **post office** *(open 8am-4pm Mon-Fri)* and a **left-luggage office** *(open 24hr)*, which charges 250/600/800Ft for one/three/six hours, 1000/5000Ft per day/week.

With much cheaper options for getting to/from Ferihegy, it would be senseless to take a taxi and risk a major rip-off. If you want to take a taxi, call one of the companies listed under Taxi later in the chapter with a mobile phone or from a phonebox at arrivals (dispatchers understand English). **Tele 5** *(☎ 355 5555)* has a flat fare of 2800Ft between the airport and Pest (3200Ft to Buda). Its taxis are just down the road, waiting for calls.

The **Airport Minibus Service** *(☎ 296 8555, fax 296 8993)* ferries passengers in eight-seater vans from the airport directly to their hotel, hostel or residence. The fare is 1800/3300Ft one way/return, and tickets are available at a clearly marked desk in the arrival halls. You need to book your journey *to* the airport 24 hours in advance but remember that, with up to seven pick-ups en route, this can be a nerve-wracking way to go if you're running late.

The cheapest – but most time-consuming – method to get into town is to take the **airport bus** (look for the stop marked 'BKV Plusz Reptér Busz' on the pavement between terminals 2A and 2B), which terminates at the Kőbánya-Kispest metro station. From there take the M3 metro into the centre. The total cost is 190Ft.

Public Transport

Budapest has an ageing but safe, efficient and very inexpensive public transport system that will never have you waiting more than five or 10 minutes for any conveyance. There are five types of vehicles in general use: metro trains on three city lines; green HÉV trains on four suburban lines; blue buses; yellow trams and red trolleybuses. All are run by **BKV** *(Budapest Transport Company; ☎ 342 2335, 06-80 406 688; ⓦ www.bkv.hu)*.

Daytime public transport in Budapest runs from about 4am to between 9pm and 11.30pm, depending on the line. From 11.30pm to 4am a network of 17 night buses (marked with an 'É' after the designated number) kicks in, running every 10 to 60 minutes, again depending on the line.

Fares & Travel Passes To ride the metro, trams, trolleybuses, buses and the HÉV (as far as the city limits, which is the Békásmegyer stop to the north) you must have a valid ticket, which you can buy at kiosks, newsstands or metro entrances. Children up to the age of six travel free when accompanied by an adult.

The basic fare for all forms of transport is 106Ft (1000/1910Ft for a block of 10/20 tickets), allowing you to travel as far as you like on the same metro, bus, trolleybus or tram line without changing. A ticket allowing unlimited stations with one change within 90 minutes costs 190Ft.

On the metro exclusively, the 106Ft base fare drops to 75Ft if you are just going three stops within 30 minutes. For 120Ft you can travel five stops and transfer at Deák tér to another metro line within one hour. Unlimited stations travelled with one change within 60 minutes costs 175Ft.

You must always travel in one continuous direction on any ticket; return trips are not allowed. Tickets have to be validated in machines at metro entrances and aboard other vehicles – inspectors will also fine you for not validating your ticket.

Life will be much simpler if you buy a travel pass. Passes are valid on all trams, buses, trolleybuses, HÉV (within the city limits) and metro lines, and you don't have to worry about validating your ticket each time you get on. The most central places to get them are at the **Deák tér metro station ticket office** *(open 6am-8pm daily)* and at the **Nyugati pályaudvar metro station ticket office** *(open 6am-8pm daily)*; see Train under Getting There & Away, earlier, for other details.

A one-day pass is poor value at 850Ft, but the three-day pass *(touristajegy, or tourist ticket)* for 1700Ft and seven-day pass *(hetijegy, or one week)* for 2100Ft are worthwhile for most people. You'll need a photo for the fortnightly/monthly passes (2650/4050Ft). All but the monthly travel passes are valid from midnight to midnight, so buy them in advance and specify the date(s) you want. The monthly pass is valid from the first day of the month until (generously) the fifth day of the following month.

Travelling 'black' (ie, without a valid ticket or pass) is risky; with increased surveillance (especially in the metro), there's an excellent chance you'll get caught. (NB: Tickets are *always* checked on the HÉV.) The on-the-spot fine is 1600Ft, which rises to 4000Ft if you pay at the **BKV office** (☎ 461 6800; VII Akácfa utca 22; open 6am-8pm Mon-Fri, 8am-2pm Sat) up to 30 days later and 8000Ft after that.

Metro Budapest has three underground metro lines that converge (only) at Deák tér: the little yellow (or Millennium) line designated M1 that runs from Vörösmarty tér to Mexikoi út in Pest; the red M2 line from Déli train station in Buda to Örs vezér tere in Pest; and the blue M3 line from Újpest-Központ to Kőbánya-Kispest in Pest. A possible source of confusion on the M1 is that one stop is called Vörösmarty tér and another is Vörösmarty utca. The HÉV suburban train line, which runs north from Batthyány tér in Buda via Óbuda and Aquincum to Szentendre, south to Ráckeve and east and northeast to Gödöllő, is almost like a fourth above-ground metro line.

Bus, Tram & Trolleybus An extensive system of trams, trolleybuses and buses serve greater Budapest. On certain bus lines the same number bus may have a black or a red number. In that case, the red-numbered bus is the express, which makes limited stops and is, of course, faster.

Buses and trams are much of a muchness, though the latter are often faster and generally more pleasant for sightseeing. Trolleybuses go along cross streets in central Pest and are of little use to most visitors, with the sole exception of the ones to City and Népliget Parks.

The most important tram lines (always marked with red lines on a Budapest map, while a broken red line is a trolleybus) are listed below.

Nos 2 & 2/a, scenic trams that travel along the Pest side of the Danube as far as Jászai Mari tér
Nos 4 & 6, extremely useful trams that start at Fehérvári út and Móricz Zsigmond körtér in district XI of south Buda respectively and follow the entire length of the Big Ring Road in Pest before terminating at Moszkva tér in Buda
No 18, which runs from southern Buda along Bartók Béla út through the Tabán to Moszkva tér

No 19, which covers part of the same route as No 18, but then runs along the Buda side of the Danube to Batthyány tér
Nos 47 & 49, linking Deák tér in Pest with points in southern Buda via the Little Ring Road
No 61, a Buda tram connecting Móricz Zsigmond körtér with Déli train station and Moszkva tér

Some buses (always shown with a blue line on a Budapest map) you might find useful include the following.

No 4 (black), which runs from northern Pest via Heroes' Square to Deák tér (the red No 4 follows the same route but crosses over Chain Bridge into central Buda)
No 6É (night bus), which follows the tram No 6 route along the Big Ring Road
No 7, which cuts across a large swathe of central Pest from Bosnyák tér and down Rákóczi út before crossing Elizabeth Bridge to Kelenföld train station in southern Buda
No 14É (night bus), which follows the M3 metro line above ground
No 86, which runs the length of Buda from Kosztolányi Dezső tér to Óbuda
No 105, which goes from Deák tér to Apor Vilmos tér in central Buda

Car & Motorcycle

Though it's not so bad at night, driving in Budapest during the day can be a nightmare: road works reduce traffic to a snail's pace; there are more serious accidents than fender-benders; and parking spots are difficult to find. The public transport system is good and cheap. Try to use it.

Parking costs between 80Ft and 180Ft on the street (8am to 6pm Monday to Friday, 8am to noon Saturday). There are 24-hour covered car parks charging around 100Ft an hour in V Szervita tér and at V Aranykéz utca 4–6 in the Inner Town, and at VII Nyár utca 20.

For assistance if you break down, ring ☎ 188. If you're trying to trace a towed vehicle, call ☎ 383 0700 or ☎ 383 0770. It's going to cost you just under 8500Ft to set your vehicle free.

Drink-driving is taken *very* seriously in Hungary; see Road Rules under Car & Motorcycle in the Getting Around chapter.

Taxi

Taxis in Budapest are still not expensive compared with other European countries, but with such an excellent public transport network available, you don't really have to use them very much. We've heard from many readers who were grossly overcharged and even threatened by taxi drivers in Budapest, so taking a taxi in this city should be approached with caution. However, the reputable firms listed later in this section have caught on to the concept of customer service and they take complaints seriously.

Avoid taxis with no name on the door and only a removable taxi light-box on the roof; these are just guys with cars and the ones most likely to rip you off. Never get into a cab that does not have a yellow licence plate and an identification badge displayed on the dashboard (as required by law), the logo of one of the reputable taxi firms (see list later) on the side doors, and a table of fares posted prominently.

Not all taxi meters are set at the same rates, and some are much more expensive than others, but there are price ceilings under which cab companies are free to manoeuvre. From 6am to 10pm the highest flag-fall fee that can be legally charged is 200Ft; the per-kilometre charge is 200Ft and the waiting fee 50Ft per minute. From 10pm to 6am the fees are 280/280/70Ft.

Budapest residents – local or foreign – rarely flag down taxis in the street. They almost always ring for them, and fares are actually cheaper if you book over the phone. Make sure you know the number of the landline phone you're calling from as that's how they establish your address (though you can, of course, call from a mobile phone, too).

The following are the telephone numbers of reliable taxi firms.

City	☎ 211 1111
Tele 5	☎ 355 5555
Fő	☎ 222 2222
Rádió	☎ 377 7777
Buda	☎ 233 3333
Est Taxi	☎ 244 4444

Bicycle

More and more cyclists are seen on the streets and avenues of Budapest these days, taking advantage of the growing network of bike paths. The main roads in the city might be a bit too busy and nerve-wracking to allow enjoyable cycling, but the side streets are fine and there are some areas (City Park, Margaret Island etc) where cycling is ideal. See Cycling under Activities earlier for ideas on where to cycle, and information on where to rent bikes.

Boat

Between May and mid-September passenger ferries run by **BKV** (☎ 369 1359; w www.ship-bp.hu) depart from IX Boráros tér (Map 7) beside Petőfi Bridge up to five times daily Friday to Sunday and head for III Rómaifürdő and Pünkösdfürdő in Óbuda, a one-hour trip with many stops along the way. Tickets (which cost 500/400Ft adult/child from end to end or 400/200Ft for intermediate stops) are sold on board. The ferry stop closest to the Castle District is I Batthyány tér, and V Petőfi tér is not far from Vörösmarty tér, a convenient place to pick up the boat on the Pest side. Note that the BKV website is in Hungarian only.

See Boat under Organised Tours earlier in this chapter for information about river cruises.

Around Budapest

Let's be honest: an awful lot in Hungary is 'around Budapest' and many of the towns and cities in the Danube Bend, Transdanubia, Northern Uplands and even the Great Plain could be day trips from the capital. You can be in Szentendre (19km) in half an hour, for example, and Gyöngyös, the gateway to the bucolic Mátra Hills, is only 80km to the east. But here are four easy day or even half-day trips from the capital.

STATUE PARK

A truly mind-blowing experience is a visit to Statue Park (Szoborpark; ☎ 424 7500, fax 337 5050; w www.szoborpark.hu; XXII Szabadkai út & Balatoni út; adult/student or child 300/200Ft; open 10am-dusk daily Mar-Nov; 10am-dusk Sat & Sun Dec-Feb), home to three dozen busts, statues and plaques of Lenin, Marx, Béla Kun and 'heroic' workers that have ended up on rubbish heaps in other former socialist countries. Ogle at the socialist realism and try to imagine that at least four of these monstrous monuments were erected as recently as the late 1980s; many were still in place when one of us moved to Budapest in early 1992. The museum shop sells fabulously kitsch communist memorabilia – statues, pins, CDs of revolutionary songs – as well as a worthwhile guide in English (600Ft).

To reach this socialist Disneyland, take tram No 19 or 49 (or a red-numbered bus No 7 from Ferenciek tere in Pest) to the terminus at

XI Etele tér. From there catch a yellow Volán bus from stand No 2 or 3 to Diósd-Érd (ask the driver to tell you where the stop is). They leave every 15 minutes and the trip takes 20 minutes.

From June to August a direct bus (1250Ft, including admission to the park) leaves from in front of the Hotel Le Meridien at V Erzsébet tér 9–10 at 9am, 10am and 11am and again at 3pm, 4pm and 5pm.

SZÁZHALOMBATTA
☎ 23 • postcode 2440 • pop 16,575
Some 28km southwest of Budapest in the town of at Százhalombatta is the new **Archaeological Park** (Régészeti Park; ☎ 350 537, 354 591; István király út 4; park & museum adult/child/family 600/300/1600Ft; open 10am-6pm Tues-Sun Apr-Oct), the only open-air prehistoric museum in Hungary. The six-hectare park sits in the middle of Iron Age tumuli – Százhalombatta means '100 mounds' – and is still undergoing excavation and expansion. What is seen at present are reconstructed Bronze Age and Iron Age settlements, plus replicas of pottery, cooking utensils, musical instruments and clothing. The highlight of the park is a reconstructed 2700-year-old oak-timber burial mound which houses an incredibly detailed burial chamber, rebuilt from archaeological finds and floor plans. An 18-minute film (in Hungarian, English or German) briefly delves into the history of the Iron and Bronze Age in Central Europe, before moving onto the burial process and a step-by-step explanation of the reconstruction of the burial crypt.

The **Matrica Museum** (☎ 354 591, fax 540 069; ⓦ www.matrica.battanet.hu; Gesztenyés út 1-3; adult/child/family 300/150/800Ft; open 10am-6pm Tues-Sun Apr-Oct; 10am-5pm Tues-Fri, 1pm-5pm Sat & Sun Nov-Mar), part of the Archaeological Park, traces the history of the settlement from prehistoric times till today.

Getting There & Away
Over two dozen trains leave Budapest's Déli and Kelenföld train stations for Százhalombatta daily; the last train returns at 9.55pm. A bus links the train station at Százhalombatta with the park, but it's rather infrequent – the last leaves for the station at 4.35pm.

Buses bound for Százhalombatta leave frequently throughout the day from the station at XI Etele tér in southern Buda.

RÁCKEVE
☎ 24 • postcode 2300 • pop 8575
The lures of this town on the southeastern end of Csepel Island, the long island in the Danube south of Budapest, are its pretty riverside park and strand, a Gothic Serbian Orthodox church (rác is the old Hungarian word for 'Serb') and the former Savoy Mansion, now a lovely hotel. **Tourinform** (☎/fax 429 747; ⓔ rackeve@tourinform.hu; Kossuth Lajos utca 51; open 9am-6pm daily mid-June–mid-Sept; 8am-4pm Mon-Fri mid-Sept–mid-June) is in the cultural centre, about 1km south of the train station.

Savoy Mansion
From the HÉV station in Ráckeve, walk south along Kossuth Lajos utca to the Savoy Mansion (Savoyai-kastély; Kossuth Lajos utca 95), now a 30-room hotel facing the Ráckeve-Danube River branch. The domed manse with two wings was built in 1720 in the baroque style for Prince Eugene of Savoy by an Austrian architect who would later go on to design Schönbrunn Palace in Vienna. The mansion was completely renovated and turned into a pricey hotel and conference centre in 1982. Concerts are held here in June and July.

Árpád Museum
This small museum (☎ 485 364; Kossuth Lajos utca 34; admission 300Ft; open 10am-6pm Tues-Sun Mar-Oct; 10am-4pm Mon-Fri Nov-Feb), south of the mansion, has exhibits focusing on the Danube along with a lot of old photographs.

Serbian Orthodox Church
As you carry on south toward the centre of town, you can't miss the blue belfry of the Serbian Orthodox Church (Görög-keleti szerb templom; Viola utca 1; open 10am-noon, 2pm-5pm Tues-Sat, 2pm-5pm Sun) to the southeast. The late Gothic church was originally built in 1487 by Serbs who fled their town of Keve ahead of the invading Turks, and many street signs in this area are in Serbian. It was enlarged in the following century. The free-standing clock tower was added in 1758.

The walls and ceiling of the church interior are covered with colourful murals painted by a Serbian master from Albania in the mid-18th century. The walls depict scenes from the Old and New Testaments and were meant to teach

BUDAPEST

the Bible to illiterate parishioners. The first section of the nave is reserved for women; the part beyond the separating wall is for men. Only the priest and his servers enter the sanctuary beyond the iconostasis, the richly carved and gilded gate festooned with icons.

Places to Eat

The **Kastély** (☎ 485 253, 424 189; Kossuth Lajos utca 95; mains 1200-2500Ft; open noon-11pm daily) is one of the better restaurants in Ráckeve, and is a good way to get a look at the mansion. **Cadran** (☎ 485 470; Hősök tere 1; pizza 440-980Ft; open 10am-10pm Mon-Sat, 12.30pm-10pm Sun) is a popular pizzeria and pub in the centre of town.

Getting There & Away

The easiest way to reach Ráckeve, 40km south of Budapest, is on the HÉV suburban train departing from the Vágóhíd HÉV terminus in district IX on the Pest side. You can get to that station from the Inner Town on tram No 2 or from Keleti train station on tram No 24. The HÉV trip takes about 1¼ hours. The last HÉV train back to Budapest leaves Ráckeve at 10.30pm.

MARTONVÁSÁR

☎ 22 • postcode 2462 • pop 4840

Lying almost exactly halfway between Budapest and the city of Székesfehérvár (in the Lake Balaton region) and easily accessible by train, Martonvásár is the site of the former **Brunswick Mansion** (Brunszvik-kastély; Brunszvik út 2), one of the loveliest summertime concert venues in Hungary. The mansion was built in 1775 for Count Antal Brunswick (Magyarised as Brunszvik), the patriarch of a family of liberal reformers and patrons of the arts (Teréz Brunszvik established Hungary's first nursery school in Pest in 1828).

Beethoven was a frequent visitor to the mansion, and it is believed that Jozefin, Teréz's sister, was the inspiration for his *Appassionata* and *Moonlight* sonatas, which the great Ludwig van composed here.

Brunswick Mansion was rebuilt in the neo-Gothic style in 1875 and restored to its ivory and sky-blue glory a century later. It now houses the Agricultural Research Institute of the Academy of Sciences, but you can see at least part of the mansion by visiting the small **Beethoven Memorial Museum** (Beethoven Emlékmúzeum; ☎ 569 500; adult/student or child 120/60Ft; open 10am-noon & 2pm-4pm Tues-Fri, 10am-6pm Sat & Sun May-Oct; 10am-noon & 2pm-4pm Tues-Fri, 10am-4pm Sat & Sun Nov-Apr) to the left of the main entrance.

A walk around the **park grounds** (adult/student or child 250/120Ft; open 8am-6pm daily summer; 8am-4pm daily winter) – one of Hungary's first 'English parks' to be laid out when these were all the rage here in the early 19th century – is a pleasant way to spend a warm summer's afternoon. The highlight of the so-called **Martonvásár Days** (Martonvásár Napok), a 10-day festival in July, are the Beethoven Evenings (Beethoven-estjei) on Saturday, when concerts are held on the small island in the middle of the lake (reached by a wooden footbridge).

The baroque **Catholic church**, attached to the mansion but accessible from outside the grounds, has frescoes by Johannes Cymbal. There's also a small **Nursery Museum** (Óvodamúzeum; ☎ 569 500; admission adult/child 120/60Ft; open 10am-4pm Tues-Sun May-Sept; 11am-3pm Tues, Fri & Sun Oct-Apr) in the park.

Places to Eat

Postakocsi (☎ 460 013; Fehérvári utca 1; mains 900-1700Ft; open 10am-10pm daily) in the centre is a convenient place for lunch and has courtyard seating. The restaurant at the **Macska pension** (Cat; ☎ 460 127; Budai út 21; mains about 1000Ft), just north of town, serves not feline under glass but the standard Hungarian *csárda* dishes.

Getting There & Away

Dozens of trains between Déli and Kelenföld train stations in Budapest and Székesfehérvár stop at Martonvásár every day and, if you attend a concert, you can easily make your way back to Velence town and Székesfehérvár or on to Budapest on the last trains (11.16pm and 11.35pm respectively). The station is a 10-minute walk along Brunszvik út, northwest of the main entrance to the mansion.

GÖDÖLLŐ

☎ 28 • postcode 2100 • pop 29,900

Just 27km northeast of the Inner Town and easily accessible on the HÉV, Gödöllő (**good**-duh-ler) is an easy day trip from Budapest. The main draw here is the Royal Mansion, which rivalled Esterházy Palace at

Fertőd in Western Transdanubia (see Fertőd in the Western Transdanubia chapter) in splendour and size when it was completed in the 1760s and is the largest baroque manor house in Hungary. But the town itself, full of lovely baroque buildings and monuments and home to the seminal Gödöllő Artists Colony (1901–20) is alone worth the trip. For information contact **Tourinform** (☎ 415 403, fax 415 402; e godollo@tourinform.hu; open 10am-5pm Tues-Sun Apr-Oct; 10am-4pm Tues-Sun Nov-Mar) just inside the entrance to the Royal Mansion.

Royal Mansion
The Royal Mansion (Királyi Kastély; ☎ 410 124, fax 423 159; W www.kiralyikastely.hu; Szabadság tér 1; adult/child/family 1000/ 350/1800Ft Apr-Oct, 750/350/1200Ft Nov-Mar; open 10am-6pm Tues-Sun Apr-Oct; 10am-5pm Tues-Sun Nov-Mar), sometimes called the Grassalkovich Mansion after its commissioner, Antal Grassalkovich (1694–1771), count and confidante of Empress Maria Theresa, was designed by Antal Mayerhoffer in 1741. After the formation of the Dual Monarchy, the mansion (or palace) was enlarged as a summer retreat for Emperor Franz Joseph, and soon became the favoured residence of his consort, the much beloved Habsburg empress and Hungarian queen, Elizabeth (1837–98) affectionately known as Sissy. Between the two world wars, the regent, Admiral Miklós Horthy, also used it as a summer residence, but after the communist came to power, part of the mansion was used as a Soviet barracks, as an old people's home and then as temporary housing. The rest was left to decay.

Partial renovation of the mansion began in 1994 and today more than a dozen rooms are open to the public on the 1st floor. The rooms have been restored (some would say too heavily) to when the imperial couple were in residence, and Franz Joseph's suites (done up in manly greys and golds) and Sissy's

lavender-coloured private apartments are impressive, if not as evocative of the past as the rooms at the Esterházy Palace. Check out the **Decorative Hall**, all gold tracery and chandeliers, where chamber-music concerts are held throughout the year but especially in late June and early July during the **Palace Concerts Chamber Music Festival**; the **Queen's Salon**, with a Romantic-style oil painting of Sissy patriotically repairing the coronation robe with needle and thread; and the **Study Annexe**, with a restored ceiling painting and an 18th-century tapestry of the huntress Diana.

A guided tour that also includes rooms and outbuildings not yet reconstructed (the palace chapel, theatre, stables etc) costs 1200/500/ 2200Ft per adult/child/family. A guide costs 4000Ft for up to 10 people.

Places to Eat
Tourinform at the palace has sample menus from restaurants around town and distributes discount vouchers.

Palazzo (Szabadság tér; pizzas 450-900Ft; open 11am-11pm daily) is conveniently attached to the HÉV station.

Pelikán (☎ 412 658; Kossuth Lajos utca 31-33; mains 600-1480Ft; open noon-11pm Sun-Thur, noon-midnight Fri & Sat), to the northwest, serves decent Hungarian fare.

Galéria (☎ 418 691; Szabadság tér 8; mains 695-1200Ft; open 11am-11pm daily) is a more upmarket restaurant attached to a pleasant pension.

Getting There & Away
HÉV trains from Örs vezér tere at the terminus of the M2 metro link Budapest with Gödöllő (40 minutes) about once every half-hour throughout the day. Make sure you get off at the Szabadság tér stop, which is the third from the last. The last train leaves at 10.40pm daily. In addition, buses leave Népstadion bus station in Budapest about every 30 minutes for Gödöllő. The last bus back is just after 7pm (8.15pm on Sunday).

Danube Bend

The Danube (Hungarian: Duna), the second-longest river in Europe after the Volga, rises in the Black Forest in southwestern Germany and flows eastward until it reaches a point about 40km north of Budapest. Here the Börzsöny Hills on the left bank and the Pilis Hills on the right force it to bend sharply southward through Budapest and the rest of Hungary for just more than 400km before it again resumes its easterly flow, finally emptying into the Black Sea in Romania.

The Danube Bend (Dunakanyar) is, strictly speaking, the S-shaped curve that begins just below Esztergom and twists for 20km past Visegrád to where it splits in two, forming the long and narrow Szentendre Island. But the name has come to describe the entire region of peaks, resorts and river towns to the north and northwest of the capital. The Bend is one of the most beautiful stretches of the Danube along its entire course of almost 3000km and should not be missed.

The right bank (that is, the area south and west of the Danube) has the lion's share of the Bend's historical towns and parkland. This was the northernmost region of Rome's colonies; Esztergom was the first seat of the Magyar kings and has been the centre of Roman Catholicism in the region for more than a millennium.

Visegrád was Central Europe's 'Camelot' and the royal seat during Hungary's short-lived flirtation with the Renaissance in the 15th century. Szentendre, which has its origins in Serbian culture, is an important centre for art and culture. And then there's the Pilis Park Forest, once a royal hunting ground, and the Visegrád Hills which, together with the Börzsöny Protected Area on the opposite bank, form the 60,000-hectare Danube-Ipoly National Park.

The river's left bank (north and east of the Danube) is far less developed, though the ancient town of Vác and, of course, the hills, gorges and trails of the Börzsöny have much to offer visitors.

SZENTENDRE
☎ 26 • postcode 2000 • pop 21,400
Just 19km north of Budapest, Szentendre (St Andrew) is the southern gateway to the Danube Bend. As an art colony that turned

Highlights

- The medieval hilltop citadel at Visegrád with its wonderful views of the Danube
- A trip by ferry from Budapest to Szentendre, Visegrád or even Esztergom
- The splendid Gothic altarpieces and paintings at the Christian Museum in Esztergom
- The sheer size of Esztergom's Basilica, plus its wonderful treasury, crypt and cupola
- The Margit Kovács Museum of ceramic art in Szentendre
- Any of a number of hikes in the Börzsöny or Pilis Hills

DANUBE BEND

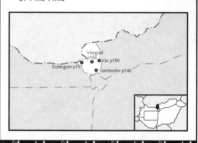

into a lucrative tourist centre, Szentendre strikes many as a little too 'cute', and the town can be crowded and relatively expensive. Still, it's an easy train trip from the capital, and the town's dozens of art museums, galleries and churches are well worth the trip. Just try to avoid it at weekends in summer.

Like most towns along the Danube Bend, Szentendre was home first to the Celts and then the Romans, who built an important border fortress here called Ulcisia Castra (Wolf's Castle). The area was overrun by a succession of tribes during the Great Migrations until the Magyars arrived late in the 9th century and established a colony here. By the 14th century, Szentendre was a prosperous estate under the supervision of the royal castle at Visegrád.

It was about this time that the first wave of Serbian Orthodox Christians came from

DANUBE BEND

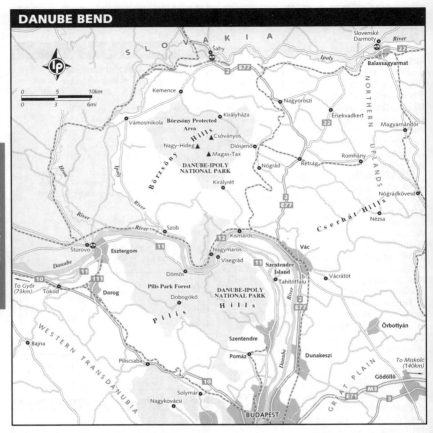

DANUBE BEND

the south in advance of the Turks (a group of people that would go on to build most of Szentendre's churches and give the town its unique Balkan feel). They settled here, and many were employed as boatmen and border soldiers under King Matthias Corvinus. But the Turkish occupation of Hungary brought this peaceful coexistence to an end, and by the end of the 17th century Szentendre was deserted. Though Hungary was liberated from the Ottomans not long afterward, fighting continued in the Balkans and a second wave of Serbs, together with Greeks, Dalmatians and others, fled to Szentendre. Believing they would eventually return home, but enjoying complete religious freedom under the relatively benevolent rule of the Habsburgs (a right denied Hungary's Protestants at the time), a half-dozen Orthodox clans each built their own wooden churches.

Szentendre's delightful location began to attract day-trippers and painters from Budapest early in the 20th century; an artists colony was established here in the 1920s. It has been known for its art and artists ever since.

Orientation

The HÉV commuter train and bus stations lie side by side south of the town centre at the start of Dunakanyar körút (Danube Bend Ring Road). From here walk through the subway and north along Kossuth Lajos utca, and veer right into Dumtsa Jenő utca onto Fő tér, the heart of Szentendre. The Duna korzó promenade along the Danube and the ferry to Szentendre Island are a few minutes' walk east and northeast, respectively, of Fő tér. The Mahart ferry pier is about a kilometre northeast on Czóbel Béla sétány, which runs off Duna korzó.

Information

There is a helpful **Tourinform** (☎ 317 965, fax 317 966; e szentendre@tourinform.hu; Dumtsa Jenő utca 22; open 9.30am-4.30pm Mon-Fri year-round, 10am-2pm Sat & Sun mid-Mar–Oct). Visitors should note that between November and mid-March much of Szentendre shuts down on weekdays. Szentendre's website is at w www.szentendre.hu.

There's an **OTP bank** (Dumtsa Jenő utca 6) just off Fő tér. The main **post office** (Kossuth Lajos utca 23-25) is across from the HÉV and bus stations; you'll also find a branch (Fő tér 15) in the centre. An **Internet café** (☎ 500 420; Bogdányi utca 40) is north of Fő tér, with access for 500Ft an hour.

Things to See

On the way from the stations, you'll pass **Požarevačka Church** (☎ 310 554; Kossuth Lajos utca 1; admission 100Ft; open 11am-5pm Fri-Sun mid-Mar–mid-Nov) just before you cross the narrow Bükkös Stream. This Serbian Orthodox church was dedicated in 1763; the lovely iconostasis inside (1742) is the oldest in Szentendre.

To the north, the **Sts Peter and Paul Church** (Péter-Pál utca 6; admission free) off Dumtsa Jenő utca began life as the Čiprovačka Orthodox Church in 1753, but was later taken over by Dalmatian Catholics. The **Barcsay Collection** (Barcsay Gyüjtemény; ☎ 310 244; Dumtsa Jenő utca 10; adult/student & child 300/150Ft; open 10am-6pm Wed-Sun Apr-Sept; 10am-4pm Fri-Sun Oct-Mar), to the east, contains the work of one of the founders of Szentendre's art colony, Jenő Barcsay (1900–88).

In the centre of **Fő tér**, the colourful heart of Szentendre surrounded by 18th- and 19th-century burghers' houses, stands the **Memorial Cross** (1763), an iron cross decorated with icons on a marble base. The **Kmetty Museum** (☎ 310 790; Fő tér 21; adult/student & child 300/150Ft; 10am-6pm Wed-Sun Apr-Sept; 10am-4pm Fri-Sun Oct-Mar) on the south-western side of the square displays the work of the cubist János Kmetty (1889–1975).

For a little less rational thought, you could cross over the square to **Blagoveštenska Church** (☎ 310 554; admission 100Ft; open daily mid-Mar–Oct), built in 1754. The church, with fine baroque and rococo elements, hardly looks 'eastern' from the outside (it was designed by the architect András Mayerhoffer), but once you are inside, the ornate iconostasis and elaborate 18th-century furnishings give the game away. It is interesting to examine the icons. Though the icons were painted only half a century after the ones in Požarevačka Church, they are much more realistic and seem to have lost that otherworldly spiritual feel.

If you descend Görög utca and turn right onto Vastagh György utca, you'll reach the entrance to the **Margit Kovács Ceramic Collection** (Kovács Margit Kerámiagyüjtemény; ☎ 310 244; Vastagh György utca 1; adult/student & child 450/220Ft; open 10am-6pm daily Feb-Oct; 10am-4pm Tues-Sun Nov-Jan) in an 18th-century salt house at No 1. Kovács (1902–77) was a ceramicist who combined Hungarian folk, religious and modern themes to create Gothic-like figures. Some of Kovács' works are overly sentimental, but many very are powerful, especially the later ones in which she became obsessed with mortality.

The **Ferenczy Museum** (☎ 310 790; Fő tér 6; adult/student & child 300/150Ft; open 10am-6pm Wed-Sun Apr-Sept) next to the Blagoveštenska Church is devoted to Károly Ferenczy (1862–1917), the father of plein air painting in Hungary, and his three children: a painter, a sculptor and a weaver.

Bogdányi utca, Szentendre's busiest pedestrian street, leads north from here. The **Nemzeti Wine Museum** (Nemzeti Bormúzeum; ☎ 317 054; Bogdányi utca 10; admission 100Ft, tastings 1400Ft; open 10am-10pm daily), connected to a restaurant, charges you to look at displays tracing the development of wine-making in Hungary and quite a bit more to sample various vintages. Far more challenging is the excellent **Anna-Ámos Collection** (☎ 310 790; Bogdányi utca 12; adult/student & child 300/150Ft; open 10am-6pm Wed-Sun Apr-Sept, 10am-4pm Fri-Sun Oct-Mar) displaying the symbolist paintings of husband-and-wife team, Margit Anna and Imre Ámos.

Szentendre has converted part of a 19th-century industrial complex into the **ArtMill** (MűvészetMalom; ☎ 319 128; Bogdányi utca 32; adult/student & child 350/200Ft; open 10am-6pm daily). In a bid to recapture its

DANUBE BEND

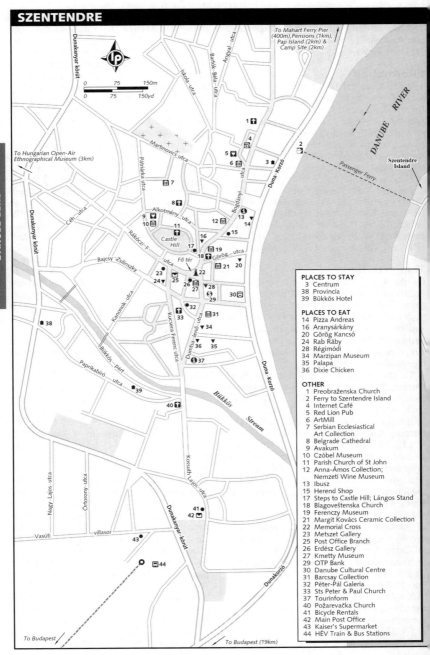

SZENTENDRE

To Mahart Ferry Pier
(400m),Pensions (1km),
Pap Island (2km) &
Camp Site (2km)

DANUBE RIVER

To Hungarian Open-Air
Ethnographical Museum (3km)

Passenger Ferry

Szentendre
Island

Castle
Hill

Fő tér

Bükkös Stream

To Budapest

To Budapest (19km)

PLACES TO STAY
3 Centrum
38 Provincia
39 Bükkös Hotel

PLACES TO EAT
14 Pizza Andreas
16 Aranysárkány
20 Görög Kancsó
24 Rab Ráby
28 Régimódi
34 Marzipan Museum
35 Palapa
36 Dixie Chicken

OTHER
1 Preobraženska Church
2 Ferry to Szentendre Island
4 Internet Café
5 Red Lion Pub
6 ArtMill
7 Serbian Ecclesiastical
  Art Collection
8 Belgrade Cathedral
9 Avakum
10 Czóbel Museum
11 Parish Church of St John
12 Anna-Ámos Collection;
   Nemzeti Wine Museum
13 Ibusz
15 Herend Shop
17 Steps to Castle Hill; Lángos Stand
18 Blagoveštenska Church
19 Ferenczy Museum
21 Margit Kovács Ceramic Collection
22 Memorial Cross
23 Metszet Gallery
25 Post Office Branch
26 Erdész Gallery
27 Kmetty Museum
29 OTP Bank
30 Danube Cultural Centre
31 Barcsay Collection
32 Péter-Pál Galeria
33 Sts Peter & Paul Church
37 Tourinform
40 Požarevačka Church
41 Bicycle Rentals
42 Main Post Office
43 Kaiser's Supermarket
44 HÉV Train & Bus Stations

past as a serious centre for artists and the arts it has some 700 sq metres of exhibition space for paintings, sculpture, graphics and applied arts. It is still expanding and will quadruple its size when the next phases are completed. Call to find out what's on.

Castle Hill (Vár-domb), which can be reached via the Váralja lépcső, the narrow steps between Fő tér 8 and 9, was the site of a fortress in the Middle Ages, but all that's left of it is the walled **Parish Church of St John** (Templom tér; admission free; open 10am-4pm Tues-Sun), from where you get splendid views of the town. St John's was originally built in the late 13th century but has been reconstructed several times over the centuries. The entrance to the church – the only one in town that has always been Catholic – is early Gothic; the frescoes in the sanctuary were painted by members of the artists colony in the 1930s. West of the church the **Czóbel Museum** (☎ 312 721; Templom tér 1; adult/student & child 300/150Ft; open 10am-6pm Apr-Sept), contains the works of the impressionist Béla Czóbel (1883–1976), a friend of Pablo Picasso and student of Henri Matisse.

The red tower of **Belgrade Cathedral** (Belgrád Székesegyház; Alkotmány utca; admission free; open daily), completed in 1764 and seat of the Serbian Orthodox bishop in Hungary, rises from within a leafy, walled courtyard north of St John's church. One of the church buildings beside it now contains the **Serbian Ecclesiastical Art Collection** (Szerb Egyházművészeti Gyűjtemény; ☎ 312 399; Pátriárka utca 5; adult/student & child 200/100Ft; open 10am-6pm Tues-Sun May-Oct; 10am-4pm Tues-Sun Mar & Apr; 10am-4pm Fri-Sun Jan & Feb), a treasure trove of icons, vestments and other sacred objects in precious metals. A 14th-century glass painting of the crucifixion is the oldest item on display; a 'cotton icon' of the life of Christ from the 18th century is unusual. Take a look at the defaced portrait of Christ upstairs on the right-hand wall. The story goes that a drunken kuruc (anti-Habsburg) mercenary slashed it and, told what he had done next morning, drowned himself in the Danube.

Hungarian Open-Air Ethnographical Museum

This collection of buildings (Magyar Szabadtéri Néprajzi Múzeum; ☎ 502 500; **w** www.sznm.hu; Sztaravodai út; adult/student & child 600/300Ft, guided tours in English, French & German 7000Ft; open 9am-5pm Tues-Sun Apr-Oct; 9am-7pm Tues-Sun July & Aug), about 3km northwest of the centre, is Hungary's most ambitious open-air museum (skanzen). Situated on a 46-hectare tract of rolling land, the museum was founded in 1967 to introduce urban Hungarians and tourists alike to traditional Magyar culture by bringing bits and pieces of villages, farms and towns to one site. The plans call for some 300 farmhouses, churches, bell towers, mills and so on ultimately to be set up in 10 regional units. So far there are six; the Upper Tisza area of Northeast Hungary, the Kisalföld and Őrség regions of Western Transdanubia, the Bakony area and Balaton Uplands of the Lake Balaton region and a market town from the Alföld region of the Great Plain.

The houses and other buildings have been carefully reassembled and are all in good condition; highlights include the Calvinist church and 'skirted' belfry from the Erdőhát of the Northeast, the German 'long house' from Harka outside Sopron, the curious heart-shaped gravestones from the Buda Hills and the lovely whitewashed facade of the thatched house from Sükösd on the Great Plain. Craftspeople and artisans do their thing on random days from late March to early November excluding July (generally Sunday and holidays), and the open-air museum hosts festivals throughout the season. For information call it or visit its website.

Activities

Pap Island (Pap-sziget), 2km north of the centre, is Szentendre's playground and has a grassy strand for sunbathing, a **swimming pool** (open 8am-7pm daily May-Sept) where a dip costs 200/100Ft (adult/student & child), **tennis courts** and **rowing boats** for hire.

You can rent **bicycles** from the **Holdas Udvar** (Kossuth Lajos utca 19), next to the post office, for 400/2500Ft per hour/day; take the hourly ferry across to Szentendre Island to enjoy kilometres of uncrowded cycling paths. **Canoes** and **motor boats** can be rented from **Dunabogdány** (☎/fax 390 086) for 1700/6000Ft per day, respectively; boats are delivered to a place you request on the river, and a minimal fee is charged for the delivery.

Places to Stay

Szentendre is so close to Budapest that there's no point in spending the night here unless you want to continue on to other towns on the Danube Bend without backtracking. What little is on offer in the centre of town can be expensive in season.

Pap-sziget Camping (☎ 310 697, fax 313 777; camping per adult/child/tent 900/500/ 1900Ft, bungalows & motel rooms for up to 4 persons 6000Ft; open May–mid-Oct) is some 2km north of Szentendre on Pap Island. It also has a hostel with single rooms for 2600Ft and doubles for 3800Ft, and pension rooms costing 5000Ft for a double. Prices include admission to the swimming pool next door. Other facilities include a small supermarket, a snack bar and a restaurant.

If you're after a **private room**, look for Zimmer frei (room for rent) signs on the Dunakanyar körút ring road; prices start at around 3000Ft per person.

St Andrea (☎ 311 989, fax 500 804; Egres utca 22; singles/doubles €20/25) has more than 15 simple rooms but is on a quiet street.

Cola (☎ 310 410, fax 500 539; Dunakanyar körút 50; singles/doubles €23/32), near St. Andrea, has 12 rooms (some with terrace) and a hunting lodge feel.

Centrum (☎/fax 302 500; Bogdányi utca 15; singles/doubles 10,000/12,000Ft) is just a few minutes' walk from Fő tér and overlooks the Danube and Duna korzó (where the main entrance is). It's expensive but its six rooms are bright, large and filled with antique furniture.

Bükkös Hotel (☎ 312 021, fax 310 782; ⓔ bukkosh@matavnet.hu; Bükkös part 16; singles/doubles €40/45) is a friendly 16 room place halfway between the bus and HÉV stations and Fő tér, and is more like a pension than a hotel – but what's in a name?

Provincia (☎ 301 082, fax 301 085; Paprikabíró utca 21-23; singles/doubles €50/ 61) is a not unattractive, 24-room modern hotel with sauna and pool hard up against the noisy ring road. Prices quoted apply from May to September.

Places to Eat

There are **food stalls** at the bus and HÉV stations – very convenient if you're going directly on to the open-air museum, where the choice is limited to a pricey restaurant called the **Skanzen** (☎ 315 723; mains 1200-1800Ft). In town, a small **lángos stand** (lángos from 150Ft) is situated under a shady tree, halfway up the steep steps from Fő tér to Castle Hill.

Dixie Chicken (Dumtsa Jenő utca 16, burgers from 240Ft) is your standard fast-food joint, but it does have a salad bar.

Régimódi (☎ 311 105; Dumtsa Jenő utca 2, set menu 1500Ft), just down from the Margit Kovács museum, occupies an old Szentendre house. Its lunch-time set menu is good.

Rab Ráby (☎ 310 819; Péter-Pál utca 1; mains 1000-2000Ft), housed in an 18th-century smithy and wine press, is another old stand-by.

Pizza Andreas (☎ 310 530; Duna korzó 5, pizzas from 700Ft) is a simpler affair close to the Danube.

Görög Kancsó (Greek Jug; ☎ 301 729, Görög utca 1; mains 1200-2500Ft) is ambitiously named and manages tzatziki and Greek salads but serves mostly standard (and pricey) Hungarian fare.

Palapa (Batthyány utca 4; mains 1000-1500Ft), a colourful Mexican restaurant on a quiet street, is a good place to go if you want a change from heavy Hungarian fare.

Aranysárkány (Golden Dragon; ☎ 301 479, Alkotmány utca 1/a; mains around 1800Ft, may sound Chinese but this place serves superb Hungarian and Austrian dishes for an above-average price. The current First Lady of the USA has graced this place with her presence, so it must be good.

The **Marzipan Museum** (☎ 310 931; Dumtsa Jenő utca 12; admission to museum 250Ft) is a good place to stop for a bit of cake and ice cream.

Entertainment

Danube Cultural Centre (☎ 312 657; Duna korzó 11/a) stages theatrical performances, concerts and folk dance gatherings and can tell you what's on elsewhere in Szentendre.

Dive into **Avakum** (Alkotmány utca 14), a cellar bar near Castle Hill, to escape the tourist hordes and rehydrate. **Red Lion** (Szerb utca 2/1), a pub just off Bogdányi utca, is more raucous and has five beers on tap.

Shopping

Szentendre is a shopper's town – from souvenir embroidery to the latest fashions - and although prices are at Budapest levels not everything you see is available in the capital. For ceramics and lace, try the **Péter-Pál Galeria** (Péter-Pál utca 1). The **Metsze Gallery** (Fő tér 15) has wonderful old engravings, prints and a handful of maps. Fo fine art, try the **Erdész Gallery** *(Fő tér 20)*, where there's a wonderful collection of avante-garde Eastern European art of the 1920s and '30s. If you don't make it to Herend (see the Lake Balaton Region chapter), you can pick up an expensive piece of porcelain at the **Herend Shop**, on the corner of Bogdányi utca and Bercsényi utca.

Getting There & Away
Bus Buses from Budapest's Árpád híd station, which is on the blue metro line, run to Szentendre at least once an hour throughout the day. Onward service to Visegrád (eight buses daily) and Esztergom (17) is good.

Train The easiest way to reach Szentendre from Budapest is to catch the HÉV suburban train from Batthyány tér in Buda, which takes just 40 minutes. You'll never wait longer than 20 minutes (half that in rush hour), and the last train leaves Szentendre for Budapest at 11.10pm. Remember that a yellow city bus/metro ticket is good only as far as the Békásmegyer stop on the way up; you'll have to pay extra to get to Szentendre. Also, many HÉV trains run only as far as Békásmegyer, where you must cross the platform to board the train for Szentendre.

Boat From late May to early September, one daily Mahart ferry plies the Danube to/from Budapest's Vigadó tér (830/1660Ft one-way/return), departing from Budapest at 9am and Szentendre at 11.45am. From mid-June to early September two extra ferries depart from Budapest at 10.30am (Express hydrofoil; 1300Ft one-way; Tues-Sun only) and 2pm and Szentendre at 5.45pm (Express hydrofoil; Tues-Sun only) and 5.55pm. From April to late May and September until seasonal shutdown, one boat operates daily, leaving Budapest at 9am and Szentendre at 5.15pm. There is one departure (10.40am) to Visegrád in the low season and two (10.40am and 3.30pm) in the high season. The 3.30pm departure continues on to Esztergom. The river-boat terminal is 1km north of town at the end of Czóbel Béla sétány.

Getting Around
Any bus heading north on route No 11 to Visegrád and Esztergom will stop near some of the pensions and the camp site on Pap Island mentioned earlier. Ring the bell after

you pass the Danubius hotel at Ady Endre utca 28 on the left. Between 14 and 16 buses daily leave bus stop No 7 for the Open-Air Ethnographical Museum.

Ferries run hourly to Szentendre Island (7am to 7.30pm daily from March to October) and cost 130/65Ft for an adult/child one way.

You can book a taxi by calling ☎ 311 111 or ☎ 301 111.

VÁC
☎ 27 • postcode 2600 • pop 35,500
Vác (German: Wartzen) lies 34km north of Budapest on the left (east) bank of the Danube opposite Szentendre Island. To the northwest and stretching as far as Slovakia are the Börzsöny Hills, the start of Hungary's mountainous northern region. The Cserhát Hills are to the east.

Unlike most Hungarian towns, Vác can prove its ancient origins without putting a spade into the ground: Uvcenum – the town's Latin name – is mentioned by Ptolemy in his 2nd-century *Geographia* as a river crossing on an important road. King Stephen established an episcopate here in the 11th century, and within 300 years Vác was rich and powerful enough for its silver mark to become the realm's legal tender. The town's medieval centre and Gothic cathedral were destroyed during the Turkish occupation; reconstruction under several bishops in the 18th century gave Vác its present baroque appearance.

No more than a sleepy provincial centre in the middle of the 19th century, Vác was the first Hungarian town to be linked with Pest by train (1846), but development didn't really come until after WWII. Sadly, for many older Hungarians the name Vác conjures up a single frightening image: the notorious prison on Köztársaság út, where political prisoners were incarcerated and tortured both before the war under the rightist regime of Miklós Horthy and in the 1950s under the communists.

Today you'd scarcely know about that as you enjoy the breezes along the embankment of the Danube, a more prominent feature here than in the Bend's other towns. Vác is also far less touristy than Szentendre, Visegrád or Esztergom – perhaps the strongest recommendation for stopping over.

Orientation
The train station is at the northeastern end of Széchenyi utca, the bus station a few steps

heading southwest on Galcsek utca. Following Széchenyi utca toward the river for about 500m will take you across the ring road (Dr Csányi László körút) and down to Március 15 tér, the main square. The Mahart ferry pier is at the northern end of Liszt Ferenc sétány; the car and passenger ferry to Szentendre Island just south of it.

Information

The helpful **Tourinform** (☎ 316 160, fax 316 464; e vac@tourinform.hu; Március 15 tér 16-18; open 9am-6pm Mon-Fri, 9am-5pm Sat & Sun mid-Jun–mid-Sept; 8am-4pm Mon-Fri, 9am-1pm Sat May–mid-June; 8am-4pm Mon-Fri mid-Sept–Apr) is on the main square.

There's an **OTP bank** in the Dunakanyar shopping centre and a there's a **Budapest Bank** (Köztársaság út 10) south of Március 15 tér. The **main post office** (Posta Park 2) is off Görgey Artúr utca.

For Internet access, head to **DunaWeb** (☎ 301 571; Széchenyi utca 8) where it charges 320/400Ft per half-hour/hour.

Things to See

Március 15 tér (also known as Fő tér) has the most colourful buildings in Vác. The **Dominican church** (Fehérek temploma) on the south side is 18th-century baroque; there's a lively **market** to the east. The seals held by the two figures on the gable of the magnificent baroque **Town Hall** (1764) at No 11 represent Hungary and Bishop Kristóf Migazzi, the driving force behind Vác's reconstruction more than 200 years ago. The building next

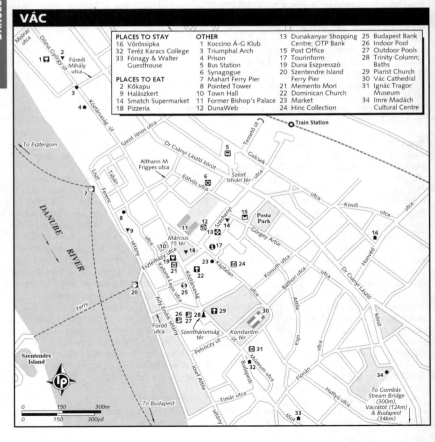

VÁC

PLACES TO STAY
16 Vörössipka
32 Teréz Karacs College
33 Főnagy & Walter Guesthouse

PLACES TO EAT
2 Kőkapu
9 Halászkert
14 Smatch Supermarket
18 Pizzeria

OTHER
1 Koccino Á-G Klub
3 Triumphal Arch
4 Prison
5 Bus Station
6 Synagogue
7 Mahart Ferry Pier
8 Pointed Tower
10 Town Hall
11 Former Bishop's Palace
12 DunaWeb
13 Dunakanyar Shopping Centre; OTP Bank
15 Post Office
17 Tourinform
19 Duna Eszpresszó
20 Szentendre Island Ferry Pier
21 Memento Mori
22 Dominican Church
23 Market
24 Hinc Collection
25 Budapest Bank
26 Indoor Pool
27 Outdoor Pools
28 Trinity Column; Baths
29 Piarist Church
30 Vác Cathedral
31 Ignác Tragor Museum
34 Imre Madách Cultural Centre

door at No 9 has been a hospital since the 18th century. Opposite at Március 15 tér 6, the former **Bishop's Palace**, parts of which belong to the oldest building in Vác, is now a school. Also on Március 15 tér, at No 19, is **Memento Mori** (☎ 316 160; Március 15 tér 19; adult/student or child 300/150Ft; open 10am-6pm Tues-Sun Apr-Oct), a rather macabre display of finds from the Dominican church's crypt.

If you walk north along Köztársaság út to No 62-64, you'll see the enormous 18th-century school that was turned into the town's infamous **prison** in the 19th century. It's still in use, as you'll gather from the armed guard staring down from the glassed-in tower. The commemorative plaque to the victims of the Horthy regime is now gone, replaced by one to those who suffered under the communists.

A little farther north is the **Triumphal Arch** (Diadalív-kapu), the only such structure in Hungary. It was built by Bishop Migazzi in honour of a visit by Empress Maria Theresa and her husband Francis of Lorraine (both pictured in the arch's oval reliefs) in 1764. From here, dip down one of the narrow side streets (such as Molnár utca) to the west for a stroll along the Danube. The **old city walls** and Gothic **Pointed Tower** (now a private home) are near Liszt Ferenc sétány 12.

If you climb up Fürdő utca near the pool complex, you'll reach tiny Szentháromság tér and its renovated **Trinity Column** (1755). The **Piarist church** (Piarista templom; admission free), completed in 1741, with a stark white interior and marble altar, is to the east across the square.

Tree-lined Konstantin tér to the southeast is dominated by colossal **Vác Cathedral** (Váci székesegyház; admission free), which dates from 1775 and was one of the first examples of neoclassical architecture to appear in Hungary. This imposing grey church designed by the French architect Isidore Canevale is not to everybody's liking, but the frescoes on the vaulted dome and the altarpiece by Franz Anton Maulbertsch are worth the look inside. There's a display of stone fragments from the medieval cathedral in the **crypt** but it is normally closed; Tourinform can arrange tours.

If you continue walking south along Budapesti főút, you'll reach the small stone **Gombás Stream Bridge** (Gombás-patak hídja), from 1757, lined with the statues of seven

saints – Vác's modest response to Charles Bridge in Prague.

The weed-choked, decrepit **synagogue** (Eötvös utca 5) off Széchenyi utca was designed by an Italian architect in the Romantic style in 1864.

There are a couple of museums in Vác of only marginal interest to visitors, including the **Ignác Tragor Museum** (☎ 315 064; Múzeum utca 4; 300/150Ft; open 10am-6pm Tues-Sun Apr-Oct) and the related **Hinc Collection** (Hinc Gyűjtemény; ☎ 313 463; Káptalan utca 16; 300/150Ft; open 10am-6pm Tues-Sun Apr-Oct), which trace the history of Vác from earliest times.

Activities
The Vác Strandfürdő (Literally 'Beach-baths') behind the Trinity statue at Szentháromság tér 3 has **outdoor pools** (adult/student or child 600/300Ft; open 7am-7pm daily June-Sept). The **indoor pool** (adult/student or child 350/200Ft; open 5.30am-3pm & 6pm-7.30pm Mon-Fri, 6am-7pm Sat, 7am-5pm Sun year-round) is on the southern edge of the 'beach', accessible from Ady Endre sétány.

Places to Stay
The **Teréz Karacs College** (☎ 315 480; Budapesti főút 2/8; dorm beds 1000Ft) opposite Migazzi tér sometimes lets out dormitory rooms in July and August. You'll see lots of szoba kiadó (room for rent) and Zimmer frei signs along Budapesti főút.

Fónagy & Walter (☎/fax 310 682; e fon wal@freemail.hu; Budapesti főút 36; rooms 7500Ft) has three rooms that are more like apartments, about 850m southeast of Március 15 tér.

Vörössipka (☎ 501 055; Honvéd utca 14; singles/doubles from 5200/6500Ft) is the newest place in town. As you'd expect, the 16 rooms at this hotel are quite immaculate and almost sparkle.

Places to Eat
Barlang Bar (Március 15 tér; dishes 700-1000Ft; open until 11pm Sun-Thur, until 1am Fri & Sat) is an interesting place for pizza and is situated in a medieval wine cellar below the street (entrance in the centre of the square).

Kőkapu (☎ 315 920; Dózsa György út 5; mains 1000-2000Ft), near the Triumphal Arch, is one of the finer restaurants in Vác with solid Hungarian fare on offer.

Halászkert (☎ *315 985; Liszt Ferenc sétány 9; mains 700-1600Ft)* is a fine place for fish soup in warm weather when you can sit outside and watch the ferries cross over to Szentendre Island.

Entertainment

The circular **Imre Madách Cultural Centre** (☎ *316 411, Dr Csányi László körút 63)* can help you with what's on in Vác. Concerts are sometimes held in **Vác Cathedral** and the **Dominican church** and at the arboretum in **Vácrátót** at 7pm on certain Sundays in June, July and August (1000-2000Ft). Don't miss the chance to hear the Vox Humana, Vác's award-winning mixed choir.

Koccino Á-G Klub (*Dózsa György út 8)* is a divey little pub opposite the Kőkapu restaurant that attracts a mixed crowd.

Duna Eszpresszó (*Eszterházy utca 2)* is a popular place for coffee during the day and something a little stronger at night; its outdoor seating overflows with people in summer.

Getting There & Away

Bus Buses depart for Árpád híd Bridge station in Budapest every half-hour or so. From Vác count on up to 16 a day to Vácrátót, at least a dozen to Balassagyarmat, between two and eight to Diósjenő and Nógrád and almost one every half-hour to Rétság. You can also reach the county capital, Salgótarján, four times a day. Two buses a week (on Wednesday and Saturday at 7.35am) leave for the Polish city of Kraków.

Train Trains depart from Nyugati station in Budapest almost every half-hour for Szob via Vác, and four of these continue along the eastern bank of the Danube to Štúrovo, across the Danube from Esztergom in Slovakia. Slow trains north to Balassagyarmat (up to 10 a day) from Vác stop at Nógrád and Diósjenő in the Börzsöny Hills.

From the first Saturday in May to the last one in September **MÁV Nostalgia** (☎ *1-317 1665;* ⓦ *www.miwo.hu/old_trains; Belgrád rakpart 26)* runs a vintage steam train (nosztalgiavonat) from Nyugati station in Budapest (departing at 9.45am) to Szob (two hours) via Vác and Nagymaros-Visegrád and returning from Szob at 4.15pm (Nagymaros-Visegrád at 4.39pm, Vác at 5.03pm). But verify this service

and schedule with MÁV Nostalgia or check its website before making plans.

Car & Motorcycle Car ferries (700/200Ft per car/bicycle) cross over to Szentendre Island hourly from 6am to 9pm; a bridge connects the island's west bank with the mainland at Tahitótfalu. From there hourly buses run to Szentendre, about 10km south.

Boat From late May to August, one daily Mahart river boat sails between Pest's Vigadó tér (at 7.30am; 7.35am from Batthyány tér in Buda) and Vác (970/1550Ft one way/ return), continuing on to Visegrád and Esztergom at 9.55am. From April to late May and late September till winter shutdown, the boat leaves Budapest at 8am on Saturday and Sunday only and departs from Vác for Visegrád and Esztergom at 10.25am.

AROUND VÁC
Börzsöny Hills

These hills begin the series of six ranges that make up Hungary's Northern Uplands, and – along with the Pilis Park Forest and the Visegrád Hills on the opposite bank of the Danube – form Hungary's 60,000-hectare Danube-Ipoly National Park. Vác is the best starting point for a visit to the Börzsöny. There's very good hiking, but make sure you get hold of Cartographia's 1:40,000 map *A Börzsöny* (No 5; 600Ft).

Nógrád, with the ruins of a hilltop castle dating back to the 12th century, could be considered the gateway to the Börzsöny; at Diósjenő, 6km north, there's **Diósjenő Camping** (☎ *35-364 134; open May-Sept; camping per tent/adult/child 600/400/300Ft, bungalows 6000-6600Ft)* with four-bed bungalows. From here you can strike out west along marked trails to 864m **Nagy Hideg** or 739m **Magas-Tax**. The Börzsöny's highest peak, 938m, lies to the west of Diósjenő and is a much more difficult climb.

If you're under your own steam, take the beautiful restricted road (a small fee may be charged) from Diósjenő to Kemence via Királyháza, where you'll find the **Matthias** (☎ *27-365 139; rooms from 5000Ft)*, a well-known 10-room riding pension with varying priced accommodation. The road follows the Kemence Stream almost the entire way – a great place for a cool dip or a picnic in summer. Just before you reach Kemence, there is a turn south into the **Fekete-völgy**, the beautiful 'Black Valley', and the 18-room **Feketevölgy Pension** (☎ 27-365 153, fax 587 140; e info@feketevolgy.hu; singles/ doubles 3500/7000Ft), a peaceful spot set well into the forest. Otherwise, head onto Kemence, where you'll find a number of pensions and camp sites.

An easy and excellent excursion is the 5km walk southwest from Nógrád to **Királyrét**, the royal hunting grounds of King Matthias Corvinus. Here a **narrow-gauge train** runs 11km south to Kismaros, where you can catch a train back to Vác, Budapest or even Štúrovo in Slovakia. The train departs twice daily on weekdays and five times daily at the weekend from April to October, but only three times daily on Saturday and Sunday the rest of the year.

VISEGRÁD
☎ 26 • postcode 2025 • pop 1540
Situated on the Danube's abrupt loop, Visegrád (from the Slavic words for 'high castle') is the most beautiful section and the very symbol of the Bend. As you approach Visegrád from Szentendre, 23km to the south, keep your eyes open for the citadel high up on Castle Hill. With the palace its base, the hill was once the royal centre of Hungary.

The Romans built a border fortress on Sibrik Hill just north of the present castle in the 4th century, and it was still being used by Slovak settlers 600 years later. After the Mongol invasion in 1241, King Béla IV began work on a lower castle by the river and then on the hilltop citadel. Less than a century later, King Charles Robert of Anjou, whose claim to the local throne was being fiercely contested in Buda, moved the royal household to Visegrád and had the lower castle converted into a palace.

For almost 200 years, Visegrád was Hungary's 'other' (often summer) capital and an important diplomatic centre. But Visegrád's real golden age came during the reign of King Matthias Corvinus (r. 1458–90) and Queen Beatrice, who had Italian Renaissance craftsmen rebuild the Gothic palace. The sheer size of the residence, its stonework, fountains and hanging gardens were the talk of the 15th century throughout Europe.

The destruction of Visegrád came with the Turks and later in 1702 when the Habsburgs blew up the citadel to prevent Hungarian

independence fighters from using it as a base. All trace of the palace was lost until the 1930s when archaeologists, following descriptions in literary sources, uncovered the ruins.

Orientation & Information
The Mahart ferry pier on route No 11, just south of the city gate and opposite the Vár hotel, is one of two stops where the bus from Szentendre or Budapest will drop you off. Across the street to the right of the Vár hotel are steps to Salamon-torony utca, which leads to the lower castle and the citadel. There is also a bus stop near the village centre and the car ferry about a kilometre south on Fő utca. **Visegrád Tours** (☎ 398 160; Rév utca 15; open 9am-5pm daily) is near the Nagymaros ferry pier, but the staff aren't exactly overjoyed about handing out information. Visegrád's website is at w www.visegrad.hu. There's a small **OTP bank** (Rév utca 9) branch (but no ATM) and a **post office** (Fő utca 77) in the village centre.

Things to See
The first thing you'll see as you walk north up Salamon-torony utca to the lower castle is the 13th-century **Solomon's Tower** (☎ 398 233; adult/student or child 400/200Ft; open 9am-4.30pm Tues-Sun May-Sept), a stocky, hexagonal keep with walls up to 8m thick. Once used to control river traffic, it now houses many of the precious objects unearthed at the royal palace.

North of the tower, a trail marked 'Fellegvár' turns southeast at a fork and leads up to **Visegrád Citadel** (☎ 398 101; adult/ student & child 500/250Ft; open 9.30am-6pm daily mid-Mar–mid-Oct, weekends only rest of year), sitting atop a 350m hill and surrounded by moats hewn from solid rock. Completed in 1259, the citadel was the repository for the Hungarian crown jewels until 1440, when Elizabeth of Luxembourg, the daughter of King Sigismund, stole them with the help of her lady-in-waiting and hurried off to Székesfehérvár to have her infant son László crowned king. (The crown was returned to the citadel in 1464 and held here – under a stronger lock, no doubt – until the Turkish invasion.)

There's a small pictorial exhibit in the residential rooms on the west side of the citadel and two smaller displays near the east gate: one on hunting and falconry, the other on

DANUBE BEND

traditional occupations in the region (stone-cutting, charcoal-burning, beekeeping and fishing). There's also a small **wax museum** of fairly lifelike torture victims. Restoration work on the three defensive levels of the citadel will continue for many years, but it's great fun just walking along the ramparts of this eyrie, admiring the views of the Börzsöny Hills and the Danube.

If you're walking to the citadel from the village centre, Kálvária sétány, a trail beginning from behind the 18th-century Catholic church on Fő tér, is less steep than the trail from Solomon's Tower. You can also reach it by minibus (see Getting Around later).

The **Visegrád Royal Palace** (*Visegrádi királyi palota;* ☎ 398 026; *Fő utca 29; adult/child 400/200Ft; open 9am-4.30pm Tues-Sun)*, the

15th-century seat of King Matthias, once had 350 rooms and was said to be unrivalled in Europe. Everything you see at the terraced palace today – the Court of Honour with its working Renaissance Hercules Fountain in the centre, the arcaded Gothic hallways, the Lion Fountain and the foundations of St George's Chapel (1366) – are reconstructions or replicas. The history of the palace and its reconstruction is told in the **King Mathias Museum** inside the palace. Also on display are architectural finds, including richly carved stones dating from the 14th century.

Activities

There are some easy **walks** and **hikes** in the immediate vicinity of Visegrád Citadel – to the 377m high Nagy-Villám Lookout Tower,

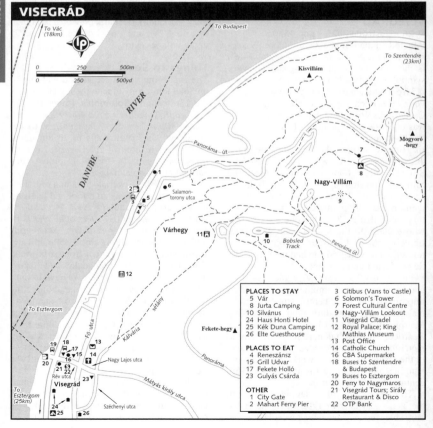

PLACES TO STAY
5 Vár
8 Jurta Camping
10 Silvánus
24 Haus Honti Hotel
25 Kék Duna Camping
26 Elte Guesthouse

PLACES TO EAT
4 Reneszánsz
15 Grill Udvar
17 Fekete Holló
23 Gulyás Csárda

OTHER
1 City Gate
2 Mahart Ferry Pier
3 Citibus (Vans to Castle)
6 Solomon's Tower
7 Forest Cultural Centre
9 Nagy-Villám Lookout
11 Visegrád Citadel
12 Royal Palace; King Mathias Museum
13 Post Office
14 Catholic Church
16 CBA Supermarket
18 Buses to Szentendre & Budapest
19 Buses to Esztergom
20 Ferry to Nagymaros
21 Visegrád Tours; Sirály Restaurant & Disco
22 OTP Bank

for example. Across from the Jurta camping ground is the sod and wood Forest Cultural Centre designed by Imre Makovecz. It contains a small wildlife exhibit.

A 750m **bobsled track** *(bob-pálya; ☎ 397 397; adult/child 320/250Ft; open 10am-5pm daily Apr-Sept; 11am-4pm public holidays Oct-Mar)* on which you wend your way down a metal chute while sitting on a felt-bottomed cart, is on the hillside below the lookout.

Places to Stay
Jurta Camping *(☎ 398 217; camping per adult/child/tent 550/350/420Ft; open May-Sept)*, is up on Mogyoró-hegy (Hazelnut Hill), about 2km northeast of the citadel. It's nicely situated but far from the centre (and bus service is infrequent).

Kék Duna Camping *(☎ 398 102, Fő utca 70; camping per adult/child up to 14/tent 700Ft/free/600Ft, bungalows per person 2500Ft; open May-Sept)* is a rather bland camp site by the highway south of the Nagymaros ferry. Bungalows sleep up to five.

Visegrád Tours *(☎ 398 160; Rév utca 15; open 9am-5pm daily)* can organise private rooms from 4000/5900Ft for singles/doubles. Many houses along Fő utca (eg, Nos 60 and 107) and Széchenyi utca (Nos 16/a, 21 and 39) have signs advertising rooms.

Elte *(☎/fax 398 165; Fő utca 117; singles/doubles 3200/5900Ft; open Apr-Sept)* is a four-storey guesthouse with accommodation that is almost as cheap as a private room. There are 33 basic rooms available as singles or doubles.

Haus Honti *(☎ 398 120, fax 397 274; Fő utca 66; singles/doubles 9000/10,000Ft)* is a friendly, 30-room hotel with a new building just off the main road to Esztergom and an older one next to a picturesque little stream *(singles/doubles 7000/8000Ft)*.

Vár *(☎ 397 522, fax 397 572; e varhotel visegrad@axelero.hu; Fő utca 9; rooms €61)*, a 21-room hotel in a lovely, renovated old building, is convenient to the Mahart boat pier but also faces busy, noisy route No 11.

Silvánus *(☎ 398 311, fax 597 516; e ho telsilvanus@mail.matav.hu; singles/doubles from 11,000/12,000Ft)*, a 94-room hotel on Fekete-hegy (Black Hill), a few minutes' walk east of the citadel, has a great location, terrace restaurant and bar, swimming pool, tennis and squash courts and tenpin bowling.

Places to Eat
Grill Udvar *(Rév utca 6; pizzas & mains from 500Ft)*, opposite the bank, is a simple, inexpensive place with sturdy pizzas and Hungarian dishes.

Reneszánsz *(☎ 398 081; Fő utca 11; mains 900-1500Ft)*, a medieval banquet–themed restaurant with men in tights and silly hats, can be a lot of fun.

Fekete Holló *(Rév utca 12; mains around 1000Ft)* is a somewhat touristy fish restaurant opposite the Nagymaros ferry pier in the village.

Gulyás Csárda *(☎ 398 329, Nagy Lajos utca 4; mains around 1000Ft)*, across from the church, is a more relaxed affair with terrace seating.

Sirály *(☎ 398 376; Rév utca 15; mains 1200-2000Ft)* is a popular restaurant with tourists and locals alike, but it's expensive. This place often has live music and a disco at the weekend.

Getting There & Away
Bus & Train Buses are very frequent (up to 16 daily) to/from Budapest's Árpád híd station, Szentendre and Esztergom. No railway line reaches Visegrád, but you can take one of two dozen daily trains to Szob from Nyugati station in Budapest. You'll need to get off at Nagymaros-Visegrád, and you can then hop on the ferry to Visegrád.

Boat Between mid-June and early September, three daily Mahart ferries (the times are 7.30am, 9am, and 2pm) leave Budapest for Visegrád (870/1740Ft one way/return, 3½ hours). Two of these ferries continue on to Esztergom at 10.55am and 5pm. Ferries to Budapest depart from Visegrád at 10.30am, 4.30pm and 5.30pm; only the first two ferries stop in Szentendre on the way. On Saturday and Sunday from July to mid-August a high-speed hydrofoil runs from Budapest to Visegrád (1790/2990Ft, one hour), departing from Budapest at 9.30am and from Visegrád at 3.55pm.

Hourly ferries cross the Danube to Nagymaros (170/170/700Ft per person/bicycle/car) from around 5.30am to 8.30pm. The ferry operates all year except when the Danube freezes over or fog descends. From Nagymaros-Visegrád train station, just inland from the ferry pier, there are trains to Budapest's Nyugati station about every hour.

Getting Around

Citibus (☎ 311 996), a taxi van service, leaves from the Mahart boat pier three times daily (9.26am, 12.26pm and 3.26pm) from April to September, stopping at the Nagymaros ferry pier two minutes later before carrying on to Jurta Camping via the citadel.

AROUND VISEGRÁD
Pilis Hills

If you want to explore the protected forest in the Pilis, the limestone and dolomite hills southwest of Visegrád, take the Esztergom bus for 6km to Dömös, where there is an excellent river beach and **Dömös Camping** (☎ 33-482 319; W www.domoscamping.hu; camping per adult/child/tent/caravan 700/ 550/700/800Ft; open May–mid-Sept), with tent sites, and includes well-equipped cottages (11,000Ft) that sleep up to four.

If you follow Duna utca across from the camp site for 3km, you'll reach the entrance to the 25,000-hectare **Pilis Park Forest**, where Matthias Corvinus once hunted and Hungary's first hiking trails were laid in 1869. It now forms part of the Danube-Ipoly National Park. Marked trails lead to **Prédikálószék** (Pulpit Seat), a 639m crag for experienced hikers and climbers only, and to **Dobogókő** (699m), a much easier ascent of about three hours via the **Rám-szakadék** (Rám Precipice). Some of the best bird-watching in western Hungary is in these hills.

At Dobogókő there's an excursion centre with further trails mapped out, or you can catch a bus to Esztergom (there are four or five a day) or to the HÉV station in Pomáz, two stops before Szentendre.

Alternatively, you can take the small ferry (300Ft; runs on demand) across the Danube from Dömös to Dömösi átkelés (on the train line two stops from Nagymaros-Visegrád, then climb to the caves that are visible on the hillside and hike back into the hills behind Nagymaros.

Cartographia's 1:40,000 *A Pilis és a Visegrádi-helység* (The Pilis and Visegrád Hills) map (No 16; 650Ft) outlines the many hiking possibilities for the entire area.

ESZTERGOM

☎ 33 • postcode 2500 • pop 29,300

Esztergom, 25km from Visegrád and 66km from Budapest via route No 11, is one of Hungary's most historical and sacred cities. For more than 1000 years it has been the seat of Roman Catholicism – the archbishop of Esztergom is the primate of Hungary. The country's first king, St Stephen, was born here in 975, and it was a royal seat from the late 10th- to mid-13th centuries. For these and many other reasons, Esztergom has both great spiritual and temporal significance for most Hungarians.

Esztergom lies on a high point above a slight curve of the Danube across from the Slovakian city of Štúrovo (Hungarian: Párkány), which can be reached by the rebuilt Mária Valéria Bridge (see Other Attractions). Vár-hegy (Castle Hill) was the site of the Roman settlement of Solva Mansio in the 1st century, and it is thought that emperor-to-be Marcus Aurelius finished his *Meditations* in a camp nearby during the second half of the 2nd century.

Prince Géza chose Esztergom as his capital, and his son Vajk (as he was known before his baptism) was crowned King Stephen here in 1000. Stephen founded one of the country's two archbishoprics and a basilica at Esztergom, bits of which can be seen in the palace.

Esztergom (German: Gran) lost its political significance when King Béla IV moved the capital to Buda following the Mongol invasion in 1241. It remained an important trading centre and the ecclesiastical seat, however, vying with the royal court for power and influence. Esztergom's capture by the Turks in 1543 interrupted the church's activities, and the archbishop fled to Nagyszombat (now Trnava in Slovakia).

The church did not re-establish its base here – the 'Hungarian Rome' – until the early 19th century. It was then that Esztergom went on a building spree that transformed it into a city of late baroque and, in particular, neo-classical buildings.

Orientation

The modern centre of Esztergom is Rákóczi tér, a few steps east of the Kis-Duna (Little Danube), the tributary that branches off to form Prímás-sziget (Primate Island). Along Bajcsy-Zsilinszky utca to the northwest is Castle Hill. To the southwest of Rákóczi tér is Széchenyi tér, the town centre in the Middle Ages and site of the rococo Town Hall.

Esztergom's bus station is near the street market on Simor János utca, 700m south of Rákóczi tér. The train station is another 1.2km farther south on Bem József tér. Mahart boats dock at the pier just south of Mária Valéria Bridge on Primate Island.

Information

Gran Tours (☎/fax 502 000; e grantours@vnet.hu; Széchenyi tér 25; open 8am-6pm Mon-Fri, 9am-noon June-Aug; 8am-4pm Mon-Fri Sept-May) is the visitor centre run by the city of Esztergom and is very helpful. You could also try **Cathedralis Tours** (☎ 415 260; cnr Bajcsy-Zsilinszky utca & Batthyány Lajos utca; open 8am-5pm Mon-Fri, 9am-noon Sat) for information.

There's an **OTP bank** (Rákóczi tér) and a branch of a **K&H bank** (Rákóczi tér) diagonally opposite each other on the main square. The **post office** (Arany János utca 2) is entered from Széchenyi tér.

Internet access is available at the **Leisure-Time Centre** (Szabadidő központ; ☎ 313 888; Bajcsy-Zsilinszky utca 4; open 8am-9pm Mon-Fri, 8am-5pm Sat, 8am-noon Sun) for 300Ft per half-hour.

Esztergom Basilica

The Basilica (Főszékesegyház; ☎ 411 895; admission free; open 7am-6pm daily), centre of Hungarian Catholicism and the largest church in the country, is in Szent István tér on Castle Hill, and its 72m-high central dome can be seen soaring up for many kilometres around. The building of the present neoclassical church was begun in 1822 on the site of a 12th-century one destroyed by the Turks. József Hild, who designed the cathedral at Eger, was involved in the final stages, and the

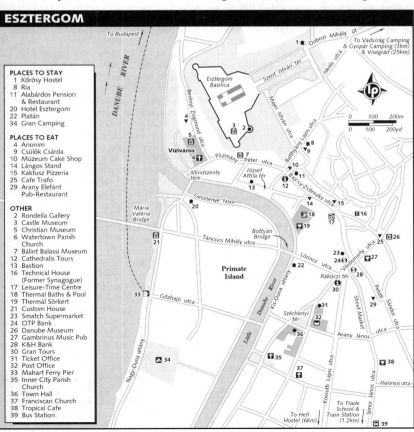

ESZTERGOM

PLACES TO STAY
1 Kőrösy Hostel
8 Ria
11 Alabárdos Pension & Restaurant
20 Hotel Esztergom
22 Platán
34 Gran Camping

PLACES TO EAT
4 Anonim
9 Csülök Csárda
10 Múzeum Cake Shop
14 Lángos Stand
15 Kaktusz Pizzeria
25 Cafe Trafo
29 Arany Elefánt Pub-Restaurant

OTHER
2 Rondella Gallery
3 Castle Museum
5 Christian Museum
6 Watertown Parish Church
7 Bálint Balassi Museum
12 Cathedralis Tours
13 Bastion
16 Technical House (Former Synagogue)
17 Leisure-Time Centre
18 Thermal Baths & Pool
19 Thermál Sörkert
21 Custom House
23 Smatch Supermarket
24 OTP Bank
26 Danube Museum
27 Gambrinus Music Pub
28 K&H Bank
30 Gran Tours
31 Ticket Office
32 Post Office
33 Mahart Ferry Pier
35 Inner City Parish Church
36 Town Hall
37 Franciscan Church
38 Tropical Cafe
39 Bus Station

Cardinal Mindszenty

Born József Pehm in the village of Csehimind-szent, near Szombathely, in 1892, Mindszenty was politically active from the time of his ordination in 1915. Imprisoned under the short-lived regime of communist Béla Kun in 1919 and again when the fascist Iron Cross came to power in 1944, Mindszenty was made archbishop of Esztergom (and thus primate of Hungary) in 1945 and cardinal the following year.

When the new cardinal refused to secularise Hungary's Roman Catholic schools under the new communist regime in 1948, he was arrested, tortured and sentenced to life imprisonment for treason. Released during the 1956 Uprising, Mindszenty took refuge in the US Embassy on Szabadság tér when the communists returned to power. There he would remain until 1971.

As relations between the Kádár regime and the Holy See began to thaw in the late 1960s, the Vatican made several requests for the cardinal to leave Hungary, which he refused. Following the intervention of US President Richard Nixon, Mindszenty left for Vienna, where he continued to criticise the Vatican's relations with the regime in Hungary. He retired in 1974 and died the following year. But as he had vowed not to return to Esztergom until the last Soviet soldier had left Hungarian soil, Mindszenty's remains were not returned until May 1991 – several weeks before the last soldier had actually left.

basilica was consecrated in 1856 with a sung Mass composed by Franz Liszt.

The grey church is colossal (118m long and 40m wide) and rather bleak inside, but the white and red marble **Bakócz Chapel** on the south side is a splendid example of Italian Renaissance stone-carving and sculpture. It was commissioned by Archbishop Tamás Bakócz who, failing in his bid for the papacy, launched a crusade that turned into the peasant uprising under György Dózsa in 1514 (see History in the Facts about Hungary chapter). The chapel escaped most – though not all – of the Turks' axes; notice the smashed-in faces of Gabriel and other angels above the altar. It was dismantled into 1600 separate pieces and then reassembled in its present location in 1823. The copy of Titian's *Assumption* over

the cathedral's main altar is said to be the world's largest painting on a single canvas.

On the northwest side of the church, to the left of the macabre relics of three priests martyred in Košice early in the 17th century and canonised as saints by Pope John Paul II in 1995, lies the entrance to the **treasury** *(kincstár; adult/child 250/150Ft; open 9am-4.30pm daily mid-Mar–Oct; 11am-3.30pm daily Nov–mid-Mar)*, an Aladdin's cave of vestments and religious plates in gold and silver and studded with jewels. It is the richest ecclesiastical collection in Hungary and contains Byzantine, Hungarian and Italian objects of sublime workmanship and great artistic merit. Watch out for the 13th-century Coronation Oath Cross, the Garamszentbenedek Monstrance (1500), the Matthias Calvary Cross of gold and enamel (1469) and the large baroque Maria Theresa Chalice.

Before you leave the cathedral, go through the door on the left and down to the **crypt** *(admission 50Ft; open 9am-5pm daily)* a series of spooky vaults with tombs guarded by monoliths representing Mourning and Eternity. Among those at rest down here are János Vitéz, Esztergom's enlightened Renaissance archbishop, and József Mindszenty, the conservative primate who holed up in the US Embassy in Budapest from 1956 to 1971 (see the boxed text 'Cardinal Mindszenty'). It's worth making the twisting climb up to the **cupola** *(admission 100Ft)* for the outstanding views over the city – this is not for the faint-hearted, particularly when it's windy. The stairs leading to the cupola are to the left of the crypt entrance.

Castle Museum

This small museum *(Vármúzeum; ☎ 415 986; Szent István tér 1; adult/student & child 400/200Ft; open 9am-4.30pm Tues-Sun Apr-Oct; 10am-4pm Tues-Sun Nov-Mar)* at the southern end of Castle Hill is housed in half a dozen rooms of the former Royal Palace, which was built mostly by French architects under Béla III (r. 1172–96) during Esztergom's golden age. The palace was the king's residence until the capital was relocated to Buda – at which time the archbishop moved in. Most of the palace was destroyed and covered with earth for defensive purposes under the Turks; it did not see the light of day again until excavations began in the 1930s.

The museum concentrates on archaeological finds from the town and its surrounding area, the majority of which is pottery dating from the 11th century onwards. Other points of interest include some of the Basilica's original ornate capitals and a fantastic view across the Danube to Slovakia. Unfortunately everything is labelled in Hungarian only.

The **Rondella Gallery** to the east is housed in a corner bastion with rotating exhibits and hosts touristy song and dance performances in summer.

Other Attractions

Below Castle Hill on the banks of the Little Danube is **Víziváros**, the colourful 'Watertown' district of pastel town houses, churches and museums. The easiest way to get there is to walk over the palace drawbridge and down the grassy hill to Batthyány Lajos utca. Turn west onto Pázmány Péter utca.

The **Bálint Balassi Museum** (*☎ 413 185; Pázmány Péter utca 13; adult/student & child 100/50Ft; open 9am-5pm Tues-Sun*), in an 18th-century baroque building, has objects of local interest, with much emphasis on the churches and monasteries of medieval Esztergom. The museum is named in honour of the general and lyric poet who was killed during an unsuccessful attempt to retake Esztergom Castle from the Turks in 1594.

Past the Italianate **Watertown parish church** (Víziváros plébániatemplom) from 1738, which is vaguely reminiscent of the glorious Minorite church in Eger, you'll come to the former Bishop's Palace at Mindszenty hercegprímás tere 2. Today it houses the **Christian Museum** (*☎ 413 880; Mindszenty hercegprímás tere 2; adult/student & child 250/150Ft; open 10am-6pm Tues-Sun*), the finest collection of medieval religious art in Hungary and one of the best museums in the country. Established by Archbishop János Simor in 1875, it contains Hungarian Gothic triptychs and altarpieces, later works by German, Dutch and Italian masters, tapestries, and what is arguably the most beautiful object in the nation: the sublime **Holy Sepulchre of Garamszentbenedek** (1480). It's a sort of wheeled cart in the shape of a cathedral with richly carved figures of the 12 Apostles (above) and Roman soldiers (below) guarding Christ's tomb. It was used at Easter Week processions and was painstakingly restored in the 1970s.

Be sure to see Tamás Kolozsvári's *Calvary* altar panel (1427), which was influenced by Italian art, the late Gothic *Christ's Passion* by 'Master M S', the gruesome *Martyrdom of the Three Apostles* (1490) by the so-called Master of the Martyr Apostles, and the *Temptation of St Anthony* (1530) by Jan Wellens de Cock, with its drug-like visions of devils and temptresses. The museum's displays are labelled in five languages, and a guided tour in English (2500Ft) can be booked by ringing the museum in advance.

Cross the bridge south of Watertown Parish Church and around 100m farther south is the recently completed **Mária Valéria Bridge**. Destroyed during WWII, it once again connects Esztergom with the Slovakian city of Štúrovo. The bridge's original **Custom House** (*admission free; open 9am-6pm Tues-Sun*) has also undergone extensive repairs, and now contains an exhibition on the bridge's history on the 1st floor.

The so-called **Technical House** (*Technika Háza; Imaház utca 4*) built in 1888, once served as a synagogue for Esztergom's Jewish community, the oldest in Hungary, and now houses a science association. It was designed in Moorish Romantic style by Lipót Baumhorn, the master architect who also engineered the synagogues in Szeged, Szolnok and Gyöngyös. Close by is the **Danube Museum** (*☎ 500 250; Kölcsey utca 2; adult/student & child 300/100Ft; open 10am-6pm Wed-Mon May-Oct; 10am-4pm Wed-Mon Nov-Apr*) with displays on – you guessed it – life on the river.

Activities

Between the still vacant Fürdő hotel and the Little Danube there are **outdoor thermal pools** (*☎ 312 249; Bajcsy-Zsilinszky utca 14; adult/child 350/150Ft; open 9am-6pm May-Sept*). You can use the **indoor pool** (*open 6am-6pm Mon & Sat, 6am-7pm Tues-Fri, 9am-4pm Sun*) year-round.

Esztergom also provides good opportunities for hiking.

Places to Stay

Camping The small but central **Gran Camping** (*☎ 411 953, fax 402 513; e for anex@elender.hu; Nagy-Duna sétány 3; camping per adult/child/tent/car 950/500/950/1000Ft, bungalows 9000-13,000Ft, doubles 6500Ft; open May-Sept*), on Primate Island, also has a hostel with dorm beds for 1700Ft. The bungalows have four to six beds.

Gyopár Camping (☎ 311 401, Vaskapui út; camping per adult/child/tent/car 550/360/450/450Ft; open mid-Apr–mid-Oct) is on Sípoló-hegyy, some 3km to the east (bus No 1) and has views of the Basilica and Slovakia.

Vadvirág Camping (☎ 312 234, fax 310 753; route No 11, 63km stone; camping per adult/child/tent/car 700/300/700/600Ft; bungalow/motel/apartment rooms per person 1100/1500/3500Ft; open May-Sept) has accommodation to suit most travellers and can be found at Bánomi dűlő, 3km on the way to Visegrád (bus No 6).

Private Rooms & Hostels See Gran Tours (☎/fax 502 000; e grantours@vnet.hu; Széchenyi tér 25; open 8am-6pm Mon-Fri, 9am-noon June-Aug; 8am-4pm Mon-Fri Sept-May) for private rooms (2000Ft per person) or apartments (6000Ft).

The **trade school** (☎ 411 746; Budai Nagy Antal utca 38; dorm beds 1200Ft) near the train station, has dormitory rooms available during the summer break.

Kőrösy (☎ 400 005; Szent István tér 16; dorm beds 2700Ft per person), hostel is usually the László Kőrösy College opposite the basilica but becomes a hostel during the college's summer break.

Hell (☎/fax 319 144; Wesselényi utca 40-42; bed in 3-bed/4-bed dorm 3000/2500Ft) is the unfortunate name given to this hostel, otherwise known as the József Károly Hell College. It is 6km south of the centre in Esztergom-Kertváros and, like the other colleges, becomes a hostel during the summer months.

Pensions & Hotels Friendly **Platán** (☎ 411 355; Kis-Duna sétány 11; rooms from 4200Ft) is more like a small, budget hotel with 23 well-used rooms. The entrance is to the right as you walk into the courtyard.

Alabárdos (☎/fax 312 640; Bajcsy-Zsilinszky utca 49; singles/doubles 6000/9000Ft) is closer to the sights than Platán and its 22 rooms are in a much better state.

Another place, which is a short distance north on a quiet street, is **Ria** (☎ 313 115, fax 401 429; Batthyány Lajos utca 11; singles/doubles 8500/ 10,500Ft). It has 13 homy rooms and bicycles to rent.

The modern block of **Hotel Esztergom** (☎ 412 555, fax 412 853; e hotelesz@elen der.hu; Nagy-Duna sétány; singles/doubles €42/56) is on Primate Island, close to Mária Valéria bridge. As well as 36 rooms there's a rather fancy restaurant, a roof terrace and a sports centre with a tennis court and canoes for rent.

Places to Eat

The cheapest place in town to grab a bite to eat is the small **lángos stand** at the entrance to the thermal pools.

Csülök Csárda (☎ 312 420; Batthyány Lajos utca 9; mains from 850Ft) is a charming eatery that's popular with both visitors and locals and serves good home cooking and huge main courses.

Anonim (☎ 411 880; Berényi Zsigmond utca 4; mains 1000-2400Ft; open until 10pm daily), in an attractive old town house, serves small but excellent dishes.

Arany Elefánt (☎ 411 592; Petőfi Sándor utca 15; mains 500-1000Ft; open until 10pm daily) is an attractive pub-restaurant just east of the market area.

Kaktusz Pizzeria (Bajcsy-Zsilinszky utca 25-27; pizzas from 450Ft; open until 10pm daily) is a place to head for pizza, pasta and salads.

Cafe Trafó (Vörösmarty utca 15; coffee from 100Ft) is a modern little island oasis (literally) – a great place to take a breather, sit back and relax.

Múzeum (cnr Bajcsy-Zsilinszky utca & Batthyány utca; cakes from 100Ft) is one of the better cake shops in Esztergom.

Entertainment

Organ concerts take place in the cathedral in summer, the Esztergom Chroniclers sometimes perform ancient Hungarian music at the palace, and a bunch of concerts and plays are held in the town from mid-July to mid-August; check with the **ticket office** (☎ 412 637; Széchenyi tér 7; open 9am-4pm Mon-Fri May-Sept; 9am-1pm Mon-Fri Oct-Apr) or visit w www.esztergominyarijatekok.hu.

The **Leisure-Time Centre** (Szabadidő központ; ☎ 313 888; Bajcsy-Zsilinszky utca 4; open 8am-9pm Mon-Fri, 8am-5pm Sat, 8am-noon Sun) has a cinema and rotating exhibits.

Thermál Sörkert, in the outdoor thermal pool grounds (see Activities earlier for details), is the place to be on a balmy summer evening; its outdoor seating area is jam-packed with a young crowd trying to be heard over the music.

Tropical Cafe *(Simor János utca 44)* is popular with students from the nearby trade school.

Gambrinus Music Pub *(Vörösmarty utca 3; open until 3am Fri & Sat)* is a popular place with live acts, and like many bars in Hungary, has a Wild West theme.

For up-to-date entertainment information, check the listings in the bi-weekly *Komárom-Esztergomi Est.*

Getting There & Away

Bus Buses to/from Budapest's Árpád híd station run about every half-hour from 4am or 4.30am to 6.30pm; count on as many as 20 buses on Sunday. The buses may go via Dorog (75 minutes) or Visegrád (two hours). Buses to Visegrád and Szentendre depart almost hourly between 6am and 8.40pm. Other important destinations served are limited: Balatonfüred (one bus daily), Dobogókő (two), Komárom (two), Pilisszentlélek (one); Sopron (one), Tata via Tatabánya (two), and Veszprém (one).

Train Trains to Esztergom depart from Nyugati train station in Budapest up to 13 times daily. To get to Western Transdanubia from Esztergom, you could take one of the three daily trains to Komárom, where you can change for Győr, Székesfehérvár and Vienna.

Boat Mahart river boats travel from Budapest's Vigadó tér in Pest and Batthyány tér in Buda to Esztergom (910/1820Ft one way/return, half-price for children aged four to 14, five hours) once daily from late May to mid-June, and twice daily from mid-June to late September. From April to late May and September to seasonal shutdown, there's only one boat that runs on Saturday and Sunday. A speedy hydrofoil makes the run from Budapest to Esztergom (1990/3390Ft, 1½ hours) on Saturday and Sunday only between early July and mid-August. The boats depart from Budapest at 9.30am and from Esztergom at 3.30pm.

DANUBE BEND

Western Transdanubia

As its name suggests, Western Transdanubia (Nyugat-Dunántúl) lies 'across the Danube' from Budapest, stretching west and southwest to the borders with Austria and Slovenia. It is a region of hills and plains, with some of the most historically important towns, castles, churches and monuments in Hungary. As the nation's 'window on the West', it has always been the richest and most developed region of Hungary, and remains popular with Austrian day-trippers in search of cheaper goods and services.

The Danube River was the limit of Roman expansion in what is now Hungary, and most of Western Transdanubia formed the province of Upper Pannonia. The Romans built some of their most important military and civil towns here – Arrabona (Győr), Scarbantia (Sopron), Savaria (Szombathely), Adflexum (Mosonmagyaróvár) and Brigetio (Komárom). Because of their positions on the trade route from northern Europe to the Adriatic and Byzantium, and the influx of Germans, Slovaks and other ethnic groups, these towns prospered in the Middle Ages. Episcopates were established, castles were built and many of the towns were granted special royal privileges.

A large part of Western Transdanubia remained in the hands of the Habsburgs during the Turkish occupation, and it was thus spared the ruination suffered in the south or on the Great Plain. As a result, some of the best examples of Romanesque and Gothic architecture can be found here. Because of the influence of Vienna continued throughout the 16th and 17th centuries, Western Transdanubia received Hungary's first baroque churches and public buildings. That domination by Austria continued, with parts of the region changing hands several times over the following centuries.

Western Transdanubia took a pounding during WWII, and though many of the town centres were spared, the outlying districts were demolished. As a result, they have distinctly similar appearances: a medieval or baroque core ringed with concrete housing blocks, factories and sometimes farmland. The region was industrialised after the war, especially around Tatabánya and Győr. Agriculture is less important here, though Sopron and Mór are wine centres.

Highlights

- The Imre Patkó Collection of Asian and African art and the Herm of László reliquary at the cathedral in Győr
- The colourful Jurisics tér in Kőszeg
- The opulent Esterházy Palace at Fertőd
- The neoclassical Széchenyi Manor at Nagycenk
- The impressive collection of weapons and armour in Sárvár's Nádasdy Castle
- The massive Benedictine abbey complex and its treasures at Pannonhalma

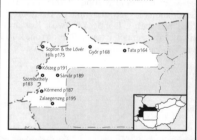

TATA
☎ 34 • postcode 2890 • pop 24,800

Tata (in German, Totis), situated west of the Gerecse Hills, is a pleasant town of springs, canals and lakes, a castle and a lot of history. Tatabánya, on the other hand, is a heavily industrial city 14km to the southeast whose only real claim to fame is a giant statue of the symbolic *turul* (see the boxed text 'Blame it on the Bird' later in this section).

Much of the action in Tata has focused in and around the 14th-century Öregvár (Old Castle) perched on a rock at the northern end of a large lake. It was a favourite residence of King Sigismund, who added a palace in the 15th century. His daughter, Elizabeth of Luxembourg, lingered here in 1440 with the purloined crown of St Stephen, en route to Székesfehérvár where her newly born son would be crowned king. King Matthias Corvinus turned Tata into a royal hunting reserve attached to Visegrád, and his successor, Vladislav (Úlászló) II, convened the Diet here

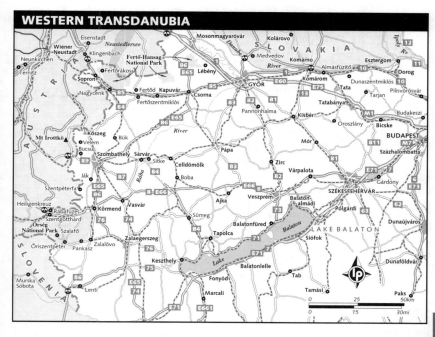

WESTERN TRANSDANUBIA

to escape from plague-ravaged Buda. Tata Castle (Öregvár) was badly damaged by the Turks in 1683, and the town did not begin its recovery until it was acquired by a branch of the aristocratic Esterházy family in the 18th century. They retained the services of Moravian-born architect Jakab Fellner, who designed most of Tata's fine baroque buildings.

Tata is as much a town of recreation as of history. Tata's two lakes offer ample opportunities for sport, and there's a spa complex to the north. Tata is also a convenient gateway to Budapest and the Danube Bend for other Western Transdanubian towns.

Orientation & Information

Tata's busy main street (Ady Endre utca), a section of route No 1, separates the larger Öreg-tó (Old Lake) from Cseke-tó (Tiny Lake). The bus station is northwest of the castle on Május 1 út. The main train staton is a couple of kilometres north of city centre. The second station, Tóvároskert, which is used only by local trains, is to the southeast and closer to the Fáklya utca camp site and hotel.

Tourinform (☎/fax 586 045; ⓔ koma rom-m@tourinform.hu; Ady Endre utca 9; open 8am-6pm Mon-Fri, 9am-5pm Sat & Sun mid-June–mid-Sept; 8am-4pm Mon-Fri mid-Sept–mid-June) is helpful, and located in the city centre.

There's a branch of the **OTP bank** (Ady Endre utca 17) opposite the Spar supermarket. The main **post office** (Kossuth tér 19) is west of the Old Lake.

You can find out more about this place by visiting the town's website (ⓦ www.tata.hu).

Öregvár

The remains of the medieval Old Castle – one of four original towers and a palace wing – were rebuilt in neo-Gothic style at the end of the 19th century just before Emperor Franz Joseph came to visit. Today they house the **Domokos Kuny Museum** (☎ 487 888; adult/concession 300/150Ft; open 10am-6pm Tues-Sun mid-Apr–Oct; 10am-2pm Wed-Fri 10am-4pm Sat & Sun Nov–mid-Apr). On the ground floor are archaeological finds from nearby Roman settlements, bits of the 12th-century Benedictine monastery near Oroszlány, and contemporary drawings of the castle in its heyday. The 'Life in the Old Castle' exhibit on the 1st floor is interesting; don't miss

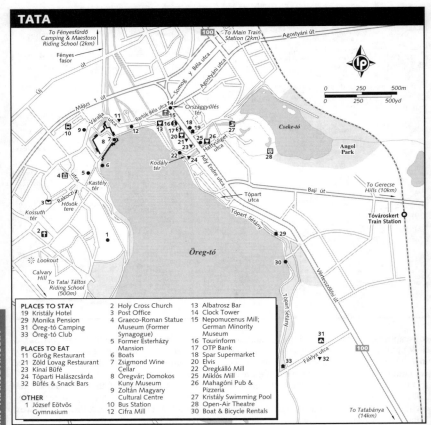

TATA

PLACES TO STAY
19 Kristály Hotel
29 Monika Pension
31 Öreg-tó Camping
33 Öreg-tó Club

PLACES TO EAT
11 Görög Restaurant
21 Zöld Lovag Restaurant
23 Kínai Büfé
24 Tóparti Halászcsárda
32 Büfés & Snack Bars

OTHER
1 József Eötvös
  Gymnasium

2 Holy Cross Church
3 Post Office
4 Graeco-Roman Statue
  Museum (Former
  Synagogue)
5 Former Esterházy
  Mansion
6 Boats
7 Zsigmond Wine
  Cellar
8 Öregvár; Domokos
  Kuny Museum
9 Zoltán Magyary
  Cultural Centre
10 Bus Station
12 Cifra Mill

13 Albatrosz Bar
14 Clock Tower
15 Nepomucenus Mill;
   German Minority
   Museum
16 Tourinform
17 OTP Bank
18 Spar Supermarket
20 Elvis
22 Öregkálló Mill
25 Miklós Mill
26 Mahagóni Pub &
   Pizzeria
27 Kristály Swimming Pool
28 Open-Air Theatre
30 Boat & Bicycle Rentals

the cathedral-like Gothic stove that takes pride of place in the **Knights' Hall**. Material on the 2nd floor examines the work of a dozen 18th-century artisans, including Kuny, a master ceramist. Tata porcelain was well known for centuries (the lobster or crayfish was a common decoration here) and the craft indirectly led to the foundation of the porcelain factory at Herend near Veszprém (see the boxed text 'Herend Porcelain' in the Lake Balaton Region chapter). The castle's neoclassical **chapel** (1822) is also open to the public.

Mills

Öregvár, attractively reflected in the lake, is surrounded by a moat, and a system of locks and sluices regulates the flow of water into nearby canals. Tata made good use of this water power; it was once known as the 'town of mills'. The shell of the 16th-century **Cifra Mill** (Cifra-malom; Bartók Béla utca 3), east of the castle, is interesting only for its red marble window frames and five water wheels visible from the north side.

The magnificently restored **Nepomucenus Mill** (Alkotmány utca 1), a bit further on, was built in 1758 and now houses the **German Minority Museum** (☎ 487 682; adult/student or child 120/60Ft) with the same opening times as Öregvár. Like Pécs and Székesfehérvár, Tata was predominantly German-speaking for several centuries and all aspects of the German experience in Hungary are explored here. The collections of festive clothing and musical instruments are in very good condition. Other mills on or around the lake include the

Öregkálló Mill on Tópart sétány and the **Miklós Mill** (*Ady Endre utca 26*), which can only be inspected from the outside.

Other Attractions

Walking southwest from the castle for a few minutes through leafy Kastély tér to Hősök tere, you'll pass the Zopf-style former **Esterházy Mansion** designed by Jakab Fellner (built 1764–69); it is just one of four in the town and served as a hospital for some years. In the old Romantic-style former synagogue (which, like so many in Hungary, is in a sad state of disrepair) is the weird **Graeco-Roman Statue Museum** (*☎ 381 251; Hősök tere 3; adult/student or child 100/50Ft; open 10am–6pm Tues-Sun mid-Apr–Oct*). Here you'll find displays of plaster copies of stone sculptures that lined the walkways of Cseke-tó in the 19th century. At Bercsényi utca 1, just before you enter Kossuth tér, stands the birthplace of Mór Farkasházi Fischer, founder of the Herend porcelain factory and Tata's most famous son. Dominating the square is another of Fellner's works, the 18th-century **Holy Cross Church** (Szent Kereszt-templom), also called the Great Church. If you're up to it, a sadly neglected crucifixion shrine, 14th-century Gothic chapel and a dodgy-looking 45m-high **lookout tower** (*adult/student or child 140/100Ft; open 9am–5pm Tues-Sun*) await at the top of **Calvary Hill** (Kálvária-domb), a short distance to the south. You can look east to the Gerecse Hills, north into Slovakia and south to the urban wasteland of Tatabánya.

Cseke-tó, surrounded by the protected 200-hectare Angolpark, built in 1780 and Hungary's first 'English park', is a relaxing place walking or a day of fishing.

The octagonal wooden **clock tower** (*óratorny; Országgyűlés tér*) is a lot older than it looks. It was designed by – guess who? – Fellner in 1763, and at one time it housed the town's tiny prison.

Activities

As odd as it may seem with a main highway only 100m away, Öreg-tó (a nature conservation area) attracts a considerable number and variety of waterfowl; see 'The Birds of Hungary' boxed text in the Facts about Hungary chapter. The best spot for **bird-watching** in winter is at the southern end of the lake, where a warm spring prevents that part of the lake from freezing over.

Blame it on the Bird

The ancient Magyars were strong believers in magic and celestial intervention, and the *táltos* (shaman) enjoyed an elevated position in their society. Certain animals – for example, bears, stags and wolves – were totemic, and it was taboo to mention them directly by name. Thus the wolf was 'the long-tailed one' and the stag the 'large-antlered one'. In other cases the original Magyar word for an animal deemed sacred was replaced with a foreign loan word: *medve* for 'bear' comes from the Slavic *medved*.

No other totemic animal is better known to modern Hungarians than the *turul*, an eagle or hawk-like bird that had supposedly impregnated Emese, the grandmother of Árpád. That legend can be viewed in many ways: as an attempt to foster a sense of common origin and group identity in the ethnically heterogeneous population of the time; as an effort to bestow a sacred origin on the House of Árpád and its rule; or just as a good story.

The lake has several **swimming beaches**, and **pleasure boats** (300/200Ft) depart from the pier just southwest of the castle and on the eastern shore of the lake, where you can also rent **bicycles** (*☎ 06-204 320 420; open 1pm–9pm daily in season*). Two **riding schools** operate in Tata; Maestoso (*☎ 485 039; Fényes-dűlő*) is north of the city centre near Fényes spa, and Tatai Táltos (*☎ 381 018; Fekete utca 2*) is south of Calvary Hill.

The **Kristály swimming pool** (*adult/ student or child 300/150Ft; open 9am-7pm daily mid-May–Sept*) is near Angolpark, but you'll probably prefer the complex at **Fényesfürdő** (*adult/student or child 600/ 400Ft*) north of the city centre (see Places to Stay). It is open the same hours and has thermal spas and several huge pools.

If you plan on doing any **hiking** in the Gerecse Hills east of Tata, get a head start by taking a bus to Tardos, Tarján or Dunaszentmiklós. Cartographia publishes a 1:40,000 map of the area with clear trail markings entitled *A Gerecse* (No 10; 650Ft).

Places to Stay

Fényesfürdő Camping (*☎/fax 481 208; e fen yescamping@axelero.hu; Fényes fasor; camping per tent/person 400/700Ft, bungalows* *sleeping 4/6 6400/9000Ft; open May-Sept)* is about 2km north of the city centre and connected to the spa complex. It also has motel rooms for 4000Ft per person and apartments which sleep four for 17,000Ft.

Öreg-tó Camping *(☎/fax 383 496;* e *oreg to@mail.matav.hu; Fáklya utca 1; camping per tent/adult/child 800/900/500Ft, bungalows with/without shower per person 2200/ 1700Ft; open May-Sept)* is south of the city centre, and is handy to the big lake.

Öreg-tó Club *(☎/fax 487 960, Fáklya utca 4; bungalows per person 950Ft, singles/ doubles 3700/6900Ft, apartments 9000Ft)* is right near the big lake and has 19 basic bungalows with shared facilities, and a 24-room hotel.

You'll find **private rooms** available near the Kristály swimming pool at Hattyúliget utca 2.

Monika *(☎/fax 383 208; Tópart sétány; rooms 7900Ft)* is not the most modern pension, but it's right on the big lake and it has a good price for couples. Ask for a room with balcony facing the lake.

Kristály *(☎ 383 577, fax 383 614; Ady Endre utca 22; singles/doubles with bathroom 9500/10,500Ft; doubles with shower 7000Ft)* is in a 200-year-old former Esterházy holding. It has a restaurant, bar and quiet courtyard, but the rooms can be rather noisy.

Places to Eat

There are lots of **büfés** and **snack bars** near Öreg-tó Camping.

Kínái Büfé *(Ady Endre utca 29; buffet from 800Ft)* is not the most salubrious place in town, but its Chinese buffet is cheap and a change from Hungarian cuisine.

Mahagóni *(Ady Endre utca 28; pizzas from 600Ft)* takes a stab at real Italian dishes (mainly pizzas) and misses just by a hair.

Görög *(Váralja utca 20; mains 950-1300Ft)*, in a restored Esterházy mansion, serves Greek-ish food in pseudo-Hellenic splendour.

Tóparti Halászcsárda *(☎ 380 136; Tópart sétány 10; open until 10pm Mon-Fri, until midnight Sat & Sun; mains from 1000Ft)*, south of Kodály tér, is a quaint little lakeside eatery serving fish.

Zöld Lovag *(Green Knight; ☎ 481 681; Ady Endre utca 17; mains from 1200Ft; open until midnight daily)* is another one of those 'medieval-style' restaurants, with colourful banners, large rough-hewn tables and chairs,

a menu in Old Hungarian script and men in tights. But the food ain't half bad at this one.

Entertainment

Zoltán Magyary Cultural Centre *(☎ 380 811; Váralja utca 4)*, between the castle and the bus station, will provide you with up-to-date information on what's going on. Venues include the atmospheric but cramped **Knights' Hall** in the castle, **Holy Cross Church** and the **József Eötvös Gymnasium** on Eötvös utca near the lake's western shore. Concerts are sometimes held in summer at the **open-air theatre** in Angolpark.

Albatrosz *(Tópart utca 3; open until midnight)*, a lively bar in an attractive old house near the castle, draws a youthful crowd.

Zsigmond *(open until midnight Tues-Sat, until 10pm Sun)*, a wine cellar in the castle, is a great place for a glass of Hungarian grape.

Elvis *(Ady Endre utca 19-21)*, in the Zsigmond Király courtyard, is a modern joint with outdoor seating, but the crowd can often be young and rowdy.

Getting There & Away

Buses leave very frequently for Tatabánya and Dunaszentmiklós, and there are up to eight departures a day to Komárom, Tarján in the Gerecse Hills and Oroszlány, the gateway to the Vértes Hills. There is one daily bus to Győr, two to Budapest (via Visegrád or Tatabánya) and seven to Esztergom.

Tata is on the railway line linking Déli, Kelenföld or Keleti stations in Budapest with Győr and Vienna. Four daily trains go directly to Sopron and Szombathely via Tata, but you usually have to change at Győr. If you're travelling by train to Esztergom, change at Almásfüzitő. To get to Slovakia, take the train to Komárom and walk across the border.

Getting Around

Bus No 1 links the main train station with the bus station and Kossuth tér. Bus No 3 will take you to Fényesfürdő; No 5 gets you close to Tóvároskert train station and Fáklya utca.

You can book a local taxi by calling on ☎ 489 808 or ☎ 489 080.

GYŐR

☎ 96 • postcode 9000 • pop 129,800

Most travellers see no more of Győr (in German: Raab) than what's visible in the distance from the highway between Vienna and

Budapest. It's usually pegged as 'that big industrial city with the funny name' (it's pronounced something like 'jyeur') and, well, neither can be denied. An important producer of trucks, rolling stock and textiles, Győr is the nation's third-largest industrial centre.

But Győr is also a historical city; in fact, after Budapest and Sopron, no place in the country can boast as many important buildings and monuments. Stroll 100m up pedestrian Baross Gábor utca and you'll enter a world that has changed little since the 17th and 18th centuries.

Situated in the heart of the so-called Little Plain (Kisalföld) at the meeting point of the Mosoni-Duna and Rába Rivers, Győr was settled by the Celts and later the Romans who called it Arrabona. The Avars came here, too, and built a circular fort (called *gyűrű* from which the town took its name) before the arrival of the Magyars.

King Stephen established a bishopric at Győr in the 11th century, and 200 years later the town was granted a royal charter, allowing it to levy taxes on goods passing through.

A castle was built here in the 16th century and, being surrounded by water, was an easily defended outpost between Turkish-held Hungary and Vienna, the seat of the Habsburg Empire, until late in the century. When the Ottomans managed to take Győr, they were able to hold on for only four years and were evicted in 1598. For that reason Győr has been praised as the 'dear guard', watching over the nation through the centuries.

Orientation & Information

Győr's train station lies south of Honvéd liget (Soldier Park) on Révai Miklós utca. To reach the bus station in Hunyadi utca on the other side of the railway line go through the subway (underpass) east of the main entrance. Baross Gábor utca leads to Belváros, the historic Inner Town, and the river runs to the north.

Tourinform (☎/fax 311 771; ⒠ gyor@tour inform.hu; *Árpad út 32; open 8am-8pm Mon-Fri, 9am-6pm Sat & Sun June–mid-Sept, 8am-6pm Mon-Fri, 9am-2pm Sat Apr & May; 9am-4pm Mon-Fri, 9am-2pm Sat mid-Sept–Mar)* is in a small glass pavilion, and **Ibusz** (☎ 311 700; *Kazinczy utca 3; open 8am-5pm Mon-Fri, 8am-noon Sat)* has an office in town, too.

OTP has a bank branch at No 16, on the main pedestrian street of Baross Gábor utca.

The **main post office** (*Bajcsy-Zsilinszky út 46)* is opposite the Győr National Theatre. There's a branch near the train station.

A small **Internet café** (*Czuczor Gergely utca 6)*, bizarrely located above a clothes shop, charges 200Ft per hour.

You can also find out more about this town on its website (W www.gyor.hu).

Things to See & Do

Almost everything worth seeing in Győr is in or around three areas just minutes apart on foot. Museums in Győr usually cost 200Ft or 400Ft for adults and 100Ft or 200Ft for students and children.

Bécsi kapu tér Baroque 'Viennese Gate Square' is dominated by the **Carmelite church**, built in 1725. On the northwest side of the square and cutting it off from the river are the fortifications built in the 16th century to stop the Turkish onslaught, and a bastion that has served as a prison, a chapel, a shop and now a restaurant. Just east is **Napoleon House** (*Király utca 4)*. One of the more unusual footnotes in Hungarian history is that Napoleon entered Hungarian territory very briefly in 1809, and actually spent the night of 31 August in this house as Győr was near a battle site. An inscription on the Arc de Triomphe in Paris recalls 'la bataille de Raab'.

The **archaeology museum** (*Bécsi kapu tér 5; open 10am-6pm Tues-Sun Apr-Oct)*, made up of cellars containing a rich collection of Roman and medieval bits and pieces (the majority of which is stone remains), is a branch of the János Xánthus Museum.

Káptalan-domb From the archaeology museum, walk up Káptalan-domb (Chapter Hill) to Apor Vilmos püspök tere, the oldest part of the city. The **cathedral** (*Székesegyház; admission free; open 10am-noon & 2pm-5pm daily)*, whose foundations date back to the 11th century, is an odd amalgam of styles, with Romanesque apses (have a look from the outside), a neoclassical facade and a Gothic chapel riding piggyback on the south side. But most of what you see inside, including the stunning frescoes by Franz Anton Maulbertsch, the main altar and the bishop's throne, is baroque from the 17th and 18th centuries.

The Gothic **Hédervary Chapel** contains one of the most beautiful (and priceless) examples of medieval gold work in Hungary,

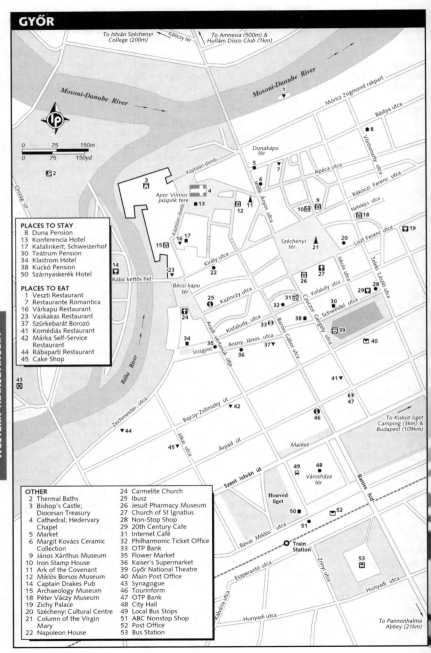

GYŐR

To István Széchenyi College (200m)
Kálóczy tér
To Amnesia (500m) &
Hullám Disco Club (1km)

Mosoni-Danube River

Mosoni-Danube River

Móricz Zsigmond rakpart

Bástya utca

Vörösmarty utca

Dunakapu tér

Apáca utca

Rákóczi Ferenc utca

Nefelejcs utca

Káptalan-domb

Apor Vilmos püspök tere

Liszt Ferenc utca

Széchenyi tér

Kazinczy utca

Iskola utca

Telaki László utca

Király utca

Bécsi kapu tér

Kisfaludy utca

Czuczor Gergely utca

Baross Gábor utca

Schweidel utca

Kisfaludy utca

Aradi vértanúk útja

Arany János utca

Virágpiac

Zechmeister utca

Rába River

Bajcsy-Zsilinszky út

Jókai utca

Árpád út

Market

Szent István út

Honvéd liget

Városháza tér

Révai Miklós utca

Train Station

Esperantó utca

Szent István út

Baross híd

Zrínyi utca

Hunyadi utca

Kálvária utca

Hunyadi utca

To Kisküt-liget Camping (3km) & Budapest (109km)

To Pannonhalma Abbey (21km)

Ország út

Rába kettős híd

0   75   150m
0   75   150yd

PLACES TO STAY
- 8 Duna Pension
- 13 Konferencia Hotel
- 17 Katalinkert; Schweizerhof
- 30 Teátrum Pension
- 34 Klastrom Hotel
- 38 Kuckó Pension
- 50 Szárnyaskerék Hotel

PLACES TO EAT
- 1 Veszti Restaurant
- 7 Restaurante Romantica
- 16 Várkapu Restaurant
- 23 Vaskakas Restaurant
- 37 Szürkebarát Borozó
- 41 Komédiás Restaurant
- 42 Márka Self-Service Restaurant
- 44 Rábaparti Restaurant
- 45 Cake Shop

OTHER
- 2 Thermal Baths
- 3 Bishop's Castle; Diocesan Treasury
- 4 Cathedral; Hedervary Chapel
- 5 Market
- 6 Margit Kovács Ceramic Collection
- 9 János Xánthus Museum
- 10 Iron Stamp House
- 11 Ark of the Covenant
- 12 Miklós Borsos Museum
- 14 Captain Drakes Pub
- 15 Archaeology Museum
- 18 Péter Váczy Museum
- 19 Zichy Palace
- 20 Széchenyi Cultural Centre
- 21 Column of the Virgin Mary
- 22 Napoleon House
- 24 Carmelite Church
- 25 Ibusz
- 26 Jesuit Pharmacy Museum
- 27 Church of St Ignatius
- 28 Non-Stop Shop
- 29 20th Century Cafe
- 31 Internet Café
- 32 Philharmonic Ticket Office
- 33 OTP Bank
- 35 Flower Market
- 36 Kaiser's Supermarket
- 39 Győr National Theatre
- 40 Main Post Office
- 43 Synagogue
- 46 Tourinform
- 47 OTP Bank
- 48 City Hall
- 49 Local Bus Stops
- 51 ABC Nonstop Shop
- 52 Post Office
- 53 Bus Station

the **Herm of László**. It's a bust reliquary of one of Hungary's earliest king-saints and dates from around 1400. If you're looking for miracles, though, move to the north aisle and the **Weeping Icon of Mary**, a 17th-century altarpiece brought from Galway by the Bishop of Clonfert in Ireland who had been sent packing by Oliver Cromwell. Some 40 years later – on St Patrick's Day no less – it began to cry tears of blood and is still a pilgrimage site.

West of the cathedral is the **Bishop's Castle** (Püspökvár), a fortress-like structure with parts dating from the 13th century; the foundations of an 11th-century Romanesque chapel are on the south side. It now houses the **Diocesan Treasury** (☎ 312 153; admission 300/100Ft; open 10am-4pm Tues-Sun), one of the richest in Hungary and labelled in English. Marvel at the heavy chasubles in gold thread, the bishops' crooks of solid silver and pieces of the True Cross, but the collection of manuscripts (some illuminated) is ultimately more impressive.

In a restored courthouse east of the cathedral you'll find the **Miklós Borsos Museum** (☎ 316 329; Apor Vilmos püspök tere 2; open 10am-6pm Tues-Sun Mar-Oct; 10am-5pm Tues-Sun Nov-Feb). Borsos lived in Győr between the two world wars. He was a prominent sculptor in Hungary throughout much of the 20th century.

Széchenyi tér A couple of blocks southeast of Káptalan-domb is Széchenyi tér, a large square in the heart of Győr. Once the market in the Middle Ages, it's currently being excavated for archaeological treasures. Along the way, at the bottom of the hill on Jedlik Ányos utca, you'll pass the outstanding **Ark of the Covenant** (Frigyláda emlékmű), a large statue dating from 1731. Local tradition has it that the king erected the city's finest baroque monument to appease the angry people of Győr after one of his soldiers accidentally knocked the Eucharist out of a priest's hands during a Corpus Christi procession.

The renovated **Column of the Virgin Mary** (Mária-oszlop; Széchenyi tér) was raised in 1686 to honour the recapture of Buda Castle from the Turks. The Jesuit and later Benedictine **Church of St Ignatius**, the city's finest, dates from 1641. The 17th-century white-stucco side chapels and the ceiling frescoes painted by the Viennese artist Paul Troger in 1744 are worth a look. Next door, the

Szécheny Pharmacy Museum (Széchenyi Patikamúzeum; ☎ 320 954; Széchenyi tér 9; admission free; open 7.30am-4pm Mon-Fri) was established by the Jesuits in 1667 and is a fully operational baroque institution. You can inspect the rococo vaulted ceiling and the frescoes with religious and herbal themes.

If time is limited, skip the main branch of the **János Xánthus Museum** (☎ 310 588; Széchenyi tér 5; open 10am-6pm Tues-Sun) across the square (Győr history, stamps and coins, antique furniture, natural history) and head for the **Imre Patkó Collection** (☎ 310 588; open 10am-6pm Tues-Sun) in the 17th-century **Iron Stump House** (Vastuskós Ház) at No 4, a former caravanserai that still sports the log into which itinerant artisans would drive a nail to mark their visit. The museum is one of the best of its size anywhere in Hungary and has an excellent collection of 20th-century fine art on the first two floors; the 3rd floor is given over to objects collected by the journalist and art historian Imre Patkó during his travels in India, Tibet, Vietnam and west Africa.

Just off Széchenyi tér is the **Margit Kovács Ceramic Collection** (Kovács Margit kerámiagyűjtemény; ☎ 326 739; Apáca utca 1; open 10am-6pm Tues-Sun Mar-Oct; 10am-5pm Tues-Sun Nov-Feb), a branch of the more famous one in Szentendre (Margit Kovács was born in Győr).

Other Attractions

Győr's atmospheric old streets are an attraction in themselves. Take a stroll down Bástya utca, Apáca utca, Rákóczi Ferenc utca, Liszt Ferenc utca and Király utca (east and northeast of Széchenyi tér), where you'll see many fine buildings. The late Renaissance **palace** (Rákóczi Ferenc utca 6), once a charity hospital, now houses the **Péter Váczy Museum** (☎ 318 141; admission free; open 10am-6pm Tues-Sun Mar-Oct; 10am-5pm Tues-Sun Nov-Feb). Váczy, a history professor and avid antiques collector, managed to assemble quite an eclectic assortment of pieces, from Greek and Roman relics to Chinese terracotta figures, all of which are on display. The museum also hosts temporary contemporary art exhibitions. Enter round the back at Nefelejcs utca 3.

Across the river the richly decorated octagonal cupola, galleries and tabernacle of the city's 1869 **synagogue** (Kossuth Lajos utca 5), are well worth a look if you can get into the decrepit old building; try at the entrance to the

WESTERN TRANSDANUBIA

music academy (formerly a Jewish school) next door.

Have a look at the colourful **flower market** held most mornings on Virágpiac south of Bécsi kapu tér.

Activities

On the left bank of the Rába River are Győr's **thermal baths** (☎ 522 646; Ország út 4; adult/child 500/400Ft; open 9am-6pm daily May-Sept, covered pool open 6am-8pm Mon-Fri year-round). They were getting a major face-lift at the time this went to print, but should be ready by the end of 2003. To get there, cross Rába kettős híd (Rába Double Bridge) over the little island and walk north along Radó sétány.

Places to Stay

Camping Some 3km northeast of town in Kiskútliget (Little Well Park) is **Kiskútligeti Camping** (☎ 318 986; camping including tent & person 1470Ft, bungalows for up to 4 persons 4300Ft; open mid-Apr–mid-Oct for bungalows), near the stadium. It also has a motel with doubles for 3800Ft, which is open year-round. The little bungalows are horrid.

Private Rooms & Hostels Private rooms for two are available from Ibusz for about 4000Ft. Dormitory accommodation is available year round at the huge **István Széchenyi College** (☎ 503 447; Héderváry út 3; dorm beds around 1000Ft) north of the city centre. Contact Tourinform for other possibilities.

Pensions Unusually for a Hungarian city, Győr is full of small private pensions and, while not the cheapest places to stay, they are usually very central and in some of the city's most colourful old buildings.

Kuckó (☎ 316 260, fax 312 195; Arany János utca 33; singles/doubles 5900/7490Ft) is a comfy pension in an old townhouse with nine rooms.

Katalinkert (☎/fax 542 088; ⓔ katalin kert@matavnet.hu; Sarkantyú köz 3; singles/ doubles 5800/7500Ft) is the new kid on the block and has six modern rooms tucked away above a pleasant courtyard restaurant.

Both excellent choices, the **Teátrum** (☎ 310 640, fax 328 827; Schweidel utca7; singles/ doubles/triples 6200/7900/9500Ft), on an attractive pedestrian street, and its sister pension, the Regency-blue **Duna** (☎/fax 329 084;

Vörösmarty utca 5; singles/doubles/triples 6200/7900/9500Ft), with 14 rooms and antique furniture in some of the common rooms.

Hotels Stumbling distance from the train and bus stations is **Szárnyaskerék** (☎ 314 629; Révai Miklós utca 5; doubles with/ without bathroom 6900/4650Ft), a four-storey, 30-room hotel that could do with a bit of love and care. Rooms without private baths have washbasins.

Klastrom (☎ 516 910, fax 327 030; ⓔ klas trom@arrabonet.gyor.hu; Zechmeister utca 1; singles/doubles/triples €49/66/76) is a three-star hotel south of Bécsi kapu tér and one of the best options in the city. The 250-year-old Carmelite convent has 42 rooms with bath, and boasts a sauna, a solarium, a pub with a vaulted ceiling, and a restaurant with courtyard seating. Rates vary according to the room and the season. The best rooms face the inner courtyard.

Konferencia (☎ 511 450, fax 511 453; ⓔ konferencia.hotel@axelero.hu; Apor Vil-mos püspök tere 3; singles/doubles 12,200/ 15,600Ft) is the modern carbuncle on Káptalan-domb next to the cathedral. This 20-room hotel was once a company guest-house and boasts underground parking, sauna, pool and solarium.

Schweizerhof (☎ 329 172, fax 326 544; ⓔ info@schweizerhof.hu; Sarkantyú köz 11-13; singles/doubles from 17,900/18,800Ft) is about as plush as you get in Győr, and so it should be for the price. There's a wellness centre, wine cellar, quality restaurant and bar within the hotel.

Places to Eat

Márka (Bajcsy-Zsilinszky út 30; buffet open 11am-5pm Mon-Sat; salads & mains around 430Ft) is a modernised place and is good for a cheap self-service meal.

Rábaparti (Zechmeister utca 15; mains from 700Ft) serves decent Hungarian fare in an unpretentious (though rather gloomy) restaurant at very reasonable prices.

Szürkebarát Borozó (☎ 311 548; Arany János utca 20; mains from 600Ft) is a decent wine cellar restaurant in a small courtyard. In the same courtyard you'll also find a popular ice cream shop.

Vaskakas (☎ 322 655; Bécsi kapu tér 2; mains 900-1500Ft), a cellar-like place in the former castle casemates near the Rába River, has loads of atmosphere as long as you don't mind long tables of German-speaking pensioners to your left and right.

Várkapu *(Bécsi kapu tér 7; dishes 800-2000Ft)*, overlooking the Carmelite church, is a charming little place to try instead. It has a limited but excellent menu.

Komédiás *(☎ 527 217; Czuczor Gergely utca 30; mains around 1000Ft)*, a cellar eatery decorated in postmodern greys and blacks, is opposite the cultural centre.

Veszti *(☎ 337 700; Móricz rakpart 3; open 11am-1pm daily; pizza from 390Ft, mains from 760Ft)*, situated in an atmospheric spot on an old paddle-steamer on the river, has a huge range of pizzas and Tex-Mex and American mains.

The **Ristorante Romantica** *(☎ 314 127; Dunakapu tér 5; pastas 1000-1500Ft, mains 1500-4000Ft)* is an upmarket place with superb Italian cuisine and an eye for detail. The only draw-back is the price.

For cakes, don't go past the tiny **cake shop** *(Jókai utca 6)*. It's so popular people line up along the footpath.

A colourful **open-air market** unfolds on Dunakapu tér most mornings. There's a **Nonstop shop** on the corner of Teleki László utca and Schweidel utca, and an **ABC Nonstop Shop** at the train station.

Entertainment

A good source of information for what's on is the free fortnightly mag *Győri Est*.

Győr National Theatre *(Győri Nemzeti Sziönház; ☎ 314 800; Czuczor Gergely utca 7)* is a modern, technically advanced, though unattractive, structure covered in Op Art (Optical Art) tiles by Victor Vasarely. The celebrated Győr Ballet and the city's opera company and philharmonic orchestra all perform here.

In June the **Hungarian Dance Festival**, the nation's most prestigious festival of dance, is held in Győr.

Zichy Palace *(Zichy-palota; ☎ 512 690; Liszt Ferenc utca 20)* is another important venue for classical music. The box office at the theatre is open from 10am till noon and 1pm to 6pm Tuesday to Friday, mornings only on Monday. For reservations to see the philharmonic, contact it's ticket office *(☎ 326 323; Kisfaludy utca 25)*.

Captain Drakes Pub on Radó sétány is a relaxing spot for a drink. It's on the little island in the Rába River.

Amnesia *(Hédervári utca 16)* is a club/bar north of the city centre that attracts a student crowd, as does the **Hullám Disco Club** *(Hédervári utca 22)*, a few hundred metres farther north.

The central **20th Century Cafe** *(Schweidel utca 25)* promotes itself as a cocktail bar and caters to a more mature crowd.

Getting There & Away

Bus There are at least a dozen departures a day to Budapest, Kapuvár and Pannonhalma, and about half as many to Pápa and Veszprém, and Székesfehérvár. Other destinations from Győr include Balatonfüred (four buses daily), Dunaújváros (five), Esztergom (one), Hévíz (two), Keszthely (five), Lébény (from eight to 12), Mosonmagyaróvár (two), Pécs (two), Szombathely (three), Tapolca (three), Tata (three), and Zalaegerszeg (five). One bus runs to Vienna at 8.40am daily, and there is an extra bus at 7.20pm Monday to Friday and at 6.25pm Saturday.

Train Győr is the main junction after Budapest. It has convenient connections with Budapest's Keleti, Kelenföld and Déli stations, and Vienna via Hegyeshalom. Trains to Ebenfurth in Austria via Sopron, which are run by a private company called GySEV and are not part of the MÁV system, are less frequent.

From Győr, you can also reach Szombathely by train via Pápa and the gateway to the Balaton region, Veszprém, via Pannonhalma and Zirc. If you're heading for Slovakia, change at Komárom.

Getting Around

You can reach the Kiskútligeti camp site on bus No 8 from beside the colossal city hall on Városház tér.

You can book a local taxi service by calling ☎ 444 444.

AROUND GYŐR
Lébény
☎ 96 • postcode 9155 • pop 3300

This village 15km northwest of Győr contains the most important example of Romanesque architecture still standing in Hungary: the Benedictine **Abbey Church of St James** *(Szent Jakab apátsági templom; Fő út 60; admission free; open daily)*. Though not as intimate or evocative of medieval Hungary as the Abbey Church at Ják near Szombathely, it is nonetheless worth a visit for its sheer size and superb condition.

The church's construction was begun by two Győr noblemen in 1199 and it was consecrated in 1212 under the authority of Pannonhalma Abbey. Though the Lébény church managed to escape destruction during the Mongol invasion, it was set aflame twice by the Turks. The abbey hired Italian stonemasons to raze the structure in 1563, but apparently they were so impressed with it that they refused to carry out the task. In the 17th century the church passed into the hands of the Jesuits, who renovated it in the baroque style in the 18th century. In the late 19th century, when neo-Romanesque and neo-Gothic architecture was all the rage in Transdanubia, the church was restored by a German architect.

Between eight and 12 buses make the run every day from Győr. The bus stop is on Fő utca, a two-minute walk east of the church.

PANNONHALMA
☎ 96 • postcode 9090 • pop 3500

Since late in the 10th century, this small village 21km southeast of Győr has been the site of a Benedictine abbey, which has even managed to continue functioning during the darkest days of Stalinism. Its secondary school, attended by some 360 students, is tops in the nation. Oddly, the only other Hungarian Benedictine monastery in operation today is in the Brazilian city of São Paolo. The abbey celebrated its millennium to great fanfare in 1996 and was added to Unesco's World Heritage List in that year.

The monastery was founded by monks from Venice and Prague with the assistance of Prince Géza. The Benedictines were considered a militant order, and Géza's son, King Stephen, made use of them to help Christianise Hungary.

The abbey and associated buildings have been razed, rebuilt and restored many times over the centuries; under the Turks, the basilica did not sustain as much damage as it could have for the simple reason that it faced east and was turned into a mosque. As a result the complex is a crazy patchwork of architectural styles.

Orientation & Information
The village is dominated by the 282m high Castle Hill (Várhegy), and the abbey. The bus from Győr stops in the centre of the village;

from here follow Váralja up to the abbey. Some buses – between four and five daily – continue up the eastern side of the hill and stop at the abbey's main entrance.

The train station is a couple of kilometres west of the village off Petőfi utca in the direction of route No 82.

The **Tourinform** (*☎/fax 471 733; e pannonhalma@tourinform.hu; Petőfi utca 25; open 9am-6pm daily June-Aug, 10am-6pm daily Sept-May*) is inconveniently located about 600m south of Szabadság tér and is quite often closed during its opening hours. A much better bet is **Pax Tourist** (*☎ 570 191, fax 570 192; e pax@osb.hu; Vár utca 1*), the only agency here, just south of the abbey's main entrance. There's an **OTP bank** (*Dózsa György utca 1*) opposite the Pax hotel. The **main post office** (*Dózsa György utca 7*) is on the same street.

Pannonhalma Abbey
Pannonhalma Abbey (*Pannonhalmi főapátság; ☎ 570 191; Vár utca 1; tours in Hungarian with foreign language text adult/child 1000/300Ft, tours in foreign languages 2000/1000Ft; open 8.30am-6pm daily June-Sept; 9.30am-4.30pm Tues-Sun Oct-May*) was thoroughly spruced up for its 1000th birthday in 1996 and is now one of the most impressive historical complexes in Hungary. You'll begin your guided tour in the central courtyard, where there is a statue of the first abbot, Asztrik, who brought the crown of King Stephen to Hungary from Rome, and a relief of King Stephen presenting his son Imre to the tutor Bishop Gellért. To the north you can observe dramatic views over the Kisalföld, while looming behind you are the abbey's modern wings and neoclassical clock tower built in the early 19th century. The abbey cannot be visited without a guide.

The entrance to **St Martin's Basilica** (Szent Márton-bazilika), built early in the 12th century, is through the **Porta Speciosa**. This arched doorway in red limestone was recarved in the mid-19th century by the Stornos, a controversial family of restorers who imposed 19th-century Romantic notions of Romanesque and Gothic architecture on ancient buildings (see the Sopron section later in this chapter). It is beautiful despite the butchery. The fresco above the doorway by Ferenc Storno depicts the church's patron, St Martin of Tours, giving half his cloak to a crouching beggar. Look down to the right below the columns and you'll see what is perhaps the oldest graffiti in Hungary: 'Benedict Padary was here in 1578', in Latin.

The interior of the long and sombre church contains more of the Stornos' handiwork, including the neo-Gothic pulpit and raised marble altar. The Romanesque niche in the wall of the 13th-century crypt is called the **Seat of St Stephen**; legend says that it contains the saint-king's throne.

As you walk along the cloister arcade, you'll notice the little faces carved in stone on the wall. They represent human emotions and vices, such as wrath, greed and conceit. In the cloister garden a Gothic sundial offers a sobering thought: 'Una Vestrum, Ultima Mea' (One of you will be my last).

The most beautiful part of the abbey is the neoclassical **abbey library** (főapátság könyvtára) built in 1836 by János Packh, who helped design the cathedral at Esztergom. It contains some 300,000 volumes – many of them priceless historical records – making it the largest private library in Hungary. But the rarest and most important document is in the **abbey archives**. It is the *Deed of Foundation* of Tihany Abbey and dates from 1055. It is written in Latin, but also contains about 50 Hungarian place names and is the earliest surviving example of written Hungarian. The library's interior may look like marble, but it is made entirely of wood. An ingenious system of mirrors within the skylights reflects and directs natural light throughout the room.

The **gallery** (képtár) off the library contains works by Dutch, Italian and Austrian masters from the 16th to 18th centuries. The oldest work, however, goes back to 1350. The most valuable piece is the 17th-century *Dead Christ* by Teniers the Younger. Below the library are the rooms of the **Millennium Exhibition** tracing the development of the abbey in Hungarian, German and English, as well as liturgical objects from the abbey treasury.

Because it still functions as a monastery, the abbey must be visited with a guide. Tours in Hungarian go on the hour between 9am to 5pm daily, from June to September; from late March to May and October to mid-November they leave on the hour between 9am and 4pm Tuesday to Sunday. Tours in English and four other languages (Italian, German, French and Russian) are only available at 11am and 1pm during these times. In winter, tours in Hun-

garian occur five times Tuesday to Sunday (10am to 3pm); those in other languages are by request only. If there's no guide available in your language, the ticket office will provide you with a leaflet to follow.

After you've admired the abbey follow the paved path south of Pax Tourist and the ticket office up the hill to two lovely **chapels** and a **lookout tower**, which offers expansive views of the region.

Special Events
There are six organ and choral concerts scheduled between April and December in the basilica – always at the same time, 3.30pm, and on the same dates: Easter Monday, Whit Monday, St Stephen's Day (20 August), Virgin Mary's Birthday (the Saturday before/after 8 September), National Day (23 October) and 26 December.

Places to Stay & Eat
The **Panoráma Camping** (☎ 471 240; Fenyvesalja utca 4/a; camping per tent/adult/child 800/600/300Ft; bungalows up to 4 persons 5000Ft; open May-Sept) to the east of Castle Hill, has a good location for visiting the abbey – just go through the gate at the back and climb the hill to the car park. The camp site itself is quite basic but it has a small büfé and salad bar.

Família (☎ 470 192, fax 570 592; Béke utca 61; doubles 5000Ft) is a four-room pension with a homy feel and a small kitchen and lounge for guests. You'll find it on route No 82 as you enter the town from the north.

Pannon (☎/fax 470 041; Hunyadi út 7/c; singles/doubles 5700/7200Ft) is larger with 20 rooms, all of which have TV and bath. It's on the way up to the abbey.

Pax (☎ 470 006, fax 470 007; e pax hotel@axelero.hu; Dózsa György utca 2; singles/doubles from €30/41) is a welcoming 24-room hotel in the centre of town. All rooms have a bathroom, and staff can organise a plethora of activities, including horse riding, wellness centre trips and walking excursions.

Both Pannon and Pax have decent, affordable restaurants.

Szent Márton (☎ 470 793; Vár utca 1; mains from 1000Ft), below the abbey near the car park, has a snack bar, restaurant, pub and gift shop.

While in town be sure to try some of the wine from the nearby Mór region, which has gained greater status over the past few years. A good place to start is **Borpince** *(Wine Cellar; Szabadság tér 27; open 11am-7pm daily)*, in the town centre, which has an extensive selection. Otherwise take a trip into the surrounding countryside; many wine makers throw open their cellar doors for tastings.

Getting There & Away

Buses to/from Győr are frequent, with almost one an hour making the trip daily. Six trains stop daily at Pannonhalma on their way to Veszprém from Győr.

SOPRON

☎ 99 • postcode 9400 • pop 55,000

Sopron (in German, Ödenburg), at the foot of the Lővér Hills and a mere 6km from the Austrian border, is one of the most charming medieval cities in Hungary. With its preponderance of Gothic and early baroque architecture, Sopron is the closest city the country has to Prague and exploring the backstreets and courtyards of the Inner Town is like a step back in time.

Sopron has had a long and tumultuous past, with more wars, difficult decisions and political rulings thrust upon its population than most cities. Indeed, as recently as 1921 the citizens of Sopron had to vote whether to stay in Austria's Bürgenland as a result of the Trianon Treaty or be re-annexed by Hungary. They resoundingly chose the latter, which explains the little knot of Hungarian territory that juts into Austria.

First to arrive in the area were the Celts, then came the Romans, who lived in a settlement called Scarbantia (now Sopron's Inner Town) between the 1st and 4th centuries. The Germans, Avars, Slavs and the Magyars followed. In medieval times, Sopron was ideally situated for trade along the so-called Amber Route from the Baltic Sea to the Adriatic and Byzantium. By the 1300s, after a century of struggle between the Hungarians and the Austrians for hegemony over the city, Sopron had been made a royal free town – its mixed population able to pursue their trades without pressure from feudal landlords. Thus a strong middle class of artisans and merchants emerged here, and their wealth contributed to making Sopron a centre of science and education.

Neither the Mongols nor Turks were able to penetrate the heart of Sopron, which is why so many old buildings still stand. But damage during WWII was severe – the area saw much restoration work done in the 1960s.

Sopron is an anomaly in Hungary – a city with a Gothic heart and a modern mind. It's true that it attracts enormous amounts of tourists, but most of the visitors who flock to the streets on a Saturday are Austrians in search of bargin haircuts, dental work and enough sausage to open their own delicatessens. Come nightfall the city is once again in the hands of the loyal citizens of Sopron.

Orientation

The medieval Belváros (Inner Town) contains almost everything of interest in Sopron, though there are a few worthy sights across the narrow Ikva Stream to the northeast, just beyond the city walls. The Lővér Hills start about 4km southwest of the city.

Sopron's main train station is on Állomás utca, south of the shoeprint-shaped Inner Town. From there walk north along Mátyás király utca, then past Széchenyi tér to reach Várkerület and Hátsókapu (Back Gate), one of the few entrances to the Inner Town. Várkerület and Ógabona tér beyond it form a ring around the Inner Town, roughly following the city's Roman and medieval walls. Sopron-Déli train station, through which trains to/from Szombathely also pass, is to the northwest of the Sopron train station. The bus station is just northwest of the Inner Town on Lackner Kristóf utca.

Information

The excellent **Tourinform** *(☎/fax 338 892; e sopron@tourinform.hu; Előkapu utca 11; open 9am-5pm daily June-Aug, 9am-4pm daily Sept-May)* is just north of the Inner Town. **Ciklámen Tourist** *(☎ 312 040; Ógabona tér 8; open 8am- or 8.30am-4.30pm Mon-Fri, 8am-1pm Sat)* is on the road leading to the bus station.

For further information on Sopron, see the town's website (w www.sopron.hu).

There's a central **OTP bank** *(Várkerület 96/a)*, and the **main post office** *(Széchenyi tér 7-10)* is south of the Inner Town, but there's a more convenient branch *(Várkerület 37)* just north.

For Internet access go to **Internet Sopron** *(Új utca 3; open 11am-8pm Mon-Fri, 10am-5pm Sat)*, which charges 400Ft for an hour's surfing.

SOPRON & THE LŐVÉR HILLS

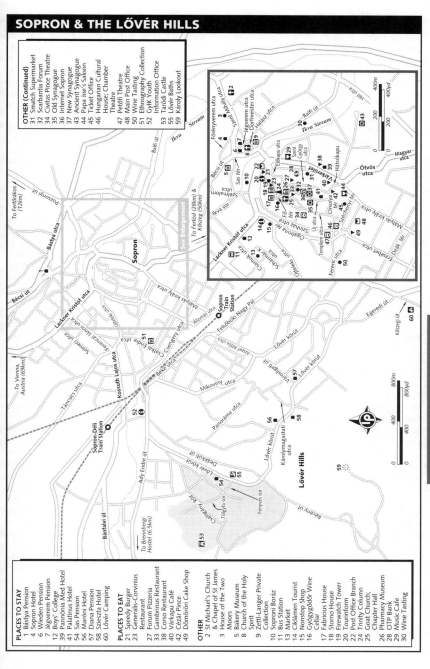

WESTERN TRANSDANUBIA

OTHER (Continued)
31 Smatch Supermarket
32 Scarbantia Forum
34 Civitas Pince Theatre
35 Old Synagogue
36 Internet Sopron
37 New Synagogue
43 Ancient Synagogue
44 Papa Joe's Saloon
45 Ticket Office
46 Hungarian Cultural House; Chamber Theatre
47 Petőfi Theatre
48 Main Post Office
50 Wine Tasting
51 Ethnography Collection
52 GyIK Youth Information Office
53 Taródi Castle
55 Lővér Baths
59 Károly Lookout

PLACES TO STAY
1 Bástya Pension
4 Sopron Hotel
6 Wieden Pension
7 Jégverem Pension
12 Boys' College
39 Pannónia Med Hotel
41 Palatinus Hotel
54 Sas Pension
56 Maróni Hotel
57 Diana Pension
58 Szieszta Hotel
60 Lővér Camping

PLACES TO EAT
21 Speedy Burger
23 Generális-Corvinus Restaurant
27 Forum Pizzeria
33 Gambrinus Restaurant
38 Corso Restaurant
40 Várkapu Café
42 Cézár Pince
49 Dömörői Cake Shop

OTHER
2 St Michael's Church & Chapel of St James
3 House of the Two Moors
5 Bakery Museum
8 Church of the Holy Spirit
9 Zettl-Langer Private Collection
10 Soproni Boráz
11 Bus Station
13 Market
15 Ciklámen Tourist
15 Nonstop Shop
16 Gyógygödör Wine Cellar
17 Fabricius House
18 Storno House
19 Firewatch Tower
20 Tourinform
22 Post Office Branch
24 Trinity Column
25 Goat Church; Chapter Hall
26 Pharmacy Museum
28 OTP Bank
29 Music Cafe
30 Wine Tasting

WESTERN TRANSDANUBIA

Inner Town

The best place to begin a tour of Sopron is to climb the narrow circular staircase to the top of the 60m-high **firewatch tower** *(tűztorony; ☎ 311 327; Fő tér; adult/child 300/150Ft; open 10am-6pm Tues-Sun Apr-Oct)* at the northern end of Fő tér. The tower affords excellent views over the city, the Lővér Hills to the southwest and the Austrian Alps to the west. Below are Fő tér and the four narrow streets that make up the Inner Town.

The tower, from which trumpeters would warn of fire, mark the hour (now done by chimes) and greet visitors to the city in the Middle Ages, is a true architectural hybrid. The 2m-thick square base, built on a Roman gate, dates from the 12th century, and the cylindrical middle and arcaded balcony from the 16th century. The baroque spire was added in 1681. **Fidelity Gate** at the bottom of the tower shows Hungary receiving the *civitas fidelissima* (Latin for 'the most loyal citizenry') of Sopron. It was erected in 1922 after that crucial referendum.

Though virtually every building in the Inner Town is of interest, Sopron has relatively few specific monuments of importance. Fő tér contains the lion's share of what there is, and also has most of the museums.

The focal points of this graceful square are the **Trinity Column** (1701), the best example of a 'plague pillar' in Hungary, and, on the south side of the square, the old **Goat Church** *(Kecsketemplom; Templom utca 1; admission free; open daily)*, whose name comes from the heraldic animal of its chief benefactor. The church was originally built in the late 13th century, but many additions and improvements have been made over the centuries. The interior is mostly baroque, the red marble pulpit in the centre of the south aisle dates from the 15th century and there is a lovely little Gothic domed tabernacle. Beneath the Goat Church is **Chapter Hall** *(Káptalan-terem; ☎ 338 843; Templom utca 1; admission free; open 10am-noon, 2pm-5pm Tues-Sun May-Sept)*, part of a 14th-century Benedictine monastery with frescoes and stone carvings.

The **Pharmacy Museum** *(Patikamúzeum; ☎ 311 327; Fő tér 2; adult/child 200/100Ft; open 10am-6pm Tues-Sun Apr-Sept, 10am-2pm Tues-Sun Oct-Mar)* is in a Gothic building beside the Goat Church.

Across to the square are **Fabricius House** at No 6 and **Storno House** at No 8; both contain several exhibits. Fabricius House contains a comprehensive **history museum** *(☎ 311 327; adult/child 300/150Ft; open 10am-6pm Tues-Sun Apr-Sept, 10am-2pm Tues-Sun Oct-Mar)*, with rooms on the upper floors devoted to domestic life in Sopron in the 17th and 18th centuries. There are a few kitchen mock-ups and exhibits explaining how people made their beds and washed their dishes in those days, but the highlights are the rooms facing the square that are crammed with priceless antique furniture. The lower floors play host to an archaeological exhibition covering Celtic, Roman and Hungarian periods of history. Be sure to look out for the Cunpald Goblet, a small, rusting drinking vessel over 1200 years old. You can follow the exhibits at your leisure with a photocopied fact sheet while old women 'guides' sit by the window making lace in the afternoon sunlight. Scarbantia-era statues reconstructed from fragments found in the area (including enormous statues of Juno, Jupiter and Minerva), guard the lapidarium (kőtar) in the cellar of house No 7 (which is between Fabricius House and Storno House), once a Gothic chapel, with vaulted ceilings 15m high.

On the 1st floor of Storno House (built 1417), there's a less-than-enthralling exhibit on Sopron's more recent history, but on the floor above is the wonderful **Storno Collection** *(Storno Gyűjtemény; ☎ 311 327; adult/child 500/250Ft; open 10am-6pm Tues-Sun Apr-Sept, 10am-2pm Tues-Sun Oct-Mar)*, which belonged to a 19th-century Swiss-Italian family of restorers whose recarving of Romanesque and Gothic monuments throughout Transdanubia is frowned upon today. To their credit, the much maligned Stornos did rescue many altarpieces and church furnishings from oblivion, and their house is a Gothic treasure trove. Highlights include the beautiful enclosed balcony with leaded windows and frescoes, leather chairs with designs depicting Mephisto with his dragons, and door frames made from pews taken from 15th-century St George's Church on Szent György utca. Franz Liszt played a number of concerts in this house in the mid-19th century.

The **Scarbantia Forum** *(Új utca 1)* is an underground original marketplace dating from Roman times. If you continue walking down Új utca – known as Zsidó utca (Jewish Street) until the Jews were evicted from Sopron in 1526 – you'll reach the **Old Synagogue** *(Ózsinagóga; ☎ 311 327; Új utca 22; adult/*

child 200/100Ft; open 9am-5pm Wed-Mon Mar-Sept) at No 22 and the **New Synagogue** (Új Zsinagóga) across the street at No 11. Both were built in the 14th century and are among the greatest Jewish Gothic monuments in Europe and unique in Hungary. The Old Synagogue, now a museum, contains two rooms, one for each sex (note the women's windows along the west wall). The main room contains a medieval 'holy of holies' with geometric designs and trees carved in stone, and some ugly new stained-glass windows. The inscriptions on the walls date from 1490. There's a reconstructed *mikvah* (ritual bath) in the courtyard. The New Synagogue forms part of a private house and offices, and cannot be visited.

Other Attractions
Sopron's sights are not entirely confined to the Inner Town. Walk back to Fő tér, past the old Roman walls, under Előkapu and over a small bridge leading to Ikva, once the district of merchants and artisans. At Balfi út 11 the excellent **Zettl-Langer Private Collection** *(Zettl-Langer Magángyűjtemény; ☎ 335 123; Balfi út 11; admission 200Ft; open 10am-noon Tues-Sun)* contains ceramics, paintings and furniture.

Heading northwards, on Dorfmeister utca, is the 15th-century **Church of the Holy Spirit** (Szentlélek-templom). Further north at Szent Mihály utca 9 is the **House of the Two Moors** (Két mór ház). It was fashioned from two 17th-century peasant houses and is guarded by two large statues – ironically now painted white.

At the top of the hill, along Szent Mihály utca is **St Michael's Church** (Szent Mihály-templom), built between the 13th and 15th centuries, and behind it the Romanesque-Gothic **Chapel of St James** (Szent Jakab-kápolna), the oldest structure in Sopron. Not much escaped the Stornos' handiwork when they 'renovated' St Michael's – they even added the spire.

If you return to the House of the Two Moors and walk west along Fövényverem utca you'll soon reach Bécsi út and the **Bakery Museum** *(Pékmúzeum; ☎ 311 327; Bécsi út 5; adult/child 200/100Ft; open 10am-2pm Tues-Sun May-Aug)*, a fantastic reminder of a bygone era. It's actually the completely restored home, bakery and shop of a successful 19th-century bread and pastry maker named Weissbeck, and contains some interesting gadgets and work-saving devices.

The city museum's **Ethnography Collection** *(Néprajzi Gyűjtemény; ☎ 311 463; Deák tér 1; adult/child 200/100Ft; open 10am-6pm Tues-Sun May-Aug)* has an interesting array of implements used in winemaking, baking and weaving.

There's an ancient **synagogue** *(Paprét 14)* all bordered up, east of the Inner Town.

Special Events
Sopron is a musical town, and the highlights of the season are the **Spring Days** in late March, the **Festival Weeks** from mid-June to mid-July and the **International Choir Festival** in early July. There's even an **International Accordion Meeting** in mid-October. Tickets to the various events are available from the ticket office *(☎ 511 730; Széchenyi tér 17-18; open 9am-5pm Mon-Fri, 9am-noon Sat)*.

Places to Stay
Camping With more than 100 bungalows **Lővér Camping** *(☎/fax 311 715; Kőszegi út; camping adult/child 600/300Ft; bungalow doubles 2688Ft; open mid-Apr–mid-Oct)*, 5km south of the city centre on Pócsi-domb, also has plenty of shaded tent sites.

Hostels The **Brennbergi Hostel** *(☎/fax 313 116; Brennbergi út; bus No 3; dorm beds 1200Ft, bungalows per person 2000FT; open mid-Apr–mid-Oct)* is pretty far west of the city centre, but the dorm is cheap.

A half-dozen different colleges and schools in the Sopron area offer accommodation in July and much of August for about 1200Ft (Tourinform can supply a list), including the **Boys' College** *(☎ 312 105; Lackner Kristóf utca 7)* near the bus station.

Private Rooms Enquire at Ciklámen Tourist for **private rooms** (2000Ft per person). You can also find quite a few private rooms by taking bus No 1 from the train station to the **Szieszta hotel** *(Lővér körút 37)*, then walking back down the hill looking for houses with *szoba kiadó* and *Zimmer frei* signs.

Pensions The central **Jégverem** *(☎/fax 510 113; e haspart@axelero.hu; Jégverem utca 1; singles/doubles 4000/8000Ft)* is an excellent bet with five suite-like rooms in an 18th-century ice cellar in the Ikva district.

Bástya *(☎ 325 325, fax 334 061; Patak utca 40; singles/doubles 6000/8000Ft)* is a modern pension, just a 10-minute walk north of the Inner Town up Szélmalom utca.

Wieden (☎ 523 222, fax 523 223; e wie den@fullnet.hu; Sas tér 13; singles/doubles 6000/8900Ft, apartments 13,900-18,000Ft) is in a lovingly renovated old townhouse and the most plush of the three. There are seven rooms and two apartments sleeping four to six people.

Hotels Prices quoted here are for the high season; expect them to drop during winter.

Palatinus (☎/fax 349 144; Új utca 23; singles/doubles €40/52) is extremely central but it's in a badly renovated building and its 30 rooms are small and dark.

Sopron (☎ 512 261, fax 311 090; w www .hotelsopron.hu; Fövényverem utca 7; singles/ doubles 14,000/16,000Ft) is up on Coronation Hill with views of the city and the Lővér Hills. It is a sprawling 100-room place, with bars, a restaurant, clay tennis courts and an outdoor swimming pool.

Pannónia Med (☎ 312 180, fax 340 766; w www.pannoniahotel.com; Várkerület 73; singles/doubles 16,800/18,900Ft) is Sopron's grand 100-year-old hotel. It has 60 renovated rooms and a pool, sauna and gym.

Places to Eat

The burgers at **Speedy Burger** (Várkerület 36; burgers 260-380Ft) are big, filling and arrive in front of you before you know it.

Cézár Pince (Hátsókapu 2; open until 11pm daily; dishes 330-690Ft), in a medieval cellar in a historical building off Orsolya tér, is the best place in Sopron for an inexpensive lunch or light meal. The platter of sausages and salad for under 700Ft attracts locals; chase it with a glass of Soproni Kékfrankos (a red) or the young white Zöldveltelini.

Generális-Corvinus (☎ 314 841; Fő tér 7-8; mains 1000-1900Ft), with its café tables on the Inner Town's main square, is a great place for a pizza in the warmer months.

Gambrinus (☎ 339 966; Fő tér 3; open until midnight daily; mains 800-1500Ft), also on the main square, has a solid Hungarian and Austrian menu.

Forum (Szent György utca 3; dishes under 1000Ft) is a popular spot for pizza.

Corso (☎ 340 990; Várkerület 73; mains 1000-1500Ft), in the Korona shopping arcade next to the Pannónia Med hotel, serves Hungarian fare. Its set menu (1290Ft) after 4pm is good value.

Várkapu Café (Várkerület 108/a; cakes from 50Ft) is excellent for cakes and coffee, and the queues at **Dömöröri** (Széchenyi tér 13; icecream 60Ft per scoop) testify to the quality of its ice cream.

There's a **Non-stop shop** at Ógabona tér 12.

Entertainment

The **Hungarian Cultural House** and **Chamber Theatre** on Széchenyi tér, both undergoing renovation at the time of writing, will host music and other cultural events. Contact Tourinform for details.

Petőfi Theatre (☎ 511 700; Petőfi tér 1), a beautiful theatre with National Romantic-style decor, is just around the corner from the Chamber Theatre.

Civitas Pince Theatre (☎ 332 098; Templom utca 16) has cabaret on Friday and Saturday nights. For more up-to-date entertainment, check the listings in the freebie biweekly Soproni Est or the monthly Soproni Program Ajánló. The **GyIK youth information office** (☎ 511 200; Ady Endre utca 10) also has information on concerts, clubs etc.

The Sopron region is noted for red wines, such as Kékfrankos and Merlot. They're pretty cheap even in restaurants, but particularly high in acid and tannin, so watch your intake if you don't want a massive macskajaj ('cat's wail' – the Hungarian term for a hangover) the next day. A convenient place to sample them is in the **Gyógygödőr** (Fő tér 4; open until 10pm Tues-Sun; wine per glass around 550Ft), a deep cellar, but there are smaller places around town with bunches of leaves hanging outside to signify they're serving wine. Look for them at Balfi út 16 and III Rákóczi Ferenc utca 17, or head directly to Sopron's biggest wine shop **Soproni Borház** (☎ 510 022; Várkerület 15).

The **Music Cafe** (Várkerület 49) is a good spot to catch some live music, particularly jazz. If you're feeling a bit more raucous, head for **Papa Joe's Saloon** (☎ 340 933; Várkerület 108; mains 900-1500Ft), which isn't bad for a bite to eat as well.

Getting There & Away

Bus The bus service is good to/from Sopron. Buses leave up to twice an hour for Fertőd, Győr, Kapuvár and Nagycenk, and departures are frequent to Kőszeg (eight daily) and Szombathely (nine). Other destinations to/ from Sopron include: Balatonfüred (two),

Budapest (four), Esztergom (two), Lake Fertő (nine), Hévíz and Keszthely (three), Kaposvár (one), Komárom (two), Nagykanizsa (two), Pécs (one), Sárvár (three), Székesfehérvár (two), Tapolca (one), Tatabánya (one), Veszprém (five) and Zalaegerszeg (two).

There is an 8am bus to Vienna daily, plus extra departures at 9.25am Monday and Thursday, and 8.55am and 9.25am on Friday. Two weekly buses make the trip to Munich and Stuttgart (8.05pm Thursday and 9.05pm Sunday).

Train Express trains en route to Vienna's Südbahnhof via Ebenfurth pass through Sopron between three and nine times daily; five local trains go to Wiener Neustadt (where you can transfer for Vienna) daily. There are up to eight express trains daily to Keleti station in Budapest via Győr and Komárom, and seven to nine local trains daily to Szombathely.

Getting Around
Bus No 12, from both the bus and train stations, circles the Inner Town then stops directly in front of Lővér Camping. For the Brennbergi Hostel take bus No 3 from the bus station.

You can book a local taxi service by calling ☎ 555 555 or ☎ 333 333.

AROUND SOPRON
Lővér Hills
This range of 300m- to 400m-high foothills of the Austrian Alps, some 5km south and southwest of the city centre, is Sopron's playground. It's a great place for hiking and walking, but is not without bitter memories, for it was here that partisans and Jews were executed by Nazis and the fascist Hungarian Arrow Cross during WWII. You can climb to the top of **Károly Lookout** (Károly kilátó) on the hill (394m) west of the Lővér hotel, to **Taródi Castle** (Csalogány köz 8) to the northwest, or you could visit the **Lővér Baths** (☎ 510 964; Lővér körút 82; adult/child 350/150Ft; covered pools, sauna & solarium open 6am-8pm Mon-Fri, 9am-8pm Sat & Sun year-round, outside pools open 9am-8pm daily late May–mid-Sept).

Places to Stay A good choice in the hills is **Diana** (☎/fax 329 013; Lővér körút 64; singles/doubles 5400/8000Ft), with eight large, comfortable rooms.

Sas (☎ 316 183, fax 341 068; Lővér körút 69; singles/doubles 4000/8000Ft) is a friendly nine-room pension that has a rural feel to it.

Maroni (☎ 312 549, fax 341 182; e res erve@hotelmaroni.hunguesthotels.hu; Lővér körút 74; singles €24-36, doubles €34-50) is one of several big hotels here. Its 190 rooms come in several different categories and are more expensive in the high season.

Szieszta (☎ 314 260, fax 316 923; e res erve@hotelszieszta.hunguesthotels.hu; Lővér körút 37; singles €34-58, doubles €46-77), a huge former trade-union holiday house, is now a 288-room hotel. Like Maroni, room rates rise in the high season.

FERTŐD
☎ 99 • postcode 9431 • pop 2700
Some 27km east of Sopron, Fertőd has been associated with the aristocratic Esterházy family since the mid-18th century when scion Miklós, proclaiming that 'Anything the (Habsburg) emperor can afford, I can afford too', began construction of the largest and most opulent summer palace in central Europe. When completed in 1766, it boasted 126 rooms, a separate opera house, a hermitage (complete with a cranky old man in a sack cloth who wanted to be left alone), temples to Diana and Venus, a Chinese dance house, a puppet theatre and a 250-hectare garden laid out in the French manner. Fertőd – or Esterháza as it was known until the middle of the 20th century – had made it onto the map.

Much has been written about the Esterházy Palace and many hyperbolic monikers bestowed on it (the 'Hungarian Versailles' is the most common). But the fact remains that this baroque and rococo structure – its architects unknown except for the Austrian Melchior Hefele – is the most beautiful palace in Hungary (although some corners could do with a lick of paint). While the rooms are mostly bare, history is very much alive here. Many of the works of composer Franz Joseph Haydn (a 30-year resident of the palace) were first performed in the Concert Hall, including the *Farewell Symphony*. In the Chinoiserie Rooms, Empress Maria Theresa attended a masked ball in 1773 and in the French Garden, Miklós 'the Splendour Lover' threw some of the greatest parties of all time for friends like Goethe, complete with fireworks and tens of thousands of Chinese lanterns.

WESTERN TRANSDANUBIA

After a century and a half of neglect (it was used as a stables in the 19th century and a hospital during WWII), the palace has been partially restored to its former glory.

Orientation & Information

The palace and its gardens on Bartók Béla utca dominate the town; the bus will let you off almost in front of the main gate. The town centre is a few minutes' walk to the west. The closest train station (on the Sopron–Győr line) is at Fertőszentmiklós 4km to the south.

Tourinform (☎/fax 370 544; @ fertod@ tourinform.hu; Joszef Hayden utca 3; open 9am-6pm Mon-Fri, 9am-5pm Sat, 9am-1pm Sun mid-June–mid-Sept; 9am-4pm Mon-Fri mid-Sept–mid-June) is in the east wing of the Grenadier House, the former living quarters of the grenadier guards, directly opposite the palace's main entrance. There's a branch of the **OTP bank** (Fő utca 7), and a **post office** (Fő utca 6), in the small town centre.

Log on to the town's website (w www.fer tod.hu) for more information.

Esterházy Palace

Some 26 renovated rooms at the horseshoe-shaped Esterházy Palace (☎ 537 640; adult/ child 1000/600Ft; open 10am-6pm Tues-Sun mid-Mar–Oct; 10am-4pm Fri-Sun Nov–mid-Mar) are open to the public; the rest of the complex houses a hotel, a secondary school and a horticultural research centre.

As you approach the main entrance to the so-called **Courtyard of Honour**, notice the ornamental wrought-iron gate, a rococo masterpiece. You can only tour the palace with a guide, but armed with a fact sheet in English (available from the ticket office), lag behind and explore the rooms away from the crowds.

On the ground floor of the palace you'll pass through several rooms decorated in mock Chinese style (all the rage in the late 18th century); the pillared **Sala Terrena**, with its floor of glimmering marble and Miklós Esterházy's initials in floral frescoes on the ceiling; and the Prince's Bed Chamber, with paintings of Amor. On the 1st floor are more sumptuous baroque and rococo salons, as well as the lavish **Concert Hall** and **Ceremonial Hall**, which lead on to each other. There's also an exhibit dedicated to the life and times of Haydn.

The apartment where Haydn lived, off and on, from 1761 to 1790 in the west wing of the baroque **Music House** (Madach sétány 1;

adult/child 200/100Ft; open 9.30am-5pm Tues-Fri, 10am-3pm Sat & Sun May–mid-Oct), southwest of the palace, has been turned into a temple to the great composer.

Special Events

From May to mid-October there are piano and string quartets performing in the palace Concert Hall at 7pm on most Fridays and Saturdays, and some Sundays.

The **Haydn Festival** in early September is usually booked out months in advance, but try your luck at Tourinform.

Places to Stay & Eat

Dori Hotel & Camping (☎/fax 370 838; Pomogyi út 1; camping per tent €2-2.60, camping per person €1.20-1.70, singles bungalows €17-21, doubles bungalows €30-34, singles hotel rooms €15-19, doubles hotel rooms €27-30) has a good range of accommodation possibilities 100m north of the palace. Prices depend on the season.

There are plenty of pensions in and around Fertőd, including the **Újvári** (☎/fax 537 097; Kossuth Lajos utca 57/a; singles/doubles 5000/7000Ft) which has a massage and reflexology studio downstairs. It's in Sarród, just 130m north of the post office.

Kastély (☎ 537 640; doubles/triples/quads 4200/5800/6600Ft), a 19-room hotel in the east wing of the palace, is one of the main reasons people come to Fertőd. You won't be sleeping in anything like the Prince's Bed Chamber but for a palace the price is right; book well in advance.

Gránátos and **Kastélykert** (mains around 1000-1500Ft), each occupying one half of the Grenadier House, are pleasant enough restaurants for a bite to eat. In summer, **food stalls** dispensing lángos (deep-fried dough with toppings) and the like fill the nearby car park.

Getting There & Away

Some two dozen daily buses link Sopron with Fertőd on weekdays and 15 or so on Saturday and Sunday. There are also buses to Győr and Kapuvár. Nine daily trains link Sopron and Győr with Fertőszentmiklós to the south.

NAGYCENK

☎ 99 • postcode 9485 • pop 1700

Only 14km west of Fertőd and the Esterházy Palace, but light years away in spirit, lies Nagycenk, site of the ancestral mansion of

The Greatest Hungarian

The contributions Count István Széchenyi made to Hungary were enormous and extremely varied. In his seminal 1830 work *Hitel* (meaning 'credit' and based on *hit*, or 'trust'), he advocated sweeping economic reforms and the abolition of serfdom (he himself had distributed the bulk of his property to landless peasants two years earlier).

The Chain Bridge, the design of which Széchenyi helped push through Parliament, was the first link between Buda and Pest, and for the first time everyone, nobles included, had to pay a toll.

Széchenyi was instrumental in straightening the serpentine Tisza River, which rescued half of Hungary's arable land from flooding and erosion, and his work made the Danube navigable as far as the Iron Gates in Romania.

He arranged the financing for Hungary's first railway lines (from Budapest in the north and east to Vác and Szolnok and west to what is now Wiener Neustadt in Austria), and launched the first steam transport on the Danube and Lake Balaton.

A lover of all things English, Széchenyi got the upper classes interested in horse racing with the express purpose of improving breeding stock for farming.

A large financial contribution made by Széchenyi led to the establishment of the nation's prestigious Academy of Science.

Széchenyi joined Lajos Batthyány's revolutionary government in 1848, but political squabbling and open conflict with Vienna caused him to lose control and he suffered a nervous breakdown. Despite a decade of convalescence in an asylum, Széchenyi never fully recovered and tragically took his own life in 1860.

For all his accomplishments, Széchenyi's contemporary and fellow reformer, Lajos Kossuth, called him 'the greatest Hungarian'. This dynamic but troubled visionary retains that accolade to this day.

the Széchenyi clan. No two houses – or families – could have been more different than these. While the privileged, often frivolous Esterházys held court in their imperial palace, the Széchenyis – democrats and reformers – all went about their work in a sombre neoclassical manor house that aptly reflected their temperament and sense of purpose. The mansion has been completely renovated and part of it has been turned into a superb museum dedicated to the Széchenyis.

The family's public-spiritedness started with Ferenc Széchenyi, who donated his entire collection of books and *objets d'art* to the state in 1802, laying the foundations for the National Library named in his honour. But it was his son, István (1791–1860), who made the greatest impact of any Hungarian on the economic and cultural development of the nation (see the boxed text 'The Greatest Hungarian').

Orientation

The train station is near the centre of Nagycenk, not far from the neo-Romanesque St Stephen's Church, designed by Miklós Ybl in 1864, and the Széchenyi family's mausoleum. The bus from Sopron stops close to the mansion's main gate.

Széchenyi Manor

The entrance to the **István Széchenyi Memorial Museum** (☎ 360 023; Kiscenki utca 3; adult/child 400/200Ft; open 10am-6pm Tues-Sun Apr-Sept; 10am-5pm Tues-Sun Oct-Mar) is in the mansion through the Sala Terrena – it's almost austere compared with the one at the Esterházy Palace in Fertőd. Guided tours on cassette in several languages (including English) are included in the admission price.

The rooms on the ground floor of the museum, furnished with period pieces, deal with the history of the Széchenyi family and their political development, from typical baroque aristocrats in the 18th century to key players in the 1848 War of Independence and István's involvement in the ill-fated government of Lajos Batthyány. A sweeping baroque staircase leads to the exhibits on the 1st floor – a veritable temple to István's many accomplishments – from Budapest's Chain Bridge and the Danube and Tisza River engineering works to steamboat and rail transport.

It is fitting that the mansion of a railway developer like István Széchenyi lies near an open-air **Train Museum** (admission free; open 10am-5pm daily), with steam engines that were still in use on main lines as late as 1950. You can actually ride a 100-year-old **narrow-gauge steam train** for 5.5km to Fertőboz and back *(one way adult/child 136/68Ft, return adult/child 272/136Ft)*. Departures between April and September from the Kastély train station at Nagycenk are at 10.05am, 11.18am and 3.30pm on Saturday and Sunday only. All turn around at Fertőboz in less than half an hour for the return trip to Kastély. There are also shorter trips to Barátság (3.3km), which are more frequent but cost the same.

A 2.5km **row of linden trees** opposite the mansion and planted by István's grandmother in 1754, leads to a **hermitage**. Like the Esterházys, the Széchenyi family had a resident loner who, in this case, was expected to earn his keep by ringing the chapel bell and tending the garden.

The **Széchenyi Mausoleum**, the final resting place of István and other family members, is in the village cemetery across the road from St Stephen's Church.

Cross-country riding, show-jump training and riding camps are available at the **Széchenyi Riding School** (☎ 360 196; Dózsa körút 52) in the village.

Places to Stay & Eat

Kastély (☎/fax 360 061; e reserve@hotel kastely.hunguesthotels.hu; Kiscenki utca 3; singles €28-62, doubles €32-84, suites for 2 €64-120), in the west wing of the mansion, is the only spot in town nowadays. It is a beautifully appointed 19-room inn, and rates vary depending on the season and room type. If you can afford it opt for room Nos 106 or 107, which are large suites with period furniture and restful views of the six-hectare garden. Rates include entrance to the museum and a thermal spa in Balffürdő, 6km northwest of Nagycenk.

The splendid dining room at the **Kastély** *(mains 1000-1500Ft)* hotel is *the* place for lunch in these parts, and there are outdoor tables in the courtyard in summer. The **Terrace** café, also at the Kastély, has a beautiful interior and serves excellent cakes and ice cream. The **Kert** *(mains around 1000Ft)*, in the renovated little train station near the Train Museum, is a more affordable restaurant and has a lovely garden. If these are full (which could be the case on weekends), snack at one of the **food stalls** in the Train Museum car park.

Getting There & Away

Nagycenk is accessible from Sopron by bus every half-hour. The village is on the railway line linking Sopron and Szombathely, and seven to nine trains arrive and depart each day.

If you time it right, you can reach Nagycenk by the toy train (the old steam trains). Take the bus from Sopron to Fertőboz and board the train for Kastély at 10.45am, 12.20pm or 4.25pm.

SZOMBATHELY

☎ 94 • postcode 9700 • pop 85,600

Szombathely (in German, Steinamanger) is a major crossroads in western Hungary. Its name (**som**-bot-hay) translates as 'Saturday place' and refers to the important weekend markets held here in the Middle Ages. For many Austrians who cross the border in search of cheap edibles and services, it remains just that.

Szombathely got an earlier start than most. In 43 AD the Romans established a trade settlement called Savaria here on the all-important Amber Route. By the start of the 2nd century it was important enough to become the capital of Upper Pannonia. Over the next few centuries, Savaria prospered and Christianity arrived; Martin of Tours, the patron saint of France, was born here in 316. But attacks by Huns, Longobards and Avars weakened its defences and then, in 455, it was destroyed by an earthquake.

Szombathely began to develop again in the early Middle Ages, but the Mongols, then the Turks and the Habsburgs, put a stop to that. It was not until 1777, when János Szily was appointed Szombathely's first bishop, that the city really began to flourish economically and culturally. The building of the railway line to Graz brought further trade. In 1945 Allied bombers levelled much of the town, which has since been rebuilt (though not very successfully in many parts).

The town's website (ⓦ www.szombathely .hu) is in Hungarain only.

Orientation & Information

Szombathely is made up of narrow streets and squares with the centre at enormous, leafy Fő tér. To the west are Berzsenyi Dániel tér and Templom tér, the administrative and ecclesiastical centres of town. The train station is on Éhen Gyula tér, five blocks northeast of Mártírok tere at the end of Széll

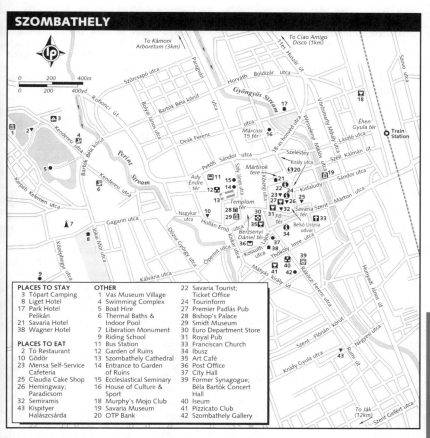

SZOMBATHELY

PLACES TO STAY
3 Tópart Camping
8 Liget Hotel
17 Park Hotel Pelikán
21 Savaria Hotel
38 Wagner Hotel

PLACES TO EAT
2 Tó Restaurant
10 Gödör
23 Mensa Self-Service Cafeteria
25 Claudia Cake Shop
26 Hemingway; Paradicsom
32 Semiramis
43 Kispityer Halászcsárda

OTHER
1 Vas Museum Village
4 Swimming Complex
5 Boat Hire
6 Thermal Baths & Indoor Pool
7 Liberation Monument & Riding School
11 Bus Station
12 Garden of Ruins
13 Szombathely Cathedral
14 Entrance to Garden of Ruins
15 Ecclesiastical Seminary
16 House of Culture & Sport
18 Murphy's Mojo Club
19 Savaria Museum
20 OTP Bank

22 Savaria Tourist; Ticket Office
24 Tourinform
27 Premier Padlás Pub
28 Bishop's Palace
29 Smidt Museum
30 Euro Department Store
31 Royal Pub
33 Franciscan Church
34 Ibusz
35 Art Café
36 Post Office
37 City Hall
39 Former Synagogue; Béla Bartók Concert Hall
40 Iseum
41 Pizzicato Club
42 Szombathely Gallery

Kálmán út. The bus station is on Petőfi Sándor utca, northwest of Fő tér.

North of Fő tér there's a very helpful **Tourinform** (☎/fax 520 316; e szombathely@tourinform.hu; Király utca 11; open 9am-6pm Mon-Fri, 9am-5pm Sat & Sun June–mid-Sept; 9am-5pm Mon-Fri mid-Sept–May), which may have moved to the City Hall on Kossuth Lajos utca by the time you read this.

Two commercial travel agencies are in the town centre: **Savaria Tourist** (☎ 511 435; Mártírok tere 1; open 8.30am-4.30pm Mon-Fri, 8am-noon Sat) and **Ibusz** (☎ 314 141; Fő tér 44; open 8.30am-4.30pm Mon-Fri).

There's a branch of the **OTP bank** (Király utca 10) diagonally opposite Savaria Tourist and the **main post office** (Kossuth Lajos utca 18) is southwest of Fő tér.

Things to See
Allied bombing in the final days of WWII did not spare the Zopf-style **Szombathely Cathedral** (1797) on Templom tér. Designed by Melchior Hefele for Bishop Szily in 1791, the cathedral was once covered in stucco work and frescoes by Franz Anton Maulbertsch and supported by grand marble columns. They're now gone, of course, though a couple of Maulbertsch originals and a glorious red and white marble pulpit remain, breaking the monotony of this sterile place.

Maulbertsch frescoes in the upstairs Reception Hall at the 1783 **Bishop's Palace** (Püspöki Levéltár; ☎ 312 056; Berzsenyi Dániel tér 3; admission free; open 9am-1pm Mon-Thur), south of the cathedral, miraculously survived the air raids, but these are not usually open to the public. You can, however, admire the frescoes of Roman ruins and gods painted in 1784 by István Dorffmeister. They're in the Sala Terrena on the ground floor. Other rooms contain more prewar photographs of the cathedral and the **Diocesan Collection** (Egyházmegyei Gyüjtemény), including missals and Bibles from the 14th to 18th centuries, Gothic vestments and a beautiful 15th-century monstrance from Kőszeg. The late-baroque **Ecclesiastical Seminary** *(Papi szeminárium; Szily János utca 1)* contains a library of some 70,000 volumes, including incunabula and medieval codices, but is open to groups only.

The **Smidt Museum** *(☎ 311 038; Hollán Ernő utca 2; adult/child 300/150Ft; open 10am-5pm Tues-Sun Mar-Dec; 10am-5pm Tues-Fri Jan & Feb)*, in a baroque mansion behind the Bishop's Palace, contains the private collection of one Lajos Smidt, a pack-rat physician who spent most of his adult life squirreling away antique weapons, furniture, fans, pipes, clocks, Roman coins and so on. None of it looks like it's worth very much, but the volume and zaniness of it all makes the museum worth a visit.

Szombathely has some of the most important Roman ruins in Hungary, and many of them are on display. The **Garden of Ruins** *(Romkert; ☎ 313 369; Templom tér; 300/150Ft; open 9am-5pm Tues-Sun Mar-Nov)*, behind the cathedral and accessible from Templom tér, contains a wealth of Savaria relics excavated here since 1938. Don't miss the beautiful mosaics of plants and geometrical designs on the floor of what was **St Quirinus Basilica** in the 4th century. There are also remains of Roman road markers, a customs house, shops and the medieval castle walls.

The **Iseum** *(Rákóczi Ferenc utca 12)* south of Fő tér is part of a grand 2nd-century complex of two temples dedicated to the Egyptian goddess Isis by Roman legionnaires. When the smaller temple was excavated in the 1950s, the city decided to reconstruct it – with cement blocks. Fortunately, someone has had the sense to right this wrong, and the temples are undergoing a facelift, which should be finished by 2005.

The **Szombathely Gallery** *(☎ 508 800; Rákóczi Ferenc utca 12; adult/child 300/150Ft; open 10am-5pm Tues & Fri-Sun, 10am-7pm Thur)* overlooking the temple is one of the best modern art galleries in Hungary. The lovely twin-towered Moorish building

across the street at No 3 is the former **synagogue** designed in 1881 by the Viennese architect Ludwig Schöne. Today it houses a music school and the **Béla Bartók Concert Hall**. A plaque marks the spot from which '4228 of our Jewish brothers and sisters were deported to Auschwitz on 4 July 1944'.

The **Savaria Museum** *(☎ 500 720; Kisfaludy Sándor utca 9; adult/child 400/200Ft; open 10am-5pm Tues-Fri, 10am-4pm Sat & Sun mid-Apr–mid-Oct; 10am-5pm Tues-Fri mid-Oct–mid-Apr)*, fronting a little park east of Mártírok tere, is worth a short look around. The ground floor is devoted to highly decorative but practical items carved by 19th-century shepherds to while away the hours; the cellar is full of Roman altars, stone torsos and blue-glass vials found at Savaria excavation sites. There's a local history exhibit on the 1st floor.

The **Vas Museum Village** *(Vasi Múzeumfalu; ☎ 311 004; Árpád utca 30; adult/child 400/200Ft; open 10am-5pm Tues-Sun Apr–mid-Nov)*, on the western bank of the fishing lake, is an open-air museum with some three-dozen 18th- and 19th-century *porták* (farmhouses) moved from various villages in the Őrség region. They are arranged around a semicircular street, as was usual on the western border. The most interesting of these are the Croatian, German and 'fenced' houses. Nettles from a strange plant called *kővirózsa* (stone rose) growing on the thatch were used to pierce little girls' ears.

About 3km northeast of the town centre is the 27-hectare **Kámoni Arboretum** *(☎ 311 352; Szent Imre herceg útja 102; 200/150Ft; open 8am or 9am-6pm Tues-Sun Apr–mid-Oct; 8am-4pm mid-Oct–Mar)*. Established in the 19th century, it has some 3000 species of trees and shrubs.

Activities

The rowing and fishing lakes northwest of the town centre along Kenderesi cover 12 hectares and make up Szombathely's playground; **boats** can be hired from the western side of the little island in the middle from March to mid-September. The huge **swimming complex** *(☎ 505 690; Kenderesi utca; adult/child 400/200Ft; open 9am-8pm daily mid-May–mid-Oct)* close by has a new pool and a bunch of slides for both big and small kids. The city's **thermal baths and indoor pools** *(☎ 314 336; adult/child 400/250Ft; open 2pm-9.30pm*

Mon, 6am-9.30pm Tues-Fri, 9am-6pm Sat & Sun) are just to the south.

A well-established **riding school** *(☎ 313 461; Középhegyi út)* lies southwest of the Liget hotel.

Places to Stay

Camping Northwest of town, **Tópart Camping** *(☎ 509 038, fax 509 039; Kenderesi utca 14; camping per person/tent 600/300Ft; double/quad bungalows 3000/5000Ft; open May-Sept)* is near the lakes and swimming complex. From the bus stop (bus No 27) walk along the causeway between the lakes.

Hostels & Private Rooms Tourinform has a list of student hostels available over summer; beds generally cost between 800Ft and 1400Ft. Try Savaria Tourist and Ibusz for **private rooms** (doubles from 3000Ft).

Hotels West of the town centre, **Liget** *(☎ 509 323, fax 314 168;* e *hliget@ax.hu; Szent István park 15; singles/doubles from 5000/ 6000Ft)* has 38 rooms that aren't that modern, but it's a quiet place, and is convenient to the lakes, museum village and riding school. The monstrous *Liberation* monument – the two concrete 'wings' on the hill to the northwest – was once topped with a big red star.

Savaria *(☎ 311 440, fax 324 532; Mártírok tere 4; singles with bathroom 7900-12,900Ft, without bathroom 4900Ft, doubles with bathroom 10,900-15,900Ft, without bathroom 6900Ft)* is Szombathely's old world hotel. It's a 92-room Art Nouveau gem built in 1917, and its restaurant, with antique *kocsma* (saloon) furniture and Winter Garden function room, are easy places to conjure up ghosts of a more elegant past. Rates vary depending on the size of the room and facilities. Unfortunately the rooms don't match the splendour of the restaurant and Winter Garden; room No 218 with bathroom and views of the square is the best.

Wagner *(☎/fax 322 208;* w *www.hotel wagner.hu; Kossuth Lajos utca 15; singles/ doubles 8800/14,600Ft)* is a lovely hotel with a sunny inner courtyard and a dozen rooms just southwest of Fő tér. The hotel's restaurant is excellent.

Park Hotel Pelikán *(☎ 513 800, fax 513 801;* w *www.hotelpelikan.hu; Deák Ferenc utca 5; singles/doubles 15,000/19,000Ft)*, a brand new four-star hotel north of the town centre, occupies a former orphanage and

children's hospital. Its 36 spacious rooms have everything you need, and there's an indoor pool, spa, sauna and fitness room. The attached restaurant is top-notch.

Places to Eat

For its size, Szombathely has surprisingly few restaurants – good, bad or otherwise. The cheapest place around is **Mensa** *(Mártírok tere 5/b; meals from 300Ft; open 9am-7pm Mon-Fri, 7am-2pm Sat)* with basic but filling meals.

Gödör *(☎ 510 078; Hollán Ernő utca 12; mains around 1000Ft)* is an inexpensive restaurant serving Hungarian fare in an authentic wine cellar.

Hemingway *(☎ 344 978; Belső Uránia Udvar; mains around 1000Ft)*, another lovely cellar restaurant, is closer to Fő tér. Practically next door is locally recommended **Paradicsom** *(☎ 342 012; Belső Uránia Udvar; mains 600-1500Ft)*, an above average Italian restaurant with a good vegetarian selection. Belső Uránia Udvar is accessible from either Mártírok tére or Fő tér.

Kispityer Halászcsárda *(☎ 508 010; Rumi út 18; mains 1000-1500Ft)*, 1.5km southwest of Fő tér, is worth the trip if you're in search of fish. Portions are large.

If you're messing around in boats on the lake or visiting the museum village and get hungry, head for **Tó** *(Lake; Rajki sétány; mains 600-1000Ft)*, a restaurant on the narrow isthmus separating the two lakes, and grab a table on the terrace.

Semiramis *(Uránia Udvar; coffee from 100Ft)* is a place that easily fits the bill of a downtown Manhattan café and serves the best coffee in Szombathely.

Claudia *(Savaria tér 1; ice cream from 60Ft)* has decent cakes and ice cream.

Entertainment

Béla Bartók Concert Hall *(Bartók Terem; ☎ 313 747; Rákóczi Ferenc utca 3)* is where the Savaria Symphony Orchestra performs throughout the year.

House of Culture & Sport *(☎ 312 666; Március 15 tér 5)* is an ugly 1960s building, but is another important venue. Head to the **ticket office** *(☎ 312 579; Király utca 11)* for information on forthcoming shows.

For a less-mannered evening, start at the **Royal**, a pub with sidewalk tables on the northern side of Fő tér, or head to the more sedate **Art Café** *(Fő tér 10)*, opposite.

Premier Padlás *(open until 4am)* is a café-pub with pool tables in the Uránia Udvar shopping arcade and is open most nights until late.

Pizzicato Club *(Thököly Imre utca 14)* regularly attracts a large student crowd.

Ciao Amico *(Arad utca; open until at least 4am daily)*, north of the centre just off 11es Huszár út, sees in the wee hours nightly. **Murphy's Mojo Club** *(Semmelweis út 28)* does not stay open as late at Ciao Amico, but it's just as popular and also serves reliable food. A good source of information is the free biweekly entertainment guide *Szombathelyi Est*.

If you are in town in June check out the Savaria International Dance Competition Ballroom, it's dancing at its tackiest best.

Getting There & Away

Bus The bus service is not so good to/from Szombathely, though up to 16 buses leave daily for Ják, every half-hour for Kőszeg and every hour for Körmend. Other destinations to/from Szombathely include Budapest (three departures daily), Győr (six), Kaposvár (three), Keszthely via Hévíz (two), Pécs (three), Sárvár (12), Sopron (four), Sümeg (seven), Szeged (one), Szentgotthárd (four), Velem (eight), Veszprém (three) and Zalaegerszeg (seven). One weekly bus departs for Graz (7am Friday) and three to Vienna (6.40am Wednesday, 7am Friday and 3.55am Saturday).

Train Express trains to Déli and Kelenföld stations in the capital go via Veszprém and Székesfehérvár. Up to four express trains run to Győr via Celldömölk. There are frequent local trains to Kőszeg, Sopron and Körmend and three express trains a day to/from Pécs. There are also up to five direct trains to/from Graz.

Getting Around

Szombathely is simple to negotiate on foot, but bus No 27 will take you from the train station to the museum village, lakes, camp site and the Liget hotel. No 1 or 1/a are good for the Kámoni Arboretum. You can order a taxi by calling ☎ 312 222.

AROUND SZOMBATHELY
Ják
☎ 94 • postcode 9798 • pop 2100

Try to visit Ják, 12km south of Szombathely and an easy half-day trip by bus. This sleepy village boasts the **Benedictine Abbey Church**

(Bencés apátsági templom; ☎ *356 217; adult/child 200/100Ft; open 8am or 9am-5pm daily)*, one of the finest examples of Romanesque architecture in Hungary. Its main feature, a magnificent portal carved in geometric patterns 12 layers deep and featuring carved stone statues of Christ and his Apostles, on the west side, was renovated for Hungary's millennium celebration in 1996. The decorative sculptures on the outside wall of the sanctuary and the church's interior are also worth a look.

The two-towered structure was begun as a family church in 1214 by Márton Nagy and dedicated to St George four decades later in 1256. Somehow the partially completed church managed to escape destruction during the Mongol invasion, but it was badly damaged during the Turkish occupation. The church has had many restorations, the most important three being in the mid-17th century, between 1896 and 1904 (when most of the statues in the portal were recut or replaced, rose windows added and earlier baroque additions removed) and from 1992 to 1996.

Enter through the south door, once used only by the monks based here. The interior, with its single nave and three aisles, has a much more graceful and personal feel than most later Hungarian Gothic churches. To the west and below the towers is a gallery reserved for the benefactor and his family. The faded rose and blue frescoes on the wall between the vaulting and the arches below could very well be of Márton Nagy and his progeny. If you slip a coin into the machine nearby, you'll illuminate the church, transforming the cold grey stone to soft yellow.

To the west of the Romanesque church is the tiny clover-leaf **Chapel of St James** (Szent Jakab-kápolna) topped with an onion dome. It was built around 1260 as a parish church since the main church was monastic. Note the paschal lamb (symbolising Christ) over the main entrance, and the baroque altar and frescoes inside.

In the unlikely event that you've missed the last bus and need a place to stay, two **private rooms** *(*☎ *356 305; singles/doubles 1400/2800Ft)* are available at the house on Széchenyi utca 16. There's a **snack bar** at the ticket office, and a **supermarket** on Szabadság tér, near where the bus stops.

Buses from Szombathely are frequent and will drop you off at the bottom of the hill a few minutes' walk from the church. From Ják you can return to Szombathely on one of up to 16 daily buses or continue to Szentpéterfa (15 daily), Körmend (one) or Szentgotthárd (one).

Körmend

☎94 • postcode 9900 • pop 12,100

Though certainly not worth a detour, this town 25km south of Szombathely is considered the gateway to the Őrség (see later in this chapter), a region on the border with Austria and Slovenia that retains many of its folk traditions and characteristics. It's also home to the **Batthyány Manor** (*Batthyány-kastély;* ☎ 410 107; Dr Batthyány-Strattmann utca 3), once the residence of the Batthyány family, an aristocratic clan that owned much of the Őrség. The manor now houses the **Rába Local History Museum** (*Rába Helytörténeti Múzeum; adult/child 300/150Ft; open 9am-noon & 1pm-5pm Tues-Sun Apr-Oct; 10am-3pm Sat & Sun Nov–mid-Mar*), which focuses on town history through old photographs (the splendid synagogue was bombed to bits in WWII), the successes of local sons and daughters, and the work of local artisans, including clockmakers, metalworkers and blue dyers. The interesting

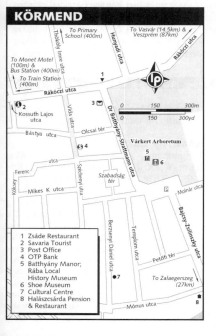

KÖRMEND

1 Zsáde Restaurant
2 Savaria Tourist
3 Post Office
4 OTP Bank
5 Batthyány Manor;
  Rába Local
  History Museum
6 Shoe Museum
7 Cultural Centre
8 Halászcsárda Pension
  & Restaurant

Shoe Museum (*Cipőmúzeum; admission free; open 9am-5pm Tues-Sun, 8am-noon Sat*) in the manor's 18th-century archives building looks exclusively at the cobbler's trade and is still producing footwear from the small Marc factory there.

If you need to stay overnight there is the **Monet** (☎ 414 282; Arany János utca 8; singles/doubles 2800/4460Ft), a motel near the bus and train stations, or the **Halászcsárda** (☎/fax 410 069; Bajcsy-Zsilinszky utca 20; singles/doubles €20/30), a pension 400m south of the Batthyány Manor. There is also a large **restaurant** here that specialises in fish and wild-game dishes; otherwise fill up at **Zsáde** (*Rákóczi utca 4; pizzas & burgers from 600Ft*), north of the manor.

Körmend's bus and train stations are five minutes apart north of the town centre on Vasútmellék utca. Bus services to/from Körmend are relatively limited, although the eight daily departures to Zalaegerszeg and 10 to Szombathely cut travel time considerably. It's better to take the train; up to 17 daily trains link Körmend with Szombathely.

SÁRVÁR

☎ 95 • postcode 9600 • pop 15,800

Some 27km east of Szombathely on the Rába River, the quiet town of 'Mud Castle' has experienced some good and some very bad times. During the Reformation, Sárvár's fortified castle was a centre of Calvinist culture and scholarship, and its owners, the Nádasdy family, were a respected dynasty in statecraft and military leadership. In 1537 Tamás Nádasdy set up a press that published the first two printed books in Hungarian – a Magyar grammar in Latin and a translation of the New Testament. Ferenc Nádasdy II, the so-called Black Captain, fought heroically against the Turks, and his grandson Ferenc III, a lord chief justice, established one of the greatest libraries and private art collections in central Europe.

But everything began to sour at the start of the 17th century. It seems that while the Black Captain was away at war, his wife Erzsébet Báthory, as mad as a hatter and bloodthirsty to boot, was up to no good (see the boxed text 'The Blood Countess' later in this section). Then Ferenc III's involvement in a plot led by Ferenc Wesselényi to overthrow the Habsburgs was exposed. He was beheaded in Vienna in 1671.

The Blood Countess

It was the scandal of the 17th century. On the night of 29 December 1610, the Lord Palatine of Hungary, Count György Thurzó, raided the castle at Csejta (now Čachtice in western Slovakia) and caught the lady of the house, Countess Erzsébet Báthory, literally red-handed – or so he and history would later claim. Covered in blood and screaming like a demon, the widow of the celebrated Black Captain was in the process of eating (as in chomp-chomp) one of her servant girls.

Yet another one, or so it would seem... By the time Thurzó had finished collecting evidence from household staff and the townspeople at Čachtice and at Sárvár, some 300 depositions had accused the countess of torturing, mutilating, murdering and – worst of all – disposing of the bodies of more than 600 girls and young women without so much as a Christian burial.

The case of the so-called Blood Countess has continued to catch the imagination of everyone from writers (Erzsébet is believed to have been the model for Bram Stoker's *Dracula*) and musicians (remember the Goth group Bathory?) to filmmakers and fetishists over the centuries, and some pretty crazy theories as to why she did it have emerged. Some say she considered the blood of young maidens to be an *elixir vitae* and bathed in it to stay young. Others claim she suffered from acute iron deficiency and just had to have those red corpuscles. Still others point to the high incidence of lunacy in the two, much intermarried branches of the Báthory dynasty. Most likely, however, Erzsébet Báthory herself was the victim of a conspiracy.

When the Black Captain died in 1604, his widow inherited all his estates – properties coveted by both Thurzó and Erzsébet's son-in-law Miklós Zrínyi, the poet and great-grandson of the hero of Szigetvár, who themselves were linked by marriage. Worse, the election of the countess' nephew Gábor Báthory as prince of Transylvania, a vassal state under Ottoman rule, threatened to unite the two Báthory families and strengthen the principality's position. It was in the interest of the Palatine – and the Habsburgs – to get this matriarch of the Báthorys out of the way.

Gábor was murdered in a power struggle in 1613 and the 'Báthory faction' in Hungary ceased to be a threat. The case against the Blood Countess never came to trial, and she remained interned 'between stones' (ie, in a sealed chamber) at the castle until she died in 1614 at the age of 54.

Was Erzsébet as bloodthirsty as history has made her out to be? Did she really bite great chunks out of the girls' necks and breasts and mutilate their genitals? Much of the villagers' testimony does appear to be consistent, but to form your own conclusions read Tony Thorne's well-researched *Countess Dracula*.

Sárvár is also well known for its 44°C thermal waters, discovered in the 1960s during experimental drilling for oil.

Orientation & Information

The train station is on Selyemgyár utca. To reach the town centre, walk south along Hunyadi János utca and turn east on Batthyány Lajos utca, which leads to Kossuth tér and the castle. The bus station is at the western end of Batthyány Lajos utca.

Helpful **Savaria Tourist** (☎/fax 320 578; e savariatourist.sarvar@enternet.hu; Várkerület 33; open 8.30am-4.30pm Mon-Fri, 8.30am-11.30am Sat) is almost opposite the castle entrance.

You'll find a branch of the **OTP bank** (Batthyány Lajos utca 2) and a **main post office** (Várkerület 32) in the small town centre.

Check out the town's website at W www .sarvar.hu for more information.

Nádasdy Castle

The entrance to the **Ferenc Nádasdy Museum** (☎ 320 158; Várkerület 1; adult/child 400/200Ft; museum & castle open 9am-5pm Tues-Sun) in pentagonal Nádasdy Castle (Nádasdy-vár) is across a brick footbridge from Kossuth tér and through the gate of a 14th-century tower. Though parts of the castle date from the 13th century, most of it is in 16th-century Renaissance style and in remarkably good condition despite Erzsébet Báthory's shenanigans and all the plundering by the Habsburgs. As punishment for the Nádasdy family's involvement in the rebellion of 1670, their estate was confiscated by the Austrian crown and the castle's contents –

including much of the library – were carted off to Vienna. As a result, many of the furnishings, tapestries and *objets d'art* you see in the museum's three wings today were collected from other sources.

One thing the Habsburgs could not take away was the magnificent ceiling frescoe in the **Knight's Hall** picturing Hungarians – the Black Captain included – doing battle with the Turks at Tata, Székesfehérvár, Győr, Pápa, Kanizsa and Buda. They were painted by Hans Rudolf Miller in the mid-17th century. The biblical scenes on the walls, depicting Samson and Delilah, David and Goliath, Mordechai and Esther and so on were painted in 1769 by István Dorffmeister. There's a particularly beautiful 16th-century cabinet of gilded wood and marble to the right of the hall as you enter.

The museum also contains one of the finest collections of weapons and armour in Hungary, and almost an entire wing is given over to the Hussars, a regiment of which was named after the family. The uniforms, all buttons, ribbons and fancy epaulets, would do any Gilbert & Sullivan operetta proud.

Among the exhibits about the castle and Sárvár is the printing press established here, and some of the then inflammatory Calvinist tracts it published. One work in Hungarian, emphatically entitled *The Pope Is Not the Pope – That's That* and dated 1603, was later vandalised by a Counter-Reformationist who defiantly wrote 'Lutheran scandal' across it in Latin.

A superb (and priceless) collection of some 60 antique Hungarian maps donated by

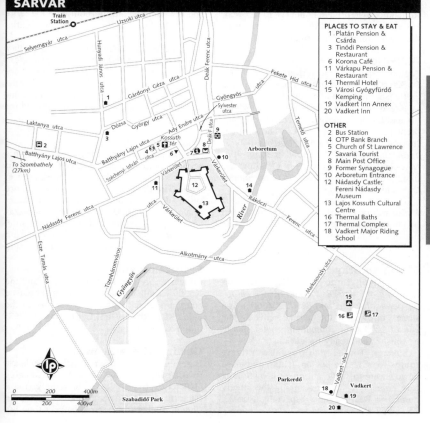

SÁRVÁR

PLACES TO STAY & EAT
1. Platán Pension & Csárda
3. Tinódi Pension & Restaurant
6. Korona Café
11. Várkapu Pension & Restaurant
14. Thermál Hotel
15. Városi Gyógyfürdő Kemping
19. Vadkert Inn Annex
20. Vadkert Inn

OTHER
2. Bus Station
4. OTP Bank Branch
5. Church of St Lawrence
7. Savaria Tourist
8. Main Post Office
9. Former Synagogue
10. Arboretum Entrance
12. Nádasdy Castle; Fereni Nádasdy Museum
13. Lajos Kossuth Cultural Centre
16. Thermal Baths
17. Thermal Complex
18. Vadkert Major Riding School

an Oxford-based expatriate Magyar in 1986 is on exhibition in a room at the end of the west wing.

Other Attractions

The **arboretum** *(Várkerület 30/a; admission free; open 9am-7pm daily Apr–mid-Oct, 9am-5pm daily mid-Oct–Mar)*, east of the castle and bisected by the Gyöngyös (a tributary of the Rába River), was planted by the Nádasdys' successors, the royal Wittelsbach family of Bavaria (the castle's last royal occupant was Ludwig III, who died in exile in 1921).

The **Church of St Lawrence** *(Szent Lőrinctemplom; Kossuth tér)*, originally medieval but rebuilt in the 19th century, is of little interest, though there are some contemporary frescoes inside.

Only the circular window and ornamentation around the door and windows of the Romantic-style private home (1850) at Deák Ferenc utca 6 north of the castle betray it as the town's former **synagogue**.

Activities

A brand spanking new **thermal complex** *(☎ 326 501; Vadkert utca 2)*, southeast of the castle, should be up and running by the time you read this, and will include indoor and outdoor hot pools, a wellness centre and comprehensive medical facilities. The original **thermal baths** *(☎ 326 501; Vadkert utca 1; adult/child 450/300Ft; open 8.30am-7pm May-Sept, 8.30am-6pm daily Oct-Apr)* are directly opposite and also have both indoor and outdoor hot pools.

There are **tennis courts** and the **Vadkert Major riding school** *(☎ 320 045)* at the end of Vadkert utca. Ask the staff at the Vadkert inn about horse hire (1500Ft an hour and 4500Ft with a coach seating up to three).

Places to Stay

Városi Gyógyfürdő Kemping *(City Spa Camping; ☎ 320 228; Vadkert utca 1; camping per adult/child/tent 800/500/660Ft)* is a stone's throw from the thermal baths. By the end of 2003 its accompanying hotel should be finished and ready for guests.

Savaria Tourist can organise **private rooms** for €15 per person. If they're closed or you want to strike out on your own, look for '*Zimmer frei*' signs among the stately homes on Rákóczi utca (especially Nos 23, 25 and 57/a).

There are two pensions with decent restaurants situated between the train station and the castle. **Platán** *(☎ 320 623, fax 326 484; e platans@elender.hu; Hunyadi János utca 23; rooms 9800Ft)* has 19 large rooms in a neoclassical building, while **Tinódi** *(☎/fax 323 606; Hunyadi János utca 11; singles/doubles 5500/6500Ft)* is smaller with nine colourful rooms, and a quiet, leafy courtyard.

Várkapu *(☎/fax 320 475; W www.varkapu.hu; Várkerület 5; singles/doubles 5400/6900Ft)*, just west of the castle, has nine clean and accommodating rooms. It also has a sauna and an excellent restaurant.

Vadkert *(☎/fax 320 045; Vadkert utca; singles/doubles with bath 6000/8000Ft)* inn is the most atmospheric place to stay. It's a 19th-century royal hunting lodge with 25 rooms in an old building and a newer annexe. The older rooms are furnished in rustic pine, and the common sitting room with the large hearth looks straight out of an Agatha Christie whodunnit.

Thermál *(☎ 323 999, fax 320 406; e thermal@savaria.hu; Rákóczi utca 1; singles/doubles €96/128)* is Sárvár's poshest hostelry with 136 rooms. It boasts all the mod cons, indoor and outdoor thermal pools and complete curative facilities – but so it should for the price.

Places to Eat

Dining options are incorporated in the town's accommodation. The *csárda* at the **Platán** *(mains 700-1500Ft)* has an inviting terrace, while **Tinódi** *(mains 700-1500Ft)* is more cellar-like. Pick of the bunch is **Várkapu** *(mains around 1000Ft)*, with excellent pizzas and Hungarian dishes, and views of the castle.

Korona *(Kossuth tér 3; ice cream from 55Ft)* is a great choice for cakes and ice cream.

Entertainment

Concerts are occasionally held in the Knight's Hall in the castle or in the castle courtyard; check with Savaria Tourist or the **Lajos Kossuth Cultural Centre** *(☎ 320 063)* in the castle for dates.

Getting There & Away

Buses that run to/from Sárvár include: Budapest (two departures daily), Bük (8), Celldömölk (10), Győr (one or two), Keszthely (two), Pápa (three), Pécs (one), Sitke (12), Sopron (three), Sümeg (four), Szombathely (hourly),

Veszprém (three) and Zalaegerszeg (two or three). Buses to Vienna leave at 3.35am on Friday and at 7.50am Saturday.

Sárvár is on the railway line linking Szombathely with Veszprém, and Székesfehérvár and Budapest's Déli, Kelenföld and Keleti stations. You can expect up to 25 trains a day to Szombathely, from where up to five continue to Graz in Austria via Szentgotthárd. Between five and 10 trains reach the other three cities daily.

KŐSZEG
☎ 94 • postcode 9730 • pop 11,900

The tranquil little town of Kőszeg (in German, Güns) is sometimes called 'the nation's jewellery box', and as you pass under the pseudo-Gothic Heroes' Gate into Jurisics tér, you'll understand why. What opens up before you is a treasure trove of colourful Gothic, Renaissance and baroque buildings that together make up one of the most delightful squares in Hungary.

In the shadow of Mt Írottkő – at 882m, the highest point in Transdanubia – and just 3km from the Austrian border, Kőszeg has played pivotal roles in the nation's defence. The best known story is the storming of the town's castle by Suleiman the Magnificent's troops in August 1532, which sounds all too familiar but has a surprise ending. Miklós Jurisics' 'army' of fewer than 50 soldiers and the town militia held the fortress for 25 days against 100,000 Turks. An accord was reached when Jurisics allowed the Turks to run up their flag over the castle in a symbolic declaration of victory provided they left town immediately thereafter. The Turks kept their part of the bargain (packing their bags at 11am on 30 August), and Vienna was spared the treatment that would befall Buda nine years later. To this day church bells in Kőszeg peal an hour before noon to mark the withdrawal.

Orientation & Information
Kőszeg's historic district, the Belváros (Inner Town), is ringed by the Várkör, which follows the old castle walls. The city's bus 'station' is a half-dozen stands on Liszt Ferenc utca a few minutes' walk to the southeast. The train station is about 1.5km in the same direction on Alsó körút.

There's a helpful **Tourinform** (☎ 563 120, fax 563 121; e koszeg@tourinform.hu;

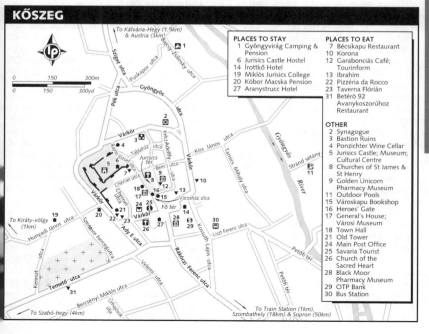

KŐSZEG

PLACES TO STAY
1 Gyöngyvirág Camping & Pension
6 Jurisics Castle Hostel
14 Írottkő Hotel
19 Miklós Jurisics College
20 Kóbor Macska Pension
27 Aranystrucc Hotel

PLACES TO EAT
7 Bécsikapu Restaurant
10 Korona
12 Garabonciás Café; Tourinform
13 Ibrahim
22 Pizzéria da Rocco
23 Taverna Flórián
31 Betérő 92 Avanykoszorúhoz Restaurant

OTHER
2 Synagogue
3 Bastion Ruins
4 Ponzichter Wine Cellar
5 Jurisics Castle; Museum; Cultural Centre
8 Churches of St James & St Henry
9 Golden Unicorn Pharmacy Museum
11 Outdoor Pools
15 Városkapu Bookshop
16 Heroes' Gate
17 General's House; Városi Museum
18 Town Hall
21 Old Tower
24 Main Post Office
25 Savaria Tourist
26 Church of the Sacred Heart
28 Black Moor Pharmacy Museum
29 OTP Bank
30 Bus Station

To Kálvária-Hegy (1.5km) & Austria (3km)

To Király-völgy (1km)

To Szabó-hegy (4km)

To Train Station (1km), Szombathely (18km) & Sopron (50km)

WESTERN TRANSDANUBIA

Jurisics tér 7; open 8am-6pm Mon-Fri, 10am-6pm Sat & Sun mid-June–mid-Sept, 8am-4pm Mon-Fri mid-Sept–mid-June) on the main square in the same building as Garabociá's cafe. **Savaria Tourist** (☎ 563 048; Várkör 69; open 8am-4pm Mon-Fri, 8am-noon Sat) is near Fő tér, as is the branch of the **OTP bank** (Kossuth Lajos utca 8), which has a foreign currency exchange machine. The **main post office** (Várkör 65) is just west of Savaria Tourist. **Városkapu bookshop** (☎ 362 430; Városház utca 4) has a decent English-language section.

Things to See

The **Heroes' Gate** (Hősök kapuja), leading into Jurisics tér, was erected in 1932 (when these nostalgic portals were all the rage in Hungary) to mark the 400th anniversary of Suleiman's departure. The tower above is open to visitors and offers wonderful views (and photo opportunities) of the square. The **General's House** (Tábornokház; Jurisics tér 4–6), next to the gate, contains a branch of the **Városi Museum** (adult/child 100/50Ft; open 10am-5pm Tues-Sun), with exhibits on folk art, trades and guilds, and the natural history of the area.

Almost all of the buildings on Jurisics tér are interesting. The red and yellow **town hall** (Városháza) at No 8 (a mixture of Gothic, Renaissance, baroque and neoclassical styles) has oval paintings on its facade of worldly and heavenly worthies. The Renaissance house at No 7, built in 1668 and now housing a pub, is adorned with graffiti etched into the stucco. Nearby is the **Golden Unicorn Pharmacy** (Arany Egyszarvú Patikaház; ☎ 360 337; Jurisics tér 11; open 10am-5pm Tues-Sun) – one of two pharmacy museums in little Kőszeg. For those of you who can't get enough of controlled substances under glass, the other is the **Black Moor Pharmacy** (Fekete Szerecseny Patikaház; ☎ 360 980; Rákóczi Ferenc utca 3; open 1pm-5pm Tues-Fri).

A statue of the Virgin Mary (1739) and the town fountain (1766), in the middle of Jurisics tér adjoin two fine churches. The Gothic **Church of St James** (Szent Jakabtemplom), built in 1407, is to the north and contains very faded 15th-century frescoes on the east wall of a giant St Christopher carrying the Christ Child, Mary Misericordia sheltering supplicants under a massive cloak, and the Three Magi with their gifts. The altars and pews are masterpieces of baroque wood-

carving, and Miklós Jurisics and two of his children are buried in the crypt. The baroque **Church of St Henry** (Szent Imre-templom) with the tall steeple has two art treasures: a painting of the church's patron by István Dorffmeister above the altar, and one of Mary visiting her cousin Elizabeth by Franz Anton Maulbertsch, on the north wall.

Just off Rajnis József utca to the northwest is a path leading to **Jurisics Castle** (Rajnis utca 9). Originally built in the mid-13th century, but reconstructed several times (most recently in 1962), the four-towered fortress is now a hotchpotch of Renaissance arcades, Gothic windows and baroque interiors. The **Castle Museum** (Vármúzeum; ☎ 360 240; adult/child 100/60Ft; open 10am-5pm Tues-Sun) on the 1st floor has exhibits on the history of Kőszeg from the 14th century (with the events of 1532 taking up most of the space) and on local wine production. Among the latter is the curious Szőlő jővésnek könyve (Arrival of the Grape Book), a kind of gardener's log of grape shoot and bud sketches begun in 1740 and updated yearly on St George's Day (23 April). You can climb two of the towers, from which a brass ensemble entertained the townspeople in the Middle Ages.

Walking south along narrow Chernel utca with its elegant baroque facades and sawtoothed rooftops (which allowed the defenders a better shot at the enemy), you'll pass the remains of the **old castle walls** and the **Old Tower** (Öreg Zwinger) at No 16, an 11th-century corner bastion.

The neo-Gothic **Church of the Sacred Heart** (Jézus Szíve-templom; Fő tér), built in 1894, is unexceptional save for its refreshingly different geometric frescoes and those 'midday' bells at 11am. The circular **synagogue** (Várkör 38), built in 1859, with its strange neo-Gothic towers, once served one of the oldest Jewish communities in Hungary, but now sits abandoned and in decay to the northeast of Jurisics tér.

Activities

Walking up to the baroque chapel on 393m-high Kálvária-hegy (Calvary hill) northwest of the town centre, or into the vineyards of Királyvölgy (King's valley) west of the Jurisics Castle, is a very pleasant way to spend a few hours. You can also follow Temető utca southwest and then south up to 458m-high Szabó-hegy (Tailor's hill). A copy of Cartographia's

Leafy Margaret Island (Margit-sziget), in the middle of the Danube River, Budapest

The Széchenyi Chain Bridge and the Royal Palace illuminated at night, Budapest

Castle Hill's colourful architecure and facades, Budapest

Esztergom Basilica and Primate Island, viewed from Mária Valéria Bridge, Esztergom

Detail of ceramic work by Margit Kovács

Beautiful architecture on Fő tér, Szentendre

A *Kőszegi-hegység és környéke* (The Kőszeg Hills & Surrounds) 1:40,000 map (No 13; 650Ft) will prove useful if you plan to do more adventurous hiking or visit the **Írottkő Nature Park** (contact Tourinform for information) to the west. The Kőszeg Hills are known for their rare Alpine flora.

There's a **small pool and 'beach'** *(Strand sétány; open 10am-6pm mid-June–Aug)* east of the town centre.

Special Events
Events to watch out for include the **Arrival of the Grape Book Festival** (see Things to See earlier for details) in late April, the **Kőszeg Castle Games** held in the castle yard throughout the summer and the **Kőszeg Vintage festival** in late September.

Places to Stay
Camping By the little Gyöngyös River is **Gyöngyvirág Camping** *(☎ 360 454, fax 364 574; Bajcsy-Zsilinszky utca 6; camping per adult/child/tent/car 500/300/300/300Ft; pension rooms 3500Ft; open year-round)*, with basic camp sites and 12 clean, modern rooms in its pension.

Hostels & Private Rooms A cheap, central option is **Jurisics Castle** *(☎ 360 113; Rajnis József utca 9; doubles 3000Ft)*, a hostel in a small building near the entrance to the castle. It's well worn, but the location makes it attractive.

Miklós Jurisics College *(☎ 361 404; Hunyadi János utca 10; dorm beds 900-1200Ft)* has dormitory accommodation in summer.

Savaria Tourist can arrange private rooms for about 2000Ft per person.

Pensions & Hotels Just west of the Inner Town is **Kóbor Macska** *(Stray Cat; ☎/fax 362 273; Várkör 100; singles/doubles 5000/6300Ft)*, a charming nine-room place with a bar downstairs that can sometimes be noisy.

Gyöngyvirág Camping (see camping earlier for details) also has a pension.

Aranystrucc *(Golden Ostrich; ☎ 360 323, fax 563 330; Várkör 124; singles/doubles 4700/7700Ft)* is one of the best places to stay at in Kőszeg. It is a 15-room hotel in an 18th-century building, near the entrance to the Inner Town. Room No 7, on the corner with balcony views over the main square, is the biggest and the best.

Írottkő *(☎/fax 360 373; e info@hotelirot tko.hu; Fő tér 4; singles/doubles 7400/9900Ft)*, with 48 rooms, is Kőszeg's main hotel. It's large and central, but both the building and its rooms are rather uninspiring.

Places to Eat
Pizzéria da Rocco *(☎ 362 379; Várkör 55; pizzas 400-1500Ft; open 10am-midnight daily)*, with its huge garden inside the old castle walls, is a great place for pizza, or indeed just a drink. For fine dining, head next door to **Taverna Flórián** *(☎ 563 072; Várkör 59; pasta around 700Ft, mains around 1500Ft)*, which serves quality Mediterranean food in beautiful cellar-like surroundings.

Bécsikapu *(☎ 360 297; Rajnis József utca 5; mains around 800Ft)*, almost opposite the Church of St James, is a pleasant little place with a back garden looking towards the castle.

Garabonciás *(Jurisics tér 7; pizzas 700Ft)* is a café in a lovely historical building in the main square.

Betérő az Aranykoszorúhoz *(Visitor at the Sign of the Golden Wreath; Temető utca 59; mains around 800Ft; open daily)* has excellent food and is definitely not a tourist haunt.

Korona *(Várkör 18; open 8am-6pm daily)*, a little *presszó* (coffee shop), can't be beat for coffee and cakes. For ice cream don't go past **Ibrahím** *(Fő tér 15; ice cream from 60Ft)*.

Entertainment
The city's **cultural centre** *(☎ 360 113)* is in the castle.

For wine (generally common Sopron vintages), go to the old wine cellar **Ponzichter** *(Rajnis József utca 10)*, which has vaulted ceilings, high Gothic windows and an inviting garden.

Getting There & Away
At least half a dozen buses run daily to Sopron, Szombathely, Sárvár and Velem, but there are only two daily services to Nagykanizsa and one each to Körmend and Keszthely. Three weekly buses (7.05am Wednesday, 8.10am Friday and 4.45am Saturday) head for Oberpullendorf and Vienna in Austria. There's also a daily bus to Lenti, the gateway to Slovenia.

Kőszeg is at the end of an 18km railway spur from Szombathely; there are 14 to 15 arrivals and departures daily (the only express – at 7.36pm – takes just 18 minutes to get to Szombathely).

WESTERN TRANSDANUBIA

ŐRSÉG REGION

This westernmost region, where Hungary, Austria and Slovenia come together, has for centuries been the nation's 'sentry' *(őrség)*, and its houses and villages, spaced unusually far apart on the crests and in the valleys of the Zala foothills, once served as the national frontier. For their service as guards, the inhabitants of the region were given special privileges by the king, which they were able to retain until the arrival of the Batthyány family.

Much of the area now forms the new 44,000-hectare **Őrség National Park**, which borders both Austria and Slovenia. The park is criss-crossed with marked hiking trails that link many of Őrség's villages, including Őriszentpéter, Szalafő, Velemér and Pankasz. Topo's 1:50,000 map *Őrség* (600Ft) is a handy reference, available at the small stationer's shop by Őriszentpéter's bus stop. For more information consult the **information centre** (☎ 548 034; Siskaszor 26/a; open 8am-4.30pm Mon-Fri), at the turn-off to Szalafő in Őriszentpéter.

Őriszentpéter

☎ 94 • postcode 9941 • pop 1200

Őriszentpéter, the centre of the Őrség, is a pretty village of timber and thatch-roofed houses and large gardens; it is the best Őrség town in which to base yourself. Its most interesting sight, a remarkably well-preserved 13th-century **Romanesque church** *(Templomszer 15)*, is an easy 2km walk northwest of the village centre. On the southern extension of the church is a wonderful carved portal and small fragments of 15th-century frescoes. The writings on the south walls inside are Bible verses in Hungarian from the 17th century. The 18th-century altarpiece was painted by a student of Franz Anton Maulbertsch.

Szalafő

☎ 94 • postcode 9942 • pop 280

Energetic travellers may want to continue another 4km along Templomszer, past arcaded old peasant houses and abandoned crank wells to Szalafő, the oldest settlement in the Őrség. In Szalafő-Pityerszer, 2km west of the village, is the **Open-Air Ethnographical Museum** *(Szabadtéri Néprajzi Múzeum; adult/child 300/150Ft; open 10am-6pm Tues-Sun mid-Mar–Oct)*, the grandiose name given to a mini-*skanzen* of three folk compounds unique to the Őrség. Built around a central courtyard,

the houses have large overhangs which allowed neighbours to chat when it rained – a frequent occurrence in this very wet area. The **Calvinist church** in the village centre has murals from the 16th century.

Places to Stay & Eat

The park's information centre has a comprehensive list of accommodation possibilities in the area.

Őrségi (☎ 428 046; Városszer 57; camping per adult/child/tent 700/550/500Ft; doubles with washbasin/shower 3000/3500Ft; camp site open mid-June–Aug) inn offers the cheapest accommodation in Őriszentpéter. It is a simple tourist hostel with eight rooms and a camp site on the road to Szalafő. The manager can also book you a **private room** or accommodation at one of the **peasant houses** (2500Ft per person) in Szalafő. Outside of opening hours you can find her at Kovácsszer 16 (☎ 428 044).

Domino (☎ 428 115; Siskaszer 5/a; singles/doubles 3000/5000Ft) has a number of lovely bungalows complete with kitchen and separate bathroom.

Bognár *(Kovácsszer 96; mains 700-1500Ft)* in Őriszentpéter is a reliable place for a meal. It's about 500m up the hill, north of the bus station.

Pitvar Presszó *(Városszer 101)*, in the centre of the village, serves snacks and drinks.

Getting There & Away

Őriszentpéter and Szalafő can be reached by one of six daily buses from Körmend and from Zalaegerszeg via Zalalövő. Other destinations include Kőszeg (one or two buses daily), Szentgotthárd (four), Sopron (one) and Lenti (three). Three daily (more from mid-May–Sept) buses leave Őriszentpéter for Szalafő.

ZALAEGERSZEG

☎ 92 • postcode 8900 • pop 62,400

Zala (as the locals call their long-named city) is an oil town, and the Zala fields to the south have contributed enormously to this county's development since the 1930s, bringing with it such modern eyesores as the ever-present TV tower and an expensive sport centre.

However, the other part of Zalaegerszeg's name speaks of a very different world: *éger* are the moisture-loving alder trees of the Göcsej Hills to the west, an area that gets the most rainfall and has some of the worst soil in all of Hungary. Sitting side by side, the city's two open-air museums (one devoted to oil, the other to traditional village life) illustrate all too well the dichotomy that is Zalaegerszeg.

Orientation & Information
The bus station is a few minutes' walk east of Széchenyi tér on Balatoni út, while the train station is about 1.5km south, at the end of Zrínyi Miklós utca, on Bajcsy-Zsilinszky tér.

Tourinform (*☎/fax 316 160;* e *zalae gerszeg@tourinform.hu; Széchenyi tér 4-6; open 10am-4pm Mon-Fri)* is quite helpful; **Zalatour** (*☎ 311 443, fax 311 469; Kovács Károly tér 1; open 9am-5pm Mon-Fri, 9am-noon Sat)* is not.

There's a branch of the **Budapest Bank** *(Kossuth Lajos utca 2)* here, and a **K&H bank** on Dísz tér, a bit further south, with an exchange machine. There's the **main post office** *(Ispotály köz 1)*, and Internet access is available at **Zalaszám** *(Kossuth Lagos utca 36; one hour 500Ft; open 10am-8pm daily)*.

Things to See & Do
The 1904 rose-coloured **synagogue** *(Ady Endre utca 14)*, with its enormous Torah-shaped organ and stained-glass rose windows, now serves as a **concert hall** and **gallery**. On Szabadság tér there's an interesting baroque **parish church** (plébániatemplom), built in 1760. Nearby are the ruins of a 15th-century **chapel**, with lovely frescoes by the Austrian painter Johannes Cymbal.

Zalaegerszeg is best known for its museums. The **Göcsej Museum** (*☎ 314 537; Batthyány Lajos utca 2; adult/child 200/100Ft; open 9am-5pm Tues-Fri, 10am-4pm Sat & Sun)*, north of Szabadság tér, is divided into two parts. The first examines the work of painter-sculptor Zsigmond Kisfaludy Strobl (1884–1975), whose earlier work included portraits and busts of Somerset Maugham, the Duke of Kent and other socialites of the 1920s and 1930s. He moved away from these to focus on socialist themes after the war. He also designed the striking *Independence* statue atop Gellért Hill in Budapest for Admiral Miklós Horthy's son during WWII. After the war, when heroic monuments were in short supply, Kisfaludy Strobl passed it off as a memorial to the Soviets – he very much deserved his nickname, the 'Side-Stepper'. The next section of the museum concerns

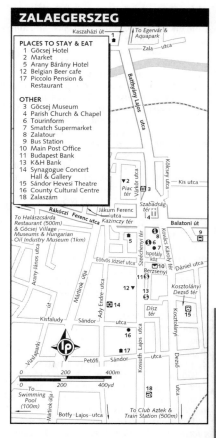

local history and folk art and is very well presented; the Roman finds from nearby Zalalövő are especially interesting, but labelled only in Hungarian.

The **Göcsej Village Museum** *(Göcseji Falumúzeum; ☎ 313 494; Falumúzeum utca 2; adult/child for both open-air museums 200/100Ft; open 10am-6pm Tues-Sun May-Sept, 10am-4pm Tues-Sun Apr & Oct)*, near a backwater of the Zala River off Ola utca, northwest of the centre, is the oldest *skanzen* in Hungary and it shows; of the three dozen structures, a good one-third are shut tight or rotting into oblivion. Still, the museum is a realistic depiction of a Göcsej traditional village 100 years ago, with its unique U-shaped farmhouses that lead to a central courtyard *(kerített házak)*, pálinka stills and smokehouses. The five carved and painted house facades date from the late 19th century. The open-air **Hungarian Oil Industry Museum** *(Magyar Olajipari Múzeum;* ☎ *311 081)*, which keeps the same hours as Göcsej Village Museum (see earlier), is a few steps to the west.

Zalaegerszeg's new **Aquapark** *(Martinovics utca; admission full day/after 2pm 3000/1060Ft; open 10am-7pm Mon, 9am-7pm Tues-Fri, 9am-8pm Sat & Sun late-May–Sept)* covers a massive 7.5 hectares and has enough pools, beaches and slides to accommodate half of the town's population.

There are also indoor and outdoor **pools** and a **sauna** at Mártírok útja 78 *(adult/child 430/280Ft; open 10am-7pm Mon, 9am-7pm Tues-Fri, 9am-8pm Sat & Sun).*

Places to Stay

Ask Zalatour about **private rooms** for 4000Ft per double. They can also book you into old **peasant houses** that accommodate between three and five people in the Göcsej Hills southwest of Zalaegerszeg (7000Ft per double), but you'll have to travel under your own steam to get there.

Várkastély *(☎/fax 364 015; Vár utca 1; dorm bed around 1500-2000Ft)* hostel is housed in the romantic 18th-century 'Castle Palace' in Egervár, 10km north of Zalaegerszeg. It has six dormitory rooms.

Göcsej *(☎ 511 924, fax 311 469; Kaszaházi utca 2; singles/doubles from 3400/4000Ft)* is a 20-room hotel with adequate rooms, but is not very conveniently located.

Piccolo *(☎ 510 055, fax 320 100;* ⓔ *info@ piccolo.hu; Petőfi Sándor utca 16; rooms 6500Ft)* is an eight-room pension on a quiet street off Kossuth Lajos utca.

Arany Bárány *(☎ 314 100, fax 320 347;* ⓦ *www.aranybarany.hu; Széchenyi tér 1; singles/doubles 8900/11,100Ft)* is a friendly, 50-room hotel and has both a new and an old wing (built in 1898).

Places to Eat

A decent place for a meal in Zalaegerszeg is the homy restaurant at the **Piccolo Pension** *(mains around 1000Ft)*; for details see Places to Stay.

Belgian Beer Cafe *(☎ 511 140; Kossuth Lagos utca 5; mains 1000-1500Ft)* may be a chain restaurant, but the food is still top quality, as is the beer.

Halászcsárda *(☎ 511 882; Rákóczi utca 47; mains from 1000Ft)* is an excellent fish restaurant near the open-air museums, with garden seating in summer.

Zalaegerszeg's lively **fruit & vegetable market** is on Piac tér, west of Szabadság tér.

Entertainment

County Cultural Centre *(☎ 314 580; Kisfaludy Sándor utca 7-10)* is a good source for what's on in Zalaegerszeg. Check the listings in the freebie bi-weekly *Zalai Est* for clubs, theatre, parties and sporting events.

Sándor Hevesi Theatre *(☎ 314 405; Kosztolányi Dezső tér 1)* is well known for its drama and musical productions (though they will be in Hungarian). The city's symphony orchestra may be playing here or at the **concert hall** in the former synagogue.

Club Aztek *(Zrínyi Miklós utca 6)*, south of the town centre, is the big club in Zala.

Getting There & Away

More than a dozen buses head for Egervár, Keszthely, Lenti and Nagykanizsa daily. Other destinations include Balatonfüred (five buses daily), Budapest (six), Győr (five), Kaposvár (three), Körmend (seven), Pécs (five), Sárvár (three), Sopron (two), Sümeg (eight or nine), Székesfehérvár (three), Szombathely (seven), Tapolca (five) and Veszprém (eight or nine).

Zalaegerszeg was bypassed during railway construction in the 19th century; today few places of any interest are serviced by trains from here. Up to four trains a day leave for Szombathely, but generally you'll have to change at Zalaszentiván. For Budapest you'll have to change at Boba.

Getting Around

Bus No 10 runs from the train station to Széchenyi tér and then west along Rákóczi utca and Ola utca to the open-air museums. To reach the Göcsej hotel take bus No 3 or 5.

You can book a local taxi service by calling ☎ 333 333 or ☎ 336 699.

Lake Balaton Region

Hungary may not have majestic mountains or ocean beaches but it does have Lake Balaton, the largest body of freshwater in Europe outside Scandinavia. This oblong lake is 78km long, 15km across at its widest point and covers an area of almost 600 sq km.

Lake Balaton (Balaton-tó), 'Hungary's inland sea', is bounded by hills to the north and gentle slopes to the south, and its surface seems to change colour with the seasons and the time of day. The lake has been eulogised in songs, poems and paintings for centuries, and the surrounding region produces some of Hungary's best wines.

But Balaton is not everyone's cup of tea. The resorts (especially those on the southern side) can be overrun in summer. The lake is shallow, averaging about 3m in depth, and on the southern shore you'll paddle for a kilometre before the water gets above your waist. The water is silty and alkaline – almost oily – and not very refreshing, averaging 26°C throughout winter and summer. Then there are the reed beds, especially on the western and northwestern shores, which suggest a swampy marsh. Indeed, the lake's name comes from the Slavic root word *blatna*, which means just that.

Lake Balaton is fed by about 40 canals and streams, but its main source is the Zala River to the southwest. The lake's only outflow is the Sió Canal, which connects it at Siófok with the Danube River east of Szekszárd.

History

The area around Lake Balaton was settled as early as the Iron Age and the Romans, who called the lake Pelso, built a fort at Valcum (now Fenékpuszta), south of Keszthely, in the 2nd century AD. Throughout the Great Migrations (see History in the Facts about Hungary chapter for details), Lake Balaton was a reliable source of water, fish, reeds for thatch, and ice in winter. The early Magyars found the lake a natural defence line, and many churches, monasteries and villages were built in the vicinity. In the 16th century the lake served as the divide between the Turks, who occupied the southern shore, and the Habsburgs to the northwest, but before the Ottomans were pushed back they had already crossed the lake and razed many of the

Highlights

- Castle Hill in Veszprém and its wonderful architecture
- Tihany's ochre-coloured Abbey Church
- The Festetics Palace at Keszthely
- Famed sunworship and local wine at one of Balaton's lakeside towns
- Europe's largest thermal lake (Gyógy-tó) at Hévíz
- Franz Anton Maulbertsch's wonderful frescoes at the Church of the Ascension, and the hill-top Sümeg Castle, both in Sümeg

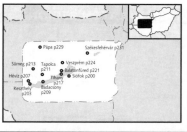

towns and border castles in the northern hills. Croats, Germans and Slovaks resettled the area in the 18th century, and the subsequent building booms gave towns such as Sümeg, Veszprém and Keszthely their baroque appearance.

Balatonfüred and Hévíz developed early as resorts for the wealthy, but it wasn't until the late 19th century that landowners, their vines destroyed by phylloxera lice, began building summer homes to rent out to the burgeoning middle classes. The arrival of the southern railway in 1861 and the northern line in 1909 increased the tourist influx, and by the 1920s resorts on both shores welcomed some 50,000 holiday-makers each summer. Just before the outbreak of WWII, that number had increased fourfold. After the war, the communist government expropriated private villas and built new holiday homes for trade unions. Many of these have been turned into hotels, greatly increasing the accommodation options.

Orientation

The two shores of Lake Balaton are like chalk and cheese. The southern coast is essentially one long resort: from Siófok to Fonyód, there are high-rise hotels, concrete embankments to prevent flooding, and minuscule grassy 'beaches' packed with sunbathers in summer. Here the water is at its shallowest and safest for children, and the beaches are not reedy as they often are on the northern shore.

Things change dramatically as you round the bend from Keszthely, a pretty town hugging the westernmost end of the lake, to the northern shore. The north has many more historical towns, mountain trails and better wine. The resorts at Badacsony, Tihany and Balatonfüred have more grace and atmosphere and are far less commercial than, say,

Siófok or Balatonboglár to the south. See also Lake Balaton's website (**W** www.balaton.hu).

Activities

The main pursuits for visitors at Lake Balaton – apart from **swimming**, of course – are **boating** and **fishing**. (See Activities in the Facts for the Visitor chapter for more details about each of these activities.) Motorboats running on fuel are banned entirely, so 'boating' here means sailing, rowing and windsurfing. Fishing is good – the indigenous *fogas* (pike-perch) and the young version, *süllő*, being the prized catch – and edible *harcsa* (catfish) and *ponty* (carp) are in abundance.

You can get a fishing licence for 500/2000Ft per day/week from **Siotour** (**☎** *310 900, fax 310 009; Szabadság tér 6*), in Siófok,

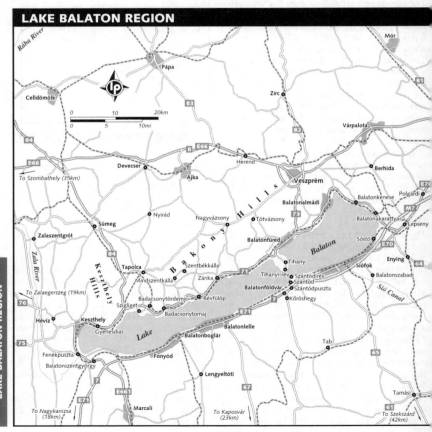

or the **National Federation of Hungarian Anglers** *(Mohosz; ☎ 1-319 9790, fax 319 9792; ⓦ www.mohosz.hu; XII Korompai utca 17)* in Budapest.

One of the big events of the year at the lake is the **Cross-Balaton Swimming Race** from Révfülöp to Balatonboglár in late July.

If you can get into the swing of it, the lake is a good place to meet people as it is one of the few places where Hungarians really do let their hair (and most everything else) down. Bear in mind, though, that during the low season (roughly late October to early April) much of the place virtually shuts down.

Getting There & Away

Trains to Lake Balaton usually leave from Déli or Kelenföld train stations in Budapest,

and buses depart from Népliget bus station. If you're travelling north or south from the lake to towns in Western or Southern Transdanubia, buses are usually preferable to trains (see the Getting Around chapter for details).

Getting Around

Railway service on both the northern and southern sides of the lake is fairly frequent. A better way to see the lake up close, though, is on a ferry run by the **Balaton Shipping Co** *(Balatoni Hajózási Rt; ☎/fax 84-310 050; ⓦ www.balatonihajozas.hu; Krúdy sétány 2)* based in Siófok. Ferries operate on the Siófok–Balatonfüred–Tihany–Balatonföldvr route, and from Fonyód to the Badacsony, up to four times daily in April/May and September/October, with much more frequent sailings from June to August. From late May to early September, ferries ply the lake from Balatonkenese to Keszthely and Révfülöp to Balatonboglár. There is also a regular car ferry between Tihanyi-rév and Szántódi-rév (from early March to late November). There are no passenger services on the lake in winter, ie, from November to March.

Fares are cheap. Adults pay 480Ft for distances of one to 10km, 760Ft for 11km to 20km, 840Ft for 21km to 40km and 900Ft for 41km to 70km. Children pay half-price, and return fares are slightly less than double the one-way fare. To transport a bicycle it costs 360/500Ft one way/return.

The car ferries charge 280/230/460/920Ft per person/bicycle/motorcycle/car.

SIÓFOK
☎ 84 • postcode 8600 • pop 22,200

Siófok, 106km southwest of Budapest, typifies the resorts of the southern shore: it's loud, brash and crowded in summer. Dedicated pursuits here are eating, drinking, sunbathing, swimming and sleeping – and whatever comes in between. It is the largest of the lake's resorts and is jammed at the height of summer – so much so that since 1997 it's allowed to call itself 'Hungary's summer capital'.

Siófok didn't start out this way. In the 19th century it was just as elegant as Balatonfüred, and the lovely villas on Batthyány Lajos utca near Jókai Park and the lakeside promenade recall those days. But late in the 20th century, after the southern railway line had reached Siófok, more and more people began to holiday here. Today many of the villas have been converted to hotels or offices, and the promenade, with its mock gas lamps, has been paved.

The regional white wine in these parts comes from Balatonboglár and is usually light and not very distinctive (though the Chardonnay isn't bad).

Orientation

Greater Siófok stretches for some 17km, as far as the resort of Balatonvilágos (once reserved exclusively for communist honchos) to the east and Balatonszéplak to the west. The dividing line between the so-called Gold Coast (Aranypart) in the east, where most of the big hotels are, and the less-developed Silver Coast (Ezüstpart) to the west is the lake-draining Sió Canal, which runs in a southeasterly direction to the Danube River.

Szabadság tér, the centre of Siófok, is to the east of the canal and about 500m southeast of the ferry pier. The bus and train stations are on Váradi Adolf tér just off Fő utca, the main drag.

Information

Tourinform (☎/fax 310 117; e siofok@tour inform.hu; Szabadság tér; open 8am-8pm Mon-Sat, 10am-6pm Sun mid-June–mid-Sept; 9am-4pm Mon-Fri mid-Sept–mid-June) has an office at the base of the old water tower (víztorony).

Commercial agencies include **Siotour** (☎ 310 900, fax 310 009; Szabadság tér 6), and **Ibusz** (☎/fax 311 213; Fő utca 176). Generally they're open from 8am to 4pm Monday to Friday, but in summer they also stay open as late as 8pm and are open on Saturday morning.

There's an **OTP bank** (Szabadság tér 10/A) with a currency-exchange machine near Tourinform, but you'll find exchange offices all over town. The **main post office** (Fő utca 186) is opposite the bus and train stations.

See the town's website w www.siofok.hu for more information.

Things to See

There's not a whole lot to see of cultural or historical importance in a place where the baser instincts tend to rule. The shark aquarium at the **Coral Aquarium** (☎ 313 917; Batthyány Lajos utca 22; adult/child 500/ 300Ft, shark show extra 200Ft; open 10am-6pm daily Apr-Oct, 10am-4pm Nov-Mar) is the largest of its kind in Hungary, but it seems out of place next to shallow Lake Balaton.

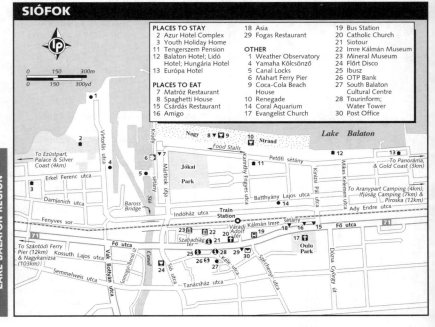

SIÓFOK

PLACES TO STAY
2 Azur Hotel Complex
3 Youth Holiday Home
11 Tengerszem Pension
12 Balaton Hotel; Lidó Hotel; Hungária Hotel
13 Európa Hotel

PLACES TO EAT
7 Matróz Restaurant
8 Spaghetti House
15 Csárdás Restaurant
16 Amigo

18 Asia
29 Fogas Restaurant

OTHER
1 Weather Observatory
4 Yamaha Kölcsönző
5 Canal Locks
6 Mahart Ferry Pier
9 Coca-Cola Beach House
10 Renegade
14 Coral Aquarium
17 Evangelist Church

19 Bus Station
20 Catholic Church
21 Siotour
22 Imre Kálmán Museum
23 Mineral Museum
24 Flört Disco
25 Ibusz
26 OTP Bank
27 South Balaton Cultural Centre
28 Tourinform; Water Tower
30 Post Office

The **canal locks** system, which was partly built by the Romans in 292 AD and used extensively by the Turks in the 16th and 17th centuries, can be seen from Krúdy sétány, the walkway near the ferry pier, or Baross Bridge to the south. Nearby are the headquarters of the Hungarian navy. The tower on the western tip of the canal entrance is the **weather observatory** of the National Meteorological Service (Országos Meteorológiai Szolgálat). Believe it or not, Lake Balaton can actually get quite rough when the wind picks up, and there's a system of warning signals.

The wooden **water tower** on Szabadság tér dates from 1912. If you walk north on narrow Hock János köz, you'll reach the **Imre Kálmán Museum** (☎ 311 287; Kálmán Imre sétány 5; adult/child 200/100Ft; open 9am-5pm Tues-Sun Apr-Oct, 9am-4pm Tues-Sun Nov-Mar). It is devoted to the life and works of the composer of popular operettas, Imre Kálmán, who was born in Siófok in 1882.

Nearby is an uninspiring **Mineral Museum** (Ásványmúzeum; ☎ 350 038; Kálmán Imre utca 10; adult/child 200/100Ft; open 10am-6pm Tues-Sun Apr-Oct), which is quite small and doesn't have much on display.

East of Szabadság tér in Oulu Park, Hungary's maverick architect Imre Makovecz strikes again with his winged and 'masked' **Evangelist church** (Evangélikus templom), which bears a strong resemblance to an Indonesian *garuda* (mythical bird).

Activities
Nagy Strand, Siófok's 'Big Beach' is east of the observatory and just north of Petőfi sétány, and is open to the public. There are many more 'managed' **swimming** areas along the Gold and Silver Coasts where it costs 400/200Ft per adult/child for a day pass and 2000/1000Ft for a weekly pass.

There are rowing boats and sailing **boats** for hire at various locations along the lake, including the Nagy Strand. On the canal's western bank you'll find **Yamaha Kölcsönzö** (☎ 06-20 945 1279; Virtorlás utca; open daily mid-May–mid-Oct) where you can hire bicycles for 400/1600Ft per hour/day and mopeds for 1500/5000Ft.

Places to Stay
Siófok is one of the few places on the lake where you might have trouble finding accommodation during the high season – Siófok

gets some 100,000 visitors in late July and August. During this time, it is worth booking ahead.

Camping There are over two dozen camp sites along the Balaton's southern shore, and Siófok has nine, most with bungalows sleeping up to four people. They are open from May to September; the highest rates apply during most of July and August.

Aranypart Camping (☎ 352 519, fax 352 801; Szent László utca 183-185; camping per tent €3.30-4.20, adult €3.90-5.50, child €1.95-2.75, bungalows €28.20-91.60), 4km east of the centre in Balatonszabadi, has its own beach; if you're coming from Budapest by train, get off at the Szabadi-fürdő station, one stop before Siófok.

Ifjúság Camping (☎/fax 352 571; Pusztatorony tér 1; camping per tent €2.90-3.80, adult €2.20-3.20, child €1.45-1.90, bungalows €22.90-68) is in Sóstó, 7km east of Siófok between tiny 'Salt Lake' and Lake Balaton. The correct train station for this camp site is Balatonszabadi–Sóstó.

For those who like to camp *au naturel*, there's a nudist site at Balatonakarattya at the northeastern end of the lake about 12km northeast of Siófok. **Piroska** (☎ 584 521, fax 584 522; Aligai út 15; camping per tent 820-990Ft, adult 750-970Ft, child 600-780Ft, bungalows 3000-4050Ft) is within easy walking distance of the Balatonakarattya train station, which is on the line running along the lake's northern shore.

Private Rooms, Hostels & Pensions
Tourinform, Siotour and Ibusz (see Information earlier) can find you a private room for €12 to €18 per person and an apartment for slightly more. Singles are rare and those staying only one or two nights are generally unwelcome; if you want to do it alone, check for 'Zimmer frei' signs along Erkel Ferenc utca and Damjanich utca on the Silver Coast and Petőfi sétány and Beszédes József sétány on the Gold Coast.

Ifjúság (☎/fax 352 571; Pusztatorony tér 1; beds per person €3.25-6.50) has small, wooden cabins that sleep two people. Kitchen and toilet facilities are shared with the campers.

Youth Holiday Home (Ifjúsági Üdülö; ☎/fax 310 131; Erkel Ferenc utca 46; beds 1500-2000Ft; open mid-June–Aug) is a hostel northwest of the town centre.

Tengerszem (π/fax 310 146; Karinthy Frigyes utca 4; singles/doubles 5500/8000Ft; open May-Sept) is a pension just south of the Nagy Strand, in a comfy old house close to the beach and a number of restaurants.

Hotels The Accor-Pannonia chain (fax 310 304; w www.pannoniahotels.hu) has four hotels with more than 560 rooms collectively along Petőfi sétány (at Nos 9 to 17) and along a narrow beach at the start of the Gold Coast: the **Balaton** (π 310 655); **Lidó** (π 310 633); **Hungária** (π 310 677); and the **Európa** (π 313 411). All are three-star and each has about 130 rooms. Rooms in the high season start at around 9000Ft, whether it's single or double occupancy.

Panoráma (π 311 638, fax 510 226; e panoramahotel@axelero.hu; Beszédes József sétány 80; singles 8600-12,300Ft, doubles 11,000-15,900Ft) is a large four-star hotel with 154 rooms.

Ázur (π 312 419, fax 312 105; Vitorlás utca 11; singles 4400-8500Ft, doubles 5800-11,200Ft), a hotel complex on the western side of the canal mouth, is friendly and reasonably priced, and has a fitness centre and private beach – but it's not in the nicest part of Siófok. It has over 400 rooms in four buildings; the main building (No 4) is the nicest one.

Ezüstpart (π 350 622, fax 350 358; e reserve@balaton.huguesthotels.hu; Liszt Ferenc sétány 2-4; singles €26-63, doubles €36-79) is an enormous hotel that has more than 800 rooms in five different buildings. Rates depend on room type and the season.

Places to Eat

Siófok is one place you won't starve, but the food quality is not always the best.

There are a number of **food stalls** by the Nagy Strand along Petőfi sétány, but if you want to sit down try **Spaghetti House** (Nagy Strand; mains around 100Ft), which is popular with students in summer and faces the lake.

Amigo (Fő utca 99; pizzas 400-700Ft) is incredibly popular for its large and tasty pizzas.

Asia (Fő utca 93; mains around 1000Ft), a few steps west of Amigo, has a mixed Asian menu.

Matróz (Krúdy sétány; mains from 700Ft) is a bar-restaurant with outdoor tables facing the canal's lock system and moored boats. It's also convenient to the ferry.

Csárdás (Fő utca 105; mains 900-1500Ft) near Kinizsi Pál utca is a reliable place in an old townhouse with a pleasant garden.

Fogas (Fő utca 184; mains 900-1800Ft), next to the post office, has one of the largest selections of fish dishes in town.

Entertainment

South Balaton Cultural Centre (π 311 855; Fő tér 2), Siófok's main cultural venue, stages concerts, dance performances and plays. Organ recitals can be enjoyed in the **Catholic church** on Váradi Adolf tér.

Two popular discos are **Flört** (Sió utca 4; open until 6am daily in summer) and the huge **Palace** (Deák Ferenc utca 2) on the Silver Coast, which is accessible by free bus from outside Tourinform between 9pm and 5am daily from May to mid-September.

Coca-Cola Beach House (Nagy Strand), with free concerts on Wednesday and Saturday nights from mid-June to mid-August, is more informal than Palace or Flört – and livelier for that.

Renegade, which is a pub a short distance to the east of Coca-Cola Beach House, is where everyone moves on to for drinking and bopping.

Getting There & Away

Bus Buses serve a lot of destinations from Siófok, but compared with the excellent train connections, they're not very frequent. The exceptions are to Kaposvár, with hourly departures. Other destinations include Budapest (seven daily), Gyula (one), Győr (one), Harkány (one), Hévíz and Keszthely (two to three), Kecskemét (one), Pécs (four), Szeged (one), Szekszárd (five), Tapolca (one), Tatabánya (one), Veszprém (five) and Zalaegerszeg (one). A bus bound for Hamburg departs at 7.15pm daily except Tuesday and Thursday and two depart for Rotterdam at 11am and 7pm daily from late June to mid-September. There are also buses to Dortmund at 7pm Monday, Tuesday, Friday and Saturday, and Köln at 7pm Thursday and Sunday during the same period.

Train The main railway line running through Siófok carries trains to Székesfehérvár, to Déli and Kelenföld train stations in Budapest, to the other resorts on the lake's southern shore and Nagykanizsa up to 26 times daily in each direction. Up to four trains daily from

Budapest to Zagreb and one to Venice stop at Siófok. Local trains run south from Siófok to Kaposvár four times daily.

Boat From late March to late October, four daily Mahart ferries link Siófok with Balatonfüred, three of which carry on to Tihany. Up to seven ferries follow the same route in July and August. See also Getting Around in the introductory section of this chapter for more details about other routes and frequencies for ferry services.

Getting Around

Departing from outside the train station and from the bus station, bus Nos 1 and 2 for the Silver Coast and Gold Coast, respectively. For a local taxi ring ☎ 312 240.

KESZTHELY

☎ 83 • postcode 8360 • pop 23,000

Keszthely (**kest**-hay), at the western end of Lake Balaton about 70km from Balatonfüred, is the only town on the lake not entirely dependent on tourism. As a result, Keszthely does not have the melancholy, ghost-town feel to it that Siófok does in the low season.

The Romans built a fort at Valcum (now Fenékpuszta) 5km to the south, and their road north to the colonies at Sopron and Szombathely is today's Kossuth Lajos utca. The town's former fortified monastery and Franciscan church on Fő tér were strong enough to repel the Turks in the 16th century.

In the middle of the 18th century, Keszthely and its surrounds (including Hévíz) came into the possession of the Festetics family,

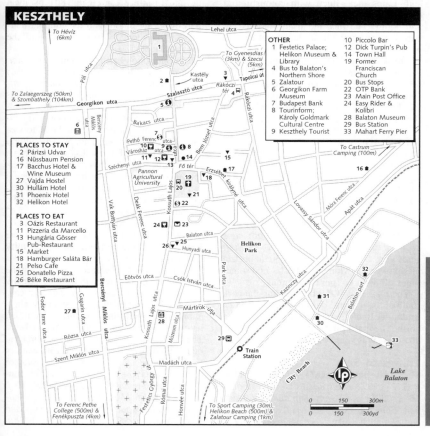

KESZTHELY

OTHER
1 Festetics Palace; Helikon Museum & Library
4 Bus to Balaton's Northern Shore
5 Zalatour
6 Georgikon Farm Museum
7 Budapest Bank
8 Tourinform; Károly Goldmark Cultural Centre
9 Keszthely Tourist
10 Piccolo Bar
12 Dick Turpin's Pub
14 Town Hall
19 Former Franciscan Church
20 Bus Stops
22 OTP Bank
23 Main Post Office
24 Easy Rider & Kolibri
28 Balaton Museum
29 Bus Station
33 Mahart Ferry Pier

PLACES TO STAY
2 Párizsi Udvar
16 Nüssbaum Pension
17 Bacchus Hotel & Wine Museum
27 Vajda Hostel
30 Hullám Hotel
31 Phoenix Hotel
32 Helikon Hotel

PLACES TO EAT
3 Oázis Restaurant
11 Pizzeria da Marcello
13 Hungária Gösser Pub-Restaurant
15 Market
18 Hamburger Saláta Bár
21 Pelso Cafe
25 Donatello Pizza
26 Béke Restaurant

LAKE BALATON REGION

progressives and reformers very much in the tradition of the Széchenyis. In fact, Count György Festetics (1755–1819), who founded Europe's first agricultural college, the Georgikon, here in 1797, was an uncle of István Széchenyi.

Today, Keszthely is a pleasant town of grand houses, trees, cafés and enough to see and do to hold you for a spell. It has a unique view of both the northern and southern shores of Lake Balaton, and the large student population contributes to the town's nightlife.

The biggest annual cultural event in Keszthely is the **Balaton Festival** (music and street theatre) held throughout May.

Orientation

The centre of town is Fő tér, from where Kossuth Lajos utca, lined with colourful old houses, runs to the north (pedestrian only) and south. The bus and train stations are opposite one another near the lake at the end of Mártírok útja. From the stations, follow Mártírok útja up the hill, then turn north into Kossuth Lajos utca to reach the centre. The ferry docks at a stone pier within sight of the Hullám hotel. From here, follow the path past the hotel. Erzsébet királyné utca, which flanks Helikon Park, leads to Fő tér.

Information

Tourinform (☎/fax 314 144; e keszthely@tourinform.hu; Kossuth Lajos utca 28; open 9am-8pm Mon-Fri, 9am-6pm Sat mid-June–mid-Sept; 9am-5pm Mon-Fri, 9am-1pm Sat mid-Sept–mid-June) is an excellent source of information on Keszthely and the entire Balaton area. Other agencies include **Keszthely Tourist** (☎ 314 288; Kossuth Lajos utca 25) and **Zalatour** (☎ 312 560; Kossuth Lajos utca 1), which are open 8.30am or 9am till 4pm or 5pm Monday to Friday and sometimes till noon or 1pm on Saturday.

There's a huge **OTP bank** facing the park south of the former Franscican church and a **Budapest Bank** (Pethő Ferenc utca 1) to the north. The **main post office** (Kossuth Lajos utca 46-48) is south of OTP.

Things to See

The **Festetics Palace** (Festetics kastély; ☎ 312 190; Kastély utca 1; adult/student 1500/750Ft; open 9am-6pm daily July-Aug, 9am-5pm Tues-Sun Sept-May), built in 1745 and extended 150 years later, contains 100 rooms in two sprawling wings. The 19th-century northern wing houses a music school, city library and conference centre; the **Helikon Palace Museum** (Helikon Kastélymúzeum) and the palace's greatest treasure, the renowned **Helikon Library** (Helikon Könyvtar) are in the baroque south wing. The admission fee is outrageous and a one-hour guided tour of the palace in one of four languages costs 'only' 5000Ft.

The museum's rooms (about a dozen in all, each in a different colour scheme) are full of portraits, bric-a-brac and furniture, much of it brought from England by Mary Hamilton, a duchess who married one of the Festetics men in the 1860s. The library is renowned for its 90,000-volume collection, but just as impressive is the golden oak shelving and furniture carved in 1801 by local craftsman János Kerbl. Also worth noting are the Louis XIV Salon with its stunning marquetry, the rococo Music Room and the private chapel (1804).

The **Georgikon Farm Museum** (Georgikon Majormúzeum; ☎ 311 563; Bercsényi Miklós utca 67; adult/child 300/150Ft; open 10am-5pm Mon-Sat, 10am-6pm Sun May-Oct) is housed in several early-19th-century buildings of what was the Georgikon's experimental farm. It contains exhibits on the history of the college and the later Pannon Agricultural University (now a few blocks to the southeast on the corner of Széchenyi utca and Deák Ferenc utca), viniculture in the Balaton region and traditional farm trades such as those performed by wagon builders, wheelwrights, coopers and blacksmiths.

Fő tér is a colourful square with some lovely buildings, including the late-baroque **Town Hall** on the northern side, the **Trinity Column** (1770) in the centre and the former **Franciscan church** (Ferences templom) in the park to the south. The church was originally built in the Gothic style in the late 14th century for Franciscan monks, but many alterations were made in subsequent centuries, including the addition of the steeple in 1898. The Gothic rose window above the porch remains, though, as do some faded 15th-century frescoes in the sanctuary and on the southern wall. Count György and other Festetics family members are buried in the crypt below.

The **Balaton Museum** (☎ 312 351; Múzeum utca 2; adult/child 200/150Ft; open 10am-6pm Tues-Sat May-Oct, 10am-5pm

Nov-Apr), on the corner of Mártírok útja and Kossuth Lajos utca, was purpose-built in 1928 and contains much on the Roman fort at Valcum (Fenékputza) and traditional life around Lake Balaton. Also of interest are exhibits depicting the history of navigation on the lake and the photographs of summer frolickers at the start of the 20th century.

There's a bird-ringing camp run by the **Hungarian Ornithological & Nature Conservation Society** *(MME; ☎ 1-275 6247 in Budapest)* with very knowledgable staff in Fenékpuszta near the delta of the Zala River, which is part of the Felvidéki National Park, south of Keszthely. The camp is just one stop on the train heading for Balatonszentgyörgy; if you're driving from Keszthely, the exit is at the 111km stone on route No 71.

Activities

Keszthely has two beaches that are OK for **swimming** or **sunbathing**: City Beach (Városi Strand), close to the ferry pier, and reedy Helikon Beach farther south. There's a **windsurfing** and **kitesurfing** school at City Beach in summer and another one at Vonyarcvas-hegy Strand across the bay in Gyenesdiás.

There are several **horse-riding** schools, including **Szécsi** *(☎ 315 732)* in Sömögyedűlő, northeast of Keszthely.

The **Bacchus Wine Museum** *(☎/fax 314 097; ⓦ www.bacchushotel.hu; Erzsébet királyné utca 18; open noon-10pm daily)*, part of the Bacchus hotel (see Places to Stay), offers wine tasting from 2200Ft.

Places to Stay

Camping There are three camp sites near the lake, two of which have bungalows and are open from May to September. As you leave the train station, head south across the tracks and you'll soon reach **Sport Camping** *(☎/fax 313 777; Csárda utca; camping per tent 600Ft, adult 650-750Ft, child 300-400Ft)*, wedged between the railway tracks and a road. It's noisy and not very clean.

Carry on south for another 1km to **Zalatour Camping** *(☎/fax 312 782; Ernszt Géza sétány; camping per tent 650-790Ft, adult 650-790Ft, child 270-300Ft, bungalows 3000-4200Ft, apartments 7900-9300Ft)*, a much bigger place with large bungalows for four people and smaller holiday houses. There are tennis courts, and the site has access to Helikon Beach.

Castrum Camping *(☎ 312 120; Móra Ferenc utca 48; camping per tent 560Ft, adult 700-840Ft, child 420-560Ft; open Apr-Oct)*, north of the stations, has its own beach but no bungalows, and is really for caravans.

Hostels Like most towns in Hungary, the colleges of Keszthely open their doors to travellers from mid-June to August. Options include **Ferenc Pethe College** *(☎ 311 290; Festetics György út 5; rooms 2154Ft)* and **Vajda Hostel** *(☎ 311 361; Gagarin utca 4; dorm beds 1000-1200Ft)*, the summer break version of Janos Vajda College.

Private Rooms Zalatour and Keszthely Tourist (see Information earlier for details) can help find private rooms for about 2000Ft to 2500Ft per person.

If you're only staying one night, the agencies may levy heavy surcharges, making it worthwhile to forgo their services and go directly to houses with signs reading '*szoba kiadó*' or '*Zimmer frei*' (Hungarian and German, respectively, for 'room for rent'), where you may be able to bargain with the owners. There are lots along Móra Ferenc utca.

Pensions A good choice near Festetics Palace is **Párizsi Udvar** *(☎/fax 311 202; Kastély utca 5; rooms from 6900Ft)*. Its 14 large rooms were originally part of the palace complex, and there are a couple of huge apartments.

Nüssbaum *(☎/fax 314 365; ⓔ nussbaum@axelero.hu; Móra Ferenc utca 15; doubles from €40)* is a comfortable pension in a quiet, leafy residential area close to the lake.

Hotels If you want to stay near the lake, the following three places are good options. Rates vary depending on the season. **Hullám** *(☎ 312 644, fax 315 950; Balaton-part 1; singles €29-51, doubles €40-61; open Apr-Oct)* is the most charming of the three and is a renovated 50-room hotel built in 1892, straight up from the ferry pier.

Phoenix *(☎ 312 631, fax 314 225; Balaton-part 5; singles €20-24, doubles €25-40)* is a two-star 73-room hotel in the park near the Hullám. It has more of a woodsy feel to it and is much cheaper.

Helikon *(☎ 311 330, fax 315 403; ⓔ dh helikon@axelero.hu; Balaton-part 5; singles €30-83, doubles €48-110)*, by far the biggest hotel in Keszthely with 224 rooms, is a few minutes' walk northeast of the pier through the park. The Helikon has its own island for swimming, an indoor swimming and sports centre with covered clay tennis courts and anything else you could imagine.

Bacchus *(☎/fax 314 097;* W *www.bacchus hotel.hu; Erzsébet királyné utca 18; singles €28-41, doubles €36-54)* is an attractive 26-room hotel where wine reigns supreme (see Activities earlier). It also serves quality food to go with its quality wine.

Places to Eat

Hamburger Saláta Bár *(Erzsébet királyné utca; burgers from 300Ft)* offers burgers, a selection of salads and outdoor seating.

Pizzeria da Marcello *(☎ 313 563; Városház utca 4; pizzas from 650Ft)*, in a cellar with rustic furniture, serves made-to-order pizzas and salads.

Another option is **Donatello Pizza** *(Balaton utca 1/a; pizzas from 530Ft)*, where the *Teenage Ninja Turtles* are very much alive and kicking. There's a small playground for the kids.

Oázis *(☎ 311 023; Rákóczi tér 3; open 11am-4pm Mon-Fri; mains 650-950Ft)*, a 'reform' restaurant east of Festetics Palace, serves vegetarian dishes such as felafel, salads and pickles.

Hungária Gösser *(☎ 312 265; Kossuth Lajos utca 35; mains from 800Ft)* is a pub-restaurant near the corner of Fő tér, in a historical building with stained-glass windows. It has a selection of German and Hungarian dishes and a salad bar.

Béke *(Kossuth Lajos utca 50; mains from 1000Ft)* has a reasonable menu including several fish dishes, an attractive outdoor seating area and a decent café.

Pelso Cafe *(coffee & cake from 200Ft; open till 9pm or 10pm)*, in a two-level modern tower-like structure in the park just south of the Catholic church, is a wonderful place to sit over cake and coffee and watch the world go by.

Keszthely's lively **food market** is off Bem Jószef utca.

Entertainment

Károly Goldmark Cultural Centre *(☎ 314 286; Kossuth Lajos utca 28)* is where you can see Hungarian folk dancing in the courtyard at 8.30pm on Sunday from July to mid-August.

Concerts are often held in the Music Room of **Festetics Palace** during the summer.

There are several interesting places for a drink south of the centre on Kossuth Lajos utca. **Easy Rider** at No 79 attracts the local young bloods, while **Kolibri** cocktail bar at No 81 is for an older crowd.

Dick Turpin's Pub *(Városház utca 2)* is a central local that has great music.

Piccolo *(Városház utca 9)* is a small pub with beer from around the world that attracts friendly students and soldiers.

Getting There & Away

Bus Important destinations served by more than 10 daily buses from Keszthely are Hévíz, Sümeg, Tapolca, Veszprém and Zalaegerszeg; there are about six to Nagykanizsa. Other towns served by bus include Badacsony (three daily), Baja (one), Budapest (six), Győr (two), Pápa (one), Pécs (three), Székesfehérvár (six) and Szombathely (one). Some of these buses – including those to Hévíz, Zalaegerszeg, Nagykanizsa and Sümeg – can be boarded at the bus stops in front of the Catholic church on Fő tér.

For buses to the lake's northern shore (Badacsony, Nagyvázsony and Tapolca), you can catch the bus along Tapolcai út.

Train Keszthely is on a branch line linking Tapolca and Balatonszentgyörgy, from where up to nine daily trains continue along the southern shore to Székesfehérvár and to Keleti or Déli train stations in Budapest. To reach Szombathely or towns along Lake Balaton's northern shore by train, you must change at Tapolca and sometimes at Celldömölk too, but the connections are quick. For Pécs take a train to Kaposvár, then change to a bus.

From mid-June to late August, **MÁV Nostalgia** *(☎ 1-317 1665;* W *www.mavnosztal gia.hu; Belgrád rakpart 26, Budapest)* runs a vintage steam-train *(nosztalgiavonat)* from Keszthely to Badacsonytomaj at 10am from Tuesday to Sunday. Verify this service with MÁV Nostalgia by phone or check the website before making plans.

Getting Around

Bus Nos 1 and 2 run from the train and bus stations to the Catholic church on Fő tér, but unless there's one waiting on your arrival it's just as easy to walk. You can make a booking for a taxi by calling ☎ 333 333.

HÉVÍZ
☎ 83 • postcode 8380 • pop 4400

If you enjoy visiting spas and taking the waters, you'll love Hévíz, site of Gyógy-tó, Europe's largest thermal lake. The people of this town some 7km northwest of Keszthely have made use of the warm mineral water for centuries, first in a tannery in the Middle Ages and later for curative purposes. The lake was first developed as a private resort by Count György Festetics of Keszthely in 1795.

Orientation & Information
The centre of Hévíz is Parkerdő (Park Wood), and its thermal lake. The bus station is on Deák tér a few steps from the northern entrance to the lake; the small commercial centre lies to the west of the station. Kossuth Lajos utca, where most of the big hotels are located, forms the western boundary of the Parkerdő.

There are two tourist agencies northwest of the bus station: **Hévíz Tourist** (☎ 341 348; Rákóczi utca 2; open 8.30am-5.30pm Mon-Fri, 9am-1pm Sat) and **Zalatour** (☎ 341 048; Rákóczi utca 8; open 8am-5pm Mon-Fri, 9am-1pm Sat). You can also source information online (**w** www.heviz.hu).

A branch of the **OTP bank** (Erzsébet királynő utca 7) is near the bus station and a **post office** (Kossuth Lajos utca 4) is west of the small town centre.

Thermal Lake
Gyógy-tó (Parkerdő; 3 hrs/whole day/10-day ticket 600/1200/5200Ft; open 8.30am-5pm in summer, 9am-4.30pm in winter) is an astonishing sight: a surface of almost five hectares in the Parkerdő, covered for most of the year in pink and white lotuses. The source is a spring spouting from a crater some 40m below ground that disgorges up to 80 million litres of warm water a day, renewing itself every 48 hours or so. The surface temperature averages 33°C and never drops below 26°C in winter, allowing bathing throughout the year, even when there's ice on the fir trees of the Parkerdő.

A covered bridge leads to the lake's fin-de-siècle central pavilion, from where catwalks and piers fan out. You can swim protected beneath these or make your way to the small rafts and 'anchors' farther out. There's a couple of piers along the shore for sunbathing as well.

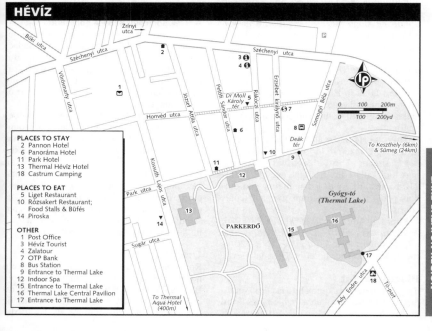

HÉVÍZ

PLACES TO STAY
2 Pannon Hotel
6 Panoráma Hotel
11 Park Hotel
13 Thermal Hévíz Hotel
18 Castrum Camping

PLACES TO EAT
5 Liget Restaurant
10 Rózsakert Restaurant; Food Stalls & Büfés
14 Piroska

OTHER
1 Post Office
3 Hévíz Tourist
4 Zalatour
7 OTP Bank
8 Bus Station
9 Entrance to Thermal Lake
12 Indoor Spa
15 Entrance to Thermal Lake
16 Thermal Lake Central Pavilion
17 Entrance to Thermal Lake

The **indoor spa** *(adult/child 490/270Ft; open 7am-4pm year-round)* is at the entrance to the park.

Places to Stay
Castrum Camping *(☎ 343 198, fax 314 422; e castrum@matavnet.hu; Tó-part; camping per tent 580-860Ft, adult 720-1150Ft, child 430-720Ft; pension singles 5800-10,100Ft, doubles 7200-11,500Ft; open year-round)*, at the lake's southern end, is the most central of Hévíz's several camp sites.

Zalatour and Hévíz Tourist can find you a private room for around €20 to €25 per double, though things could be tight in summer. You'll see a lot of signs reading '*Zimmer frei*' and '*szoba kiadó*' along Kossuth Lajos utca and Zrínyi utca, where you can make your own deals directly.

Most hotels have specials for stays of one week or more, and the rates quoted vary depending on the season.

Pannon *(☎ 340 482, fax 540 111; e pannonhotels@matavnet.hu; Széchenyi utca 23; singles €29, doubles €40-54)* has 46 colourful rooms and is housed in a former trade-union holiday home with an attractive garden.

Panoráma *(☎ 341 074, fax 343 136; e reserve@hotelaquamarin.heviz.hu; Petőfi Sándor utca 9; singles €29-39, doubles €38-46)*, a 13-storey hotel with 208 rooms in two buildings, isn't as attractive an option as Pannon.

Park *(☎ 341 190, fax 341 193; Petőfi Sándor utca 26; singles €39-59, doubles €55-79)*, in elegant Kató Villa (1927), is the loveliest hotel in Hévíz and just a few steps up from the Parkerdő. The Park has 30-rooms and a small pool, sauna and spa complex for guests.

Thermal Hévíz *(☎ 341 180, fax 340 666; e dhtheviz@axelero.hu; Kossuth Lajos utca 9-11; singles €55-98, doubles €92-144)* may look rather dire from the outside, but its 210 rooms are good. It has indoor and outdoor pools, a sauna, solarium, gym and tennis courts.

Thermal Aqua *(☎ 500 700, fax 340 970; e dhtaqua@axelero.hu; Kossuth Lajos utca 13-15; singles €48-82, doubles €78-120)* is the 224-room sister hotel of Thermal Hévíz.

Places to Eat
The best place for a quick bite is at the southern end of Rákóczi utca, which has **food stalls** and **büfé** (snack bars) selling snacks from 180Ft, including *lángos* (deep-fried dough with toppings), sausages, fish and hamburgers.

For a proper Hungarian meal try any of the following places.

Piroska *(☎ 343 942; Kossuth Lajos utca 10; mains 700-1400Ft)* occupies a quiet spot west of the lake and has a shady terrace.

Rózsakert *(Rákóczi utca 3; mains from 1000Ft)* is quite touristy but it's convenient to the lake and the bus station.

Liget *(Dr Moll Károly tér; pizzas & mains around 1000-1200Ft)* has a terrace with tables on the steps down to Rákóczi utca.

Getting There & Away
Hévíz isn't on a railway line, but buses travel east to Keszthely almost every half-hour from stand No 3 at the bus station. There are at least a dozen daily departures to Sümeg and Zalaegerszeg and there are about half as many to Badacsony, Balatonfüred, Nagykanizsa and Veszprém. Other buses run to Baja (one daily), Budapest (five), Győr (three), Kaposvár (four), Kecskemét (one), Pápa (six), Pécs (two), Sopron (two), Székesfehérvár (four), Szekszárd (one) and Szombathely (three).

BADACSONY
☎ 87 • postcode 8261 • pop 2600

Four towns make up the Badacsony region: Badacsonylábdihegy, Badacsonyörs, Badacsonytördemic and Badacsonytomaj. But when Hungarians say Badacsony, they usually mean the little resort at the Badacsony train station, near the ferry pier southwest of Badacsonytomaj.

Badacsony is thrice-blessed. Not only does it have the lake for swimming and the mountains for wonderful walks and hikes, but it has produced wine – lots of it – since the Middle Ages. Badacsony was one of the last places on Balaton's northern shore to be developed and has more of a country feel to it than most other resorts here. Only Tihany vies for supremacy in the beauty stakes (both places are 'landscape protection reserves'), and you might stop here for a day or two to relax.

Orientation
Route No 71, the main road along the lake's northern shore, runs through Badacsony as Balatoni út; this is where the bus will let you off. The ferry pier is on the eastern side of this road; almost everything else is to the

west. Above the village, several pensions and houses with private accommodation ring the base of the hill on Római út, which debouches into Balatoni út at Badacsonytomaj, a few kilometres to the northeast. Szegedi Róza utca branches off to the north from Római út and runs through the vineyards to the Kisfaludy House restaurant (see Places to Eat later) and the base of the hill.

Information

Tourinform (☎/fax 431 046; ⓔ badacsony-tomaj@tourinform.hu; Park utca 6; open 9am-6pm Mon-Fri, 9am-1pm Sat & Sun June-Aug, 8am-4pm Mon-Fri Sept-May) has an office in the centre of town.

Miditourist (☎ 431 028; Egry sétány 3; open 8.30am-5pm Mon-Fri, 8.30am-noon Sat May-Oct) is also in the centre of the village, and has a branch (☎ 431 028; Park utca 53; open 9am-7pm daily May-Oct) to the northeast.

Balatontourist (☎ 531 021; Park utca 4; open 9am-5pm Mon-Fri, 9am-noon Sat May-Oct) is next to Tourinform.

You can change money at the **post office** (Park utca 3).

Things to See & Do

The **József Egry Museum** (Egry sétány 12), in town, is normally devoted to the Balaton region's leading painter (1883–1951) but it was in meltdown mode at the time of writing, and no one is sure when it will reopen.

The dramatic slopes and vineyards above the town centre are sprinkled with little

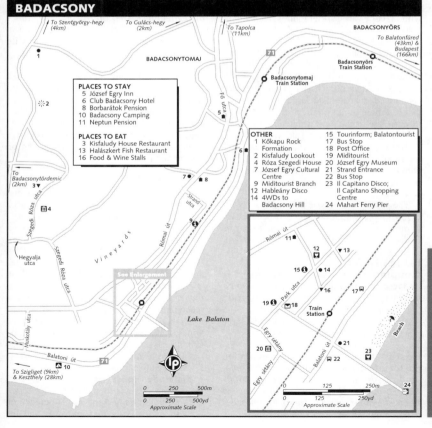

BADACSONY

PLACES TO STAY
5 József Egry Inn
6 Club Badacsony Hotel
8 Borbarátok Pension
10 Badacsony Camping
11 Neptun Pension

PLACES TO EAT
3 Kisfaludy House Restaurant
13 Halászkert Fish Restaurant
16 Food & Wine Stalls

OTHER
1 Kőkapu Rock Formation
2 Kisfaludy Lookout
4 Róza Szegedi House
7 József Egry Cultural Centre
9 Miditourist Branch
12 Hableány Disco
14 4WDs to Badacsony Hill
15 Tourinform; Balatontourist
17 Bus Stop
18 Post Office
19 Miditourist
20 József Egry Museum
21 Strand Entrance
22 Bus Stop
23 Il Capitano Disco; Il Capitano Shopping Centre
24 Mahart Ferry Pier

To Szentgyörgy-hegy (4km)
To Gulács-hegy (2km)
To Tapolca (11km)
BADACSONYÖRS
To Balatonfüred (43km) & Budapest (166km)
BADACSONYTOMAJ
Badacsonyörs Train Station
Badacsonytomaj Train Station
To Badacsonytördemic (2km)
Hegyalja utca
Szegedi Róza utca
Muskotály utca
Vineyards
Római út
Strand utca
See Enlargement
Lake Balaton
To Szigliget (9km) & Keszthely (28km)
Balatoni út

Római út
Park utca
Train Station
Egry sétány
Balatoni út
Beach

0   250   500m
0   250   500yd
Approximate Scale

0   125   250m
0   125   250yd
Approximate Scale

wine-press houses and 'folk baroque' cottages. One of these is the **Róza Szegedi House** (☎ 430 906; adult/child 300/100Ft; open 10am-6pm Tues-Sun, May-Sept), which belonged to the actress wife of the poet Sándor Kisfaludy from Sümeg. Established in 1790, it contains a literature museum.

The flat-topped forested massif overlooking the lake is just the place to escape the tipsy herds. If you'd like to get a running start on your hike, catch one of the open 4WDs marked 'Badacsony-hegyi járat' (600/1000Ft one way/return). They depart from diagonally opposite Tourinform between 9am and 7pm (or 8pm between May and September) whenever at least six paying passengers climb aboard. The driver will drop you off at the Kisfaludy House restaurant (see Places to Eat later) where a large map of the marked trails is posted by the car park. Or you might arm yourself in advance with a copy of Cartographia's *A Balaton* 1:40,000 topographical map (No 41; 650Ft).

Several paths lead to lookouts – at 437m, **Kisfaludy Lookout** (Kisfaludy kilátó) is the highest – and to neighbouring hills like **Gulács-hegy** (393m) and **Szentgyörgy-hegy** (415m) to the north. The landscape includes abandoned quarries and large basalt towers that resemble organ pipes; of these, **Kőkapu** (Stone Gate) is the most dramatic. Several of the trails take you past **Rózsakő** (Rose Rock). A 100-year-old plaque explains an unusual tradition: 'If a lad and a lass sit here together with their backs to the lake, they will be married in a year.' Good luck – or regrets (as the case may be).

The postage-stamp-size **beach** (300/150Ft) is reedy; you would do better to head a few kilometres northeast to Badacsonytomaj or Badacsonyörs for a swim.

Places to Stay

Camping The closest camping ground is **Badacsony Camping** (☎ 531 041; camping per tent 655-990Ft, adult 655-930Ft, child 520-700Ft; open May–early Sept) at the water's edge about 1km west of the ferry pier. Price depends on the season.

Hostels Offering budget accommodation the **József Egry Inn** (☎/fax 471 057; Római út 1; beds in 1–5-person rooms 1300-1800Ft; open mid-Apr–mid-Oct) is near the Badacsonytomaj train station. Its rates depend on the season.

Neptun (☎/fax 431 293; Római út 156; beds 850Ft; open year-round) offers two- to four-person rooms with shared showers.

Private Rooms Miditourist has a particularly good list of private rooms for the entire Badacsony area. Balatontourist charges €18 to €25 per double, depending on the season. It generally costs more for stays of less than three nights. If you want to strike out on your own there are plenty of places along Római út and Park utca.

Pensions There are several small pensions among the vineyards on the road north of the railway line, including the 16-room **Neptun** (☎/fax 431 293; Római út 156; rooms 5500-7000Ft; open Apr-Dec), which is a 10-minute walk from the station. See also Hostels earlier.

Borbarátok (☎/fax 471 597; **e** borbarat@matavnet.hu; Római út 78; singles/doubles 5500/6000Ft) is Neptun's sister pension in Badacsonytomaj, and is a friendly place with a dozen modern, very comfortable rooms.

Hotels The 70-room **Club Badacsony** (☎ 471 040, fax 471 059; **e** biro-manyai@axelero.hu; Balatoni út 14; rooms €47-106; open mid-May–Oct) includes a sauna and lies on the shore in Badacsonytomaj with its own beach. It's the biggest and most expensive place in the area. Rates vary depending on season and facilities.

Places to Eat

There are **food stalls** with picnic tables dispensing sausage, fish soup, *lángos* and *gyros* (meat skewers), as well as **wine stalls** (60Ft per glass, 450Ft to 600Ft per litre) between the train station and Park utca.

Halászkert Fish Restaurant (☎ 431 054; Park utca 5; mains around 1500Ft) is crowded and touristy, but the fish dishes are excellent.

Borbarátok (☎/fax 471 597; Római út 78; mains 1000-1500Ft) pension has a bar and restaurant that is very lively. This is the place to try a glass of Badacsony's premier white wines, Kéknyelű (Blue Stalk) or Szürkebarát (Pinot Gris). Its sister pension **Neptun** also has a good restaurant with a large terrace (see Places to Stay earlier).

Kisfaludy House (☎ 431 016; Szegedi Róza utca 87; mains 1000-2500Ft; open until midnight daily Apr-Nov) is perched on the hill overlooking the vineyards and the lake. This place (built in 1798) was once a press house of the Kisfaludy family. The al fresco terrace at this restaurant is the best place in Badacsony for a meal or a drink. To the west is Szigliget Bay, the loveliest bay on the lake, and directly across to the south lie what Hungarians call the two 'breasts' of Fonyód: the Sípos and Sándor Hills.

Entertainment

József Egry Cultural Centre (☎ 571 070; Római út 55) is opposite Borbarátok pension.

Il Capitano is a big disco in the shopping centre by the beach, which heaves in summer (it's closed over winter).

Hableány (Park utca 12) is a restaurant that sometimes hosts a weekend disco during the summer.

Getting There & Away

Three daily buses head for Balatonfüred and Székesfehérvár; other buses run to Budapest (one daily), Hévíz (one), Keszthely (one), Nagykanizsa (one), Tapolca (two), Várpalota (one), Veszprém (one) and Zalaegerszeg (three).

Badacsony is on the rail line linking all the towns on Lake Balaton's northern shore with Déli and Kelenföld train stations in Budapest and with Tapolca. To get to Keszthely you must change at Tapolca, but there's often an immediate connection by train.

Passenger ferries between Badacsony and Fonyód run at least four times daily from late April to late October; eight ferries daily in June and September and nine daily in July and August. In Fonyód you can get a connection to Southern Transdanubia by taking a train direct to Kaposvár.

A boat ride to Badacsony from Siófok (see Getting There & Away under Siófok earlier), Balatonfüred or Keszthely is the best way to get the feel of Lake Balaton. Boats operate from late May to early September and are more frequent from July to late August.

For information on the MÁV Nostalgia steam-train service between Keszthely and Badacsony, see the Keszthely Getting There & Away section earlier.

TAPOLCA

☎ 87 • postcode 8300 • pop 18,900

This pleasant town has a particularly fine setting wedged between the Balaton Highlands and the Southern Bakony Hills some 14km northeast of Badacsony. To the southeast lies the Kál Basin and such picturesque towns as Mindszentkálla and Szenbékkálla, with Romanesque church ruins, gentle landscapes and bountiful vineyards.

Tapolca has always been an important crossroads; under the Romans both the road between Rome and Aquincum and the road that linked Savaria (Szombathely) and Arrabona

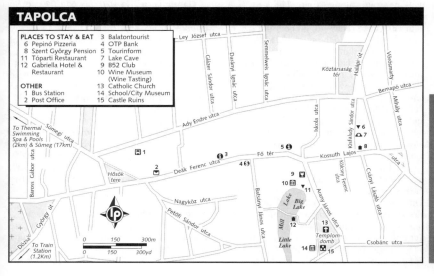

TAPOLCA

PLACES TO STAY & EAT	
6	Pepinó Pizzeria
8	Szent György Pension
11	Tóparti Restaurant
12	Gabriella Hotel & Restaurant

OTHER	
1	Bus Station
2	Post Office
3	Balatontourist
4	OTP Bank
5	Tourinform
7	Lake Cave
9	B52 Club
10	Wine Museum (Wine Tasting)
13	Catholic Church
14	School/City Museum
15	Castle Ruins

(Győr) passed through here. The Romans were followed by the Avars and, in turn, by the early Slavs, who called the area Topulcha, from the Slavic root word for 'hot springs'. Tapolca's original source of wealth was wine – a legacy of the Romans – but the town only really appeared on the map when the Bakony bauxite mining company set up its headquarters here.

Orientation & Information

Tapolca's main thoroughfare is Deák Ferenc utca, which runs west from Hősök tere, where the bus station is located, and east to Fő tér, just north of Mill Lake. The train station is on Dózsa György út, about 1.2km southwest of the centre.

Tourinform (☎ 510 777, fax 510 778; e tapolca@tourinform.hu; Fő tér 17; open 9am-6pm Mon-Fri, 10am-5am Sat mid-June–mid-Sept; 8.30am-4.30pm Mon-Fri mid-Sept–mid-June) is just north of Mill Lake.

Balatontourist (☎/fax 321 179; Deák Ferenc utca 7; open 8am-3.30pm Mon-Fri, 9am-11.30am Sat) is in the Postaudvar shopping centre.

There's a branch of the **OTP bank** (Fő tér 2) near Balatontourist and the **post office** (Deák Ferenc utca 19) is near the bus station.

Mill Lake

Mill Lake (Malom-tó), just south of Fő tér is reached through the gateway at No 8 or by walking south along Arany János utca. A small footbridge divides it in two: to the north is the **Big Lake** (Nagy-tó) – about the size of a big puddle – and to the south the **Little Lake** (Kis-tó). Created in the 18th century to power a water mill, the lake has been artificially fed since the nearby bauxite mine lowered the level of the karst water. But it remains a picturesque area, with pastel-coloured houses reflected in the water of the Big Lake, a church and a museum near the Little Lake choked with water lilies. In the centre is the slowly turning blades of the mill house, which is now the Gabriella hotel; see Places to Stay later.

The **Catholic church** on Templom-domb just east of the lake has a Gothic sanctuary but the rest of the church is 18th-century baroque. The ruins of Tapolca's **medieval castle**, destroyed during the Turkish occupation, can be seen to the southwest. Nearby is the small **School Museum** (Iskola Múzeum; ☎ 413 415; Templom-domb 15; adult/child 150/50Ft; open 9am-4pm Mon-Fri mid-Apr–mid-

Oct; 9am-4pm Mon-Fri mid-Oct–mid-Apr), which also doubles as the **City Museum**.

Lake Cave

Tapolca's second big attraction, the Lake Cave (Tavasbarlang; ☎ 412 579; Kisfaludy utca 3; adult/child 300/200Ft; open 10am-6pm daily June-Aug; 10am-5pm Tues-Sun Apr, May, Sept & Oct) is a short distance to the northeast. You can visit about 100m of the cave and even row a boat (400Ft) on a small underground pond, which has returned since mining ended here in 1990.

Activities

There's a **thermal spa and open-air swimming pool** (Sümegi út; adult/child 450/300Ft; open 10am-8pm Mon-Fri, 9am-8pm Sat & Sun May-Sept) northwest of the centre. You can sample various Bakony wines at the **Wine Museum** (Bormúzeum; open 9am-6pm Mon-Fri) at the northern end of the Big Lake; admission to the museum costs 350/150Ft per adult/child.

Places to Stay & Eat

Accommodation in Tapolca is limited to one pension and one hotel.

Szent György (☎/fax 413 593; Kisfaludy Sandor utca 1; singles/doubles 6500/8000Ft) is an attractive and well-run eight-room pension next to the Lake Cave.

Gabriella (☎ 511 070, fax 511 077; e ho telgab@elender.hu; Batsányi tér 7; singles/doubles from 4500/6500Ft) has 15 newly renovated hotel rooms housed in the original mill in the centre of the lake.

The setting of the Gabriella hotel's **restaurant** (mains 1000-2000Ft) is delightful, with tables on the footbridge in warm weather, but the food at the **Szent György** (mains 1000-1500Ft) is much better.

Elsewhere in town, **Pepinó** (☎ 414 133; Kisfaludy utca 9; pizzas from 500Ft), near the Lake Cave, has decent pizzas.

Tóparti (pizzas/mains from 550/700Ft), opposite Gabriella hotel (see its entry earlier), has plenty of outdoor seating next to the Big Lake.

Entertainment

Gabriella hotel and **Tóparti** restaurant are both perfect places to sit back, sip a beer, and watch the mill blades turn hypnotically. Head to the club **B52** (Arany János utca 3; open *until 5am Fri & Sat)* when you require something more raucous.

Getting There & Away

Bus Tapolca is an important transport hub with buses departing at least hourly for Keszthely, Nagyvázsony, Sümeg and Veszprém. Other important destinations serviced by bus include Balatonfüred (two buses daily), Badacsonytomaj (five to six), Budapest (four), Győr (two), Hévíz (six), Kaposvár (one), Nagykanizsa (two), Pápa (three), Sárvár (one), Sopron (one), Szombathely (one) and Székesfehérvár (three).

Train Tapolca is the main terminus for the rail line linking most of the towns along Lake Balaton's northern shore with Székesfehérvár and Budapest. Another line heads for Balatonszentgyörgy, from where up to 14 daily trains continue along the southern shore to Székesfehérvár and to the Keleti, Kelenföld or Déli train stations in Budapest. A third rail line goes northwest to Sümeg and Celldömölk, from where up to three daily trains continue on to Szombathely in Western Transdanubia.

SÜMEG
☎ 87 • postcode 8330 • pop 7100

This small town, some 19km northwest of Tapolca between the Bakony and Keszthely Hills, has a few pleasant surprises. Sümeg was on the map as early as the 13th century, when an important border fortress was built by King Béla IV in the aftermath of the Mongol invasion. The castle was strengthened several times during the next three centuries, repelling the Turks but falling to the Habsburg forces, which torched it in 1713. (It was later restored.)

Sümeg's golden age came later in the 18th century when the all-powerful bishops of Veszprém took up residence here and commissioned some of the town's fine baroque buildings. Sümeg declined in later years, but those glory days live on in its fine architecture and hill-top castle.

Orientation & Information

Kossuth Lajos utca is the main street running north–south through Sümeg. The bus station is on Béke tér, a continuation of Kossuth Lajos utca south of the town centre. The train station is a 10-minute walk northwest, at the end of Darnay Kálmán utca.

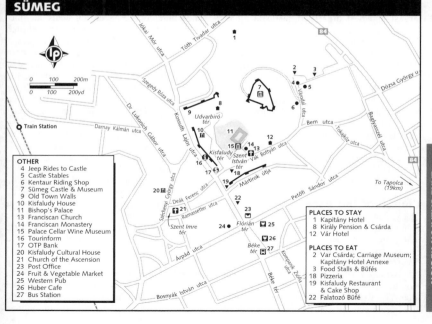

Tourinform (☎/fax 351 908; e sumeg@ tourinform.hu; Kossuth Lajos utca 25; open 9am-6pm Mon-Fri, 9am-5pm Sat & Sun mid-June–mid-Sept; 8am-4pm Mon-Fri mid-Sept–mid-June) is on the main drag.

An **OTP bank** (Kossuth Lajos utca 17) with a currency-exchange machine is in a townhouse and the **post office** (Kossuth Lajos utca 1) is close to Florian tér.

Sümeg Castle

This imposing castle (☎ 352 598; adult/child 600/300Ft; open 8am-8pm daily Apr-Sept, 8am-4pm daily Oct-Mar) sits on a 270m-high cone of limestone above the town – a rare substance in this region of basalt. You can reach it by climbing Vak Bottyán utca, which is lined with lovely baroque kúriák (mansions), from Szent István tér and then following Vároldal utca past the **Castle Stables** (Váristálló) at No 5, which now house a riding school (see Activities later). The castle is also accessible from the northeast via route No 84 and by hitching a ride in a jeep (which costs 1000Ft per car) from the parking lot at the end of Várodal utca.

Sümeg Castle fell into ruin after the Austrians abandoned it early in the 18th century, but was restored in the 1960s. Today it is the largest and best preserved castle in all of Transdanubia and well worth the climb for the views east to the Bakony Hills and south to the Keszthely Hills. There's a small **Castle Museum** (Vármúzeum) of weapons, armour and castle furnishings in the 13th-century **Old Tower** (Öregtorony); pony rides and archery in the castle courtyard; a snack bar; and a restaurant. Medieval tournaments and feasts within the castle walls are organised throughout the year. You can still see bits of the **old town walls** below the castle at the northern end of Kossuth Lajos utca (Nos 13 to 33). A 16th-century tower is now the living room of the house at No 31.

Church of the Ascension

The castle may dominate the town, but for many people it is not Sümeg's most important sight. For them that distinction is reserved for the Church of the Ascension (church office ☎ 352 003; Szent Imre tér; admission free; open daily), which is west of Kossuth Lajos utca and just off Deák Ferenc utca. You would never know it from the outside; architecturally, the building (1756) is unexceptional. But step inside and marvel at what has been called the 'Sistine Chapel of the rococo'.

That's perhaps an overstatement, but it's true that Franz Anton Maulbertsch's frescoes (1757–58) are the most beautiful baroque examples in Hungary and by far the prolific painter's best work. The frescoes, whose subjects are taken from the Old and New Testaments, are brilliant expressions of light and shadow. Pay special attention to the Crucifixion scene in Golgotha on the northern wall in the nave; the Adoration of the Three Kings, with its caricature of a Moor opposite Golgotha; the Gate of Hell, across the aisle under the organ loft on the western side under the porch; and the altarpiece of Christ ascending airily to the clouds. Maulbertsch managed to include himself in a couple of his works, most clearly among the shepherds in the first fresco on the southern wall (he's the one holding the round cheeses and hamming it up for the audience). The commissioner of the frescoes, Márton Padányi Bíró, bishop of Veszprém, is shown on the western wall near the organ. Drop a coin in the machine to illuminate the frescoes and to view them at their best.

Other Attractions

The Church of the Ascension steals the limelight from the 17th-century **Franciscan church** (Ferences templom; Szent István tér 7; admission free; open daily), which has modern frescoes, a beautifully carved baroque altar and a pietà that has attracted pilgrims for 300 years. Don't miss the ornate pulpit with the eerie dismembered hand grasping a crucifix. The baroque **Franciscan monastery** (Ferences kolostor; Szent István tér 9; admission free; open daily), built in 1657, is next door.

The former **Bishop's Palace** (Püspöki palota) at No 8-10 of the same square was a grand residence when completed in 1755. It is now in an advanced state of decay, but you can still admire the two Atlases holding up the balcony at the entrance, and the copper rain-spouts in the shape of sea monsters.

Kisfaludy House (Kisfaludy szülőháza; ☎ 352 020; Kisfaludy tér 4; adult/child 100/50Ft; open 10am-6pm Tues-Sun Mar-Sept; 8am-4pm Mon-Fri Oct-Feb) is the birthplace of Sándor Kisfaludy (1772–1844), the Romantic 'poet of the Balaton'. Together with a history of his life and work, the museum contains further exhibits on Sümeg

Castle and the area's geology. Outside along a wall is the **Sümeg Pantheon** of local sons and daughters who made good.

The small **Carriage Museum** *(Várodal utca; admission free)*, next to the Kapitány hotel's annexe, has well-restored horse carriages and a small array of medieval weapons and armour. Ask for the key at the Vár Csárda restaurant on Várodal utca.

Activities

There is some excellent **hiking** east of Sümeg into the Bakony Hills (known as 'Hungary's Sherwood Forest'), but get yourself a copy of Cartographia's *Bakonye-hegység – déli rész* (Bakony Hills – Southern Part) 1:40,000 map (No 3; 650Ft).

If you want to go horse riding, visit the **Castle Stables** *(☎ 550 087; e varistallo@ matavnet.hu; Vároldal utca 5)*. There's also information available at the **Kentaur riding shop** *(☎ 351 836; Vároldal utca 10; open 9am-6pm daily)*. Both places charge around 2000Ft per hour.

You can taste wine at the **Palace Cellar Wine Museum** *(Palota Pince Bormúzeum; open 1pm-6pm daily)* at the Bishop's Palace.

Places to Stay

Tourinform can help with private rooms for about 2000Ft per person (see Orientation & Information earlier for contact details).

Vár *(☎/fax 352 352; e hotelvar@matavnet .hu; Vak Bottyán utca 2; singles/doubles from 4000/5000Ft)* is a 29-room hotel that's quite sterile, but it is modern, cheap and has views of the town and castle.

Király *(☎/fax 352 605; Udvarbíró tér 5; singles/doubles 4000/6000Ft)* is a six-room, family-run pension in an old farmhouse behind Kisfaludy House on Szent István tér. This is a cosy, flower-bedecked place with a sauna, fitness room, wine cellar and a *csárda* (Hungarian-style restaurant).

Kapitány *(☎ 352 598, fax 351 101; w www .hotelkapitany.hu; Tóth Tivadar utca 19; singles €30-35, doubles €35-40)*, a modern, well-designed 45-room hotel north of the castle, has a swimming pool, sauna, tennis court, horses for rent and a wine cellar. It also has an annexe near the Carriage Museum.

Places to Eat

The access road to the castle from route No 84 is lined with **snack stands** and **büfé**.

Falatozó *(Kossuth Lajos utca 7; dishes from 300Ft; open 7am-5pm Mon-Fri, 6.30am-noon Sat)*, south of the castle, is a cheap stand-up büfé at a butcher's shop.

Pizzéria *(Szent István tér 1; pizzas from 600Ft)* is an extremely popular place with a huge garden; it serves pizza, Hungarian dishes and has a salad bar.

Kisfaludy *(☎ 352 128; Kossuth Lajos utca 13; mains 1000-1500Ft)* restaurant at the former Kisfaludy hotel remains open and is one of the few places in the centre of town where you can have a sit-down meal. The *cukrászda* (cake shop) here is popular for ice cream and cakes.

Vár Csárda *(☎ 550 166; Várodal utca; mains 1000-1500Ft)*, closer to the castle, is touristy with Gypsy music and lots of German tourists but it's very pleasant in warmer weather to sit under the walnut trees in full view of the hill-top fortress.

The **fruit and vegetable market** on Árpád utca is just west of Kossuth Lajos utca.

Entertainment

Kisfaludy Cultural House *(☎ 352 332; Széchenyi György utca 9-11)*, near the Church of the Ascension, will let you know what's on in Sümeg. Popular watering holes include the **Huber Cafe** *(Béke tér 8)* and the **Western Pub** *(Petőfi Sándor utca 1)*, with split-log tables and jukebox rave music.

Getting There & Away

Hourly buses leave Sümeg each day for Hévíz, Keszthely, Tapolca; departures to Pápa, Veszprém and Zalaegerszeg are also frequent. Other buses go to Budapest (four buses daily), Győr (five), Kaposvár (two), Köszeg (one), Nagykanizsa (three), Sopron (three), Pécs (one), Szombathely (one) and Lenti (one), which is near the border with Slovenia.

Sümeg is on the railway line linking Tapolca and Celldömölk, from where up to three daily trains continue on to Szombathely. For Budapest and other points to the east and west along the northern shore of Lake Balaton, change at Tapolca.

NAGYVÁZSONY

☎ 88 • postcode 8291 • pop 1860

When you grow tired of the Balaton hubbub, take an easy excursion north to Nagyvázsony, a sleepy little market town in the southern Bakony Hills. The drive from Badacsony via Tapolca or from Tihany, 15km to the southeast, takes you through some of the prettiest countryside in the Lake Balaton region, and it's here you'll find the important 15th-century Vázsonykő Castle.

Orientation & Information

In the centre of town you'll find Nagyvázsony's three bus-stops and a branch of the **OTP bank** (Kinizsi utca 82), which has no ATM, all on the same street. The **post office** (Kinizsi utca 59) is opposite the bank.

Vázsonykő Castle

This castle (☎ 264 786; Vár utca; adult/child 400/300Ft; open 8am-5pm Mon-Fri, 9am-5pm Sat & Sun Apr-Oct), at the end of the street on a gentle slope north of the tiny town centre, was begun early in the 15th century by the Vezsenyi family, but in 1462 was presented to General Pál Kinizsi by King Matthias Corvinus in gratitude for the brave general's military successes against the Turks. It became an important border fortress during the occupation and was used as a prison in the 1700s.

The castle is essentially a rectangle with a horseshoe-shaped barbican. The 30m-high, six-storey keep is reached via a bridge over the dry moat. A large crack runs from the top of the tower to the bottom, but it must be secure enough: the upper rooms contain the **Kinizsi Castle Museum** (Kinizsi Vármúzeum), while the lower room displays dummies torturing one another. Part of General Kinizsi's red-marble sarcophagus sits in the centre of the restored chapel, and there's a collection of archaeological finds in the crypt.

Other Attractions

The **Post Office Museum** (Postmúzeum; ☎ 264 300; Temető utca 3; adult/child 100/50Ft; open 10am-6pm Tues-Sun Mar-Oct, 10am-2pm Tues-Sun Nov-Feb) is just south of the castle. Nagyvázsony was an important stop along the postal route between Budapest and Graz in the 19th century (horses were changed here). The museum is a lot more interesting than it sounds, particularly the section on the history of the telephone in Hungary beginning with the installation of the first switchboard in Budapest in 1890. Opposite is an 18th-century **Evangelist church** with a free-standing belfry.

Nearby is a small **Open-Air Folk Museum** (Szabadtéri Néprajzi Múzeum; ☎ 264 724; Bercsényi utca 21; adult/child 130/70Ft;

open 10am-6pm Tues-Sun May-Oct) at a farmhouse dating from 1825. It was once the home of a coppersmith, and his workshop remains.

The **Church of St Stephen** (Szent István templom; Rákóczi utca) was built by General Kinizsi in 1481 on the site of an earlier chapel. Most of the interior, including the richly carved main altar, is baroque.

Places to Stay

Vázsonykő (☎ 264 344, fax 264 707; Sörház utca 2; singles/doubles 3500/5000Ft) is a seven-room pension, which is both friendly and welcoming.

Malomkő (☎/fax 264 165; e malomko@mail.uti.hu; Kinizsi utca 47-49; singles/doubles €20/36) is a flashier, more modern pension in the town centre and has 15 rooms.

Kastély (☎/fax 264 109; Kossuth Lajos utca 16) is an 18th-century mansion on six hectares of parkland that once belonged to the aristocratic Zichy family. At the time of writing, this hotel was undergoing renovations; call ahead to see if it has reopened.

Places to Eat

The thatched **Vár Csárda** (Temető utca 5; mains around 900Ft), overlooking the castle, has a relaxing garden but is open during summer only. Try the good home cooking at the **Vázsonykő** (☎ 264 344; Sörház utca 2; mains around 900Ft) or **Malomkő** (☎/fax 264 165; Kinizsi utca 47-49; mains 900-1500Ft) pensions at other times. The latter also has a good cukrászda.

Castillo (Kinizsi utca 86; pizzas from 600Ft), in the town centre, is an option for pizza.

Getting There & Away

Some 12 buses a day link Nagyvázsony and Veszprém, 23km to the northeast, and up to eight run to Tapolca daily to the southwest. Other buses go to Keszthely (two or three daily), Ajka (two), Budapest (one) and Zalaegerszeg (one) via Sümeg. You can also reach Balatonfüred via Tótvázsony.

TIHANY

☎ 87 • postcode 8237 • pop 1300

The place with the greatest historical significance on Lake Balaton is Tihany, 11km southwest of Balatonfüred. Tihany village is on a peninsula of the same name that juts

5km into the Balaton, almost linking the lake's two shores. The entire peninsula is a nature reserve of hills and marshy meadows; it has an isolated, almost wild, feel to it that is unknown around the rest of the lake. The village, on a hill top on the eastern side of the peninsula, is one of the most charming in the Balaton region.

There was a Roman settlement in the area, but Tihany first appeared on the map in 1055, when King Andrew I (ruled 1046–60), a son of King Stephen's great nemesis, Vászoly, founded a Benedictine monastery here. The *Deed of Foundation* of the Abbey Church of Tihany, now in the archives of the Benedictine abbey at Pannonhalma, south of Győr, is one of the earliest known documents bearing any Hungarian words – some 50 place names within a mostly Latin text. It's a linguistic treasure in a country where, until the 19th century, the vernacular in its written form was spurned – particularly in schools – in favour of the more 'cultured' Latin and German.

In 1267 a fortress was built around the church and was able to keep the Turks at bay when they arrived 300 years later. But the castle was demolished by Habsburg forces in 1702, and all you'll see today are ruins.

Tihany Peninsula is a popular recreational area with beaches on its eastern and western coasts and a big resort complex on its southern tip. The waters of the so-called Tihany Well, off the southern end of the peninsula, are the deepest – and coldest – in the lake, reaching an unprecedented 12m in some parts.

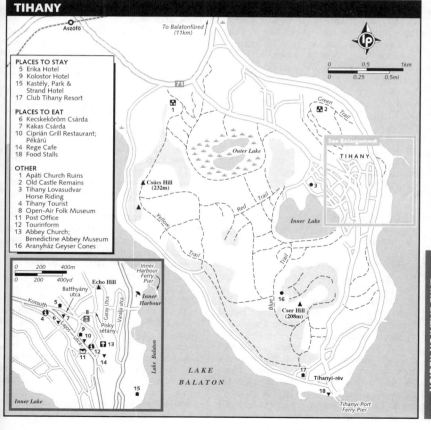

TIHANY

PLACES TO STAY
5 Erika Hotel
9 Kolostor Hotel
15 Kastély, Park &
   Strand Hotel
17 Club Tihany Resort

PLACES TO EAT
6 Kecskeköröm Csárda
7 Kakas Csárda
10 Ciprián Grill Restaurant;
   Pékárú
14 Rege Cafe
18 Food Stalls

OTHER
1 Apáti Church Ruins
2 Old Castle Remains
3 Tihany Lovasudvar
   Horse Riding
4 Tihany Tourist
8 Open-Air Folk Museum
11 Post Office
12 Tourinform
13 Abbey Church;
   Benedictine Abbey Museum
16 Aranyház Geyser Cones

Orientation

Tihany village, perched on an 80m-high plateau along the peninsula's eastern coast, is accessible by two roads when you turn south off route No 71. The Inner Harbour (Belső kikötő), where ferries to/from Balatonfüred and Siófok dock, is below the village. Tihanyi-rév (Tihany Port), to the southwest at the tip of the peninsula, is Tihany's recreational area. From here, car ferries run to Szántódi-rév and passenger ferries to Balatonföldvár.

Two inland basins on the peninsula are fed by rain and ground water. The Inner Lake (Belső-tó) is almost in the centre of the peninsula and visible from the village, while the Outer Lake (Külső-tó), to the northwest, has almost completely dried up and is now a tangle of reeds. Both basins attract bird life.

Information

The bus from Balatonfüred stops on Kossuth Lajos utca below the Abbey Church. There are a number of places to go for information, including **Tourinform** (☎/fax 448 804; e ti hany@tourinform.hu; Kossuth Lajos utca 20; open 9am-8pm Mon-Fri, 9am-6pm Sat & Sun June-Aug; 9am-5pm Mon-Fri, 9am-3pm Sat May & Sept; 9am-3pm Mon-Fri Oct-Apr) and **Tihany Tourist** (☎/fax 448 481; Kossuth Lajos utca 11; open 9am-5pm daily Apr-Oct). You can also try the website w www .tihany.hu for more information.

The **post office** (Kossuth Lajos utca 37) has an ATM and an exchange bureau. There's another ATM at the Club Tihany resort at Rév utca 3 (see Places to Stay later).

Abbey Church

This twin-spired, ochre-coloured church (☎ 448 405; adult/child/family 260/130/650Ft; open 9am-6pm daily May-Sept, 10am-5pm daily Apr & Oct, 10am-3pm daily Nov-Mar) was built in 1754 on the site of King Andrew's church and contains fantastic **altars**, **pulpits** and **screens** carved between 1753 and 1779 by an Austrian lay brother named Sebastian Stuhlhof. They are baroque-rococo masterpieces and all are richly symbolic.

With your back to the sumptuous main altar (the saint with the broken chalice and snake is Benedict, the founder of Western monasticism) and the Abbot's Throne, look right to the side altar dedicated to Mary. The large angel kneeling on the right is said to represent Stuhlhof's fiancée, a fisherman's daughter who died in her

youth. On the Altar of the Sacred Heart across the aisle, a pelican (Christ) nurtures its young (the faithful) with its own blood. The besotted figures atop the pulpit beside it are four doctors of the Roman Catholic Church: Sts Ambrose, Gregory, Jerome and Augustine. The next two altars on the right- and left-hand sides are dedicated to Benedict and his twin sister, Scholastica; the last pair, a baptismal font and the Lourdes Altar, date from the 20th century.

Stuhlhof also carved the magnificent choir rail above the porch and the organ with all the cherubs. The frescoes on the ceilings by Bertalan Székely, Lajos Deák-Ébner and Károly Lotz were painted in 1889, when the church was restored.

The remains of King Andrew I lie in a limestone sarcophagus in the Romanesque **crypt**. The spiral sword-like cross on the cover is similar to ones used by 11th-century Hungarian kings.

The **Benedictine Abbey Museum** (Bencés Ápátsági Múzeum), next door to the Abbey Church in the former Benedictine monastery, is entered to the right of the main altar in the Abbey Church. It contains exhibits about Lake Balaton, liturgical vestments, a library of manuscripts and a bedroom where the deposed Habsburg Emperor Charles IV and his wife Zita spent a week in October 1921. ('They filled the house with their sacred presence,' reads the plaque.) In the cellar there's a small museum of Roman statues and ghastly modern sculptures.

The admission fee includes entry to the museum and crypt; guided tours are conducted for 5000Ft per person.

Other Attractions

Pisky sétány, a promenade running along the ridge north from the church to Echo Hill, passes a cluster of folk houses that have now been turned into a small **Open-Air Folk Museum** (Szabadtéri Néprajzi Múzeum; ☎ 714 960; adult/child 200/100Ft; open 10am-6pm Tues-Sun May-Sept).

You'll find **Echo Hill** (Visszhang-hegy) at the end of Pisky sétány. At one time, up to 15 syllables of anything shouted in the direction of the Abbey Church would bounce back but, alas, because of building in the area (and perhaps climatic changes) you'll be lucky to get three nowadays. From Echo Hill you can descend Garay utca and Váralja utca to the Inner Harbour and a small beach, or continue on to the hiking trails that pass this way.

Activities

Hiking is one of Tihany's main attractions; there's a good map outlining the trails near the front of the Abbey Church. Following the Green Trail northeast of the church for an hour will bring you to the **Russian Well** (Oroszkút) and the ruins of the **Old Castle** (Óvár) at 219m, where Russian Orthodox monks, brought to Tihany by Andrew I, hollowed out cells in the soft basalt walls.

The 232m-high **Csúcs Hill**, with panoramic views of Lake Balaton, is about two hours west of the church via the Red Trail. From here you can join up with the Yellow Trail originating in Tihanyi-rév, which will lead you north to the ruins of the 13th-century **Apáti Church** (Ápáti templomrom) and to route No 71. The Yellow Trail crosses with the Blue Trail, which then actually leads you south to the **Inner Lake** and **Aranyház**, a series of geyser cones formed by warm-water springs and resembling (somewhat) a 'Golden House'.

Horses are available for hire at the **Tihany Lovasudvar** (☎ 714 747, Kiserdőtelepi utca 10; open 9am-6pm daily year-round) just north of the Inner Lake.

Places to Stay

Accommodation in Tihany is limited and expensive; you could consider making it a day trip from Balatonfüred by bus, which takes only 20 minutes. Also, most of the hotels listed in this section are closed between mid-October or November and March or April.

Tihany Tourist (☎/fax 448 481; Kossuth Lajos utca 11; open 9am-5pm daily Apr-Oct) can find private rooms from 4000Ft per double in the low season and 5000Ft in the high season. Many houses along Kossuth Lajos utca and on the little streets north of the Abbey Church have 'Zimmer frei' signs.

Kolostor (☎/fax 448 009; Kossuth Lajos utca 14; rooms from 6000Ft) is a six-storey hotel above a popular restaurant. There are a couple of rooms with low ceilings under the eaves that are a little cheaper than the usual doubles.

Erika (☎ 448 010, fax 448 646; Batthyány utca 6; doubles €60) is a swish, 16-room hotel where doubles come with bath and all the mod cons. It has a small swimming pool.

Kastély, Park & Strand (☎ 448 611, fax 448 409; e hotel.fured@matavnet.hu; Fürdőtelepi út 1; Kastély singles 11,000-19,600Ft, doubles 13,500-22,200Ft; Park singles 10,700-17,800Ft, doubles 12,900-20,000Ft; Strand singles 5400-7500Ft, doubles 7000-10,700Ft) is a hotel on the Inner Harbour that has 26 rooms in a former Habsburg summer mansion (the Kastély), 44 rooms in an ugly modern wing (the Park) and 21 rooms in a small one-level building (the Strand). Rates depend on the season and room facilities. The hotels have a five-hectare garden and their own beach.

Club Tihany (☎ 538 500, fax 448 083; w www.clubtihany.hu; Rév utca 3; singles/doubles from €45/56; bungalows from €50), just up from the car-ferry pier, is a 13-hectare resort with 160 bungalows and a 330-room hotel – and every sporting, munching and quaffing possibility imaginable. It has two-person bungalows while some rooms in the high-rise hotel have lake views and balconies.

Places to Eat

The cheapest place to eat on the Tihany peninsula is at the **food stalls** at Tihanyi-rév. Note that most of the restaurants listed here are closed between mid-October or November and March or April.

Rege Cafe (☎ 448 280; Kossuth Lajos utca 22; mains 1000-2000Ft), in the former monastery stables next to the church and museum, serves expensive light meals and cakes and offers a panoramic view from its terrace.

You would do better to eat at the atmospheric **Kecskeköröm** (Fossil Shell; Kossuth Lajos utca 13; mains around 1200Ft), a csárda a few hundred metres northwest of the Rege Café on the main road; or at the **Kakas Csárda** (☎ 448 541; Batthyány utca 1; mains around 1500Ft), in a rambling basalt house almost opposite Kecskeköröm.

The restaurant at **Kolostor** (☎/fax 448 009; Kossuth Lajos utca 14; mains from 1000Ft) has German-Hungarian pub grub, and at the height of summer it puts on medieval banquets in the restaurant's lower level.

Ciprián Grill (☎ 448 515; mains from 1000Ft), next door to the Kolostor hotel, is another decent choice.

Pékárú, a small hole in the wall between Kolostor and Ciprián, is a popular bakery with tasty snacks.

Getting There & Away

Buses cover the 11km from Balatonfüred's train station to and from Tihany about 20 times daily. The bus stops at both ferry landings before climbing to Tihany village.

The Balaton passenger ferries from Siófok, Balatonfüred and elsewhere stop at Tihany from late April to late October. Catch them at the pier below the abbey or at Tihanyi-rév. From March to mid-November the car ferry takes 10 minutes to cross the narrow stretch of water between Tihanyi-rév and Szántódi-rév and departs every 40 minutes to an hour.

BALATONFÜRED
☎ 87 • postcode 8230 • pop 13,200

Balatonfüred is the oldest and most popular resort on the northern shore of Lake Balaton. It has none of the frenzy or brashness of Siófok, partly because of its aristocratic origins and partly because the thermal waters of its world-famous heart hospital attract a much older crowd.

The thermal water here, rich in carbonic acid, had been used as a cure for stomach ailments for centuries, but its other curative properties were only discovered by scientific analysis in the late 18th century. Balatonfüred was immediately declared a spa with its own chief physician in residence.

Balatonfüred's golden age was in the 19th century, especially the first half, when political and cultural leaders of the Reform Era (roughly 1825–48) gathered here in the summer. The town became a writers colony of sorts. Balatonfüred was also the site chosen by István Széchenyi to launch the lake's first steamship *Kisfaludy* in 1846.

By 1900 Balatonfüred was a popular place for increasingly wealthy middle-class families to escape Budapest's heat. Wives would base themselves here all summer along with their children while husbands would board the 'bull trains' in Budapest at the weekend. The splendid promenade and a large wooden bath were built on the lake to accommodate the increasing crowds.

Orientation

Balatonfüred has two distinct districts: the lakeside resort area and the commercial centre in the older part of town around Szent István tér to the northwest. Almost everything to see and do is down by the lake.

The train and bus stations are on Dobó István utca, about a kilometre northwest of Vitorlás tér, where the ferry pier is located. The quickest way to get to the lake from either station is to walk east on Horváth Mihály utca and then south on Jókai Mór utca.

Information

Tourinform (e *balatonfured@tourinform.hu*) has two offices in Balatonfüred. One is inconveniently located 1km northeast of the centre (☎ *580 480, fax 580 481; Petőfi Sándor utca 68; 9am-4pm Mon-Fri May-Oct, 9am-2pm Mon-Fri Nov-Apr*) and another annoyingly placed 1.5km to the southwest (☎ *580 480; Széchenyi utca 47; open 9am-5pm Mon-Fri, 9am-1pm Sat May-Sept, 9am-3pm Mon-Fri Oct-Apr*). From July to August an **information booth** can be found on Zákonyi Ferenc utca.

There's a main office for **Füred Tourist** (☎ *481 605; Petőfi Sándor utca 2; open 9am-6pm Mon-Fri in winter, 9am-6pm Mon-Fri, 9am-3pm Sat, 9am-1pm Sun in summer*) and a branch at Tagore sétány 1.

You can also log on to the website at w www.balatonfured.hu for more information.

The **OTP bank** (*Petőfi Sándor utca 8*) and **post office** (*Zsigmond utca 14*) are northwest of the ferry pier.

Things to See

The **Jókai Memorial Museum** (*Jókai Emlék-múzeum;* ☎ *343 426; 200/100Ft; open 10am-6pm Tues-Sun May-Oct*) is housed in the summer villa of the prolific writer Mór Jókai, just north of Vitorlás tér. In his study here, Jókai churned out many of his 200 novels under the stern gaze of his wife, the actress Róza Laborfalvi.

Across the street is the tiny neoclassical **Round Church** (*Kerek templom;* ☎ *343 029; Blaha Lujza utca 1; admission free*) completed in 1846. The *Crucifixion* (1891) by János Vaszary sits above the altar on the western wall and is the only notable thing inside.

If you walk down Blaha Lujza utca you'll pass the villa (now a hotel) at No 4 where the 19th-century actress-singer Lujza Blaha spent her summers from 1893 to 1916. A short distance farther along is Gyógy tér, the heart of the spa. In the centre of this leafy square, **Kossuth Pump House** (1853) dispenses slightly sulphuric, but drinkable, thermal water. This is as close as you'll get to the hot spring. Although Balatonfüred is a major spa, the mineral baths are reserved for patients of the State Hospital of Cardiology.

The late baroque **Horváth House** (*Gyógy tér 3*), for many years a hotel, was the site of the first **Anna Ball** in 1825 (see Activities, later). The ball has since become the big

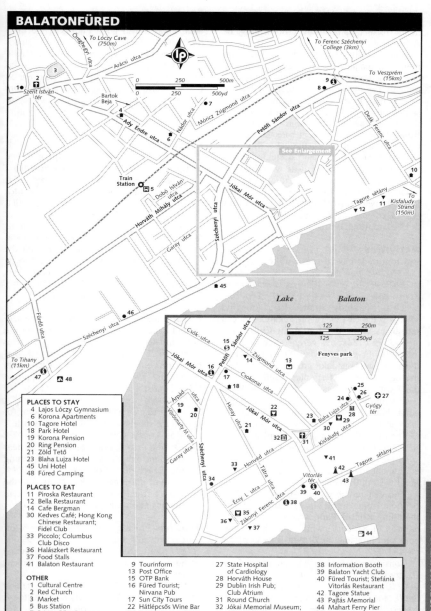

BALATONFÜRED

To Lóczy Cave (750m)
To Ferenc Széchenyi College (3km)
To Veszprém (15km)
Szent István tér
Bartok Beja
To Kisfaludy Strand (150m)
Train Station
Lake   Balaton
To Tihany (11km)
Fenyves park
Gyógy tér
Vitorlás tér

PLACES TO STAY
4 Lajos Lóczy Gymnasium
6 Korona Apartments
10 Tagore Hotel
18 Park Hotel
19 Korona Pension
20 Ring Pension
21 Zöld Tető
23 Blaha Lujza Hotel
45 Uni Hotel
48 Füred Camping

PLACES TO EAT
11 Piroska Restaurant
12 Bella Restaurant
14 Cafe Bergman
30 Kedves Café; Hong Kong
    Chinese Restaurant;
    Fidel Club
33 Piccolo; Columbus
    Club Disco
36 Halászkert Restaurant
37 Food Stalls
41 Balaton Restaurant

OTHER
1 Cultural Centre
2 Red Church
3 Market
5 Bus Station
7 Bringa-Bike Centrum
8 Kristóf Papp Bicycle
   Rentals

9 Tourinform
13 Post Office
15 OTP Bank
16 Füred Tourist;
    Nirvana Pub
17 Sun City Tours
22 Hátlépcsős Wine Bar
24 Former Sanatorium
25 Balaton Pantheon
26 Kossuth Pump House

27 State Hospital
    of Cardiology
28 Horváth House
29 Dublin Irish Pub;
    Club Átrium
31 Round Church
32 Jókai Memorial Museum;
    Jókai Café
34 Fontaine Room Service
35 Galéria Disco

38 Information Booth
39 Balaton Yacht Club
40 Füred Tourist; Stefánia
    Vitorlás Restaurant
42 Tagore Statue
43 Pajtás Memorial
44 Mahart Ferry Pier
46 Roland Garros Tennis
    Centre
47 Tourinform

LAKE BALATON REGION

event in Balatonfüred and every July it's held in the former **Sanatorium** (1802), now the Árkád Hotel, opposite.

Nearby is the **Balaton Pantheon**, with memorial plaques from those who took the cure at the hospital. The Bengali poet Rabindranath Tagore was one of them. A bust of this Nobel Prize-winning man of letters stands on Tagore sétány before a lime tree that he planted in 1926 to mark his recovery from illness after treatment here. Diagonally opposite and closer to the lake there's a bizarre memorial of a hand stretching out of the water in memory of those who drowned in the lake when the *Pajtás* boat sank in 1954.

On the eastern side of the tér is the sprawling, 600-bed **State Hospital of Cardiology** *(Országos Szívkórház; Gyógy tér 2)*, which put Balatonfüred on the map.

Activities

Balatonfüred has **three public beaches** *(adult/child per day 260/160Ft, per week 1680/960Ft; open 8.30am or 9am-6pm or 7pm daily mid-May–mid-Sept)*. The best beach is **Kisfaludy Strand** along Aranyhíd sétány to the east of Tagore sétány. You can rent boats at the **Balaton Yacht Club** *(BYC; ☎ 343 955; Zákonyi Ferenc utca 2)* from 7000/9000Ft per hour/day. During summer there are one-hour **lake cruises** *(☎ 342 230)* that depart from the ferry pier at 2pm and 4pm daily with an extra sailing at 11am on Wednesday and Sunday, which cost 900/600Ft per adult/child. Cruises (2½ hours; 1900/1200Ft) leave at 10am on Wednesday and Sunday.

The **Roland Garros Tennis Centre** *(☎ 343 824; Széchenyi utca 27; open 6am-11pm in summer)*, with clay courts, instruction and equipment for hire is next to the Margaréta hotel west of the centre.

You can rent **bicycles** for around 350Ft per hour from several places in Balatonfüred, including **Kristóf Papp** *(☎ 343 937; Petőfi Sándor utca 62/b)*, which also has tennis courts for hire, and the **Bringa-Bike Centrum** *(☎ 481 077; Nádor utca 37)*.

Consider walking or cycling to **Lóczy Cave** *(Lóczy-barlang; Öreghegyi utca; adult/child 200/100Ft; open 10am-5pm Tues-Sun May-Sept)*, north of the old town centre. It is the largest cave in the Lake Balaton region and accessible from Szent István tér. Just walk east a couple of minutes on Arácsi utca past the excellent **market** (which sells everything from

food to shoes) and then north on Öreghegyi utca. There's also good **hiking** in the three hills with the names Tamás (Thomas), Sándor (Alexander) and Péter (Peter) to the northeast.

In July the **Anna Ball** is held in the Sanatorium, near Gyogy ter; it's a prime event on the Hungarian calendar. Tickets cost from 25,000Ft. Concerts and other events accompany the ball; keep your eyes peeled if you're here during July.

Places to Stay

Camping There's only one camping ground at Balatonfüred, but it can accommodate 3500 people. **Füred Camping** *(☎ 580 241; e cfured@balatontourist.hu; Széchenyi utca 24; camping 2900-4900Ft, adult 600-1300Ft, child 500-1050Ft, 3–4 person bungalows 5460-22,490Ft; 3–4 person motel rooms 5460-22,490Ft; open Apr–mid-Oct)* is about 1.5km southeast of the train station on the lakeshore. To get a bungalow you have to arrive during reception office hours (reception is open 8am to 1pm and from 3pm to 7pm daily). Rates skyrocket during July and August.

Private Rooms & Hostels As elsewhere around Lake Balaton, private room prices are rather inflated. The staff at Füred Tourist offer them for €25 to €30 per double. Another good place for booking rooms is **Sun City Tours** *(☎/fax 481 798; Csokonai utca 1)* opposite Füred Tourist. **Fontaine Room Service** *(☎ 343 673; Honvéd utca 11)* claims to be open 24 hours. There are lots of houses with rooms for rent on the streets north of Kisfaludy Beach.

Lajos Lóczy Gymnasium *(☎ 343 428; Bartók Béla utca 4; dorm beds 1500Ft)* near the train and bus stations and the far-flung **Ferenc Széchenyi College** *(☎ 343 844; Hősök tere; dorm beds 1500Ft)*, 3km to the northeast of the resort town of Balatonfüred, usually have accommodation in summer.

Pensions Friendly **Ring** *(☎ 342 884; Petőfi Sándor utca 6/a; singles/doubles from 7200/8000Ft)* is a 12-room pension and is so named because the owner was a champion boxer. Rooms are neat and clean.

Korona *(☎ 343 278, fax 580 712; e majer@koronapanzio.hu; Vörösmarty Mihály utca 4; singles from €27-37, doubles from €32-46)* is near Ring and has 20 rooms. They also have a separate house with five apartments and a garden at Nádor utca 5.

Zöld Tető (☎/fax 341 701; e zoldteto@net quick.hu; Huray utca 4; singles/doubles from €35.50/45.50, apartments from €50) is closer to the lake and an excellent choice. Its newly renovated rooms are a cut above the rest and there's a lovely garden and huge apartments.

Hotels Prices for accommodation fluctuate throughout the year and usually peak between early July and late August.

Blaha Lujza (☎ 581 210, fax 581 219; w www.hotelblaha.hu; Blaha Lujza utca 4; singles 7300-8200Ft, doubles 9300-12,300Ft), with 22 rooms, is one of the loveliest hotels to stay in. It's the most central place in town and was the summer home of the much loved 19th-century actress-singer from 1893 to 1916.

Tagore (☎/fax 342 603; Deák Ferenc utca 56; singles €22-35, doubles €29-50) hotel has 36 rooms by Kisfaludy Strand. The rooms aren't modern but they're big and reasonably comfortable.

Park (☎ 343 203, fax 342 005; e park hotel@sednet.hu; Jókai Mór utca 24; singles €24-42, doubles €30-50) is a rather posh old-world 32-room hotel, complete with swimming pool.

Uni (☎ 581 360, fax 581 361; e hotel uni@sednet.hu; Széchenyi utca 10; singles 4520-9880Ft, doubles 5610-11,850Ft) is one of the best (and cheapest) of the dozen or so high-rise hotels lining the lake in Balatonfüred. It has 48 rooms, a private beach and car parking is included in the price.

Places to Eat

For cheap eats, head west along the lake and Zákonyi Ferenc utca where you'll come across a plethora of **food stalls**.

Stefánia Vitorlás (Tagore sétány 1; mains around 1500Ft), with its central location, is expensive and touristy but has an extensive selection of fish dishes.

Balaton (☎ 481 319; Kisfaludy utca 5; mains 1000-2000Ft) is a cool, leafy oasis amid all the hubbub. It serves huge portions and is a better choice than Vitorlás.

Halászkert (☎ 343 039; Zákonyi Ferenc utca 3; mains 800-1000Ft) serves some of the best korholy halászlé (drunkard's fish soup) in Hungary on its large terrace.

The eastern end of Tagore sétány is a strip of pleasant bars and terraced restaurants including the **Bella** (☎ 481 815; pizzas 600-800Ft), with good pizzas, Hungarian staples

and the wonderful Panorama terrace facing the lake. The **Piroska** (mains around 1500Ft) is a very popular restaurant with local residents.

Piccolo (Honvéd utca 3; mains 1000-2000Ft) is another restaurant with a lovely terrace, perfect for summer evenings. It serves Hungarian/Central European fare.

Hong Kong (Blaha Lujza utca 7; mains 750-1000Ft) is a cheap, Chinese restaurant with a small terrace.

Kedves (Blaha Lujza utca 7) is a café downstairs from Hong Kong where Lujza Blaha herself took tea.

Escape the crowds down by the lake and head to popular **Cafe Bergman** (☎ 341 087; Zsigmond utca 3), near the post office, for cake and ice cream.

Entertainment

The staff at the **cultural centre** (☎ 481 187; Kossuth Lajos utca 3) near Szent István tér can tell you what's on.

Hatlépcsős (Six Steps; Jókai Mór utca 30) is a cheap wine bar that attracts students and dipsomaniacs, but it's not a bad place to sample one of Balatonfüred's famous Rieslings.

If you prefer a beer, carry on north to the Wild West-themed **Nirvana Pub** (Petőfi Sándor utca 2) or the popular **Dublin Irish Pub** (Blaha Lujza utca 9).

There are clubs all over town in summer, including **Galéria**, a disco on Zákonyi Ferenc utca. Other hot spots are the **Columbus Club** (Honvéd utca 7), **Club Átrium** (Blaha Lujza utca 9) at the Dublin Irish pub and **Fidel Club** (Blaha Lujza utca 7) next door.

Getting There & Away

Bus Buses for Tihany and Veszprém leave continually throughout the day. Other daily departures are to Budapest (four), Esztergom (one), Győr (seven), Hévíz (six), Kecskemét (one), Nagykanizsa (one), Sopron (two), Székesfehérvár (seven), Tatabánya (one) and Zalaegerszeg (four).

Train Frequent express and local trains travel northeast to Székesfehérvár and to Déli and Kelenföld stations in Budapest, and southwest to Tapolca and lakeside towns as far as Badacsony.

Boat From April to late October, daily Mahart ferries link Balatonfüred with Siófok and Tihany.

LAKE BALATON REGION

Up to nine daily ferries serve the same ports from late May to mid-September; one ferry just before 9am goes on to various ports, terminating at Badacsony.

Getting Around

You can reach Vitorlás tér and the lake from the train and bus stations on bus Nos 1, 1/a and 2; bus No 1 continues on to Füred Camping.

You can book the local taxi service by calling ☎ 444 444.

VESZPRÉM

☎ 88 • postcode 8200 • pop 63,900

Spreading over five hills between the northern and southern ranges of the Bakony Hills, Veszprém has one of the most dramatic locations in the Lake Balaton region. The walled castle district, atop a plateau, is a living museum of baroque art and architecture. Though not as rich as, say, Sopron (Western Transdanubia) in sights or historical buildings, Veszprém's buildings are generally in better condition. It's a delight to stroll through the windy Castle Hill district's single street, admiring the embarrassment of fine churches. As the townspeople say, 'Either the wind is blowing or the bells are ringing in Veszprém'.

The Romans did not settle in what is now Veszprém but 8km to the southeast at Balácapuszta, where important archaeological finds have been made. Prince Géza, King Stephen's father, founded a bishopric in Veszprém late in the 10th century, and the city grew as a religious, administrative and educational centre (the university was established in the

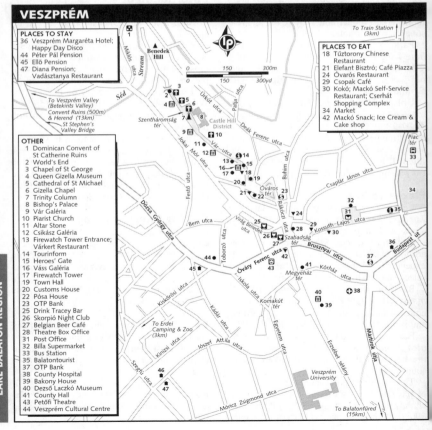

VESZPRÉM

PLACES TO STAY
36 Veszprém Margaréta Hotel; Happy Day Disco
44 Péter Pál Pension
45 Ellö Pension
47 Diana Pension; Vadásztanya Restaurant

PLACES TO EAT
18 Tűztorony Chinese Restaurant
21 Elefant Bisztró; Café Piazza
24 Óváros Restaurant
29 Csopak Café
30 Kokó; Mackó Self-Service Restaurant; Cserhát Shopping Complex
34 Market
42 Mackó Snack; Ice Cream & Cake shop

OTHER
1 Dominican Convent of St Catherine Ruins
2 World's End
3 Chapel of St George
4 Queen Gizella Museum
5 Cathedral of St Michael
6 Gizella Chapel
7 Trinity Column
8 Bishop's Palace
9 Vár Galéria
10 Piarist Church
11 Altar Stone
12 Csikász Galéria
13 Firewatch Tower Entrance; Várkert Restaurant
14 Tourinform
15 Heroes' Gate
16 Váss Galéria
17 Firewatch Tower
19 Town Hall
20 Customs House
22 Pósa House
23 OTP Bank
25 Drink Tracey Bar
26 Skorpió Night Club
27 Belgian Beer Café
28 Theatre Box Office
31 Post Office
32 Billa Supermarket
33 Bus Station
35 Balatontourist
37 OTP Bank
38 County Hospital
39 Bakony House
40 Dezsö Laczkó Museum
41 County Hall
43 Petöfi Theatre
44 Veszprém Cultural Centre

Views of Sopron from the firewatch tower

A charming medieval courtyard, Sopron

The 60m-high firewatch tower, Sopron

Esterházy Palace ('Hungary's Versailles'), Fertőd

Birdlife 'taking the waters' at Keszthely

Evening stroll at Keszthely, Lake Balaton

Sailing, a popular Hungarian activity

Statues of King Stephen and Queen Gizella at the World's End in Veszprém, near Lake Balaton

13th century). It also became a favourite residence of Hungary's queens.

The castle at Veszprém was blown up by the Habsburgs in 1702, and lost most of its medieval buildings during the Rákóczi War of Independence (1703–11) shortly thereafter. But this cleared the way for Veszprém's golden age, when the city's bishops and rich landlords built most of what you see today. The church's iron grip on Veszprém prevented it from developing commercially, however, and it was bypassed by the main railway line in the 19th century.

Orientation

The bus station is on Piac tér, a few minutes' walk northeast from Kossuth Lajos utca, a pedestrian street of shops and travel agencies. If you turn north at the end of Kossuth Lajos utca at Szabadság tér, and walk along Rákóczi utca you'll soon reach the entrance to Castle Hill (Vár-hegy) at Óváros tér.

The train station is 3km north of the bus station at the end of Jutasi út.

Information

Tourinform (☎/fax 404 548; e veszprem@ tourinform.hu; Vár utca 4; open 9am-6pm Mon-Fri, 11am-3pm Sat, 11am-4pm Sun June-Aug, 9am-5pm Mon-Fri Sept-May) has lots of information on the city and the surrounding villages.

The head office of **Balatontourist** (☎ 544 400; w www.balatontourist.hu; Kossuth Lajos utca 25; open 8.30am-4.30pm Mon-Fri year-round; 8.30am-noon Sat in summer) is between the bus station and the Castle Hill district.

Find out more about Veszprém by logging on to its website (w www.veszprem.hu).

You can change money at a branch of the **OTP bank** (Óváros tér 25) or at the much bigger branch (cnr Brusznyai utca & Mártírok útja) with a currency-exchange machine. There is a **post office** (Kossuth Lajos utca 19) near Balatontourist.

Internet access is available at **Kokó** (Kossuth Lajos utca; open 9am-10pm Mon-Thur, 9am-midnight Fri & Sat, 2pm-10pm Sun), a cake shop on the 1st floor of the Cserhát shopping complex, which charges 500Ft per hour.

Castle Hill

You should begin any tour of Veszprém in Óváros tér, the medieval market place at the bottom of Castle Hill. Of the many fine 18th-century buildings in the square, the most interesting is the late baroque **Pósa House** (1793) with an iron balcony at No 3, now a bank. The buildings at Nos 7 and 9 are the former **customs house** (also a bank) and the **town hall**.

As you begin to ascend Castle Hill and its sole street, Vár utca, you'll pass through **Heroes' Gate** (Hősök kapuja), an entrance built in 1936 from the stones of a 15th-century castle gate.

To your left is the **firewatch tower** (tűztorony; ☎ 425 204; Vár utca 9; adult/child 100/50Ft; open 10am-6pm daily mid-Mar–Oct), which, like the one in Sopron, is an architectural hybrid of Gothic, baroque and neoclassical styles. The chimes heard on the hour throughout Veszprém emanate from here, and you can climb to the top for excellent views of the rocky hill and the Bakony Hills.

The extremely rich **Piarist church** (Piarista templom; ☎ 426 088; Vár utca 12; admission free; open 9am-5pm daily May-Oct) was built in 1836 in the neoclassical style. The red marble **altar stone** (1467) diagonally opposite outside the parish office at No 27 is the oldest piece of Renaissance stonework in Hungary.

The U-shaped **Bishop's Palace** (Püspöki palota; Vár utca 16), is where the queen's residence stood in the Middle Ages. It faces Szentháromság tér, named for the **Trinity Column** (1751) in the centre. The palace, designed by Jakab Fellner of Tata in the mid-18th century, is not open to the public.

Next to the Bishop's Palace is the early Gothic **Gizella Chapel** (Gizella-kápolna; ☎ 426 088; Vár utca 18; adult/child 100/ 50Ft; open 9am-5pm daily May-Oct), named after Gizella, the wife of King Stephen, who was crowned near here early in the 11th century. The chapel was discovered when the Bishop's Palace was being built in the mid-18th century. Inside the chapel are Byzantine-influenced 13th-century frescoes of the Apostles. The **Queen Gizella Museum** (☎ 426 088; Vár utca 35; adult/child 200/100Ft; open 9am-5pm daily May-Oct) of religious art is opposite the chapel.

Parts of the dark and austere **Cathedral of St Michael** (székesegyház; ☎ 426 088; Vár utca 18-20; admission free; open 9am-5pm daily May-Oct), which is the site of the first bishop's palace, date from the beginning of the 11th century, but the cathedral has been rebuilt many times since then – the early Gothic crypt is original, though. Beside the cathedral, the octagonal foundation of the 13th-century **Chapel of St George** *(Szent György kápolna; ☎ 426 088; adult/child 100/50Ft; open 10am-5pm daily May-Oct)* sits under a glass dome.

From the rampart known as **World's End**, at the end of Vár utca, you can gaze north to craggy Benedict Hill (Benedek-hegy) and the Séd Stream, and west to the concrete viaduct (now St Stephen's Valley Bridge) over the Betekints Valley. In Margit tér, below the bridge, are the ruins of the medieval **Dominican Convent of St Catherine** and to the west is what little remains of the 11th-century **Veszprém Valley Convent**, whose erstwhile cloistered residents are said to have stitched Gizella's crimson silk coronation robe in 1031. The **statues of King Stephen and**

Reach Out & Touch

It could have been a chapter from a Mills & Boon novel for the macabre. The year was 1996 and the millecentenary celebrations honouring the arrival of the Magyars in the Carpathian Basin in 896 were under way in Hungary. People were in the mood to mark dates and one of those people was the archbishop of Veszprém.

He knew that it had been in Veszprém that the future king, Stephen, and a Bavarian princess, Gizella, were married in 996. Just suppose, he thought, that the bishop of the Bavarian city of Passau, where Gizella's remains had been resting these nine centuries, agreed to send her hand to Hungary. The Holy Dexter, St Stephen's revered right hand, could be brought down from the Basilica in Budapest and they could... Well, the mind boggled.

All parties agreed (the bishop of Passau even threw in Gizella's arm bone) and the date was set. On 4 May, in the square in front of the Cathedral of St Michael in Veszprém, the hands were laid together and – 1000 years to the day – coyly touched in marital bliss once again.

The world did not change as we know it that fine spring morning – the No 2 tram raced along the Danube in Budapest; Mr Kovács dished out steaming *lángos* from his stall somewhere along Lake Balaton; schoolchildren in Sárospatak recited their *ábécé*. But all true Magyars knew, deep in their hearts, that all was right with the world.

Queen Gizella at World's End were erected in 1938 to mark the 900th anniversary of King Stephen's death. See also the boxed text 'Reach Out & Touch').

Vár utca is lined with **art galleries**, including the **Váss Galéria** at No 7, the **Csikász Galéria** at No 17 and the **Vár Galéria** at No 29, which exhibit everything from religious paintings to postmodernist sculpture. A ticket costing 300/2000Ft per adult/child gets you into all three galleries as well as the firewatch tower; the galleries generally open from 10am to 6pm daily.

Dezső Laczkó Museum

The Dezső Laczkó Museum *(Bakony Museum; ☎ 564 330; Erzsébet sétány 1; adult/child 200/100Ft; open 10am-6pm Tues-Sun mid-Mar–mid-Oct; noon-4pm Tues-Sun mid-Oct–mid-Mar)* is south of Megyeház tér. It has archaeological exhibits (the emphasis is on the Roman settlement at Balácapuszta), a large collection of Hungarian, German and Slovak folk costumes and superb wooden carvings, including objects made by the famed outlaws of the Bakony Hills in the 18th and 19th centuries. Next to the main museum is **Bakony House** *(Bakonyi ház; ☎ 564 330; adult/child 130/70Ft; open 10am-6pm Tues-Sun May-Sept)*, a copy of an 18th-century thatched peasant dwelling in the village of Öcs, southwest of Veszprém. It has the usual three rooms found in Hungarian peasant homes, and the complete workshop *(kamra)* of a flask maker has been set up.

Petőfi Theatre

Take a peek inside this theatre *(☎ 424 235; Óváry Ferenc utca 2; open 9am-1pm & 2pm-5pm Mon-Fri)* even if you're not attending a performance. It's a pink, grey and burgundy gem of Hungarian Art Nouveau architecture and its decoration was designed by István Medgyaszay in 1908. It's also important structurally, as the theatre was the first building in Hungary to be made entirely of reinforced concrete. The large round stained-glass window entitled *The Magic of Folk Art* by Sándor Nagy is exceptional.

Places to Stay

Erdei Camping *(☎ 326 751; Kittenberger utca 14; camping per tent/person 700/750Ft, 4-person bungalows 8400-9000Ft; motel rooms per person 1900-2500Ft; open* *mid-Apr–mid-Oct)* is a small place quite far west of town near the zoo. The motel at the camp site is one of the cheapest places to stay in Veszprém; rooms have shared facilities. The smaller **pension** *(singles 2700-3200Ft, doubles 5400-6200Ft)*, next door, is more expensive. Rates depend on the season.

Balatontourist can help you with private rooms (2500Ft per person) and flats (from 7000Ft).

There are two pensions in attractive villas on József Attila utca southwest of the centre. **Diana** *(☎/fax 567 350; József Attila utca 22; singles/doubles 5500/7500Ft)*, with 10 accommodating rooms and a restaurant (see Places to Eat later), is the better deal. **Éllö** *(☎ 420 097, fax 329 711; József Attila utca 25; singles/doubles 10,000/12,000Ft)* has 18 large rooms but is overpriced.

Péter Pál *(☎ 567 790;* e *info@peter pal.hu; Dózsa György utca 3; singles/doubles/triples 6000/7700/10,000Ft)* is far and away the best pension in town, with 12 very well kept rooms, a lovely garden, an excellent restaurant and very friendly and helpful staff.

Veszprém Margaréta *(☎ 424 876, fax 424 076; Budapest út 6; singles/doubles 8300/12,300Ft)* is a 75-room hotel and is the most central, but its on a very busy thoroughfare, quite ugly and not particularly appealing.

Places to Eat

Mackó *(Kossuth Lajos utca 6; meals around 500Ft; open 5.30am-7.30pm daily)*, is one of the cheapest places in town for a bite. It's a self-service restaurant that also offers little pizzas, salads and cakes in the Cserhát shopping complex. **Mackó Snack** *(Szabadság tér; burgers & pizza slices from 240Ft)* is another cheap place for a bite to eat. Next door is a popular ice cream and cake shop.

Elefánt Bisztró *(Óváros tér 6; mains from 1000Ft)* doesn't exactly serve gigantic portions like the name would suggest, but the food, from steaks to salads, is altogether top notch.

Café Piazza *(Óváros tér 4; pizzas from 700Ft)* is next door to Elefánt and has decent pizza. Both Piazza and Elefánt have seating splayed out on the tér.

There are very few places to eat on Castle Hill, but you could try either of the following: **Tüztorony** *(☎ 326 220; Vár utca 1; most mains under 1000Ft)*, between the firewatch tower and Heroes' Gate, is a friendly Chinese restaurant with a cheap lunch menu (480Ft)

while **Várkert** *(☎ 442 992; Vár utca 17; set menu 990Ft)* has a three-course set menu throughout the day.

Óváros *(☎ 326 790; Szabadság tér 14; mains 1000-2000Ft)* is a restarant in a lovely baroque building with outdoor seating on various levels.

The restaurant at the pension **Péter Pál** *(☎ 567 790; Dózsa György utca 3)* gets rave reviews from local people and readers, and the restaurant at the Diana pension, **Vadásztanya** *(☎/fax 567 350; József Attila utca 22)*, is very good as well.

The café **Csopak** *(Kossuth Lajos utca 5)*, near Szabadság tér, is a popular student hang-out and a decent place for cakes.

The large **covered market**, where you can buy food among other things, is on Piac tér south of the bus station.

Entertainment

Veszprém Cultural Centre *(☎ 429 111; Dózsa György utca 2)* is where the city's symphony orchestra is based. **Petőfi Theatre** *(☎ 424 235; Óváry Ferenc utca 2)* is magnificent and stages both plays and concerts; tickets are available from the box office *(☎ 422 440; Szabadság tér 7; open 9am-1pm & 2pm-5pm Mon-Fri)*. Concerts are often held in July and August in front of the **Bishop's Palace** in Szentháromság tér, which is said to have perfect acoustics, and from time to time at the **Piarist church**.

Belgian Beer Café *(Szabadság tér 5)* has a wide selection of beers and a big courtyard away from busy Szabadság tér.

Skorpió Night Club *(Virág Benedek utca 1; open until 2am Mon-Thur, until 4am Fri & Sat, until 1am Sun)* is a good place for a pint or to kick up your heels.

Drink Tracey Bar *(Virág Benedek utca 4)*, opposite Skorpió, blasts out techno music and attracts a *very* young crowd.

Happy Day Disco *(Budapest út 7; open until 4am Fri-Sun)* is another popular club with an unfortunate name. It's opposite the Veszprém Margaréta hotel.

Getting There & Away

Bus Connections with Veszprém are excellent, with half-hourly departures to Budapest (including five express buses and many more via Székesfehérvár), Herend, Nagyvázsony, Keszthely via Balatonfüred, Pápa, Sümeg and Tapolca. Other destinations include Esztergom (three buses daily), Győr (nine), Kaposvár (two), Kecskemét (three), Nagykanizsa (four), Pécs (two), Siófok (nine), Szeged (three), Szekszárd (three), Szombathely (three) and Zalaegerszeg (four).

Train Three railway lines meet at Veszprém. The first connects Veszprém with Szombathely and Budapest's stations via Székesfehérvár (up to eight/10 daily to Budapest/Szombathely). The second line carries up to six trains daily north to Pannonhalma and Győr, where you can transfer for Vienna (see Train in the Getting There & Away chapter for details on getting to/from Vienna). The third, southeast to Lepsény, links Veszprém with the railway lines on the northern and southern shores of Lake Balaton up to six times daily.

Getting Around
Bus Nos 1 and 2 run from the train and bus stations to Szabadság tér. You'll need your own transport to Erdei. To book a local taxi ring ☎ 444 444.

AROUND VESZPRÉM
Herend
☎ 88 • postcode 8440 • pop 3300
The porcelain factory at Herend (W www .herend.hu), 13km west of Veszprém, has been producing Hungary's finest handpainted chinaware for over 150 years. There's not a lot to see in this dusty one-horse village, and prices at the outlet don't seem any cheaper than elsewhere in Hungary, but the **Porcelánium** (☎ 523 100; W www.porcelanium.com; Kossuth Lajos utca 140; adult/child factory & museum 1000/400Ft, museum only 300/100Ft; open 9am-5.30pm daily Apr-Oct; 9am-4.30pm Mon-Sat Nov-Mar) is worth the trip. It consists of a museum which displays the most prized pieces of the rich Herend collection, and a mini-factory (closed on Monday), where you can witness first-hand how ugly clumps of clay become delicate porcelain. It's a five-minute walk northeast from the bus station. Labels are in four languages, including English, which makes it easy to follow the developments and changes in patterns and tastes (see the boxed text 'Herend Porcelain'), and there's a short film tracing the history of Herend porcelain.

The complex has a **shop** selling antique pieces; otherwise scout around the few shops close to the Porcelánium for new pieces. Should you feel hungry, Porcelánium has a

Herend Porcelain

A terracotta factory, set up at Herend in 1826, began producing porcelain 13 years later under Mór Farkasházi Fischer of Tata in Western Transdanubia.

Initially it specialised in copying and replacing the nobles' broken chinaware settings imported from Asia. You'll see some pretty kooky 19th-century interpretations of Japanese art and Chinese faces on display in the Porcelánium museum here (see Porcelánium in the Herend section for details). But the factory soon began producing its own patterns; many, like the *Rothschild bird* and *petites roses*, were inspired by Meissen and Sèvres designs from Germany and France. The Victoria pattern of butterflies and wild flowers of the Bakony was designed for Queen Victoria after she admired a display of Herend pieces at the Great Exhibition in London in 1851.

To avoid bankruptcy in the 1870s, the Herend factory began mass production; tastes ran from kitschy pastoral and hunting scenes to the ever-popular animal sculptures with the distinctive scale-like triangle patterns. In 1993, three quarters of the factory was purchased by its 1500 workers and became one of the first companies in Hungary privatised through an employee stock-ownership plan. The state owns the other quarter.

cheapish bistro, a café and an expensive restaurant. **Lila Akác** (Kossuth Lajos utca 122; mains from 800Ft) is a restaurant west of the museum and across Vasút utca, and a more relaxing place for something to eat.

There's an MKB bank branch on Kossuth Lajos utca, just east of the museum.

Getting There & Away
You can reach Herend by bus from Veszprém at least every 30 minutes; other destinations include Sümeg (three buses daily) and Balatonfüred (two). Five local trains run through Herend daily on their way to Ajka. Change there for Szombathely.

PÁPA
☎ 89 • postcode 8500 • pop 34,400
This attractive town some 50km northwest of Veszprém has been called the 'Athens of Transdanubia' largely because of its Calvinist

school. It was attended by such literary greats as the poet Sándor Petőfi and the novelist Mór Jókai in the 19th century. Religious tolerance has been a hallmark of Pápa for centuries.

Protestantism gained ground swiftly in the area in the 16th century and the first Hungarian translation of the Heidelberg Catechism was published here in 1577. During the late Middle Ages, Pápa was the third-most important Protestant stronghold in Transdanubia after Sopron and Sárvár.

Pápa flourished after liberation from the Turks, with Bishop Károly Esterházy overseeing the construction of many of its fine baroque buildings, and whose family effectively owned the town from 1648 to after WWII (1939–45). His brother Ferenc encouraged trade by allowing Jews to settle in Pápa. Pottery, broad cloth and paper-making industries were mainly run by Jews and by the end of the 19th century Pápa had one of the largest Jewish populations in Hungary. The railways – and large-scale industrialisation – passed Pápa by, allowing it to retain much of its lovely architecture.

Orientation & Information

Pápa's main drags are Fő tér and Fő utca, which run southeast from Kastély-park to Március 15 tér. Pedestrian Kossuth Lajos utca runs southward from the large parish church on Fő tér. The bus station is on Szabadság utca, a short distance east of the church. The train station is in Béke tér, north of the centre at the end of Esterházy Károly utca.

Tourinform (☎/fax 311 535; e papa@ tourinform.hu; Fő utca 5; open 9am-5pm Mon-Fri, 9am-noon Sat June-Sept; 9am-4pm Mon-Fri Oct-May) is next to the **OTP bank** (Fő utca 5). A **K&H bank** (Kossuth Lajos utca 27) branch is opposite the **main post office** on the same street. There's a well-stocked **foreign language bookshop** (Fő utca 6) opposite Tourinform.

Find out more about Pápa by going online to its website (w www.papa.hu).

Things to See

The enormous U-shaped yellow building at the entrance to Kastély-park is the former **Esterházy Palace** (Esterházy kastély; ☎ 313 584) built in 1784 on the foundations of an older castle. Russian soldiers were billeted here as late as 1990. The palace contains a small regional museum, which is currently

undergoing renovation – check with Tourinform (see Information earlier) for opening times – a music school and a library.

South of the palace on Fő tér is the Catholic **Great Church** (Nagytemplom) built by Jacob Fellner in 1786 and dedicated to St Stephen. It contains wonderful frescoes (1781–82) of St Stephen's life and martyrdom by Franz Anton Maulbertsch (the same artist who did the frescoes in Sümeg) and Hubert Mauer. The spooky remains of the Roman martyr St Martialis are preserved in a see-through coffin below the altar in the Virgin's Chapel to the left as you enter.

The **Calvinist Church History Museum** (Református Egyhátörténeti Múzeum; Fő utca 6; adult/child 100/50Ft; open 9am-5pm Tues-Sun May-Oct) may not sound like a crowd-pleaser but it puts in perspective Protestantism and the role of the **Calvinist College** (Reformátis Kollégium; ☎ 324 420; Március 15 tér 9; open 8am-4pm Tues-Fri, 9am-5pm Sat May-Oct). The college is a little farther south and its **library**, containing 75,000 valuable tomes, can be visited.

Arguably the most popular museum in Pápa is the **Blue Dyeing Museum** (Kékfestő

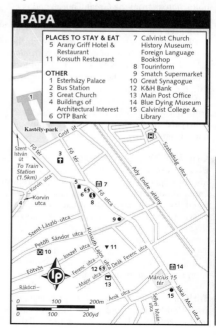

PÁPA

PLACES TO STAY & EAT
5 Arany Griff Hotel & Restaurant
11 Kossuth Restaurant

OTHER
1 Esterházy Palace
2 Bus Station
3 Great Church
4 Buildings of Architectural Interest
6 OTP Bank
7 Calvinist Church History Museum; Foreign Language Bookshop
8 Tourinform
9 Smatch Supermarket
10 Great Synagogue
12 K&H Bank
13 Main Post Office
14 Blue Dying Museum
15 Calvinist College & Library

Kastély-park

Grof út

Szent István út

To Train Station (1.5km)

Korvin utca

Korvin utca

Fő tér

Fő utca

Szabadság utca

Ady Endre sétány

Szent László utca

Petőfi Sándor utca

Eötvös

Rákóczi

József utca

Kossuth Lajos utca

Ferenc utca

Major utca

Deák Ferenc utca

Árok utca

Március 15 tér

Jókai Mór utca

Sellye István utca

0   100   200m
0   100   200yd

Múzeum; ☎ *324 390; Március 15 tér 12; adult/child 300/150Ft, free on Sun for families & students over 18; open 9am-5pm Tues-Sun Apr-Dec)*, which showcases a method of colouring cotton fabric deep blue that was a famous Pápa export throughout Hungary. The museum is housed in a factory that stopped operating in 1956, but the machines remain in perfect working order, demonstrations are sometimes held and there's an interesting display of samples and old photographs.

The streets running west off Kossuth Lajos utca are particularly rich architecturally, especially along Korvin utca; check out the Gothic, baroque and rococo gems at Nos 4, 9, 7 and 13 on Korvin utca, most of which are now offices. To the south the **Great Synagogue** *(Nagyzsinagóga; Petőfi Sándor utca 24-26)*, a romantic structure built in 1846 with some 100,000 bricks donated by the Esterházy family, barely stands.

Places to Stay & Eat
Arany Griff *(☎ 312 000, fax 312 005;* e *au griff@enternet.hu; Fő tér 15; singles 5984-7480Ft, doubles 8704-11,288Ft)* is a 25-room hotel, across from the Great Church and is as central as you'll find. Rates vary depending on the season.

Places to eat are rather scarce though the restaurant at the back of **Arany Griff** *(mains 800-1200Ft)* and its *cukrászda*, with outdoor seating out front in the warmer months, is a safe bet for reliable food.

Kossuth *(Kossuth Lajos utca 22; mains around 750-1200Ft)*, a restaurant in a quiet courtyard in the Kossuth Udvar shopping mall, is an option.

Getting There & Away
Bus Bus service to/from Pápa is good with hourly departures to Győr and Veszprém. Other important destinations include Balatonfüred (two buses daily), Budapest (three), Kaposvár (one), Keszthely (eight), Nagykanizsa (two), Sárvár (two), Sopron (three), Sümeg (seven), Szeged (one), Szombathely (one), Tapolca (four) and Zalaegerszeg (three).

There is a bus to Vienna at 6.55am on Monday, Thursday and Friday.

Train Pápa is on the rail line linking Győr with Celldömölk, from where you can carry on to Szombathely up to eight times daily.

The only other place you can reach by rail from Pápa is Csorna, which is on the main line between Győr and Sopron.

SZÉKESFEHÉRVÁR
☎ 22 • postcode 8000 • pop 107,000
Székesfehérvár may look like just another big city off the M7 between Budapest and Lake Balaton (35km to the southwest) but this city (German: Stuhlweissenburg) is traditionally known as the place where the Magyar chieftain Árpád first set up camp, making this the oldest town in Hungary.

Although Székesfehérvár is not on Lake Balaton, everyone travelling between Budapest and the lake passes this way. Székesfehérvár can also be seen as a day trip from Budapest.

Close to the city is Velence, a much smaller and more subdued lake than the Balaton. The lake is the third largest in Hungary at 10.5km long. Almost a third of its surface is covered in reeds, so it's a good place to observe birdlife. Other activities include swimming, water sports and fishing.

History
As early as the 1st century, the Romans had a settlement at Gorsium near Tác, 17km to the south. When Árpád arrived late in the 9th century, the surrounding marshes and the Sárvíz River offered protection – the same reason Prince Géza built his castle here less than 100 years later. But it was Géza's son, King Stephen I, who raised the status of Székesfehérvár by building a fortified basilica in what he called Alba Regia. Hungary's kings (and some of its queens) would be crowned and buried here for the next 500 years. In fact, the city's seemingly unpronounceable name (**sake**-kesh-fehair-vahr) means 'Seat of the White Castle', as it was the royal capital and white was the king's colour.

With Visegrád, Esztergom and Buda, Székesfehérvár served as an alternative royal capital for centuries, and it was here in 1222 that King Andrew II was forced by his *servientes* (mercenaries) to sign the *Golden Bull*, an early bill of rights. The Turks captured Székesfehérvár in 1543 and used Stephen's basilica to store gunpowder. It exploded during a siege in 1601; when the Turks left in 1688, the town, the basilica and the royal tombs were in ruins.

SZÉKESFEHÉRVÁR

PLACES TO STAY
1 Magyar Király Hotel
18 Alba Regia Hotel
35 Rév Hotel

PLACES TO EAT
3 Castrum Restaurant
4 Vörösmarty Cake Shop
12 Korzó Pub
16 Food Stalls
17 Ristorante Rinascimento
29 Bástya Pizzeria

OTHER
2 Vörösmarty Theatre
5 OTP Bank
6 King Stephen Museum (Branch)
7 Black Eagle Pharmacy
8 Theatre Ticket Office
9 King Stephen Museum
10 Cistercian Church

11 István Csók Gallery
13 Cathedral & Coronation Church Foundations
14 Garden of Ruins
15 Skála Department Store; Kaiser's Supermarket
19 Kávé Színház
20 Viewing Platform
21 Bishop's Palace
22 National Orb
23 Franciscan Church
24 'Broken Bell' Memorial
25 Tourinform; Town Hall
26 St Anne's Chapel
27 Ibusz
28 St Stephen's Cathedral
30 Market
31 Bus Station
32 Udvárház Shopping Centre; Isolabella Pizzeria
33 Post Office
34 St Stephen Monument

Stephen, and much less Árpád, would hardly recognise today's Székesfehérvár. The stones from his basilica were used to construct the Bishop's Palace in 1801; several decades later, the marshland was drained and the Sárvíz was diverted. The city had been at a crossroads since the 11th century, when crusaders (on a budget) from Western Europe passed through Székesfehérvár on their way to the Adriatic Sea. The arrival of the railway in the 1860s turned the city into a transport hub.

In March 1945 the Germans launched the last big counteroffensive of WWII near Székesfehérvár. Though the fighting razed the city's outskirts (the historic centre was left more or less intact), it opened the way for postwar industrial development.

Orientation

Városház tér and Koronázó tér together form the core of the old town. Pedestrian Fő utca – what the Romans called Vicus Magnus – runs north from here. The train station is a 15-minute walk southeast in Béke tér and can be reached via József Attila utca and its continuation, Deák Ferenc utca. The bus station is in Piac tér near the market, just outside the old town's western wall.

Information

Tourinform (☎ 312 818, fax 502 772; e fejer-m@tourinform.hu; Városház tér 1; open 9am-7pm Mon-Fri, 9am-6pm Sat & Sun May–mid-Sept; 9am-4pm mid-Sept– May) has an office next to the town hall. Another agency in town is **Ibusz** (☎ 329 393;

Táncsics Mihály utca 5; open 8am-4pm or 4.30pm Mon-Fri) south of Koronázó tér.

There's a branch of the **OTP bank** *(Fő utca 6)* at the northern end of town and the **main post office** *(Kossuth Lajos utca 16)* is at the southern end. The **West Side Music Club** *(Vörösmarty tér 1)* has a couple of terminals for Internet access and charges 500Ft per hour.

For more details about this city check out its website (W www.szekesfehervar.hu).

St Stephen's Cathedral

St Stephen's Cathedral *(Szent István székesegyház; Géza nagyfejedelem tér; admission free)*, just off Arany János utca, was constructed in 1470 and originally dedicated to Sts Peter and Paul, but what you see today is essentially an 18th-century baroque church. The ceiling frescoes inside were painted by Johannes Cymbal in 1768. On the paving stones in front of the cathedral are foundation outlines of an earlier (perhaps 10th-century) church. The wooden crucifix on the cathedral's northern wall is dedicated to the victims of the 1956 Uprising. Generally the church is locked but you can get a glimpse of the inside through its glass doors; check the services timetable to take a closer look.

Just north of the cathedral is **St Anne's Chapel** *(Szent Anna kápolna; Arany János utca; admission free)* built around the same time, with additions (the tower, for example) made some centuries later. The Turks used the chapel as a place of worship; you can still see the remains of a painting from that era.

Around Városház tér & Koronázó tér

Arany János utca debouches into the double square of Városház tér to the west and Koronázó tér to the east. The single-storey block of the **town hall** *(Városház tér)* dates from 1690; the larger northern wing was formerly the Zichy Palace built in the 18th century. Opposite is the austere 1745 **Franciscan church** *(Ferences templom; admission free)*. The stone ball with the crown in the centre of the square is the **National Orb** (Országalma – which means 'national apple' in Hungarian) dedicated to King Stephen. The monument that looks like a **broken bell** (1995) lying on its side is dedicated to the victims of WWII.

The most imposing building on Koronázó tér is the Zopf-style **Bishop's Palace** (Püspöki palota), which is built with the rubble from the medieval basilica and royal burial chapels. The basilica and royal burial chapels stood to the east, in what is now the **Garden of Ruins** *(Romkert; ☎ 315 583; adult/child 200/100Ft; open 9am-5pm Tues-Sun Apr-Oct)*. The site is particularly sacred to Hungarians – some three dozen of their kings and queens were crowned and 15 buried here. The dolefullooking white-marble sarcophagus in the chamber to the right as you enter the main gate is thought to contain the remains of Géza, Stephen or his young son, Prince Imre. Decorative stonework from the basilica and royal tombs lines the walls of the loggia, and in the garden are the foundations of the **cathedral** and the **Coronation Church**. A small amount of excavation of the site continues. The Garden of Ruins is open for paying visitors but you get to see most of it from the street or the **viewing platform** to the west on Koronázó tér.

Around Fő utca

Lying to the north of the town centre, the **Black Eagle** *(Fekete Sas; ☎ 315 583; Fő utca 5; admission free; open 9am-4.30pm Mon-Fri)* is a pharmacy set up by the Jesuits in 1758, with beautiful rococo furnishings. A few steps to the west, on Oskola utca, the **István Csók Gallery** *(Bartók Béla tér 1; ☎ 314 106; adult/child 200/100Ft; open 10am-7pm Mon-Fri 10am-6pm Sat & Sun)* has a good collection of 19th and 20th-century Hungarian art. Note that the gallery is closed on the first Monday of each month.

The **King Stephen Museum** *(István Király Múzeum; ☎ 315 583; Fő utca 16; adult/child 200/100Ft; open 10am-4pm Tues-Sun May-Sept, 10am-2pm Tues-Sun Oct-Apr)* has a large collection of Roman pottery (some of it from Gorsium), an interesting folk-carving display and an exhibit covering 1000 years of Székesfehérvár history. The museum branch *(Országzászló tér 3; open 2pm-6pm Tues-Sun May-Sept, 2pm-4pm Tues-Sun Oct-Apr)* has temporary exhibits.

Places to Stay

College accommodation options for July and August are available from Tourinform. Try Ibusz for private rooms (from 2500Ft per person). **Rév** *(☎ 314 441, fax 450 042; József Attila utca 42; singles/doubles 3600/3900Ft)* is a workers' residence-cum-hotel with rooms available to tourists. It looks a little rough, but it's cheap and the rooms are clean.

Magyar Király (☎ *311 262, fax 327 788; Fő utca 10; singles/doubles 7500/10,000Ft)* is a 150-year-old hotel with 57 rooms that in its heyday must have been very grand.

Szárcsa Hotel (☎ *325 700, fax 506 818; Szautca 1; air-con singles/doubles 8500/ 10,500Ft)* is a fair distance south from the town centre but it's worth the trip. Each of its nine rooms are individually decorated with antique furniture and have a safe and large bathrooms. There's a quality restaurant here, too.

Alba Regia (☎ *313 484, fax 316 292;* e *reserve@hotelalbaregia.hunguesthotels .hu; Rákóczi út 1; singles/doubles 14,200/ 19,100Ft)*, near the Garden of Ruins, is a modern hotel with 104 expensive rooms.

Taurus Kastély (☎ *447 030, fax 447 032;* e *kastelyszallo@mail.datatrans.hu; Kastély utca 1; singles/doubles €73/78, suites €134)* is great if you fancy staying in a stately home. Originally the Zichy family's country manor (1821) at Seregélyes, some 16km southeast of Székesfehérvár, it now houses a hotel, complete with frescoed dining hall, tennis court, pool and sauna, on 22 hectares of parkland.

Places to Eat

There are a bunch of decent **food stalls** *(Kégi György utca)* in the square in front of the Skála department store.

Korzó (*Fő utca 2; mains 700-900Ft)* is a decent pub for lunch or dinner, and cheap.

Bástya (☎ *315 091; Kossuth Lagos utca 3; pizzas from 500Ft)* is a lovely pizzeria near St Stephen's Cathedral that serves large pizzas and has outdoor seating.

Isolabella (☎ *328 318; Kossuth Lajos utca 12; pizzas from 500Ft)*, in the courtyard of the Udvárház Shopping Centre, is a good pizzeria.

Ristorante Rinascimento *(Távírda utca 15; mains 700-1200Ft)*, in the small Ferenc shopping mall, claims to have 'real Italian food'.

Castrum (☎ *505 719; Várkörút 3; mains from 1700Ft)*, an atmospheric cellar restaurant, has excellent food but it's quite expensive.

Vörösmarty *(Fő utca 6; open until 9pm daily)* is a popular cake shop with outdoor seating.

Entertainment

Vörösmarty Theatre *(Fő utca 8)*, near the Magyar Király hotel, hosts cultural performances. You can buy tickets from the box office (☎ *327 056; Fő utca 3; open 8am-5.30pm Mon-Fri)* in the courtyard here.

The wine to try in these parts is Ezerjó (which means 'a thousand good things') from Mór, 27km to the northwest in the Vértes Hills. It's an acidic, greenish-white tipple that is light and fairly pleasant. Tourinform (see Information earlier for details) has a list of wine cellars to visit in Mór.

Kávé Színház *(Coffee Theatre; Táncsics Mihály utca 1)* is a fantastic place for a quiet drink, day or night. Its huge terrace overlooks Koronázó tér and the Garden of Ruins.

Bahnhof Fehérvár, a club on Takarodó utca, east of the train station, revs (and raves) up at the weekend. It's easy to spot – someone has parked a locomotive into the side of the building.

West Side Music Club *(Vörösmarty tér 1)*, southeast of the bus station, is another popular place, but it is rather small and pokey.

For more information on what's on, check the free bi-weekly *Fehérvári Est* magazine.

Getting There & Away

Bus Buses depart for Budapest, Veszprém and the vineyards near Mór at least once every 30 minutes, and you can reach Lake Velence towns like Sukoró, Velence and Gárdony (via Agárd) frequently throughout the day.

Other destinations from Székesfehérvár include Baja (two buses daily), Balatonfüred (six), Esztergom (two), Győr (seven), Hévíz (two or three), Kalocsa (two), Kecskemét (two), Kaposvár (two), Keszthely (three), Martonvásár (nine), Pápa (two), Pécs (two to four), Siófok (six), Sopron (two), Sümeg (five), Szeged (two), Szekszárd (five), Tapolca (four), Tata (three) and Zalaegerszeg (two).

Train Székesfehérvár is an important rail junction, and you can reach most destinations in all of Transdanubia from here. One line splits at Szabadbattyán some 10km to the south, leading to Lake Balaton's northern shore and Tapolca on one side of the lake and to the southern shore and Nagykanizsa on the other.

Trains every half-hour link Székesfehérvár with Kelenföld and Déli train stations in Budapest; five to seven run daily to Szombathely via Veszprém. A local train runs north to Mór and Komárom (where you cross over to Slovakia) seven times daily.

Getting Around

Bus No 12/a runs close to Szárcsa Hotel. You can book local taxis on ☎ 222 222 or ☎ 343 343.

Southern Transdanubia

Southern Transdanubia (Dél-Dunántúl) is bordered by the Danube to the east, the Dráva River and Croatia to the south and west, and Lake Balaton to the north. It is generally flatter than Western Transdanubia and the Lake Balaton region, with the Mecsek and Villány Hills rising in isolation from the plain, milder and considerably wetter.

Although there are some large towns here, Southern Transdanubia is not nearly as built-up or industrial as the rest of Transdanubia. In general, it is thickly settled with villages, most of these are small in population. Agriculture is still the main industry – from the fruit orchards of the Zselic region south of Kaposvár and the almonds of Pécs to the wines of Szekszárd and the Villány-Siklós region.

Southern Transdanubia was settled by the Celts and then the Romans, who built important towns at Alisca (Szekszárd) and Sophianae (Pécs) and introduced grape-growing. The north-south trade route passed through here, and many of the settlements prospered during the Middle Ages.

The region was a focal point of the Turkish occupation. The battle that led to the Ottoman domination of Hungary for more than a century and a half was fought at Mohács in 1526, and one of the most heroic stands taken by the Hungarians against the invaders took place at Szigetvár some 40 years later. Pécs was an important political and cultural centre under the Turks.

Late in the 17th century, the abandoned towns of Southern Transdanubia were resettled by Swabian Germans and Southern Slavs, and after WWII ethnic Hungarians came from Slovakia and Bukovina in Romania as did Saxon Germans. These people left a mark that can still be seen and felt today, namely in the local architecture, food and certain traditions.

This part of Transdanubia has a lot to offer the traveller – from the art museums of Pécs and the castles of Siklós and Szigetvár to the thermal spas of Harkány and Zalakaros. Once you have soaked up as much art, history and curative water as you can possibly hold, top it all off with some of the country's best wines from Szekszárd and Villány (in competition for the best red wines in the country).

Highlights

- The Zsolnay and Csontváry museums, the old synagogue and the early Christian chapel in Pécs
- A ride on the narrow-gauge train through the Gemenc Forest in the Sárköz region
- The wines of Villány and the wine cellars of Villánykövesd
- A dip in the cure-all thermal baths at Harkány, especially in winter
- The Castle Museum's collection of gloves, fans and umbrellas at Siklós
- A performance at Kaposvár's splendid Gergely Csiky Theatre

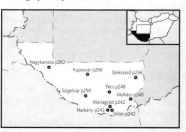

SZEKSZÁRD
☎ 74 • postcode 7100 • pop 37,000

Szekszárd lies south of the Sió River, which links Lake Balaton with the Danube, among seven of the Szekszárd Hills. It is the capital of Tolna County and the centre of the Sárköz folk region, but more than anything else Szekszárd is the gateway to Southern Transdanubia. In fact, you can see the region start in the town's main square (Garay tér), where the Great Plain, having crossed the Danube, rises slowly, transforming into the Szekszárd Hills.

Szekszárd was a Celtic and later a Roman settlement called Alisca. The sixth Hungarian king, Béla I, conferred royal status on the town and founded an important Benedictine abbey here in 1061.

The Turkish occupation left Szekszárd desolated, but the area was repopulated late in the 17th century by immigrant Swabians from Germany, and the economy was

234

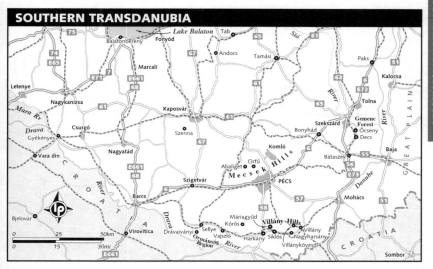

SOUTHERN TRANSDANUBIA

revitalised in the next century by wheat cultivation and viticulture. For more information on Szekszárd's fabulous reds, see the 'Wines of Hungary' special section.

Orientation & Information

The bus and train stations are opposite one another on Pollack Mihály utca. From here, follow pedestrian Bajcsy-Zsilinszky utca west through the park to the city centre. Garay tér ascends to the old castle district, today's Béla tér. Munkácsy Mihály utca runs southwest from Béla tér to Kálvária utca and Calvary Hill.

The straight-faced but helpful **Tourinform** (☎ 511 263, fax 511 264; e szekszard@tour inform.hu; Garay tér 18; open 9am-6pm Mon-Fri, 9am-5pm Sat & Sun May-Sept; 9am-5pm Mon-Fri Oct-Apr) staff have loads of information on the town and Tolna County. Otherwise **Tolna Tourist** (☎ 412 144; Széchenyi utca 38; open 8am-4.30pm Mon-Thur, 8am-4pm Fri, 8am-noon Sat) can help out.

There's an **OTP bank** (Mártírok tere 5-7) in the centre and the **main post office** (Széchenyi utca 11-13) is northwest of OTP.

Things to See

You can get a good overview of Szekszárd by following Kálvária utca from outside the Alisca hotel and up the grassy steps to the 205m **Calvary Hill** (Kálvária-hegy). The

hill's name recalls the crucifixion scene and chapel erected here in the 18th century by grief-stricken parents who had lost their child (still remembered thanks to a famous poem by Mihály Babits, a native son of Szekszárd). The Danube and the Great Plain are visible to the east, the Sárköz region beyond the hills to the south and the Szekszárd Hills to the west; on a clear day, you can just see the nuclear power station at Paks, 30km to the north.

The little village – the so-called Upper Town (Felsőváros) – in the valley to the northwest is full of vineyards and private cellars. Walk along Bartina utca, which becomes Remete utca, to **Remete Chapel** (Remete kápolna; 1778), an important pilgrimage site, at the end; return via Bocskai utca to the north of Szekszárd Stream.

The neoclassical **County Hall** (vármegyeháza; ☎ 419 667; Béla tér 1; open 9am-5pm Tues-Sun Apr-Sept; 9am-3pm Tues-Sun Oct-Mar), designed by Mihály Pollack in 1828, sits on the site of Béla's abbey and an earlier Christian chapel; you can see the excavated foundations in the central courtyard. On the upper floor of the building, there is the **Franz Liszt Exhibition** (adult/child 100/50Ft) and across the hall the **Eszter Mattioni Gallery** (adult/child 100/50Ft), whose works in striking mosaics of marble, glass and mother-of-pearl invoke peasant themes with a twist. The square's baroque yellow **Inner City Catholic**

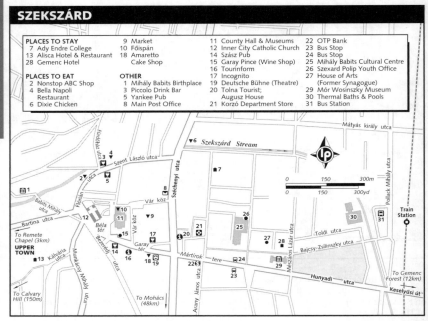

SZEKSZÁRD

PLACES TO STAY	9 Market	11 County Hall & Museums	22 OTP Bank
7 Ady Endre College	10 Főispán	12 Inner City Catholic Church	23 Bus Stop
13 Alisca Hotel & Restaurant	18 Amaretto	14 Szász Pub	24 Bus Stop
28 Gemenc Hotel	Cake Shop	15 Garay Pince (Wine Shop)	25 Mihály Babits Cultural Centre
		16 Tourinform	26 Szexard Polip Youth Office
PLACES TO EAT	OTHER	17 Incognito	27 House of Arts
2 Nonstop ABC Shop	1 Mihály Babits Birthplace	19 Deutsche Bühne (Theatre)	(Former Synagogue)
4 Bella Napoli	3 Piccolo Drink Bar	20 Tolna Tourist;	29 Mór Wosinszky Museum
Restaurant	5 Yankee Pub	Augusz House	30 Thermal Baths & Pools
6 Dixie Chicken	8 Main Post Office	21 Korzó Department Store	31 Bus Station

Church (Belvárosi templom; 1805), is the largest single-nave church in Hungary.

The **Mór Wosinszky Museum** (☎ 316 222; Szent István tér 26; adult/child 100/50Ft; open 10am-6pm Tues-Sun Apr-Sept; 10am-4pm Tues-Sun Oct-Mar) was purpose-built in 1895 and is now named after a local priest and archaeologist who discovered the remains of a Neolithic culture in the town of Lengyel to the northwest. The finds, artefacts left by various peoples who passed through the Danube Basin ahead of the Magyars, are among the best anywhere (don't miss the fine Celtic and Avar jewellery), as is the large folk collection of Serbian, Swabian and Sárköz artefacts. Three period rooms – that of a well-to-do Sárköz farming family and their coveted spotted-poplar furniture, another from the estate of the aristocratic Apponyi family of Lengyel, and a poor gooseherd's hut – illustrate very clearly the different economic brackets that existed side by side in the region a century ago. Also interesting are the exhibits relating to the silk factory that was started in Szekszárd in the 19th century with Italian help.

The Moorish flourishes of the **House of Arts** (Művészetek Háza; ☎ 511 247; Szent István tér 28; changing exhibitions adult/child 300-400/150-200Ft; open 10am-6pm Tues-Fri), behind the museum, reveal its former life as a synagogue. It is now used as a gallery and concert hall. Four of its original iron pillars have been brought outside and enclosed in an arch, suggesting the tablets of the 10 Commandments, and there's a striking 'tree of life' monument a short distance south to 'Szekszárd's heroes and victims of WWII'.

Franz Liszt performed several times at the pink neo-Gothic **Augusz House** (Széchenyi utca 36-40); today it houses a music school and Tolna Tourist.

Szekszárd produced two of Hungary's most celebrated poets: Mihály Babits (1883–1941) and the lesser-known János Garay. The **Mihály Babits' Birthplace** (szülőháza; ☎ 312 154; Babits Mihály utca 13; adult/child 100/50Ft; open 9am-5pm Tues-Sun Apr-Oct; 9am-3pm Tues-Sat Nov-Mar) has been turned into a memorial museum. Although the poet's avant-garde, deeply philosophical verse may be obscure, even in Hungarian, it's a good chance to see how a middle-class family lived in 19th-century provincial Hungary.

Activities

Try the covered **thermal baths and outdoor pools** (Toldi utca 6; adult/child 300/160Ft; pools open 9am-6pm daily mid-May–Aug; baths open 2pm-8pm Mon, 6am-8pm Tues-Sun year-round) near the train and bus stations.

For horse riding, head to the **Gemenc Excursion Centre** (see Around Szekszárd later for details), some 12km east of Szekszárd.

Szekszárd has a few places scattered around town in which to sample the local vintage. One of the best venues is the **Garay Pince** (☎ 412 828; Garay tér 19; open 10am-6pm Mon-Fri, 8am-2pm Sat, 8am-noon Sun), opposite the Szász pub (see Entertainment later), with some of Szekszárd's best wines for tasting and purchasing. Tourinform has a full list of wine cellars in town, and a Wine Road map of the surrounding area.

Special Events

Among the big events staged annually in Szekszárd are the **Alisca Wine Days** in early June, the **Danube Folklore Festival**, jointly sponsored with Kalocsa and Baja in mid-July, and the **Szekszárd Vintage Festival** in late September.

Places to Stay

Ady Endre College (☎ 311 288; Augusz Imre utca 15; dorm beds €3 per person), near Szekszárd Stream, has dormitory rooms available in July and August.

Tolna Tourist and Tourinform have **private rooms** for around 1500Ft per person.

Alisca (☎ 312 228, fax 511 242; Kálvária utca 1; singles/doubles 4000/6000Ft) is a 19-room hotel and is a pleasant place up in the hills, with almost a country feel to it.

Gemenc (☎ 311 722, fax 311 335; Mészáros Lázár utca 1; singles 5850-7750Ft, doubles 8300-11,000Ft) is an ugly hotel, but many of its 92 rooms have recently been renovated. It's centrally located and has all the usual outlets – restaurant, coffee shop, nightclub etc. Rates vary depending on the season.

Places to Eat

Dixie Chicken (Széchenyi utca; meals from 300Ft), north of Szekszárd Stream, is the cheapest place to eat in town.

Bella Napoli (Szent László utca; dishes from 600Ft; open 11am-10.30pm or 11pm Mon-Sat), in a small shopping centre northwest of Garay tér, is decent for pasta and pizzas.

Főispán (☎ 312 139; Béla tér 1; mains from 900Ft), a cellar restaurant in the basement of the County Hall, has fine Hungarian dining that goes easy on the wallet. There's a small collection of assorted wine-making implements which they purport to be a wine museum, but it's interesting all the same.

Amaretto (Garay tér 6; ice cream from 60Ft) is a cake shop with the best ice cream in town.

Food supplies can be bought from a large **market** in Piac tér along Vár köz, just down the steps from Béla tér. The **ABC** shop (Flórián utca 4), north of Béla tér, is open round the clock.

Entertainment

Mihály Babits Cultural Centre (☎ 316 722; Szent István tér 10) is a modern place and has information about concerts and other cultural events taking place in the county hall courtyard, the New City Church (Újváros templom) on Pázmány tér and the House of Arts. For alternative culture, contact the **'Szexard' Polip youth office** (☎ 315 022; open 1pm-6pm Mon-Sat) in the same building, to the rear. Otherwise consult the free biweekly Szekszárdi Est magazine.

For a quiet drink, plop yourself down on the colourful stools at the **Piccolo Drink Bar** (Fürdőház utca 3) or across the road at the **Yankee Pub** (Szent László utca 5). Better yet, try the more central **Szász** (Garay tér 20), the 'Saxon' pub just a few metres west of the Romantic-style Deutsche Bühne (Német Színház; ☎ 510 257; Garay tér 4), a German theatre dating from the early 20th century and still staging performances.

Incognito (Garay tér; open 8pm-4am Thur-Sat) is the most central place for a night out clubbing.

Getting There & Away

Bus There are between nine and 14 daily departures for Budapest, Paks and Pécs, and at least six buses leave daily for Baja, Decs, Tamási, Siófok, and Mohács. From Szekszárd you can reach Harkány (via Pécs; three buses daily), Székesfehérvár (five), Kecskemét (one), Balatonfüred (two), Kaposvár (two), Szeged (two), Győr (two) and Veszprém (two). Some of these buses are boarded on Mártírok tere south of the cultural centre.

Buses bound for Keselyűs (between two and five daily) will drop you off near the Gemenc Excursion Centre in Bárányfok.

Train Only two direct trains leave Budapest's Déli station every day for Szekszárd. Otherwise, take the Pécs-bound train from Budapest's Deli, Kelenföld or Keleti stations and change at Sárbogárd. To travel east (eg, to Baja), west (to Kaposvár) or south (to Pécs), you must change trains at Bátaszék, 20km to the south. Öcsény and Decs, 4km and 8km to the south respectively, are on the train line to Bátaszék.

Getting Around

Bus No 1 goes from the stations through the centre of town to Béla tér and then on to the Upper Town as far as Remete Chapel. Local taxis can be ordered on ☎ 555 555.

AROUND SZEKSZÁRD
Gemenc Forest

The Gemenc, an 18,000-hectare flood forest of poplars, willows, oxbow lakes and dikes 12km east of Szekszárd, is part of the Danube-Drava National Park. Until engineers removed some 60 curves in the Danube in the mid-19th century, the Gemenc would flood to such a degree that the women of the Sárköz region would come to the market in Szekszárd by boat. Under the old regime, it was the favourite hunting ground of former communist leaders, who came here to shoot its famous red deer.

Today the backwaters, lakes and ponds beyond the earthen dams, which were built by wealthy landowners to protect their farms, offer sanctuary to red deer, boar, black storks, herons and woodpeckers. Hunting is restricted to certain areas, and you can visit the forest all year, but not on foot.

The main entrance is at the **Gemenc Excursion Centre** (☎ 312 552; open 10am-5pm daily) in Bárányfok, about halfway down Keselyűsi út between Szekszárd and the forest. It offers activities such as horse riding; it costs 1500Ft per person per hour, and a coach ride 700Ft. (Keselyűsi út was once the longest stretch of covered highway in the Austro-Hungarian Empire, and in the late 19th century mulberry trees were planted along it to feed the worms at the silk factory in Szekszárd.)

A **narrow-gauge train**, which once carried wood out of the Gemenc Forest, is a fun – but difficult – way to go; all in all, it's probably easier to organise a tour of the forest through Tolna Tourist in Szekszárd (see Orientation & Information earlier for that town). The train runs from Bárányfok to Pörböly (adult one way/return 500/840Ft, child 500/300Ft, two hours), some 30km to the south (see Gemenc Forest under Around Baja in the Great Plain chapter for details), once a day at 3.35pm from May to October. Two others – at 10.30am and 1.35pm (Sunday only) – go only as far as the Gemenc-Dunapart (adult/child 570/340Ft; 12km), where you need to change trains for Pörböly. The abridged trip in itself is worthwhile, weaving and looping around the Danube's remaining bends, but make sure you double-check the times with **Tourinform** (see Orientation & Information earlier) in Szekszárd or with the train station at **Pörböly** (☎ 491 483; ᴡ www .gemencrt.hu) before you set out.

Near the centre, an ornate wooden hall, built without nails for Archduke Franz Ferdinand to house his hunting trophies in the late 19th century, now houses a **Forest museum**. The hall was exhibited at the 1896 Millenary Exhibition in Budapest and is now in its fourth location – most recently reassembled from Mártírok tere in Szekszárd by Polish labourers who – this is *not* a Polish joke – used nails.

It's possible to stay at the centre in **wooden bungalows** (☎ 410 151; bungalows up to 3 persons 7500Ft), which have all the amenities of a hotel. The centre also organises boat excursions of the park; the price depends on the length of trip and the amount of people.

The **Trófea** (mains 900-1600Ft) is a *csárda* (Hungarian-style restaurant) near the entrance to the centre and opens daily till 10pm. See Getting There & Away under Szekszárd for information on transport.

Sárköz Region

The folkloric region of Sárköz, consisting of five towns southeast of Szekszárd between route No 56 and the Danube, is the centre of folk weaving in Hungary. **Öcsény** is the largest town, but for the visitor the most interesting is **Decs**, with its high-walled cottages, late Gothic Calvinist church and folk houses.

The Sárköz became a very rich area after flooding was brought under control in the mid-19th century. In a bid to protect their wealth and land, most families limited themselves to having one child and, judging from the displays at the **Regional Museum** (Tájház; Kossuth utca 34-36; adult/child 100/50Ft; open 9am-1pm Tues-Sun), in a peasant house in Decs, they spent a lot of their money on lavish interior decoration and some of the most ornate (and Balkan-looking)

Traditions Alive

The isolation of areas like the Sárköz region near Szekszárd and the Ormánság region south of Szigetvár – places 'somewhere behind the back of God', as the Hungarians call them – helped preserve folk customs and crafts not found elsewhere in Hungary.

In the Sárköz, be on the lookout for local pottery decorated with birds, the distinctive black- and-red striped woven fabric so common that it was once used as mosquito netting in this bug-infested region, and the unique *írókázás fazékok* (inscribed pots) usually made as wedding gifts.

In the Ormánság, shepherds have always been famed for the everyday items they'd carve from horn or wood, including crooks, pocket mirror frames and shaving kits. The oaken trousseau chests made to hold the distinctive Ormánság bridal brocaded skirts and 'butterfly' head-dresses, and decorated with geometrical shapes, are unique and superior to the 'tulip chests' *(tulipán láda)* found in prosperous peasant houses elsewhere in Hungary.

embroidered folk clothing in Hungary. The house was built in 1836 from earth and woven twigs, so that when the floods came only the mud had to be replaced; check out the ingenious porcelain 'stove with eyes' (concave circles) to radiate more heat.

In August mock Sárköz-style weddings are staged at the **Village House** *(Faluház; for information ☎ 495 040; Ady Endre utca)*; it also has information on the region. See Getting There & Away under Szekszárd for information on transport.

MOHÁCS

☎ 69 • postcode 7700 • pop 20,700

The defeat of the Hungarian army by the Turks here on 29 August 1526 was a watershed in the nation's history. With it came partition and foreign domination that would last almost five centuries. It is not hyperbole to say that the effects of the battle at Mohács can still be felt in Hungary today.

Mohács is a sleepy little port on the Danube that wakes up only during the annual **Busójárás festival**, which is a pre-Lent free-for-all late in February or March when devils come out to play. The town is also a convenient gateway to Croatia and the beaches of the Adriatic, with the border crossing at Udvar some 12km to the south.

Orientation & Information

The centre of Mohács lies on the west bank of the Danube; residential New Mohács (Újmohács) is on the opposite side. Szabadság utca, the main street, runs west from the river, beginning and ending with large war memorials in decay.

The bus station is on Rákóczi utca, south of leafy Deák tér. Catch trains about 1.5km north of the city centre near the Strandfürdő at the end of Bajcsy-Zsilinszky utca.

Tourinform *(☎/fax 505 504; e mohacs@tourinform.hu; open 7.30am-6pm Mon-Fri, 10am-6pm Sat & Sun mid-June–mid-Sept; 7.30am-4pm Mon-Thur, 7.30am-1pm Fri mid-Sept–mid-June)* is in the Moorish Town Hall. **Mecsek Tours** *(☎ 511 020, fax 511 023; Szent Mihály tér 6-7; open 8am-4.30pm Mon-Fri)*, in the Csele hotel, doesn't have a lot of information on the town.

You'll find an **OTP bank branch** *(Jókai Mór utca 1)* and a **K&H bank** *(Szabadság utca 23)*, at opposite ends of the main drag. The **post office** *(Széchenyi tér 2)* is in the southern wing of the Town Hall.

Mohács Historical Memorial Site

The Mohács Historical Memorial Site *(Mohácsi Történelmi Emlékhely; ☎ 382 130; adult/child 330/170Ft; open 9am-5pm Tues-Sun May-Sept; 10am-4pm Wed-Sun Apr & Oct)*, west of route No 56 at Sátorhely (literally 'encampment') about 6km southwest of Mohács, was opened in 1976 to mark the 450th anniversary of the battle. It's a fitting memorial to the dead: over 100 carved wooden markers in the shape of bows, arrows, lances and heads lean this way and that over a common grave that was only discovered in the early 1970s. Explanations of the battle are in Hungarian, but free audio tapes in English and German are available.

Dorottya Kanizsai Museum

This museum *(☎ 311 536, Városház utca 1; adult/child 150/80Ft; open 10am-5pm daily Apr-Oct; 10am-4pm Tues-Sat Nov-Mar)*, named after the heroic noblewoman from Siklós who presided over the burial of the dead after the battle at Mohács, has two branches, both open the same hours.

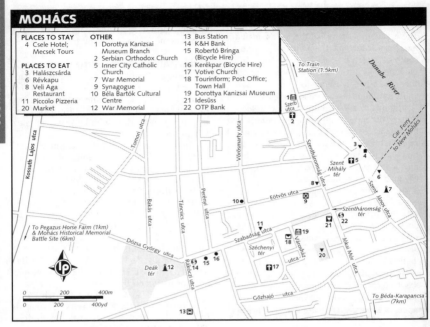

MOHÁCS

PLACES TO STAY
4 Csele Hotel;
   Mecsek Tours

PLACES TO EAT
3 Halászcsárda
6 Révkapu
8 Veli Aga
   Restaurant
11 Piccolo Pizzeria
20 Market

OTHER
1 Dorottya Kanizsai
   Museum Branch
2 Serbian Orthodox Church
5 Inner City Catholic
   Church
7 War Memorial
9 Synagogue
10 Béla Bartók Cultural
   Centre
12 War Memorial

13 Bus Station
14 K&H Bank
15 Robertó Bringa
   (Bicycle Hire)
16 Kerékpar (Bicycle Hire)
17 Votive Church
18 Tourinform; Post Office;
   Town Hall
19 Dorottya Kanizsai Museum
21 Idesüss
22 OTP Bank

The smaller branch at Szerb utca 2 (get the key at museum's other branch), next to the Serbian Orthodox church, is devoted entirely to the 1526 battle and is a well-balanced exhibit, with both the Turks and the Hungarians getting the chance to tell their side of the story. The museum's other branch, next to the town hall at Városház utca 1, has a large collection of costumes worn by the Sokác, Slovenes, Serbs, Croats, Bosnians and Swabians who repopulated this devastated area in the 17th century. The distinctive (and, to some, ugly) grey-black pottery of Mohács and the various devil's or ram's-head masks worn at the Busójárás festival are also on display.

Other Attractions

The city's other sights amount to a handful of churches and a synagogue. The Byzantine-style **Votive Church** (Fogadalmi templom; Széchenyi tér) was erected in 1926 for the 400th anniversary of the battle and looks not unlike a mosque. It has some contemporary frescoes of the event and inspired modern stained-glass windows in its large dome.

The pulpit in the baroque **Inner City Catholic Church** (1776), on Szent Mihály tér near the Csele hotel, is interesting, and from here it's a short walk north to the **Orthodox church** (Szentháromság utca 33), which was built in 1732 and until WWI served a very large local congregation of Serbs. The church's icons and ceiling frescoes date from the 18th century.

In the courtyard of the old **synagogue** (Eötvös utca 1), a large monument featuring stars of David, menorahs, tablets and inscriptions in Hungarian and Hebrew honours the Jewish victims of fascism.

Activities

The **Béda-Karapancsa**, a 10,000-hectare woodland some 7km southeast of Mohács, is where locals head to fish, hike and bike. Like the Gemenc Forest, it's part of the Danube-Drava National Park. Purchase a good map of the area, such as Béda-Karapancsai tájegység (Béda-Karapancsa Region; 600Ft), from Tourinform. **Bicycles** are available for hire from a shop called **Robertó Bringa** (Szabadság utca 21) or from **Kerékpar** (Szabadság utca 19).

You can rent horses at the **Pegazus Horse Farm** (☎ 301 244; open year-round) south of the centre at Eszéki út No 2, the road to the

Mohács battle site. If you're into **wine**, pick up a copy of the *Mohács-Bóly White Wine Route* leaflet from Tourinform, which pinpoints about a dozen villages in the area where you can sample the local drop.

Places to Stay
Accommodation options are limited to one hotel, one motel and one pension. For **private rooms** see Mecsek Tours.

Csele *(☎ 511 020, fax 511 023; Szent Mihály tér 6-7; singles 4700-7900Ft, doubles 8000-11,000Ft)* is a modern, 49-room hotel fronting the Danube. Rates vary depending on the floor; rooms on the 1st and 2nd floor have TV, minibar and balcony, and are therefore more expensive.

Places to Eat
Piccolo *(Szabadság utca 24; pizzas 500-850Ft)*, in a small courtyard, is an upbeat, friendly and popular pizzeria.

Révkapu *(☎ 322 228; Szent János utca 1; mains 700-1000Ft)*, in a motel of the same name, has a great spot right on the Danube; in fact its terrace almost juts out over the river.

Veli Aga *(☎ 311 417; Szentháromság utca 7; mains 800-1000Ft)* tries to cash in on the past – but not very successfully. It purports to serve 'real Turkish and Hungarian food' but delivers only the latter.

Halászcsárda *(☎ 322 542; Szent Mihály tér 5; mains around 1000Ft)* is the best place in town to dine. It has a beautiful terrace overlooking the Danube and a dozen different fish dishes on the menu; the only drawback is the resident band churning out tacky folk music.

The **market** is in a courtyard just west of Jókai Mór utca.

Entertainment
Béla Bartók Cultural Centre *(☎ 511 120; Vörösmarty utca 3)*, north of Széchenyi tér, has staff who can tell you what's on offer in Mohács.

Most restaurants in town have outdoor seating, which is the best place to be on a humid summer evening. A good choice is **Idesüss** *(Jókai Mór utca 2)*, a decent place for a *korsó* (pint) or two, with seating in a glassed-in pavement pavilion.

Getting There & Away
Bus services from Mohács aren't as frequent as other towns, but buses to Pécs, Bátaszék,

Baja and Budapest leave almost hourly. Other destinations include Villány, Siklós, and the spa at Harkány (three buses a day), Békéscsaba (one), Kaposvár (two), Kalocsa (one Monday to Saturday), Kecskemét via Baja (two), Szeged (seven), Szekszárd (five) and Székesfehérvár (one).

Mohács is linked by rail with Villány and Pécs (up to seven departures a day), but to get anywhere else, the bus is the best – indeed, often the only – option.

Getting Around
Buses headed for any of the following towns will let you off at the Mohács battle site: Nagynyárád, Majs, Lippó, Bezedek and Magyarbóly. A year-round car ferry (80/1000Ft per person/car) links Szent Mihály tér south of the Csele hotel with residential New Mohács – and the start of the Great Plain – across the Danube to the east. The trip takes only a few minutes. You can book the local taxi service by calling ☎ 303 303.

SIKLÓS
☎ 72 • postcode 7800 • pop 10,900
Protected from the north, east and west by the Villány Hills, Siklós, Hungary's southernmost town, has been making wine (mostly whites) since the Romans settled here at a place they called Seres. Siklós is also close to Villány (which is in competition with Szekszárd for producing Hungary's best red wines) and the spa centre at Harkány. Today the town is a favourite destination for shoppers south of the border, and you'll see almost as much Croatian in shops as you will Hungarian.

Orientation & Information
The town centre of Siklós runs from the bus station on Szent István tér along Felszabadulás utca to Kossuth tér. Siklós Castle stands watch over the town from the hill to the west. The main train station is northeast of Kossuth tér at the end of Táncsics Mihály utca. The town's other train station, Siklósi-szőlők, northwest of the centre on the road to Máriagyűd, is more convenient to the bus station.

Siklos can claim the dubious distinction of being one of the few towns in Hungary without a tourist information office; wait till you get to Harkány. At least there are banks: **OTP** at Felszabadulás 60-62 and **K&H** at No 46-48. The **post office** *(Flórián tér 1)* has pretty folkloric motifs in front.

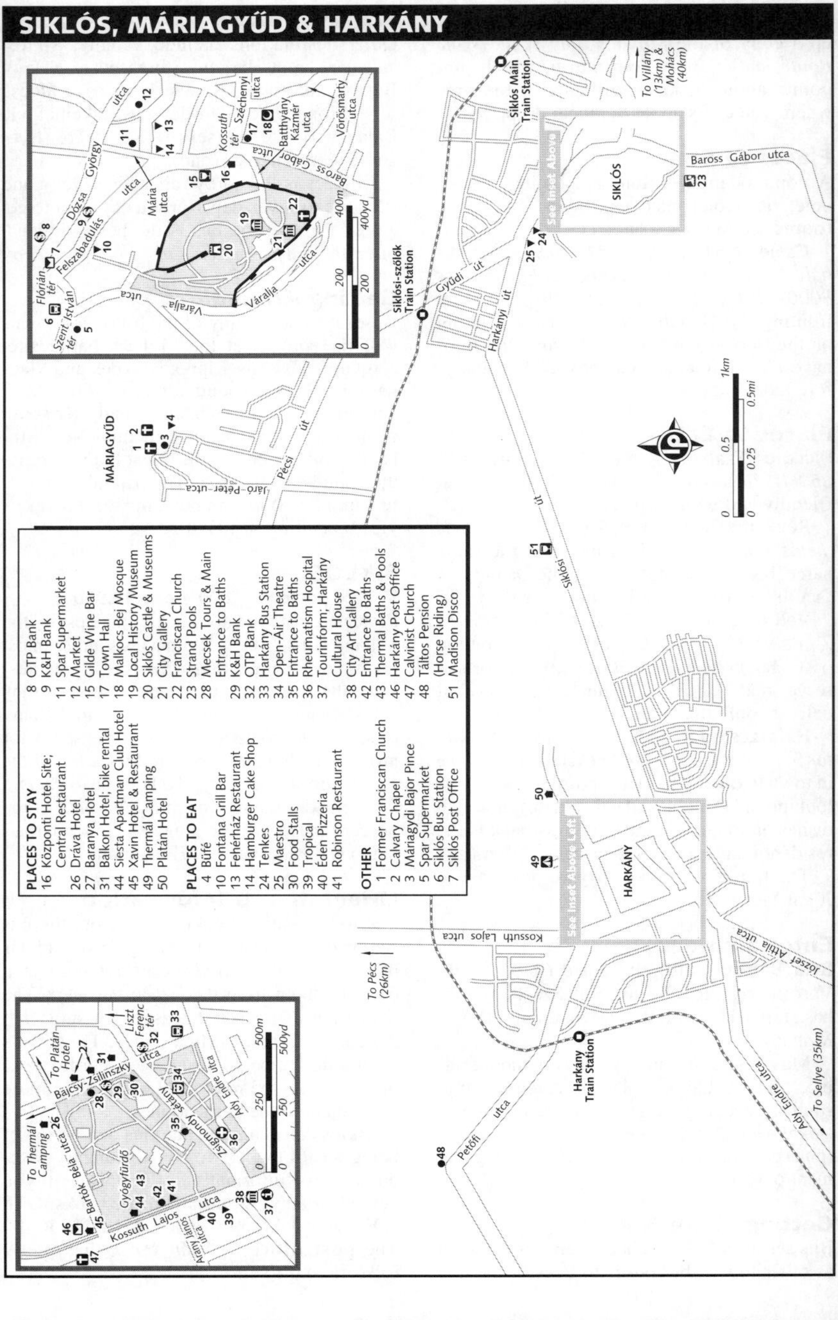
SIKLÓS, MÁRIAGYŰD & HARKÁNY
PLACES TO STAY
16 Központi Hotel Site; Central Restaurant
26 Dráva Hotel
27 Baranya Hotel
31 Balkon Hotel; bike rental
44 Siesta Apartman Club Hotel
45 Xavin Hotel & Restaurant
49 Thermál Camping
50 Platán Hotel
PLACES TO EAT
4 Büfé
10 Fontana Grill Bar
13 Fehérház Restaurant
14 Hamburger Cake Shop
24 Tenkes
25 Maestro
30 Food Stalls
39 Tropical
40 Éden Pizzeria
41 Robinson Restaurant
OTHER
1 Former Franciscan Church
2 Calvary Chapel
3 Máriagyűdi Bajor Pince
5 Spar Supermarket
6 Siklós Bus Station
7 Siklós Post Office
8 OTP Bank
9 K&H Bank
11 Spar Supermarket
12 Market
15 Gilde Wine Bar
17 Town Hall
18 Malkocs Bej Mosque
19 Local History Museum
20 Siklós Castle & Museums
21 City Gallery
22 Franciscan Church
23 Strand Pools
28 Mecsek Tours & Main Entrance to Baths
29 K&H Bank
32 OTP Bank
33 Harkány Bus Station
34 Open-Air Theatre
35 Entrance to Baths
36 Rheumatism Hospital
37 Tourinform; Harkány Cultural House
38 City Art Gallery
42 Entrance to Baths
43 Thermal Baths & Pools
46 Harkány Post Office
47 Calvinist Church
48 Táltos Pension (Horse Riding)
51 Madison Disco
MÁRIAGYŰD
SIKLÓS
HARKÁNY
Siklósi-szőlők Train Station
Siklós Main Train Station
Harkány Train Station
To Pécs (26km)
To Villány (13km) & Mohács (40km)
To Sellye (35km)
See Inset Above
See Inset Above Left

Siklós Castle

Though the original foundations of Siklós Castle (☎ 351 433; Vár körút; 450/250Ft; open 9am-4pm or 6pm Tues-Sun) date from the mid-13th century, what you see when you look up from the town is an 18th-century baroque palace girdled by 15th-century walls and bastions. The castle has changed hands many times since it was built by the Siklósi family and, until very recently, it was the longest continuously inhabited castle in the country. Its most famous occupant was the re-former Count Kázmér Batthyány (1807–54), among the first of the nobility to free his serfs. He joined the independence struggle of 1848 and was named foreign minister by Lajos Kossuth at Debrecen.

Walk to the castle either from Kossuth tér via Batthyány Kázmér utca or up Váralja from Szent István tér near the bus station. The drawbridge leads to the entrance at the **barbican**, which is topped with loopholes and a circular lookout. You can also explore the castle and enjoy some fine views of the Villány Hills from along the promenade linking the four mostly derelict towers.

The three-storey palace in the central court-yard housed a hotel and a hostel in three of its wings until 1993; the **Castle Museum** (Vár-múzeum) is in the south wing. To the right as you enter the main door is an unusual exhibit devoted to the manufacture and changing styles of gloves, fans and umbrellas since the Middle Ages, with much emphasis on the Hamerli and Hunor factories at Pécs, which produced some of Europe's finest kid gloves in the 19th century. The **cellar** contains barely recognisable stone fragments from Roman, Gothic and Renaissance times. Most of the 1st floor is now a modern art gallery, but don't miss the wonderful **Sigismund Hall** (Zsigmond-terem) with its Renaissance fire-place and star-vaulted, enclosed balcony.

To the right of the museum entrance, two doors lead to the dark and spooky **cells** – a real dungeon if ever there was one. The walls are several metres thick, and up to five grilles on the window slits discouraged would-be escapees. Woodcuts on the walls of the upper dungeon explain how various torture devices were put to use. After this, the Gothic **chapel** is a vision of heaven itself, with its brilliant arched windows behind the altar, web vaulting on the ceiling and 15th-century frescoed niches.

Other Attractions

The 15th-century Gothic **Franciscan church** on Vajda János tér is south of the castle but still within its walls. The Franciscan cloister is now the **City Gallery** (Városi Galéria; Vajda János tér 4; adult/child 150/75Ft; open 10am-4pm Tues-Sun), and at No 6 the small **Local History Museum** (Helytörténeti Mú-zeum; adult/child 150/75Ft; open 10am-4pm Tues-Sun mid-Apr–mid-Oct) contains lack-lustre exhibits on the town's history.

If you walk down Batthyány Kázmér utca past the little statue of the heroic Dorottya Kanizsai (see Mohács), you'll come to the 16th-century **Malkocs Bej Mosque** (Malkocs bej dzsámija; Vörösmarty utca 14; adult/child 150/75Ft; open 8am-5pm Tues-Sun mid-Apr–mid-Oct; 9am-5pm Sat & Sun mid-Oct–mid-Apr). Now beautifully restored, the mosque houses temporary exhibits.

The busy **market**, with everything from knock-off jeans and trainers to čevapčiči (spicy meatballs) is south of Dózsa György utca.

Places to Stay & Eat

Accommodation and eating options are slim on the ground.

With the Központi hotel on Kossuth Lajos tér *still* undergoing extensive renovations, Siklós can also boast being one of the few towns in the country with no real hotel, though you will see quite a few houses advertising **private rooms** along Harkány út northwest of the centre. Otherwise, make Siklós a side-trip from Harkány, 6km to the west, or book a private room through one of the agencies there.

Fehérház (mains around 600Ft) restaurant, near the market, is a cheap place to eat.

Fontana Grill Bar (Felszabadulás utca 45; mains from 600Ft) has plenty of 'grilled' op-tions but not much else. It does have a quiet courtyard back from busy Felszabadulás utca.

For something close to the bus and train stations, try **Tenkes** (Felszabadulás utca 65/a; mains 850-1500Ft), a pleasant restaurant that specialises in fish, or the nearby **Maestro** (Felszabadulás utca 69; pizzas & pasta from 400Ft) is more basic, and deals mainly with pizza and pasta.

Centrál (☎ 352 513; Kossuth tér 5; mains 800-1500Ft), in the Központi hotel, is a large eatery with simple Hungarian fare.

Hamburger (Felszabadulás utca 22) cake shop serves delicious sweet things, despite its savoury name.

Entertainment

You should really save the wine tasting for Villány and the cellars at Villánykövesd, but if you want to sample a glass here, try the little **borozó** (wine bar) in the castle courtyard or the divey **Gilde** *(Felszabadulás utca 7; open 5pm-midnight)* near Kossuth tér.

Madison *(open 9pm-4am Fri & Sat)*, halfway between Siklós and Harkány, about 3km west of Siklós, is a more popular disco.

Getting There & Away

Generally you won't wait more than 30 minutes for buses to Pécs or Harkány; hourly buses leave for Máriagyűd and Villány. For Mohács, count on between five and 10 buses a day. Other destinations include Budapest and Székesfehérvár (one bus each daily), Szigetvár (one to three), Szekszárd (two) and Sellye (up to four).

Trains link Siklós with Villány (change here for Mohács or Pécs), Máriagyűd, Harkány, Sellye and Barcs. But trains are infrequent, and only two of them run the full line daily.

AROUND SIKLÓS
Máriagyűd
☎ 72 • postcode 7818

The erstwhile **Franciscan church** *(admission free)* in this village at the foot of 408m-high Mt Tenkes, northwest of Siklós, has been a place of pilgrimage for 800 years, and you can make your own by walking (or hopping on a Máriagyűd or Harkány-bound bus) for about 3km along Gyűdi út and Pécs út and turning north on Járó Péter utca when the church's two towers come into view.

Máriagyűd was on the old trade route between Pécs and Eszék (now Osijek in Croatia), and a church has stood here since the mid-12th century. Today's church is a large 18th-century affair with modern frescoes on the ceiling, baroque painted altars, some beautifully carved pews and the main object of devotion: Mary and the Christ Child in gold and silver over the main altar. The most interesting time to visit is on Sunday or on a *búcsú* (a patron's festival – the Virgin Mary has lots of them) when merchants set up their stalls beside the church (see the boxed text 'Farewell to All That' later in this chapter). Mass is conducted in Hungarian at the Calvary Chapel, but at the outdoor altar on the hill above it, just as many people attend German-language services, often with accompanying oompah band music.

Máriagyűdi Bajor Pince *(☎ 351 143; Tenkes utca 14)*, in an old cellar in the square just below the church, is a good place to sample some of Siklós' white wines. For a quick snack, head to the nearby **büfé**. From here, you can start a 6km hike up and around Mt Tenkes.

HARKÁNY
☎ 72 • postcode 7815 • pop 3500

It's a wonder that no statue stands in honour of János Pogány in this spa town 6km west of Siklós and 26km south of Pécs. He was the poor peasant from Máriagyűd who cured himself of swollen joints early in the 19th century by soaking in a hot spring he had discovered here. The Batthyány family recognised the potential almost immediately, erecting bathing huts in 1824 near the 62°C spring, which has the richest sulphuric content in Hungary.

Of course, all that means crowds (well over 100,000 Hungarian, German, Croatian and Yugoslavian visitors in the high season), *lángos* (deep-fried dough with toppings) and gyro stalls in spades and an occasionally strong whiff of rotten eggs. But you might like it. People come to Harkány to socialise, and the town is on the western edge of the Villány-Siklós region, so there is plenty of wine about.

Orientation

Harkány is essentially the Gyógyfürdő, a 12-hectare green square filled with pools, fountains and walkways, and bordered by hotels and holiday homes of every description. The four streets defining the thermal complex are Bartók Béla utca to the north, Ady Endre to the south, Bajcsy-Zsilinszky utca (with most of the hotels) to the east, and Kossuth Lajos utca, with several restaurants, to the west. The bus station is on Bajcsy-Zsilinszky utca at the southeast corner of the park. The train station is to the northwest on Petőfi utca, which branches off from Kossuth Lajos utca.

Information

Tourinform *(☎ 479 624, fax 479 989; e harkany@tourinform.hu; Kossuth Lajos utca 2/a; open 9am-6pm Mon-Fri, 10am-6pm Sat & Sun mid-June–mid-Sept; 9am-4pm Mon-Fri mid-Sept–mid-June)* has an office at the Harkány Cultural House. The small **City Art Gallery** is next door. **Mecsek Tours** *(☎ 480 332, fax 479 045; Bajcsy-Zsilinszky utca 2; open 9am-4pm or 5pm Mon-Fri, 9am-noon Sat summer; 9am-4pm Mon-Fri rest of the* *year)* is at the main entrance to the baths, north of the bus station.

K&H bank has a *bureau de change* at the main entrance to the spa; there's an **OTP bank branch** on Bajcsy-Zsilinszky utca, just north of the bus station, and a **post office** *(Kossuth Lajos utca 57)* at the northwest corner of Gyógyfürdő. The town's website is at w www.harkany.hu.

Thermal Spa
The main entrance to the **thermal baths** *(gyógyfürdő;* ☎ 480 251; adult/child €5.80/3.30; open 9am-11pm daily mid-June–Aug; 9am-5pm or 6pm daily Sept–mid-June) and **outside pools** (adult/child €2.30/1.70; open 9am-11pm daily mid-June–Aug; 9am-5pm Mon-Thur, 9am-10pm Fri-Sun Sept-Dec; 7pm-11pm Fri-Sun Dec–mid-June), which are meant to cure just about everything, is on Bajcsy-Zsilinszky utca. Services range from drinking cures and mud massage to the enticing 'wine foam bath', but it's a treat just to swim in the 38°C outdoor pool, especially in cool weather.

Activities
You can ride **horses** or hire a coach at the **Táltos pension** (☎ 479 067; Széchenyi tér 30d) northwest of the centre, off Petőfi utca. **Bike rental** is available for 300/1200Ft per hour/day in the garden of the Balkon hotel during summer.

Places to Stay
Camping Along with tent sites, **Thermál Camping** (☎ 480 117; Bajcsy-Zsilinszky utca 6; camping per tent/person 700/700Ft, bungalows for up to 4 persons 8000Ft; open mid-Mar–mid-Oct) has a 20-room motel (rooms 3500Ft), a hotel (rooms 5000Ft) with 26 rooms and two dozen bungalows with two double rooms and kitchen.

Private Rooms Tourinform has a comprehensive list of **private rooms** and **apartments** from 3000Ft, but it doesn't make bookings. Try your luck with Mecsek Tours. For a one-night stay you may be better off going to a hotel or investigating the possibilities yourself by strolling east on Bartók Béla utca, where *Zimmer frei* (room for rent) signs proliferate.

Hotels Harkány has an incredible array of hotels and pensions to suit all budgets.

Baranya (☎/fax 480 160; Bajcsy-Zsilinszky utca 5; singles/doubles €18/36) hotel occupies three buildings with a total of 150 rooms opposite the baths' entrance.

Dráva (☎ 580 810, fax 580 813; Bartók Béla utca 1; non-renovated singles/doubles €18-21/26-30, renovated singles/doubles €22-29/31-40), with 68 rooms (23 not yet renovated) in two buildings, is in a pretty park just short of the camp site. Rates for rooms vary depending on the month.

Platán (☎ 480 507, fax 480 411; e palzol@axelero.hu; Bartók Béla utca 15; singles 4000-6000Ft, doubles 6200-9300Ft) is a quiet, 60-room hotel in two former trade union holiday houses to the east, with rates that depend on the season, the building and whether the room has a balcony.

The 49 room **Balkon** (☎ 580 830, fax 580 833; Bajcsy-Zsilinszky utca 3; singles/doubles 6800/9300Ft, 2-person room with balcony 10,400Ft) is housed in an Art Deco sanatorium once used by Communist Party honchos. It has a certain charm and lovely grounds, but the clientele is composed almost entirely of pensioners on health cures.

The fanciest places to stay are on the west side of the spa park and include the following two places.

Siesta Apartman Club (☎ 480 611, fax 480 302; Kossuth Lajos utca 17; singles €23.50-31.30, doubles €28-38.30) has 83 spotless rooms, but the staff can sometimes be a little snooty. Rates vary depending on the season.

Xavin (☎/fax 479 399; e xavin@freemail .hu; Kossuth Lajos utca 43; singles/doubles 5600/8900Ft) is a pension-like hotel.

Places to Eat
You won't starve or die of thirst in this town of sausage stands and wine kiosks, but if you want to sit down while eating, try the island-themed **Robinson** (Kossuth Lajos utca 7; mains 1000-1500Ft), with pizza and other dishes.

Éden (Kossuth Lajos utca 14; pizzas 750-1000Ft; open 11am-11pm Tues-Sun), in a beautiful pink Eclectic building across the street, serves pizza.

Xavin (☎/fax 479 399; e xavin@freemail .hu; Kossuth Lajos utca 43; mains 1200-2000Ft) is on the expensive side, but it has a lovely silver-service restaurant and an extensive wine list.

Tropical (Kossuth Lajos utca 12; ice cream from 60Ft) is popular for ice cream and cake.

Entertainment

You can find out what's on at the **Harkány Cultural House** (*Harkányi Művelődési Ház;* ☎ 480 459, *Kossuth Lajos utca 2a*) but you shouldn't expect too much in the way of high-brow entertainment here.

Getting There & Around

For a local taxi ring ☎ 480 123.

Bus While buses depart once or twice an hour for Siklós and Pécs, other destinations are not so well served, with only one bus a day to Baja (June to September only), Kecskemét, Kalocsa (on weekends), Sellye (weekdays), Veszprém, Szeged (June to August) and Székesfehérvár. Other destinations include Budapest (two buses a day), Szekszárd (one), Szigetvár and Máriagyűd (one or two each) and Mohács (up to three).

In summer, buses to Stuttgart via Munich leave Harkány on Thursday at 1.30pm and Sunday at 2.30pm, and arrive in the German city at 6.30am on Friday and 7.30am on Monday respectively. Buses also go to Frankfurt via Pécs and Nuremberg at 1.30pm on Sunday, arriving there at 8am on Monday. Three buses a day link Harkány to Croatia: two go to Osijek (at 12.30pm and 5.30pm) and one goes to Našice (10am weekdays).

Train By rail from Harkány, you can reach Sellye (up to five times daily) and Barcs (up to three) to the west, and Siklós and Villány to the east (up to seven). Change at Villány for Mohács or Pécs.

VILLÁNY

☎ 72 • postcode 7773 • pop 3550

Some 13km northeast of Siklós and dominated by cone-shaped Mt Szársomlyó (422m) to the west, Villány is a village of vineyards, vines and grapes. In 1687 it was the site of what is known as the 'second battle of Mohács', a ferocious confrontation in which the Turks got their comeuppance and were driven southward by the Hungarians and slaughtered in the Dráva marshes. Serbs and Swabians moved in after the Turkish occupation and viticulture resumed. Today, Villány is one of Hungary's principal producers of wine. For more details see the 'Wines of Hungary' special section.

You might consider visiting Villány (German: *Wieland*) during the September harvest,

when the town is a beehive of activity: human chains pass buckets of almost black grapes from trucks to big machines that chew off the vines, reduce the fruit to a soggy mass and pump the must – the unfermented grape juice – into enormous casks.

Orientation & Information

Villány is essentially just one main street, Baross Gábor utca, and the bus stops in the centre of the village near the ABC supermarket and the town hall. The train station is about 1200m to the north on Ady Endre fasor, en route to Villánykövesd.

The **Villány-Siklós Wine Route Association** (☎/fax 492 242; W *www.borut.hu; Deák Ferenc utca 22*), just north of the bus station, produces a handy information booklet (250Ft) covering places to buy and sample local wines in the region. It also organises wine tours.

There's an **OTP bank** (*Baross Gábor utca 27*) and a **post office** (*Vörösmarty utca 2*) opposite the Oportó restaurant.

Wine Museum & Wine Tasting

The Wine Museum (*Bormúzeum;* ☎ 492 130; *Bem József utca 8; admission free, wine tastings for groups only; open 9am-5pm Tues-Sun*), housed in a 200-year-old tithe cellar, has a collection of 19th-century wine-producing equipment, such as barrels, presses and hand corkers. Downstairs in the sand-covered cellars, Villány's celebrated wines age in enormous casks, and vintage bottles dating from 1895 to 1971 are kept in safes. There's a small shop at the entrance selling Villány and Siklós wines, some of them vintage and among the best labels available in Hungary.

You can sample wines in many of the family **cellars** that line Baross Gábor utca, including Pólya at No 58, Költő at No 71, Szende at No 87 and Fritsch at No 97. They're normally open 9am to 6pm daily; expect to pay around 1100/2200Ft to sample four/eight wines.

The best place for tasting is in the cellars cut into the loess soil at **Villánykövesd** (German: *Growisch*), about 3.5km northwest of town along the road to Pécs. Cellars line the main street (Petőfi út) and the narrow lane (Pincesor) above it. Along the former, try the deep Polgár cellar at No 51 or Baschta at No 63. On Pincesor, No 14-15 is the cellar of master vintner Imre Tiffán, while Schwarzwalter is at No 20-21 and Blum at No 24. The cellars keep difficult hours, so it's a hit-or-miss proposition. For advice on what to try, see the 'Wines of Hungary' special section.

Places to Stay & Eat

There are plenty of signs advertising **private rooms** in Villány.

Gere (☎/fax 492 195; Diófás tér 4; rooms 8000Ft) is an eight-room pension and you shouldn't miss the chance to stay here. They have more rooms in another location some 300m south at Fáy András utca 17, plus wine tastings in their cellar.

Júlia (☎ 492 710; Baross Gábor utca 41; rooms 8500Ft), a pension with six rooms, is just down the road from Gere and a good option should Gere be full. It has an intimate little restaurant (mains 1000-2000Ft) that serves some of the best veal pörkölt (stew) in Hungary. It also does wine tastings.

Cabernet (☎ 493 200, fax 493 222; ⓦ www .hotelcabernet.hu; Petőfi utca 29; singles/ doubles €35-38/43-47) in Villánykövesd, is worth considering if you really want to stay in the centre of the wine area. It has 25 rooms, a restaurant, and once again, does wine tastings.

Oportó (Baross Gábor utca 33; mains around 1000Ft) is a large, pleasant restaurant with a terrace near the town centre and close to where the bus lets you off.

Villány also has a simple **pizzeria** (Baross Gábor utca 71a; mains & pizzas from 600Ft) that includes Hungarian dishes on its menu.

Fülemüle Csárda (Nightingale Inn; Ady Endre fasor; mains 900-1800Ft), a lovely old farm house a couple of hundred metres past the train station, is a good place to stop for a bite on your way to/from Villánykövesd.

Getting There & Away

There are infrequent buses to Pécs, Siklós, Harkány, Budapest, Mohács and Villány-kövesd (five on weekdays, two on Saturday), but for most destinations, you must go to Siklós first. Trains run east to Mohács, west to Siklós and Harkány, north to Pécs and south to Sarajevo.

ORMÁNSÁG REGION

About 30km west of Harkány, this plain was prone to flooding by the Dráva River for centuries. That and the area's isolation is reflected in its unusual architecture, folk ways and distinct dialect. Couples usually limited themselves to having just one child since, under the land-tenure system here, peasants were not allowed to enlarge their holdings. That's not the only reason why the area's 'footed' talpás házak are so small: these 'soled' houses were built on rollers so that they could be dragged to dry land in the event of flooding.

Sellye

☎ 73 • postcode 7960 • pop 3200

In Sellye, the 'capital' of the Ormánság region, a representative footed house of mortar, lime and a wooden frame sits behind the **Géza Kiss Ormánság Museum** (☎ 480 201; Köztársaság tér 6; adult/child 100/70Ft; open 10am-4pm Tues-Sun Apr-Oct; 10am-2pm Nov-Mar). The house has the typical three rooms and some big differences: the parlour was actually lived in; the front room was a 'smoke kitchen' without a chimney; and, to keep mosquitoes at bay, what few windows the house had were kept very small. The museum's rich collection contains Ormánság costumes and artefacts.

There's an **arboretum** with rare trees and plants surrounding the Draskovich family mansion (now a school) behind the museum.

Mátyás király utca, the main drag, is southwest of the bus station, and the train station is to the southeast on Vasút utca.

Other Ormánság Villages

The Calvinist church at **Drávaiványi** (Dózsa utca 1/b; admission free), with a colourful panelled ceiling and choir loft dating from the late 18th century, is 5km southwest of Sellye and can be reached by bus. **Vajszló**, an Ormánság village 11km southeast of Sellye with several footed houses, is on the same train line as Sellye. Buses travel eastward from Vajszló to **Kórós** (Kossuth Lajos utca 40; admission free), whose folk-decorated Calvinist church (1795) is among the most beautiful in the region.

Getting There & Away

Harkány is the easiest starting point for any excursion into the Ormánság, but the area is also accessible by public transport from Szigetvár – in fact, it is closer to that city. However, the infrequent milk-run buses from Szigetvár take almost two hours to cover 25km (admittedly passing through some very attractive little villages), and if you catch the train, you must change at Szentlőrinc. The train from Harkány to Vajszló and Sellye (up to five a day) involves no change and takes only an hour and 20 minutes. See Getting There & Away under Harkány, earlier, for more information.

PÉCS
☎ 72 • postcode 7600 • pop 166,500

Blessed with a mild climate, an illustrious past and a number of fine museums and monuments, Pécs is one of the most pleasant cities to visit in Hungary. For those reasons and more, many travellers put it second to Budapest on their 'must-see' list.

Lying equidistant from the Danube River to the east and the Dráva River to the south on a plain sheltered from northern winds by the Mecsek Hills, Pécs enjoys an extended summer and is an ideal place for viticulture, fruit and nut growing, especially almonds. But for the visitor, the capital of Baranya County, Pécs, is more than anything else a 'town of art', beating Szentendre on the Danube Bend hands down.

History

The Romans may have settled in Pécs for the region's weather, fertile soil and abundant water, but more likely they were sold by the protection offered by the Mecsek Hills. Calling their settlement Sophianae, it quickly grew into the commercial and administrative centre of Lower Pannonia. The Romans brought Christianity with them, and reminders of it can be seen in the early clover-shaped chapels unearthed at several locations here.

Pécs' importance grew in the Middle Ages, when it was known as Quinque Ecclesiae after its five churches (it is still called Fünfkirchen in German). King Stephen founded a bishopric here in 1009, and the town was a major stop along the trade route to Byzantium. Pécs developed as an intellectual and

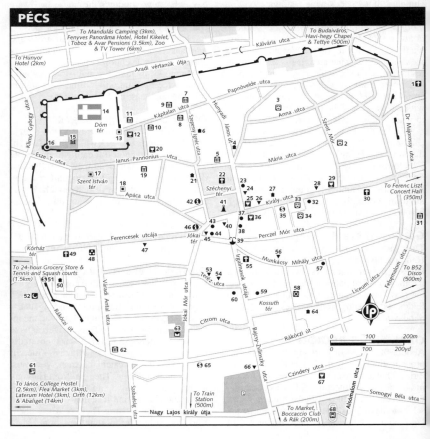

PÉCS

humanist centre with the founding of a university – Hungary's first – in 1367. The 15th-century bishop Janus Pannonius, who wrote some of Europe's most celebrated Renaissance poetry in Latin, was based in Pécs.

The city was fortified with walls after the Mongol invasion of the early 13th century, but they were in such poor condition three centuries later that the Turks took the city with virtually no resistance in 1543. The Turks moved the local populace outside the walls and turned Pécs into their own administrative and cultural centre. When they were expelled almost 150 years later, Pécs was virtually abandoned, but still standing were monumental souvenirs that now count as the most important Turkish structures in the nation. The resumption of wine production by German and Bohemian immigrants and the discovery of coal in the 18th century spurred Pécs' development. The manufacture of luxury goods (gloves, Zsolnay porcelain, Pannonvin sparkling wine, Angster organs), and the exploitation of nearby uranium mines, came later.

Orientation

The oval-shaped inner town, virtually all of it now pedestrian-only, has as its heart Széchenyi

tér, where a dozen streets converge. One of these is Király utca, a promenade of restored shops, pubs and restaurants to the east. To the northwest lies Pécs' other important square, Dóm tér. Here you'll find the cathedral, several early Christian chapels and Káptalan utca, the 'street of museums'. Pécs' train station is in Indóház tér – follow Jókai Mór utca north to reach the inner town. The bus station is close to the big market on Zólyom utca. Walk north along Bajcsy-Zsilinszky utca and Irgalmasok utcája to the centre.

Information

The knowledgable staff at **Tourinform** (☎ 213 315, fax 212 632; e baranya-m@tourinform.hu; Széchenyi tér 9; open 9am-7pm Mon-Fri, 9am-6pm Sat & Sun mid-June–mid-Sept; 8am-4pm Mon-Fri, 9am-2pm Sat mid-Sept–mid-June) has copious amounts of information on Pécs and for the Baranya County. Also, two helpful travel agencies for information in town are **Mecsek Tours** (☎ 513 376; Széchenyi tér 1; open 9am-5pm Mon-Fri, 9am-1pm Sat year-round) and **Ibusz** (☎ 212 157, fax 211 011; Apáca utca 1; open 8.30am-5.30pm Mon-Thur, 8.30am-4pm Fri).

PÉCS

PLACES TO STAY
4 Főnix Hotel; Cellárium Restaurant
6 Centrum Motel
21 Mátyás College
27 Palatinus
50 Pátria
64 Diana

PLACES TO EAT
24 Mecsek Cake Shop
26 Dóm
28 Oázis
40 Virág Cake Shop
45 Az Elefánthoz & Morik Caffé
47 Hellas Taverna
53 Tex-Mex Café
54 Aranykacsa
56 Vörös Sárkány
66 Spar supermarket

OTHER
1 St Augustine Church
2 Bóbita Puppet Theatre
3 Croatian Theatre
5 Janus Pannonius Archaeology Museum

7 Zsolnay Porcelain Museum; Mecsek Mine Museum
8 Vasarely Museum
9 Modern Hungarian Art Gallery
10 Endre Nemes Museum; Utca Exhibit
11 Ferenc Martyn Museum
12 Kioszk Café
13 Jug Mausoleum
14 Basilica of St Peter
15 Bishop's Palace
16 Barbican
17 Tomb Chapel
18 Roman Tomb Site
19 Csontváry Museum; Dante Cafe; Mac Café
20 Kaptalani
22 Mosque Church
23 Former Nádor Hotel
25 Royal Café
29 Arizona Ranch Pub
30 Church of St Stephen
31 City History Museum
32 Theatre Ticket Office
33 Pécs National Theatre
34 Chamber Theatre
35 M&M Exchange

36 The Murphy's Pub
37 Pécs Cultural Centre; ATM
38 Mecsek Tours
39 Zsolnay Fountain
41 Trinity Column
42 Tourinform
43 House of Artists; Corvina Art Bookshop
44 Zsolnay Porcelain Outlet
46 Ibusz
48 Pasha Memi Baths (Ruins)
49 Franciscan Church
51 OTP Bank
52 Pasha Hassan Jakovali Mosque
55 Church of the Good Samaritan
57 Lenau House
58 Synagogue
59 Town Hall
60 Blazek Leather Shop
61 Hullám pools
62 Ethnography Museum
63 Main Post Office
65 OTP Bank
67 Soul 6
68 Bus Station

The **main OTP bank** on Rákóczi út has a currency exchange machine. It also has an **ATM** (Széchenyi tér 1) at the Pécs Cultural Centre. **M&M Exchange** (Király utca 16; open 8.30am-5pm Mon-Fri, 8.30am-1pm) offers a decent rate.

The **main post office** (Jókai Mór utca 10) is in a beautiful Art Nouveau building dating from 1904 (note the angels in relief writing, mailing and delivering the post). The **Corvina Art Bookshop** (Széchenyi tér 7-8) in the Artists House (Művészetek Háza) has an excellent selection of English-language books.

Mac Café (☎ 210 661; Janus Pannonius utca 11), inside Dante Café (see Entertainment), charges 500Ft for Internet connection.

Most of Pécs' museums and other sites are open 10am to 6pm Tuesday to Saturday and to 4pm Sunday from April to October and till 4pm the rest of the year; they cost 200Ft to 450Ft per adult and 100Ft to 200Ft per child. Opening times and admission are listed here only when they differ from these.

For more information try Pécs' website at ⓦ www.pecs.hu.

Széchenyi tér

This lovely square of mostly baroque buildings backed by the Mecsek Hills is where you should start a walking tour of Pécs. Dominating the square – indeed, the very symbol of the city – is the former Pasha Gazi Kassim Mosque. Today it's the Inner Town Parish Church (Belvárosi plébánia templom) but more commonly known as the **Mosque Church** (☎ 321 976; admission free; open 10am-4pm Mon-Sat, 11.30am-4pm Sun mid-Apr–mid-Oct; 10am-noon Mon-Sat, 11.30am-2pm Sun mid-Oct–mid-Apr). It is the largest building still standing in Hungary from the time of the Turkish occupation.

The square mosque with a green copper dome was built with the stones of the ruined medieval church of St Bertalan in the mid-16th century; after the expulsion of the Turks, the Catholic Church repossessed it. The northern semicircular part was added in the 20th century. The Islamic elements on the south side are easy to spot: windows with distinctive Turkish ogee arches; the prayer niche (*mihrab*) carved into the interior southeast wall; faded verses from the Koran to the southwest; lovely geometric frescoes on the corners. The mosque's minaret was pulled down in 1753 and replaced with a tower.

The **Janus Pannonius Archaeology Museum** (Janus Pannonius Régészeti Múzeum; ☎ 312 719; Széchenyi tér 12; adult/child 200/100Ft; open 10am-4pm Tues-Sun Apr-Oct; 10am-2pm Tues-Sun Nov-Mar), behind the Mosque Church in the 17th-century home of a janissary commander, traces the history of Baranya County up to the time of Árpád and contains many examples of Roman stonework from Pannonia, a model of St Bertalan's Church and medieval porcelain.

The **Trinity Column** in the lower part of Széchenyi tér is the third one to grace the spot and dates from 1908. The **porcelain Zsolnay Fountain** with a lustrous glaze, to the southeast in front of the rather gloomy **Church of the Good Samaritan**, was donated to the city by the Zsolnay factory in 1892.

Kossuth tér

This square southeast of Széchenyi tér has two important buildings: the Eclectic **town hall** (1891) to the north and the restored **synagogue** (☎ 315 881; Kossuth tér; 150/50Ft; open 9am-5pm Sun-Thur, 9am-5pm Fri May-Oct) to the east. The synagogue was built in the Romantic style in 1869. Fact sheets in a dozen languages are available. Shortly after the fascist Hungarian government established a ghetto in Pécs in May 1944, most of the city's 3000 Jews were deported to the Nazi death camps.

Around Dóm tér

The foundations of the four-towered **Basilica of St Peter** (☎ 513 030; Dóm tér; adult/child 1000/500Ft; open 9am-5pm Mon-Fri, 9am-2pm Sat, 1pm-5pm Sun Apr-Oct; 10am-4pm Mon-Sat, 1pm-4pm Sun Nov-Mar) – or simply the cathedral (székesegyház) – date back to the 11th century and the side chapels are from the 1300s. But most of what you see today of the neo-Romanesque structure is the result of renovations carried out in 1881.

The entry fee to the basilica includes entry to the Jug Mausoleum, the early Christian tomb chapel and the Roman tomb site. Guided tours in are conducted in Hungarian and German and cost 2000Ft.

The basilica is very ornate inside; the elevated central altar is a reproduction of a medieval one. The most interesting parts of the basilica are the four chapels under the towers and the crypt, the oldest part of the structure. The **Chapel of Mary** on the northwest side and the **Chapel of the Sacred Heart** to the northeast contain works by the 19th-century painters Bertalan Székely and Károly Lotz. The **Mór Chapel** to the southeast has more works by Székely as well as magnificent pews. The **Corpus Christi Chapel** on the southwest side (enter from the outside) boasts a 16th-century red marble tabernacle, one of the finest examples of Renaissance stonework in the country.

The **Bishop's Palace** (Püspöki palota; 1770), to the southwest is not generally open to the public, but have a look at the curious **statue of Franz Liszt** (Imre Varga; 1983), peering over from a balcony. On the southern side of the baroque Ecclesiastical Archives (Egyházi levéltár) is the entrance to the **Jug Mausoleum** (Korsós sírkamra; closed Nov-Mar), a 4th-century Roman tomb whose name comes from a painting of a large drinking vessel with vines found here. The **early Christian tomb chapel** (Ókeresztény sírkápolna; ☎ 312 719; adult/child 500/250Ft), across Janus Pannonius utca in Szent István tér, dates from about 350 AD and has frescoes of Adam and Eve, and Daniel in the lion's den. The admission fee to the chapel includes entry to Roman tomb site. There's another, later **Roman tomb site** containing 110 graves a little farther south at Apáca utca 8. The three tombs gained the status of a World Heritage Site in 2000.

The **Csontváry Museum** (☎ 310 544; Janus Pannonius utca 11) exhibits the major works of Tivadar Kosztka Csontváry (1853–1919), a unique symbolist painter whose tragic life is sometimes compared with that of Vincent van Gogh, who was born in the same year. Many of Csontváry's oversized canvases are masterpieces, especially *Storm on the Great Hortobágy* (1903), *Solitary Cedar* (1907) and *Baalbeck*, an artistic search for a larger identity through religious and historical themes.

To the west and north of Dóm tér is a long stretch of the **old city wall** that enclosed an area far too large to defend properly. The circular **barbican** (Esze Tomás utca 2), the only stone bastion to survive in Pécs, dates from the late 15th century and was restored in the 1970s.

Káptalan utca

Káptalan utca, running east from Dóm tér to Hunyadi János út, contains a plethora of museums, all of them in listed buildings.

The **Ferenc Martyn Museum** (☎ 324 822; Káptalan utca 6; adult/child 350/100Ft; open 10am-2pm Tues-Sun Apr-Oct) displays works by the Pécs-born painter and sculptor (1899–1986) and sponsors special exhibits of local interest. The entry fee to the museum includes entry to the Endre Nemes exhibition and Schaár's Utca (☎ 310 172; open 10am-2pm Tues-Sun Apr-Oct) is devoted to paintings by the surrealist **Endre Nemes** (1908–85) and the sculptures of **Amerigo Tot** (1909–84). In a separate pavilion behind it is Erzsébet Schaár's *Utca* (Street), a complete artistic environment in which the sculptor set her whole life in stone. The **Modern Hungarian Art Gallery** (Modern Magyar Képtár; ☎ 324 822; Káptalan utca 4) is the best place for an overview of art in Hungary from between 1850 till today. For work up to 1950 pay special attention to the works of Simon Hollósy, József Rippl-Rónai and Ödön Márffy. For more abstract and constructionist art, watch out for the names András Mengyár, Tamás Hencze, Béla Uitz and Gábor Dienes. The **Péter Székely Gallery** behind the museum has large stone and wood sculptures.

The two most interesting museums are at the eastern end of the street: the **Vasarely Museum** (☎ 324 822) at No 3 and the **Zsolnay Porcelain Museum** (☎ 324 822) at No 2. Victor Vasarely was the father of Op Art and, although some of the works on exhibit by him and his disciples are dated, most are evocative, very tactile and just plain fun.

The Zsolnay porcelain factory was established in Pécs in 1853 and was at the forefront of art and design in Europe for more than half a century. Many of its majolica tiles were used to decorate buildings throughout the country and contributed to establishing a new pan-Hungarian style of architecture. Zsolnay's darkest period came when the postwar communist government turned it into a plant for making ceramic electrical insulators. It's producing art again (in very limited quantities), but contemporary Zsolnay can't hold a candle to the chinoiserie pieces from the late 19th century and the later Art Nouveau and Art Deco designs done in the lustrous eosin glaze. The museum, housed in a residence dating from the Middle Ages, was the home of the Zsolnay family and contains many of their furnishings and personal effects.

The 400m cellar labyrinth of the Vasarely Museum hosts the **Mecsek Mine Museum**, which consists of mineral stones and mining traditions from Southern Transdanubia.

Other Attractions

Southwest of the inner town and opposite the Pátria hotel is the **Pasha Hassan Jakovali Mosque** *(Jakováli Hasszán Pasa dzsámija;* ☎ *313 853; Rákóczi út 2; adult/child 140/ 80Ft; open 10am-1pm & 2pm-6pm Thur-Tues Apr-Sept)*, wedged between a trade school and a hospital. The 16th-century mosque – complete with minaret – is the most intact of any Turkish structure in Hungary and contains a small museum of Ottoman *objets d'art*. The **Ethnography Museum** *(Néprajzi Múzeum;* ☎ *315 629; Rákóczi út 15)* to the southeast, examines ethnic Hungarian, German and South Slav folk art in the region.

One of Pécs' most enjoyable pedestrian streets, Ferencesek utcája (lots of funky clothes and jewellery shops, restaurants and cafés) runs east from Rákóczi út to Széchenyi tér, and then Király utca also becomes pedestrian. You'll pass the ruins of the 16th-century **Pasha Memi Baths** *(Ferencesek utcája 35)*, three beautiful old churches and, on Király utca, the neo-rococo **Pécs National Theatre**. Just beyond the **Church of St Stephen** *(Király utca 44a)*, built in 1741, turn south (right), where you'll find the excellent **City History Museum** *(Várostörténeti Múzeum;* ☎ *310 165; Felsőmalom utca 9; open 10am-4pm Tues-Sat)*.

The suburb of Budaiváros to the northeast of the town centre is where most Hungarians settled after the Turks banned them from living within the city walls. The centre of this community was the **All Saints' Church** *(*☎ *324 937; Tettye utca 14; admission free)*. Originally built in the 12th century and reconstructed in Gothic style 200 years later, it was the only Christian church allowed in Pécs during the occupation and was shared by three sects – who fought bitterly for every square centimetre. Apparently it was the Muslim Turks who had to keep the peace among the Christians.

To the northeast up on a hill is **Havi-hegy Chapel** *(*☎ *314 715; Havihegyi utca 7; admission free)*, built in 1691 by the faithful after the town was spared the plague. The church is an important city landmark and offers wonderful views of the inner town and the narrow streets and old houses of the Tettye Valley.

You can get a taste of the Mecsek Hills by walking northeast from the centre of Pécs to Tettye and the **Garden of Ruins** (Romkert), what's left of a bishop's summer residence built early in the 16th century and later used by Turkish dervishes as a monastery. To the northwest, up Fenyves sor and past the **zoo** *(állatkert;* ☎ *312 788; adult/student/child 360/330/280Ft; open 9am-5pm daily Apr-Oct)*, a winding road leads to **Misina Peak** (535m) and a **TV tower** *(*☎ *336 900; adult/ student/child 280/240/180Ft; open 9am-9pm Sun-Thur, 9am-11pm Fri & Sat June-Aug; 9am-7pm rest of year)*, an impressive 194m structure with a viewing platform and café-bar. But these are just the foothills; from here, trails lead to the lovely towns of **Orfű** and **Abaliget**, on a plateau 15km and 20km to the northwest respectively, and to Southern Transdanubia's highest peak, **Mt Zengő** (682m). See Mecsek Hills later in this chapter for more details.

The Sunday **flea market** (Vásár tér), about 3km southwest of the inner town on Megyeri út, attracts people from the countryside, especially on the first Sunday of the month.

Activities

The closest swimming complex to the centre is **Hullám** *(*☎ *512 935; Szendrey Júlia utca 7; adult/child 500/250Ft; indoor pool open 6am-10pm daily, outdoor pool open 9am-7pm daily in summer)*. The Makár Tanya Sportmotel *(*☎ *224 400; Középmakár dűlő 4)*, west of the inner town, has **tennis and squash courts** and gives lessons from 7am to dusk.

Special Events

Among the big annual events in this party town are the **International Music Festival** from late June to early July; **Pécs Days** in late September, a 10-day festival of dance and music with a couple of alcohol-related events; and the **European Wine Song Festival** in late September, Europe's only festival exclusively for male singers.

Places to Stay

Camping Up in the Mecsek Hills near the zoo is **Mandulás Camping** *(*☎ *315 981, fax 315 961;* e *mandulas@mecsektours.hu; Ángyán János utca 2; bus No 34; tent sites 600Ft, bungalows 1600Ft per person; open mid-Apr–mid-Oct)*, which, along with tent and campervan sites, has 28 bungalows with shared shower, a motel (doubles 3500Ft) and a 20-room hotel (doubles with bathroom 6000Ft).

Hostels & Private Rooms In July and August, central **Mátyás College** (☎ 315 846; Széchenyi tér 11; dorm beds around 1200Ft) and **János College** (☎ 251 234; Szántó Kovács János utca 1/c; dorm beds around 1000Ft) to the west, accommodate travellers in dormitories with two to five beds. Ask Tourinform about other college dorms.

Mecsek Tours and Ibusz may be able to arrange **private rooms** from 2000Ft per person; apartments range from 4000Ft to 6000Ft.

Pensions As in Budapest, most of the pensions in Pécs are sprinkled in the surrounding hills and rather difficult to get to without your own transport. **Toboz** (☎ 510 555, fax 510 556; e toboz@dravenet.hu; Fenyves sor 5; singles/doubles 7600/10,200Ft) is a 12-room pension on a tree-lined street just south of the zoo. It's set in among trees and has a retreat feel to it.

Avar (☎ 510 766, fax 510 767; w www.avar panzio.hu; Fenyves sor 2; singles/doubles from 5000/7000Ft), with seven cramped rooms, is cheaper than nearby Toboz but a distant second choice. Its website is in Hungarian only.

Centrum (☎/fax 311 707; Szepessy Ignác utca 4; singles/doubles 4500/5600Ft) is one of the few central places. Its seven rooms are not particularly modern, but they're comfortable.

Hotels A cheap, central option and only a stone's throw from the Mosque Church is **Főnix** (☎ 311 682, fax 324 113; Hunyadi János út 2; singles/doubles 4790/7290Ft), with 16 rooms.

Diana (☎ 328 594, fax 333 373; Tímár 4/a; dorm beds 2000Ft per person, singles/doubles 5600/8600Ft), with eight excellent hotel-style rooms and dorm rooms that sleep up to four, is a great choice just south of the synagogue.

Laterum (☎ 252 108, fax 252 131; bus No 4; Hajnóczy utca 37-39; dorm beds 2000-2500Ft, doubles 5500-8000Ft) hotel is an excellent (though far-flung) place to stay and is enormous, with 133 rooms on the far west side of town. Room rates vary depending on whether you sleep in a dorm room or a room with shared or private bath bath, and there's an inexpensive self-service restaurant (dishes around 300Ft) just off the hotel lobby.

Hunyor (☎ 512 640, fax 512 643; e huny or@mecsektours.hu; Jurisics Miklós utca 16; singles/doubles from 8000/12,000Ft) is in the Mecsek foothills and a bit out of the way but has excellent views of the city and almost a resort feel. There's a pleasant restaurant attached and all 52 rooms have TV, minibar, telephone and bathroom.

Kikelet (☎ 512 900, fax 512 901; e re serve@hotelkikelet.hunguesthotels.hu; Károlyi Mihály utca 1; singles/doubles from €55/67), a hotel farther out still into 'them thar' hills and near the TV tower, is in a couple of erstwhile trade-union holiday houses and offers 33 rooms.

Fenyves Panoráma (☎/fax 315 996; Szőlő utca 64; singles/doubles from 6800/9800Ft), south of the Kikelet, is a 20-room hotel and, as its name suggests, has great views. All rooms have a balcony.

Palatinus (☎ 514 260, fax 514 738; e pala tinuspatria@mail.matav.hu; Király utca 5; singles €51-75, doubles €58-82) is Pécs' old-world hotel. It is swamped by tour groups and its 94 rooms are way overpriced. Rates vary depending on the season and whether the rooms have been renovated.

Pátria (☎ 514 280, fax 514 778; e palati nuspatria@mail.matav.hu; Rákóczi út 3; singles/doubles €47/54), is in an ugly, 117-room block and has cheaper rooms. Its recently renovated rooms have been recommended by readers.

Places to Eat
Oázis (Király utca 17; kebabs and dishes 500-800Ft) is a small takeaway spot (they also have streetside seating) serving Middle Eastern dishes at the right price.

Vörös Sárkány (Red Dragon; Munkácsy Mihály utca 9; lunch specials 60Ft; open 11am-7pm Mon-Fri, 11am-5pm Sat) is good for a cheap and filling Chinese meal.

Hellas Taverna (Ferencesek utcája 9; mains 600-1000Ft) has Greek dishes like dolmades, pastitsio and moussaka along with the requisite gyros (250Ft).

Tex-Mex Café (☎ 215 427; Teréz utca 10; mains 900-1500Ft), one of the best places in Pécs, is an attractive cellar restaurant with tacos, enchiladas and a bit of tequila to wash it all down with.

Cellárium (☎ 314 453; Hunyadi Jánis út 2; mains 800-1200Ft), just below the Főnix hotel, is a reliable choice for a meal and is close to the centre.

Az Elefánthoz (☎ 215 026; Jókai tér 6; mains around 1000Ft) is a bustling Italian restaurant with excellent pizza, pasta and meal-sized salads. Occupying the same building and sharing the same terrace is **Morik Caffé** (☎ 215 026), a great place to people-watch.

Aranykacsa (☎ 518 860; Teréz utca 4; mains around 2000Ft), south of Széchenyi tér, has silver service dining and an expensive menu.

Dóm (☎ 210 088; Király utca 3; mains 800-1600Ft), is a small loft restaurant in a courtyard with wonderful fin-de-siècle paintings and stained-glass windows.

There's an ongoing debate in Pécs over which cukrászda (cake shop) serves better cakes and ice cream: the **Mecsek** (☎ 315 444; Széchenyi tér 16) near the old Nádor hotel or the **Virág** (☎ 313 793; Irgalmasok utcája). The best bet is to try them both.

There's a **Spar supermarket** south of the town centre on Bajsy-Zsilinszky utca. Pécs' **fruit and vegetable market** is near the bus station on Zólyom utca.

Entertainment

House of Artists (☎ 315 388; Széchenyi tér 7-8; open noon-5pm Mon-Fri), advertises its many cultural programmes outside, including classical music concerts. For tickets visit the **Pécs Cultural Centre** (☎ 336 622, Széchenyi tér 1). These are the places to ask about classical music concerts. Other musical venues include the **Ferenc Liszt Concert Hall** (☎ 311 557; Király utca 83), east of the town centre and **Lenau House** (☎ 332 515; Munkácsy Mihály utca 8).

Pécs is also renowned for its opera company and the Sophianae Ballet, which perform at the **Pécs National Theatre** on Király utca. If you're told that tickets to this theatre are sold out, try for a cancellation at the box office an hour before the performance. Advance tickets can be purchased from the **theatre office** (☎ 310 539; Király utca 18).

Other stages are the **Chamber Theatre** next door to the National Theatre, the **Croatian Theatre** (Anna utca 17) and the **Bóbita Puppet Theatre** (Mária utca 18) – somewhere John Malkovich would be proud to perform.

Pécs is a big university town and that is reflected in the city's nightlife. Some of Pécs' most popular discos and music clubs include **Boccaccio** (Bajcsy-Zsilinszky utca 45), a huge place with three floors; the small and popular

Soul 6 (Czindery utca 6); **Rák** (Ipar utca 7), the place to go for rock; and the **B52 Disco** (Universitás út 35).

There are pubs and bars almost the entire length of Király utca, many of them with outdoor tables in summer. The **Royal Café** at No 1, **Murphy's Pub** at No 2 and the **Arizona Ranch** at No 29 are all good bets.

Dante Café (Janus Pannonius 11), occupying the ground floor of the Csontváry Museum, is a good place to meet local students, and has a huge garden and occasional live music.

Kaptalani on Janus Pannonius utca is a lovely little borozó (wine bar) with outdoor seating near the cathedral. It's also a great spot to try the local wine – white Cirfandli, a speciality of the Mecsek Hills.

While visiting the cathedral or the museums along Káptalan utca, stop in for a drink or a coffee at the **Kioszk** in the little park between Káptalan utca and Janus Pannonius utca. It's probably the only chance you'll ever have to drink in what was once a baptistry.

The biweekly freebie Pécsi Est is a great source for information on what's on in Pécs and the surrounding towns.

Shopping

Pécs has been renowned for its leatherwork since Turkish times, and you can pick up a few bargains in several shops around the city; try one called **Blázek** (Teréz utca 1). There's a **Zsolnay** (Jókai tér 2) porcelain outlet here.

Getting There & Away

Bus Departures are frequent (once or even twice an hour) to Siklós, Mohács, Harkány, Kaposvár, Vajszló, Szigetvár and Szekszárd. You can also reach Budapest (five buses a day), Békéscsaba (one), Győr (two), Hévíz (two), Kecskemét (two), Sellye (two to five), Siófok (four), Székesfehérvár (three), Sopron (one), Szeged (seven), Veszprém (two or three), Villány (one to two) and Zalaegerszeg (four to five).

There are hourly buses in summer to Abaliget and Orfű in the Mecsek Hills, but only seven to 10 in winter.

Buses run three to four times a day between Barcs and Zagreb. There are also three buses a day (11.50am, 4.30pm and 4.45pm) from Pécs to Osijek in Croatia.

Train Up to 13 trains a day connect Pécs with Budapest. You can reach Nagykanizsa and other points northwest via a rather circuitous but scenic 148km line along the Dráva River. From Nagykanizsa, up to eight trains a day continue on to Szombathely. One early morning express (5.35am) follows that route from Pécs all the way to Szombathely. Two daily trains run from Pécs (10.50am and 1pm) to Osijek.

Getting Around
To get to the Hunyor hotel, take bus No 32 from the train station or from opposite the Mosque Church. Bus Nos 34 and 35 run direct to the Kikelet and Fenyves hotels from the train station. Bus No 34 goes on to the camp site, while bus No 35 continues to the TV tower. For the Laterum hotel, take bus No 4 from the train station or the market near the bus station to the end of the line at Uránváros. Bus Nos 3 and 50 from the train station are good for the flea market on Vásár tér.

You can order a local taxi by calling ☎ 222 222 or ☎ 333 333.

MECSEK HILLS
Buses from Pécs reach most towns in the Mecsek Hills, but if you plan to do a lot of hiking, get a copy of Cartographia's 1:40,000 *A Mecsek* map (No 15; 650Ft) before setting out.

Orfű
☎ 72 • postcode 7677 • pop 740
The most accessible of the Mecsek resorts and the one with the most recreational facilities is Orfű, a series of settlements on four artificial lakes where you can swim, row, canoe and fish. There's a riding school at the **Tekeresi Lovaspanzió** (*Tekeres Horse Pension; mobile ☎ 06-30 227 1398; Petőfi utca 3*) at Tekeres to the northwest. From Széchenyi tér you can walk south along tiny Lake Orfű to the **Mill Museum** (*Malommúzeum; ☎ 498 440; adult/child 250/150Ft; open 10am-5pm daily May-Sept*), a series of old pump houses.

Places to Stay & Eat Panoráma Camping (*☎ 378 501; e campingorfu@freemail .hu; Dollár utca 1; camping per adult/child/tent from 550/250/400Ft, hostel beds 1200Ft, bungalows from 4400Ft; open mid-Apr–mid-Oct*), above the large public beach in the lake's southwestern corner, has dinghies, sailboards and bicycles for rent. Rates increase over the summer period. Other places to stay in Orfű include the four-room

Vaskakas pension (*☎ 498 219; Mecsekárosi utca 29; rooms from 4000Ft*) on the lake's eastern shore and the eight-room **Molnár** pension (*☎/fax 378 563; Széchenyi tér 18/a; singles/doubles 4000/6000Ft*).

Muskátli (*Széchenyi tér; mains around 1000Ft*), close to Molnár pension in the small village centre, is a pleasant little restaurant.

Abaliget
☎ 72 • postcode 7678 • pop 650
Abaliget, 3km northwest of Orfű and accessible by bus or on foot via a trail up and over the hill behind Panoráma Camping, is quieter but not as attractive. There are some **private rooms** and **pensions** along Kossuth Lajos utca, the main street, or you could try **Barlang Camping** (*☎ 498 730; camping per adult/child/tent 500/300/500Ft, motel/hotel rooms per person 2200Ft, bungalows 5000Ft*) on the town's tiny lake. The site also has a nine-room motel, a 14-room hotel and bungalows for up to four people.

Barlang Camping is near the 450m-long **Abaliget Cave** (*☎ 498 766; adult/child 450/220Ft; open 8am-6pm daily Apr-Oct*), which can be visited in season.

KAPOSVÁR
☎ 82 • postcode 7400 • pop 68,500
Somogy County is usually associated with the Balaton and rightly so: it controls the entire money-spinning southern shore of the lake from Siófok to Balatonberény. Kaposvár, the county seat some 55km to the south, does not generally spring to mind.

It's not an unattractive city, it must be said, situated in the Zselic foothills along the valley of the Kapos River. But don't come to 'Kapos Castle' looking for a fortress like the one at Siklós or Szigetvár; the Turks and then the Habsburgs dispatched that long ago. In fact, so heavy and constant was the fighting here over the centuries that few buildings date from before 1900. Instead, visit Kaposvár for its art (the city is associated with three great painters: the postimpressionists József Rippl-Rónai and János Vaszary, as well as Aurél Bernáth) and theatre, among the best in provincial Hungary.

Orientation & Information
The train and bus stations are a block apart south of the city centre, on Budai Nagy Antal utca. From here, walk up Teleki utca to

SOUTHERN TRANSDANUBIA

Kossuth tér and Fő utca, a lovely pedestrian street where most of the action is.

For information about Kaposvár and surrounds, see **Tourinform** (☎/fax 320 404; e kaposvar@tourinform.hu; Fő utca 8; open 9.30am-5.30pm Mon-Fri, 9.30am-1.30pm Sat mid-June–mid-Aug; 8.30am-5pm Mon-Fri, 8.30am-noon Sat mid-Aug–mid-June). **Siotour** (☎ 320 537, fax 312 459; w www.sio tour.hu; Fő utca 1; open 8am-4.30pm Mon-Fri) is in the same building as the Csokonai hotel.

The **OTP bank** (Széchenyi tér 2) has several ATMs. The **main post office** (Bajcsy-Zsilinszky utca 15) is west of Széchenyi tér. The town's website is at w www.kaposvar.hu.

Things to See

In among the pretty, pastel-coloured buildings lining Fő utca is the former county hall (1820) at No 10, which now houses two museums: the **Somogy County & Rippl-Rónai Museums** (☎ 314 114; adult/child 200/100Ft; open 10am-6pm Tues-Sun Apr-Oct; 10am-4pm Tues-Sun Nov-Mar).

The Somogy County Museum contains a large ethnographical collection and a gallery of contemporary art on the ground floor. There is a grand collection of paintings on the first floor, which include works by Vaszary Bernáth and Béla Kádár.

The folk collection is noteworthy for its wood and horn carvings (at which the swineherds of Somogy County excelled), examples of famous indigo-dyed cotton fabrics (kékfestő), an exhibition on the county's infamous outlaws (including the paprika-tempered 'Horseshoe Steve'), and costumes of the Croatian minority, who dressed and decorated their houses in white fabric during mourning periods as the Chinese do. The top floor is full of paintings by Ödön Rippl-Rónai, the brother of Kaposvár's most celebrated – and arguably Hungary's best – painter, József Rippl-Rónai (1861–1927).

József Rippl-Rónai, was born at Fő 19, above the lovely **Golden Lion Pharmacy** (Aranyoroszlán patika; admission free; open 7.30am-6pm Mon-Fri), built in 1774 and now a museum. Most of his work is exhibited in the **Rippl-Rónai Memorial Museum** (Rippl-Rónai Emlékmúzeum; ☎ 422 144; Róma-hegy 88; adult/child 200/100Ft; open 10am-6pm Tues-Sun Apr-Oct; 10am-4pm

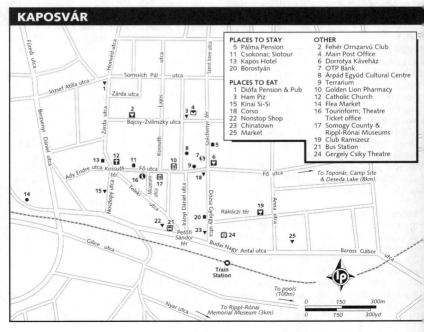

KAPOSVÁR

PLACES TO STAY
5 Pálma Pension
11 Csokonai; Siotour
13 Kapos Hotel
20 Borostyán

PLACES TO EAT
1 Diófa Pension & Pub
3 Ham Piz
15 Kinai Si-Si
18 Corso
22 Nonstop Shop
23 Chinatown
25 Market

OTHER
2 Fehér Orrszarvú Club
4 Main Post Office
6 Dorrotya Kávéház
7 OTP Bank
8 Árpád Együd Cultural Centre
9 Terrarium
10 Golden Lion Pharmacy
12 Catholic Church
14 Flea Market
16 Tourinform; Theatre Ticket office
17 Somogy County & Rippl-Rónai Museums
19 Club Ramszesz
21 Bus Station
24 Gergely Csiky Theatre

Shopping on the Király utca promenade in Pécs, Southern Transdanubia

Art at the Zsolnay Porcelain Museum, Pécs

Open for business, Villány

The Ferenc Móra Museum, housed in the historic 1896 Palace of Education, Szeged

Lily pads blanket Lake Tisza on the Great Plain

The Reformed College's library, Debrecen – preserving around 650,000 volumes

Nov-Mar), a graceful 19th-century villa, about 3km southeast of the city centre.

Built in 1911, the cream and lemon-coloured Secessionist **Gergely Csiky Theatre** (Rákóczi tér 2), with its hundreds of arched windows, is worth a look even if you are not attending a performance.

If you can handle it, step down into the **Terrarium** (☎ 424 460; Fő utca 31; adult/child 400/300Ft; open 9am-6pm daily May-Aug; 9am-5pm Mon-Fri, 9am-noon Sat, 2pm-5pm Sun Sept-Apr) in a humid cellar. Cobras, caymans, boas and a python as thick as a stevedore's forearm are all there to greet you.

There's a small daily **flea market** (Vásárteri út), west of the bus station.

Activities

The Zselic region (Zselicség) south of Kaposvár, some 9000 hectares of which is under a nature-conservation order, is webbed with trails for easy **hikes** through villages, forests and low hills. Get a copy of Cartographia's 1:60,000 A Zselic map (No 17; 650Ft) before you go.

The artificial Deseda Lake at Toponár, 8km northeast of the city, offers **swimming**, other **water sports** and **tennis**. More convenient to the centre, though, are the **outdoor pools** (adult/child 350/250Ft; open 9am-7pm daily mid-May–Aug) and the **thermal baths** (Csík Ferenc sétány; open 6am-9pm Tues-Sun Sept–mid-May). The admission fee for the outdoor pools includes entry to the thermal baths.

Places to Stay

Deseda Camping (☎ 312 020, fax 312 854; open mid-June–late Aug; camping per adult/child/tent 900/450/700Ft) in Toponár does not have bungalows, but travellers armed with a tent can take bus No 8 or the train headed for Siófok and get off at the second stop.

Siotour can book you a **private room** for around 2000Ft per single (difficult to find, as always) and from around 4000Ft per double.

Pálma (☎/fax 420 227; Széchenyi tér 6; rooms 6800Ft) pension is a homy place with six comfortable rooms, and has a great cake and ice-cream shop below it.

Diófa (☎/fax 422 504; József Attila utca 24; singles/doubles 5000/6000Ft) is a slightly bigger pension with eight rooms. There's a sauna on site and a restaurant downstairs.

Csokonai (☎ 312 011, fax 316 716; e sio tour@mail.datanet.hu; Fő utca 1; singles/ doubles without bathroom 2300/3400Ft, doubles with bathroom from 4200Ft), in an 18th-century house, is a very cheap option if you don't mind sharing the bathroom.

Borostyán (☎ 512 475, fax 512 474; Rákóczi tér 3; singles/doubles 4900-8100/7900-10,000Ft), an upmarket six-room Art Nouveau extravaganza, is one of provincial Hungary's most interesting caravanserais. Rates vary depending on the room size.

Kapos (☎/fax 316 022; w www.kapos hotel.hu; Kossuth tér; singles 5900-8900Ft,

Farewell to All That

The word búcsú (church patronal festival) derives from the ancient Turkish for 'absolution' or 'the forgiveness of sins'. From medieval times it has taken on the additional meaning of 'pilgrimage' in Hungarian.

Búcsúk were usually linked with an icon or statue in a particular church, such as the Black Madonnas at Andocs, north of Kaposvár in Southern Transdanubia, and Máriapócs, near Nyírbátor in the Northeast. They could also honour the name of a church's patron saint. People would march, often for days, to the holy place carrying banners and singing. Local people would accommodate and feed the pilgrims for little or nothing. Often the faithful would spend the night in the church itself, believing that the absolution – or the cure – was more likely to occur in sleep.

Over the centuries búcsúk took on a more secular tone. Merchants would set up their stalls around the church, selling not only relics and religious articles but clothing, food and drinks as well. Showmen, buskers and musicians entertained the crowds and, in some places, there was even a 'bride market' with hopeful young women appearing with their full dowries. While the old and infirm congregated in the church to touch and venerate the holy picture or statue, the young remained outside for the entertainment.

As it happens, búcsú has yet another meaning in Hungarian: 'farewell'. Thus the Budapest Búcsú (Budapest Goodbye) every June marking the departure of the last Soviet soldier from Hungarian soil in 1991 has a double meaning: it is both a raging party paying homage to hedonism and a 'goodbye' to the last of the much despised occupiers.

doubles 7700-11,600Ft) is an unattractive, modern 79-room affair but friendly and very centrally located. Rates depend on the room category.

Places to Eat

Ham Piz *(Bajcsy-Zsilinszky utca 13; burgers and pizzas from 300Ft; open until 11pm daily)* next to the post office, is a studenty place that serves the two fast foods of choice in Hungary these days.

Chinatown *(Budai Nagy Antal utca 9; mains 650-1000Ft)*, has its entrance on Dózsa György utca opposite the Gergely Csiky Theatre. The food is almost American-Chinese; indeed, members of the US Army Europe National Support Element Operation Joint Guard (a mouthful in itself) from NATO's base at Taszár awarded Chinatown a 'scroll of appreciation' in 1998, which is still proudly displayed in the front window.

Kínai Si-Si *(Noszlopy Gáspár utca 6; mains 800-1900Ft)* in a lovely old blue house, also does good Chinese food, but has the addition of Japanese dishes on the menu.

Corso *(cnr Fő utca & Dózsa György utca; mains 900-1000Ft)* is a relaxed place with a Hungarian menu and outdoor seating on colourful Fő utca.

Borostyán *(☎ 512 475; Rákóczi tér 3; mains 1000-1600Ft; open until 11pm Mon-Sat)*, in the hotel of the same name, has a fancy dining room and a quiet courtyard.

There's a **24-hour shop** at the bus station on Budai Nagy Antal utca. The **fruit and vegetable market** is east of Rákóczi tér.

Entertainment

The **Árpád Együd Cultural Centre** *(☎ 512 229; Csokonai utca 1)* has information on things cultural on offer in Kaposvár.

Gergely Csiky Theatre *(☎ 528 450; Rákóczi tér 2)*, along with being a masterpiece of Art Nouveau (or Secessionist) architecture, has a great reputation and was at the forefront of Hungarian artistic innovation in the 1970s. The **booking office** *(☎ 511 208; Fő utca 8; open 8.30am-12.30pm & 1pm-5pm Mon-Fri, 8.30am-noon Sat)* is at Tourinform.

Kaposvár is known for its choral groups, and concerts are given in venues around the city, including the **Catholic church** on Kossuth tér.

Dorottya Kávéház *(Széchenyi tér 8)* at Dorottya House, where most of the action in playwright Mihály Csokonai Vitéz's comic epic *Dorottya* (1804) takes place, is a good spot for a beer or game of pool.

Diófa *(Zárda utca 39)*, a pub north of Kossuth tér, is another good drinking hole.

Fehér Orrszarvú *(White Rhinoceros; Bajcsy-Zsilinszky utca 1c; open 10pm-4am Thur-Sun)* is the place to go if you're looking for a 'nostalgia' (read oldies) disco. It's housed in a big old dusky pink mansion northeast of Kossuth tér.

For something more up-to-date try **Club Ramszesz** *(Rákóczi tér 9-11)* near the train and bus stations.

For up-to-date entertainment, check the listings in the freebie biweekly *Kapos Est.*

Getting There & Away

Bus Between eight and 11 daily buses link Kaposvár with Barcs, Pécs and Gálosfa. Other destinations include Baja (one bus a day), Budapest (three), Győr (two), Hévíz (two), the thermal spa at Igal (two to seven), Mohács (two), Nagykanizsa (two to four), Siófok (three), Sopron (one), Szeged (one), Szekszárd (one), Szenna (two from stop No 11), Szigetvár (two), Szombathely (three), Tapolca (two) and Zalaegerszeg (one).

Train You can reach Kaposvár by train from both the eastern (Siófok) and western (Fonyód) ends of Lake Balaton's southern shore. Another line links Kaposvár with Budapest (via Dombóvár) to the northeast up to four times a day and, to the west, with Gyékényes, from where international trains depart for Zagreb (three a day) and Venice (one).

Getting Around

Bus No 8 terminates near the lake and the camp site in Toponár. For the Rippl-Rónai Memorial Museum in Róma-hegy, take bus No 15.

Local taxis are available by calling ☎ 313 333 or ☎ 555 555.

SZIGETVÁR

☎ 73 • postcode 7900 • pop 11,700

Szigetvár, 33km west of Pécs and 40km south of Kaposvár, was a Celtic settlement and then a Roman one called Limosa before the Magyar conquest. The strategic importance of the town was recognised early on, and in 1420 a fortress was built on a small island – Szigetvár means 'island castle' – in the marshy areas of the Almás River. But Szigetvár would be indistinguishable today from other Southern

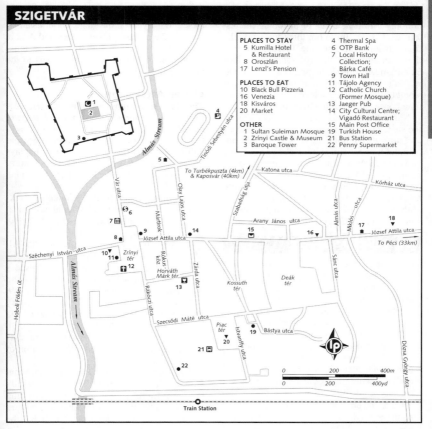

SZIGETVÁR

PLACES TO STAY
5 Kumilla Hotel & Restaurant
8 Oroszlán
17 Lenzl's Pension

PLACES TO EAT
10 Black Bull Pizzeria
16 Venezia
18 Kisváros
20 Market

OTHER
1 Sultan Suleiman Mosque
2 Zrínyi Castle & Museum
3 Baroque Tower

4 Thermal Spa
6 OTP Bank
7 Local History Collection; Bárka Café
9 Town Hall
11 Tájolo Agency
12 Catholic Church (Former Mosque)
13 Jaeger Pub
14 City Cultural Centre; Vigadó Restaurant
15 Main Post Office
19 Turkish House
21 Bus Station
22 Penny Supermarket

Transdanubian towns had the events of September 1566 not taken place (see the boxed text 'Big Sally of Szigetvár' later).

Today you can visit what remains of the town's celebrated castle, and there are a handful of Turkish-era monuments to gawk at. The opening of the Park of Turkish-Hungarian Friendship, north of the city, has helped to cement the friendly ties between the two former enemies.

Orientation & Information

The bus and train stations are close to one another a short distance south of the town centre at the end of Rákóczi utca. To reach the centre follow this road north into lovely Zrínyi tér. Vár utca on the northern side of the square leads to the castle.

Tájolo Agency (☎/fax 312 654; Zrínyi tér 3; open 9.15am-1pm & 1.45pm-4pm Mon-Fri, 9am-noon Sat) can supply you with a small amount of information on the town. There's a branch of **OTP** (Vár utca 4) on the way to the castle, and a **main post office** (József Attila utca 27-31) east of Zrínyi tér.

For more information try logging on to the town's website (🖳 www.szigetvar.hu).

Zrínyi Castle

Our hero Miklós Zrínyi would probably not recognise the four-cornered castle (☎ 311 442; adult/child 250/150Ft; open 9am-6pm Tues-Sun May-Sept; 9am-3pm Tues-Sun Apr & Oct) he so valiantly fought to save more than 400 years ago. The Turks strengthened the bastions and added buildings; the Hungarians rebuilt it again in the 18th century. Today there are only a few elements of historical interest left: walls from 3m to 6m thick linked by the four bastions; the **Baroque Tower** crowning the southern wall; the 16th-century **Sultan Suleiman Mosque** (Szulejmán pasa dzsámija) with a truncated minaret; and a summer mansion built by Count Andrássy in 1930, which now houses the **Castle Museum**.

Naturally, the museum's exhibits focus on the siege and its key players. Zrínyi's praises are sung throughout, there's a detailed account of how Suleiman built a bridge over the Dráva in 16 days to attack Szigetvár, and the miniatures of Hungarian soldiers being captured, chopped up and burned are still quite horrifying. Sebestyén Tinódi, the beloved 16th-century poet and wandering minstrel who was born in Szigetvár, also rates an altar

Big Sally of Szigetvár

For more than a month at Szigetvár in late 1566, Captain Miklós Zrínyi and the 2500 Hungarian and Croatian soldiers under his command held out against Turkish forces numbering up to 80,000. The leader of the Turks was Sultan Suleiman I, who was making his seventh attempt to march on Vienna and was determined to take what he derisively called 'this molehill'. When the defenders' water and food supplies were exhausted – and reinforcements from Győr under Habsburg Emperor Maximilian II were refused – Zrínyi could see no other solution but a suicidal sally. As the moated castle went up in flames, the opponents fought hand to hand, and most of the soldiers on the Hungarian side, including Zrínyi himself, were killed. An estimated one-quarter of the Turkish forces died in the siege; Suleiman died of a heart attack and his corpse was propped up on a chair during the fighting to inspire his troops and avoid a power struggle until his son could take command.

More than any other heroes in Hungarian history, Zrínyi and his soldiers are remembered for their self-sacrifice in the cause of the nation and for saving Vienna – and thereby Europe – from Turkish domination. *Peril at Sziget*, a 17th-century epic poem by Zrínyi's great-grandson and namesake, Miklós Zrínyi (1620–64), immortalises the siege and is still widely read in Hungary.

of worship. The mosque next door, completed in the year of the siege, contains an art gallery; the arches, prayer niches and Arabic inscriptions on the walls are worth a look. There's also a small *büfé* (snack bar) to the north of the mosque.

Other Attractions

The tiny **Local History Collection** (Helytörténeti Gyűtemény; Vár utca 1; adult/child 100/50Ft; open 9am-4pm Tues-Sat) is a hotchpotch of folk carvings, embroidery and valuables from local churches, but it displays a great collection of 18th- and 19th-century shop signs as well as locks and keys from the castle.

The ogee-arched (called 'donkey's back' arches in Hungarian) windows and hexagonal roof of the baroque **Catholic church** (Zrínyi tér 9; admission free) are the only exterior signs that this was once the Pasha Ali Mosque, built in 1589. The altarpiece of the Crucifixion and the muted ceiling frescoes depicting the deaths of Zrínyi and Suleiman were painted by István Dorffmeister in 1789.

Near the bus station, the 16th-century **Turkish House** (Török-ház; ☎ 311 407; Bástya utca 3; admission 100Ft; open 10am-2pm Tues-Sun May-Sept) was a caravanserai during the occupation and contains an exhibit of Turkish miniatures.

The Catholic church at Turbékpuszta, about 4km northeast of Szigetvár, was originally built as a **tomb for Suleiman**. But according to local tradition, only the sultan's heart lies within; his son and successor, Selim II, had the body exhumed and returned to Turkey.

Some 4km north of Szigetvár on route No 67 to Kaposvár, a Turkish-era battlefield has been turned into the **Park of Turkish-Hungarian Friendship** (Török-Magyar barátság parkja) with interesting stone memorials in the shape of domes and turbans and statues commemorating both Suleiman and Zrínyi.

You can't miss the flamboyant **City Cultural Centre** (Városi Művelődési Ház; József Attila utca), which was designed – surprise, surprise – by maverick architect Imre Makovecz (using his own 'organic' style).

Activities

Szigetvár's **thermal spa** (☎ 312 840; Tinódi Sebestyén utca 23; adult/child 480/240Ft; open 9am-5pm or 7pm daily year-round) is not far from the Kumilla hotel.

Places to Stay

The Tájolo Agency may be able to help you find a **private room**.

Lenzl's pension (☎ 413 045; e lenzls@ dravanet.hu; József Attila utca 63; singles/ doubles from 3000/6000Ft) has attractive rooms, but they are a bit on the small size.

Oroszlán (☎ 310 116, fax 312 817; Zrínyi tér 2; singles/doubles from 6100/8000Ft) has 34 purely functional rooms, and its only redeeming feature is that it's central to everything.

Kumilla (☎/fax 510 288; e szik.kft@ axelero.hu; Olay Lajos utca 6; singles 5000-6700Ft, doubles 6700-7800Ft) is a cosy, 29-room hotel housed in an old music school and takes its name from the beloved daughter of Suleiman and his Russian wife. Rates vary depending on the season, and include entrance to the nearby thermal pools.

Places to Eat

There are a lot of food stalls at the **market** on Piac tér near the bus station.

Venezia (József Attila utca 41; pizzas from 500Ft; open 11am-11pm daily) is a simple place but is deservedly popular for its tasty pizzas.

Black Bull Pizzeria (Széchenyi utca 2; pizzas from 600Ft) is more central than Venezia and serves similar fare.

Kisváros (☎ 312 514; József Attila utca 81; mains 700-1400Ft) serves basic Hungarian dishes in very appealing surroundings.

Vigadó (József Attila utca; mains from 700Ft) in the cultural centre, is another good place for lunch or dinner.

Kumilla's (☎/fax 510 288; e szik.kft@ axelero.hu; Olay Lajos utca 6; mains 700-1200Ft) is a quiet but pleasant restaurant, especially on the terrace in warm weather.

Entertainment

The **Black Bull** (Széchenyi utca 2) is not only popular for its pizzas, but also for a beer in the evenings. Another option is **Bárka** (Vár utca 1), a small coffee shop/bar in the Local History Collection.

On Horváth Márk tér, a small square linking Zrínyi tér with Zárda utca is **Jaeger**, a pub with outdoor tables that attracts a youngish crowd.

Getting There & Away

Bus Between nine and 13 daily buses depart from Szigetvár for Pécs, while two to four run to Kaposvár. Otherwise, there are departures to Barcs (four daily), Hévíz (one), Mohács (one or two), Szentlőrinc (one), Veszprém (one), Zalaegerszeg (two) and Nagykanizsa and Siklós (three). From Barcs, on the border with Croatia 32km to the southwest, three or four buses head for Zagreb daily.

Sellye and the Ormánság folk region are accessible from Szigetvár, but there is only one excruciatingly slow bus at 12.40pm on weekdays and at 12.20pm on Saturday. By train, you must travel east for 15km and change at Szentlőrinc.

Train Szigetvár is on a rail line linking Pécs and Nagykanizsa. The 84km stretch from Barcs to Nagykanizsa follows the course of the Dráva River and is very scenic, especially around Vízvár and Bélavár. If you're trying to leave Hungary from here, get off at Murakeresztúr (two stops before Nagykanizsa), through which trains pass en route to Zagreb, Ljubljana, Trieste and Venice.

NAGYKANIZSA
☎ 93 • postcode 8800 • pop 56,000

Lying on a canal linking the Zala River to the north with the Mura River on the Croatian border, Nagykanizsa hosted a succession of settlers, including Celts, Romans, Avars and Slavs, before the arrival of the Magyars. Early in the 14th century, King Charles Robert ceded the area to the Kanizsay family, who built a castle in the marshes of the canal west of what is now the town centre. The castle was fortified after the fall of Szigetvár in 1566 but, despite the heroics of one Captain György Thury, it too was taken by the Turks and remained an important district seat for 90 years. Development didn't really begin until a few centuries later with the construction of the Budapest-Adriatic rail line through the town and the discovery of the Zala oil fields to the west.

Nagykanizsa is not especially noted for its sights (nothing remains of the castle that was blown to smithereens by the Habsburgs in the 18th century); the town is almost totally focused on drilling for oil, making light bulbs and furniture, and brewing beer. But if you think of it as a convenient stepping stone, you'll literally be on the right track. From Nagykanizsa you can easily reach Western Transdanubia, both shores of Lake Balaton, Italy, Slovenia, Croatia and the beaches of the Adriatic.

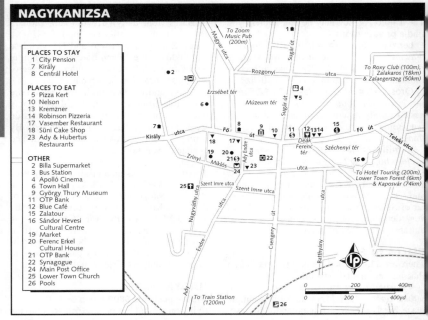

NAGYKANIZSA

PLACES TO STAY
1 City Pension
7 Király
8 Centrál Hotel

PLACES TO EAT
5 Pizza Kert
10 Nelson
13 Kremzner
14 Robinson Pizzeria
17 Vasember Restaurant
18 Süni Cake Shop
23 Ady & Hubertus Restaurants

OTHER
2 Billa Supermarket
3 Bus Station
4 Apolló Cinema
6 Town Hall
9 György Thury Museum
11 OTP Bank
12 Blue Café
15 Zalatour
16 Sándor Hevesi Cultural Centre
19 Market
20 Ferenc Erkel Cultural House
21 OTP Bank
22 Synagogue
24 Main Post Office
25 Lower Town Church
26 Pools

Orientation & Information

The train station is south of the city centre on Ady Endre utca. To reach the centre walk north along this road for about 1200m, and you'll be on Fő út, the main street. The bus station is in the centre to the west of Erzsébet tér.

There is a **Zalatour** (☎ 311 185, fax 313 303; Fő út 13; open 8am-5pm Mon-Fri, 8am-noon Sat) office, and an **OTP bank branch** (Deák Ferenc tér 15) is on the corner of Sugár út, and there's another OTP branch (Ady Endre utca 6) to the southwest. The **main post office** (Ady Endre utca 10) is next door.

Things to See

The **György Thury Museum** (☎ 314 596; Fő út 5; adult/child 200/100Ft; open 10am-5pm Tues-Sun) has an interesting standing exhibit called *The Forest and the People in Zala*; absolutely nothing connected with wood, the woods and forestry is overlooked – from antique saws and charcoal-burning equipment to household utensils made of bark and exquisite hunting knives and rifles. The contemporary illustrations of Kanizsa Castle are fascinating, especially the idealised Turkish one from 1664 showing 14 minarets within the castle walls.

The neoclassical **synagogue** (admission free; open 2pm-6pm Tues-Sat), built in 1810 in a courtyard behind Fő út 6 (once a Jewish school), is in appalling condition, though it is occasionally used for concerts and lectures. Outside the western entrance a cenotaph remembers the 2700 Jews who were rounded up here in late April 1944 and deported to the death camps at Auschwitz.

The Franciscan **Lower Town Church** (Alsóvárosi templom; cnr Szent Imre utca & Nagyváthy utca; admission free), begun in 1702 but not completed for 100 years, has ornate stucco work and a rococo pulpit. You can't miss the holy-water font, carved from the burial stone of the Turkish general Pasha Mustafa.

Have a look at the **Apolló Cinema** (Sugár út 5), in a small garden south of Rozgonyi utca. Formerly the Municipal Theatre, it's a unique example of Art Nouveau and Hungarian folk architecture designed in 1926 by István Medgyaszay. Unfortunately it no longer screens films and is in a state of disrepair.

Activities

The so-called Lower Town Forest (Alsóvárosi erdő), 6km east of the town centre, has a large rowing lake with **boats** available in summer.

There are **outdoor pools** (adult/child 260/150Ft; open 9.30am-6.30pm daily June–mid-Sept) and an **indoor pool** (open 11am-8pm Mon, 6am-8pm Tues-Fri, 9am-6pm Sat & Sun year-round) in the Kiskert, south of the centre at Csengery út 49. But if you want to take the (thermal) waters, you'll have to go to the spa at Zalakaros, 18km to the northeast near the Little Balaton (Kis-Balaton). The Zalakaros spring, which gushes out of the ground at an incredible 92°C, was discovered by workers drilling for oil in the early 1960s.

Places to Stay
Zalatour can organise **private rooms** for about 2000Ft per person.

Hotel Touring (☎ 318 800, fax 320 194; e khotelsb@elender.hu; Attila utca 4; rooms €20-31) is not the most salubrious place in town but it has 47 cheap rooms (rates depend on facilities) in a quiet suburban area and is a few hundred metres east of the town centre.

Király (☎ 325 489; cnr Király utca & Kalmár utca; singles/doubles 5400/8200Ft) is a pleasant pension on the 1st floor of a small shopping and office complex, with nine large, bright modern rooms.

City (☎ 318 800, fax 320 194; e khotelsb@elender.hu; Sugár út 26; rooms 9000Ft) pension is the better-groomed sister of Touring, but has only four rooms.

Centrál (☎ 314 000, fax 310 111; Erzsébet tér 23; singles/doubles 11,000/15,000Ft), a hotel built in 1912, tries to corner the business market, making it a rather expensive place to stay. There are 30 rooms here, all with mod cons.

Places to Eat
There are a number of cheap places on Ady Endre utca, including **Ady** at No 5 and **Hubertus** at No 7; both have mains from 700Ft.

Pizza Kert (Sugár út 5; pizzas around 700Ft) is great on summer evenings; there's a big front courtyard here fronted by a small park.

Vasember (cnr Ady Endre utca & Erzsébet tér; mains 700-1500Ft) restaurant in the Iron Man House, has Hungarian main courses.

For more upmarket options, try any one of a string of restaurants along Fő utca and Deák tér. **Nelson** (☎ 315 304; Fő utca 7; steaks 1250-1800Ft) is a cellar pub-restaurant with a great steak menu. **Robinson** (Deák tér 9; pizzas from 700Ft) is a rather dark but fashionable pizzeria popular with Nagykanizsa's young bloods and open till late.

Kremzner (☎ 313 057; Deák Ferenc tér 11; mains from 800Ft) is a clean, modern place with a Germanic twist.

Süni (Erzsébet tér 2; ice cream from 60Ft) is a good place for cakes and ice cream.

Entertainment
Sándor Hevesi Cultural Centre (☎ 310 456; Széchenyi tér 5-9) can tell you what's on in Nagykanizsa. It and the **Ferenc Erkel Cultural House** (☎ 312 325; Ady Endre utca 8) behind the post office host weekend discos.

The local Kanizsai beer flows as freely throughout the year as it does at the **Kanizsai Days festival** and there are a lot of decent pubs and bars, including the **Nelson** (☎ 315 304; Fő utca 7t) and **Blue Café** (Deák tér 13), with a cool glass brick bar and neon lighting.

For clubbing take your pick between **Roxy Club** (Balatoni utca 2) and **Zoom Music Pub** (Magyar utca 19), northwest and northeast of Fő út respectively.

Getting There & Away
There's a bus running every 30 minutes to the Zalakaros spa and also hourly ones to Zalaegerszeg. Otherwise, there are departures to Budapest (two daily), Keszthely (six), Sopron (one), Szeged (one), Pápa (two), Kaposvár (up to eight), Balatonmagyaród (up to 11) on the Little Balaton, Pécs (six) and Szombathely (up to eight).

From Nagykanizsa, up to nine daily trains go north to Szombathely, at least two head south for Zagreb and one continues onto Ljubljana, Trieste and Venice. Trains run direct to Déli, Kelenföld and Keleti stations in Budapest and the southern shore resorts, but if you're headed for the western or northern sides (such as Keszthely or Balatonfüred), you must change at Balatonszentgyörgy.

Getting Around
Nagykanizsa is an easy walking city, but you may prefer to wait and ride. From the train station, bus No 18 goes to the bus station and city centre. Bus No 17/b terminates near the rowing lake in the Lower Town Forest, or you can take the Budapest-bound local train and get off at the first stop (Nagyrécse).

You can book for the local taxi service by calling ☎ 312 222.

Great Plain

The Great Plain (Nagyalföld) is Hungary's 'Midwest', an enormous prairie that stretches for hundreds of kilometres east and southeast of Budapest. It covers nearly half of the nation's territory – some 45,000 sq km – but only about a third of all Hungarians live here.

After Budapest and Lake Balaton, no area is so well known outside Hungary as the Great Plain. Like Australians and their Outback, many Hungarians tend to view the Great Plain romantically as a region of hardy shepherds fighting the wind and the snow in winter and trying not to go stir-crazy in summer as the notorious *délibáb* (mirages) rise off the baking soil, leading them, their mop-like *puli* dogs and flocks astray. This mythology of the Great Plain can be credited to 19th-century paintings like *Storm on the Puszta* and *The Woebegone Highwayman* by Mihály Munkácsy, and the nationalist poet Sándor Petőfi, who described the Plain as 'My world and home…The Alföld, the open sea'.

But that's just a part of the story of the Great Plain; like the USA's Midwest, it defies such an easy categorisation. Grassland abounds in the east but much of the south is given over to agriculture, and there's industry in the centre. The graceful architecture of Szeged and Kecskemét, the recreational areas along the Tisza River, the spas of the Hajdúság region, the paprika fields around Kalocsa – all are as much a part of the Great Plain as the whip-cracking *csikós* (cowboy).

Five hundred years ago the region was not a steppe but forest land – and at the constant mercy of the flooding Tisza and Danube Rivers. The Turks chopped down most of the trees, destroying the protective cover and releasing the topsoil to the winds; villagers fled north or to the market towns and *khas* (towns under the sultan's jurisdiction). The region had become the *puszta* (meaning 'deserted' or 'uninhabited'), and it was home to shepherds, fisherfolk, runaway serfs and outlaws. The regulation of the rivers in the 19th century dried up the marshes and allowed for methodical irrigation, paving the way for intensive agriculture, particularly on the Southern Plain.

Hungarians generally divide the Great Plain in two: the area 'between the Danube and the Tisza Rivers', stretching from the foothills of the Northern Uplands to the border

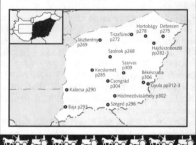

with Yugoslavia, and the land 'beyond the Tisza' from below Hungary's Northeast region to Romania. But this does not really reflect the lie of the land, the routes that travellers usually take or, frankly, what's of interest. Instead, it can be divided into the Central Plain, the Eastern Plain and the Southern Plain.

Central Plain

The Central Plain, stretching eastward from the capital and including Szolnok, Jászberény and the Tisza River, is the smallest of the Great Plain's divisions. Though it offers the least of the three areas to travellers, there are still some attractions: the spas and resorts on Lake Tisza attract visitors by the busload every year. But the Central Plain (Közép-Alföld) is usually crossed without a second glance en route to 'richer' areas.

Though it had been a crossroads since Neolithic times, the Central Plain only came into its own after the Mongol invasion of the early 13th century, which left it almost completely depopulated. In a bid to strengthen his position, King Béla IV (r. 1235–70) settled the area with Jász, or Jazygians, an obscure pastoral people of Persian origin whose name still appears in towns throughout the region, and Kun (or Cumans) from western Siberia, known for their equestrian skills.

The area suffered under the Turks and during the independence wars of the 18th and 19th centuries. But Transylvanian salt and timber from the Carpathians had brought commerce to the region and, with the construction of the Budapest–Szolnok railway line (1847) and river drainage, industry developed.

SZOLNOK
☎ 56 • postcode 5000 • pop 81,500

A 'deed of gift' issued by King Géza I makes mention of what was then called Zounok as early as 1075, and it has remained the most important settlement in the Central Plain since that time. Szolnok has had its own share of troubles: it was laid to waste more than a dozen times over the centuries. The last disaster came in 1944, when Allied bombing all but flattened the city and the retreating German troops blew up the bridge over the Tisza. The appearance of present-day Szolnok dates from after WWII, but a few old monuments, the city's thermal spas and the Tisza (a river Daniel Defoe once described as 'three parts water and two parts fish') give it a calm, almost laid-back feel.

Orientation
Szolnok is situated on the confluence of the Tisza River and the narrow Zagyva River. Its main street, Kossuth Lajos út, runs roughly west–east a few blocks north of the Tisza. Across the Tisza Bridge (Tisza híd), rebuilt in 1963, is the city's recreational area, Tiszaliget (Tisza Park), with a camp site and other accommodation as well as swimming pools. A backwater of the Tisza (Alcsi-Holt-Tisza) lies southeast of the park.

The city's busy train station is on Jubileumi tér, a couple of kilometres west of the city centre at the end of Baross Gábor út (the continuation of Kossuth Lajos út). The bus station is a few minutes' walk north of Kossuth Lajos út on Ady Endre utca.

Information
The **Tourinform** (☎ 424 803, fax 341 441; e szolnok-m@tourinform.hu; Ságvári körút 4; open 8am-6pm Mon-Fri, 10am-6pm Sat & Sun mid-June–Sept; 8am-4pm Mon-Thur, 8am-3pm Fri Oct–mid-June) is around the corner from the bus station. **Ibusz** (☎ 423 602, fax 420 039; Szapáry út 24; open 8am-5pm Mon-Fri) is farther south. The city's website is at w www.szolnok.hu.

The **OTP bank** (Szapáry út 31), **MKB bank** (cnr Baross Gábor út & Sütő utca) and **main post office** (Baross Gábor út 14) are to the south and southwest of Tourinform.

Things to See
Like so many fortresses on the Great Plain, Szolnok Castle was blown to bits by the Habsburgs in 1710, and the rubble was later used to rebuild the city centre. What little is left of the **castle ruins** – just a bit of wall – can be seen near Gutenberg tér across the Zagyva River. Gutenberg tér is also the site of Hungary's most famous **artists' colony** (művésztelep; ☎ 425 549; Gutenberg tér 4), founded in 1902 and once counting among its members the realist painters Adolf Fényes, István Nagy and László Mednyánszky. Fronting the Zagyva northeast of Szabadság tér is the **Tabán district** with the last remaining peasant houses in Szolnok.

The **János Damjanich Museum** (☎ 421 602; Kossuth tér 4; open 9am-5pm Tues-Sun May-Oct; 10am-4pm Nov-Apr) is divided into three sections: archaeological finds from the Bronze Age and Roman times (adult/child 100/50Ft); an extensive ethnographical collection (100/50Ft); and exhibits relating to Szolnok's history, especially the artists' colony (50/25Ft). Damjanich, a great hero during the siege of Szolnok in 1849, was one of the Martyrs of Arad – 13 generals executed by the Austrians there later that year (see The 1848–49 War of Independence & the Dual Monarchy under History in the Facts about Hungary chapter).

The **Szolnok Gallery** (☎ 378 023; Templom utca 2; adult/child 100/50Ft; open 9am-5pm Tues-Sun May-Oct; 10am-4pm Nov-Apr) shows works by contemporary artists from the region. The primary reason for visiting the gallery is to see the building itself – a Romantic-style **synagogue** that was designed by Lipót Baumhorn in 1898. (Baumhorn also did the glorious temples in

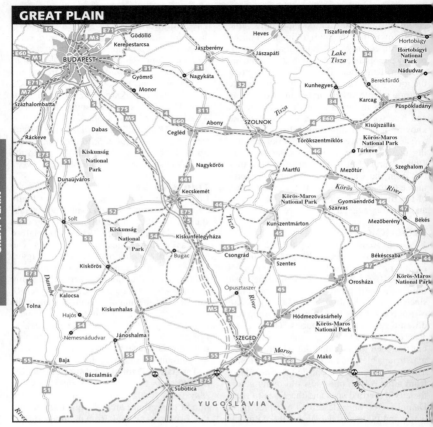

Szeged and Gyöngyös.) West of the gallery are the baroque **Franciscan church and monastery** *(Ferences templom és kolostor; Templom utca 8; admission free)* completed in 1757 – the city's oldest buildings.

Architecture buffs should walk up Szapáry út from the Szolnok Gallery to No 19 for a look at a fine example of a **Hungarian Art Nouveau building**. Today it houses a few small businesses.

Activities

Szolnok is a spa town and has several places where you can 'take the waters'. The **Tisza Park thermal pools** *(Tiszaligeti sétány; open 8am-6pm daily June-Aug)* are across the river and cost 350/230Ft (adult/child) to enter. There's a small rowing lake behind.

Closer to town, west of Tisza Bridge, the Damjanich complex has an **indoor and outdoor thermal pool** *(Damjanich utca 3; adult/ child 380/240Ft; open 6am or 7am-9pm daily May-Sept; 6am-6.30pm Mon-Sat, 7am-1pm Sun Oct-Apr)* and a large sun-bathing area. The more serious **thermal baths** *(adult/child 560/370Ft; open 7.30am-4pm daily May-Sept; 7.30am-9pm daily Oct-Apr)*, those at the Tisza hotel, are mock Turkish with a bit of Art Deco thrown in and are a great place to laze away an afternoon.

Places to Stay

Camping On the island south of the centre is **Tiszaligeti Camping** *(☎/fax 424 403; Tisza-ligeti sétány 34; camping per adult/child/tent 500/400/500Ft, 2-person bungalows from*

Pensions & Hotels Near the Tisza Bridge at the entrance to Tisza Park is **Touring** (☎ 379 805, fax 376 003; Tiszaligeti sétány; singles 5800-6800Ft, doubles 8000-9400Ft) hotel. All its 35 rooms have shower or bath.

Trojka (☎ 514 600, fax 420 486; W www .trojka.hu; Tiszaligeti sétány 5; singles/doubles 5000/8000Ft) pension is farther west than Touring and its eight rooms are more cosy. There is a restaurant on the ground floor.

Student (☎ 421688, fax 378 703; Mártírok útja 8-14; beds per person 2200Ft), a hotel on the opposite bank and closer to the centre of town, has 75 rooms available from late June to late August. This is one of the best places to stay in Szolnok if you're looking for company or a party; the small bar is a congenial meeting spot, and lively Matróz Disco is next door.

Tisza (☎ 510 850, fax 421 520; W www .hoteltisza.hu; Verseghy park 2; singles/ doubles 11,000/15,000Ft), also on the river's right bank, is Szolnok's old-world hotel built in 1928 over a thermal spring. It has 33 rooms, an attached spa, a decent pub and restaurant and loads of atmosphere. Entrance to the thermal pools, breakfast and parking are included in the room price.

Hozam (☎ 510 530, fax 420 778; Mária utca 25; singles/doubles 16,000/22,000Ft) is a very flash and expensive 11-room hotel on a quiet residential street in the centre. It comes complete with a sauna, Jacuzzi, a lovely restaurant and a chichi club.

Places to Eat
Pronto (Kossuth Lajos út 6; pizzas 380-480Ft) is a cheap, clean pizzeria that's perfect for a quick bite on the run.

Caffè Alexander (Táncsics Mihály utca 15; pizzas 450-1000Ft) is another popular place for pizza near the Szigliget Theatre.

Szapáry (Szapáry út 23; mains from 600Ft) is a studenty place that serves up cheap Hungarian dishes.

Róza (☎ 426 630; Konstantin utca 36; most mains under 1000Ft) is a bit out of the way but serves Hungarian dishes that are better than average and has a quiet courtyard.

Ristorante da Michele (☎ 421 242; Petőfi Sándor utca 6; mains from 800Ft, pizzas from 450Ft) is an upmarket choice near Róza. It has decent pizzas and salads among other things, and is largely nonsmoking.

Borlovag (Wine Knight; Baross Gábor út 6; mains 1000-2000Ft) is a medieval-themed

6000Ft; camping open May-Sept). There is an adjoining 40-room motel that offers single rooms for 5000Ft and doubles for 5600Ft; and dormitory accommodation in rooms with up to three beds for 1600Ft per person.

Private Rooms & Hostel Ibusz can organise a private room for 2000Ft to 3000Ft for a double and 4000Ft to 6000Ft for an apartment.

Tourist Centre (Turistkai Központ; ☎ 424 705, fax 424 335; e turisztkaikozpont@szol nex.hu; bed in 6-bed cottage per person 700ft, triples/quads per person 1500Ft), while not very conveniently located at the western end of Tisza Park, is a good deal, with triples and quads in bungalows. The eight little cottages with six beds are available mid-May to mid-September only.

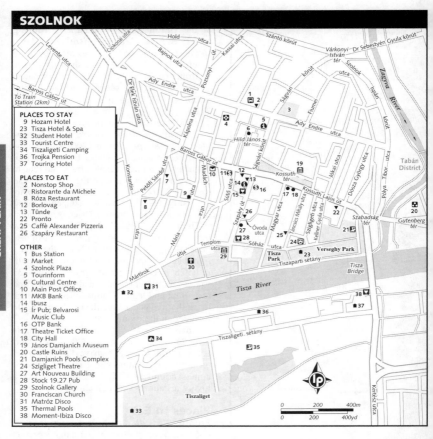

SZOLNOK

PLACES TO STAY
9 Hozam Hotel
23 Tisza Hotel & Spa
32 Student Hotel
33 Tourist Centre
34 Tiszaligeti Camping
36 Trojka Pension
37 Touring Hotel

PLACES TO EAT
2 Nonstop Shop
7 Ristorante da Michele
8 Róza Restaurant
12 Borlovag
13 Tünde
22 Pronto
25 Caffè Alexander Pizzeria
26 Szapáry Restaurant

OTHER
1 Bus Station
3 Market
4 Szolnok Plaza
5 Tourinform
6 Cultural Centre
10 Main Post Office
11 MKB Bank
14 Ibusz
15 Ír Pub; Belvarosi
   Music Club
16 OTP Bank
17 Theatre Ticket Office
18 City Hall
19 János Damjanich Museum
20 Castle Ruins
21 Damjanich Pools Complex
24 Szigliget Theatre
27 Art Nouveau Building
28 Stock 19.27 Pub
29 Szolnok Gallery
30 Franciscan Church
31 Matróz Disco
35 Thermal Pools
38 Moment-Ibiza Disco

pub-restaurant, complete with a knight in shining armour guarding the entrance.

The garden of the **Tisza hotel restaurant** (☎ 510 850; Verseghy park 2; mains 1000-1500Ft) is the most pleasant spot in town for a meal on a warm summer night, watching the crowds stroll along the river walk.

Tünde (Szapáry út 28; ice cream from 60Ft), taking up the ground floor of a decorative Art Nouveau building, is a good place for ice cream and cake.

There's a **nonstop shop** by the bus station on Ady Endre utca, and a **Spar supermarket** and **food hall** in the Szolnok Plaza nearby.

Entertainment

City Cultural Centre (☎ 514 569; Hild János tér 1), near Tourinform, can tell you whether there are concerts on at the **Franciscan church** or whether Szolnok's celebrated symphony orchestra or Béla Bartók Chamber Choir are performing.

Szigliget Theatre (Szigligeti színház; Tisza park 1), across from the Tisza hotel and one of the most attractive theatres in provincial Hungary, was at the forefront of drama in Hungary in the 1970s and '80s and was the first in Eastern Europe to stage Dr Zhivago (1988) – pretty daring at the time. Tickets are available at the **box office** (☎ 422 902; Kossuth tér 17-23; open 9am-1pm & 2pm-5pm Mon-Fri).

Szapáry út has a couple of popular pubs and clubs worth checking out. **Ír Pub** and **Belvarosi Music Club** share the building at No 24, and the strangely named **Stock 19.27 Pub** is closer to the river at No 7.

The **Moment-Ibiza** *(Tiszaligeti sétány 1)* disco next to the Touring hotel and the **Matróz** *(Tiszaparti sétány 7)* rage till the wee hours over the weekend. For up-to-date entertainment information, check the listings in the freebie biweekly *Szolnoki Est*.

Getting There & Away
Many buses run to towns around Hungary, including Jászberény (eight daily), Kecskemét (seven), Budapest (one), Baja (one), Gyula (one), Kunszentmárton (four), Szeged (six), Gyöngyös (five), Eger (four), Tiszafüred (three), Karcag (one) and Veszprém (one).

Szolnok has excellent rail service: you can travel to/from Budapest, Debrecen, Nyíregyháza, Békéscsaba, Sofia, Bucharest and dozens of points in between without changing. (For Miskolc, change at Hatvan; Cegléd is where you transfer for Kecskemét and Szeged.)

Getting Around
From the train station, bus No 6, 7 or 8 will take you to Kossuth tér. If heading for the Tourist Centre or other accommodation in Tisza Park, take bus No 15.

For a local taxi, dial ☎ 344 111.

JÁSZBERÉNY
☎ 57 • postcode 5100 • pop 30,000
Jászberény was the main political, administrative and economic centre of the Jász (Jazygian)

settlements as early as the 13th century but developed slowly as the group began to die out.

The town's biggest draw has always been the Lehel Horn, which was the symbol of power of the Jazygian chiefs for centuries. Nowadays, say 'Lehel' and most Hungarians will think of the country's largest manufacturer of household appliances, located several kilometres west of the city.

Orientation & Information
The main street is a long 'square' (Lehel vezér tér), which runs almost parallel to the narrow 'city branch' of the Zagyva River. The bus station is a two blocks to the west across the Zagyva on Petőfi tér. The train station is 1.5km southwest at the end of Rákóczi út.

Tourinform *(☎ 406 439, fax 412 163; e jaszbereny@tourinform.hu; Lehel vezér tér 33; open 8am-4.30pm Mon-Fri, 10am-4pm Sat & Sun mid-June–mid-Sept; 8am-4.30pm Mon-Fri mid-Sept–mid-June)* is in the Deryné Cultural Centre. **Ibusz** *(☎ 412 143, fax 412 820; Szövetkezet utca 7a)* is to the southwest.

There's an **OTP bank** *(Lehel vezér tér 28)* and the **main post office** *(Lehel vezér tér 8)* is to the north on the same street.

Things to See & Do
The **Jász Museum**, *(☎ 412 753; Táncsics Mihály utca 5; adult/child 100/50Ft; open 9am-5pm Tues-Sun Apr-Oct; 9am-4pm Tues-Fri,*

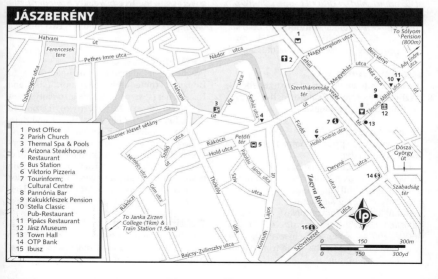

JÁSZBERÉNY

1 Post Office
2 Parish Church
3 Thermal Spa & Pools
4 Arizona Steakhouse Restaurant
5 Bus Station
6 Viktorio Pizzeria
7 Tourinform; Cultural Centre
8 Pannónia Bar
9 Kakukkfészek Pension
10 Stella Classic Pub-Restaurant
11 Pipács Restaurant
12 Jász Museum
13 Town Hall
14 OTP Bank
15 Ibusz

9am-1pm Sat & Sun Nov-Mar), housed in what was once the Jazygian military headquarters, runs the gamut of Jász culture and life – from costumes and woodcarving to language. But all aisles lead to the **Lehel Horn**, an 8th-century Byzantine work carved in ivory. Legend has it that a Magyar leader called Lehel (or Lél) fell captive during the Battle of Augsburg against the united German armies in 955 AD and, just before he was executed, killed the king by striking him on the head with the horn. The alleged murder weapon, richly carved with birds, battle scenes and anatomically correct satyrs, doesn't seem to have suffered any serious damage from the blow to the royal noggin.

The museum also spotlights local sons and daughters who made good, including the watercolourist András Sáros and the 19th-century actress Róza Széppataki Déryné. You've seen Mrs Déry before, though you may not know it. She is forever immortalised in that irritating Herend porcelain figurine you see in antique shops everywhere in Hungary of a woman in a wide organza skirt playing her *lant* (lute) and kissing the air.

Have a look at the fading ceiling frescoes inside the Roman Catholic **parish church** (*plébániatemplom; admission free*) at Szentháromság tér 4; the nave was designed in 1774 by András Mayerhoffer and József Jung, two masters of baroque architecture.

There's a **thermal spa** (☎ 412 108; Hatvani út 5; adult/child 280/200Ft; open 9am-7pm Tues & Thur, 9am-6pm Wed, Fri & Sat, 9am-5pm Sun Feb-Dec) and **outdoor pools** (Hatvani út 5; adult/child 280/200Ft; open 9am-6pm daily May-Aug) west of the Zagyva.

Special Events

If you are in town in August, try to attend the **Jászberény Summer/Csángó Festival**, which has folk dancing and music.

Places to Stay

Ibusz can arrange **private rooms** from around 2000Ft per person.

Janka Zirzen College (☎ 502 405; Rákóczi út 53; dorm beds 1700Ft) has accommodation throughout July and August and at weekends only in spring and autumn.

Kakukkfészek (Cuckoo's Nest; ☎ 412 345; Táncsics Mihály utca 8; singles/doubles 1600/3200Ft), a pension close to the museum and town centre, has nine triple rooms and is a cheap option.

Sólyom Pension (☎ 401 267, fax 406 785; Sólyom út 8; rooms from 5000Ft) is nicer than Kakukkfészek but is about 800m northeast of the centre up Ady Endre utca.

Places to Eat

The **cultural centre** has a cheap fast-food place serving gyros and hamburgers from 200Ft.

Pipács (Táncsics Mihály utca 10; mains around 1000Ft) is a traditional Hungarian restaurant with an inviting garden.

Stella Classic (☎ 400 140; cnr Táncsics Mihály utca & Réz utca; mains around 1200Ft) pub-restaurant has a much more interesting menu than nearby Pipács.

Viktorio Pizzeria (Holló András utca; pizzas 400-1000Ft), around the corner from the cultural centre, has an incredible selection of 40 pizzas to choose from.

Arizona Steakhouse (cnr Rákóczi út & Serház utca; most mains under 1000Ft), close to the bus station, has plenty of outdoor seating and is a popular place with Jászberény's young bloods.

The restaurant at the **Sólyom** (mains around 1000Ft) pension is good value and packs in the locals at midday.

Entertainment

Déryné Cultural Centre (☎ 406 439; Lehel vezér tér 33) is your best source of information. Jászberény receives a small amount of coverage in the free biweekly *Szolnoki Est*.

Pannónia (Táncsics Mihály utca 4; open until 5am Fri-Sat) bar is a disco two nights a week.

Getting There & Away

Frequent bus departures include those to Budapest (nine daily), Szolnok (six) and Kecskemét (seven). There are also daily buses to Szeged (three), Miskolc (two), Tiszafüred (one), Eger (five), Mátraháza (three), and Baja, Debrecen, Kalocsa and Karcag (one each).

Jászberény lies approximately halfway between Hatvan and Szolnok on the railway line. These two cities are on Hungary's two main trunks, and virtually all main cities in the east are accessible from one or the other. Both Hatvan and Szolnok have direct links to Budapest.

Getting Around

Bus Nos 2 and 4 connect the train station with the bus terminus, from where you can walk to the centre of town.

TISZAFÜRED
☎ 59 • postcode 5350 • pop 15,400

Tiszafüred was a rather sleepy town on the Tisza River until the early 1980s when the river was dammed and a reservoir opened up more than 125 sq km of lakes to holiday-makers. While hardly the 'Lake Balaton of the Great Plain' as the tourist brochures say (it's about one-fifth the size and has none of the facilities or life of its big sister), Lake Tisza (Tisza-tó) and its primary resort, Tiszafüred, offer swimmers and boating enthusiasts a break before continuing on to the Hortobágy region, 30km to the east, and Debrecen, or Eger and the Northern Uplands. The lake can get very crowded in the high season.

Orientation & Information
Tiszafüred lies at the northeast end of Lake Tisza. From the bus and train stations opposite one another on Vasút utca, walk 10 or 15 minutes west and then southwest to the beach and camp sites. To reach the centre of town, follow Baross Gábor utca and then Fő út south for about a kilometre.

Tourinform (☎/fax 511 123; e tiszafured@tourinform.hu; Fürdő út 21; open 8am-7pm Mon-Fri, 8am-5pm Sat & Sun mid-June–mid-Sept; 8am-4pm Mon-Fri mid-Sept–mid-June) has an office between the lake and the town's thermal spa. There is an Ibusz (☎ 511 005, fax 352 047; Fő út 30) office in the centre.

Close by are the OTP bank (Piac út 3) behind Fő út and post office (Fő út 14).

Things to See
Tiszafüred is essentially a resort town, but there are a couple of interesting sights. The Pál Kiss Museum (☎ 352 106; Tariczky sétány 6; adult/child 100/50Ft; open 9am-noon, 1pm-5pm Tues-Sun) is in a beautiful old manor house (1840) south of the city's thermal baths. Most of the collection is given over to the everyday lives of Tisza fisherfolk and the work of local potters.

The area south of Szőlősi út is chock-full of traditional houses with thatched roofs and orderly little flower and vegetable gardens – a nice respite from the hubbub of the beach. One of them, the Gáspár Nyúzó House (Nyúzó Gáspár Fazekas Tájház; Malom utca 12; adult/child 75/50Ft; open 9am-noon, 2pm-5pm Tues-Sun May-Oct), is a former potter's residence and contains antique potting wheels, drying racks, furniture and plates

in the light primary colours, and patterns of stars, and birds and flowers unique to the region. Just southwest of the village house is the working pottery of Imre Szücs (☎ 351 483; Belsőkertsor út 4/a). His pottery, with its highly decorative and colourful markings, is in stark contrast to the dark and sombre creations from Mohács or Nádudvar.

Activities
If the lake is too cold for you, Tiszafüred's thermal spa, at the northern end of town on Poroszlói út, has four open-air pools (open 7.30am-7pm daily May-Sept), as well as a sauna (open 8am-7pm mid-Mar–mid-Nov) and a wide range of medical services. Admission to the pools costs 250/210Ft (adult/child); to the sauna it's 250/200Ft.

Horgász and Fortuna camp sites and the Hableány hotel (see Places to Eat) rent out bicycles and mountain bikes for around 1000/200Ft a day/hour. Fortuna and Hableány also rent canoes/paddle boats/motorboats for 1200/1000/4000Ft a day. There's an extra charge of 1500Ft for fuel with motorboat rentals. If you prefer to let someone else do the driving while on the water, contact Kormorán boat harbour (☎ 350 350) or Hableány, both in Tiszaörvény, for information about boat tours (prices range from 3000Ft to 6400Ft for a day trip).

There's horse riding available for 2000Ft to 3000Ft per hour at the Gulyás farm (☎ 351 814) in Tiszaörvény near the Hableány hotel.

Places to Stay
There are 11 camp sites in and around Tiszafüred, open from as early as April and till as late as October.

Termál Camping (☎ 352 911, fax 351 228; Húszöles út 2; camping per person 630-720Ft, per tent 480-560Ft, bungalows 6300-7900Ft) is a very friendly, four-star place unattractively located on a busy road southwest of the thermal spa. It has bungalows for four people and clay tennis courts. Camping costs vary depending on the season.

Horgász Camping (☎/fax 352 619; Holt-Tisza part; camping per adult/child/tent 500/400/400Ft, doubles/triples/quads 3500/4200/4900Ft) is a lakeside place with snack stalls, a restaurant, recreational facilities (including tennis) and holiday homes accommodating two/three/four people with shared showers. The public beach is a short distance to the north.

GREAT PLAIN

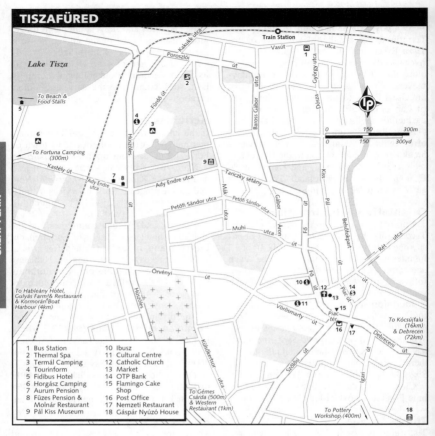

TISZAFÜRED

1 Bus Station	10 Ibusz
2 Thermal Spa	11 Cultural Centre
3 Termál Camping	12 Catholic Church
4 Tourinform	13 Market
5 Fidibus Hotel	14 OTP Bank
6 Horgász Camping	15 Flamingo Cake
7 Aurum Pension	Shop
8 Füzes Pension &	16 Post Office
Molnár Restaurant	17 Nemzeti Restaurant
9 Pál Kiss Museum	18 Gáspár Nyúzó House

Fortuna Camping (☎/fax 351 913; Holt-Tisza part; camping per adult/child/tent from 450/400/550Ft, bungalows from 3000Ft), to the southwest, is quite secluded and within easy walking distance of the lake. The bungalows are for four people.

Ibusz has **private rooms** available from 1500Ft to 2000Ft per person.

Fidibus (☎/fax 351 818; rooms from 4000Ft; open mid-Apr–mid-Sept) is a 10-room hotel on a ship moored near the public beach (szabad strand).

Füzes (☎/fax 351 854; Húszöles út 31b; singles/doubles 3500/5460Ft) is a comfortable and friendly 10-room pension, south of the camp sites. All the rooms have shower and TV, and there's a popular restaurant and busy local bar next door.

Aurum (☎ 351 338; Ady Endre utca 29; singles/doubles 6000/6600Ft) pension is a flashier, more expensive place, almost next door to Füzes.

Places to Eat
There are plenty of **food stalls** serving gyros, pizza, lángos (deep-fried dough with toppings) etc at the public beach and the camp sites.

Nemzeti (☎ 352 349; Fő út 8; mains around 1000Ft) is a restaurant just beyond Piac tér. It's open late only in summer (normally only 10am-3pm Mon-Fri) and has Gypsy music.

Molnár (mains 1000-1500Ft) is the restaurant next to the Füzes pension (see Places to Stay), and has a good fish selection. A table on the breezy terrace is a better choice than Nemzeti.

Western (☎ *350 162; Húszöles út 163; mains 1000-2000Ft*) is new kid on the block, about 1km south of the town centre. It specialises in fish, game and steak dishes.

Hableány (☎ *353 333; Hunyadi utca 2; mains 1000-2000Ft*) is, according to local people, the best restaurant in the Tiszafüred area, but you'll need to have your own wheels: it's in a hotel Tiszaörvény, about 4km to the southwest.

Gémes csárda (*Húszöles út 80a; mains from 1000Ft*) is another locally recommended place but it too is a fair way out.

Flamingo on Fő út, which is a combination '*cukrászda* and *bronzárium*' opposite the start of Szőlősi út, does some excellent baking (well, of cakes – we don't know about the quality of the tanning).

Entertainment
The best place for a lively evening in summer is down by the camp sites and food stalls lining the lakefront, or on **Fidibus**, where there is an open-air bar on top of the 'boatel' which is a great place for a sundowner.

Getting There & Away
Up to 10 buses daily link Tiszafüred with Abádszalók, another popular lake resort to the south. Other destinations served daily include Budapest (four buses daily), Szolnok (three to five), Karcag (two), Eger (five), Szeged and Jászberény (two each), Miskolc and Debrecen (at least three each) and Hajdúszoboszló (one).

Tiszafüred is on the railway line linking Füzesabony (from where you can carry on to Eger or Miskolc), and Debrecen, which passes through the Hortobágy region. Another line heads south to Karcag (the transfer point from Szolnok and once the seat of the Kun chiefs).

Eastern Plain

The Eastern Plain (Kelet-Alföld) includes Debrecen, the towns of the Hajdúság region, and the Hortobágy, the birthplace of the *puszta* (Great Plain) legend. This part of the Great Plain was important for centuries as it was on the Salt Road – the route taken by traders in that precious commodity – from Transylvania via the Tisza River and across the Eastern Plain by bullock cart to the wealthy city of Debrecen. When the trees were chopped down and the river was regulated, the water in the soil evaporated, turning the region into a vast, saline grassland suitable only for grazing. The myth of the lonely *pásztor* (shepherd) in billowy trousers, the wayside *csárdas* (inns) and Gypsy violinists was born – to be kept alive in literature, fine art and the imagination of the Hungarian people.

DEBRECEN
☎ 52 • postcode 4000 • pop 213,700

Debrecen, Hungary's second-largest city, has been synonymous with wealth and conservatism since the 16th century. That may not be immediately apparent on Piac utca on a Saturday night as you collide with drunks and kids on inline skates, but you don't have to go far to find either.

The area around Debrecen had been settled since the earliest times, and when the Magyars arrived late in the 9th century they found a colony of Slovaks here who called the region Dobre Zliem for its 'good soil'. Debrecen's wealth, based on salt, the fur trade and cattle-raising, grew steadily through the Middle Ages and increased during the Turkish occupation; the city kept all sides happy by paying tribute to the Ottomans, the Habsburgs and Transylvanian princes at the same time.

Most of the large estates on the Eastern Plain were owned by Debrecen's independent-minded burghers, who had converted to Protestantism in the mid-16th century. These *cívis* (from the Latin for 'citizen') lived in the city while the peasants raised horses and cattle in the Hortobágy. *Hajdúk* (from *hajt*, 'to drive') – landless peasants who would later play an important role in the wars with the Habsburgs as Heyduck mercenaries (see the boxed text 'The Heyducks') – drove the animals on the hoof westward to markets as far as France.

Debrecen played a pivotal role in the 1848–49 War of Independence and, late in the 19th century and early in the 20th, it experienced a major building boom. Today it is the capital of Hajdú-Bihar County and an important university city.

Orientation
Debrecen is an easy city to negotiate. A ring road, built on the city's original earthen walls, encloses the Belváros (Inner Town). This is bisected by Piac utca, which runs northward from the train station at Petőfi tér to Kálvin tér, site of the Great Church and Debrecen's centre. With the exception of Nagyerdei Park,

GREAT PLAIN

The Heyducks

The Hajdúság region was settled in the 15th century predominantly by the *hajdúk* (English: Heyducks or Haiduks), a community of Magyar and Slav drovers and brigands turned mercenaries and renowned both for their skill in battle and their bisexuality. When the Heyducks helped István Bocskai (1557–1606), prince of Transylvania, rout the Habsburg forces at Álmosd, southeast of Debrecen, in 1604, they were raised to the rank of nobility, and some 10,000 were granted land – as much to keep the ferocious, randy brigands in check as to reward them.

The Heyducks built towns with walled fortresses around the region. Many of the streets in today's Hajdú towns trace the concentric circles of these walls, the outermost forming ring roads. The Hajdúság continued as a special administrative district until 1876, when it was incorporated into Hajdú-Bihar County and the Heyducks' privileges were terminated.

the recreational 'Big Forest Park' some 3km north, almost all of Debrecen's attractions are within easy walking distance of Kálvin tér.

The bus station is on Külső-Vásártér, the 'outer marketplace' at the western end of Széchenyi utca.

Information

The very helpful **Tourinform** (☎ 412 250, fax 535 323; e debrecen@tourinform.hu; Piac utca 20; open 8am-8pm daily mid-May–Sept; 9am-5pm Mon-Fri Sept-May) office is in the town hall. **Hajdútourist** (☎ 415 588, fax 319 616; e hajdutourist@debrecen.com; Kálvin tér 2a; open 8am-5pm Mon-Fri, 8am-noon Sat) is at the entrance to the Udvarház shopping mall across from the Great Church while **Ibusz** (☎ 415 555, fax 410 756; Révész tér 2; open 8am-5pm Mon-Fri, 8am-noon or 12.30pm Sat) is near the Little Church.

There's an **OTP bank** (Hatvan utca) opposite the **main post office** (Hatvan utca 5-9). You'll find other ATMs at Piac utca 16 and 45. **Hajdú Net Cafe** (☎ 536 724; Kossuth utca 8; open 9am-midnight daily) has Internet access for 300Ft to 400Ft an hour. The **Csokonai Bookshop** (Piac utca 45) has good foreign language and map selections.

Things to See

The yellow neoclassical **Great Church** (☎ 412 694; Kálvin tér; adult/child 60/30Ft; open 9am-4pm Mon-Fri, 9am-1pm Sat, noon-4pm Sun), built in 1821, has become so synonymous with Debrecen that mirages of its twin clock towers were reportedly seen on the Great Plain early in the last century. Accommodating some 3000 people, the Nagytemplom is Hungary's largest Protestant church, and it was here that Lajos Kossuth read the Declaration of Independence from Austria on 14 April 1849. Don't miss the magnificent organ in the loft behind the pulpit.

North of the church stands the **Reformed College** (Református Kollégium; ☎ 414 744; Kálvin tér 16; adult/child 160/80Ft, guided tours 2000Ft; open 9am-5pm Tues-Sat, 9am-1pm Sun), built in 1816, the site of a prestigious secondary school and theological college since the Middle Ages. Downstairs, there are exhibits on religious art and sacred objects (including a 17th-century chalice made from a coconut) and on the school's history; be sure to visit the 650,000-volume **library** and the **oratory**, where the breakaway National Assembly met in 1849 and Hungary's postwar provisional government was declared in 1944.

Folklore exhibits at the **Déri Museum** (☎ 322 207; Déri tér 1; adult/child 500/ 300Ft; open 10am-6pm Tues-Sun Apr-Oct; 10am-4pm Tues-Sun Nov-Mar), a short walk west of the Reformed College, offer excellent insights into life on the *puszta* and among the bourgeois citizens of Debrecen up to the 19th century. Mihály Munkácsy's mythical interpretations of the Hortobágy and his *Christ's Passion* take pride of place in a separate art gallery. The museum's entrance is flanked by four superb bronzes by sculptor Ferenc Medgyessy, a local boy who merits his own **Medgyessy Museum** (☎ 413 572; Péterfia utca 28; adult/child 100/50Ft; open 10am-4pm Tues-Sun) in an old burgher house to the northeast.

Just walking along Piac utca and down some of the side streets, with their array of neoclassical, baroque and Art Nouveau buildings, is a treat. Kossuth utca and its continuation, Széchenyi utca, where the baroque Calvinist **Little Church** (Kistemplom; ☎ 342 872; Révész tér 2; admission free; open daily), completed in 1726, stands with its bastion-like tower, is especially interesting. The **Status**

Que Conservative Synagogue *(Kápolnási utca)*, just south of Bajcsy-Zsilinszky utca, dates from 1909 and is worth a look if the caretaker will let you in. The derelict **Orthodox synagogue** *(Pászti utca 6)* is nearby.

Tímárház *(☎ 368 013; Nagy Gál István utca 6; open 10am-6pm Tues-Fri, 10am-2pm Sat)* is a folk-craft centre and workshop, where embroiderers, basket weavers, carvers and so on do their stuff in rotation.

Definitely worth the trip is the colourful **flea market** near the large sports complex on Vágóhíd utca, served by bus Nos 9, 15, 30 and 30/a from the train station. In the morning it attracts a motley group of Ukrainians, Poles, Romanians, Roma and Hungarians from Transylvania who hawk everything from socks to live animals.

Activities

The city's Nagyerdei Park offers boating and walks along leafy trails, but the main attraction here is the **thermal bath** *(☎ 514 100)*, a complex offering a half-dozen indoor and open-air pools of brownish mineral and fresh water, sauna and every type of therapy imaginable. There is an **indoor spa** *(open 8am-4pm Mon-Fri May-Aug; 6am-7pm Mon-Fri Sept-Apr)* and **outdoor pools** *(open 6am-7pm daily May-Sept)*. Admission to the complex costs 500/430Ft (adult/child).

If you want to see more of the great outdoors, head for the **Erdőpuszta** (Puszta Forest), a protected area of pine and acacia forests, lakes and trails a few kilometres to the east and southeast of Debrecen. Bánk, the centre, has a splendid **arboretum** *(Fancsika*

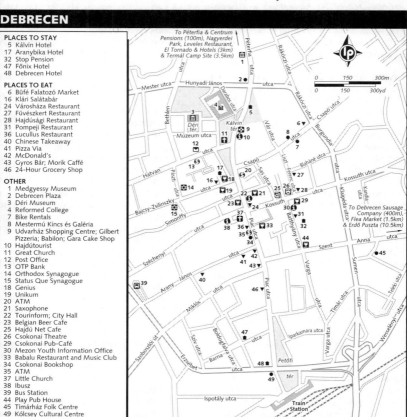

DEBRECEN

PLACES TO STAY
5 Kálvin Hotel
17 Aranybika Hotel
32 Stop Pension
47 Főnix Hotel
48 Debrecen Hotel

PLACES TO EAT
6 Büfé Falatozó Market
16 Klári Salátabár
24 Városháza Restaurant
27 Füvészkert Restaurant
28 Hajdúsági Restaurant
31 Pompeji Restaurant
36 Lucullus Restaurant
40 Chinese Takeaway
41 Pizza Via
42 McDonald's
43 Gyros Bár; Morik Caffé
46 24-Hour Grocery Shop

OTHER
1 Medgyessy Museum
2 Debrecen Plaza
3 Déri Museum
4 Reformed College
7 Bike Rentals
8 Mestermű Kincs és Galéria
9 Udvarház Shopping Centre; Gilbert
    Pizzeria; Babilon; Gara Cake Shop
10 Hajdútourist
11 Great Church
12 Post Office
13 OTP Bank
14 Orthodox Synagogue
15 Status Que Synagogue
18 Genius
19 Unikum
20 ATM
21 Saxophone
22 Tourinform; City Hall
23 Belgian Beer Cafe
25 Hajdú Net Cafe
26 Csokonai Theatre
29 Csokonai Pub-Café
30 Mezon Youth Information Office
33 Babalu Restaurant and Music Club
34 Csokonai Bookshop
35 ATM
37 Little Church
38 Ibusz
39 Bus Station
44 Play Pub House
45 Tímárház Folk Centre
49 Kölcsey Cultural Centre

To Péterfia & Centrum Pensions (100m), Nagyerdei Park, Leveles Restaurant, El Tornado & Hotels (3km) & Termál Camp Site (3.5km)

To Debrecen Sausage Company (400m), Flea Market (1.5km) & Erdő Puszta (10.5km)

Train Station

GREAT PLAIN

utca 93a) and there are **boats for rent** on
Vekeri Lake (Vekeri-tó).

You can rent bikes from the **bicycle shop**
(☎ 456 220; Csapó utca 19; open 9am-5pm
Mon-Fri, 9am-1pm Sat) in Debrecen for
700Ft a day.

Special Events
Annual events to watch out for include the
Hajdúság Carnival in February, the **Spring
Festival** of performing arts in March, **Jazz
Days** in June and the famous **Floral Carnival**
held around 20 August.

Places to Stay
Camping The best of the three camp sites in
Debrecen is **Termál** (☎/fax 412 456; Nagyerdei körút 102; camping per adult/child/
tent 500/260/550Ft, bungalows with/with-
out shower from 4400/2800Ft; open May-
Sept), northeast of Nagyerdei Park. Tents are
available for rent, and bungalows here can
accommodate four people.

Private Rooms & Hostels Hajdútourist
and Ibusz can arrange **private rooms** from
2000Ft per person and apartments for four
people from 6000Ft. With so many univer-
sities and colleges in town, there's plenty of
dormitory accommodation in summer (and
sometimes at the weekend, year-round), costing under 1000Ft per person. Tourinform can
provide you with a list.

Pensions Not far north of the centre is
Péterfia (☎/fax 423 582; Péterfia utca 37b;
rooms 6400Ft), a 20-room establishment in a
charming row house.

Centrum (☎ 416 193, fax 442 843; e cen
trumpanzio@axelero.hu; Péterfia utca 37a;
singles 6500Ft, doubles 6900-7600Ft) is a
flashier and more expensive 20-room place
next door to Péterfia, complete with private
garden.

Stop (☎ 420 301; Batthyány utca 18;
singles/doubles 5400/6400Ft), a more central
pension with 14 rooms, is a friendly place in
a courtyard off a pedestrians-only street
(though there is parking at the back).

Hotels The **Debrecen** (☎/fax 410 111; Petőfi
tér 9; singles/doubles from 2800/3500Ft) is a
cheap 85-room hotel opposite the train station
that's more for resident students and workers,
but there are always a few rooms spare.

Főnix (☎ 413 355, fax 413 054; Barna utca
17; singles/doubles 5100/6500Ft) is a better
choice than Debrecen, with 52 rooms on a
fairly quiet side street northwest of Petőfi tér.

Nagyerdő (☎ 410 588, fax 319 739; e re
serve@hotelnagyerdo.hunguesthotels.hu; Pallagi út 5; singles/doubles from €40/54) is a
huge, 100-room spa hotel in Nagyerdei Park.

Termál (☎ 514 111; fax 311 730; w www
.termalhotel.hu; Nagyerdei park 1; singles/
doubles €69/79) has 96 rooms and rates here
include entry to the baths and breakfast.

Aranybika (☎ 508 600, fax 421 834;
e aranybika@civishotels.hu; Piac utca 11-
15; singles 9250-17,250Ft, doubles 11,000-
21,500Ft) is a landmark Art Nouveau hotel
with 200 very different rooms and is still *the*
place to stay in Debrecen. Rates at the Aranybika vary depending on whether you stay in
the charming old wing or garish new building, and on the season.

Kálvin (☎/fax 418 522; e kalvin@civisho
tels.hu; Kálvin tér 4; singles 11,000-12,500Ft,
doubles 13,000-15,500Ft) is a modern, flashy
62-room place near the Great Church. Lower-
priced rooms face busy Kálvin tér.

Places to Eat
Büfé Falatozó (Csapó utca; 100g for 180Ft),
in the fruit and vegetable market, has more
sausage varieties than you can shake a long
roll of meat at. Try the inviting liver and blood
sausage; as they say, 'When in Rome…'

Gyros Bár (cnr Piac utca & Miklós utca;
gyros from 390Ft) is excellent value for hamburgers and gyros and has outdoor seating.

Babilon (Kálvin tér 5; gyros from 360Ft), in
the Udvarház shopping mall, is another popular gyros place.

Gilbert (Kálvin tér 5; pizzas 400-800Ft)
pizzeria, also in the Udvarház shopping mall,
has people lining up for the pizza and pasta.

Hajdúsági (cnr Liszt Ferenc utca & Kossuth utca; lunch set menu 900Ft) is a rather
bland place but its ever-changing set menu is
a magnet to what seems like half the city
workers in Debrecen.

Füvészkert (Liszt Ferenc utca 11; mains
700-1500Ft) is also a lunch-time favourite,
which has Hungarian dishes, a salad bar and
a cake/ice cream shop.

Városháza (☎ 444 767; Piac utca 20;
mains 1000-1700Ft) may look a little tacky
but the local cuisine at this cellar restaurant
is top-notch.

Pizza Via (☎ 310 800; Arany János utca 2; pizzas from 500Ft), a bright, modern pizzeria on the 1st floor, has preferable surroundings to Gilbert.

The **Chinese takeaway** (☎ 588 479; Arany János utca 28; mains 400-600Ft; open until 10pm) is a genuine takeaway place and good for Asian food.

Klári Salátabár (Bajcsy-Zsilinszky utca; mains around 600Ft; open 9am-7pm Mon-Fri) is a rare breed indeed in provincial Hungary – it caters to vegetarians.

Pompeji (416 988; Batthyány utca 4; mains from 800Ft) is a flashy, cluttered restaurant with fine Italian dishes.

Lucullus (☎ 418 513; Piac utca 41; mains 1000-1700Ft) cellar restaurant is consistently good and popular with locals.

Leveles (Leafy; ☎ 324 482; Medgyessy sétány; mains 900-1700Ft) is close to the thermal pools in a quiet park. Its German/Hungarian menu comes locally recommended, as does its large, outdoor patio.

Gara (Kálvin tér; ice cream from 55Ft; open 9am-6pm daily) in the Udvarház mall has some of the best cakes and ice cream (made with real fruit and loads of it) outside Budapest.

Morik Caffè (cnr Piac utca & Miklós utca) harks back to a bygone era; it's a place for serious coffee drinkers where the waitresses wear blue frocks and frilly white bonnets.

There's a **24-hour grocery shop** (Piac utca 75) within walking distance of the train station and the bustling covered **fruit & vegetable market** in Csapó utca is open daily.

Entertainment

Debrecen prides itself on its cultural life; check with staff at the delightful **Csokonai Theatre** (☎ 455 075; Kossuth utca 10) or the **Kölcsey Cultural Centre** (☎ 525 270; Petőfi tér 10), near the train station, for event schedules.

Bartók Hall (Bartók terem) in the Aranybika hotel, sometimes holds concerts, as does the **Great Church**.

Mezon youth information office (☎ 415 498; Batthyány utca 2b; open 10am-6pm Mon-Fri, 9am-1pm Sat) can fill you in on the popular music scene, or you can check the listings in the biweekly entertainment freebie Debreceni Est.

Csokonai (Kossuth utca 21) is a cellar pub-café attracting a young crowd and serving decent food to boot.

Play Pub House (Batthyány utca 24-26) on a pedestrians-only street has outside tables that are very pleasant in the warm weather.

Unikum (Bajcsy-Zsilinszky utca 2) is a simple, cheap cellar-pub that attracts plenty of students.

Saxophone (Piac utca 18) is far more upmarket than Unikum and caters to a more fashionable and affluent crowd.

Babalu Restaurant and Music Club (☎ 536 414; Piac utca 26a; open noon-midnight) is one of the better spots to catch some live jazz.

Belgian Beer Cafe (Piac utca 29) is proof again that Belgian beer is taking over the world; plenty of locals can be seen swilling litres of the amber liquid here every night.

Popular clubs include **Genius** (open 10pm-4am), in the Aranybika hotel, which often has live music and English-speaking students, and **El Tornado** (Pallagi út 2; open 5pm-4am), another popular student hangout, near the thermal baths.

Shopping

You can't leave the city without buying – or at least trying – some of the famous Debrecen sausage available at butcher shops (eg, on Kossuth utca) and grocery stores everywhere; the market is also a good place to procure some. If that's not enough to satisfy your taste buds, tours are available at **Debrecen Sausage Company** (☎ 437 531; Vágóhid utca 9) itself; call ahead to make an appointment.

There's a lovely antique-cum-curio shop called **Mestermü Kincs és Galéria** (Csapó utca 22) near the market.

Getting There & Away

From Debrecen you can catch a direct bus to any of the following destinations: Bánk (five daily), Békéscsaba (10), Berettyóújfalu (hourly), Eger (five), Gyöngyös (two), Gyula (three), Hajdúböszörmény (half-hourly), Hajdúnánás (10), Hajdúszoboszló (half-hourly), Hódmezővásárhely and Szeged (three), Kecskemét (one), Mátészalka (two), Miskolc (hourly), Nádudvar (seven), Nyírbátor and Nyíregyháza (three each), Sátoraljaújhely (two), Szarvas (two) and Tokaj (two).

Foreign destinations served by bus include Košice (Kassa) in Slovakia at 7am Monday to Thursday and, in Romania, Baia Mare (Nagybánya) at 5.30am on Friday and Oradea (Nagyvárad) at 6.30am on Tuesday and Thursday and at 5am on Saturday.

GREAT PLAIN

Debrecen is served by around 20 trains daily from Nyugati (and sometimes Keleti) station in Budapest via Szolnok, including eight 2½-hour expresses. Cities to the north and northwest – Nyíregyháza, Tokaj and Miskolc – can be reached most effectively by train. For Eger, take the train to Füzesabony and change. For points south, use the bus or a bus/train combination.

Daily international departures from Debrecen to Satu Mare and Baia Mare in Romania leave at 11.45am and 5.31pm.

Getting Around

Tram No 1 – the only line in town – is ideal both for transport and sightseeing. From the train station, it runs north along Piac utca to Kálvin tér and then carries on to Nagyerdei Park, where it loops around for the same trip southward.

Most other city transport can be caught at the southern end of Petőfi tér. Bus Nos 12 and 19 link the train and bus stations.

For a local taxi, you can ring ☎ 444 444 or ☎ 444 555.

HORTOBÁGY

☎ 52 • postcode 4071 • pop 1800

This village, some 40km west of Debrecen, is the centre of the Hortobágy region, once celebrated for its sturdy cowboys, inns and Gypsy bands. But you'll want to come here to ex-

plore the 81,000-hectare Hortobágy National Park and wildlife preserve – home to hundreds of birds as well as plant species that are usually found only by the sea. Its importance as a cultural landscape has not just been noted in Hungary – in 1999 Unesco promoted the park to a world heritage site.

It's true that the Hortobágy has been milked by the Hungarian tourism industry for everything it's worth, and the stage-managed horse shows, costumed *csikósok* and tacky gewgaws on sale are all over the top. Still, dark clouds appearing out of nowhere to cover a blazing sun and the possibility of spotting a mirage may have you dreaming of a different Hortobágy – the mythical one that only ever existed in paintings, poems and the imaginations of the people.

Orientation & Information

Buses – as few as there are – stop on the main road (route No 33) near the village centre or on Petőfi tér near the shopping centre; the train station is to the northeast at the end of Kossuth utca. **Tourinform** (☎/fax 589 321; e hortobagy@tourinform.hu; Petőfi tér 1; open 8am-6pm Mon-Fri, 9am-5pm Sat & Sun May–mid-Sept; 8am-4pm Mon-Fri mid-Sept–May) has an office in the Herder Museum. The national park's **head office** (☎ 529 935; Sumen utca 2; w www.hnp.hu; open 8am-1pm Mon-Thur, 8am-noon Fri) is in Debrecen.

There's an **OTP bank** in the shopping complex and the **post office** (Kossuth utca 2) is opposite the Hortobágy inn.

Hortobágy National Park

With its varied terrain and water sources, the park (admission to restricted area 800Ft) offers some of the best bird-watching in Europe. Indeed, some 344 species (of the continent's estimated 400) have been spotted here in the past 20 years, including many types of grebes, herons, shrikes, egrets, spoonbills, storks, kites, warblers and eagles. The great bustard, one of the world's largest birds, standing a metre high and weighing in at 20kg, has its own reserve with limited access to two-legged mammals (see 'The Birds of Hungary' boxed text in the Facts about Hungary chapter).

Visitor passes, available from Tourinform, allow entry to four restricted areas of the park. To see the best parts of the park, though – the closed areas north of route No 33 and the

HORTOBÁGY

1 Hortobágy Inn
2 Post Office
3 Shopping Centre; OTP; Pizza Sfera
4 Bus Stop
5 Hortobágy Gallery
6 Hortobágy Csárda
7 Tourinform; Herder Museum
8 Round Theatre
9 Puszta Camping

Móricz Zsigmond utca

Arany János utca

Erdei F. utca

körut

To Train Station (200m)

To Sándor Petőfi Collége (400m)

Kossuth utca

Petőfi tér

To Máta & Hortobágy Club (2km)

Hortobágy

Nine-Hole Bridge

River

33

To Czinege János utca (250m), Hortobágy Hotel (2km) & Debrecen (39km)

To Pásztortanya Inn & Macskatelek Airfield (3km), Öregtavi Guesthouse (7km) & Tiszafüred (36km)

To Rare Breed Park (800m)

0   100   200m
0   100   200yd

saline swamplands south of it – you must have a guide and travel by horse, carriage or special 4WD. Contact **Tourinform, Aquila Nature Tours** (☎/fax 456 744; W www.hungary bird.hu; Péterfia utca 46), a Debrecen-based travel agency with specialised bird-watching and nature tours, or **Birdwatching Hortobágy** (☎/fax 561 101; W www.birdwatching.hu; Bocskai tér 2) a group of local tour guides and interpreters in Hajdúböszörmény. Trips from three to six hours cost around 24,000Ft for up to three persons; day trips cost around 28,000Ft, or 16,000Ft per person if less than three people. Tours lasting a few days cost 12,000Ft per day for a guide, 12,000Ft for an interpreter and 70Ft per kilometre.

The national park office offers infrequent tours (adult/child 600/300Ft) of the park – call ☎ 529 935 for times, dates and details. Otherwise contact Tourinform for information on private companies offering a variety of excursions (adult/child 1700/800Ft) into the *puszta*.

Other Attractions

The **Nine-Hole Bridge** (Kilence-lyukú híd), built in 1833 and spanning the marshy Hortobágy River, is the longest stone bridge (and certainly the most sketched, painted and photographed) in Hungary. Just before it stands the **Hortobágyi Csárda** (Petőfi tér 2) one of the original eating houses (1781) used by salt traders on their way from the Tisza River to Debrecen. The going was rough along the muddy trails, and bullock carts could only cover about 12km a day. That's why you'll still find inns spaced at those intervals today at, for example, Látókép, Nagyhegyes and Hortobágy. The inns provided itinerant Roma fiddlers with employment, though they did not originally live in this part of Hungary. Gypsy music and *csárdas* have been synonymous ever since.

The **Hortobágy Gallery** (adult/child 100/50Ft; open 10am-5pm daily Apr-Oct; 10am-3pm Nov-Mar), just behind the restaurant, has a potpourri of art styles and media with a Hortobágy theme, some of them saccharine-sweet, others quite evocative. Check the big skies in some of the works by László Holló or Arthur Tölgyessy and see if they don't match the real one.

The **Herder Museum** (Pásztormúzeum; Petőfi tér 1; adult/child 200/100Ft; open 9am-6pm daily May-Sept, 10am-4pm Mar, Apr, Oct & Nov), housed in an 18th-century

carriage house across from the *csárda*, has good exhibits on how riders, cowherds, shepherds and swineherds fed and clothed themselves and played their music. Spare some time for a close look at the finely embroidered jackets and elaborate long capes (*szűr*) they wore.

The **Round Theatre** (Körszín; adult/child 200/100Ft; open 9am-4pm daily Apr-Sept; 10am-4pm Oct & Nov), next to the Herder Museum, is a mixture of the gallery, the museum and a little bit extra – its ever-changing exhibitions range from art from the region to informative displays on bird life in the park.

The new **Rare Breed Park** (☎ 589 321; adult/child 200/100Ft, horse-show 1000/500Ft; open 9am-6pm daily Mar-Nov), about 400m southwest of the Herder Museum across the Hortobágy River, is a fun place for kids of all ages. Here you'll get up close and personal with animals unique to the *puszta*, including the heavy-set black-eyed Hungarian Grey cattle, the curly-haired *mangalica* pig, the permed *kuvasz* dog, and the *racka* sheep, whose corkscrew-like horns are particularly devilish.

Máta, about 2km north of Hortobágy village, is the centre of the Hortobágy horse industry, and the mighty Nonius is bred here. State-owned until the early 1990s, the horses, carriages, herds of Hungarian Grey cattle and *racka* sheep have been taken over by a German-Hungarian riding and hotel company called Hortobágy Club. But even if you don't ride and aren't interested in staged 'rodeos', it's worth a walk over for a look at the stables, the horses and the fine old carriages.

Activities

At Máta, the **Hortobágy Club** (☎ 589 369) offers any number of **horse-related activities**: riding and roping displays by the *csikósok*, with a two-hour tour of the *puszta* by carriage (adult/child 1700/800Ft) to see the cattle, sheep and perhaps something a little wilder; horse riding (2300Ft); and riding lessons (1800Ft per hour) and carriage driving (6000Ft).

The national park office organises scenic **flights** (☎ 529 920) over the region, but they're not cheap; flights cost 1500Ft per minute for up to three people. Planes take off from the airfield at Macskatelek, about 3km west of the village at the 70km stone.

Special Events

The area is busiest in July when Máta hosts the **International Equestrian Days** and during the

Hortobágy Bridge Fair on 19–20 August, an attempt to recreate the old 'outlaw' fairs held here in the last century.

Places to Stay

Puszta Camping (☎ 369 488; camping per adult/child/tent 550/400/500Ft, bungalows per person 1500Ft; open May-Sept), about 300m south of the Herder Museum, has a quiet spot near the river, and even has a tiny thermal pool.

Róna Camping (☎ 369 071; camping per person/tent 400/400Ft) at the Hortobágy hotel in Borsós, 2km to the east, is a less convenient site.

Sándor Petőfi College (☎ 369 488; József Attila utca 1; dorm beds under 1500Ft), run by Puszta Camping, has four-bed dormitory rooms available in summer.

Tourinform has a list of **private rooms** from 2000Ft per person, or try the houses at Czinege János utca 3 and 21 (400m east of Petőfi tér) or Arany János utca 14 and 17.

Hortobágy Inn (☎ 369 137; Kossuth utca 1; singles/doubles 3500/6000Ft) is the most central place to stay. It's a basic but pleasant place with 10 large rooms and friendly staff.

Hortobágy Hotel (☎ 369 071; singles/doubles/triples 4500/6000/8000Ft) is a good choice if there's no room at the inn. It's an attractive enough place with a central garden and 20 rooms in an old building and a newer concrete shoebox in Borsós.

Two other possibilities are a bit far out, but each has its own attractions.

Öregtavi (☎/fax 369 119; singles/doubles 6000/8000Ft), a nine-room guesthouse by the Hortobágy Fish Pond (Hortobágyi halastó), 7km northwest of the village, is an excellent spot for some informal bird-watching. Unfortunately it's not signposted; look for the big lime-green house.

Pástortanya (☎ 369 127; singles/doubles with shared bathroom 2800/4000Ft, apartment 5000Ft) inn is a traditional Hortobágy-style farmhouse with four rooms and an apartment sleeping up to four. It's next to the Macskatelek airfield and has its own restaurant.

Hortobágy Club (☎ 369 020, fax 369 027; ⓦ www.hchotel.hu; singles 16,200-17,550Ft, doubles 22,950-25,650Ft, suite 25,650-28,350Ft, house 21,600-29,700Ft), the resort hotel in Máta, has 58 deluxe rooms, 20 individual houses (complete with private stables), swimming pool, fitness centre and

two restaurants and is a world apart. The prices are out of this world too and vary depending on the season. The separate houses accommodate four to six people.

Places to Eat

Hortobágyi Csárda (☎ 589 144; mains 1000-2000Ft; open 8am-10pm daily) is touristy and a little pricey, but you've got to have a meal at Hungary's most celebrated roadside inn. Order a duck dish, relax to the Gypsy standards and admire the Hortobágy kitsch taking up every square centimetre of wall space.

There ain't much else around. **Pizza Sfera** (pizzas 550-700Ft), in the shopping complex, is the cheapest place to eat in town, the **Hortobágy Inn** (mains 600-900Ft) has a small, rather rough restaurant, **Pástortanya** (mains 1000Ft) also has its own restaurant and the **Magyaros** and **Hajdú** restaurants at the Hortobágy Club are open late. The **Nyerges** near the paddocks and stables is pleasant for a drink – if the wind is in your favour.

Getting There & Away

Four daily buses between Debrecen (via Hajdúszoboszló) and Eger stop in Petőfi tér. Hortobágy is on the railway line linking Debrecen and Füzesabony and is served by between eight and 10 trains daily, with the last train leaving for Debrecen about 8pm. Trains headed for Füzesabony (last one at 8.38pm) also stop at the Hortobágyi halastó station near the Öregtavi guesthouse and Tiszafüred.

HAJDÚSÁG REGION

The Hajdúság region is a loess (silt) area of the Eastern Plain west of Debrecen that was settled by the Heyducks, a medieval community of drovers and outlaws turned mercenaries and renowned for their skill in battle (see boxed text 'The Heyducks' under Debrecen, earlier in this chapter).

The Hajdúság continued as a special administrative district until the late 19th century but lost its importance after that. Today it is one of the most sparsely populated areas of Hungary – dusty and forlorn, but evocative.

Hajdúszoboszló

☎ 52 • postcode 4200 • pop 24,500

Hajdúszoboszló, 20km southwest of Debrecen, was a typical Hajdúság town until 1925, when springs were discovered during drilling for oil and natural gas. Today, with its huge spa complex, park, pools, grassy 'beaches' and other recreational facilities, it is Hungary's Coney Island, Blackpool and Bondi Beach all rolled into one – for better or for worse.

It may indeed be the 'poor man's Balaton', as one holiday-maker described it, but Hajdúszoboszló has its serious side too. A large percentage of the hundreds of thousands of visitors who flock here every year are in search of a cure from its therapeutic waters.

Orientation Almost everything you'll want or need can be found on the broad street (route No 4) running through town and changing names four times: Debreceni útfél, Szilfákalja út, Hősök tere and Dózsa György utca. The thermal baths and park, lumped together as the Holiday Area (Üdülőterület), occupy the northeastern portion of Hajdúszoboszló. Hősök tere – the town centre – lies to the southwest.

The bus station is on Fürdő utca, just north of Debreceni útfél. The train station lies about 3km south on Déli sor. Reach Hősök tere by walking northwest along Rákóczi utca.

Information Housed in the cultural centre building is **Tourinform** (π/fax 558 929; e hajduszoboszlo@tourinform.hu; Szilfákalja út 2; open 8am-6pm daily June–mid-Sept; 9am-4.30pm Mon-Fri, 9am-noon mid-Sept–May). **Hajdútourist** (π 557 751; József Attila utca 2; open 9am-5pm Mon-Fri, 9am-1pm Sat) is just up from the spa's main entrance. There's a large **OTP bank** (Szilfákalja út 10) with a currency exchange machine next to the ABC supermarket and the **main post office** (Kálvin tér 1) is farther west.

Things to See & Do The main attraction here is the **thermal baths complex** (π 360 344; adult/child 750/650Ft; open 8am-6pm daily year-round; outdoor pools open summer only) comprising a dozen mineral and fresh-water pools, saunas, solarium and treatment centre. The centre is open all year, with the exception of the summer-only outdoor pools. There are weekly, two-week and three-week passes available and entry is cheaper after 4pm. You can rent rowing boats for 600Ft per hour. Just to the north of the baths is the new **Aqua-park** (adult/child 3800/1900Ft), which, considering it only has nine slides, is overpriced. If you plan on zipping down the speed slides, remember to keep your feet together.

Near the **Calvinist church** (Kálvin tér 9; admission free), built in 1717, is a 20m stretch of wall and a small tower – all that remains of a 15th-century Gothic **fortress** destroyed by the Turks in 1660. Across Hősök tere a statue of István Bocskai stands not so proud – a pint-sized prince out of all proportion to his snorting stallion and great deeds.

Down Bocskai utca, past the 18th-century baroque **Catholic church** at No 6, where Pope John Paul II prayed as Karol Wojtyla, bishop of Kraków, in the early 1970s, is the **Bocskai Museum** (π 362 165; Bocskai utca 12; adult/child 300/150Ft; open 9am-1pm & 2pm-6pm Tues-Sun May-Sept; 9am-1pm & 2pm-4pm Tues-Sun Oct-Apr), a temple to the memory of Prince István and his Heyduck helpers. Among the saddles, pistols and swords hangs Bocskai's banner, the standard of the Heyduck cavalry, picturing the prince doing battle with a leopard (which mysteriously changes into a lion in later versions). There are also exhibits of the city's cultural achievements and of the development of the thermal baths, with some curious Art Deco spa posters and medical instruments that could have come from a medieval dungeon.

A lovely thatched cottage houses the **István Fazekas Pottery House** (Ady Endre utca 2; open 8am-4pm Mon only), featuring the distinctive black pottery produced by the Fazekas family in neighbouring Nádudvar (see Nádudvar a little later in this chapter). But unless you're in Hajdúszoboszló on a Monday you'll miss it.

There's a striking monument called **Forest of Bells** near the entrance to the spa, honouring the dead of wars throughout Hungarian history.

Special Events The main event here is the **Szoboszló Summer festival** in mid-July.

Places to Stay The choice of accommodation in this tourist-oriented town is enormous, and prices vary according to the season.

Hajdútourist Camping (π/fax 557 851; e hajdutourist@axelero.hu; Debreceni útfél 6; camping per adult/child/tent 500/260/550Ft, cabins 4400-6000Ft; open May-Sept) in the park along the noisy motorway to Debrecen also has hotel rooms for 3000-5000Ft. The cabins sleep four.

Thermal Camping (π/fax 365 991; Böszörményi út 35a; camping per person/tent

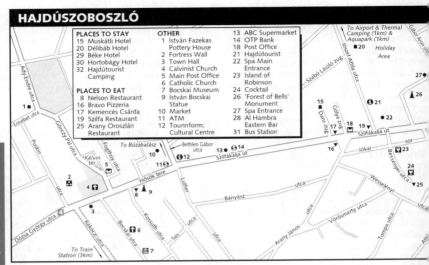

HAJDÚSZOBOSZLÓ

PLACES TO STAY
15 Muskátli Hotel
20 Délibáb Hotel
29 Béke Hotel
30 Hortobágy Hotel
32 Hajdútourist
   Camping

PLACES TO EAT
8 Nelson Restaurant
16 Bravo Pizzeria
17 Kemencés Csárda
25 Szilfa Restaurant
25 Arany Oroszlán
   Restaurant

OTHER
1 István Fazekas
   Pottery House
2 Fortress Wall
3 Town Hall
4 Calvinist Church
5 Main Post Office
6 Catholic Church
7 Bocskai Museum
9 István Bocskai
   Statue
10 Market
11 ATM
12 Tourinform;
   Cultural Centre

13 ABC Supermarket
14 OTP Bank
18 Post Office
21 Hajdútourist
22 Spa Main
   Entrance
23 Island of
   Robinson
24 Cocktail
26 'Forest of Bells'
   Monument
27 Spa Entrance
28 Al Hambra
   Eastern Bar
31 Bus Station

700/700Ft) is another camping ground, north-east of the thermal spa at the edge of town.

Virtually every third household in Hajdúszoboszló lets out **private rooms** in the high season, and *szoba kiadó* (room for rent) signs sprout like mushrooms after a rain along the city's quiet backstreets. Tourinform has a long list of possibilities, otherwise Hajdútourist can arrange a place for around 2500Ft per person.

Hortobágy *(☎/fax 271 431; e hortobagy hot@freemail.hu; Mátyás király sétány 3; singles/doubles 6200/8500Ft),* a complex of four guesthouses near the baths, has good-sized modern rooms and a huge garden.

Muskátli *(☎ 363 744, fax 361 027; e muskatlihajduszoboszlo@matavnet.hu; Daru zug 5a; singles €30-40, doubles €43-50)* has 78 large and small rooms, a swimming pool, a thermal bath and a pleasant restaurant with outside seating in front.

Délibáb *(☎ 360 366, fax 362 059; e delibab@civishotels.hu; József Attila utca 4; singles €37-58, doubles €46-74),* with a massive 250 rooms, is one of the larger spa hotels (many of which offer one and two-week 'cure' packages). Rates vary depending on the season and facilities of the room.

Béke *(☎ 361 411, fax 361 759; e reserve@ hotelbeke.huguesthotels.hu; Mátyás király sétány 10; singles €35-54, doubles €60-74),* with 194 rooms in the park to the east of the thermal baths, has its own swimming pool and sauna.

Places to Eat There are plenty of sausage, *lángos* and ice-cream **stalls** along Szilfákalja út and in the park. For pizza try the Szabadság hotel's **Bravo** *(Szilfákalja út 54; pizzas from 500Ft),* which also has good salads.

Szilfa *(József Attila utca 2; mains 800-1500Ft)* is a pleasant eatery with a covered terrace on the corner of Szilfákalja út and is less touristy (it still puts on traditional dancing shows, though) than Kemencés.

Kemencés *(Szilfákalja út 40/a; mains 900-1200Ft)* is a flashier *csárda*-like place a few paces to the southwest of Szilfa.

Arany Oroszlán *(Golden Lion; Bessenyei utca 14; mains 900-1200Ft)* is a quiet, relaxing place on a leafy residential street.

Nelson *(☎ 270 226; cnr Hősök tere & Kossuth utca; mains 1000-2000Ft)* is on the expensive side but the food is good and there's street-side seating.

Entertainment The City Cultural Centre *(☎ 557 693; Szilfákalja út 2)* offers tips on what's on in town, including organ and choral concerts in the Calvinist church.

Al Hambra Eastern Bar *(Mátyás király sétány 8)* is an alfresco bar and a suitable place to rehydrate after a long day soaking in steamy brown mineral water.

Take your pick of two popular clubs just south of the thermal baths: **Cocktail** (Bessenyei utca 12; open 8pm-3am daily) and **Island of Robinson** (cnr Bessenyei utca & Jókai sor; open till 11pm Tues, Thur & Sun, 2am Wed & Fri & 4am Sat).

Getting There & Away Buses from Hajdúszoboszló depart for Miskolc five times daily and buses for Eger (via Hortobágy), Kecskemét and Szeged once each daily. Up to two dozen head to Debrecen daily. There's direct service twice daily to Hortobágy and an extra one at 7.30am added on from mid-June to September. International destinations served by bus include Oradea (Tuesday and Thursday at 6am) and Baia Mare (Friday at 5am), both in Romania.

Trains headed for Szolnok and Budapest from Debrecen stop at Hajdúszoboszló a couple of times an hour throughout the day.

Nádudvar
☎ 54 • postcode 4181 • pop 8720

This town, 18km west of Hajdúszoboszló and easily reached by one of up to seven daily Debrecen–Hajdúszoboszló buses, is the centre of the black-pottery cottage industry.

From the bus station on Kossuth Lajos tér (the **post office** is on the south side), turn left onto Fő utca and walk 800m in a westerly direction past the neoclassical **Catholic church**,

graves of Soviet soldiers killed in WWII, and a huge modern cultural centre, to No 152, where Ferenc Fazekas maintains his **pottery workshop** (☎ 480 569; open 8am-6pm Mon-Fri). The potter's clay, rich in iron, is gathered and stored for a year before it is turned on a wheel into vases, jugs, pitchers and candlesticks, then decorated, smoked in a kiln and polished, giving the objects their lovely and quite distinctive black glossy appearance. Ferenc is usually on hand to give visitors a demonstration, and his wares are available in the small shop next door. There is also a small **museum** (admission free) containing 18th-century pottery made by the Fazekas family and an old foot-operated potter's wheel. Do not confuse this workshop with the touristy Fazekasház almost opposite at Fő utca 159.

There are a few small **eateries** on Fő tér near the bus station, and the **Regina Cafe** (Fő utca 128) near the workshop is fine for snacks and drinks.

Southern Plain

The Southern Plain spans the lower regions of the Danube and Tisza Rivers and contains many of the most interesting towns and cities on the Great Plain. Even so, at times the plain seems even more endless here, with large farms and the occasional tanya (homestead) breaking the monotony. The Southern Plain (Dél-Alföld) was even less protected than the rest of the region, and its destruction by the Turks was complete. With little precipitation and frequent drought, the area is the hottest part of the Great Plain and, summer lasts well into October.

KECSKEMÉT
☎ 76 • postcode 6000 • pop 108,500

Lying halfway between the Danube and the Tisza Rivers in the heart of the Southern Plain, Kecskemét is ringed with vineyards and orchards that don't seem to stop at the limits of this 'garden city'. Colourful architecture, fine museums, apricot groves and the region's excellent barackpálinka (apricot brandy) beckon, and the Kiskunság National Park, the puszta of the Southern Plain, is right at the back door.

History has been kind to Kecskemét, now the capital of Hungary's largest county (Bács-Kiskun). While other towns on the Ottoman-occupied Great Plain were administered by the dreaded *spahis* (the name given to a member of the Turkish irregular cavalry), who had to pay their own way and took what they wanted when they wanted it, Kecskemét – like Szeged farther south – was a *khas* town, under the direct rule and protection of the sultan. In the 19th century the peasants in the region planted vineyards and orchards to bind the poor, sandy soil. When phylloxera struck in 1880, devastating vineyards throughout Hungary, Kecskemét's vines proved immune: apparently the dreaded lice didn't like the sand. Today the region is responsible for one-third of Hungary's total wine output, though it must be said that this thin, rather undistinguished 'sand wine' is not the best. It's also a major producer of *foie gras*, and the large goose farms – some of them with tens of thousands of the cranky creatures – have increased the Plain's fox population substantially.

Kecskemét's agricultural wealth was used wisely – it was able to redeem all its debts in cash in 1832 – and today the city can boast some of the most spectacular architecture in the country. Art Nouveau and the so-called Historical Eclectic (or Hungarian Romantic) style predominate, giving the city a turn-of-the-20th-century feel. It also was – and still is – an important cultural centre: an artists' colony was established here in 1912, and the composer Zoltán Kodály chose Kecskemét as the site for his world-famous Institute of Music Education. Two other local boys who made good were László Kelemen, who formed Hungary's first provincial travelling theatre here late in the 18th century, and József Katona (1791–1830), the father of modern Hungarian drama.

Orientation

Kecskemét is a city of multiple squares that run into one another without warning and can be a little confusing at first. The bus and main train stations are opposite one another near József Katona Park. A 10-minute walk southwest along Nagykőrösi utca will bring you to the first of the squares, Szabadság tér. The city's other train station, Kecskemét KK, from where narrow-gauge trains head for Bugac, is on Halasi út, which is the southern continuation of Batthyány utca.

Information

Tourinform (*☎/fax 481 065; **e** kecskemet@tourinform.hu; Kossuth Lajos tér 1; open 8am-8pm Mon-Fri, 9am-1pm Sat & Sun* July-Aug; 8am-5pm Mon-Fri, 9am-1pm Sat May, June & Sept; 8am-5pm Mon-Fri Oct-Apr)* is on the northeast side of the town hall. **Ibusz** (*☎ 486 955, fax 480 557; Kossuth tér 3; open 9am-5pm Mon-Fri, 9am-noon Sat)* is in the Aranyhomok hotel. You can visit the city's website at **w** www.kecskemet.hu.

The **OTP bank branch** (*Szabadság tér 1/a)*, on the corner of Arany János utca, does foreign exchange. The **main post office** (*Kálvin tér 10-12)* is near the centre of town. **Piramis Internet Café** (*Csányi utca 1-3; 480Ft per hour; open 10am-8pm Mon-Fri, noon-8pm Sat & Sun)* is upstairs in a small shopping mall.

Things to See

Kecskemét has many museums, churches and other interesting buildings, all within easy walking distance of the town centre.

Around Kossuth tér On the eastern side of Kossuth tér is the **Franciscan Church of St Nicholas** (*Szent Miklós ferences templom; admission free)*, dating in parts from the late 13th century; the **Zoltán Kodály Institute of Music Education** (*Kodály Zoltán Zenepedagógiai Intézet; ☎ 481 518; Kéttemplom köz 1; adult/child 100/50Ft; open noon-1pm & 4pm-6pm Mon-Fri, 10am-6pm Sat & Sun)* occupies the baroque monastery behind it to the east. Inside is a very small museum, well, a corridor, devoted to the composer the institute is named after. The main building in the square, however, is the sandy-pink **town hall**, a lovely late 19th-century building designed by Ödön Lechner, who mixed Art Nouveau/Secessionist with folkloric elements to produce a uniquely Hungarian style. Another beautiful example of this style is the restored **Otthon Cinema** (*Széchenyi tér 4)*, on the corner of pedestrian Görögtemplom utca. The town hall's carillon chimes out strains of works by Ferenc Erkel, Kodály, Mozart, Handel and Beethoven several times during the day, and groups are allowed into the spectacular **Council Chamber** (*☎ 483 683 for information)*. The floral ceilings and the frescoes of Hungarian heroes and historical scenes were painted by Bertalan Székely, who tended to romanticise the past. Just outside and hidden by a rhododendron bush, the **József Katona Memorial** marks the spot where the young and much loved playwright dropped dead of a heart attack in 1830.

You can't miss the tall tower of the Catholic **Great Church** (Nagytemplom; admission free) just north of the town hall and built in 1806. The big tablets on the front honour (from left to right) a mounted regiment of Hussars that served in WWI; citizens who died in the 1848–49 War of Independence; and the Kecskemét victims of WWII.

Szabadság tér Walking northeast into Szabadság tér, you'll pass the 17th-century **Calvinist church** and the **Calvinist New College** (Református újkollégium) from 1912, a later version of the Hungarian Romantic style that looks like a Transylvanian castle and is now a music school. Two other buildings in the square are among the city's finest. The Art Nouveau **Ornamental Palace** (Cifrapalota),

which dates from 1902 and is covered in multicoloured majolica tiles, now contains the **Kecskemét Gallery** (Kecskeméti Képtár; ☎ 480 776; Rákóczi út 1; adult/child 260/130Ft; open 10am-5pm Tues-Sat, 1.30pm-5pm Sun). Don't go in so much for the art; climb the steps to the aptly named **Decorative Hall** (Díszterem) to see the amazing stucco peacock, bizarre windows and more tiles. The **House of Technology** (Technika Háza; ☎ 487 611; Rákóczi út 2; admission free; open 10am-6pm Mon-Fri), a Moorish structure dating from 1871, was once a synagogue. Today it is used for conferences and exhibitions.

Museums Arguably the city's most interesting museum and one of the few of its kind in

KECSKEMÉT

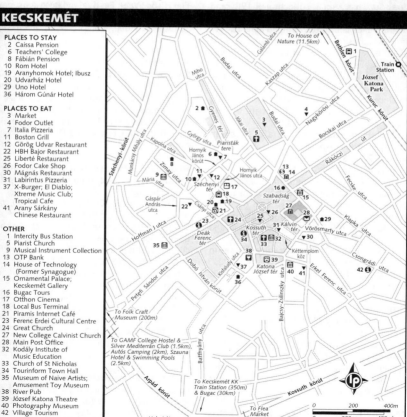

PLACES TO STAY
2 Caissa Pension
6 Teachers' College
8 Fábián Pension
10 Rom Hotel
19 Aranyhomok Hotel; Ibusz
20 Udvarház Hotel
29 Uno Hotel
36 Három Gúnár Hotel

PLACES TO EAT
3 Market
4 Fodor Outlet
7 Italia Pizzeria
11 Boston Grill
12 Görög Udvar Restaurant
22 HBH Bajor Restaurant
25 Liberté Restaurant
26 Fodor Cake Shop
30 Mágnás Restaurant
31 Labirintus Pizzeria
37 X-Burger; El Diablo;
   Xtreme Music Club;
   Tropical Cafe
41 Arany Sárkány
   Chinese Restaurant

OTHER
1 Intercity Bus Station
5 Piarist Church
9 Musical Instrument Collection
13 OTP Bank
14 House of Technology
   (Former Synagogue)
15 Ornamental Palace;
   Kecskemét Gallery
16 Bugac Tours
17 Otthon Cinema
18 Local Bus Terminal
21 Piramis Internet Café
23 Ferenc Erdei Cultural Centre
24 Great Church
27 New College Calvinist Church
28 Main Post Office
32 Kodály Institute of
   Music Education
33 Church of St Nicholas
34 Tourinform Town Hall
35 Museum of Naive Artists;
   Amusement Toy Museum
38 River Pub
39 József Katona Theatre
40 Photography Museum
42 Village Tourism

Europe the **Hungarian Museum of Naive Artists** (*Magyar Naiv Müvészek Múzeuma;* ☎ 324 767; *Gáspár András utca 11; adult/child 150/50Ft; open 10am-5pm Tues-Sun mid-Mar–Oct*) is in the Stork House (1730), surrounded by a high white wall, just off Petőfi Sándor utca. Lots of predictable themes here, but the warmth and craft of Rozália Albert Juhászné's work, the drug-like visions of Dezső Mokry-Mészáros and the paintings of András Süli (Hungary's answer to Henri Rousseau) will hold your attention. There's a gallery in the cellar where you can purchase original paintings almost as good as those on display upstairs.

Next door, the **Amusement Toy Museum** (*Szórakaténusz Játékmúzeum;* ☎ 481 469; *adult/child 200/100Ft; open 10am-5pm Tues-Sun*) has a small collection of 19th- and early-20th-century dolls, wooden trains, board games and so on, dumped haphazardly in glass cases. But the museum spends most of its time and money on organising events and classes for kids (workshops 10am to noon and 2.30pm to 5pm Wednesday and Saturday, 10am to noon Sunday, mid-March to December). Much is made of Ernő Rubik, the Hungarian inventor of that infuriating Rubik cube from the 1970s.

The **Hungarian Folk Craft Museum** (*Magyar Népi IsparmÜvészet Múzeuma;* ☎ 327 203; *Serfőző utca 19a; adult/child 200/100Ft; open 10am-5pm Tues-Sat*), the granddaddy of all museums in Kecskemét, is farther southwest and a block in from Dózsa György út. Some 10 rooms of an old farm complex are crammed with embroidery, woodcarving, furniture, agricultural tools and textiles, so don't try to see everything.

The **Hungarian Photography Museum** (*Magyar Fotográfiai Múzeum;* ☎ 483 221; *Katona József tér 12; adult/child 150/100Ft; open 10am-5pm Wed-Sun*) is not very impressive but is housed in an Art Deco former Orthodox synagogue.

The **Leskowsky Musical Instrument Collection** (*Leskowsky Hangszergyüjtemény;* ☎ 486 616; *Zimay László utca 6/a; admission free; open by appointment*) traces the development of music-making over the centuries and has a decent collection of instruments from five continents.

Market Kecskemét's lively **flea market** is southeast of the city on Kulső Szegedi út.

Activities

Kecskemét has an abundance of **thermal water**, and in summer the four Szék-tó pools on Izsáki út, the continuation of Dózsa György út, or the lake in Leisure Time Park (Szabadidőpark) just north of them, are packed with local frolickers. Throughout the year you can take to the waters in the large **indoor swimming pool** (*Izsáki út 1; adult/child 400/260Ft; open 6am-9pm daily*).

Special Events

Special events in Kecskemét include both the **Bohém Ragtime & Jazz Festival** and the cultural **Spring Festival** in March, the **Kodály International Music Festival** from mid-June to mid-August and the **Kecskemét Animated Film Festival**, held every even year in June. The **Hirős Week Festival** in late August pays homage to the richness of Kecskemét agricultural produce, notably the golden *sár gabarack* (apricot).

Places to Stay

Camping Autós Camping (☎ 329 398 *Csabai Géza körút 5; camping per person/tent 600/500Ft; bungalows 5500Ft; open Apr-Oct*) is nearly 5km from the train station on the southwestern side of Kecskemét. It's generally crammed with German and Dutch tourists in caravans.

Hostels & Private Rooms Tourinform has an extensive list of college accommodation in town.

GAMF Ságvári College (☎ 510 300, fax 516 399; e koll@gamf.hu; *Izsáki út 10; beds from 1250Ft open mid-June–Aug*) is about three blocks from the camp site, and has accommodation in a four-bed room and single and doubles are also available. You can sometimes get a bed in other months, outside the 'official' open season.

Teachers' College (☎ 486 977, fax 486 767; *Piaristák tere 4; beds 1600Ft*) is right in the centre of town and has accommodation from mid-June to August.

Ibusz charges from 1500Ft to 2500Ft per person for a **private room**.

Farm Accommodation If you want a quiet break, have your own transport and can stay put in one place for a minimum of three nights, a farmhouse stay is a great option. The area outside Kecskemét is called the *tanya világ*, or 'farm world', and is very picturesque, with isolated thatch-roofed farmhouses and distinctive shahoofs *(gémeskút)*, the distinctive sweep-pole wells set amid orchards and mustard fields. **Village Tourism** *(Falusi Turizmus; ☎/fax 486 230; Csongrádi utca 25)* has lists of houses for rent throughout the county, but many are within a 30km radius of Kecskemét at Bugac, in the Helvécia vineyards to the southwest, and at Lajosmizse, a horse-riding centre to the northwest.

Pensions & Hotels A fab place to stay is **Fábián** *(☎ 477 677, fax 477 175; Kápolna utca 14; singles/doubles 5500/7500Ft)*, a pension with 10 modern, clean rooms with bath. The friendly staff speak a multitude of languages.

Caissa *(☎/fax 481 685;* e *caissa@matav net.hu; Gyenes tér 18; singles/doubles 5000/ 5800Ft)* is an eight-room pension on the 5th floor of a residential building (thankfully there's a lift) and has larger rooms for up to five people also available.

Rom *(☎/fax 483 174; Széchenyi tér 14; rooms 5000Ft, apartment 10,000Ft)* is a four-room 'mini-hotel' above a solarium in a small shopping plaza and across from the local bus station. The apartment, which sleeps four and has a small kitchen, is great value.

Aranyhomok *(Golden Sands; ☎ 486 286, fax 481 174;* e *aranyhomok@axelero.hu; Kossuth tér 3; singles/doubles 8100/15,000Ft)* is the city's largest and ugliest hotel, with 111 rooms and a slew of outlets.

Uno *(☎ 480 046, fax 476 697;* w *www .hoteluno.hu; Benuczky Ferenc utca 4; singles/ doubles €43/46)* is a modern, 24-room hotel east of the centre.

Udvarház *(☎ 413 912, fax 413 914; Csányi utca 1-3; singles/doubles 10,800/11,500Ft)* tucked away in a courtyard with 17 rooms, is small, quiet and central.

Három Gúnár *(☎ 483 611, fax 481 253;* w *www.hotelharomgunar.hu; Batthyány utca 1-7; singles/doubles 10,900/12,000Ft)*, a charming, friendly and small hotel formed by cobbling four old townhouses together, has 46 smallish rooms (the best are Nos 306 to 308). The hotel has a so-so restaurant and a popular bar called the **President Club** with pool tables and pizza, open till 2am daily. Some of the rooms are nonsmoking.

Szauna *(☎ 501 190, fax 501 199; Csabai Géza körút 2; singles/doubles 6500/8500Ft)*

is a vast, modern but friendly place in a quiet location next to the thermal spa. It has 38 rooms, a restaurant, a gym and, naturally enough, a sauna.

Places to Eat

Kecskemét has its fair share of cheap burger joints. Good choices include **Boston Grill** *(☎ 484 444; Kápolna utca 2)* and **X-Burger** *(Kisfaludy utca 4)*, in a small mall, both with burgers from around 250Ft and open late daily.

El Diablo *(☎ 500 922; Kisfaludy utca 4; mains 1000-2000Ft)* is a Mexican place next door to X-Burger with fine dishes and bizarre decor – mind the plastic snakes.

Italia *(☎ 484 627; Hornyik János körút 4; pizzas from 400Ft)* serves up acceptable pizza.

Görög Udvar *(☎ 492 513; Széchenyi tér 9; mains 950-1500Ft)* is a classy Greek restaurant worth crossing the street for and serves gyros (950Ft), souvlaki (1100Ft) and moussaka (1100Ft).

Labirintus *(Kéttemplom köz 2; pizzas from 270Ft)* is a cellar restaurant popular with students that has a vast array of pizza and pastas.

Arany Sárkány *(☎ 320 037; Erkel Ferenc utca 1a; mains around 1000Ft)* is a Chinese place southeast of Katona József tér.

HBH Bajor *(Csányi utca 4; mains 900-1500Ft)*, in a sheltered courtyard behind the cultural centre, is worth trying for well-prepared German-Hungarian food.

Magnás *(☎ 417 640; Csongrádi utca 2; mains 800-1500Ft)* cellar restaurant is an upmarket place and a better choice than HBH Bajor for similar food.

Liberté *(☎ 480 350; Szabadság tér 2; mains 1000-2000Ft)* is the place to go if you wanted to splurge. It's in a historical building east of the Great Church.

Fodor, in the same building as Liberté, has the best ice cream and cakes in Kecskemét. Fodor has another outlet at Nagykőrösi utca 15.

Kecskemét's large **market**, with both a covered and an open section, is located on Jókai utca north of Szabadság tér behind the Piarist church.

Entertainment

Kecskemét is a city of music and theatre; you'd be crazy not to see at least one performance here.

Ferenc Erdei Cultural Centre *(☎ 484 594; Deák Ferenc tér 1)*, which sponsors some

GREAT PLAIN

events, is a good source of information and should be the first place you head to.

József Katona Theatre (*Katona József tér 5*) is a 19th-century theatre that stages dramatic works as well as operettas and concerts by the Kecskemét Symphony Orchestra; check with the **ticket office** (☎ 483 283; open 10am-1pm & 3pm-6pm Tues-Fri) for details.

Kecskemét, like so many Hungarian towns, has a plethora of Wild West–themed pubs. One convivial example is **River Pub** (*Lestár tér 1*), west of the József Katona Theatre.

A chilled-out place for a drink in the evenings is the **Tropical Cafe** (*Kisfaludy utca 4*); once you're ready to go clubbing head next door to the **Xtreme Music Club** or to the student-friendly **Silver Mediterrán Club** (*Izsáki út 2*) near GAMF college. Both stay open till the wee small hours.

Pick up a free copy of biweekly *Kecskeméti Est* for more information on clubs, films, events and parties.

Getting There & Away

Bus Kecskemét is well served by buses, with frequent departures for the most far-flung destinations. Buses depart twice hourly to Kiskunfélegyháza, hourly to Budapest, every couple of hours to Szeged and twice daily to Pécs. Other destinations include Baja (four buses daily), Békéscsaba (one), Debrecen (one), Eger (two), Gyula (one) and Szolnok (seven).

Train Kecskemét is on the railway line linking Nyugati station in Budapest with Szeged, from where trains cross the border to Subotica and Arad. To get to Debrecen and other towns on the Eastern Plain, you must change at Cegléd. A very slow narrow-gauge train leaves Kecskemét KK train station south of the city centre three times daily for Kiskőrös. Transfer there for Kalocsa. Kecskemét KK is also the station from which trains leave for Bugac (see Kiskunság National Park).

Getting Around

Bus Nos 1, 5, 11 and 15 link the bus and train stations with the local bus terminus behind the Aranyhomok hotel. From Kecskemét KK station, catch the No 2 or 2/a to the centre. For the pools, hotels and camp site on Csabai Géza körút, bus Nos 1, 11 and 22 are good. The No 13 goes past the flea market.

You can order the local taxi service by calling ☎ 484 848.

KISKUNSÁG NATIONAL PARK
☎ 76

Kiskunság National Park (*adult/child 1100/ 550Ft, includes museum & horse show*) consists of half a dozen 'islands' of land totalling more than 76,000 hectares. Much of the park's alkaline ponds, dunes and grassy 'deserts' are off-limits to casual visitors, but you can get a close look at this environmentally fragile area – and see the famous horse herds go through their paces to boot – at **Bugac** on a sandy steppe 30km southwest of Kecskemét.

The best source of information on attractions at the park, transport possibilities and the park in general is **Bugac Tours** (☎ 482 500; e bugac@mail.datanet.hu; Szabadság tér 5; open 8am-4.30pm Mon-Fri) in Kecskemét. They also have a small office at the park entrance. The **House of Nature** (☎ 482 611; w www.knp.hu; Liszt Ferenc utca 19; open 9am-4pm Tues-Fri, 10am-2pm Sat), the park's official office in Kecskemét, is another good source of information. Here you'll also find a small exhibition on the flora and fauna found throughout Kiskunság (adult/child 100/50Ft).

At the park entrance you can board a **horse-driven carriage** (the adult/child fare of 2200/1100Ft includes entry to the museum and horse show, and carriages depart at 2.15pm daily from June to August and 12.15pm in May and September) or walk 1.5km along the sandy track to the **Herder Museum** (*Pásztormúzeum; open 10am-5pm daily May-Oct*), a circular structure designed to look like a horse-driven dry mill. It's filled with stuffed fauna and pressed flora of the Kiskunság, as well as branding irons, carved wooden pipes, embroidered fur coats and a tobacco pouch made from a gnarled old ram's scrotum.

There will still be a few minutes to inspect the stables before the **horse show,** which happens at 3.15pm daily from June to August and 1.15pm daily in May and September. Outside, you may come across a couple of noble Nonius steeds being made to perform tricks that most dogs would be disinclined to do (sit, play dead, roll over). The real reason for coming, though, is to see the horseherds crack their whips, race one another bareback and ride 'five-in-hand', a breathtaking performance in which one *csikós* gallops five horses around the field at full speed while standing on the backs of the last two.

Bathers at Egerszalók open-air hot spring, near Eger – Bűkk Hills, Northern Uplands

Neoclassical basilica (designed in 1836 by József Hild), Eger

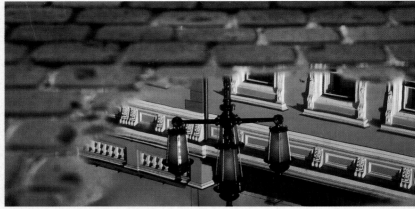
Nyíregyháza's Korona Hotel reflected in a cobblestone puddle

Calvinist church bell tower, Nyírbátor

All aboard at the train station, Nyírbátor

Nyíregyháza Catholic Church, built in 1904

Bugaci Karikás Csárda *(mains from 1000Ft)* with its *gulyás* (a thick beef soup cooked with onions and potatoes) and folk-music ensemble, can be a lot more fun than first appears, and has horses for riding (2000Ft per hour). Bugac Tours has a **camp site** *(☎ 482 500; camping per person 500Ft)* accommodating 60 people and rustic **cottages** *(☎ 482 500; doubles 8000Ft)* for rent nearby.

The best way to get there on your own is by bus from Kecskemét. The 11am bus from the main terminal gets you to the park entrance around noon. After the show, the bus back to Kecskemét passes by the park entrance at 4pm Monday to Friday, and 6.35pm Saturday and Sunday (a change at Jakabszállás is required). More convenient (and generally a lot more fun) on the weekend is the narrow-gauge train; it leaves from Bugac felső station, a 15 minute walk south of the park entrance, at 6.20pm and will get you to Kecskemét KK train station (south of the town centre) around 7.45pm. If you want to take the train to Bugac you'll have to wait a while for the horse show – trains leave Kecskemét KK at 8am, getting you to Bugac felső around 9.15am.

KALOCSA
☎ 78 • postcode 6300 • pop 18,600

With Esztergom, Kalocsa was one of the two episcopal seats founded by King Stephen in 1009 from the country's 10 dioceses. The town had its heyday in the 15th century when, fortified and surrounded by swamps and the river, it could be easily protected. But Kalocsa was burned to the ground during the Turkish occupation and was not rebuilt until the 18th century.

While never as significant as Esztergom, Kalocsa played an important role after the 1956 Uprising. For 15 years, while the ultra-conservative József Mindszenty, archbishop of Esztergom and thus primate of Hungary, took refuge in the US Embassy in Budapest (see the boxed text 'Cardinal Mindszenty' in the Danube Bend chapter), the prelate of Kalocsa was forced to play a juggling game with the government to ensure the church's position – and, indeed, existence – in a nominally atheistic communist state.

Today Kalocsa is a quiet town, as celebrated for its paprika (see the boxed text 'Hungary's Red Gold') and folk art as for its turbulent history.

Orientation & Information

The streets of Kalocsa fan out from Szentháromság tér, site of Kalocsa Cathedral and the Archbishop's Palace. The bus station lies at the southern end of the main avenue, tree-lined Szent István király út. The train station is to the northeast on Mártírok tere, a 20-minute walk from Szentháromság tér along Kossuth Lajos utca.

Korona Tours *(☎ 461 819, fax 462 186; Szent István út 6; open 8am-5pm Mon-Fri)*, below the Paprika Museum, is the best source of information on the town and its surrounding area. They also offer a range of guided tours, including trips to Bakodpuszta, a scaled-down version of Bugac (see Kiskunság National Park earlier); Hajós, a small wine village to the south of Kalocsa; and the inevitable 'Travels in Paprikaland'. The town's website (in Hungarian only) is at ⓦ www.kalocsa.hu. An **OTP bank branch** *(Szent István király út 43-45)*, a **K&H bank** *(Szent István király út 28)* and a **post office** *(Szent István király út 44)* are all along the main street.

Kalocsa Cathedral

Almost everything of interest in Kalocsa is on or near Szent István király út, beginning at Szentháromság tér, where the **Trinity Column** (1786) is corroding into sand. Kalocsa Cathedral *(☎ 462 641; admission free)*, the fourth church to stand on the site, was completed in 1754 by András Mayerhoffer and is a baroque masterpiece, with a dazzling pink and gold interior full of stucco, reliefs and tracery. Some believe that the sepulchre in the crypt is that of the first archbishop of Kalocsa, Asztrik, who brought King Stephen the gift of a crown from Pope Sylvester II, thereby legitimising the Christian convert's control over Hungary. A plaque on the south side outside memorialises this event. Franz Liszt was the first one to play the cathedral's magnificent 3560-pipe organ.

The **Cathedral Treasury** *(Főszékesegyházi kincstár; ☎ 462 641; Hunyadi János utca 2; adult/child 300/150Ft; open 9am-5pm daily May-Oct)*, just east of the cathedral across Kossuth Lajos utca, is a trove of gold and bejewelled objects and vestments. In case you were wondering, the large bust of St Stephen was cast for the Millenary Exhibition in 1896 and contains 48kg of silver and 2kg of gold. Among the other valuable objects is a 16th-century reliquary of St Anne and a gold and crystal baroque monstrance.

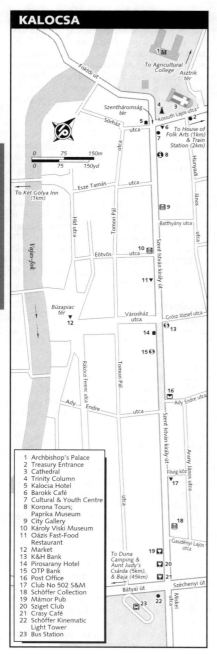

KALOCSA

To Agricultural College

Szentháromság tér

Sörház utca

To House of Folk Arts (1km) & Train Station (2km)

0   75   150m
0   75   150yd

To Két Gólya Inn (1km)

Esze Tamás utca

Hid utca

Tomori Pál

Eötvös utca

Vajas-fok

Rákóczi Ferenc utca

Ady Endre utca

Búzapiac tér

Városház utca

Grósz József utca

Tomori Pál

Szent István király út

Ady Endre utca

utca

Szent István király út

Arany János utca

Filvig köz

To Duna Camping & Aunt Judy's Csárda (5km), & Baja (45km)

Gaudényi Lajos utca

Bátyai út

Miskei utca

Széchenyi út

1 Archbishop's Palace
2 Treasury Entrance
3 Cathedral
4 Trinity Column
5 Kalocsa Hotel
6 Barokk Café
7 Cultural & Youth Centre
8 Korona Tours;
   Paprika Museum
9 City Gallery
10 Károly Viski Museum
11 Oázis Fast-Food
   Restaurant
12 Market
13 K&H Bank
14 Pirosarany Hotel
15 OTP Bank
16 Post Office
17 Club No 502 S&M
18 Schöffer Collection
19 Mámor Pub
20 Sziget Club
21 Crasy Café
22 Schöffer Kinematic
   Light Tower
23 Bus Station

Archbishop's Palace

The Great Hall and the chapel of the Archbishop's Palace *(Érseki palota; ☎ 462 166; Szentháromság tér 1)* (1766), contain magnificent **frescoes** by Franz Anton Maulbertsch, but you won't get to see these unless there's a concert on. The **Episcopal Library** *(Érseki könyvtár; adult/child 300/150Ft; open 8am-5pm Tues-Sun Apr-Oct)*, however, is open to visitors. The library contains more than 100,000 volumes, including 13th-century codices, a Bible that belonged to Martin Luther and is annotated in the reformer's hand, illuminated manuscripts, and verses cut into palm fronds from what is now Sri Lanka.

Museums

The **Károly Viski Museum** *(☎ 462 351; Szent István király út 25; adult/child 250/150Ft, explanation sheet in English 300Ft; open 9am-5pm Tues-Sun)* is rich in folklore and art and highlights the life and ways of the Swabian (Sváb), Slovak (Tót), Serbian (Rác) and Hungarian peoples of the area. It's surprising to see how plain the interiors of peasant houses were early in the 19th century and what rainbows they became 50 years later as wealth increased: walls, furniture, doors – virtually nothing was left undecorated by the famous 'painting women' of Kalocsa. Yet at a marriage the wedding party wore black while the guests were dressed in clothes gaily embroidered (a craft at which the women of Kalocsa also excel). The museum also has a large collection of coins dating from Roman times to today. The **City Gallery** *(Városi Képtár; Szent István király út 12-14; admission free; open 10am-5pm Tues-Sun Apr-Oct)* is diagonally opposite.

Along with Szeged, Kalocsa is the largest producer of paprika, the 'red gold' *(piros arany)* so important in Hungarian cuisine (see the boxed text 'Hungary's Red Gold' later in this section). You can learn a lot more than you need to know about its development, production and beneficial qualities at the **Paprika Museum** *(☎ 461 819; Szent István király út 6; adult/child 500/300Ft; open 10am-5pm daily Mar-Nov)*, which is set up like the inside of a barn used for drying the pods in long garlands. If you happen to be in Kalocsa in September, get out to any of the nearby villages to see the green fields transformed into red carpets.

Other places to see examples of wall and furniture painting include the **House of Folk**

Arts *(Népmüvészeti tájház;* ☎ *461 560; Tompa Mihály utca 5-7; adult/child 500/ 300Ft; open 10am-5pm Tues-Sun mid-Apr– mid-Oct)* and **Juca néni csárdája** *(Aunt Judy's Csárda;* ☎ *461 469),* a touristy restaurant near the Danube 6km southwest of Kalocsa. Some people find today's flower and paprika motifs twee and even garish; compare the new work with that in the museums and see what you think.

An exhibition of the futuristic work of the Paris-based artist Nicholas Schöffer, who was born in Kalocsa in 1912, can be seen at the **Schöffer Collection** *(☎ 462 253; Szent István király út 76; adult/child 200/100Ft; open 10am-noon & 2pm-5pm Tues-Sun).* If you can't be bothered, have a look at his **kinematic light tower** *Chronos 8* (1982) near the bus station – a Meccano-set creation of steel beams and spinning, reflecting mirrors that was supposed to portend the art of the new century two decades ago. Guess not.

Special Events

The **Danube Banks Folklore Festival** is jointly sponsored with Szekszárd and Baja and held in mid-July. **Kalocsa Paprika Days** in September celebrate the harvest of the town's 'red gold'.

Places to Stay

Duna Camping *(☎ 462 534; Meszesi út; camping per person/tent 600/700Ft, bungalows 6000Ft; open mid-June–mid-Sept)* is about 5km southwest of town. **Private rooms** are quite rare; try your luck along Kossuth Lajos utca.

Pirosarany *(Red Gold;* ☎ *462 220, fax 462 621; Szent István király út 37; singles/doubles 6900/7200Ft),* a 20-room, dusky pink hotel, is an odd place – half hotel, half office building.

Két Gólya *(☎/fax 462 259; Móra Ferenc utca 17; singles/doubles 4800/8800Ft),* an inn across the little Vajas stream has eight basic doubles.

Kalocsa *(☎/fax 461 244;* e *beta@mail. externet.hu; Szentháromság tér 4; singles/ doubles/triples 8000/11,250/14,250Ft),* a hotel housed in beautifully restored episcopal offices built in 1780, has 30 rooms in a main building and a courtyard annexe.

Places to Eat

Oázis *(Szent István király út 31; light meals from 200Ft)* is a simple place but good for something fast (pizza, gyros, burgers).

Hungary's Red Gold

Paprika, the 'red gold' *(piros arany)* so essential in many Hungarian dishes, is cultivated primarily around Szeged and Kalocsa. About 10,000 tonnes of the spice are produced annually, 55% of which is exported. Hungarians themselves consume about 0.5kg of the spice per capita every year.

Opinions vary on how and when the *Capsicum annum* plant first arrived in Hungary – from India via Turkey and the Balkans or from the New World – but mention of it is made in documents dating from the 16th century.

There are many types of fresh or dried paprika available in Hungarian markets and shops, including the rose, apple and royal varieties. But as a ground spice it is most commonly sold as *csipős* or *erős* (hot or strong) paprika and *édes* (sweet) paprika.

Capsicum annum is richer in vitamin C than citrus fruits, and it was during experimentation with the plant that Dr Albert Szent-Györgyi of Szeged first isolated the vitamin. He was awarded the Nobel Prize for medicine in 1937.

Club No 502 S&M *(Szent István király út 64; mains & pizzas from 600Ft)* is an oddly named place with basic main courses.

If you happen to be heading for the Danube ferry crossing over to Gerjen southwest of Kalocsa or staying at the camp site, the **Juca néni csárdája** *(Aunt Judy's Csárda;* ☎ *461 469; mains 700-1500Ft)* is in the vicinity.

Kalocsa's **market** on Búzapiac tér has a lot more than just grain.

Entertainment

Kalocsa Cultural & Youth Centre *(☎ 462 200; Szent István király út 2-4)* is housed in an 18th-century baroque seminary; inquire about any concerts scheduled in the **Great Hall** *(Nagy Terem)* of the Archbishop's Palace or the **cathedral**.

Barokk, a café in the same building as the Youth Centre and facing Szentháromság tér, attracts the town's many students.

Several popular bars – this is a garrison town – can be found along Szent István király út in the direction of the bus station, including the **Crasy Cafe** at No 89, the **Sziget Club** at No 87, the **Mámor** pub in a small house behind No 85, and the **Club No 502 S&M** at No 64. All

GREAT PLAIN

except Crasy Cafe have outside seating in the warmer months, but it does have the advantage of a pool table and air-hockey.

Getting There & Away

There are very frequent buses to/from Budapest, Baja and Solt, a horse-breeding centre with many riding and carriage-driving opportunities. There are also buses to Hajós (four daily), Kiskunhalas (four), Szeged (four), Székesfehérvár (two), Nagykőrös (one) and Eger (one). Buses to Arad in Romania leave at 5.40am Monday to Saturday.

Kalocsa is at the end of a rail spur to Kiskőrös, the birthplace of Hungary's greatest poet, Sándor Petőfi (1823–49); there are five departures daily. From Kiskőrös you can make connections to Budapest. A very slow (2¼-hour) narrow-gauge train links Kiskőrös with the smaller of Kecskemét's two train stations, Kecskemét KK, three times daily.

BAJA

☎ 79 • postcode 6500 • pop 39,300

On the Danube about 45km south of Kalocsa, Baja was a fortified town during the Turkish occupation but suffered greatly and had to be repopulated with Germans and Serbians in the 18th century. Today it is an important commercial centre and river port, but it is perhaps best known as a holiday and sports centre – the perfect place to relax for a spell before heading on.

Baja has one of the loveliest locations of any town on the Southern Plain. One of its main squares (Szentháromság tér) gives on to a branch of the Danube, and just across are two recreational islands with beaches and floodbank forests. The bridge across the river to the north is an important one. There's only one other crossing between here and Budapest (at Dunaföldvár, 78km to the north), and the Baja Bridge serves as a gateway to Transdanubia.

Orientation & Information

Vörösmarty utca and pedestrians-only Eötvös utca link Baja's three main squares: Vörösmarty tér, Szent Imre tér and Szentháromság tér. The last one lies on the Kamarás-Duna (or Sugovica as it is known locally), a branch of the Danube River that cuts Petőfi and Nagy Pandúr Islands off from the mainland before emptying into the main river downstream. The bus station is on Csermák Mihály tér northeast of the centre; the train station is

a few minutes to the north across Vonat kert (Train Garden).

Tourinform (☎ 420 792; e baja@tourin form.hu; Szentháromság tér 5; open 9am-5pm Mon-Fri) has an office close to the Duna Hotel. There's a **K&H bank branch** (Szentháromság tér 10) with a currency exchange machine and an **OTP bank** (cnr Szentháromság tér & Deák Ferenc utca). The main **post office** (Oroszlán utca 5) is just off Vörösmarty tér. There's a small **Internet café** (Bartók Béla utca 7; open noon-9pm Mon-Fri, 9am-4pm Sat) with access costing 500Ft per hour.

Things to See

The enormous **Szentháromság tér**, a colourful square of baroque and neoclassical buildings marred only by the multitude of parked cars, is dominated on the east side by the city's **town hall** and its 'widow's walk' looking out towards the Danube.

South of the town hall at Deák Ferenc utca 1 stands the **István Türr Museum** (☎ 324 173; enter from Roosevelt tér; adult/child 200/100Ft; open 10am-4pm Wed-Sat mid-Mar–mid-Dec), named after a local hero who fought in the 1848–49 War of Independence and alongside Garibaldi in southern Italy in 1860. The museum's prime exhibit, entitled 'Life on the Danube', covers wildlife, fishing methods and boat building. Another deals with the folk groups of Baja and its surrounds: the Magyars, Germans, South Slavs (Bunyevác, Sokac) and – surprisingly for Hungary – Roma; all have lived together in this region for several centuries. The rarely seen Roma woodcarving is good, but don't miss the exquisite South Slav black lace, the gold work for which Baja was once nationally famous, and the weavings from Nagybaracska to the south.

The museum couldn't possibly ignore the city's famous sons, including Türr, the painter István Nagy and András Jelky (1738–83), an apprentice tailor who set out for Paris in the mid-18th century but headed in the wrong direction and ended up wandering around China, Japan, Ceylon and Java for 10 years before returning to Hungary to write his memoirs. You'll find a statue of this peripatetic Magyar dressed in his Chinese best on Jelky András tér.

The **István Nagy Gallery** (☎ 325 649; Arany János utca 1; adult/child 200/100Ft; open 10am-4pm Wed-Sat mid-Mar–mid-Dec) – once the mansion of the Vojnich family, built in 1820, and an artists' colony after

WWII – is named after the leading painter of what is known as the Alföld School. Other members are featured, including Gyula Rudnay, as well as 'outsiders' such as the cubist Béla Kádár and sculptor Ferenc Medgyessy.

Buildings of architectural note include the **Franciscan church** (Ferences templom; Bartók Béla utca; admission free) behind the town hall, which was built in 1728 and has a fantastic baroque organ; and the late baroque **Serbian Orthodox church** (☎ 423 199; Táncsics Mihály utca 21; admission free; open 9am-noon Wed & Thur) in a quiet square. The iconostasis is definitely worth a detour.

But the neoclassical **synagogue** (☎ 322 741; Munkácsy Mihály utca 7-9; open 1pm-6pm Mon-Thur, 10am-6pm Fri, 8am-noon Sat), from 1845, beats them both. On the right

as you enter the gate, you'll pass a sheltered memorial to the victims of fascism. Above the columns on the synagogue's tympanum (the facade below the roof) on the west side, the Hebrew inscription reads: 'This is none other than the house of God and the gate to heaven.' The tabernacle inside, with its Corinthian pilasters, is topped with two lions holding a crown while four doves pull back a blue and burgundy curtain. Now a public library, it holds a massive 180,000 volumes, including a first full edition of the 18th-century French Diderot & D'Alembert's Encyclopaedia.

The **Bunyevác Village House** (Bunyevác tájház; ☎ 324 173; Pandúr utca 51; admission 100Ft; open 10am-2pm Wed-Sat mid-Mar–mid-Dec) displays South Slav furniture, clothing, decorative items and tools in an old

GREAT PLAIN

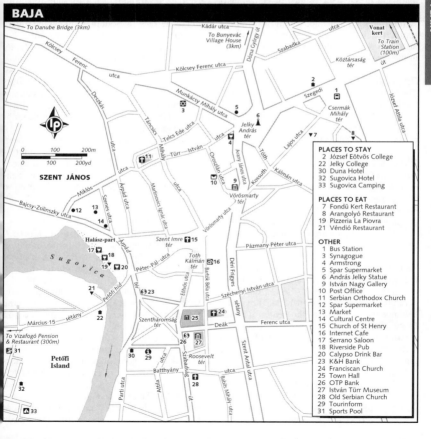

BAJA

PLACES TO STAY
2 József Eötvös College
22 Jelky College
30 Duna Hotel
32 Sugovica Hotel
33 Sugovica Camping

PLACES TO EAT
7 Fondű Kert Restaurant
8 Arangolyó Restaurant
19 Pizzeria La Piovra
21 Véndió Restaurant

OTHER
1 Bus Station
3 Synagogue
4 Armstrong
5 Spar Supermarket
6 András Jelky Statue
9 István Nagy Gallery
10 Post Office
11 Serbian Orthodox Church
12 Spar Supermarket
13 Market
14 Cultural Centre
15 Church of St Henry
16 Internet Cafe
17 Serrano Saloon
18 Riverside Pub
20 Calypso Drink Bar
23 K&H Bank
24 Franciscan Church
25 Town Hall
26 OTP Bank
27 István Türr Museum
28 Old Serbian Church
29 Tourinform
31 Sports Pool

cottage in Baja-Szentistván, a half-hour walk from the city centre.

One of the liveliest **markets** in Hungary, full of Serbs, Romanians and Hungarians from Transylvania, takes place on Wednesdays and Saturdays north of Árpád tér just beyond the bridge over to Petőfi Island.

Activities

The Sugovica resort on Petőfi Island has **fishing**, **boating**, **mini-golf** and **tennis** on offer to anyone willing to pay, and there's a covered swimming pool – the **Sports Pool** (Sportuszoda; adult/child 450/300Ft; open 6am-7.30pm Mon, Tues, Thur, Fri; 8am-7.30pm Sat & Sun) – across the walkway on Petőfi hid.

Avoid the **public beaches** on Petőfi Island in favour of the less crowded ones on the mainland in Szent János east of Halász-part or on Nagy Pandúr Island. But be prepared to swim to the latter or face a long walk to the southern suburb of Homokváros, across the bridge to Nagy Pandúr Island and then north to the beach.

Special Events

The big event of the year is the **Baja Folk Festival** held on the second Saturday in July. It's more a celebration of the town's famous fish soup; 2000 stewpots of the stuff (a Guinness record) are served on the day.

Places to Stay

Sugovica Camping (☎ 321 755, fax 323 155; Petőfi-sziget 32; camping per adult 390-550Ft, per child 195-275Ft, per tent 540-880Ft, doubles 3200-9800Ft) is just south of the Sports Pool to the south and has expensive bungalows, but they are in a relatively attractive camp site. There are 19 in all, and rates vary according to the season. The two most 'remote' ones, though they're not directly on the water, are those designated R9 and R10.

There are two colleges offering dorm accommodation (beds around 1200Ft) over the summer months close to the centre of town: **Jelky College** (☎ 322 021; Március 15 sétány), on Petőfi Island, and **József Eötvös College** (☎ 321 655; Szegedi út), near the bus station.

Vizafogó (☎ 326 585, fax 321 253; Március 15 sétány 27; rooms 6000Ft), a pension on the northwest corner of Petőfi Island, has seven small but modern rooms, some with terraces overlooking the Sugovica River.

Duna (☎ 323 224, fax 324 844; e hotel duna-baja@webmail.hu; Szentháromság tér 6; singles 4400-7600Ft, doubles 5100-8200Ft) is a wonderful old place right by the Danube with 50 rooms. Many rooms have river views. If there are three of you (or money is no problem), stay in No 106, a two-room suite with bathroom and a beautiful roof terrace overlooking the river. Other good rooms to ask for are Nos 111, 239, 257, 260 and 263.

Sugovica (☎ 321 755, fax 323 155; singles/ doubles 7100/8200Ft) on Petőfi Island is Baja's most expensive hotel. The 34 rooms all have bathroom, TV, minibar and a balcony looking onto the park or river. There's even a private mooring for guests arriving by boat.

Places to Eat

Neither the restaurant nor the pub (open till midnight) at the **Duna** hotel is very agreeable, but the terrace café out the front on the square is a great place to sit in warmer months.

Aranygolyó (Golden Ball; Csermák Mihály tér 9; mains from 600Ft; open Mon-Fri only) is an inexpensive place beside the bus station.

Véndió (Old Nut; ☎ 326 585; Martinovics utca 8/b; mains from 800Ft) is a restaurant few minutes across the bridge at the northern end of Petőfi Island. For outside seating nothing beats this place.

Pizzeria La Piovra (small/large pizzas from 400/600Ft) across the river in Halász-part, is another great spot when the weather is fine.

Vizafogó (mains 750-1400Ft), at the pension of the same name, is the place to go to try Baja's famous fish soup.

Entertainment

József Attila Cultural Centre (☎ 326 633; Árpád tér 1) is your source for information about what's going on in Baja. Ask about concerts in the old Serbian church (now a music school and hall) on Batthyány utca.

There's a stretch of lively pubs and bars facing the water at Halász-part, including the **Calypso Drink Bar**, the **Riverside Pub** and the **Serrano Saloon**.

Armstrong (cnr Türr István utca & Arany János utca), a cellar bar with regular live jazz and rock, is a good place to head if the mosquitoes down by the river start to suck you dry.

Getting There & Away

Bus Buses to Kalocsa and Szeged depart at least once an hour; there are five to 10 daily departures to Mohács, Szekszárd, Pécs, Kecskemét and Budapest as well. Other destinations include: Békéscsaba and Csongrád (two each), Hévíz (one), Jászberény (one), Kaposvár (two), Szolnok (one), Veszprém (two) and Zalaegerszeg (one). International buses depart for Arad in Romania on Sunday at 6am.

Train The rail line here links Bátaszék and Kiskunhalas; you must change at the former for Budapest, Szekszárd, Pécs and other points in Southern Transdanubia. From Kiskunhalas, it's impossible to get anywhere of importance without at least another change (the one exception is the fast train to Budapest).

AROUND BAJA
Gemenc Forest

From May to October, a **narrow-gauge train** runs from Pörböly, 13km west of Baja, along some stunning hairpin turns of the Danube to the protected Gemenc Forest near Szekszárd. The reserve is incredibly beautiful and a rich hunting ground. From the terminus at Bárányfok, you can carry on to Szekszárd and other points in Southern Transdanubia.

The best way to schedule such a trip is to take the 6.43am train from Baja to Pörböly, from where you'll catch the little train at 8am to Bárányfok (adult one-way/return 500/840Ft, child 500/300Ft; two hours; 30km). From here there are two to five buses to Szekszárd. Two other trains from Pörböly (adult/child 570/340Ft; 1¼ hours; 19km) – at 9.20am and 1.15pm go only as far as the Gemenc Delta where you need to change trains for Bárányfok. The trains do not always run to schedule; check times and dates at the Baja train station or ring **United Forest Railways** (ÁEV; ☎ 74-491 483; W www.gemencrt.hu; Bajai út 100) in Pörböly before you set out. You wouldn't want to be marooned in the Gemenc with a lot of crazy hunters running wild.

For more information on the Gemenc Forest, see the Around Szekszárd section in the Southern Transdanubia chapter.

SZEGED
☎ 62 • postcode 6700 • pop 175,500

Szeged – a corruption of the Hungarian word *sziget*, or 'island' – is the largest and most important city on the Southern Plain and lies just west of where the Tisza and Maros Rivers converge. In fact, some would argue that, in terms of culture and sophistication, Szeged

(German: Segedin) beats Debrecen hands down as the 'capital' of the Great Plain as a whole.

Remnants of the Körös culture suggest that these goddess-worshipping people lived in the Szeged area 4000 or 5000 years ago, and one of the earliest Magyar settlements in Hungary was at Ópusztaszer to the north. By the 13th century, the city was an important trading centre, helped along by the royal monopoly it held on the salt being shipped in via the Maros River from Transylvania. Under the Turks, Szeged was afforded some protection since the sultan's estates lay in the area, and it continued to prosper in the 18th and 19th centuries as a free royal town.

But disaster struck in March 1879, when the Tisza swelled its banks and almost wiped the city off the map. All but 300 houses were destroyed, and Szeged, under the direction of engineer Lajos Tisza, was rebuilt with foreign assistance between 1880 and 1883. As a result, the city has an architectural uniformity unknown in most other Hungarian cities, and the leafy, broad avenues that ring the city in an almost perfect circle were named after the European cities that helped bring Szeged back to life. (The Moscow and Odessa sections appeared after the war for political reasons and the latter has since been changed to Temesvári körút in honour of Timişoara, where the Romanian revolution of 1989 began.) The Tisza still manages to wash through the town at regular intervals – the highest level to date was recorded in June 1970, the second as recently as April 2000 – but the damage caused by these floods is a fraction of the 1879 disaster.

Since WWII, Szeged has been an important university town – students marched here in 1956 before their classmates in Budapest did – and a cultural centre. Theatre, opera and all types of classical and popular music performances abound, culminating in the Szeged Open-Air Festival in summer. But the city is just as famed for its edibles: Szeged paprika, which mates so wonderfully with fish from the Tisza River in *szegedi halászlé* (spicy fish soup), and Pick, Hungary's finest salami.

Orientation

The Tisza River, joined by the Maros, flows west and then turns abruptly south through the centre of Szeged, splitting the city in two as cleanly as the Danube bisects Budapest. But comparison of the two cities and their rivers stops there. The Tisza is a rather undignified

GREAT PLAIN

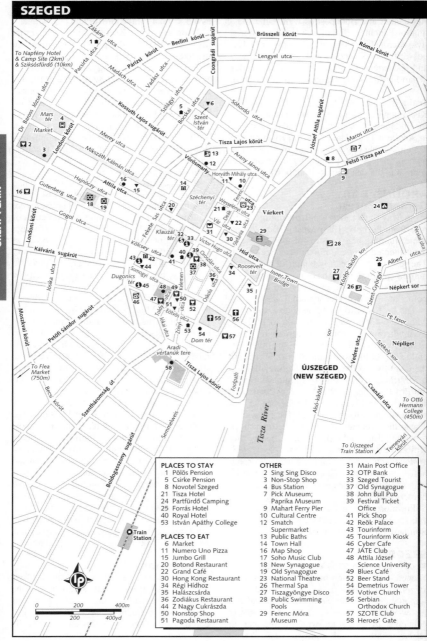

SZEGED

PLACES TO STAY
1 Pölös Pension
5 Csirke Pension
8 Novotel Szeged
21 Tisza Hotel
24 Partfürdő Camping
25 Forrás Hotel
40 Royal Hotel
53 István Apáthy College

PLACES TO EAT
6 Market
11 Numero Uno Pizza
15 Jumbo Grill
20 Botond Restaurant
22 Grand Café
30 Hong Kong Restaurant
34 Régi Hídhoz
35 Halászcsárda
36 Zodiákus Restaurant
44 Z Nagy Cukrászda
50 Nonstop Shop
51 Pagoda Restaurant

OTHER
2 Sing Sing Disco
3 Non-Stop Shop
4 Bus Station
7 Pick Museum;
  Paprika Museum
9 Mahart Ferry Pier
10 Cultural Centre
12 Smatch
  Supermarket
13 Public Baths
14 Town Hall
16 Map Shop
17 Soho Music Club
18 New Synagogue
19 Old Synagogue
23 National Theatre
26 Thermal Spa
27 Tiszagyöngye Disco
28 Public Swimming
  Pools
29 Ferenc Móra
  Museum

31 Main Post Office
32 OTP Bank
33 Szeged Tourist
37 Old Synagogue
38 John Bull Pub
39 Festival Ticket
  Office
41 Pick Shop
42 Reök Palace
43 Tourinform
45 Tourinform Kiosk
46 Cyber Cafe
47 JATE Club
48 Attila József
  Science University
49 Blues Café
52 Beer Stand
54 Demetrius Tower
55 Votive Church
56 Serbian
  Orthodox Church
57 SZOTE Club
58 Heroes' Gate

muddy channel here, and the other side of Szeged is not the city's throbbing commercial heart as Pest is to Budapest but a large park given over to sunbathing, swimming and other hedonistic pursuits.

Szeged's many squares and inner and outer ring roads make the city confusing for some, but virtually every square in the city has a large signpost with detailed plans and a legend in several languages. The main train station is south of the city centre on Indóház tér; tram No 1 connects the station with the town. The bus station, to the west of the centre on Mars tér, is within easy walking distance via pedestrians-only Mikszáth Kálmán utca.

Information

Tourinform (☎/fax 488 690; e szeged@tour inform.hu; Dugonics tér 2; open 10am-6pm Mon-Fri May-Sept; 9am-4pm Mon-Fri Oct-Apr) is tucked away in a quiet courtyard; from May to September they also have a separate pavilion on Dugonics tér (open 9am-9pm daily). Another source of information is **Szeged Tourist** (☎ 420 428; Klauzál tér 7; open 9am-5pm Mon-Fri).

There's an **OTP bank branch** (Klauzál tér 4) in the building where the revolutionary hero Lajos Kossuth gave his last speech before going into exile in Turkey in 1849. The **K&H bank** (Klauzál tér 2) next door has a foreign currency exchange machine. Szeged has a **main post office** (Széchenyi tér 1) and an excellent **map shop** (Attila utca 9; open 9am-5pm Mon-Fri, 9am-noon Sat). **Cyber Cafe** (Dugonics tér 11; open till midnight daily) is a dark basement bar where Internet use costs 480Ft per hour.

Things to See

Szeged is an easy walking city but if you'd like to sit while you see the sights **tour buses** (☎ 450 831 for information) leave Klauzál tér on the hour throughout the day in July and August (750/500Ft).

Begin an easy walking tour of Szeged in Széchenyi tér, a square so large it almost feels like a park. The neobaroque **town hall**, with its graceful tower and colourful tiled roof, dominates the square, while statues of Lajos Tisza, István Széchenyi and the *kubikosok* (navvies) who helped regulate the Tisza River take pride of place under the chestnut trees.

Pedestrian Kárász utca leads south through Klauzál tér. Turn west on Kölcsey utca and walk for about 100m to the **Reök Palace** (Reök-palota; Tisza Lajos körút), a mind-blowing green and lilac Art Nouveau structure built in 1907 that looks like a knick-knack on the bottom of an aquarium. At the time of writing it stood empty awaiting its new tenants.

Farther south, Kárász utca meets Dugonics tér, site of the **Attila József Science University** (abbreviated JATE in Hungarian), named after its most famous alumnus. József (1905–37), a much loved poet, was actually expelled from here in 1924 for writing the verse 'I have no father and I have no mother/I have no God and I have no country' during the ultraconservative rule of Admiral Miklós Horthy. A **music fountain** in the square plays at irregular intervals throughout the day.

From the southeast corner of Dugonics tér, walk along Jókai utca into Aradi vértanúk tere. **Heroes' Gate** (Hősök kapuja) to the south was erected in 1936 in honour of Horthy's White Guards, who were responsible for 'cleansing' the nation of 'Reds' after the ill-fated Republic of Councils in 1919. The fascistic murals have disappeared (replaced with some 'nice' but amateurish ones), but the brutish sculptures still send chills down the spine.

Dóm tér, a few paces to the northeast, contains Szeged's most important monuments and is the centre of events during the annual summer festival. The **National Pantheon** – statues and reliefs of 80 notables running along an arcade around three sides of the square – is a crash course in Hungarian art, literature, culture and history. Even the Scotsman Adam Clark, who supervised the building of Budapest's Chain Bridge, wins accolades, but you'll look forever for any sign of a woman.

The Romanesque **Demetrius Tower** (Dömötör-torony), the city's oldest structure, is all that remains of a church erected here in the 12th century. In its place stands the twin-towered **Votive Church** (Fogadalmi templom; ☎ 420 157; admission free; open 7am-6pm Mon-Sat, 8am-6pm Sun), a disproportionate brown brick monstrosity that was pledged after the flood but not completed until 1930. About the only things worth seeing in the church are the organ, with more than 11,500 pipes, the dome covered with frescoes and the choir. Instead, peek inside the **Serbian Orthodox church** (adult/child 100/80Ft) to the northeast, which dates from 1778, for a look at the fantastic iconostasis: a central gold 'tree' with 60 icons hanging off its 'branches'. You'll find the key at Somogyi utca 3 (flat I/5).

Oskola utca, one of the city's oldest streets, leads from Dóm tér to Roosevelt tér and the Palace of Education (1896) at No 1-3, which now houses the **Ferenc Móra Museum** *(☎ 549 040; Várkert; adult/child 300/150Ft; open 10am-3pm Tues, 10am-5pm Wed-Sun)*. The museum's strength lies in its collection of folk art from Csongrád County, bearing intelligent descriptions in several languages. That, and the unique exhibit of 7th-century Avar finds done up to look like a clan yurt, put this light years ahead of most other museums in Hungary.

For many people, Szeged's most compelling sight is the Hungarian Art Nouveau **New Synagogue** *(Új zsinagóga; ☎ 423 849; Gutenberg utca 13; adult/child 200/100Ft; open 10am-noon & 1pm-5pm Sun-Fri Apr-Sept; 9am-2pm Sun-Fri Oct-Mar)*, which was designed by Lipót Baumhorn in 1903. It is the most beautiful Jewish house of worship in Hungary and still very much in use. If the grace and enormous size of the exterior don't impress you, the blue and gold interior will. The cupola, decorated with stars and flowers (representing Infinity and Faith), appears to float skyward, and the tabernacle of carved acacia wood and metal fittings is a masterpiece. There are a few other buildings of interest in this area, the former Jewish quarter, including the neoclassical **Old Synagogue** *(Ózsinagóga; Hajnóczy utca 12)*, built in 1843, and just south of Széchenyi tér, the remains of another old **synagogue** *(Nádor utca 3)*, now a private house.

If you'd like to know more about the making of Szeged's famed salami – from hoof to shrink-wrap – the **Pick Museum** *(☎ 421 814; Felső-Tisza-part 10)*, here since 1869, can oblige, but you must call in advance to arrange a time. And if that doesn't satisfy your taste buds, head next door to the **Paprika Museum** *(☎ 421 814; Felső-Tisza-part 10; admission free; open 3pm-6pm Fri, 1pm-4pm Sat)* to burn them into submission. Pick salami can be purchased from the **Pick shop** on the corner of Kárász utca and Kölcsey utca.

Szeged's **flea market** is near Vám tér at the start of Szabadkai út southwest of the centre.

Activities

Just north of Széchenyi tér you'll find the **public baths** *(Tisza Lajos körut 24; adult/child*

550/440Ft open 6am-6pm Mon-Fri, 6am-3.30pm Sat)*. Across the Tisza River, the parkland of Újszeged (New Szeged) has **swimming pools** *(Közép-kikötő sor; open 10am-6pm daily May-Sept)* and a **thermal spa** *(☎ 431 133; Fürdő utca 1; open 7am-6pm daily)* as well as beaches along the river. Entry to the pools is 450/250Ft (300/150Ft after 3pm), and to the spa it's 650/450Ft. But the best place for swimming is in the suburb of Sziksósfürdő, about 10km to the west of town at Kiskundorozsma. Along with a conventional strand, swimming pool and rowing boats, this thermal **'Soda Salt Lake'** *(open 10am-6pm Mon-Fri, 8am-6pm Sat & Sun May-Sept)* also has a nudist beach. It's 450/250Ft to get in (300/150Ft after 3pm).

Special Events

The **Szeged Open-Air Festival** unfolds on Dóm tér from mid-July to late August with the two towers of the Votive Church as a backdrop. The outdoor theatre here seats some 6000 people. Main events include an opera, an operetta, a play, folk dancing, classical music, ballet and a rock opera. Festival tickets and information are available from the **ticket office** *(☎ 554 713; Kelemen utca 7; open 10am-5pm Mon-Fri year-round; 10am-1pm Sat & Sun July & Aug)*. But Szeged isn't all highbrow; others might prefer the annual **X Szeged Beer Festival** in mid-June or the **International Trucker Country Meeting** and **Bavarian Beer Festival** in mid-July.

Places to Stay

Camping Szeged has five camp sites, most of which operate between May and September and have bungalows. **Partfürdő** *(☎ 430 843, fax 425 559; Közép-kikötő sor; camping per adult/child/tent 600/430/600Ft, bungalows from 6000Ft)* is in New Szeged along the river opposite the city centre. Guests have free use of the swimming and thermal pools nearby.

Napfény Camping *(☎ 421 800, fax 467 579; e hotelnapfeny@mail.tiszanet.hu; Dorozsmai út 4; camping per person/tent €2.40/1.60, bungalows per person €27-36; open year-round)*, across a large bridge near the western terminus of tram No 1, is another (but much less attractive) site, convenient to the city. Bungalows are for three or four people.

There are a couple of camping grounds by Sziksósfürdő in Kiskundorozsma, including **Sziksós Camping** *(☎ 463 050; Széksósi út)* and **Naturista Camping** (☎ 463 988; *Vereshomok dűlő 1*), an *au naturel* site by the lake's beach. Both have camping for around 600/300/600Ft per adult/child/tent.

Hostels & Private Rooms Plenty of student dormitories in Szeged open their doors to travellers in July and August, including **István Apáthy College** (☎ 545 896; *Eötvös utca 4; dorm beds 1250ft, rooms per person from 2500Ft*) next to the Votive Church. **Ottó Hermann College** (☎ 544 309; *Temesvári körút 52; bus No 2; dorm beds from 700Ft, doubles 2000Ft*) is a cheaper option but is east of the town centre in New Szeged.

Your best bet for a **private room** is Szeged Tourist, which charges 2000Ft to 3000Ft per person. Flats are from 6000Ft.

Pensions Within walking distance of the bus station is **Pölös** (☎/fax 498 208; *Pacsirta utca 17/a; singles/doubles 4500/5500Ft*), a comfy, pink nine-room pension.

Csirke (☎ 426 188; *Bocskai utca 3/b; singles/doubles 5000/6000Ft*), a pension with the unlikely name of 'Chicken', has quite large rooms but they are often taken, so call ahead.

Hotels One of the best places to stay in Szeged is **Tisza** (☎/fax 478 278; **W** www .tiszahotel.hu; *Wesselényi utca 1; singles 5880-11,900Ft, doubles 8760-14,900Ft*), a fine old hotel just off Széchenyi tér. It's been given a partial overhaul, but some rooms still remain good value. It's a lovely place, with large, bright and airy rooms and friendly staff.

Napfény (*motel doubles €12, hotel singles/ doubles/triples €31/40/51*), next to the camp site, has both a motel (most rooms only open May to September) and a year-round hotel with a total of 160 rooms.

Royal (☎ 475 275, fax 420 223; **W** www .royalhotel.hu; *Kölcsey utca 1-3; singles/ doubles with bathroom 11,900/14,100Ft, with shower 9500/10,100Ft*) is the most central of Szeged's upmarket hotels with 110 rooms in renovated old and new wings.

Novotel Szeged (☎ 562 200, fax 562 221; **e** h2996@accor-hotels.com; *Maros utca 1; singles/doubles €74/81*) is a modern, 136-room hotel near a noisy stretch of road but with good views of the river, and rooms with all the trimmings.

Forrás (☎ 430 130, fax 430 866; **e** re serve@hotelforras.hunguesthotels.hu; *Szent-*

Györgyi Albert utca 16-24; singles/doubles 17,200/19,600Ft), in New Szeged, is a spa hotel with 177 rooms. The rooms in the attic are cheaper (singles/doubles 11,100/14,300Ft.)

Places to Eat

Jumbo Grill (*Mikszáth Kálmán utca 4; dishes from 270Ft*), with salads and excellent grilled chicken, is a good spot for a cheap meal.

Numero Uno Pizza (☎ 424 745; *Széchenyi tér 5; pizzas from 275Ft*) has good pizzas, and its garden is a fine place for a drink.

Botond (*Széchenyi tér 13; mains 900-1500Ft*) serves better-than-average Hungarian food with pleasant outside seating in summer.

Pagoda (*Zrínyi utca 5; mains around 900Ft*) serves mock-Chinese food amid faded vermilion, but it does have a nonsmoking room and the price is right.

Hong Kong (*Deák Ferenc utca 24; mains 700-1000ft; open until 11.30pm daily*) has better Chinese food than Pagoda.

Halászcsárda (☎ 555 980; *Roosevelt tér 14; mains around 1500Ft; open 11am-11pm daily*) is a Szeged institution and serves up *szegedi halászlé* (Szeged-style fish soup) by the cauldron.

Régi Hídhoz (☎ 420 910; *Oskola utca 4; mains 800-1200Ft*), near the Halászcsárda, serves standard Hungarian fare and has a pleasant garden.

Zodiákus (☎ 420 914; *Oskola utca 13; mains 1000-2000Ft*) is a cut above, with an excellent international menu and zodiac symbols everywhere you look.

For coffee, cake and a bit of peace and quiet, head for **Grand Café** (☎ 420 578; *Deák Ferenc utca 18*) on the 2nd floor.

Z Nagy (*Dugonics tér 2; ice cream from 60Ft*) is great old-style *cukrászda* with plenty of outside seating.

Szeged has two big **fruit & vegetable markets**, one on Mars tér, site of the notorious Star Prison for political prisoners early in the 1950s, and the other northwest of Széchenyi tér on Szent István tér. There's a **nonstop shop** at Zrínyi utca 1 and another at Mars tér 17.

Entertainment

Your best sources of entertainment information in this culturally active city are **Tourinform** or the **Gyula Juhász Cultural Centre** (☎ 479 566; *Vörösmarty utca 3*).

Szeged National Theatre (*Szegedi Nemzeti Színház;* ☎ 479 279; *Deák Ferenc utca 12-14*), built in 1886, has always been the centre of cultural life in Szeged and usually stages operas and ballet.

The **New Synagogue** (*Új zsinagóga;* ☎ *423 849; Gutenberg utca 13*) holds free organ concerts from late March to mid-September; it's a good chance to take in the splendour of the building without having to pay.

There's a vast array of bars, clubs and other night spots in this student town, especially around Dugonics tér; the **Blues Café** (*Somogyi utca 20*) is always worth a look, as is the very popular **beer stand** (*Somogyi utca; open May-Sept*) farther east.

Both **Numero Uno** (*Széchenyi tér 5*) and **Grand Café** (*Deák Ferenc utca 18*) are worth stopping in for a drink even if you're not having a meal; the latter often screens arty films at weekends.

John Bull Pub (*Oroszlán utca 6*) flies the Union Jack in Szeged; there's even a red London telephone box here.

JATE Club (*Toldy utca 1; open daily*) is the best place to meet students on their own turf; it's usually packed, except when there's exams on. **SZOTE Club** (*Dom tér 13*) is another university place with its own following.

Tiszagyöngye (Közép-kikötő sor) is a huge disco in New Szeged near the river.

Sing Sing Disco (*cnr Mars tér & Dr Baross József utca; open Wed & Sat*) occupies a huge pavilion near the bus station and hosts many rave parties.

Soho Music Club (*Londoni körút 3*) is one of the better places in town for drum and bass.

For more information about venues and events check the free biweekly entertainment guide *Szegedi Est*.

Getting There & Away

Bus Bus service is very good from Szeged, with frequent departures to Békéscsaba, Csongrád, Ópusztaszer, Makó and Hódmezővásárhely. Other destinations include Budapest's Népstadion (seven buses daily), Debrecen (two), Eger (two), Gyöngyös (two), Győr (two), Gyula (six), Kecskemét (10), Mohács (six), Pécs (seven), Siófok (two), Székesfehérvár (five), Tiszafüred (two) and Veszprém (three). Buses also head for Arad across the Romanian border daily at 6.30am with extra ones on Friday at 8.45am, Saturday at 10.10am and Sunday at 8.10am. There are buses to Timişoara on Tuesday and Friday at 6.30am and on Saturday at 10.10am.

Buses run to Novi Sad in Yugoslavia once daily and to Subotica three times daily. A 9.30am bus on Friday departs for Vienna.

Train Szeged is on a main railway line to Budapest's Nyugati station. Another line connects the city with Hódmezővásárhely and Békéscsaba, where you can change trains for Gyula or Romania. Southbound local trains leave Szeged for Subotica in Yugoslavia twice daily at 6.35am and 4.20pm.

Getting Around

The No 1 tram from the train station will take you north to Széchenyi tér. The tram turns west on Kossuth Lajos sugárút and goes as far as Izabella Bridge, where it turns around. Alight there for the Napfény hotel, motel and camp site.

You can get closer to the Napfény on bus No 75 or 78, which stops directly opposite the complex on Kossuth Lajos sugárút. Get off just after you cross the bridge over the railway tracks. The correct bus to Szentmihály and the flea market is the No 76; you can also take tram No 4. For Sziksósfürdő, take bus 7/f from the main bus station.

Local taxis can be ordered on ☎ 444 444 or ☎ 555 555.

ÓPUSZTASZER

☎ 62 • postcode 6767 • pop 2200

About 28km north of Szeged, the **Ópusztaszer National Historical Memorial Park** (*Ópusztaszeri Nemzeti Történeti Emlékpark;* ☎ *275 133;* **W** *www.opusztaszer.hu; admission park only 600Ft, park & panorama painting adult/student or child 1200/800Ft; open 9am-6pm daily Apr-Oct; 9am-4pm daily Nov-Mar*) in Ópusztaszer commemorates the single most important event in Hungarian history: the *honfoglalás*, or 'conquest', of the Carpathian Basin by the Magyars in 896.

Contrary to what many people think (Hungarians included), the park does not mark the spot where Árpád, mounted on his white charger, first entered 'Hungary'. That was actually the Munkács Valley, Hungarian territory until after WWI and now Ukrainian territory. But according to the 12th-century chronicler known as Anonymous, it was at this place called Szer that Árpád and the six clan chieftains, who had sworn a blood oath of fidelity to him, held their first assembly, and so it was decided that a **Millennium**

Monument would be erected here in 1896. (Scholars had actually determined the date of the conquest to be between 893 and 895, but the government was not ready to mark the 1000-year anniversary until 1896.)

Situated atop a slight rise in the Great Plain about a kilometre from the Szeged road, the park is an attractive though sombre place. Besides the neoclassical monument with Árpád taking pride of place, there are ruins of an 11th-century Romanesque church and monastery still being excavated, and an excellent open-air museum (skanzen; open Apr-Oct) with a farmhouse, windmills, an old post office, a schoolhouse and cottages moved from villages around southeast Hungary. In one, the home of a rather prosperous and smug onion-grower from Makó, a sampler admonishes potential gossips: 'Neighbour lady, away you go/If it's gossip that you want to know' (or words to that effect).

To the west of the park beside the little lake, a museum reminiscent of a Magyar chieftain's tent houses a huge panorama painting entitled The Arrival of the Hungarians. Completed by Árpád Feszty for the Millenary Exhibition in Budapest in 1896, the enormous work, which measures 15m x 120m, was badly damaged during WWII and was restored by a Polish team in time for the 1100th anniversary of the conquest in 1996. Two galleries (adult/child 400/300Ft for one gallery, 650/550Ft for both) above the painting are devoted to art and history of the area. Of particular interest are photos of rough-and-ready tribal Magyars dressed in their traditional 19th-century outfits.

Szeri Camping (☎ 275 123; Árpád liget 111; camping per adult/child/tent 600/300/600Ft, bungalows 4400Ft, motel rooms per person 1100Ft; open mid-Apr–mid-Oct), near the entrance to the park, has 14 bungalows sleeping four persons. The Szeri Csárda (mains 800-1500Ft) next door serves a decent gulyás.

Frequent buses travel between Szeged and Ópusztaszer.

HÓDMEZŐVÁSÁRHELY
☎ 62 • postcode 6800 • pop 51,200

Sitting on the dried-up bed of what was once Lake Hód, some 25km northeast of Szeged, the city of 'Hód Meadow Marketplace' was no more than a collection of disparate communities until the Turkish invasions, when much of the population was dispersed and the town's centre razed. The peasants of Hódmezővásárhely returned to subsistence farming in the 17th century, but the abolition of serfdom in the mid-19th century, without the redistribution of land, only increased their isolation and helped bring about an agrarian revolt led by János Kovács Szántó in 1894, an event the townspeople are justly proud of – and which the communist regime trumpeted for decades.

Folk art, particularly pottery, has a rich tradition in Hódmezővásárhely; some 400 independent artisans working here in the mid-19th century, made it the largest pottery centre in Hungary. Today you won't see much more pottery outside the town's museums than you would elsewhere, but the influence of the dynamic artists' colony here is felt well beyond Kohán György utca – from the galleries and Autumn Weeks art festival to the ceramic and bronze street signs by eminent artists.

Orientation & Information
The bus station is just off Andrássy utca on Bocskai utca, about a 10-minute walk east from Kossuth tér, the city centre. There are two train stations in town: the main one and Hódmezővásárhelyi-Népkert. The first is east of the city centre at the end of Mérleg utca, the second southwest at the end of Ady Endre utca.

For information head to Tourinform (☎/fax 249 350; e hodmezovasarhely@tourinform.hu; Szegfű utca 3; open 9am-6pm Mon-Fri, 10am-5pm Sat & Sun mid-June–mid-Sept; 8am-4pm Mon-Fri mid-Sept–mid-June). Szeged Tourist (☎ 534 915; Szőnyi utca 1; open 9am-5pm Mon-Fri), housed in an old granary next to the Old Church, is another source.

OTP bank (Andrássy utca 1) has a branch at the northeast corner of Kossuth tér. The main post office (Hódi Pál utca 2) is on the northwest corner of Kossuth tér.

Things to See
Museums & Galleries The János Tornyai Museum (☎ 344 424; Szántó Kovács János utca 16-18; adult/child 100/50Ft; open 10am-3pm Tues, 10am-5pm Wed-Sun), named after a leading member of the Alföld School of alfresco painting, displays some early archaeological finds, but its raison d'être is to show off the folk art of Hódmezővásárhely – the painted furniture, 'hairy' embroidery done with yarn-like thread, and

GREAT PLAIN

pottery unique to the region. The collection of jugs, pitchers and plates, most of them made as wedding gifts, is the finest of all and represents the many types once made here and named after city districts, including Csúcs (white and blue), Tabán (brown) and Újváros (yellow and green).

More pottery is on display at the **Csúcs Pottery House** (Csúcsi Fazekasház; Rákóczi utca 101; admission free; open 1pm-5pm Tues-Sun), once the home of master potter Sándor Vékony, and at the **Folk Art House** (Népmüvészeti tájház; ☎ 341 750; Árpád utca 21; admission free; open 9am-noon & 3pm-6pm Tues-Sun), two old thatched farmhouses standing self-consciously in the middle of a housing estate. Enter from Kaszap utca.

Outsiders are not allowed into the **artists' colony** (művésztelep; Kohán György utca 2), founded in the early part of this century, but you can view selected members' work at the **Alföld Gallery** (☎ 242 247; Kossuth tér 8, enter from Szönyi utca; adult/child 100/50Ft; open 10am-3pm Tues, 10am-5pm Wed-Sun) across from Szeged Tourist in a neoclassical former Calvinist school. Naturally the Alföld School dominates; you might go a little crazy

looking at horses and shahoof wells and cowboys on the Great Plain in every season through the eyes of Tornyai, István Nagy and József Koszta, but there are other things to enjoy such as the work of Menyhért Tóth and the impressionist János Vaszary.

Other Attractions It was said that the peasants of Hódmezővásárhely were so poor that they only found comfort in God. Judging from the number of places of worship in town (about a dozen representing half as many religions or sects), they didn't have two farthings to rub together. Few of them are outstanding monuments, but check out the Calvinist folk baroque **Old Church** (Ótemplom; Kossuth Lagos tér 8) dating from 1724 next to Szeged Tourist; the **Serbian Orthodox church** (Szántó Kovács János utca 9) from 1792; and the **synagogue** (Szeremlei utca 3), an old pile from 1857 with a later Art Nouveau facade (1906), north of Kálvin tér. It has a wonderful stained-glass rose window.

You may wonder about the long stone wall that stretches from the bus station westward for almost 4km. It's a **flood barrier** built in 1881, just two years after Szeged was inundated. The

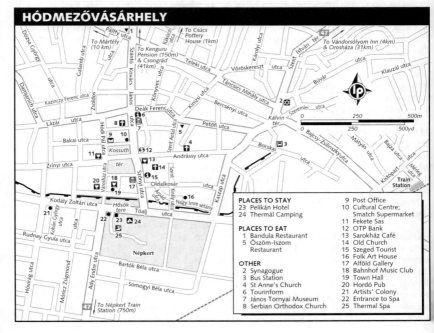

Hód-tó Canal south of Népkert Park may not look very threatening, but that's probably just what Szegeders were saying about the tranquil Tisza before 1879.

Activities

The **thermal spa** (☎ 244 238; Ady Endre utca 1; open 8am-8pm daily) in the Népkert, south of Kossuth tér, has eight hot and cold pools where you can immerse yourself for 300/120Ft (adult/child), but Mártély, about 10km to the northwest on a backwater of the Tisza, is the city's real recreational centre, with **boating**, **fishing** and **swimming** available.

István Kucsora (☎ 535 148; e hodmgrt@ hodmgrt.hu) has horses for **cross-country riding** and **carriage driving** at the Vándorsólyom Inn. It's about 4km northeast of the city on route No 47 (Kutasi út) en route to Orosháza. See Places to Stay & Eat for more information.

Special Events

If you're in the area in October, check the dates for the **Autumn Weeks**, a nationally attended arts festival. The city's other big festival – the one we had to drag Neal away from, kicking and screaming – is the **Sheep Fair** (Juhászverseny) on the last weekend of April.

Places to Stay & Eat

Thermál Camping (☎ 245 033; Ady Endre utca 1; camping per adult/child/tent 650/ 325/750Ft, bungalows with/without shower 6000/5500Ft) in the Népkert has a handful of rather uncomfortable (but convenient) bungalows for two people. There's better (but nowhere near as convenient) camping in Mártély at **Tisza-part Camping** (☎ 228 057; camping per adult/child/tent 500/300/500Ft, bungalows per person 1200-1600Ft; open May-Sept).

Szeged Tourist has **private rooms** for about 2000Ft per person.

Kenguru (☎ 534 841, fax 534 840; w www .kenguru.vasarhely.hu; Szánto Kovás János utca 78; singles/doubles 5600/6720Ft), a new pension in town, has 19 modern, bright rooms and a pool, sauna and solarium. Room 17 is the best choice; it has a balcony.

Vándorsólyom (☎ 341 900, fax 342 276; Kutasi út; singles 4600-7100Ft, doubles 5200-7700Ft), a nine-room inn in a peaceful, rural setting. Rates depend on the size of the room.

Pelikán (☎/fax 534 645; Ady Endre utca 1; singles/doubles 6200/8000Ft) is a 19-room hotel next to the spa.

Öszöm-Iszom (Szent Antal utca 8; mains 500-900Ft) – that's 'I Eat-I Drink' in Szeged dialect – is OK for a quick meal.

Bandula (☎ 244 234; cnr Szántó Kovács János utca & Pálffy utca; mains around 1000Ft) has an international menu and is a better place for a meal though it's a bit far out.

Entertainment

Petőfi Cultural Centre (☎ 241 710; Szántó Kovács János utca 7) can advise you on what's on in town.

Sarokház (cnr Andrássy utca & Szönyi utca), a café called the 'Corner House', is the best place for people-watching in Hódmezővásárhely.

Hordó (cnr Városház utca & Hősök tere), a pub near the town hall building, is fine for a glass as is the **Fekete Sas** (Hódi Pál utca), on the ground floor of the grand old Fekete Sas Hotel (currently under renovation).

Bahnhof Music Club (Kossuth tér 1), which you enter from Hősök tere, is the bopping-est venue in town.

Getting There & Away

Buses to Szeged, Békéscsaba, Makó, Szentes, Csongrád, Orosháza and the resort area of Mártély are frequent; there is a minimum of three daily departures to Kecskemét, Szolnok, Jászberény and Budapest. One or two buses daily head for Baja, Mohács, Parádfürdő, Szeghalom, Tiszafüred, Miskolc, Debrecen, Hajdúszoboszló, Gyöngyös and Pécs. One bus daily, at 6.15am, heads for Arad in Romania.

Two railway lines pass through Hódmezővásárhely, and all trains serve both train stations, which are 2km apart. The more important of the two lines connects Szeged with Békéscsaba. The smaller line links Makó, Hungary's onion capital and the birthplace of Joseph Pulitzer, with Szolnok.

CSONGRÁD

☎ 63 • postcode 6640 • pop 20,000
The 13th century did not treat the town of Csongrád (from the Slavic name Černigrad, meaning 'black castle') very well. Once the royal capital of Csongrád County, the town and its fortress were so badly damaged when the Mongols overran it that Béla IV transferred the seat to Szeged in 1247.

Csongrád never really recovered from the invasion. Its development was slow and until the 1920s it was not even a town. As a result, the Öregvár (Old Castle) district to the east looks much the way it did in the 17th century: a quiet fishing village of thatched cottages and narrow streets on the bank of the Tisza.

Orientation & Information

Csongrád lies on the right bank of the Tisza, close to where it is joined by the Körös River, some 58km north of Szeged. A backwater (Holt-Tisza) south of town is used for recreation. The bus station is on Hunyadi tér, five minutes from the main street, Fő utca. The train station lies to the southwest at the end of Vasút utca.

Tourinform *(☎/fax 481 008;* **e** *cson grad@tourinform.hu; Szentháromság tér 8; open 9am-6pm Mon-Fri, 10am-5pm Sat & Sun mid-June–mid-Sept; 8am-4pm Mon-Fri mid-Sept–mid-June)*, in the cultural centre, doesn't seem to stick to its opening hours. A better bet for information is **Csongrád Tourist** *(☎/fax 483 631;* **e** *idegenforgalom@ vnet.hu; Fő utca 3; open 9am-8pm daily)* in the lobby of the Erzsébet hotel.

There's an **OTP bank branch** *(Szentháromság tér 8)* next to the cultural centre and the **main post office** *(Dózsa György tér 1)* is northeast of the bus station.

Things to See & Do

The **László Tari Museum** *(☎ 481 052; Iskola utca 2; adult/child 200/100Ft; open 1pm-5pm Tues-Fri, 8am-noon Sat, 8am-noon & 1pm-5pm Sun)* is dedicated to the thousands of navvies who left Csongrád and vicinity in the 19th century to work on projects regulating rivers and building canals. Some travelled to sites as far away as Istanbul and Warsaw and were virtual slaves, working from 5am to 8pm with meatless meals and the occasional 'smoke' break.

Walking eastward from the museum to the Öregvár district, you'll pass the baroque **Church of Our Lady** (Nagyboldogasszony temploma), built in 1769, and the beautiful Secessionist **János Batsányi College** *(Kossuth tér)*. A bit farther on is **St Rókus Church**, built in 1722 on the site of a Turkish mosque.

The cobblestone streets of the protected **Öregvár** (Old Castle) district begin at a little roundabout three blocks east of the church.

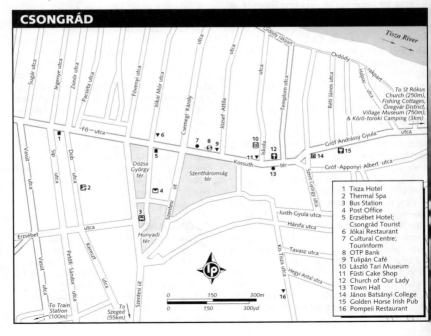

CSONGRÁD

To St Rókus
Church (250m),
Fishing Cottages,
Öregvár District,
Village Museum (750m),
& Körö-toroki Camping (3km)

To Train
Station
(100m)

To
Szeged
(55km)

1   Tisza Hotel
2   Thermal Spa
3   Bus Station
4   Post Office
5   Erzsébet Hotel;
    Csongrád Tourist
6   Jókai Restaurant
7   Cultural Centre;
    Tourinform
8   OTP Bank
9   Tulipán Café
10 László Tari Museum
11 Füsti Cake Shop
12 Church of Our Lady
13 Town Hall
14 János Batsányi College
15 Golden Horse Irish Pub
16 Pompeii Restaurant

Most of the district is made up of private homes or holiday houses, but the **Village Museum** (Tájház; Gyökér utca 1; adult/child 100/50Ft; open 1pm-5pm Tues-Sun May-Oct) gives a good idea of how the simple fisherfolk of Csongrád lived until not so long ago. It's housed in two old cottages connected by a long thatched roof and contains period furniture, household items and lots of fish nets and traps.

The **thermal spa** (Dob utca 3-5; adult/child 300/150Ft; open 7am-5pm Mon-Fri, noon-7pm Sat & Sun), fed by a spring with water that reaches 46°C, is in a large park and there are also **outdoor pools** and a **strand** (open 7am-8pm daily).

Csongrád Tourist can arrange **fishing** and **boating trips** from the Körös-toroki camp site.

Places to Stay

Körös-toroki Camping (☎ 481 185, fax 483 631; camping up to three persons with tent 2500Ft, bungalows for two 5500Ft; open mid-May–mid-Sept), on the beach near where the Körös River flows into the Tisza a couple of kilometres east of the town centre, has 19 bungalows all with kitchen and shower (mercifully on stilts – the area floods in heavy rain and the mosquitoes are unbearable).

Csongrád Tourist has **private rooms** costing 3500Ft to 5000Ft from two people, but from April to September they'll almost certainly try to book you into one of their more expensive **fishing cottages** in the Öregvár district. If you're feeling flush, this is the most atmospheric place to stay. Prices for these 200-year-old houses, some of which have kitchens and living rooms, start at about 5000Ft, though the average is about 10,000Ft. The nicest ones are at Öregvár 49, 57/b and 60.

Erzsébet (☎ 483 960, fax 483 631; Fő utca 3; singles/doubles 5500/6000Ft) is an old 13-room hotel minutes from the bus station. Rates include entry to the thermal spa.

Tisza (☎/fax 483 594; Fő utca 23; singles/doubles 8500/10,000Ft) is a modern 15-room hotel to the west.

Places to Eat

On the ground floor of the Erzsébet hotel is a cheap **café** (hamburgers from 250Ft) with hamburgers, gyros and such.

Tulipán (Szentháromság tér 2-6; mains from 600Ft; open till 8pm daily) is a simple café-restaurant in the centre of Csongrád.

Pompeii (☎ 470 160; Kis Tisza utca 6; mains around 1000Ft) is a bit out of the way, but it serves decent pizza and South Slav specialities in a renovated old house.

Jókai (☎ 475 010; Jókai Mór utca 1; mains 750-1650Ft) is the best place in town, with Hungarian and Serb main courses and a good wine list.

Füsti (Iskola utca 2; ice cream 50Ft) is a good cake shop if you're after something sweet.

Entertainment

Kossuth Cultural Centre (☎ 483 414; Szentháromság tér 8) can tell you what might be on in Csongrád.

Golden Horse Irish Pub (Gróf Andrássy Gyula utca 17/a) is about the only decent place in town for a drink, and is east of the centre on the way to the Öregvár.

Getting There & Away

Bus From Csongrád buses run Baja (two daily), Békéscsaba (three), Budapest (eight or nine), Eger (two), Gyula (two), Hódmezővásárhely (nine), Kecskemét (13), Kiskunfélegyháza (17), Lajosmizse (three), Orosháza (seven), Szentes (every 15 minutes) and Szolnok (four). The 12 daily buses to Szeged go via Ópusztaszer.

There's a daily departure for Arad in Romania at 5.30am.

Train Csongrád is on the 39km secondary railway line linking Szentes to the east with Kiskunfélegyháza to the west. You can't get very far from Szentes but Kiskunfélegyháza is a stop on the Budapest–Szeged express-train line.

BÉKÉSCSABA

☎ 66 • postcode 5600 • pop 67,600

When most Hungarians hear mention of Békéscsaba, they usually think of two very disparate things: fatty sausage and bloody riots. Csabai, a sausage not dissimilar to Portuguese *chorizo*, is manufactured here, and Békéscsaba was the centre of the Vihar Sarok, the 'Stormy Corner' of the Great Plain, where violent riots broke out among day labourers and harvesters in 1890. Ironically, the city is now the capital of Békés – 'Peaceful' – County.

Békéscsaba was an important fortified settlement as early as the 14th century, but it was razed and its population scattered under

Turkish rule. Early in the 18th century, a Habsburg emissary named János György Harruckern invited Rhinelanders and Slovaks to resettle the area, and it soon became a Lutheran stronghold.

Development began to reach Békéscsaba in the 19th century when the railway passed through the city (1858). In 1906, in response to the earlier agrarian movements, András Áchim founded his radical Peasants' Party here, an important political force in Hungary for many years. By 1950, Békéscsaba had surpassed nearby Gyula in importance and the county seat was moved here – something for which Gyula has yet to forgive her sister city.

These days Békéscsaba is very much a working city, relying on agriculture and food-processing, and although it isn't the most exciting town on the map, it's still a pleasant, friendly place to tarry on the way to the spas at Gyula or perhaps to Romania.

Orientation & Information

Békéscsaba's train and bus stations stand side by side at the southwestern end of Andrássy út, the main drag. A long stretch of this street, from Petőfi utca and Jókai utca to Szent István tér, is a pedestrian walkway, and just beyond it lies the Élővíz-csatorna, the 'Living Water Canal' that links Békéscsaba with Békes to the north, Gyula to the east, and the Körös River. To the east of the canal lies the Park-erdő, the city's cool and leafy playground.

The staff at **Békéstourist** (☎ *323 448; Andrássy út 10; open 8am-5pm Mon-Thur, 8am-4pm Fri)* are well informed and helpful.

BÉKÉSCSABA

PLACES TO STAY
15 Fiume Hotel & Restaurant

PLACES TO EAT
6 Szlovák Hotel Restaurant
23 Márvány Cake Shop
24 Halászcsárda
27 Market

OTHER
1 Peasant Houses
2 Slovakian Village House
3 Peasant Houses
4 Small Church
5 Great Church
7 Szünet
8 István Mill
9 Mihály Munkácsy Museum
10 Town Hall
11 Catholic Church
12 Cultural Centre
13 Phaedra Cinema; Babylon Terasz
14 Jókai Theatre
16 OTP Bank
17 Club Narancs
18 Csaba
19 Post Office
20 OTP Bank
21 Bacchus
22 Békéstourist
25 Thermal Baths
26 Greek Orthodox Church
28 Bus Station
29 Penny supermarket

You can visit the city's website at W www .bekescsaba.hu. There's an **OTP bank** *(Szent István tér 3)* and an OTP branch *(Andrássy út 4)* in the centre of town and the **main post office** *(Szabadság tér 1-3)* is opposite the Fiume hotel. Internet access is available at **Szünet** *(☎ 452 082; Kossuth tér 8; open 11am-10pm daily)* for 300Ft an hour.

Things to See & Do

The **Mihály Munkácsy Museum** *(☎ 323 377; Széchenyi utca 9; adult/child 100/50Ft; open 10am-6pm Tues-Sun)* has exhibits devoted to the wildlife and ecology of the Great Plain as well as to the folk culture of the region, but it's essentially a temple to the painter Munkácsy (1844–1900). Some may find his depictions of the Great Plain and its denizens a little sugar-coated, but as a chronicler of that place and time (real or imagined) he is unsurpassed in Hungarian fine art. An ethnographic exhibit traces the history of the Romanian, Slovak, German and Hungarian ethnic groups of the region. Don't miss the fine Slovak embroidery and the Hungarian painted furniture.

Present or future farmers would no doubt be interested in the **Grain Museum** *(Gabonamúzeum; ☎ 441 026; Gyulai út 65; adult/child 100/50Ft; open 10am-5pm Tues-Sun)*, housed in several old thatched barns and crammed with traditional tools and implements. The bladeless 19th-century windmill nearby is one of the best examples surviving in Hungary.

The **Slovakian Village House** *(Szlovák tájház; ☎ 327 038; Garay utca 21; adult/child 100/50Ft; open 10am-noon, 2pm-6pm Tues-Sun)*, is a wonderful Slovakian farmhouse built in 1865 and full of folk furniture and ornamentation. A lot of other typical peasant houses can be found in the neighbourhood, especially on Szigetvári utca and Sárkantyú utca.

Don't miss the **István Mill** *(István Malom; Gőzmalom tér)*, a grey-brick colossus from the early 20th century, best viewed from the small canal bridge near the Mihály Munkácsy Museum. It was the first steam mill built in Hungary and is still in operation.

The Lutheran **Great Church** *(Nagytemplom; Szeberényi tér 1; admission free)*, completed in 1824, and the 18th-century **Small Church** *(Kistemplom; Szeberényi tér 2; admission free)* facing each other across Kossuth tér attest to the city's deeply rooted Protestantism. The baroque **Greek Orthodox church** *(Bartók Béla utca 51-53; admission free)*, dating from 1838 and looking out of place amongst apartment blocks, could easily be mistaken for yet another Lutheran church from the outside.

The splendid **town hall** *(városháza; Szent István tér 7)* has a facade (1873) designed by the overworked Budapest architect Miklós Ybl. Walk east on József Attila utca to the canal and Árpád sor, which is lined with busts of Hungarian literary, artistic and musical greats and some wonderful late 19th-century mansions.

The **Árpád thermal baths** *(adult/child 450/280Ft; open 6am-7.30pm or 8.30pm daily)* and indoor and outdoor **swimming pools** are near the Halászcsárda restaurant at Árpád sor 2.

Places to Stay

János Arany College *(☎/fax 459 366; Lencsési út 136; dorm beds 800-900Ft)* in the Youth Camp (Ifjusági-tábor) near the Parkerdő has dormitory rooms available from late June to August.

Sport *(☎ 449 449; Gyulai út; rooms 4400Ft)* hostel has 14 rooms that ring the upper floors of a large stadium northwest of the Parkerdő. Sporting events and concerts are held in the huge auditorium across from the rooms, so don't expect much sleep if a rock band or a basketball game is on. Still, you couldn't ask for better seats. There's a raucous used-car market outside on Sunday.

Garzon Fényves *(☎/fax 457 377; W www .fenyveshotel.hu; rooms 7300Ft)* is a 45-room hotel split between three buildings in the Ifjusági-tábor. It's a cool and leafy oasis but not very convenient to the centre unless you have your own wheels.

Fiume *(☎ 443 243, fax 441 116; W www .fiume.viharsarok.com; Szent István tér 2; singles/doubles 7000/9900Ft)* bears the old name of the Adriatic port of Rijeka (now in Croatia) and is Békéscsaba's premier hotel and one of the nicest in Hungary. This restored 39-room hotel has a top-class restaurant and a popular pub-restaurant.

Places to Eat

For a quick bite to eat, **Babylon Terasz** *(Irány utca 10; light meals from 300Ft)*, attached to the Phaedra cinema, is a good place to stop.

Szlovák *(Kossuth tér 10; most mains under 1000Ft; open until 10pm Mon-Sat)* hotel restaurant is an inexpensive option which serves hearty Slovak and Hungarian specialities.

Fiume *(mains 700-1800Ft)* at the hotel of the same name offers some of the best food in town in clean, bright surroundings.

Halászcsárda *(☎ 327 426; Árpád sor 1; mains 900-1500Ft)* is the place to go if you're in the mood for fish; it's across the canal near the spa.

Márvány *(Andrássy út 21; ice cream from 60Ft; open until 9pm daily)* is the place to satisfy your sweet tooth. The cake shop has outside seating on a pretty square with a fountain.

There's a big food **market** *(Szabó Dezső utca; open Wed & Sat)*, which is just north of Andrássy út.

Entertainment

The beautifully restored **Jókai Theatre** *(☎ 441 527; Andrássy út 1)*, which dates from 1875, and the **Great Church** are the main cultural venues in Békéscsaba. Ask the staff at Békéstourist or the **County Cultural Centre** *(☎ 527 660; Luther utca 6)* for dates and times. Check the listings in *Békés Est*, a biweekly entertainment guide distributed for free.

Bacchus *(Andrássy út 10; open till 10pm daily)* himself would have been proud of this place – a small wine bar that keeps the wine flowing freely right up till closing time.

Club Narancs *(Szent István tér 3; open until 11pm Mon-Wed, until 4am Thur-Sat)*, opposite the Fiume hotel, makes a fun night out. It is a meeting place for students in a cellar with vaulted ceilings, cold beer and live or canned music. From Thursday to Saturday it becomes the **Rock Est Club**.

Csaba *(Szabadság tér 6)*, just south of Narancs, is another pumping joint that hosts ever-changing clubbing nights on Saturdays.

Getting There & Away

For points north such as Debrecen, take one of nine daily buses. Buses leave for Gyula and Békés every half-hour and for Szarvas once an hour. Some 14 buses daily go to Szeged and two to Budapest. Other destinations and their daily departure frequencies include Baja (one), Berettyóújfalu (10), Eger (two), Hajdúszoboszló (one), Karcag (one), Kecskemét (five), Miskolc (one), Pécs (one), Szeghalom (nine), Szolnok (one) and Vésztő (five to eight – direct, via Gyula or via Mezőberény).

Up to 11 daily trains – most of them expresses – link Békéscsaba with Szolnok and Budapest's Keleti station. Trains are frequent (up to 15 daily) to Gyula, and about half of them continue on to Vésztő (a change at Kötegyán may be required). Up to 11 trains daily depart from Békéscsaba for Szeged. As many as five international trains leave Békéscsaba daily for Bucharest via Arad and Braşov.

Getting Around

From the bus and train stations you can reach Szent István tér on foot via Andrássy út in about 20 minutes or wait for bus No 5 to Szabadság tér. Bus No 9 passes through the same square on its way past the stadium and Grain Museum. Board Bus No 7 for the college, Fényves hotel and Parkerdő.

You can order a taxi on ☎ 444 222.

VÉSZTŐ

☎ 66 • postcode 5530 • pop 8300

The **Vésztő-Mágor National Historical Monument** *(Vésztő-Mágor Történelmi Emlékhely; ☎ 477 148; adult/child 200/100Ft; open 9am-6pm daily May-Sept; 10am-4pm daily Apr & Oct)*, 4km northwest of Vésztő, contains two burial mounds of a type found throughout Hungary (see Százhalombatta in the Budapest chapter) and as far east as Korea. Such mounds are not all that rare on the Great Plain, but these are particularly rich in archaeological finds. The first is a veritable layer cake of cult and everyday objects, shrines and graves dating from the 4th century BC onward. The second contains the 10th-century **Csolt monastery** and church. It is in the centre of the patchwork 52,000-hectare **Körös-Maros National Park**, which is very rich in aquatic vegetation and wildlife. For information contact the **park directorate** *(☎ 313 855, fax 311 658; PO Box 72, Annaliget 1)* in Szarvas.

Vésztő is 36km north of Gyula (served by up to five buses daily) and roughly the same distance northeast of Békéscsaba, from where between five and eight buses depart daily for Vésztő. From the village you can walk for 4km to the site or catch one of five daily buses bound for Szeghalom, which will drop you off just outside. The last bus back leaves at 7.39pm; be sure to double-check, though. Up to nine daily trains leave Békéscsaba for Vésztő (a change at Kötegyán may be required), but be warned that they follow a circuitous route by way of Gyula and take 1½ hours to cover just 64km.

SZARVAS
☎ 66 • postcode 5540 • pop 18,800

Szarvas is a pretty, green town 45km north-west of Békéscsaba on a backwater of the Körös River (Holt-Körös). Szarvas was a market town that also suffered decimation under the Turks; Slovaks came here in large numbers late in the 18th century. But the best thing that ever happened to Szarvas was the arrival of Sámuel Tessedik, a Lutheran minister and pioneering scientist who established one of Europe's first agricultural institutes here in 1770.

Szarvas' big draws are water sports on the Holt-Körös, and the town's arboretum, easily the best in Hungary.

Orientation & Information
Szabadság út, the main street, bisects the town and leads westward to the Holt-Körös and the arboretum. On either side of Szabadság út are dozens of small squares organised in chessboard-like fashion by Tessedik, full of flower gardens and even small orchards.

The train station is in the eastern part of town at the end of Vasút utca, while the bus station is in the centre on Szabadság út at the corner with Bocskai István utca.

Tourinform (☎/fax 311 140; e szarvas@ tourinform.hu; Kossuth tér 3; open 9am-6pm Mon-Fri, 9am-5pm Sat & Sun mid-June–mid-Sept; 9am-5pm Mon-Fri May–mid-June & mid-Sept–end Sept; 9am-4pm Mon-Fri Oct-Apr) has an office in the cultural centre. For online information in Hungarian, go to ☒ www .szarvas.hu/tourinform.

There is an **OTP bank branch** on Szabadság út, just west of the Árpád hotel, while the **main post office** (Szabadság út 9) is on the other side of the street.

Things to See & Do
The **Szarvas Arboretum** (☎ 312 344; adult/child 250/200Ft; open 8am-6pm mid-Jan–mid-Dec), with some 30,000 individual plants not native to the Great Plain, is Hungary's finest. On 82 hectares it contains around 1600 species of rare trees, bushes and grasses, including mammoth pine, ginkgo, swamp cedar, Spanish pine and pampas grass. The arboretum is about 2km northwest of the centre across the Holt-Körös.

The **Sámuel Tessedik Museum** (☎ 216 608; Vajda Péter utca 1; adult/child 150/80Ft; open 10am-4pm Tues-Sun Apr-Oct; 1pm-5pm Tues-Sun Nov-Mar) has some interesting Neolithic exhibits from the goddess-worshipping Körös culture taken from burial mounds on the Great Plain, and much on Slovakian and Magyar ethnic dress and folk art. The section devoted to Tessedik and his work in making Szarvas bloom is interesting but

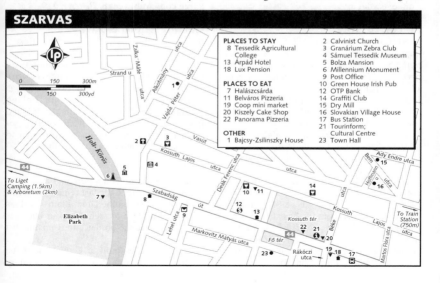

SZARVAS

PLACES TO STAY
8   Tessedik Agricultural College
13 Árpád Hotel
18 Lux Pension

PLACES TO EAT
7   Halászcsárda
11 Belváros Pizzeria
19 Coop mini market
20 Kiszely Cake Shop
22 Panorama Pizzeria

OTHER
1   Bajcsy-Zsilinszky House

2   Calvinist Church
3   Granárium Zebra Club
4   Sámuel Tessedik Museum
5   Bolza Mansion
6   Millennium Monument
9   Post Office
10 Green House Irish Pub
12 OTP Bank
14 Graffiti Club
15 Dry Mill
16 Slovakian Village House
17 Bus Station
21 Tourinform; Cultural Centre
23 Town Hall

unfortunately only in Hungarian. The **birthplace of Endre Bajcsy-Zsilinszky**, the resistance leader murdered by Hungarian fascists in 1944, is on the same street four blocks to the north.

The neoclassical **Bolza Mansion** *(Bolza-kastély; Szabadság út 2)*, facing the Holt-Körös, was built in 1819 as the homestead of a land-owning family of that name who founded the arboretum. Today it is part of the Tessedik Agricultural College but the grounds can be visited. On the steps leading down to the river stands a statue of Romulus and Remus, revealing the Bolza family's Roman origins. Directly in front of the mansion in the middle of the Holt-Körös is the new **Millennium Monument**, a rather bizarre construction that is meant to represent St Stephen's Crown flanked by two angels on top of a pole. You can make of it what you will.

The horse-driven **dry mill** *(szárazmalom;* ☎ *312 960; Ady Endre utca 1; adult/child 250/100Ft; open 1pm-5pm Tues-Sun Apr-Sept)*, dating from the early 19th century, is the best preserved in Hungary. It was still operating until the 1920s and is 100% original.

The **Slovakian Village House** *(Szlovák tájház;* ☎ *311 239; Hoffmann utca 1; adult/child 120/60Ft; open 1pm-4pm Sat, 10am-noon Sun May-Sept)* nearby has three rooms filled with hand-woven textiles and articles from everyday life.

Places to Stay

Liget Camping *(☎/fax 311 954;* W *www .ligetpanzio.hu; camping per adult/child/tent 650/450/500Ft, bungalows up to four persons 10,000-12,000Ft)*, which also has an 11-room pension with rooms from 9400 to 12,600Ft, is across the river just beyond Elizabeth Park *(Erzsébet-liget)* on route No 44. Rates vary depending on the season.

The **Tessedik Agricultural College** *(☎ 313 311; Szabadság út 1-3; beds from 2400Ft)* has a range of not-so-cheap accommodation possibilities in summer.

Lux *(☎ 313 417, fax 312 754;* e *lux@szarvas.hu; Szabadság út 35; rooms from 7500Ft)*, a pension with 11 well-kept rooms, is a stone's throw from the bus station.

Árpád *(☎ 312 120, fax 311 564; Szabadság út 32; singles/doubles 5100/7400Ft)* is an old-world hotel with 19 rooms in a partly renovated 19th-century mansion.

Places to Eat

Belváros *(Kossuth Lajos utca 23; pizzas 400-1000Ft)* is a good spot for pizza, as is **Panoráma** *(Kossuth tér; pizzas from 450Ft)*, next to Tourinform, which has the advantage of outdoor seating.

Halászcsárda *(☎ 311 164; mains 700-2000Ft; open until 11pm)* fish restaurant in the northeast corner of Elizabeth Park just over the bridge west of town is the best place for a meal in Szarvas. It has tables on a terrace by the river.

Kiszely *(cnr Szabadság út & Béke utca; ice cream from 55Ft; open 9am-9pm daily)* is a great *cukrászda* next to Tourinform and the cultural centre.

Diagonally opposite Kiszely is a small **Coop mini market** *(cnr Rákóczi utca & Szabadság út)*.

Entertainment

Péter Vajda Cultural Centre *(☎ 311 181, Kossuth tér 3)* should have updates on what might be on in Szarvas. Szarvas has a couple of excellent music clubs with live acts most weekends including the **Graffiti Club** *(☎ 214 430; Kossuth Lajos utca 50)* and the **Granárium Zebra Club** *(☎ 311 946; Kossuth Lajos utca 2)* in a splendid old town house.

Green House Irish Pub *(Kossuth Lajos utca 25)* is a sprawling place open till late daily.

For more information on what's on pick up a free copy of biweekly *Békés Est*.

Getting There & Away

Szarvas can be reached by bus from Békéscsaba (at least hourly), Debrecen (two daily), Gyula (two), Kecskemét (six), Miskolc (two), Orosháza (four), Szeged (six), Szentes (seven), Szolnok (one) and Tiszafüred (two).

Szarvas is on the train line linking Mezőhegyes and Orosháza with Mezőtúr and has services six times daily. From Békéscsaba, it's faster to take an express train to Mezőtúr and change for Szarvas there.

GYULA

☎ 66 • postcode 5700 • pop 34,100

A town of spas with the last remaining medieval brick castle on the Great Plain, Gyula is a wonderful place to recharge your batteries before crossing the border into Romania just 4km to the east.

A fortress was built at Gyula (the name comes from the title given to tribal military commanders among the ancient Magyars) in the 14th century, but it was seized by the Turks and held until 1695. Like Békéscsaba, Gyula came into the hands of the Harruckern family after the aborted Rákóczi independence war of 1703–11. They settled Germans and other groups in different sections of Gyula, and the names have been retained to this day: Big and Little Romanian Town (Nagy Románváros, Kis Románváros), German Town (Németváros) and Hungarian Town (Magyarváros).

Gyula refused to allow the Arad-bound railway to cross through the town in 1858 – a development welcomed by Békéscsaba, 20km to the west. As a result, Gyula was stuck at the end of a spur and developed at a much slower pace. In 1950 the county seat was moved from here (after 500 years, Gyulans like to point out) to its sister city. Gyula is still seething and a strong rivalry persists between the two: from who should be allocated more county money to whose football team and sausage is better.

But for better or worse, Gyula's spas, summer theatre in the castle and proximity to Romania attract far more visitors than Békéscsaba's scant offerings.

Orientation

Gyula is actually two towns: the commercial centre on Városház utca to the west and the Várfürdő (Castle Bath) in a large park to the east. The areas are within easy walking distance of each other. The Élővíz Canal runs east–west through the centre of Gyula, from a branch of the Körös River to Békéscsaba and beyond.

Gyula's bus station is south of Kossuth Lajos tér on Vásárhelyi Pál utca. Walk north through the park to the square and over the canal bridge to reach the town centre. The train station is at the northern end of Béke sugárút.

Information

Your best source of information is **Tourinform** (☎/fax 561 680; e bekes-m@tourinform.hu; Kossuth Lajos utca 7; open 9am-7pm Mon-Fri, 10am-6pm Sat & Sun mid-June–mid-Sept; 9am-5pm Mon-Fri mid-Sept–mid-June) located in a gallery. It this is closed, consult the **virtual information point** (Városház utca) – a touch-sensitive screen with general town information next to the Kézmüves cake shop. There is a **Gyula-**

tourist (☎ 463 026, fax 463 367; Eszperantó tér 1; open 8am-5pm Mon-Fri) office south of the Élővíz Canal. The town's website is at w www.gyula.hu.

There's an **OTP bank branch** (Hét vezér utca 2-6) west of Városház utca and the main **post office** (Eszperantó tér) is near Gyulatourist. A small **cyber café** (Kossuth Lajos utca 5; Internet access 600Ft per hour; open till 8pm daily) can be found above the Kis Kévmüves cake shop.

Things to See

Gothic **Gyula Castle** (Váfürdő utca; adult/child 200/100Ft; open 9am-5pm Tues-Sun), overlooking a picturesque moat near the baths, was originally built in the mid-15th century but has been expanded and renovated many times over the centuries, most recently late in the 1950s. There's not much to see inside, but you can stroll along its thick walls and climb the tower; both provide fine views of park and town. The squat 16th-century **Rondella** tower houses a café and wine bar with a delightful terrace in summer.

The **György Kohán Museum** (☎ 361 795; adult/child 150/100Ft; open 10am-6pm Tues-Sun Apr-Oct; 10am-4pm Tues-Sun Nov-Mar), in Göndöcs-Népkert, a park at Béke sugárút 35, is Gyula's most important art museum with more than 3000 paintings and graphics bequeathed to the city by the artist upon his death in 1966. The large canvases of horses and women in dark blues and greens and the relentless summer sun of the Great Plain are quite striking and well worth a look.

The baroque **Inner City Church** (Belvárosi templom; Harruckern tér; admission free) from 1777 has some interesting contemporary ceiling frescoes highlighting events in Hungarian and world history – including an astronaut in space! The Zopf **Romanian Orthodox church** (admission free) from 1812, to the east in Gróza Park, has a beautiful iconostasis (you can try and get the key from the house just south of the church entrance), but for contemporary icons at their kitschy best, no place can compare with the **Mary Museum** (Apor tér 11; adult/child 200/100Ft; open 9am-noon & 12.30pm-3pm Tues-Sun Mar-Nov; 9am-noon Tues-Sun Dec-Feb). You've never seen the Virgin in so many guises. On the same square stands the **Ferenc Erkel House** (☎ 463 552; Apor tér 7; adult/child 200/100Ft; open 10am-6pm

GREAT PLAIN

Tues-Sun), birthplace of the man who composed operas and the music for the Hungarian national anthem. The house contains memorabilia about his life and music.

The **Ferenc Erkel Museum** *(☎ 361 236; Kossuth Lajos utca 17; adult/child 200/100Ft; open 10am-6pm Tues-Sun)* has a **Dürer Room** devoted to archaeological finds – pottery, jewellery, weapons – from the region.

An interesting – and, for Hungary, very unusual – museum is **Ladics House** *(☎ 463 940; Jókai Mór utca 4; adult/child 200/ 100Ft; open 9am-6pm Tues-Sun)*, the perfectly preserved and beautifully furnished mid-19th century residence of a prosperous bourgeois family. Guided tours (in Hungarian only) start every half-hour or so and offer an excellent look into what life was like in a Hungarian market town.

Next door, the **Százéves** *(☎ 362 045; open 10am-8pm daily)* cake shop and museum facing Erkel tér is a visual and culinary delight. Established around 1840 (no doubt Mrs Ladics bought her *petits-fours* here), the Regency-blue interior is filled with Biedermeier furniture and mirrors in gilt frames. It is one of the most beautiful *cukrászdák* in Hungary.

Activities
The **Castle Baths** (Várfürdő) are in the 30-hectare Castle Garden (Várkert) east of the city centre and count a total of 20 pools. Admission is 750/650Ft (adult/child), or 400Ft after 3pm. There are nine **pools inside the spa** *(open 8am-6pm daily year-round)* and 11 **outdoor pools** *(open 8am-8pm daily May-Sept)*. **Boats** are available for rent on the small lake next to the castle over the summer months.

Special Events
The biggest event of the year is the **Gyula Theatre Festival**, with performances in the castle courtyard from late July to mid-August. There's an **All-Hungarian Folkdance Festival** in mid-August.

Places to Stay
Camping Of Gyula's three camp sites, **Márk** *(☎ 463 380; Vár utca 5; camping for two 2000Ft; open year-round)* is the friendliest and most central, but it's tiny and only for caravans and tents. There are no bungalows, but there are a couple of double rooms available (3000Ft).

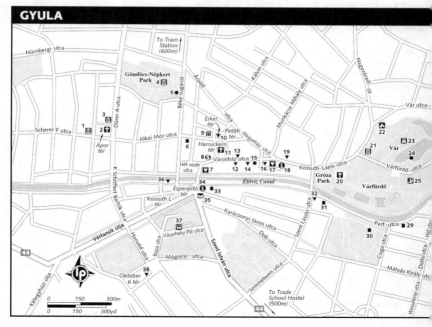

GYULA

Thermál Camping (☎ 463 704, fax 463 551; Szélső utca 16; camping per adult/child/tent 700/450/400Ft; open year-round) has a huge camp site and a motel with single rooms for 3900ft and double rooms for 5000Ft, but is a bit far out.

Private Rooms & Hostels Gyulatourist can book you a private room from 2000Ft per person or an entire apartment with kitchen and living room from 6000Ft. You'll see lots of signs advertising rooms along Szent László utca and, east of the spa, Tiborc utca and Diófa utca.

The **Girls' Trade School** (☎ 463 822, fax 463 192; e munkacs@freemail.hu; Szent István utca 69; dorm beds around 1200Ft; open mid-June–mid-Aug) turns into a 102-bed hostel with dormitory accommodation during the summer.

Hotels There are plenty of hotels in or around the Várfürdő, most of them sprawling, modern affairs with everything you could possibly need, and satellite TVs. Room rates vary widely depending on the season, but generally the most expensive times are from June to September and over the Christmas and New Year holidays.

Aqua (☎/fax 463 146; Part utca 7c; singles/doubles from 4000/7800Ft), a former trade union holiday house on a quiet bank of the canal, is a 64-room hotel and the cheapest of the hotels around the Várfürdő. The rooms on the top floor are newly renovated.

Park (☎ 463 711, fax 463 124; e park gyula@civishotels.hu; Part utca 15; singles/doubles from 5000/7500Ft), is a short distance to the west of Aqua, and has 56 rooms, a small swimming pool, solarium and sauna.

Agro (☎ 463 522, fax 561 520; Part utca 5; singles/doubles from €38/46), which has lovely gardens at the back, also has 56 rooms.

Erkel (☎/fax 463 555; e reserve@hotel erkel.hunguesthotels.hu; Várkert 1; singles/doubles from €25/41) is the closest hotel to the spa – in fact, the spa is connected by a corridor. It is a sprawling place with 315 rooms.

Aranykereszt (☎/fax 463 194; Eszperantó tér 2; singles/doubles from 4000/5000Ft), away from Várfürdő but alongside the canal, is the most charming hotel in Gyula. Its 20 rooms all have telephone, TV and minibar, and there's a popular restaurant and a bar with two tenpin bowling lanes.

Corvin (☎ 362 044, fax 362 158; Jókai utca 9-11; doubles €33-37), a 28-room hotel, is more central but less interesting than Aranykereszt.

Places to Eat

City Burger (Városház utca; gyros & burgers from 300Ft; open until 10pm Mon-Fri, until midnight Sat & Sun) is a fast-food takeaway place.

Fehér Holló (Tiborc utca 49; mains 700-1200Ft) has a nice quiet spot near the canal and is a good choice for csárda-style Hungarian meals, especially if you're staying near the castle and baths.

Őcsi & Fusek (Kossuth Lajos utca 6; mains 700-1000Ft) is not only popular for its great back courtyard but also for its excellent lunch-time set menu (470Ft).

Halászcsárda (☎ 466 303; cnr Part utca & Szent László utca; mains 600-1000Ft), next to the Agro hotel and facing the canal, offers the usual fishy dishes in pleasant surroundings.

Herkules Taverna (Bodoky utca; mains 900-1200Ft) is a colourful place overlooking the canal that serves Greek specialities.

GREAT PLAIN

PLACES TO STAY	PLACES TO EAT
6 Corvin Hotel	10 Százéves Cake Shop
22 Márk Camp Site	12 Kisködmön Restaurant
26 Erkel Hotel	13 City Burger
27 Thermál Camping	14 Kévműves Cake Shop
29 Aqua Hotel	16 Kis Kévműves Cake Shop;
30 Park Hotel	Cyber Cafe
31 Agro Hotel	19 Őcsi & Fusek
33 Aranykereszt Hotel	28 Fehér Holló Csárda
	32 Halászcsárda
	36 Herkules Taverna
	38 Market

OTHER		17 Bacardi
1 Mary Museum		18 Tourinform
2 Catholic Church		20 Romanian Orthodox
3 Ferenc Erkel House		Church
4 György Kohán Museum		21 Ferenc Erkel Museum;
5 Cultural Centre		Dürer Room
7 Macho Club		23 Castle
8 OTP Bank		24 Boat Rental
9 Ladics House		25 Castle Baths
11 Inner City Church		34 Gyulatourist
15 Virtual Information		35 Post Office
Point		37 Bus Station

Kisködmön *(Little Sheepskin;* ☎ *463 934; Városház utca 15; mains 1000-1500Ft)* is a fancy place with a solid Hungarian menu and a large, inviting garden.

You can't miss the cakes and decor at the **Százéves** *(*☎ *362 045; Erkel tér 1; open 10am-8pm daily)* cake shop – see Things to See earlier.

Kézmüves *(Artisan; Városház utca 21; ice cream from 55Ft)* cake shop is a less enchantingly decorated option than Százéves, but equally tasty. A smaller shop by the same name – **Kis Kézmüves** – is a few steps east.

Gyula's main **market** *(Október 6 tér)* for fruit, vegetables and other produce is southwest of the bus station.

Entertainment

Ferenc Erkel Cultural Centre *(*☎ *463 806; Béke sugárút 35)* in Göndöcs-Népkert has staff that can tell you what cultural events are on offer in Gyula. Organ concerts are sometimes held at the **Inner City Church**.

Decent pubs along Kossuth Lajos utca include originally named **Bacardi** at No 3 and the **Öcsi & Fusek** (see Places to Eat).

Macho *(Városház utca 1; open until 4am Sun-Thur, until 6am Fri & Sat)* is an unfortunately named club but is very popular.

Getting There & Away

With Gyula lying on an unimportant rail spur, buses are the preferred mode of transport. There are dozens each day departing for Békéscsaba and four go to Debrecen. Other destinations include Budapest (two daily), Eger (one), Kecskemét (two), Miskolc (one), Szeged (six), Szeghalom via Vésztő (two) and Vésztő direct (three).

Some 15 trains daily run west on line 128, Gyula's link to the Békéscsaba–Szolnok–Budapest rail line. Travelling north on this poky line will get you to Vésztő, Szeghalom and eventually to Püspökladány, where you can change trains for Debrecen. The only international train from Gyula leaves for the Romanian town of Salonta three times daily.

Northern Uplands

The Northern Uplands (Északi Felföld) make up Hungary's mountain region – foothills of the mighty Carpathians that roll eastward from the Danube Bend almost as far as Ukraine, some 300km away. By anyone's standards, these mountains don't amount to much: The highest peak – Kékes in the Mátra Range – 'soars' to just over 1000m. But in a country as flat as Hungary, these hills are important for environmental and recreational reasons.

The Northern Uplands include five or six ranges of hills – depending on how you count. From west to east they are: the Börzsöny, home to many of Hungary's Slovak ethnic community and best reached from Vác (see Around Vác in the Danube Bend chapter for details); the Cserhát; the Mátra; the Bükk; the Aggtelek (in reality, an adjunct to the eastern Cserhát region); and the Zemplén.

Generally, these hills are forested, though a large part of the lower regions are under cultivation (mostly grapes). Castles and ruins abound, and the last vestiges of traditional folk life are found here, especially among the Palóc people of the Cserhát Hills and the Mátyó of Mezőkövesd, just south of the Bükk Range. The ranges are peppered with resorts and camp sites, and it is a region famed for its wine.

Less idyllic are industrial Miskolc, once a socialist 'iron city that works' and now the centre of the country's widest rust belt, the polluted Sajó Valley, and the depressed towns of Nógrád County.

For general information on the Northern Uplands check out Ⓦ www.nordtur.hu.

Cserhát Hills

The Cserhát Hills are a rather unimpressive entry to the Northern Uplands. None of them reaches higher than 650m, and much of the area is cultivated and densely populated, obviating any serious hiking. But people don't visit the Cserhát for the hills; they come for folk culture, particularly that of the Palóc people (see the boxed text 'The Good Palóc People').

BALASSAGYARMAT
☎ 35 • postcode 2660 • pop 18,900

As the centre of the Cserhát region, Balassagyarmat bills itself as the 'capital of the Palóc'

Highlights

- The rich collection of folk art at the Palóc Museum in Balassagyarmat

- The town of Eger, with its grand castle, beautifully preserved architecture and legendary wine

- The restored castle and living folk traditions in Hollókő

- The narrow-gauge railway that winds its way from Miskolc through the Bükk Hills to Lillafüred

- The Rákóczi Cellar at Tokaj, where you can taste Hungary's most celebrated sweet wine

- The view of the Zemplén Hills at sunset from historic Boldogkő Castle at Boldogkőváralja

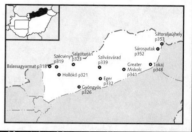

and, while other places may look more folksy, the town's excellent Palóc Museum gives it the leading edge. Lying just south of the Ipoly River and the Slovakian border, Balassagyarmat suffered more than most towns in the region during the Turkish occupation. Its castle was reduced to rubble and its houses were abandoned for decades. It regained stature late in the 18th century as the main seat of Nógrád County, but even that was taken away after WWII in favour of the 'new town' of Salgótarján. Today Balassagyarmat's few baroque and neoclassical buildings and the odd monument don't pull in the crowds; it's the town's link with Palóc culture that beckons.

Orientation & Information
The train station is about 600m south of the town centre at the end of Bajcsy-Zsilinszky

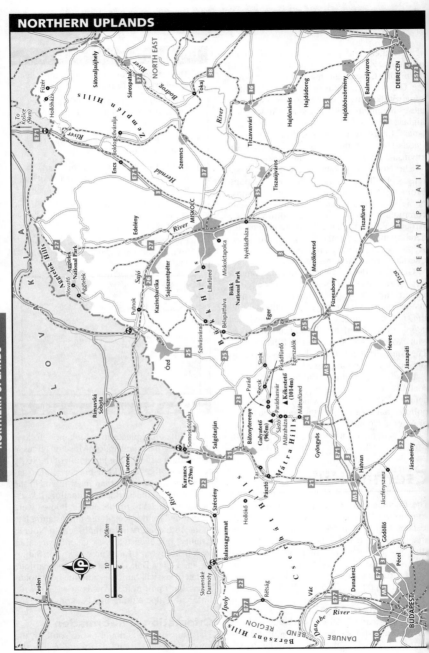

utca. The bus station is behind the town hall on Köztársaság tér, which splits Rákóczi fejedelem útja, the main drag, in two.

There's no Tourinform office here, but the staff at the City Gallery (see Other Attractions later in this section) are helpful.

There is a branch of **OTP bank** *(Rákóczi fejedelem útja 44; open 7.45am-4pm Mon-Wed & Fri, 7.45am-5pm Fri)* and there's a branch of **Budapest Bank** *(Rákóczi fejedelem útja 31; open 8am-5pm Mon-Fri)* just south of the bus station. The **post office** *(Rákóczi fejedelem útja 24; open 8am-7pm Mon-Fri, 8am-noon Sat)* is to the northeast, past the Roman Catholic church.

For general information on Balassagyarmat, see W www.balassagyarmat.hu.

Palóc Museum

The Palóc Museum *(☎ 300 168; Palóc liget 1; adult/child 240/125Ft; open 10am-4pm Tues-Sun May-Sept, 10am-4pm Tues-Sat Oct-Apr)* in Palóc Park, west of Bajcsy-Zsilinszky utca, was purpose-built in 1914 to house Hungary's richest collection of Palóc artefacts and is a must for anyone planning to visit traditional villages in the Cserhát Hills.

The standing exhibit 'From Cradle to Grave' on the 1st floor takes you through the important stages in the life of the Palóc people, and includes pottery, superb carvings, mock-ups of a birth scene, a classroom and a

The Good Palóc People

The people called the Palóc are a distinct Hungarian group living in the fertile hills and valleys of the Cserhátalja. Ethnologists are still debating whether they were a separate people who later mixed with the Magyars (their name means Cuman in several Slavic languages, suggesting they came from western Siberia) or a Hungarian ethnic group that, through isolation and Slovakian influence, developed its own ways. What's certain is that the Palóc continue to speak a distinct dialect of Hungarian (unusual in a country where language differences are virtually nonexistent) and, until recently, were able to cling to their traditional folk dress, particularly in such towns as Hollókő, Bugac, Rimóc and Örhalom. Today, with the Mátyó people of Mezőkövesd, they are considered the guardians of living folk traditions in Hungary.

wedding. There are also votive objects used for the all-important *búcsú*, or church patronal festivals (see the boxed text 'Farewell to All That' in the Southern Transdanubia chapter for details). But the Palóc women's agility with the needle – from the distinctive floral embroidery in blues and reds to the almost microscopic white-on-white stitching – leaves everything else in the dust.

An **open-air museum** *(skanzen; admission 125Ft; open 10am-4pm Tues-Sun May-Sept)*, including an 18th-century Palóc-style house, stable and church, stands in the garden behind the main museum.

Other Attractions

The **City Gallery** *(Városi Képtár; ☎ 300 186; Köztársaság tér 5; adult/child 100/50Ft; open 10am-noon, 12.30pm-5pm Tues-Sun)*, opposite the former county hall, is devoted to contemporary Nógrád painters, sculptors and graphic artists from the 1960s onward and is worth a look around. The **Local History Collection** *(Helytörténeti Gyűtemény; ☎ 300 663; Rákóczi fejedelem útja 107; adult/child 200/120Ft; open 8am-noon, 1pm-4.30pm daily)*, in an 18th-century noble's mansion called Csillagház (Star House), honours more locals, including the artist Endre Horváth, who lived here and designed some of the forint notes in circulation.

The tiny **Serbian Orthodox church** *(Szerb templom; ☎ 300 622; Szerb utca 5; admission free; open 2pm-6pm Tues-Sun)*, which you can enter through an archway at Rákóczi fejedelem útja 30, contains a gallery of paintings by local artists.

Places to Stay

There's a small **camp site** *(☎ 301 168, 300 404; Kővári út 13; open mid-June–Aug)* with tent sites for 100 people and three small cabins on the main road leading west out of town.

Szalézi College *(☎ 301 765, 301 465; Ady Endre utca 1; dorm beds 1200Ft)* has 180 dormitory beds available from mid-June to late August and maybe at weekends at other times of the year.

Club Panzió *(☎/fax 301 824; e nyirjes@axelero.hu; Teleki László utca 14; doubles 8000Ft, apartment with kitchen for 4 20,000Ft)* is an 18-room pension and the only year-round accommodation option in Balassagyarmat proper.

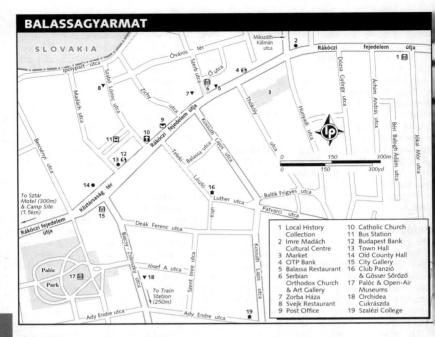

BALASSAGYARMAT

1	Local History Collection
2	Imre Madách Cultural Centre
3	Market
4	OTP Bank
5	Balassa Restaurant
6	Serbian Orthodox Church & Art Gallery
7	Zorba Háza
8	Svejk Restaurant
9	Post Office
10	Catholic Church
11	Bus Station
12	Budapest Bank
13	Town Hall
14	Old County Hall
15	City Gallery
16	Club Panzió & Gösser Söröző
17	Palóc & Open-Air Museums
18	Orchidea Cukrászda
19	Szalézi College

Sztár Motel (☎/fax 301 152, 341 152; Kővári út 12; doubles 4200Ft), with eight rooms, is 300m to the west of town and has a 24-hour restaurant.

Places to Eat

The **market** (Thököly utca) has plenty of food stalls and stand-up places to eat.

Balassa (☎ 300 418; Rákóczi fejedelem útja 32-36; set menus from 590Ft; open 10am-10pm Mon-Thur, 10am-midnight Fri & Sat) is a cheap, sit-down restaurant with a little terrace. The **Gösser Söröző** (mains 730-1860Ft; open 10am-midnight) at the Club Panzió serves food as well as suds.

If you're in the mood for something ethnic, **Svejk** (☎ 300 999; Szabó Lőrinc utca 16; meals 1500Ft; open 11am-10.30pm Mon-Sat, noon-10pm Sun) serves Czech and Slovakian dishes, while **Zorba Háza** (☎ 315 976; Rákóczi fejedelem útja 28; mains 450-750Ft; open 10am-midnight Mon-Sat, 2pm-11pm Sun), in a shopping centre off the main road, has pizza, pasta and some Greek dishes.

Orchidea Cukrászda (☎ 311 450; Bajcsy-Zsilinszky utca 12; open 9am-7pm Mon-Fri, 8am-7pm Sat & Sun), opposite Palóc Park has excellent ice cream and cakes.

Entertainment

Imre Madách Cultural Centre (☎ 300 622, Rákóczi fejedelem útja 50; open 8am-8pm Mon-Fri, 1pm-8pm Sat & Sun) is the place to find out what's on. Also check out the free bi-weekly *Nógrádi Est* magazine, which includes coverage of Balassagyarmat.

Getting There & Away

Some 12 to 15 daily buses link Budapest with Balassagyarmat via Vác and Rétság. There are two or three daily buses to Hatvan, one each to Gyöngyös and Pászto, and plenty to Salgótarján via Litke or Endrefalva. Seven buses go daily to Szécsény on weekdays (three or four at the weekend); Szécsény is the place to change for Hollókő. There are week day buses to Hont on the Slovakian border at 6am and 11.50am (4.50pm at the weekend).

Balassagyarmat can be reached throughout the day via a snaking train line from Vác. The trip takes over two hours to cover 70km; the bus will cut that time in half. If coming from Budapest or the east by train, change at Aszód

NORTHERN UPLANDS

SZÉCSÉNY

☎ 32 • postcode 3170 • pop 7000

Eighteen kilometres east of Balassagyarmat in the picturesque Ipoly Valley bordering Slovakia, Szécsény is usually given a miss by travellers headed for its tiny, but much better-known, neighbour to the southeast, Hollókő. But while Hollókő has folklore, Szécsény has history. In 1705, in a camp behind where Forgách Manor now stands, the ruling Diet made Ferenc Rákóczi II of Transylvania the prince of Hungary and the commander in chief of the *kuruc* forces fighting for independence from the Austrians.

Orientation & Information

The train station is about 1.5km north of the town centre just off Rákóczi út en route to Litke. The bus station is on Király utca, east of the Firewatch Tower on Fő tér.

Tourinform (☎ *370 777, fax 370 170;* e *szecseny@tourinform.hu; Ady Endre utca 7; open 8am-6pm Mon-Fri May-Sept, 8am-4pm Mon-Fri Oct-Apr)* has an office in the same building as the Sándor Kőrösi Csoma Memorial Exhibition (see Forgách Manor & Museums later in this section). Its website is in Hungarian only.

You'll find a branch of **OTP bank** *(Rákóczi út 86; open 7.45am-3pm Mon-Wed, 7.45am-5pm Thur, 7.45am-2pm Fri)* northwest of the town hall, and the **post office**

(Dugonics utca 1; open 8am-4pm Mon-Fri, 8am-noon Sat) to the south of it.

For general information on Szécsény, see W www.szecseny.hu.

Forgách Manor & Museums

Forgách Manor *(Ady Endre utca 7)* was built around 1760 from the remains of a medieval border fortress. In the mid-19th century it passed into the hands of the aristocratic Forgách family, who made further additions, and today it houses a motley assortment of exhibits, such as the **Ferenc Kubinyi Museum** (☎ *370 143; adult/child 200/100Ft; open 10am-6pm Tues-Sun May-Sept, 10am-4pm Tues-Sat Oct-Apr).*

On the ground floor there's a small pharmaceutical exhibit as well as a few rooms done up much the way the Forgách family would have liked to see them. Upstairs, beyond the Stone Age bones and chips, the reconstructed Neolithic house and the Bronze Age jewellery, is a ghastly hunting exhibit with any number of 'useful' items (napkin rings, cups, pistol butts, umbrella handles) carved and whittled from the carcasses and coats of our furred and feathered friends.

Only a little less frightening is the **Bastion Museum** (Bástya Múzeum) located in the northeast tower, from where part of the original 16th-century castle wall is seen to the west and south. Exhibits include an all-too-complete

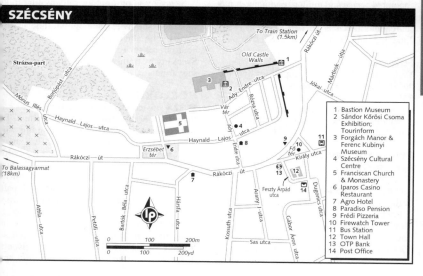

SZÉCSÉNY

1 Bastion Museum
2 Sándor Kőrösi Csoma Exhibition; Tourinform
3 Forgách Manor & Ferenc Kubinyi Museum
4 Szécsény Cultural Centre
5 Franciscan Church & Monastery
6 Iparos Casino Restaurant
7 Agro Hotel
8 Paradiso Pension
9 Frédi Pizzeria
10 Firewatch Tower
11 Bus Station
12 Town Hall
13 OTP Bank
14 Post Office

collection of torture implements: racks, yokes, stocks and a flogging bench.

Those of a nervous disposition will seek refuge in the **Sándor Kőrösi Csoma Memorial Exhibition** (Kőrösi Csoma Sándor Emlékkiállítás) in the manor's gate house. Kőrösi Csoma (1784–1842) was a Hungarian Franciscan monk who travelled to Tibet and wrote the first Tibetan-English dictionary.

Franciscan Church & Monastery

Parts of the Gothic Franciscan church and monastery (Ferences templom és kolostor; ☎ 370 880; Haynald Lajos utca 7-9; donation requested; open 9am-5pm daily) date from the 14th century, and the latter has been restored to its former glory after years of neglect. In the church sanctuary (the oldest section) a guide will point out the 500-year-old carvings of saints, flowers and fruits in the vaulted ceiling (the carvings on the pillars were destroyed by the Turks when they occupied Szécsény in 1552). You can also see where Muslims carved out a mihrab, or prayer niche, in the south wall.

In the baroque monastery (essentially dating from the 17th century, though with parts of the Gothic church incorporated into it) you'll see the monks' cells and, depending on what's open, the library, dining hall, Gothic oratory overlooking the church's interior, and/or the Rákóczi Room, where the newly appointed prince and military commander met with his war cabinet in 1705. Tours of the church and monastery depart at 10am, 11am, 2pm, 3pm and 4pm Tuesday to Saturday.

Firewatch Tower

You may think you're seeing things but, yes, the 19th-century firewatch tower (tűztorony; Rákóczi út 86), near Fő tér in the centre of town, is leaning (by three degrees) – a result of shelling and bombing in 1944, and clay subsidence.

Places to Stay & Eat

Agro (☎ 370 382, fax 370 936; Rákóczi út 90/b; dorm bed in 2-/4-bed room 2100/ 1800Ft) is a hostel-like hotel with 12 rooms in the centre of Szécsény.

Paradiso (☎ 372 427, fax 370 947; e para diso@gyaloglo.hu; Ady Endre utca 14; singles/ doubles/triples/quads with shower 4500/ 7500/10,500/14,000Ft), the only other game in town, is a comfortable, 17-room pension in

the former servants' quarters of Forgách Manor.

Iparos Casino (☎ 370 091; Erzsébet tér 1; mains 750-2600Ft; open 11.30am-10pm Tues-Sat) has basic but very cheap Hungarian dishes.

Frédi (☎ 370 372; Rákóczi út 85; pizza 590-1490Ft) is a decent pizzeria (with a wood-burning oven) and cukrászda (cake shop), and is a lot more upbeat than the other places.

The restaurant at the **Paradiso** (starters 350-1250Ft, mains 600-1800Ft; open noon-11pm Mon-Fri, noon-midnight Sat) is quite good, serves local specialities and has outside seating in a lovely courtyard with a fountain.

Entertainment

The staff at the **Szécsény Cultural Centre** (Szécsényi Művelődési Központ; ☎ 370 860; Ady Endre utca 12) may have information on what's on in Szécsény. The free biweekly Nógrádi Est magazine includes Szécsény.

Getting There & Away

Some seven buses depart for Hollókő on weekdays, with up to nine on Saturday and five on Sunday. You shouldn't have to wait more than a half-hour for buses to Balassagyarmat or Salgótarján (with a possible change for the latter at Litke, Endrefalva or Nógrádmegyer). There are nine daily buses to Budapest and up to five to Pászto.

Szécsény is on a minor railway line linking it with Balassagyarmat and Aszód to the west and southwest and Ipolytarnóc to the north on the Slovakian border, where you can board trains for Lučenec. To get to Vác from Szécsény by train, you must change at Balassagyarmat.

HOLLÓKŐ

☎ 32 • postcode 3176 • pop 465

People either love Hollókő or they hate it. To some, the two-street village nestling in a valley 16km southeast of Szécsény is Hungary's most beautiful and deserves kudos for holding on to its traditional architecture and a few old customs. Others see it as a staged tourist trap run by Budapest entrepreneurs with paid 'performers'. Unesco agreed with the former view in 1987 when it put Hollókő on its World Heritage List of cultural sites – the first village in the world to receive such an honour. What sets Hollókő (Raven Rock) apart is its restored 13th-century castle and

NORTHERN UPLANDS

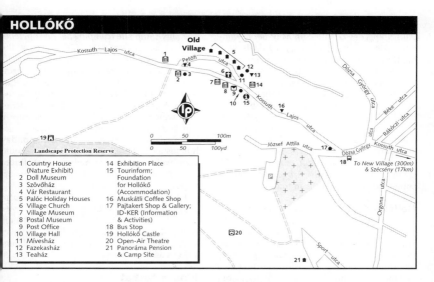

HOLLÓKŐ

1 Country House
   (Nature Exhibit)
2 Doll Museum
3 Szövőház
4 Vár Restaurant
5 Palóc Holiday Houses
6 Village Church
7 Village Museum
8 Postal Museum
9 Post Office
10 Village Hall
11 Míveshaz
12 Fazekasház
13 Teaház
14 Exhibition Place
15 Tourinform;
   Foundation
   for Hollókő
   (Accommodation)
16 Muskátli Coffee Shop
17 Pajtakert Shop & Gallery;
   ID-KER (Information
   & Activities)
18 Bus Stop
19 Hollókő Castle
20 Open-Air Theatre
21 Panoráma Pension
   & Camp Site

Landscape Protection Reserve

the architecture of the so-called Old Village (Ófalu), where some 60 houses and outbuildings have been listed as historic monuments.

The village has burned to the ground many times since the 13th century (most recently in 1909), but the villagers have always rebuilt their houses exactly to plan with wattle and daub – interwoven twigs plastered with clay and water.

These days, few women wear the traditional Palóc dress – wide, red and blue, pleated and embroidered skirts, and ornate headpieces. Still, on Sunday mornings, important feast days such as Easter and Assumption Day (15 August) or during a wedding, you may get lucky and catch some in fancy garb.

Orientation & Information

The bus will stop on Dózsa György utca at the top of Kossuth Lajos utca; from there walk down the hill to the Old Village.

Tourinform (☎ 579 011, fax 579 010; e holloko@tourinform.hu; Kossuth Lajos utca 68; open 9am-5pm Mon-Fri, 10am-4pm Sat & Sun Apr-Sept; 9am-5pm Mon-Fri, 10am-2pm Sat & Sun Mar-Oct) will supply you with as much information as you need about Hollókő. You can get a cash advance on your credit card at the **post office** (Kossuth Lajos utca 72; open 8am-4pm Mon-Fri), two doors down.

For general information (in Hungarian) on Hollókő, see w www.euroastra.com/holloko.

Things to See

The Old Village's wonderful **folk architecture** is its main attraction. Stroll along the two cobblestone streets, past the whitewashed houses with carved wooden gables and porches and red-tiled roofs. Wine is stored in the small cellars that open onto the streets.

Village Church A little wooden church, the focus of the village's spiritual and social life, is on the corner where Petőfi utca, the Old Village's 'other' street, branches off from Kossuth Lajos utca. Built as a granary in the 16th century and sanctified in 1889, it is a fairly austere affair both inside and out.

Museums Five small museums in traditional houses line Kossuth Lajos utca. The **Postal Museum** (Postamúzeum; ☎ 379 288; Kossuth Lajos utca 80; adult/child 100/50Ft; open 10am-6pm Tues-Sun Apr-Oct) is a branch of the one in Budapest. Next door, the **Village Museum** (Falumúzeum; ☎ 379 258; Kossuth Lajos utca 82; adult/child 100/50Ft; open 10am-4pm daily Apr-Oct; 10am-2pm Thur, noon-2pm Fri, 10am-4pm Sat & Sun Nov-Mar) is the usual, three-room Hungarian setup, with folk pottery, painted furniture, embroidered pillows and, in the back yard, an interesting carved wine press dated 1872. A nature exhibition at the **Country House** (Tájház; ☎ 36-412 791 in Eger; Kossuth Lajos

NORTHERN UPLANDS

utca 99-100; adult/child 150/80Ft; open 9am-5pm Tues & Thur-Sun May-Sept; 9am-3pm Tues & Thur-Sun Oct-Apr) deals with the flora, fauna and human inhabitants of the Eastern Cserhát Landscape Protection Reserve, part of which surrounds the village.

The **Exhibition Place** *(Kiállítóhely tóhely; ☎ 379 255; Kossuth Lajos utca 79; adult/child 60/30Ft; open 10am-5pm daily Apr-Oct)* spotlights the work of a local master woodcarver and a photographer. The **Doll Museum** *(Babamúzeum; ☎ 379 088; Kossuth Lajos utca 96; adult/child 120/80Ft; open 10am-5pm daily Apr-Sept)* exhibits some 200 porcelain dolls in traditional dress.

Hollókő Castle Hollókő Castle *(Hollókői Vár; adult/child 250/100Ft; open 10am-5.30pm daily Apr-Oct)* on Szár-hegy (Stalk Hill) can be reached by following the trail up the hill across from the Tájház or from the bus stop by walking up to József Attila utca and then following the west-bound trail from the car park. At 365m, the castle has a commanding view of the surrounding hills.

The castle was built at the end of the 13th century and strengthened 200 years later. It was captured by the Turks and not liberated until 1683 by the Polish king Jan Sobieski (ruled 1674–96). It was partially destroyed after the War of Independence early in the 18th century but is, in fact, one of northern Hungary's most intact fortresses. The views from the top of the pentagonal keep are stunning.

Activities

ID-KER *(☎ 379 273; Kossuth Lajos utca 46; open 9am-4pm daily Apr-Sept, 9am-3pm Mon-Fri Oct-Mar)*, based in the Pajtakert (Barnyard) shop and gallery, can organise **folk-craft lessons**, such as weaving, woodcarving, pottery and egg painting. There are some gentle **walks** into the hills and valleys of the 140-hectare **landscape protection reserve** to the west and south of the castle. *A Cserhát*, the 1:60,000 Cserhát map (No 8; 650Ft) from Cartographia, will help you plan your route.

Special Events

Hollókő marks its calendar red for the annual Easter Festival in late March or April, the **Nógrád Folklore Festival** and **Palóc Homespun Festival** held at the open-air stage in July, and the **Castle Games**, a touristy medieval tournament at the castle in August.

Places to Stay

The only **camp site** *(camping per person/tent/ caravan/car 500/500/500/200Ft)* is at the Panoráma complex (see later in this section).

Private rooms are available from Tourinform (from 1500Ft per person). The **Foundation for Hollókő** *(Hollókőért Közalapítvány, ☎/fax 579 010; e holokozal@mail.datanet .hu)*, which shares an office with Tourinform and keeps the same hours, can arrange accommodation at one of the 10 **Palóc holiday houses** along Petőfi utca (though you should book well ahead in the high season). Prices start at about 3600Ft for a double but expect to pay 5000Ft to 7000Ft.

Panoráma *(☎/fax 379 048; Orgona utca 31; doubles/quads 4000/6000Ft, bungalows 5000Ft)*, perched on the hill off Sport utca south of the village, is a holiday complex with a nine-room pension, five four-bed bungalows and a camp site.

Places to Eat

Vár *(☎ 379 029; Kossuth Lajos utca 93-95; meals around 1200Ft; open 11am-8pm daily)* is one of the few places to eat in Hollókő, but remember that this is still very much an early-to-bed, early-to-rise farming community: it closes early.

Muskátli *(☎ 379 262; Kossuth Lajos utca 61; open 11am-8pm daily Apr-Sept; 11am-5pm Wed-Fri & Sun, 11am-6pm Sat Oct-Mar)* is a coffee shop that serves meals as well.

Teaház *(Teahouse; ☎ 380 016; Petőfi utca 4)*, a little place behind the Míveszház (see Shopping), has a small wine bar in the cellar.

Shopping

Szövőház *(Loom House; ☎ 379 273; Kossuth Lajos utca 94; open 10am-5pm Tues-Sun)* is a good place for finding hand-woven and embroidered goods. It's interesting to watch the women demonstrate how their enormous loom works, and you can give it a go yourself (adult/child 100/60Ft).

Míveszház *(Craft House; ☎ 380 016; Petőfi utca 6)* has an excellent selection of Palóc folk dress and costumes. **Fazekasház** *(Pottery House; ☎ 379 252; Petőfi utca)*, behind the Teaház, has hand-thrown vases, jugs, candlesticks and decorative items. The decorated *mézeskalács* (honey cakes) for sale at **Pajtakert** *(☎ 379 273; Kossuth Lajos utca 46)* make great gifts.

Getting There & Away
Szécsény is the gateway to Hollókő, with some buses heading there twice an hour (up to 20 daily) Monday to Friday; there are 17 buses on Saturday and nine on Sunday. You can also catch one of about six weekday buses (five on Saturday, four on Sunday) to Salgótarján via Pászto.

SALGÓTARJÁN
☎ 32 • postcode 3100 • pop 48,850

After an idyllic day in Hollókő or any of the rural villages of the Cserhát, arriving in the modern city of Salgótarján, 25km east of Szécsény, is like stepping into a cold shower. Ravaged by fire in 1821 and by serious flooding 70 years later, Salgótarján can boast almost no buildings that predate this century.

The surrounding Medves Hills have been exploited for their coal since the 19th century, and it is on this that Salgótarján's success is based. As in Miskolc, the communists found the coal miners and steelworkers here sympathetic to their cause and were supported both during the Republic of Councils and after the war (though this did not stop the dreaded ÁVH secret police from shooting

down over 100 citizens here during the 1956 Uprising); see also The 1956 Uprising under History in the Facts about Hungary chapter for more information on this event. For its support, Salgótarján was made the county seat in 1950 and rebuilt throughout the 1960s.

Orientation & Information
Because it has virtually swallowed the village of Somoskőújfalu some 10km to the north, Salgótarján feels like a large city. The train and bus stations are a short distance apart to the west of the city centre.

Tourinform (☎ 512 315, fax 512 316; e salgotarjan@tourinform.hu; Fő tér 5; open 9am-6pm daily mid-June–Sept; 9am-5pm Mon-Fri, 10am-1pm Sat & Sun Oct–mid-June), in the same building as the Attila József Cultural Centre, is helpful and friendly.

Travel agencies in the centre include **Nógrád Tourist** (☎ 310 660; Erzsébet tér 5; open 8am-4pm Mon-Fri, 8am-noon Sat), on the first level of the shopping arcade, and **Ibusz** (☎ 421 200, fax 511 635; Fő tér 6; open 8am-5pm Mon-Fri).

There's a branch of **OTP bank** (Rákóczi út 12; open 7.45am-6pm Mon, 7.45am-5pm

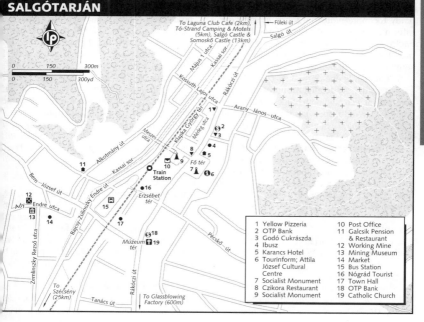

SALGÓTARJÁN

1 Yellow Pizzeria
2 OTP Bank
3 Godó Cukrászda
4 Ibusz
5 Karancs Hotel
6 Tourinform; Attila
  József Cultural
  Centre
7 Socialist Monument
8 Czikora Restaurant
9 Socialist Monument
10 Post Office
11 Galcsik Pension
   & Restaurant
12 Working Mine
13 Mining Museum
14 Market
15 Bus Station
16 Nógrád Tourist
17 Town Hall
18 OTP Bank
19 Catholic Church

Tues-Thur, 7.45am-4pm Fri) next to the Godó Cukrászda, and a second branch *(Rákóczi út 22; open 7.45am-5pm Mon, 7.45am-4pm Tues-Fri)* below the Catholic church. The main **post office** *(Fő tér 1; open 8am-8pm Mon-Fri, 8am-noon Sat)* is closer to the end of Klapka György tér despite it's official address.

For general information about Salgótarján, see W̄ www.salgotarjan.hu.

Things to See

The **Mining Museum** *(Bányászati Múzeum; ☎ 420 258; Zemlinszky Rezső utca 1; adult/child 250/125Ft; open 9am-3pm Tues-Sun Apr-Sept, 9am-2pm Tues-Sun Oct-Mar)*, the city's only real sight, is a short walk southwest of the train and bus stations. Filled with geological maps and samples, old uniforms and a statue of St Barbara, the patron of miners, standing proudly next to old communist banners calling for the nationalisation of the mines, the museum's style is somewhat outdated and is not particularly interesting. Across the street a 280m-long mine continues to be 'worked' by performers in unrealistically clean overalls; you can wander through the pits.

The production of glassware has been an important industry in Salgótarján since at least the start of the 20th century. Should you be ready for more industrial tourism, ask Tourinform about tours of the **ST Glassblowing Factory** *(ST Öblösüveggyár; ☎ 410 433; Huta utca 1; open 9am-1pm Mon-Fri)*, about 700m south of the centre along Rákóczi út.

Salgótarján is one of the few cities in Hungary that still has **socialist monuments** prominently displayed, and both of these monuments are in Fő tér – Budapest put its own collection in the 'zoo' that is Statue Park years ago (for details see Statue Park under Around Budapest in the Budapest chapter). One to the west of the square depicts a supporter of Béla Kun's 1919 Republic of Councils running with a rifle in hand; the other, to the east in front of the cultural centre, shows a couple of socialist youths looking rather guilty as they set doves free.

Special Events

The event in Salgótarján is the **International Dixieland Festival** in May.

Places to Stay

Tó-Strand Camping *(☎ 430 168, 310 660; Kemping út; camping per person/tent/caravan 500/800/1200Ft)* is about 5km northeast of

the town centre, just off the road to Somoskő. There are also two year-round **motels** *(singles/doubles with shared shower 2000/3500Ft)* with a total of 19 rooms, and an unheated **motel** *(doubles 2600Ft)* and **bungalows** *(doubles 2000Ft)* that are available from April to September. A boating lake, tennis courts and a pool are nearby. You can reach the camp site on bus No 6 from Rákóczi út.

For **private rooms** *(singles/doubles 4000/6000Ft)* in one of the city's many high-rises contact Ibusz (see under Orientation & Information earlier in this section).

Galcsik *(☎ 422 660, fax 316 524; Alkotmány út 2; singles/doubles with shower 2980/4980Ft, singles/doubles/triples with bathroom 4980/7480/9980Ft)* is a 32-room, well-maintained pension near the bus station and one of the better deals in town.

Karancs *(☎ 410 088, fax 414 994; e̲ karancshotel@mail.gabonet.hu; Fő tér 6; singles/doubles €31/38)* is a very ordinary, 46-room hotel with a restaurant and bar.

Places to Eat

Yellow *(☎ 310 480; Rákóczi út 11; pizza 380-700Ft; open 8.30am-midnight Mon-Fri, 9.30am-midnight Sat)*, at the corner with Kossuth Lajos út, is a pizzeria and pub, and a good choice for a cheap (if unexceptional) meal.

Czikora *(CZZ; ☎ 311 384; Fő tér 1; mains 690-980Ft; open 7.30am-9pm Mon-Sat)* is a small restaurant opposite the Karancs hotel. It has decent food.

Galcsik *(☎ 422 660; mains 850-1190Ft, open 7am-10pm Mon-Fri, 7am-11pm Sat 7am-9pm Sun)*, at the pension of that name serves the best food in Salgótarján.

Godó Cukrászda *(☎ 416 068; Rákóczi út 12; open 10am-9pm Mon-Sat, 9am-9pm Sun)*, just north of the Karancs Hotel, is the best cake shop in town

Entertainment

Attila József Cultural Centre *(☎ 310 503, 312 637; Fő tér 5; open 8am-8pm Mon-Fri, 10am-6pm Sat & Sun)* is Salgótarján's premier cultural venue. **Laguna Club Cafe** *(☎ 06-20 936 7072; Füleki út 58; open 9am-5am Wed-Sat)* is a popular club. Salgótarján night spots can be found in the free biweekly *Nográdi Est*.

Getting There & Away

Buses leave Salgótarján hourly for Balassagyarmat and Szécsény via Endrefalva. You can also get to Budapest (half-hourly departures, some via route No M3), Pászto (hourly), Eger (11 departures Monday to Friday, seven on Saturday, five on Sunday), Miskolc (two departures daily), Hatvan (three or four Monday to Saturday, two Sunday), Hollókő (four), Gyöngyös (six Monday to Saturday, three Sunday) and Parádfürdő (two) in the Mátra Hills and Tar (three to five daily).

A train line links Salgótarján with Hatvan and the main Budapest–Miskolc trunk to the south and, to the north, Somoskőújfalu and, in Slovakia, Lučenec.

AROUND SALGÓTARJÁN
Salgó & Somoskő Castles
Salgó Castle (admission 100Ft; open 9am-5pm Tues-Sun), 8km northeast of the city centre, was built atop a basalt cone some 623m up in the Medves Hills in the 13th century. After Buda Castle fell to the Turks in 1541, Salgó served as an important border fortress, but it too was taken 23 years later and fell into ruin after the Turks abandoned it in the late 16th century. The castle is remembered best for the visit made by Sándor Petőfi in 1845, which inspired him to write one of his best loved poems, Salgó. Today you can make out the inner courtyard, tower and bastion from the ruins, but views of Somoskő and into Slovakia are excellent from this peaceful spot.

To visit the interior of Somoskő Castle (adult/child 200/100Ft; open 8am-8pm daily Apr-Oct, 8am-4pm daily Nov-Mar), which is in Slovakian territory, you must cross the border at Somoskőújfalu – don't forget your passport – and follow a path east on foot for about 3km to the castle. Built in the 14th century from basalt blocks, Somoskő was able to hold off the Turkish onslaught longer than Salgó Castle, not falling until 1576. Ferenc Rákóczi used it during the independence war in 1706 and for that reason it was partially destroyed by the Austrians.

Adventurous souls who have time on their hands might want to follow the marked trail westward from Somoskőújfalu along the Slovakian border for 4km to 729m **Mt Karancs**; you'll see the High Tatras from the lookout tower atop what's known locally as the 'Palóc Olympus'. Cartographia's 1:60,000 A Karancs, a Medves és a Heves-Borsodi-dombság map (No 11; 650Ft) covers these hills.

To get to Salgó Castle, catch bus No 11/b anywhere along Rákóczi út to the Eresztvény recreational area; the castle is up the hill to the southwest. An easier way to reach it, though, is to stay on the same bus to the terminus in Salgóbánya, the city's old mining district, and follow the path leading off Vár út to the west. Bus No 11/a also goes to Eresztvény and then heads for Somoskő.

Buddhist Stupa
Travelling along route No 21 toward Pászto, some 22km south of Salgótarján, you might think you've driven through a black hole and arrived in South-East Asia. There, on a hillside to the north of the village of **Tar**, is a full-sized Buddhist stupa, its little chimes tinkling and coloured pendants fluttering in the gentle breeze. It's all part of **Sándor Kőrösi Csoma Memorial Park**, consecrated in 1992 by the Dalai Lama in memory of the early 19th-century Hungarian Franciscan monk who became a Hungarian Bodhisattva (Buddhist saint). The stupa, with a revolving prayer wheel containing sacred texts, has become something of a local tourist attraction and there's a **gift shop** and **snack bar** (open 9am-7pm Tues-Sun Apr-Sept, 10am-4pm Tues-Sun Oct-Mar). Buses to Tar, a couple of kilometres to the south, and to Pászto stop along the highway just below the stupa.

Mátra Hills

The Mátra Hills, which boast Hungary's highest peaks, are the most developed and easily accessible of the Northern Uplands ranges. And with all the recreational options – from hiking and picking wild mushrooms in the autumn to hunting and skiing in winter – there's enough here to satisfy all tastes.

The Mátra Hills can be reached from such cities as Eger and Pászto, but Gyöngyös is its real springboard. It is also the centre of the Mátraalja wine-growing region, noted especially for Hárslevelű (Linden Leaf), a green-tinted white wine that is spicy and slightly sweet at the same time.

For general information on the Mátra Hills (in Hungarian only), see **w** www.matrahegy.hu.

GYÖNGYÖS
☎ 37 • postcode 3200 • pop 36,200
A colourful, small city at the base of the Mátra Hills, Gyöngyös, from the Hungarian word meaning 'pearl', has been an important

trading centre since Turkish times and later became known for its textiles. Today, people come here to see the city's churches (the largest Gothic church in Hungary is here), visit its rich medieval library or have a glass or two of wine before heading for the hills.

Orientation

The bus station is on Koháry út, a 10-minute walk southeast of Fő tér, the main square. The main train station is on Vasút utca, near the eastern end of Kossuth Lajos utca. The Előre station, from where the narrow-gauge trains depart (see Activities later in the Gyöngyös section), is next to the Mátra Museum at the start of Dobó István utca.

Information

Tourinform (*☎/fax 311 155;* **e** *gyongyos@ tourinform.hu; Fő tér 10; open 10am-6pm daily mid-June–mid-Sept, 7.30am-4pm Mon-Thur, 7.30am-1.30pm Fri mid-Sept–mid-June)* is in the centre of town and particularly helpful, but its website is in Hungarian only. Among the big travel agencies in town is **Ibusz** (*☎ 311 861, fax 311 807; Kossuth Lajos utca 6; open 8am-5pm Mon-Fri)*.

You'll find a large branch of the **OTP bank** (*Fő tér 1; open 7am-5pm Mon, Tues & Thur, 7am-6pm Wed, 7am-4pm Fri)* on the other side of Fő tér from Tourinform. There's a **Budapest Bank** (*Fó tér 19; open 8am-5pm Mon-Fri)* at the southern end of the square; look for its ATM around the corner on Móricz Zsigmond utca. The main **post office** (*Páter Kiss Szaléz utca 9-11; open 8am-8pm Mon-Fri, 8am-noon Sat)* is accessed from Mátyás király utca.

City Disco Club (see Entertainment later in the Gyöngyös section) also has an **Internet café** (*w citydisco.fw.hu; 300/500Ft 30/60 min; open 11am-11pm daily)*.

For general information on Gyöngyös, check out *w* www.gyongyos.hu.

Things to See

The **Mátra Museum** (*☎ 311 447; Kossuth Lajos utca 40; adult/child 200/100Ft; open 9am-5pm Tues-Sun Mar-Oct, 10am-2pm Tues-Sun Nov-Feb)*, housed in an old manor house in Orczy Garden, contains exhibits on the history of Gyöngyös, with much emphasis on Benevár – a 14th-century castle northeast of Mátrafüred and now in ruins – and the natural

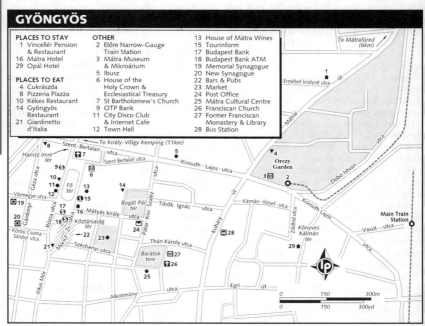

GYÖNGYÖS

PLACES TO STAY	OTHER	
1 Vincellér Pension & Restaurant	2 Előre Narrow-Gauge Train Station	13 House of Mátra Wines
16 Mátra Hotel	3 Mátra Museum & Mikroárium	15 Tourinform
29 Opál Hotel	5 Ibusz	17 Budapest Bank
	6 House of the Holy Crown & Ecclesiastical Treasury	18 Budapest Bank ATM
PLACES TO EAT		19 Memorial Synagogue
4 Cukrászda		20 New Synagogue
8 Pizzeria Piazza	7 St Bartholomew's Church	22 Bars & Pubs
10 Kékes Restaurant	9 OTP Bank	23 Market
14 Gyöngyös Restaurant	11 City Disco Club & Internet Cafe	24 Post Office
21 Giardinetto d'Italia	12 Town Hall	25 Mátra Cultural Centre
		26 Franciscan Church
		27 Former Franciscan Monastery & Library
		28 Bus Station

history of the Mátra region, including a 'baby' mammoth. City lore has it that the wrought-iron railings enclosing the garden were made from gun barrels taken during the *kuruc* (anti-Habsburg mercenaries) uprising. Downstairs is the **Mikroárium**, an aquarium-terrarium full of snakes, lizards and tropical fish.

St Bartholomew's Church *(Szent Bertalan templom; Szent Bertalan út 1)* is on the east side of Hanisz Imre tér. It was built in the 14th century and is the largest Gothic church in Hungary. You'd hardly know it, though, with the baroque restoration (including an unusual upper-storey gallery inside) that was carried out 400 years later. To the southeast the so-called **House of the Holy Crown** *(Szent Korona-ház)*, which served as a safe house for the St Stephen's Crown three times from 1806 to 1809 during the Napoleonic Wars, contains the city's **Ecclesiastical Treasury** *(Egyházi Kincstár; ☎ 311 143; adult/child 100/50Ft; open 10am-noon, 2pm-5pm Tues-Sun)*, one of the richest collections of liturgical objects and church plates in the country.

The **Franciscan church** *(Ferences templom; Barátok tere 1)* was built around the same time as St Bartholomew's, but it too has undergone some major changes, with the frescoes and baroque tower added in the 18th century. The church's most celebrated occupant – well, second most famous to the faithful – is János Vak (Blind) Bottyán, a heroic but sight-challenged commander who served under Ferenc Rákóczi II during the War of Independence. The former **monastery** (built 1730), which is attached to the church, contains the **Hungarian Franciscan Memorial Library** *(Magyar Ferencesek Műemlék Könytára; Barátok tere 2; admission free; open 2pm-4pm Tues-Fri, 10am-1pm Sat)*, the only historical archive in Hungary to have survived the Turkish occupation intact. Among its 14,000 volumes are some of the rarest books written in Hungarian.

Gyöngyös was home to a relatively large Jewish community from the 15th century to WWII, and two splendid synagogues bear witness to this history. The older of the two, the neoclassical **Memorial Synagogue** *(Műemlék zsinagóga; Vármegye utca)* built in 1820, faces Gyöngyös Stream and now houses the city's TV studios. The Moorish-Secessionist **New Synagogue** *(Új zsinagóga; Kőrösi Csoma Sándor utca)*, at the corner with Gárdonyi Géza utca, was designed by Lipót Baumhorn in 1930, two decades after he completed his masterpiece in Szeged. It is now a warehouse.

The **House of Mátra Wines** *(Mátrai Borok Háza; ☎ 302 226; Fő tér 10; open 10am-5pm Tues-Fri, 9am-1pm Sat)*, in a courtyard off the main square, showcases local and regional wines and offers tastings. If you're interested in trying the region's Rieslings, Leányka and Hárslevelű *in situ*, ask Tourinform for a copy of *A Mátraaljai Borút* (The Mátraalja Wine Road) map and a list of cellars offering tastings.

Activities

Two **narrow-gauge trains** *(☎ 312 453, 312 447)* depart from Előre station just beyond the Mátra Museum. One heads 7km northeast for Mátrafüred and is the most enjoyable way of entering the Mátra Hills. The other goes to Lajosháza, 11km north of Gyöngyös. This trip offers no real destination, except a place to begin hiking – perhaps east along the Nagyvölgy (Big Valley) past a series of water catchments or north as far as Galyatető, at 965m Hungary's second-highest peak. If you take the little train back from Mátrafüred, get off at Farkasmály-Borpincék, where there's a row of wine cellars. To return, you can wait for the train (last one at 5.27pm or 6.37pm, depending on the season) or jump onto a bus coming down route No 24, but it's an easy 4km walk (or crawl) back to Gyöngyös.

Be advised that trains to Lajosháza (adult/child 200/100Ft one way, 380/200Ft return) run only on Saturday, Sunday and holidays from May to September (maximum four trains daily in each direction) with extra ones on Wednesday and Friday from mid-June to August. Up to 10 trains daily make the run to Mátrafüred (adult/child 170/85Ft one way, 320/170Ft return) from April to October. During the rest of the year, count on seven trains on weekdays and eight at the weekend.

Places to Stay

The closest **camp site** is at Sástó, 3km north of Mátrafüred (see under Sástó later in this chapter). **Király-völgy Kemping** *(☎/fax 364 185; e info@kiralyvolgykemping.hu; Táncsics Mihály út 40; per person/tent/caravan/car 400/600/800Ft)*, 11km to the northwest in Gyöngyöspata, has some two dozen sites and rents out bicycles for 500/2500Ft an hour/day.

Both Tourinform and Ibusz can book you a **private room** in Gyöngyös or the Mátra Hills from 2000Ft per person.

Opál (☎ 505 400, fax 300 450; Könyves Kálmán tér 13; singles/doubles 5500/8300Ft), a 16-room hotel in a former college, has that cheap-veneer feel to it but offers good value.

Vincellér (☎ 311 691, fax 500 323; W www .hotels.hu/vinceller_panzio; Erzsébet királyné út 22; doubles 8900Ft, apartments 13,000Ft), northeast of the centre, is an attractive, though relatively expensive 15-room pension.

Mátra (☎ 313 063, fax 312 057; e inn-side@mail.matav.hu; Mátyás király utca 2; singles/doubles €35/45), facing Fő tér and now part of the Inn-Side chain of hotels, has some nice public areas, but the 40 guest-rooms look pretty much as they always have: dingy, dark and worn.

Places to Eat

Kékes (☎ 311 915; Fő tér 7; mains 1100-2200Ft; open 9am-10.30pm daily) has a lovely terrace on the main square and a few vegetarian dishes.

Pizzéria Piazza (☎ 313 082; Hanisz Imre tér 1; mains 550-950Ft; open 11am-11pm Mon-Thur, 11am-midnight Fri & Sat, 11am-10pm Sun) has basic and somewhat pricey Italian fare. **Giardinetto d'Italia** (☎ 300 709; Rózsa utca 8; pizza 350-980Ft; open 11am-10pm daily), with a terrace in a little park south of Fő tér, is a better choice.

Gyöngyös (☎ 311 019; Bugát Pál tér 2; mains 900-1800Ft; open 11am-11pm daily) is one of the best restaurants in town, with excellent regional specialities and local wine in a neorustic environment.

There's a nameless **cukrászda and ice-cream parlour** (Mátrai út; open 10am-7pm Mon, Wed & Thur, 9am-7pm Fri-Sun) in Orczy Garden north of the Mátra Museum.

Entertainment

Mátra Cultural Centre (Mátra Művelődési Központ; ☎ 312 281; Barátok tere 3) is, we're told, a 'Finnish functionalist-style building', with huge, colourful stained-glass windows. This is where Gyöngyös entertains itself.

There are a number of popular night spots around town, especially along Móricz Zsigmond utca, a 'strip' of bars and pubs south of Fő tér. **City Disco Club** (☎ 312 381; Fő tér 9) throbs at the weekend, with three different dance floors.

For more listings pick up a copy of the free biweekly *Gyöngyösi Est* magazine.

Getting There & Around

You can book a taxi on ☎ 313 300.

Bus You won't wait for more than 20 minutes for buses to Budapest, Eger (though only three daily via Parádfürdő), Hatvan, Mátrafüred and Mátraháza. There are about a dozen buses daily to destinations further into the Mátra, like Parád and Parádfürdő, 10 buses to Recsk and five to Sirok. You can also catch buses to Jászberény (10 daily), Szolnok (five), Salgótarján (six), Kecskemét (five), and Miskolc, Hajdúszoboszló and Tiszafüred (two each).

Train Gyöngyös is on a dead-end spur some 13km from the Vámosgyörk stop on the Budapest–Miskolc trunk line. A dozen trains a day connect the city with Vámosgyörk, 10 of which carry on to Keleti station in Budapest.

GYÖNGYÖS TO EGER

Route No 24 wends its way through the Mátra Hills north of Gyöngyös to Parádsasvár and then cuts eastward; if you're under your own steam, it's a very pretty route to Eger (60km). Buses to Mátrafüred, Mátraháza, Parád and Parádfürdő are frequent, but the best approach is by the narrow-gauge train that terminates in Mátrafüred.

Mátrafüred

☎ 37 • postcode 3232

Mátrafüred is a pleasant little resort at 340m. Though there is a small **Palóc ethnographic private collection** (Palóc néprajzi magángyűtemény; ☎ 320 137; Pálosvörösmarti út 2; adult/child 150/100Ft; open 9am-5pm daily May-Sept, 9am-4pm Oct-Apr) of dolls, textiles and carvings just south of the narrow-gauge train, the many easy **walks** in the area are the main attraction. Buy a copy of Cartographia's 1:40,000 *A Mátra* map (No 14; 650Ft) before setting out.

You can change money at the **post office** (Béke utca 5; open 8am-noon & 12.30pm-3.30pm Mon-Fri). For general information on Mátrafüred (in Hungarian only), see W www.matrainfo.hu.

Places to Stay & Eat There are lots of signs advertising **private rooms** (from 1800Ft per person) along Béke utca, which runs west off Parádi utca (route No 24).

Gyöngyvirág (☎ *520 001, fax 520 002;* e *info@gyongvirag.hu; Béke utca 8; singles 5000-6000Ft, doubles 6000-7000Ft)*, one of the nicest places to stay in these parts, has 24 tastefully furnished rooms and an outside grill restaurant in summer.

Diana (☎ *320 136, fax 323 022; Turista utca 1; singles/doubles/triples 3500/7000/ 9000Ft)* is a basic but comfortable 12-room hotel just off Béke utca.

There are plenty of **food stalls** and the like on Parádi utca opposite the train station.

Benevár (☎ *320 261; Parádi utca 13; mains 490-1350Ft; open 11am-11pm daily)*, next to the monstrous Avar hotel, is an attractive *csárda* (Hungarian-style restaurant).

Fekete Rigó (☎ *320 052; Avar utca 2; mains 620-1120Ft)*, the 'Blackbird' just off Béke utca, is a more relaxed choice than Benevár and has a lovely beer garden.

Sástó
☎ 37 • postcode 3232

Three kilometres north of Mátrafüred, **Sástó Camping** (☎ *574 002, fax 374 025;* e *sas to@elpak.hu; camping per person with tent/caravan/car 800/1000/300Ft; open mid-Apr–mid-Oct)* is the highest camp site in Hungary (520m) and certainly one of the most attractive. Centred on a small lake with rowing boats, fishing and a 54m-high lookout tower, the camp site complex offers a wide range of accommodation – from 2nd-class wooden bungalows for two/three people for 2500/3900Ft, and a double without bath in the 28-room motel for 3400Ft, to luxury bungalows or a cottage on the edge of the lake for two, three or four people with shower, fridge and TV. **Snack bars** abound, and there is the **Sásto Vendéglő** (☎ *374 061)*, quite a decent restaurant, and a small **grocery shop** here.

Mátraháza
☎ 37 • postcode 3233

Mátraháza is built on a slight incline 715m above sea level and about 5km north of Sástó. It is an attractive spot to base yourself for short walks in the immediate area or more adventurous hiking further afield. The **post office** (*open 8am-3.30pm Mon-Fri)* is at the start of the road to Kékestető, the country's highest point and centre for winter sport, and

there's an **OTP bank ATM** at the bus station along the main road through the village.

Places to Stay & Eat Along route No 24 from Sástó to Mátraháza, you'll pass two big resort hotels.

Bérc (☎ *374 102, 374 103, fax 374 095;* e *berchotel@matavnet.hu; doubles with bathroom 6300-7600Ft)* is a 128-room hotel that has a large indoor swimming pool (800Ft), 10-pin bowling and clay tennis courts (600Ft per hour). Rates vary depending on the room and the season (make sure you get an upper-floor room with a balcony looking out onto the Kékes Hills).

Ózon (☎ *374 004, fax 374 039;* e *re serve@hotelozon.hunguesthotels.hu; singles 5500-13,100Ft, doubles 7000-14,600Ft)*, the posher and more attractive option, has 59 rooms (many with balconies) in a quiet park. Rooms are either in the old ('classic') building or the new ('business') one.

The **Pagoda Pihenő Panzió** (☎ *374 023, 374 023, fax 374 022;* w *www.hotels.hu /pagoda; singles €24-28, doubles €30-35, triples €42-48)* is an old hotel with a pagoda-like roof in the centre of Mátraháza village. Currently only 29 rooms in one of four buildings (building B) are available. The website is in Hungarian only.

Opposite the car park at the start of the ascent to Kékestető, the **Borostyán** (☎ *374 090; buffet lunch around 1500Ft; open 9am-10pm daily in summer, 9am-10pm Tues-Sun winter)* has decent food and a lovely outside seating pavilion.

Kékestető
☎ 37 • postcode 3221

Next to the Pagoda pension in Mátraháza, you'll see the end of a ski trail that runs down from Kékestető and Mt Kékes. In the absence of a lift, skiers wanting another go hop on the bus, which continuously covers the 4km to the top. The modern nine-storey **TV tower** (☎ *367 086; adult/child 300/190Ft; open 9am-6pm May-Sept, 9am-5pm Oct-Apr)* at the top is open to view-seekers; the old tower in front of it houses the **Hegycsúcs** (☎ *567 004, fax 367 086;* w *www.hotels.hu/hegycsucs; doubles/ triples 7900/10,800Ft)*, a hotel with sauna and gym. Choose one of the two rooms on the 7th floor (No 13 is a twin, No 14 a double), and you'll be sleeping at the highest point in Hungary; the website is in Hungarian only.)

NORTHERN UPLANDS

You won't exactly be on top of the world but the nearby **Kékes Fogadó** (☎ 06-70 217 9954, fax 367 086; singles/doubles/triples 2000/4000/6000Ft) is a 24-room holiday house and has much cheaper (and more basic) accommodation.

Parádsasvár

☎ 36 • postcode 3242 • pop 540

Parádsasvár is where Hungary's most effective – and most odouriferous – gyógyvíz (medicinal drinking water) is bottled. Stop for a glass if you can stand the stench of this sulphuric brew. The **Parád Crystal Factory** (Parád Kristály Manufaktura; ☎ 364 353, fax 364 494; e para dkristaly@mail.datanet.hu; Rákóczi utca 46-48; open 10am-1pm, 2pm-3pm Tues-Sat), which produces Hungary's highest-quality crystal and glassware, can be visited. There are also pieces on display at the nearby **Sasvár Gallery** (Sasvár Galéria; ☎ 364 493; open 10am-3pm Tues-Fri, 9am-1pm Sat) and for sale at the **sample shop** (☎ 364 051; open 9am-3pm Mon-Fri, 9am-1pm Sat & Sun).

Parádsasvár can boast having one of provincial Hungary's most beautiful and expensive hotels: the **Sasvár Kastélyszálloda** (Sasvár Castle Hotel; ☎ 444 444, fax 544 010; w www.sasvar.hu; Kossuth Lajos utca 1; singles €135-225, doubles €155-265). It's a 58-room hotel in a restored Renaissance-style hunting lodge built in 1882 by Miklós Ybl, who was responsible for the State Opera House in Budapest and many other fine buildings. It has every mod con and facility you could possibly wish for (including Secret Service–style security) and is surrounded by 2.5 hectares of parkland.

Parád & Parádfürdő

☎ 36 • postcodes 3240 & 3244 • pop 2425

Parád and Parádfürdő run into one another and nowadays effectively make up one long town. You can't miss the **Coach Museum** (Kocsimúzeum; ☎ 364 387, 544 073; Kossuth Lajos utca 217; adult/child 300/200Ft; open 9am-5pm Tues-Sun Apr-Oct, 10am-4pm Tues-Sun Nov-May), housed in the red marble Cifra Istálló (Ornamental Stables) of Count Károlyi and one of the most interesting small museums in Hungary. (For the record, the word 'coach' comes from Kocs, a small village in Transdanubia where these lighter, horse-drawn vehicles were first used in place

of the more cumbersome wagons.) Inspect the interiors of the diplomatic and state coaches, which are richly decorated with silk brocade; the closed coach used by 19th-century philanderers on the go; and the bridles containing as much as 5kg of silver. There are **horse riding** possibilities here as well.

The **Erzsébet Királyné Park Hotel** (Queen Elizabeth Park Hotel; ☎ 444 044, fax 544 170; e erzsebethotel@axelero.hu; Kossuth Lajos utca 372; singles/doubles €69/80), a lovely 42-room hotel at the eastern end of Parádfürdő, was designed by Miklós Ybl in 1893.

Recsk

☎ 36 • postcode 3245 • pop 3200

From Parádfürdő the road continues on for 2km to Recsk, a place that lives on in infamy as the site of Hungary's most brutal forced-labour camp, set up by Mátyás Rákosi in 1950 and closed down by the reformer Imre Nagy in 1953. In honour of those who slaved and died here, the **Recsk Forced-Labour Death Camp** (Recski Kényszerminka Halál-tábor; ☎ 1-312 6105 in Budapest; admission 50Ft; open 9am-5pm daily May-Sept, 9am-3pm Sat & Sun Oct-Apr) has been partially reconstructed near the quarry, about 5km south of the village.

Sirok

☎ 36 • postcode 3332 • pop 2370

Sirok, 8km to the east of Recsk, is effectively the last town in the Mátra Hills. The ruins of an early 14th-century **castle** perched on a mountain top due north of the village provide superb views of the Mátra and Bükk Hills and the mountains of Slovakia. **Vár Camping** (☎/fax 361 558; Dobó István utca 30; open mid-May–Sept) lies at the foot of the castle ruins.

Bükk Hills

The Bükk Hills, which take their name from the many 'beech trees' growing here, are a green lung buffering Eger and the industrial city of Miskolc. Although much of the area has been exploited for its ore for the ironworks of Miskolc and other towns of the scarred Sajó Valley to the east, a large tract – over 43,000 hectares, in fact – is a national park. The Bükk teems with wildlife, and there are some 800 caves in the mountains; for information contact the **Bükk National Park**

Directorate *(Bükki Nemzeti Park Igaz-gatósága;* ☎ *36-411 581, fax 412 791; Sánc utca 6)* in Eger.

The Bükk Plateau, a 20-sq-km limestone area rising to heights of between 800m and 900m, is particularly attractive for cyclists and hikers. Cartographia's three 1:40,000 maps (650Ft each) of the Bükk region are: *A Bükk-fennsík* (Bükk Plateau; No 33); *A Bükk – északi rész* (Bükk – northern section; No 29) and *A Bükk – déli rész* (Bükk – southern section; No 30).

EGER

☎ 36 • postcode 3300 • pop 61,500

Everyone loves Eger, and it's immediately apparent why: the beautifully preserved baroque architecture gives the town a relaxed, almost Mediterranean, feel; it is the home of the celebrated Egri Bikavér (Eger Bull's Blood) wine known the world over; and it is flanked by two of the Northern Uplands most beautiful ranges. Hungarians visit Eger for those reasons and more, for it was here that their forebears fended off the Turks for the first time during the 170 years of occupation in 1552 (see the boxed text 'The Siege of Eger').

The Turks came back to Eger in 1596 and this time captured the city, turning it into a provincial capital and erecting several mosques and other buildings until they were driven out at the end of the 17th century. All that remains of this architectural legacy is a lonely little minaret pointing its long finger towards the heavens in indignation.

Eger played a central role in Ferenc Rákóczi II's attempt to overthrow the Habsburgs early in the 18th century, and it was then that a large part of the castle was razed by the Austrians. Having enjoyed the status of an episcopate since the time of King Stephen in the 11th century, Eger (Erlau in German) flourished in the 18th and 19th centuries, when the city acquired most of its wonderful baroque architecture.

Orientation

Dobó István tér, the centre of Eger, is just a few minutes on foot to the east from the renovated bus station on Pyrker János tér. To reach the centre from the main train station on Vasút utca, walk north along Deák Ferenc utca and then pedestrian Széchenyi István utca, Eger's main drag. The Egervár train station, which serves Szilvásvárad and other

---

The Siege of Eger

The story of the Turkish attempt to take Eger Castle is the stuff of legend. Under the command of István Dobó, a mixed bag of 2000 soldiers held out against more than 100,000 Turks for a month in 1552. As every Hungarian kid in short trousers can tell you, the women of Eger played a crucial role in the battle, pouring boiling oil and pitch on the invaders from the ramparts. A painting by Bertalan Székely called *The Women of Eger* in the castle's art gallery pays tribute to these brave ladies.

Also significant was Eger's wine, if we're to believe the tale. It seems that Dobó sustained his soldiers with the ruby-red vintage. When they fought on with increased vigour – and stained beards – rumours began to circulate among the Turks that the defenders were gaining strength by drinking the blood of bulls. The name Bikavér (Bull's Blood) was born.

Géza Gárdonyi's *Eclipse of the Crescent Moon* (1901), which describes the siege and is required reading for many young Hungarians, can be found in English translation (Corvina) in bookshops throughout the land.

---

points north, is on Vécseyvölgy utca, a five-minute walk north of the castle.

Information

Tourinform *(☎ 517 715, fax 518 815;* e *eger@tourinform.hu; Bajcsy-Zsilinszky utca 9; open 9am-7pm Mon-Fri, 10am-6pm Sat & Sun June-Aug; 9am-5pm Mon-Fri, 9am-1pm Sat Sept-May)* can supply all the information you need and recommend agencies dealing with private accommodation.

Commercial travel agencies in Eger include: **Egertourist** *(☎ 510 270, fax 411 225; Bajcsy-Zsilinszky utca 9; open 9am-5pm Mon-Fri, 9am-1pm Sat Jun-Sept);* **Ibusz** *(☎ 311 451, fax 312 652; Széchenyi István utca 9; open 8am-4pm Mon-Fri, 9am-1pm Sat Jun-Sept);* and **Villa Tours** *(☎ 410 215, fax 518 038; Jókai utca 1; open 8am-4pm Mon-Fri).*

An **OTP bank** *(Széchenyi István utca 2; open 7.45am-5pm Mon, Tues, Thur, Fri, 7.45am-6pm Wed)* branch is due west of Tourinform. The main **post office** *(Széchenyi István utca 20-22; open 8am-8pm Mon-Fri, 8am-1pm Sat)* is 350m to the north. Egri Est

EGER

PLACES TO STAY
2 Korona Hotel & István Cellar
3 Romantik Hotel
9 Minaret Hotel
13 Leányka út College
15 Senator Ház Hotel & Restaurant
25 Szent János Hotel
36 Panoráma Hotel
51 Tourist Motel
53 Eger & Park Hotel
    Archbishop's Garden College
57 Freddy Panzió
59 Tulipán Kemping

PLACES TO EAT
4 Mini ABC Shop
6 Elefanto Restaurant; Hippolit Club
7 Market

14 Pallas Cafe
20 Gyros
24 Express Self-Service Restaurant
29 Dobos Cake Shop
31 HBH Bajor
35 Pizza Club
38 Marján Cake Shop
52 Fehérszarvas Vadásztanya
58 Talizmán Restaurant
60 Kulacs Csárda
61 Ködmön Csárda

OTHER
1 Serbian Orthodox Church
5 Post Office
8 Minaret
10 County Cultural Centre
11 Castrum Antivitás Shop

12 Eger Castle & Museums
16 Minorita Cafe
17 Pepi Kávéház
18 Centrum Department Store
21 Ibusz
22 Egri Est Café & Internet Cafe
23 Cistercian Church
26 Archbishop's Palace
27 Ticket Office
28 Ecclesiastical Collection
30 Egri Galéria
32 Hungarian Foal Wine Bar
33 Minorite Church
34 Former Neoclassical Synagogue

37 Former Orthodox Synagogue
40 County Hall
41 Franciscan Church
42 Villa Tours
43 Tourinform
44 Egertourist
45 OTP Bank
46 Lyceum & Museums
47 Provost's Palace
48 Broadway Palace Club
49 Basilica
50 Géza Gárdonyi Theatre
54 Open-Air & Covered Pools
55 Thermal Baths
56 Aladár Bitskey Swimming Pool
62 Szépasszony-völgy Wine Cellars

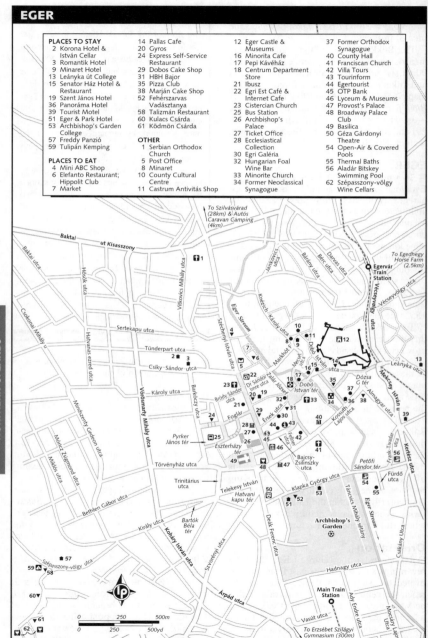

Café (see Entertainment later in the Eger section) doubles as an Internet café (300/500Ft per 30/60 minutes).

For general information on Eger, see
W www.eger.hu.

Eger Castle

The best overview of the city can be had by climbing up the cobblestone lane from Dózsa György tér to Eger Castle (Egri Vár; ☎ 312 744; Vár 1; adult/student combined ticket 500/250Ft, grounds only 200/100Ft; open 8am-8pm Tues-Sun Apr-Aug, 8am-7pm Tues-Sun Sept, 8am-6pm Tues-Sun Oct & Mar, 8am-5pm Tues-Sun Nov-Feb), erected in the 13th century after the Mongol invasion. Much of the castle is of modern construction, but you can still see the foundations of 12th-century St John's Cathedral. Models and drawings in the István Dobó Museum, housed in the former Bishop's Palace (1470), show how it once looked. On the ground floor, a statue of Dobó takes pride of place in Heroes' Hall. The 19th-century building on the northwestern side of the courtyard houses the Eger Art Gallery, with several works by Mihály Munkácsy.

Beneath the castle are casemates hewn from solid rock, which you may tour with a Hungarian-speaking guide included in the price (English-language guide 400Ft extra). Other exhibits, including the Waxworks (250/150Ft) and Minting Exhibit (100/50Ft) cost extra. You can still tour the castle grounds (200/100Ft) on Monday, when all the other exhibits are closed.

Eszterházy tér

Begin a walking tour of the city at the Basilica (Bazilika; Pyrker János tér 1), a neoclassical monolith completed in 1836 and designed by József Hild, the same architect who later worked on the cathedral at Esztergom. Despite the cathedral's size and ornate altars, the interior is surprisingly light and airy. Northeast of the cathedral in the Archbishop's Palace (Érseki Palota; Széchenyi utca 5) is the Ecclesiastical Collection (Egyházi Gyűtemény; ☎ 421 332; adult/child 200/100Ft; open 9am-5pm Tues-Sat Apr-Oct, 8am-4pm Mon-Fri Nov-Mar), with priceless vestments, church plate and liturgical objects.

Directly opposite the cathedral is the sprawling Zopf-style Lyceum (Líceum; ☎ 520 400; Eszterházy tér 1; open 9.30am-3pm Tues-Sun Apr-Sept, 9.30am-1.30pm Sat & Sun Oct-Mar), dating from 1765. The 20,000-volume library (adult/student 300/150Ft), on the 1st floor of the south wing, contains hundreds of priceless manuscripts and codices. The ceiling fresco (1778) here is a trompe l'oeuil masterpiece depicting the Counter-Reformation's Council of Trent (1545–63) and a lightning bolt setting heretical manuscripts ablaze.

The Astronomy Museum (adult/student 300/150Ft), on the 6th floor of the east wing, contains 18th-century astronomical equipment and an observatory; climb three more floors up to the observation deck for a great view of the city and to try out the camera obscura, the 'eye of Eger', designed in 1776 to spy on the town and to entertain townspeople.

Other Attractions

Walk north along Széchenyi utca to the Cistercian church (Ciszterek temploma; Széchenyi utca 15) built in 1743. The theatrical baroque altar sculpture of St Francis Borgia in gilt and white stucco is well worth a look. The Serbian Orthodox church (Ráctemplom; ☎ 320 129; Vitkovics Mihály utca 30; admission 200Ft; open 10am-4pm Tues-Sun) and its enormous iconostasis of gold leaf and braid is farther north; enter from Széchenyi utca 59.

Retrace your steps to the Cistercian church and turn east onto Dr Sándor Imre utca and Markhót Ferenc utca to the minaret (Knézich Károly utca; admission 100Ft; open 9am-6pm daily Apr-Oct), topped with a cross. Only nonclaustrophobes will brave the 97 narrow spiral steps to the top.

Mecset utca south of the minaret leads to central Dobó István tér, site of the town's market in medieval times. On the southern side of the square stands the Minorite church (Minorita templom), built in 1771 and one of the most glorious baroque buildings in the world. The altarpiece of the Virgin Mary and St Anthony of Padua is by Johann Kracker, the Bohemian painter who also did the fire-and-brimstone ceiling fresco in the Lyceum library. Statues of István Dobó and his comrades-in-arms routing the Turks in 1552 fill the square in front of the church.

From Dobó István tér cross the little Eger Stream to Dózsa György tér and turn southwest onto Kossuth Lajos utca, a fine, tree-lined street with dozens of architectural gems. At No 17 stands the former Orthodox synagogue (Ortodox zsinagóga), built in 1893 and now a furniture store backing onto a shopping mall. (A **neoclassical synagogue** dating from 1845 and now partly renovated is around the corner at Dr Hibay Károly utca 7.) You'll pass several outstanding baroque and eclectic buildings, including the **county hall** (megyeháza) at No 9 with a wrought-iron grid above the main door of Faith, Hope and Charity by Henrik Fazola, a Rhinelander who settled in Eger in the mid-18th century. Walk down the passageway, and you'll see two more of his magnificent works: baroque wrought-iron gates decorated on both sides that have taken over from the minaret as the symbol of Eger. The gate on the right shows the seal of Heves County and has a comical figure on its handle. The more graceful gate on the left is decorated with grapes. The **Franciscan church** (Ferences templom) at No 14 was completed in 1755 on the site of a mosque. The wrought-iron balcony and window grids of the rococo **Provost's Palace** (Kispréposti palota) at No 4 were also done by Fazola.

Wine Tasting
You can sample Eger's famous wines at many places around town, including the **Borkóstoló a Magyar Csikóhoz** (☎ 310 635; Dobó István tér 1; mains 650-780Ft; open 11am-11pm Sun-Thur, 11am-midnight Fri & Sat), a dive of a wine bar and self-service restaurant with a mouthful of a name that means 'Wine Tasting at the Sign of the Hungarian Foal'. You can also sample wines from around Hungary in the **István Cellar** (☎ 131 670; Tündérpart 5; open 10am-10pm daily) below the Korona hotel (see Places to Stay later in this section). But why bother drinking in town when you can do the same in the wine cellars of the evocatively named **Valley of the Women** (Szépasszony-völgy) so close by? The best time to visit the valley on a warm day is the late afternoon.

From the western end of the Basilica, walk south on Trinitárius utca to Bartók Béla tér and then west along Király utca to Szépasszony-völgy utca. Veer to the left as you descend the hill past the large Talizmán restaurant and into the valley and you'll see dozens of cellars. This is the place to sample Bull's Blood – one of very few reds produced in Eger – or any of the whites: Leányka, Olaszrizling and Hárslevelű from nearby Debrő.

The choice of wine cellars can be a bit daunting and their characters can change, so walk around and have a look yourself. Nos 16, 17, 29 and 48 are always popular; for schmaltzy Gypsy music, try No 32 or 42. But if you're interested in good wine, visit cellar Nos 5, 13, 18, 23 and 31. Be careful though; those glasses (about 50Ft) go down easily. Hours are erratic, but a few cellars are sure to be open till the early evening. The taxi fare back to Eger centre is about 600Ft.

Other Activities
You can unwind after sightseeing in the **Archbishop's Garden** (enter from Petőfi Sándor tér 2), once the private reserve of papal princes. It has **open-air swimming pools** (☎ 411 699, 412 202; adult/senior & student 500/350Ft; open 6am-8pm Mon-Fri, 8am-7pm Sat & Sun May-Sept) as well as **covered pools** (adult/senior & student 500/350Ft; open 9am-7pm daily Oct-Apr). The nearby **thermal baths** (☎ 413 356; Fürdő utca 1-3; admission 500Ft; open to women noon-6pm Wed & Fri, to men noon-6pm Tues, Thur & 10am-2pm Sat) date from Turkish times.

The stunning new **Aladár Bitskey Swimming Pool** (☎ 511 810; Frank Tivadar utca; adult/senior & student 500/300Ft; open 6am-8pm Mon-Fri, 8am-6pm Sat & Sun) nearby was designed by maverick Hungarian architect Imre Makovecz.

Horse riding is available at the **Egedhegy Lipizzaner Horse Farm** (☎/fax 312 804; open 9am-noon, 3pm-8pm daily July-Sept; 9am-noon, 1pm-3pm daily Oct-Dec; 9.30am-noon, 1pm-4pm daily Jan-Apr; 9am-6pm daily May & June) in Vécseyvölgy, northeast of the centre. Riding costs about 2000Ft per hour; instruction is 4000Ft. The bus to Noszvaj (not Novaj) goes past the farm.

Special Events
Annual events include the **Border Fortress Merrymaking Festival** and Games at the castle in July, **Baroque Weeks** in late July/August, the **Agria International Folkdance Meeting** in August and the **Bacchus Wine Festival** in mid-September.

Places to Stay
Camping You can camp at **Tulipán Kemping** (☎/fax 410 580; e tulipn-freddy@freemail.hu; Szépasszony-völgy utca 71; per person 600Ft, tent/caravan site 600/800Ft,

4-/5-bed bungalows 5000/9000Ft; open year round); it has four-bed bungalows with shared bath and five-bed bungalows with private bath, kitchen and TV.

Autós Caraván Camping (*☎/fax 428 593; Rákóczi út 79; camping per person & tent/ caravan 1000/1300Ft; open mid-Apr–mid-Oct)*, 4km north of Eger (turn left at the Shell station), has bungalows as well as camp sites.

Hostels A number of colleges offer accommodation from mid-June/July to August, including the 300-bed **Leányka út College** *(Leányka úti Kollégium; ☎ 520 430, fax 520 440; Leányka utca 6; dorm beds 1200Ft, doubles with showers 2500Ft)* east of the castle; the even more central **Archbishop's Garden College** *(Érsekkerti Kollégium; ☎ 413 661, fax 520 440; Klapka utca 12; dorm beds 1200-1400)*, with 132 beds; and the 400-bed **Erzsébet Szilágyi Gymnasium** *(Szilágyi Erzsébet Gimnázium; ☎ 410 571, fax 310 259; Mátyás király út 62; dorm beds 1100-1500Ft)*, about 1km south of the train station.

Private Rooms Egertourist, Ibusz and Villa Tours (see Information earlier in this section) can all organise private rooms for between 2000Ft and 3000Ft a night per person. You might also look for a room along Almagyar utca (Nos 7 and 19) or Mekcsey István utca (Nos 10/a, 13, 14, 14/a and 14/b). You'll also see *szoba kiadó* signs everywhere on Knézich Károly utca near the minaret and Szépasszony-völgy utca.

Guesthouses & Pensions The **Tourist Motel** *(☎ 411 101, fax 429 014; Mekcsey István utca 2; singles/doubles/triples/quads with shared bathroom 3000/5000/6000/ 7000Ft)* is a frayed, though spotlessly clean and friendly place south of the castle. It has 34 rooms; breakfast costs 500Ft extra.

Freddy Panzió *(☎ 350 600, fax 410 580; ⒺItulipan-freddy@freemail.hu; Szépasszony-völgy utca 71; doubles €32)*, with 25 rooms above Tulipán Kemping, has a swimming pool, sauna and steam room.

Hotels The family-run **Minaret** *(☎ 410 233, 410 020, fax 410 473; Ⓔ hotelminaret@ matavnet.hu; Knézich Károly utca 4; singles/ doubles/triples/quads €30/40/50/60)* offers 38 rooms, but there always seem to be noisy groups checking in or out when we visit.

Szent János *(☎ 510 350, fax 517 101; Ⓔ hotelszentjanos@hotelszentjanos.hu; Szent János utca 3; singles/doubles/triples €36/ 47/62)* is better than Minaret, although it is a somewhat antiseptic, 10-room place hewn out of a baroque townhouse.

Korona *(☎ 313 670, fax 310 261; Ⓔ korona ho@mail.agria.hu; Tündérpart utca 5; singles €30-50, doubles €45-60, triples €55-80)*, on a quiet side street off Csíky Sándor utca, has 40 rooms, with rates that vary depending on the season. It also has a 'wine museum' in its 200-year-old wine cellar called **István Pince** *(István wine cellar; open noon-10pm daily Tues-Sat)*, where you can sample wines from all regions.

Romantik *(☎ 310 456, fax 516 362; Ⓔ romantik-eger@axelero.hu; Csíky Sándor utca 26; singles €35-55, doubles €40-65, triples €50-75)* is a very friendly and cosy 16-room hotel with a pretty back garden.

Senator Ház *(☎/fax 320 466; Ⓔ hotel sen@axelero.hu; Dobó István tér 11; singles €27.50-48, doubles €39-57)* is a delightful 18th-century inn with 11 rooms in Eger's main square that many – including us – consider to be the finest small hotel in provincial Hungary.

Eger & Park *(☎ 522 222, fax 413 114; Ⓔ hotelegerpark@axelero.hu; Szálloda utca 1-3; singles €45-90 & doubles €50-92)*, with an old-world section (Park; enter from Klapka György utca 8) and an ugly modern wing (Eger), has a total of 165 rooms, but make sure you get one of the Park's three dozen. The hotels have all the facilities you'd expect at three-star prices: swimming pool, sauna, gym, tennis courts and bowling alley.

Panoráma *(☎ 412 886, fax 410 136; Ⓔ panhotel@lelender.hu; Dr Hibay Károly utca 2; singles €40-51, doubles €67-80, triples €82-96)* is Eger's flashy 'face' hotel.

Places to Eat
Express *(☎ 517 920; Barkóczy utca 4; open 7am-8pm daily)*, just northeast of the bus station, is a large, self-service restaurant where you can have a meal for less than 500Ft.

Gyros *(☎ 310 135; Széchenyi utca 10; open noon-10pm daily)* is a friendly local café-restaurant on a pedestrian street, with Greek salads (360Ft), moussaka (750Ft) and souvlakia (750Ft). **Pizza Club** *(☎ 427 606; Dr Hibay Károly utca 8; pizzas 650-1200Ft; open noon-10pm daily)*, just off Dobó István tér, can be recommended.

Elefanto (☎ 411 031; Katona István tér 2; mains 950-1800Ft; open noon-midnight daily), perched high above the market, is a great new place, with a nonsmoking interior and covered balcony for alfresco dining. The café-restaurant at the **Senator Ház** (starters 350-500Ft, mains 1050-1800Ft; open 11am-midnight daily) is a delightful place for a meal or just a snack of palacsinta (pancakes; 130Ft to 350Ft).

HBH Bajor (☎ 515 516; Bajcsy-Zsilinszky utca 19; mains 990-1990Ft; open 11.30am-10pm daily) serves reliable Hungarian-Germanic food in a bright, clean environment.

Fehérszarvas Vadásztanya (☎ 411 129; Klapka György utca 8; mains 1350-2900Ft; open noon-midnight daily), near the Park hotel, is Eger's silver-service restaurant. But the 'White Deer Hunters' Farm', with its game specialities, is really a place to enjoy in autumn and winter.

There are a couple of csárdas (Hungarian-style inns) amid the wine cellars (see Wine Tasting earlier under Eger) in Szépasszony-völgy, including the touristy **Kulacs** (☎ 311 375; mains 900-1500Ft; open noon-11pm daily) and the cheaper **Ködmön** (☎ 413 172; set menu 890Ft; open noon-11pm daily).

Marján (☎ 312 784; Kossuth Lajos utca 28; open 9am-10pm daily May-Sept; 9am-8pm daily Oct-Apr), a cake shop south of Dózsa György tér, is the place to try for something sweet. Other options include the **Pallas** (☎ 318 614; Dobó István utca 20; open 9.30am-9pm daily), a coffee shop in a small courtyard with a classical motif, and the **Dobos** (☎ 413 335; Széchenyi utca 6; open 9.30am-7pm daily).

Mini ABC (Széchenyi utca 38) is open 24 hours. The covered **market** (Katona István tér; open 6am-6pm Mon-Fri, 6am-1pm Sat, 6am-10am Sun) is by the little Eger Stream.

Entertainment

Tourinform, the **County Cultural Centre** (☎ 510 020; Knézich Károly utca 8) opposite the minaret, or the city **ticket office** (☎ 518 347; Széchenyi utca 5; open 9am-4pm Mon-Fri) can tell you what's on in Eger. Venues are the **Géza Gárdonyi Theatre** (☎ 310 026; Hatvani kapu tér 4; box office open 2pm-7pm Mon-Fri), the **Lyceum** and the **Basilica**, where there are half-hour organ concerts at 11.30am from Monday to Saturday and at 12.45pm on Sunday from mid-May to mid-October.

Dobó István tér has wine bars and cafés with outside seating in summer, including the **Pepi Kávéház** (☎ 314 001; open 10am-10pm daily) at No 3 and the **Minorita** (☎ 313 971; open 9am-10pm Sun-Fri, 9am-midnight Sat) at No 7.

Egri Est Café (☎ 411 105; Széchenyi utca 16; open 11am-midnight Sun-Thur, 11am-4am Fri & Sat) is a decent café-bar, with parties at the weekend.

The **Broadway Palace** (☎ 517 220; Pyrker tér 3; open 10pm-6am Wed, Fri & Sat) is a bizarre, cave-like place beneath the cathedral steps that rages late in the week. **Hippolit Club** (☎ 412 452; Katona István tér 2; open 10pm-5am Fri & Sat) is a dancing venue at the Elefanto restaurant.

Eger is included in the free biweekly Gyöngyösi Est listings magazine.

Shopping

The **Egri Galéria** (☎ 517 518; Érsek utca 8; open 10am-1pm & 2pm-6pm Mon-Fri, 10am-2pm Sat) has lovely jewellery, fine art, pottery and other collectibles for sale. **Castrum Antikvitás** (☎ 311 613; Harangöntő utca 2; open 9am-5pm Mon-Fri) is the place to go for antiques.

Getting There & Away

Bus services are good, with buses every 30 to 40 minutes to Felsőtárkány in the Bükk, Gyöngyös (usually via Kerecsend), Mező-kövesd, Noszvaj, Szilvásvárad and Bélapát-falva. Other destinations include: Aggtelek and Jósvafő (one bus daily), Békéscsaba (three buses daily), Budapest (hourly via the M3), Hatvan (six), Kecskemét (three), Debrecen (five), Miskolc (10) and Szeged (two) via Csongrád. Remember that the bus to Miskolc only goes through the Bükk via Felsőtárkány on Sunday at 7am and 11.25am.

Eger is on a minor railway linking Putnok and Füzesabony; you usually have to change at the latter for Budapest, Miskolc or Debrecen. There are up to five direct trains a day to and from Budapest's Keleti station (2½ hours) that do not require a change.

Getting Around

From the main train station, bus No 11, 12 or 14 will drop you off at the bus station or town centre.

You can book a taxi by calling ☎ 411 411, ☎ 411 222 or ☎ 555 555.

AROUND EGER
Egerszalók
☎ 36 • postcode 3394 • pop 1720

The open-air **hot spring** *(hőforrás;* ☎ *474 597; adult/senior & child over 10 250/ 150Ft; open 24hr)* at Egerszalók, 8km south-west of Eger, is quite a sight: cascades of *very* hot water running down from what look like steaming icebergs but what are in fact mounds of salt and other minerals. Above the main pool in the hills to the right is a naturist area (follow the signs *'nudizmus terület'*) with a small pond shaded by apple trees. The bus to Kerecsend via Demjén will drop you off 250m north of the entrance.

Mezőkövesd
☎ 49 • postcode 3400 • pop 18,500

Some 18km southeast of Eger, Mezőkövesd (Ⓦ www.mezokovesd.hu) is the centre of the Mátyó, a Magyar people famous for their fine embroidery and other folk art.

From the Mezőkövesd bus station on Rákóczi utca, walk south for 50m and then east along Mátyás király út for 600m to Szent László tér, where you'll find **Tourinform** *(*☎ *500 285, fax 500 286;* ℮ *mezokovesd@ tourinform.hu; Szent László tér 23; open 10am-4pm Mon-Fri).*

Across the square to the north is the **Mátyó Museum** *(*☎ *311 824; Szent László tér 20; adult/child 200/100Ft; open 9am-4pm Tues-Sun May-Oct, 9am-3pm Tues-Sun Nov-Apr)* in the cultural centre. The displays explain the regional differences and historical development of Mátyó needlework: from white-on-white stitching and patterns of blue and red roses, to the metallic fringe that was banned in the early 1920s because the high cost was ruining some families. Across the square is the **Church of St Ladislas** *(Szent László tér 28; open 8am-4.30pm mid-Mar–mid-Sept, 8am-3.30pm mid-Sept–mid-Mar),* with an overwrought romantic fresco of a Mátyó church service (1961) above the arch in the east transept.

From Hősök tere, a short distance south-west of Szent László tér, enter any of the small streets running southward to find the **Hadas** district, a completely different world of thatched and whitewashed cottages with old women outside stitching the distinctive Mátyó rose patterns in the sun. Interesting lanes to stroll along are Patkó köz, Kökény köz and Mogyoró köz, but the centre of ac-tivity is Kis Jankó Bori utca, named after Hungary's own 'Grandma Moses' who lived and stitched her famous '100 roses' patterns here for almost 80 years. Her 200-year-old cottage is now the **Bóri Kis Jankó Memorial House** *(Kis Jankó Bori Emlékház;* ☎ *500 134; Kis Jankó Bori utca 24; adult/child 200/ 100Ft; open 10am-4.30pm Tues-Sat, 10am-2pm Sun),* filled with needlework and brightly painted furniture. Other houses on Kis Jankó Bori utca that you can visit and watch the women at work are Nos 1, 5 (the folk-art association; ☎ 411 686), 7 *(táncpajta* or 'dance barn'), 9 and 32. Also poke your head into No 1 or No 9 of Mogyoró köz. Most of the work is for sale directly from the embroiderers; you can also buy it at the **folk-art shop** *(*☎ *505 376; open 8am-4pm Mon-Fri),* on the southwest corner of Szent László tér, or at a shop called **Gerti** *(*☎ *411 403; Mátyás király út 80; open 9am-6pm daily).*

With Eger so close, there's no point in staying overnight in Mezőkövesd. But if you miss the last bus or you want to catch an early-morning one to Miskolc, **Borsod Tourist** *(*☎ *412 614; Mátyás király út 153; open 9am-4.30pm Mon-Thur, 9am-2pm Fri)* en route to/from the bus station can organise private rooms for 1800Ft to 2000Ft per person. The **Tulipános Guesthouse** *(*☎ *228 7119, fax 500 232; Mogyoró köz 1; doubles from 3000Ft)* is in the heart of the Hadas district. The **Vigadó** *(*☎ *505 080, fax 505 089;* ℮ *vigado52@hu.inter.net; Mátyás király út 173; doubles 7000-9000Ft, triples 10,500-12,500Ft)* is a 22-room hotel a short distance east of the centre.

For something to eat, try the **Hungária** *(*☎ *416 800; Alkotmány út 2; mains 650-910Ft; open 11am-10pm Sun-Thur, 11am-midnight Fri & Sat),* next to Tourinform, for international food; the **Mátyó Csárda** *(*☎ *377 7577; Mártírok útja 4; mains 580-680Ft; open 10am-9m Mon-Thur, 11pm-2am Fri & Sat),* south of the bus station, for rustic Hungarian dishes; or **Pizza Néró** *(*☎ *415 670; Eötvös utca 9; pizza 550-1000Ft; open 10am-11pm Sun-Thur, 10am-2pm Fri & Sat),* south of Hősök tere, for pizza.

There's an **OTP bank** *(Mátyás király út 149; open 7.45am-4pm Mon-Fri)* near Borsod Tourist and the **post office** *(Mátyás király út 87; open 8am-6pm Mon-Fri, 8am-noon Sat)* is just south of the bus station. Buses run to and from Eger and Miskolc at least every half-hour. Other destinations accessible from Mezőkövesd include Budapest (two to three buses daily), Debrecen (three), Gyöngyös (up to four), Nyíregyháza (three), Szeged (two) and Tisztafüred (seven).

SZILVÁSVÁRAD
☎ 36 • postcode 3348 • pop 1950

The western Bükk region is most easily approached from Szilvásvárad, some 28km north of Eger. An easy day trip from Eger, Szilvásvárad is an ideal base for hiking into the Szalajka Valley and is the centre of horse breeding in Hungary. It is also the place to ride on one of Hungary's most delightful narrow-gauge trains.

Orientation & Information
Get off the train at the first of Szilvásvárad's two stations, Szilvásvárad-Szalajkavölgy, and walk along Egri út northeast for about 10 minutes to the centre of town. The town's main station is 3km to the north.

You can change money at the **OTP bank** *(Egri út 30/a; open 8am-4pm Mon-Fri)*. There's an ATM next to the **post office** *(Egri út 12; open 8am-4pm Mon-Fri)*.

Things to See & Do
The open-air **narrow-gauge railway** *(☎ 355 197; adult/child one way 160/80Ft, steam train 320/240Ft)* chugs its way for 5km into the Szalajka Valley seven times daily from May to September (10 times at the weekend), with three departures daily in April and October. The station is about 300m south of Egri út at Szalajka-völgy 6.

The little open-air train stops at **Szalajka-Fátyolvízesés**. From there, you can walk for 15 minutes to **Istállóskő Cave**, where Stone Age pottery shards were discovered in 1912, or climb 958m **Mt Istállóskő**, the highest peak in the Bükk. To return to Szilvásvárad, either stay on the train for the return trip or walk back for 1½ hours along shady paths, taking in trout-filled streams and the **Forestry Museum** *(Erdészeti Múzeum; ☎ 355 112, 355 109; open 8.30am-4.30pm Tues-Sun mid-Apr–Sept, 8.30am-3pm Tues-Sun Oct, 9am-2pm daily Nov–mid-Apr)*, which deals with everything the forest surrenders.

The covered and the open **racecourses** *(adult/child 150/100Ft)* in Szilvásvárad put on Lipizzaner parades and coach races on weekends throughout the summer, but times are not fixed. Learn more about these intelli-

---

The Magnificent White Stallions

Lipizzaners, the celebrated white horses bred originally for the imperial Spanish Riding School in Vienna under the Habsburgs, are considered to be the finest riding horses in the world – the *haute école* of dressage equines. And with all the trouble that's put into breeding and training them, it's not surprising. They are very intelligent, sociable animals, quite robust and graceful.

Lipizzaners are bred for riding and show at Lipica in Slovenia; at Piber, northeast of Graz in Austria, for the Spanish Riding School; and in the US state of Illinois. The Lipizzaners at Szilvásvárad are raised as carriage horses; as a result they are bigger and stronger.

Breeding, as they say, is paramount. Some six families with 16 ancestors (including Spanish, Arabian and Berber breeds) can be traced back to the early 18th century, and their pedigrees read like those of medieval nobility. When you walk around the stables at the stud farm or the Horse Museum, you'll notice charts on each horse's stall with complicated figures, dates and names like 'Maestoso', 'Neapolitano' and 'Pluto'. It's all to do with the horse's lineage.

A fully mature Lipizzaner measures about 15 hands (that's about 152cm) and weighs between 500kg and 600kg. They have long backs, short, thick necks, silky manes and expressive eyes. They live for 25 to 30 years and are particularly resistant to disease. But, like most horses, they are somewhat short-sighted (near-sighted) and will nuzzle you out of curiosity if you approach them while they graze.

Lipizzaners are not born white but grey, bay (ie, reddish brown) or even chestnut. The celebrated 'imperial white' does not come about until they are between five and 10 years old, when their hair loses its pigment; think of it as part of an old nag's ageing process. Their skin remains grey, however, so when they are ridden hard and sweat, they become mottled and aren't so attractive.

gent horses by visiting the **Horse Museum**
(*Lovas Múzeum;* ☎ *355 135; Park utca 8;
adult/child 100/80Ft; open 9am-noon, 1pm-
4pm Tues-Sun*), in an 18th-century stable.
The **Lipizzaner State Stud Farm** (*Lipicai Állami Ménesgazdaság;* ☎ *355 155; Fenyves
utca; adult/child 100/80Ft; open 8am-noon,
2pm-4pm Tues-Sun*) can also be visited. It
rents out **horses** (1800/2500Ft per hour in
the paddock/further afield) and offers **coach
rides** (from 4300/7400Ft for a two-/four-
horse coach seating three people). **Coach driving instruction** costs 5100/9000Ft an hour.

The new **Prison Museum** (*Börtön Múzeum; adult/child 300/200Ft; open 9am-
6pm daily*) in the centre of the village is
strictly kids' stuff.

The Protestant **Round Church** (*Kerektem-
plom; Aradi vértanúk útja*), with its Doric
columns and dramatic dome raised in 1841,
looks to some like a provincial attempt to
duplicate the basilica at Eger. Displays in a
17th-century farmhouse called **Orbán House**
(*☎ 355 133; Miskolci út 58-60; adult/child
150/100Ft; open 9am-5pm Tues-Sun mid-
Apr–Oct*) are devoted to the flora, fauna and
geology of Bükk National Park.

Mountain Bike Rentals (*☎ 06-30 335
2695; 700/900/1100/1300/1500Ft for 1/2/3/
4/5hrs, 1800Ft day*) has a stand opposite the
narrow-gauge train station in Szalajka-völgy.

Places to Stay & Eat

Hegyi Camping (*☎/fax 355 207;* **W** *www
.hegyicamping.com; Egri út 36/a; tent site
per person 550-750Ft, trailer/caravan site/
1800/2000Ft, 2-/3-/4-bed houses 3900/
4900/5600Ft, bungalows 3900/4900/5600Ft;
open mid-Apr–mid-Oct*) has a variety of accommodation.

Lipicai (*☎ 355 100, fax 355 200; Egri út
12-14; singles/doubles 5100/6100Ft*) is a
29-room hotel in a blockhouse-like building
with very basic accommodation.

Szilvás (*☎ 355 159, fax 355 324;* **e** *re
serve@hotelszilvas.huguesthotels.hu; Park
utca 6; singles 4600-6300Ft, doubles 6900-
9200Ft*), a 40-room hotel just beyond the
Horse Museum in an old mansion, is the most
interesting place to stay in Szilvásvárad.
Prices depend on the season and whether your
room has a bath, a shower and/or a toilet.

Szalajka-völgy is lined with **food stalls**
and **restaurants**, including **Lovas** (*☎ 355
555; mains 860-2620Ft; open 10am-10pm*

daily), with a covered terrace, and **Fenyő**
(*☎ 564 015; mains 750-990Ft; open 8am-
10pm*). Many of them serve trout (30Ft to
50Ft per kilogram), the speciality of the area

Getting There & Away

Buses to/from Eger are very frequent and,
though they stop at Bélapátfalva and sometimes Mónosbél, they're faster than the train.
Buses also go to Ózd (about 10 daily departures on weekdays, hourly at the weekend),
Budapest (three to four buses daily), Aggtelek and Jósvafő (one), Mezőkövesd (one
on weekdays), Miskolc (one), Gyöngyös (up
to four), Mátraháza (one) and Putnok (three).

Up to nine trains daily link Eger with Szilvásvárad. If heading for Szilvásvárad from
the centre of Eger, board the train at the

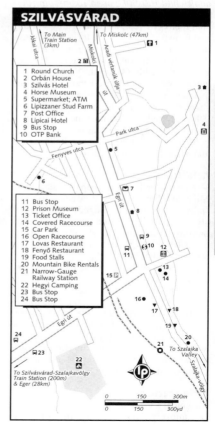

SZILVÁSVÁRAD

1 Round Church
2 Orbán House
3 Szilvás Hotel
4 Horse Museum
5 Supermarket; ATM
6 Lipizzaner Stud Farm
7 Post Office
8 Lipicai Hotel
9 Bus Stop
10 OTP Bank
11 Bus Stop
12 Prison Museum
13 Ticket Office
14 Covered Racecourse
15 Car Park
16 Open Racecourse
17 Lovas Restaurant
18 Fenyő Restaurant
19 Food Stalls
20 Mountain Bike Rentals
21 Narrow-Gauge Railway Station
22 Hegyi Camping
23 Bus Stop
24 Bus Stop

NORTHERN UPLANDS

Egervár station, north of the castle on Gárdonyi Géza utca. Four of these trains carry on to Putnok, from where you can enter Slovakia via Bánréve or head southeast for Miskolc.

AROUND SZILVÁSVÁRAD
Bélapátfalva
☎ 36 • postcode 3346 • pop 3465

On the train or bus to or from Szilvásvárad, you'll pass through the town of Bélapátfalva (W www.belapatfalva.hu), which seems to stand out for no other reason than the giant cement factory that covers everything in fine white powder.

In fact one of Hungary's most perfectly preserved Romanesque monuments is just a few minutes away. It's the **Bélháromkút Abbey Church** (☎ 354 784, 06-20 934 3665; adult/child 100/50Ft; open 10am-4pm Tues-Sun mid-Mar–Oct) built by French Cistercian monks in 1232 and reached by walking east from the village centre for 1.5km (follow the 'Apátság Múzeum' signs) along Apátság utca. Along the way you'll see another sign giving the address for the key (templom kulcsa), which is at Rozsa Ferenc utca 42 and available in season. The church, built in the shape of a cross, is set in a peaceful dell just below Mt Bélkő. Don't miss the 19th-century painted **Calvary scene** nearby.

Most of the buses and trains linking Eger and Szilvásvárad stop at Bélapátfalva.

MISKOLC
☎ 46 • postcode 3500 • pop 192,300

Miskolc, Hungary's third-largest city, is a sprawling metropolis ringed by refineries, abandoned factories and cardboard-quality housing blocks. A relatively affluent mining and steel-making town under the socialist regime, Miskolc was hit harder than most by the collapse of heavy industry here in the early 1990s.

So why come to this 'capital of the rust belt'? For one thing, its location at the foot of the Bükk Hills makes it an ideal place to start a trek or walk into the national park. The thermal waters of nearby Miskolctapolca are among the most effective in Hungary, and the western suburb of Diósgyőr boasts a well-preserved castle.

Orientation
Miskolc is a long, narrow city stretching from the unlovely Sajó Valley in the east to the Bükk foothills in the west. The main drag, Széchenyi István út, is lined with some interesting old buildings, especially those around the so-called **Dark Gate** (Sötétkapu), an 18th-century vaulted passageway.

The main train station, called Tiszai pályaudvar, lies to the southeast on Kandó Kálmán tér, a 15-minute tram ride from the centre. The huge bus station is on Búza tér, a short distance northeast of Széchenyi út.

Information
Tourinform (☎ 350 425, fax 350 439; e mis kolc@tourinform.hu; Rákóczi utca 2; open 9am-7pm Mon-Fri, 9am-6pm Sat & Sun mid-June–mid-Sept; 9am-5pm Mon-Fri, 9am-4pm Sat & Sun mid-Sept–mid-June) is in Rákóczi House on Széchenyi út. Commercial travel agencies on Széchenyi út include **Cooptourist** (☎ 328 812, fax 357 676; open 9am-5pm Mon-Fri, 10am-12.30pm Sat) at No 14; **Ibusz** (☎ 324 090, fax 326 606; open 8am-5pm Mon-Thur, 8am-4pm Fri) at No 18; and **Borsod Tourist** (☎ 350 666; fax 350 694; open 8am-4.30pm Mon-Thur, 8am-4pm Fri) at No 35.

There is a branch of the **OTP bank** (Széchenyi út 15; open 7.45-4pm Mon-Thur & Fri, 7.45am-5pm Thur) opposite the Dark Gate. The **main post office** (Kazinczy utca 16; open 8am-8pm Mon-Fri, 8am-1pm Sat) is on the eastern side of Hősök tere, but a more convenient post office branch (Széchenyi út 3-9; 8am-7pm Mon-Fri) is on the 1st floor of a shopping block opposite Tourinform.

Netgate Internet Szalon (☎ 505 832; e netgate@chello.hu; Deryné utca 18; open 10am-8pm Mon-Fri, 2pm-8pm Sat) is through a small courtyard off Deryné utca and to the right. It charges 300Ft per hour.

For general information on Miskolc, check out the website W www.miskolc.hu.

Things to See
Two houses of worship attest to the large communities of Greeks and Jews who once called Miskolc their home. The **Hungarian Orthodox church** (Magyar ortodox templom; Deák tér 7; admission 50Ft), a splendid, late-baroque structure, has an iconostasis (1793) that is 16m high with 88 icons. A guide will escort you to the **Orthodox Ecclesiastical Museum** (Ortodox Egyházi Múzeum; ☎ 415 441; adult/child 80/40Ft; open 10am-6pm Tues-Sat May-Sept, 10am-

GREATER MISKOLC

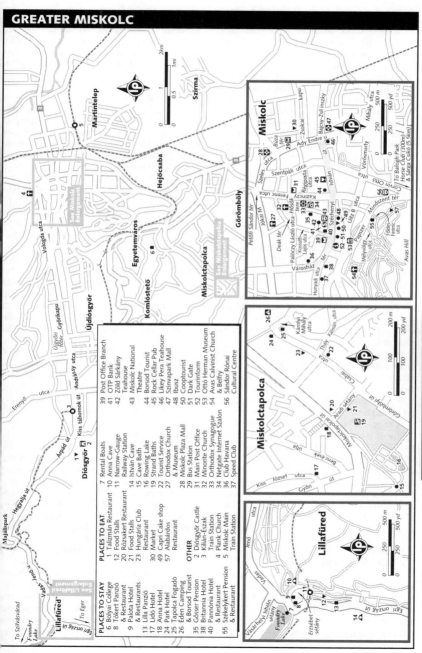

2km
1mi

Martintelep

Miskolc

Szirma

Hejőcsaba

Egyetemváros

Komlóstető

Miskolctapolca

Görömböly

Újdiósgyőr

See Miskolc Enlargement

See Miskolctapolca Enlargement

Vologda utca

Ujgyóri öter.

Gyóikapu

Andrássy utca

To Szilvásvárad
Foundry Lake
To Eger

Lillafüred

See Lillafüred Enlargement

Majálispark

Hegyalja út

Erenyő utca

Árpád út

Kiss tábornok út

Diósgyőr

To Szinva n. lake
Vadás
Egri ország út

PLACES TO STAY
6 Bolyai College
8 Tököert Panzió & Restaurant
9 Palota Hotel & Restaurants
13 Lilla Panzió
17 Lidó Hotel
18 Anna Hotel
24 Park Hotel
25 Tapolca Fogadó & Borsod Tourist
26 Éden Camping
35 Gösser Pension
38 Britannia Hotel
40 Pannónia Hotel
55 Székelykert Pension & Restaurant

PLACES TO EAT
1 Talizmán Restaurant
12 Food Stalls
20 Rózsakert Restaurant
21 Food Stalls
23 Hungária Club & Restaurants
30 Market
49 Capri Cake shop
57 Alabárdos Restaurant

OTHER
2 Diósgyőr Castle
3 Kilián-Észak Train Station
4 Plank Church
5 Miskolc Main Train Station
7 Rental Boats
10 Anna Cave
11 Narrow-Gauge Railway Station
14 István Cave
15 Cave Bath
16 Rowing Lake
19 Strand Baths
22 Tourist Service
27 Orthodox Church & Museum
28 Miskolc Plaza Mall
29 Bus Station
31 Main Post Office
32 Minorite Church
33 Orthodox Synagogue
34 Netgate Internet Szalon
36 Club Havana
37 Speed Club
39 Post Office Branch
41 OTP Bank
42 Zöld Sárkány Teahouse
43 Miskolc National Theatre
44 Borsod Tourist
45 Rock Cellar Pub
46 Likey Pera Teahouse
47 Szinvapark Mall
48 Ibusz
50 Cooptourist
51 Dark Gate
52 Touriform
53 Ottó Herman Museum
54 Avas Calvinist Church & Belfry
56 Sándor Rónai Cultural Centre

Miskolctapolca

Lillafüred

Tues-Sat Oct-Apr) near the main gate. Watch out for the Black Madonna of Kazan, presented to the church by Catherine the Great, and the jewel-encrusted Mt Athos Cross brought to Miskolc by Greek settlers in the 18th century. To the southeast stands the large and crumbling **Orthodox synagogue** *(Ortodox zsinagóga; Kazinczy utca 7)* designed in 1861 by Ludwig Förster, architect of the Great Synagogue in Budapest.

The Calvinist **Plank Church** *(Deszkatemplom)* is a 1938 replica of a 17th-century Transylvanian-style wooden church in the cemetery north of Petőfi tér. It has been completely rebuilt and renovated after having been badly damaged by fire in 1997.

The **Ottó Herman Museum** *(☎ 346 875; ⓦ www.hermuz.hu; Papszer 1; adult/child 200/100Ft; open 10am-4pm Tues-Sun)*, south of the centre, has one of Hungary's richest collections of Neolithic finds (many from the Bükk region), good ethnographical and mineral collections and an exhibit of fine art. From here, take a stroll up leafy **Avas Hill**; the best approach is via Mélyvölgy utca, off Papszer, or Földes Ferenc utca, off Mindszent tér. Veer to the right along the narrow lane past some of the more than 800 wine cellars cut into the limestone.

In a cemetery below the hill is the large Gothic **Avas Calvinist church** *(Avasi református templom)*, with a painted wooden interior (1410). The bell tower dates from the mid-16th century. The key is in the parish office at Papszer 14.

A must-see but a bit of a journey from the centre is the four-towered **Diósgyőr Castle** *(☎ 533 355; Vár utca 24; adult/child 600/250Ft; open 9am-6pm daily May-Sept, 10am-4pm Oct-Apr)*, in a suburb of the same name some 7km west of the centre. Begun in the 13th century, the castle was heavily damaged early in the 18th century and was only restored – very insensitively in some parts – in the 1950s.

Activities

The **Balogh Park Horse Club** *(☎ 411 858, fax 412 527; Görgey utca 12)* hires out horses for riding and runs a **riding school** south of Mindszent tér. Further afield, there's a horse-riding school at the **Sárga Csikó** *(☎ 303 522, fax 341 656)*, a riding hotel in Miskolc-Görömböly, south of the city on route No 3 (Pesti út). Take bus No 4 from the bus station.

Special Events

A number of special events and festivals are held at Diósgyőr Castle including the **Castle Games** in May and the celebrated open-air **Kaláka International Folk Festival** in mid-July.

Places to Stay

Bolyai College *(☎ 565 260; Egyetem utca 17; dorm beds 1200Ft)*, at the university in Egyetemváros, has hundreds of dormitory beds available in July and August. There are up to 25 available during the rest of the year.

Private rooms for two people from Ibusz or Borsod Tourist cost 2500Ft to 3500Ft, but they'll probably be in one of the housing projects ringing the city.

Gösser *(☎ 505 045, fax 344 425; ⓔ gosser .panzio@matavnet.hu; Déryné utca 7; doubles 7000Ft)* is an ordinary seven-room city pension that is not worth the price it charges, but it's central. Its sister-pension, **Székelykert** *(☎/fax 411 222; Kisavas Alsó sor, Földes Ferenc utca 4; doubles 7000Ft)*, also with seven rooms, is below Avas Hill.

Britannia *(☎/fax 351 066; Hunyadi utca 3; singles/doubles 8900/9500Ft)* is a relatively stylish, eight-room hotel in an older building.

Pannónia *(☎ 504 980, fax 504 984; ⓔ hotelpannonia@chello.hu; Kossuth Lajos utca 2; singles €71, doubles €84-94)*, very much in the centre, is Miskolc's No 1 hotel. It has a restaurant, brasserie and 41 ordinary rooms, but is way overpriced.

Places to Eat

Pannónia's pub-restaurant *(mains 750-1600Ft; open 11am-11pm daily)* has a terrace that is a pleasant place for an evening meal in summer.

Alabárdos *(☎ 412 215; Kisavas Első sor 5, open 6pm-midnight Mon-Sat)* is said by some to be Miskolc's best restaurant, but it's really just a tarted-up Hungarian restaurant serving the same old things.

The restaurant at the **Székelykert** *(☎ 411 222; open 11am-10.30pm daily)* serves Transylvanian specialities, dishes rarely encountered at restaurants in Hungary.

Talizmán *(☎ 378 627; Vár utca 14; open noon-10pm daily)* in Diósgyőr, can be recommended for its menu and pleasant location on a chestnut-tree lined pedestrian street just up from the castle.

Capri (☎ 348 928; Széchenyi út 16; open 9am-9pm daily) is a central *cukrászda* serving cakes and ice cream.

There is a large **market** (Zsolcai kapu) east of Búza tér.

Entertainment

Miskolc National Theatre (Miskolci Nemzeti Színház; ☎ 516 700, 510 736; Széchenyi út 23; box office 10am-7pm Mon-Fri, 3pm-7pm Sat & Sun) stages plays and other performances in a new purpose-built theatre behind the original theatre (built 1857), where the beloved 19th-century actress Róza Széppataki Déryné once walked the floorboards. There are also performances at the **Sándor Rónai Cultural Centre** (Rónai Sándor Művelődési Központ; ☎ 342 408; Mindszent tér 3). The baroque **Minorite church** (Minorita templom; Hősök tere), built in 1734, and the **Avas Calvinist church** have regular organ concerts.

Miskolc is a big university town: Popular places to meet include the **Zöld Sárkány** (☎ 428 134; Széchenyi út 19; open 10am-8.45pm Mon-Fri, noon-10pm Sat), a rather earnest teahouse and café in a courtyard; **Likey Pera** (☎ 06-30 206 1244; Széchenyi út 94; open 10am-10pm Sun-Thur, 10am-10pm Fri & Sat), a more relaxed teahouse with Asian brew and South American decor; **Rock Cellar Pub** (☎ 415 912; Széchenyi utca 61; open noon-midnight Mon-Thur, noon-2am Fri & Sat), with jazz, darts and billiards; and **Club Havana** (☎ 344 872; Városház tér 3; open 8am-2am daily), a lovely terraced café-bar with canned Latino music. **Speed Club** (☎ 358 849; Hunyadi utca 5; open 10pm-dawn Thur-Sat), is a popular, central dance club.

For more listings see the free biweekly *Miskolci Est* magazine.

Getting There & Away

Buses depart for Debrecen every 30 minutes to an hour. If you're heading south, it's best to take the bus, though departures are infrequent (eg, one daily bus to Békéscsaba and Gyula and two to Kecskemét). There are about 10 buses daily to Eger, but if you're travelling on a Sunday, be sure to take the 6.25am or 3.15pm bus; these follow the scenic route through the Bükk Hills via Felsőtárkány.

Miskolc is served by hourly trains from Keleti station in Budapest; about a dozen trains depart daily for Nyíregyháza via Tokaj. Two or three of these trains carry on to Debrecen, but generally you'll have to change at Nyíregyháza. About a dozen trains leave Miskolc each day for Sárospatak and Sátoraljaújhely.

Daily international trains from Miskolc include those departing for Košice in Slovakia (six) and Kraków and Warsaw in Poland (two). For Oradea and Cluj-Napoca in Romania, you'll have to change at Püspökladány. For Lviv, Kyiv and Moscow, change at Nyíregyháza or Debrecen.

Getting Around

Tram Nos 1 and 2 begin at the train station and travel the length of the city before turning around in Diósgyőr. You can also reach Diósgyőr on bus No 1.

You can order a taxi by ringing ☎ 323 323, ☎ 333 333 or ☎ 333 444.

AROUND MISKOLC
Miskolctapolca
☎ 46 • postcode 3519

The curative waters of the thermal spa in this southwestern recreational suburb, 7km from the centre of Miskolc, have been attracting bathers since the Middle Ages, though the gimmicky **Cave Bath** (Barlangfürdő; ☎ 561 361; Pazár István sétány 1; admission Mon-Fri before/after 3pm 800/600Ft, weekend 1200/900Ft; open 9am-7pm mid-July–Aug, 9am-6pm daily Sept–mid-July), with its 'mildly radioactive waters' and thrashing shower at the end, are relatively new arrivals (1959). The pretty **Strand Bath** (Strandfürdő; ☎ 368 127; Miskolctapolcai út 1), in the centre of the town's large park, has **outside pools** (adult/child 450/300Ft, after 4pm 250/200Ft; open 9am-6pm daily May-Sept). You can rent **rowing boats** and **pedal boats** (500Ft per half-hr; 10am to 6pm May-Sept) for boating on the park lake.

Éden Camping (☎ 561 510, fax 368 917; e botour@elender.hu; Károlyi Mihály utca 1; camping per person/tent/caravan 600/800/1400Ft, bungalows 8000-9800Ft; open mid-Apr–mid-Oct) has bungalows accommodating four people.

Borsod Tourist (☎/fax 368 917), which has a representative office at Éden Camping, can book you a **private room** for 2000Ft per person, though there are signs offering them at private houses everywhere (eg, Görömbölyi út 15, 36 and 42/a). You might also try the **Tourist Service** (☎ 363 970; Csabai utca 14; open 9am-7.30 daily) for private accommodation.

NORTHERN UPLANDS

Lídó (☎ 369 035, fax 369 800; e harom.g@ freemail.hu; Kiss József utca 4; singles/ doubles/triples/quads 2500/4200/5900/ 6600Ft), relatively far from the action and in an unattractive bunker-like building with 49 rooms, is about as cheap a place you'll find in Miskolctapolca.

Park (☎ 360 811, fax 369 931; e park hotel@axelero.hu; Csabai utca 35; doubles 8000Ft) is a renovated, 55-room hotel near the camp site that once served as a retreat for athletes.

Tapolca Fogadó (☎/fax 562 215; e tapol cafogado@chello.hu; Csabai utca 36; doubles/ triples 7500/9500Ft) is a new inn, with 14 rooms and lots of turrets, opposite the Park.

Anna (☎ 316 555, fax 311 606; e anna hotel@chello.hu; Miskolctapolcai út 7; doubles 8600Ft), with 15 very pleasant rooms and friendly management, is one of the more attractive places to stay in town.

There are plenty of **food stalls** and **snack bars** on Aradi sétány. The **Rózsakert** (☎ 360 033; Aradi sétány 5; mains 350-800Ft) is a cheap place for a sit-down meal. Further afield the **Hungária Club** (☎ 432 884; Csabai utca; mains 590-1180Ft) has a cheap set lunch for 380Ft.

Bus No 2 serves Miskolctapolca and the Cave Bath from Búza tér in Miskolc. Bus No 12 and – during the week – No 22 go to the university.

Lillafüred
☎ 46 • postcode 3517

At 320m above sea level, Lillafüred lies at the junction of two valleys formed by the Garadna and Szinva streams, 12km west of Miskolc. Lillafüred has been a resort since the early part of this century and 'sights' as such are few. But it is a pleasant break from Miskolc and the springboard for walks and hikes into the eastern Bükk Hills.

People travel to Lillafüred just to take the **narrow-gauge train** from Miskolc, one of the most enjoyable forest train trips in Hungary.

Caves Sometimes called Petőfi Cave, **Anna Cave** (☎ 334 130; adult/child 400/300Ft; open daily mid-Apr–mid-Oct) is below the Palota hotel and next to a cooling waterfall, and offers 25-minute tours hourly between 10am and 3pm. **István Cave** (☎ 334 131; adult/child 400/300Ft; open daily mid-Apr– mid-Oct) is about 500m up the mountain

road leading to Eger; it offers one-hour tours hourly between 10am and 3pm, with extra tours at 9am and 4pm in July and August. István Cave has stalagmites, stalactites, sink-holes and large chambers; Anna Cave has fossils – leaves, branches, even entire trees.

Hiking A number of lovely **walks** can be undertaken from the terminuses of the two lines of the narrow-gauge train at **Garadna** and **Taksalápa**, but accommodation is sparse in these parts and hikers had better be prepared to camp rough if they miss the train. Be sure to have a copy of the northern Bükk map (No 29) from Cartographia and carry extra water.

Other Activities Jade-coloured **Foundry Lake** (Hámori-tó), named after the proto-blast furnace set up here by a German named Frigyes Fazola in the early 19th century to exploit the area's iron ore, offers **fishing** (Mohosz information in Miskolc ☎ 324 702) and boating. **Rowing boats** (10am-6pm daily May-Sept) cost 300/100Ft per half-hour per adult/child, while **paddle boats** cost 500Ft per half-hour. The Palota hotel rents out **bicycles** for 300Ft per hour.

Places to Stay & Eat A tidy five-room pension in a park behind the Palota, **Lilla Panzió** (☎/fax 379 299; Erzsébet sétány 7; doubles 6000Ft) has doubles without bath.

Tókert Panzió (☎ 533 560, fax 531 202; e tokert@tokert.hu; Erzsébet sétány 3; singles/ doubles 6700/8800Ft), in the shadow (in every sense) of the Palota hotel, has 12 rooms, great views of the lake and a decent restaurant.

The **Palota** (☎ 331 411, fax 533 203; e reserve@hotelpalota.hunguesthotels.hu; Erzsébet sétány 1; singles €67-73, doubles €73-89), a mock-Gothic structure that's a 129-room hotel again after a 40-year stint as a trade-union holiday home, dominates the town. The hotel has three restaurants, including the posh **Mátyás**, with stained-glass windows, enormous fireplace and waiters who look like they're dressed to say a Mass.

There are several **food stalls** serving lángos (deep-fried dough with toppings) and sausage near the narrow-gauge train station, including the little **Falatozó** bistro, which serves cheap, decent meals and picnic tables. The restaurant at the **Tókert** (mains 780-1790Ft; open 7am-11pm) has great views and some affordable set lunches.

Getting There & Away You can reach Lillafüred by bus or the narrow-gauge train. Bus No 1 from Miskolc goes to the tram terminus at Diósgyőr. Transfer here to bus No 5 or 15, which leaves for Lillafüred every half-hour or so. Bus No 68 runs every half-hour between Újgyőri főtér on Andrássy utca, west of Miskolc's centre, and Bükkszentlászló.

Kilián-Észak train station, from where the little narrow-gauge train for Lillafüred departs, is off Kiss tábornok út in western Miskolc, almost in Diósgyőr. There are only two departures daily October to mid-April, increasing to four daily during the week and between six and nine daily at the weekend for the remainder of the year. Check the schedules at Tourinform in Miskolc or call ☎ 370 663 or ☎ 379 086 for information. From Lillafüred, the train carries on another 6km to Garadna.

Another line of the narrow gauge branches off at Papírgyár – the paper factory that polluted the Szinva Stream – and covers the 20km between Kilián-Észak station and Taksalápa. The frequency of this under-utilised line is now just two departures at the weekend between May and September (9.30am and 2.10pm out, 1pm and 6pm back).

Aggtelek Karst Region

If you thought the caves at Lillafüred were kids' stuff, head 60km north to Aggtelek National Park, a hilly karst region encompassing some 20,000 hectares. The Baradla-Domica caves network is the largest stalactite system in Europe, with 25km of passageways (6km of them in Slovakia), and was declared a dual-nation Unesco World Heritage Site in 1995. The array of red and black stalactite drip stones, stalagmite pyramids and enormous chambers is astonishing and a must-see.

A tour of the cave sections usually includes a short organ recital or some other form of music in the Concert or Giants' Halls and, if the water is high enough, a boat ride on the Styx, an underground stream.

AGGTELEK
☎ 48 • postcode 3759 • pop 650
There are three entrances to the Baradla Cave system: at Aggtelek village; at Jósvafő, 6km to the east; and at Vörös-tó (Red Lake), just

before Jósvafő. Guided tours of the Baradla Cave system depart from these points, but the most popular short and long tours can be joined at the Aggtelek entrance.

Orientation & Information
Tourinform (☎/fax 343 029, 343 073; e aggtelek@tourinform.hu; Baradla oldal 1; open 9am-6pm daily mid-June–mid-Sept; 7.30am-4pm Mon-Thur, 7.30am-1.30pm Fri mid-Sept–mid-June), at the small nature museum near the Aggtelek cave ticket office, can supply you with information and sell you a copy of the Aggteleki-karszt és környéke (Aggtelek Karst & Surrounds; No 1; 650Ft), an excellent 1:40,000 hiking map from Cartographia. For more detailed information, contact the **Aggtelek National Park Directorate** (Aggteleki Nemzeti Park Igazgatósága; ☎/fax 350 006; w www.anp.hu; Tengerszem oldal 1) in Jósvafő. The website is in Hungarian only.

The **post office** (Kossuth utca 37; open 8am-4pm Mon-Fri) in Aggtelek has an ATM. You can also change money at the Cseppkő hotel (see Places to Stay & Eat later in this section).

Baradla Cave
Baradla Cave (Baradla-barlang; open 8am-6pm daily Apr-Sept, 8am-4pm daily Oct-Mar) offers tours that depart even with one participant. Students with an international ID pay 50% of the admission fee and children under six go free. The temperature at this level is usually about 10°C with humidity over 95%, so be sure to bring a sweater along.

Short tours lasting about one hour (1km, 1200Ft) start at the Aggtelek entrance at 10am, 1pm and 3pm with an additional tour at 5pm from April to September. A one-hour tour (900Ft) that covers 1.5km of a different section is available from the Jósvafő entrance near the Tengerszem hotel at 9am and 5pm from April to September and at 10am and 3pm the rest of the year.

A two-hour 'middle tour' of the Jósvafő section (2.3km, 1400Ft) departs at 10am, noon, 1.30pm and 3pm in high season and at noon only the rest of the year from the Vörös-tó entrance; it ends at the one in Jósvafő. You can also buy reduced-price tickets that combine the two short tours (2.5km, 1600Ft) and the Aggtelek short and the Jósvafő middle tours (3.3km, 2000Ft) over two consecutive days.

A small **exhibition space** near the Aggtelek entrance to the cave has exhibits dealing with the flora and fauna of the caves and countryside.

Other Activities
You can join up with some excellent **hiking trails** above the Tourinform office in Aggtelek, affording superb views of the rolling hills and valleys. A relatively easy three-hour (7km) walk along the **Baradla Trail**, tagged yellow, will take you from Aggtelek to Jósvafő. There are other treks lasting five to six hours, and these can be used for cycling and horse riding. A 20km **bicycle route** links Aggtelek and Szögliget to the northeast, and bicycles can be rented from **Zsolt Bacsó** (☎ 350 128; open 9am-7pm daily July & Aug; 9am-6pm Sat & Sun Sept-June) in Jósvafő. The **Hucul Stud Farm** in Jósvafő has horses for hire (1200Ft per hour) and offers hour-long carriage and, in winter, sledge (sleigh) rides for 2000Ft.

The park directorate organises a number of programmes, including three-hour **guided walks** in Aggtelek and Jósvafő (600Ft each) as well as **themed tours** of the national park lasting three to six hours – from ecology (600Ft to 900Ft) to zoology and botany (1200Ft to 1700Ft).

Special Events
Main events in Aggtelek and its vicinity are the **International Choir Festival** in Baradla Cave in June, the **Gömor-Torna Festival** of folk and world music in July, and **Mountaineering Day** in late August, which attracts climbers from all over Hungary.

Places to Stay & Eat
Baradla Camping (☎/fax 343 029, 343 073; Baradla oldal 1; camping per person/tent/caravan 700/700/900Ft; 4-person/6-person bungalows 4800/10,000Ft; open mid-Apr–mid-Oct), where you can pitch a tent or rent a bungalow, is next to the Aggtelek cave entrance. **Baradla Hostel** (dorm beds per adult/student 1600/1100Ft; open year round) has dorm rooms with two, three and six beds.

Cseppkő (☎ 343 075, fax 342 181; Gyömrői út 2; doubles about 6000Ft), on a scenic hill above the entrance to the cave, is the only hotel in Aggtelek and has 70 rooms, a restaurant, bar, a terrace with splendid views, and a tennis court and sauna/solarium.

Tengerszem (☎/fax 350 006; e info.anp@ axelero.hu; Tengerszem oldal 2; doubles 7900-9900Ft, triples 8900-11,400Ft, quads 10,900-13,400Ft), a renovated 18-room hotel in Jósvafő, is worth considering if you intend to join cave tours at both the Aggtelek and Jósvafő entrances.

There are **food stalls** in the car park near the cave entrance in Aggtelek. Both **Cseppkő** and the **Tengerszem** hotels have restaurants.

Getting There & Away
Direct buses link Aggtelek with Budapest and Miskolc. They leave Jósvafő (stopping at Aggtelek about 10 minutes later) for Budapest twice daily at 5.30am and 2.45pm (with an additional bus at 4.10pm Friday to Sunday) and for Miskolc at 4.30am and 11.30am weekdays, at 5.45am Saturday and at 11.30am Sunday. There's also a daily departure to Eger via Szilvásvárad.

Aggtelek can also be reached from Miskolc (1½ hours, four to six trains daily) – you want the one heading for Tornanádaska. The Jósvafő–Aggtelek train station is some 14km east of Jósvafő (and 20km from Aggtelek village); a local bus meets each of the trains to take you to either town.

Getting Around
Five buses a day link Aggtelek (stop just outside the Cseppkő hotel) and Jósvafő (stop at the cave entrance) via Vörös-tó.

Zemplén Hills

The Zemplén region is not uniform. On the southern and eastern slopes are the market towns and vineyards of the Tokaj-Hegyalja region. The wine trade attracted Greek, Serbian, Slovak, Polish, Russian and German merchants, and their influence can be felt in the area's architecture, culture and wine to this day. The northern Zemplén on the border with Slovakia is the nation's 'wildest' region and full of castle ruins.

BOLDOGKŐVÁRALJA
☎ 46 • postcode 3885 • pop 1100
The train linking Szerencs (on the main Budapest–Miskolc–Nyíregyháza trunk line) with Hidasnémeti, near the Slovakian border, stops at a dozen wine-producing towns as it wends its way some 50km up the picturesque

Hernád Valley. Some of the towns, such as Tállya and Gönc, are interesting in themselves, while others serve as starting points for forays into the southern Zemplén Hills. But not one combines the two so well as Boldogkőváralja, a charming village with an important castle.

Orientation

Heading north from Szerencs, make sure you sit on the right-hand side of the train to see Boldogkőváralja's dramatic castle as it comes into view. The train stops on the other side of the highway about some 2.5km west of the castle.

Boldogkő Castle

Perched atop a basalt mountain, 'Happy Rock' Castle (adult/child 300/150Ft; open 9am-6pm mid-Apr–mid-Oct) commands a splendid 360° view of the southern Zemplén Hills, the Hernád Valley and nearby vineyards. Originally built in the 13th century, the castle was strengthened 200 years later but gradually fell into ruin after the kuruc revolt late in the 17th century.

There's a tiny museum here with exhibits on notable occupants and medieval weaponry, but walking through the uneven courtyard up onto the ramparts and looking out over the surrounding countryside in the late afternoon is much more satisfying. It's easy to see how the swashbuckling lyric poet Bálint Balassi (1554–94) produced some of his finest work here.

Regional History Exhibit

The little Regional History exhibit (Tajtörténeti kiállítás; ☎ 467 918; Kossuth Lajos utca 32; adult/child 100/80Ft; open 10am-4pm Fri, Sat & Sun May-Sept) has some interesting items devoted to Balassi and local sons and daughters who made it good overseas (one set up the first Hungarian-language newspaper in the USA), as well as a display of folk dress, a fully equipped smithy, and exhibits on the flora and fauna of the Zemplén.

Hiking

Marked trails lead from the castle's northern side to Regéc, about 15km to the northeast via Arka and Mogyoróska, skirting mountains and 14th-century castle ruins along the way. From here you can either retrace your steps to Boldogkőváralja or follow the road westward to the Fony train stop (some six trains a day

in each direction), which is about 10km to the west. The hardy and/or prepared may want to carry on another 8km north to Gönc, a pretty town where the wooden barrels used to age traditional Tokaj wine have been made for centuries. It's on the main train line back to Szerencs. Depending on which way you're hiking, make sure you're armed with the northern (No 22) or southern (No 23) section of Cartographia's Zempléni-hegység (Zemplén Hills) 1:40,000 map (650Ft each).

Places to Stay & Eat

Tekerjes (☎ 387 701, fax 387 742; Kossuth Lajos utca 41; doubles 2000Ft), a little inn with 11 very basic rooms, is open all year.

Parasztház (Peasant House; ☎ 387 730; Kossuth Lajos utca 75; open May–mid-Oct), a traditional little old farmhouse for rent near the history museum is another option. The house at Major utca 4 nearby has private rooms.

Aside from the restaurant at the Tekerjes, the only other place for a sit-down meal is the Bodókő (Kossuth Lajos utca) at the bottom of the road to the castle.

Getting There & Away

Boldogkőváralja is on the train line connecting Szerencs with Hidasnémeti, and some six trains per day in each direction stop at the town. Only one of these is direct; the rest require a change (no wait) at Abaújszántó.

TOKAJ

☎ 47 • postcode 3910 • pop 4650
The wines of Tokaj, a picturesque little town of vineyards and nesting storks, have been celebrated for centuries. Tokaj is, in fact, just one of 28 towns and villages of the Tokaj-Hegyalja, a 6600-hectare vine-growing region that produces wine along the southern and eastern edges of the Zemplén Hills and was declared a World Heritage Site in 2002. For more information on Tokaj wines see the Wines of Hungary special section in the Facts for the Visitor chapter.

Orientation & Information

Tokaj's centre lies west of where the Bodrog and Tisza Rivers meet. The train station is 1200m south of the town centre; walk north for 15 minutes along Baross Gábor utca and Bajcsy-Zsilinszky utca to Rákóczi út, the main thoroughfare. Buses arrive and depart from along Serház utca east of Kossuth tér.

NORTHERN UPLANDS

Tourinform (☎ 552 070, fax 352 259; 🅔 tokaj@tourinform.hu; Serház utca 1; open 9am-4pm Mon-Fri) is just off Rákóczi út and between the **OTP bank** (Rákóczi út 35; open 8am-4pm Mon-Fri) and the **post office** (Rákóczi út 24; open 8am-5pm Mon-Fri, 8am-noon Sat).

For general information on Tokaj (in Hungarian only), check out 🅦 www.tokaj.hu.

Things to See

The **Tokaj Museum** (☎ 352 636; Bethlen Gábor utca 13; adult/child 300/200Ft; open 9am-4pm Tues-Sun May-Nov), in the 18th-century Greek Trading House, leaves nothing unsaid about the history of Tokaj, the Tokaj-Hegyalja region and the production of its wines. There's also a superb collection of Christian liturgical art, including icons, medieval crucifixes and triptychs, and Judaica from the nearby Great Synagogue.

Just up the road in an 18th-century Greek Orthodox church, the **Tokaj Gallery** (☎ 352 003, 352 731; Bethlen Gábor utca 17; admission free; open 10am-4pm daily May-Oct) exhibits works by local artists; the carved wooden pulpit is particularly fine.

East of the gallery, the 19th-century Eclectic **Great Synagogue** (Nagy zsinagóga; Serház utca 55), which was used as a German barracks during WWII, is once again boarded up and falling into ruin after a partial renovation in 1992. There's a large **Orthodox Jewish cemetery** in Bodrogkeresztúr, 6km northwest of Tokaj.

Wine Tasting

Private wine cellars offering tastings (usually 4pm to 9pm) are scattered throughout town, including those at Rákóczi út 2 and 6, Óvári utca 6, 10 and 40 and Bem József utca 2 and 16.

For the ultimate in tasting venues head for the 600-year-old **Rákóczi Cellar** (Rákóczi Pince; ☎ 352 408; 🅔 rakoczi@axelero.hu, Kossuth tér 15; open 10am-7pm or 8pm daily mid-Mar–Oct), where bottles of wine mature in long corridors (one measures 28m by 10m). Tastings of six Tokaj wines cost 1800Ft to 2750Ft, depending on the wines selected. **Hímesudvar** (Decorative Court; ☎ 352 416, 🅦 www.himesudvar.hu; Bem utca 2; 1500Ft for 6 wines; open 9am-9pm daily May-Sept, 9am-7pm Oct-Apr), a 16th-century wine cellar with shop above the town centre, is another option. The website is in Hungarian only.

Start with 100mL glasses; you may swallow more than you think you can drink. The correct order for sampling a half-dozen Tokaj wines is Furmint, dry Szamorodni, sweet Szamorodni and then the Aszú wines – from three to five or four to six *puttony* (a measure of aszú essence added to base wines in making Tokaji).

Other Activities

In summer, **water tours** of the Bodrog and Tisza Rivers are available from the **Mahart ferry pier** (☎ 352 937, fax 352 108) just off Hősök tere. Contact the **Union Federation** (Unió Alapítvány; ☎/fax 352 927, 06-20 955 3604; Bodrogkeresztúri út 5) about **canoe** and **kayak** rentals. There's **swimming**

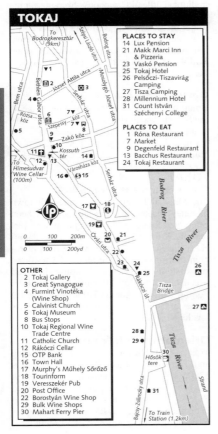

TOKAJ

PLACES TO STAY
14 Lux Pension
21 Makk Marci Inn & Pizzeria
23 Vaskó Pension
25 Tokaj Hotel
26 Pelsőczi-Tiszavirág Camping
27 Tisza Camping
28 Millennium Hotel
31 Count István Széchenyi College

PLACES TO EAT
1 Róna Restaurant
7 Market
9 Degenfeld Restaurant
13 Bacchus Restaurant
24 Tokaj Restaurant

OTHER
2 Tokaj Gallery
3 Great Synagogue
4 Furmint Vinotéka (Wine Shop)
5 Calvinist Church
6 Tokaj Museum
8 Bus Stops
10 Tokaj Regional Wine Trade Centre
11 Catholic Church
12 Rákóczi Cellar
15 OTP Bank
16 Town Hall
17 Murphy's Mühely Sörőző
18 Tourinform
19 Veresszekér Pub
20 Post Office
22 Borostyán Wine Shop
29 Bulk Wine Shops
30 Mahart Ferry Pier

from the grassy riverfront beach across the Tisza Bridge.

Kopasz-hegy (Bald Mountain) and its TV tower west of the town centre offer a stunning panorama of Tokaj and the surrounding vineyards.

Special Events

The **Tokaj Wine Festival**, held in late May, attracts oenophiles from far and wide as do the **Vintage Days** in September.

Places to Stay

Tisza Camping (☎ 352 012; Tisza-part; tent/caravan site 700/500Ft, bungalows per person 1300Ft; open Apr-Oct), across the river and just south of the bridge, offers its own restaurant, boat rentals and beach.

Pelsőczi-Tiszavirág Camping (☎ 352 626, fax 352 017; Horgász út 11; tent/caravan site 450/900Ft, per person 450Ft, 2-bed/3-bed bungalows 4000/6000Ft) is along the river just north of Tisza Bridge opposite town and a better option overall, though both sites are plagued by mosquitoes.

Count István Széchenyi College (☎ 352 355; Bajcsy-Zsilinszky utca 15-17; dorm beds 1000Ft) has at least a few beds in dormitory rooms available throughout the year.

Private rooms (doubles 2800Ft to 5000Ft) are available from Tourinform. You can also find them available around town, including along Óvári utca (Nos 36, 40 and 46), Bethlen Gábor utca (Nos 12, 20, and 20/a), Serház utca (No 26) and Bem József utca. Rooms on offer along Hegyalja utca (eg, No 21) are convenient to the train station and are surrounded by vineyards.

Vaskó (☎ 352 107, 352 689; Rákóczi út 12; doubles 6000Ft) is an eight-room, very central pension.

Makk Marci (☎ 352 336, fax 353 088; Liget köz 1; doubles 6200Ft), a seven-room inn, has a popular pizzeria attached.

Lux (☎/fax 352 145; Serház utca 14; doubles 4500Ft) is a friendly, six-room pension north of the Tourinform office and open mid-April to December.

Tokaj (☎ 352 344, fax 352 759; Rákóczi út 5; singles 4600-5700Ft, doubles 5000-6200Ft), at the confluence of the Bodrog and Tisza Rivers, has 40 basic rooms without a frill in sight.

Millennium (☎ 352 247, fax 352 437; e millennium@axelero.hu; Bajcsy-Zsilinszky utca 34; doubles 9100Ft, 2-person/4-person suites 13,800/15,800Ft), a modern new hotel with 18 rooms, is just south of the centre.

Places to Eat

Makk Marci (☎ 352 336; pizzas 430-900Ft; open 8am-10pm daily) is a cheap and friendly pizzeria.

Bacchus (☎ 352 054; Kossuth tér 17; mains 450-750Ft; open 8am-8pm Mon-Sat, 9am-8pm Sun) in Tokaj's central square is good for basic Hungarian stodge.

Tokaj (☎ 352 344; Rákóczi út 3; fish dishes 690-1390Ft, other mains 890-1990Ft), which is part of the Tokaj hotel but located next door to it, is a pleasant enough place with some decent fish dishes on the menu.

Róna (☎ 352 116; Bethlen Gábor utca 19; mains 700-1650Ft; open 11am-9pm daily) also specialises in fish.

Degenfeld (☎ 553 050; Kossuth tér 1; mains 950-2200Ft; open 11.30am-10pm daily), in a lovely 19th-century town house on the main square, is one of provincial Hungary's finest restaurants. It has inventive New Magyar cuisine, an excellent wine list and beautiful decor.

Tokaj's small **market** (Szépessy köz) is just east of the Tokaj Museum.

Entertainment

Should you get tired of all that wine, there are a couple of pubs to turn your head – or lips – to, including the **Vereszekér** (Red Cart; Rákóczi út 30-32; open 2pm-2am daily), a congenial pub in a little courtyard, and **Murphy's Műhely Söröző** (☎ 06-20 945 8562; Rákóczi út 42; open 2pm-10pm daily), the first (and we assume only) Irish 'workshop pub' in the Zemplén.

Shopping

Wine, wine and more wine – from a 10L plastic jug of new Furmint to a bottle of six-puttony Aszú – is available in shops and cellars throughout Tokaj. Buy bulk wines (200Ft to 250Ft a litre) along Bajcsy-Zsilinszky utca. For a choice of vintage wines, try the shop at the **Rákóczi cellar** (☎ 352 408; open 10am-7pm or 8pm daily); the **Borostyán wine shop** (☎ 352 313; Rákóczi út 11; open 10am-9pm Mon-Fri, 10am-10pm Sat & Sun); the **Furmint Vinotéka** (☎ 353 340, 352 919; Bethlen Gábor utca 14; open 9am-5pm daily), with both wine and folk art for sale;

and the new – and arguably the best – shop at the **Tokaj Regional Wine Trade Centre** (☎ 552 173; Ⓦ www.tokajtc.com; Kossuth tér 1; open 9am-7pm Mon-Fri, 10am-8pm Sat & Sun), next to Degenfeld restaurant.

Getting There & Away

Nine weekday buses (five on Saturday and Sunday) go to Szerencs, the chocolate capital of Hungary, but it's just as easy to get there by train. There's one bus a day to Debrecen and two to Nyíregyháza.

Up to 16 trains a day connect Tokaj with Nyíregyháza and some 14 with Miskolc; change at the former for Debrecen. To travel north to Sárospatak and Sátoraljaújhely, take the Miskolc-bound train and change at Mezőzombor.

SÁROSPATAK

☎ 47 ● postcode 3950 ● pop 14,925

The town of Sárospatak (Muddy Stream) is renowned for its college and castle, the finest example of a Renaissance fort extant in Hungary. It is also a convenient stop en route to Slovakia.

A wealthy (and free) royal wine-producing town since the early 15th century, Sárospatak soon became a centre of Calvinist power and scholarship; 200 years later it was the focal point for Hungarian resistance to the Habsburgs. The list of alumni of the town's illustrious Calvinist college, which helped earn Sárospatak the nickname 'Athens on the Boldrog', reads like a who's who of Hungarian literary and political history and includes the patriot Lajos Kossuth, the poet Mihály Csokonai Vitéz and the novelist Géza Gárdonyi.

Orientation & Information

Sárospatak is a compact town lying on the snaking Bodrog River and its attractive backwaters. The bus and train stations are cheek-by-jowl at the end of Táncsics Mihály utca, northwest of the city centre. Walk southeast through shady Iskola Park to join up with Rákóczi út, the main drag.

Tourinform (☎ 315 316, fax 511 411; ⓔ sarospatak@tourinform.hu; Eötvös utca 6; open 9am-6pm Mon-Fri, 9am-5pm Sat & Sun mid-June–mid-Sept; 7.30am-4pm Mon-Thur, 7.30am-1.30pm Fri mid-Sept–mid-June) is in the western wing of the Sárospatak Cultural Centre. An **OTP bank** (Eötvös utca

3; open 7.30am-4pm Mon-Wed & Fri, 7.30am-5pm Thur) is a short distance to the east; The **main post office** (Rákóczi út 45; open 8am-6pm Mon-Fri, 8am-noon Sat) is opposite the Bodrog department store.

For general information about the town, see Ⓦ www.sarospatak.hu.

Rákóczi Castle

This castle (☎ 311 083, 511 113; Szent Erzsébet utca 19-21; adult/child 300/150Ft; open 10am-6pm Tues-Sun Mar-Oct, 10am-5pm Tues-Sun Nov-Feb) should be your first port of call; enter the Várkert (Castle Garden) by crossing over the dry moat at the southern end of Rákóczi út or from Szent Erzsébet utca. Although the oldest part of the castle, the renovated, five-storey **Red Tower** (Vörös-torony) dates from the late 15th century. The **Renaissance palace wing** (palotaszárny) was built in the following century and later enlarged by its most famous owners, the Rákóczi family of Transylvania. They held it until 1711 when Ferenc Rákóczi II's aborted independence war against the Habsburgs drove him into exile in Turkey and put the castle in the hands of Austrian aristocrats.

Today the Renaissance wings of the palace and the 19th-century additions contain the **Rákóczi Museum**, devoted to the uprising and the castle's later occupants, with bedrooms and dining halls overflowing with period furniture, tapestries, porcelain and glass. Of special interest is the small, five-windowed bay room on the 1st floor near the **Knights' Hall**, with its stucco rose in the middle of a vaulted ceiling. It was here that nobles put their names sub rosa (literally 'under the rose' in Latin) to the kuruc uprising against the Habsburg emperor in 1670. The expression, which means 'in secret', is thought to have originated here. You should also look out for the **Fireplace Hall**, with its superb Renaissance hearth, and, outside in the courtyard, the so-called **Lorántffy Gallery**, a 17th-century loggia linking the east palace wing with the Red Tower.

The casemates of the **Italian Bastion** (Olászbástya) contain a small **waxworks** focusing on Hungarian royalty and an exhibit in the cellars of the east wing is devoted to the **history of wine** and **wine-making** in the surrounding Tokaj-Hegyalja region. There's also a mock-up of a Renaissance kitchen.

Other Attractions

The **Castle Church** (Vártemplom; ☎ 311 183; Szent Erzsébet utca 7; adult/child 100/50Ft; open 9am-5pm Tues-Sat, 11.30am-4pm Sun May-Oct), north of the castle, is one of Hungary's largest Gothic hall churches (those within castle walls) and has flip-flopped from serving Catholics to Protestants and back many times since the 14th century. The enormous baroque altar was moved here from the Carmelite church in Buda Castle late in the 18th century; the 200-year-old organ from Kassa (now Košice in Slovakia) is still used for concerts throughout the year. The statue by Imre Varga outside the church depicts a 13th-century queen of Hungary, the Sárospatak-born and much revered St Elizabeth, riding side-saddle, and her husband Louis IV on foot.

To the southwest of the church is the **Sárospatak Gallery** (☎ 511 012; Szent Erzsébet utca 4; adult/child 200/100Ft; open 10am-4pm Tues-Sun), which displays the work of the sculptor János Kurta Andrássy along with some temporary exhibits.

The history of the celebrated **Calvinist College** (Református Kollégium; ☎ 311 057; Rákóczi út 1; adult/child 200/100Ft; open 9am-5pm Mon-Sat, 9am-1pm Sun) is told in words and displays at the **Comenius Memorial Museum** in the last of the college's original buildings, an 18th-century physics classroom. The collection is named after János Amos Comenius, a Moravian humanist who organised the education system here late in the 17th century and wrote the world's first illustrated textbook for children, Orbis Pictus (World in Pictures).

The main reason for visiting the college is to see its 75,000-volume **Great Library Hall** (Nagy Könyvtárterem) in the main building, a long, oval-shaped room with a gallery and a trompe l'oeuil ceiling simulating the inside of a cupola. Guided library tours leave on the hour between 9am and 4pm Monday to Saturday and between 9am and noon on Sunday.

The former **synagogue** (Rákóczi út 43), near the post office, is now a shop selling electronics goods.

Sárospatak counts a number of buildings designed by the 'organic' architect Imre Makovecz, including the anthropomorphic cultural centre on Eötvös utca, the Hild Udvar shopping complex on Béla Király tér and the cathedral-like Árpád Vezér College at Arany János utca 3–7.

Wine Tasting

The **Rákóczi Wine Cellar** (Rákóczi Pince; ☎ 312 310, 311 902; Szent Erzsébet utca 26; open 8am-5pm Mon-Fri, 10am-8pm Sat & Sun May-Sept; 8am-4pm Mon-Fri Oct-Apr), just south of the Sárospatak Gallery, offers wine tastings. They take place on the hour and cost 400/600/770/1000/1200Ft for one/three/four/five/six wines.

Other Activities

The **thermal baths and pools** (☎ 311 639; adult/senior & child 400/250Ft, after 2pm 300/250Ft; open 8am-6pm daily May-Sept) are in the Végardó recreational complex about 2km northeast of the centre.

Special Events

Saint Elizabeth Days is a popular weekend festival in early June in the castle quarter. Sárospatak hosts some of the events of the **Zemplén Arts Days** in mid-August along with other Zemplén towns, including Sátoraljaújhely, Szerencs, Füzér and even Košice across the border in Slovakia.

Places to Stay

Termálfürdő Camping (☎ 311 510; Határ utca 2; sites per person/tent/caravan/car 550/600/900/200Ft, bungalows 4500-6000Ft; open May-Aug), near the thermal spa in Végardó, has camp sites as well as bungalows for four; prices depend on the month.

Tengerszem Camping (☎ 312 744, fax 314 527; Herceg Ferenc utca 2; sites per person/tent/caravan/car 700/650/1100/150Ft; 2-person bungalow 4200-4500Ft, 4-person bungalow 6800-8300Ft; open Apr-Oct), a much nicer site opposite the baths, has 45 bungalows.

Dezső Lajos Kollégium (☎ 312 211; Eötvös utca 7; singles/doubles 2600/4700Ft) is a college with 337 beds, offering more comfortable accommodation.

Júlia (☎/fax 312 871; Határ utca 6; doubles/triples 4400/5600Ft) is a very friendly, four-room guesthouse but a bit far from whatever action Sárospatak has to offer. **Kert** (☎/fax 311 559; Rákóczi út 31; doubles 4500Ft), a small pension in the centre, has an attractive little garden.

Bodrog (☎ 311 744, fax 511 363; e bodrog@matavnet.hu; Rákóczi út 58; singles 7500-10,500Ft, doubles 8600-11,800Ft) is in a four-storey block with 49 large rooms in

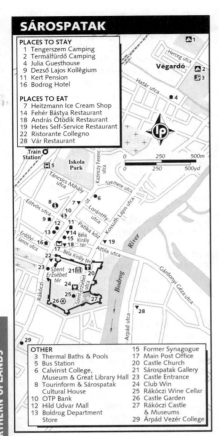

SÁROSPATAK

PLACES TO STAY
1 Tengerszem Camping
2 Termálfürdő Camping
4 Julia Guesthouse
9 Dezső Lajos Kollégium
11 Kert Pension
16 Bodrog Hotel

PLACES TO EAT
7 Heitzmann Ice Cream Shop
14 Fehér Bástya Restaurant
18 András Ötödik Restaurant
19 Hetes Self-Service Restaurant
22 Ristorante Collegno
28 Vár Restaurant

OTHER
3 Thermal Baths & Pools
5 Bus Station
6 Calvinist College, Museum & Great Library Hall
8 Tourinform & Sárospatak Cultural House
10 OTP Bank
12 Hild Udvar Mall
13 Boldrog Department Store
15 Former Synagogue
17 Main Post Office
20 Castle Church
21 Sárospatak Gallery
23 Castle Entrance
24 Club Win
25 Rákóczi Wine Cellar
26 Castle Garden
27 Rákóczi Castle & Museums
29 Árpád Vezér College

the centre of town. All rooms have shower or bath and air-conditioning, and there's a nice restaurant and a beer bar.

Places to Eat
Hetes (☎ 311 228; Kossuth Lajos utca 57; mains 380-470Ft; open 10am-3pm Mon-Fri) is a very cheap, self-service restaurant.

Fehér Bástya (☎ 312 400; Rákóczi út 39; mains 680-1100Ft; open 8am-10pm daily) is an intimate little Hungarian restaurant in a pension.

András Ötödik (Andrew V; ☎ 312 415; Béla Király tér 3; mains 415-2060Ft; open 11am-9pm Mon, 11am-10pm Tues-Thur & Sun, 11am-midnight Fri & Sat) has metamorphosed into a full Hungarian restaurant from a popular café and cake shop.

Ristorante Collegno (☎ 314 494; Szent Erzsébet utca 10; pizza 450-1450Ft; open 11am-midnight Mon-Sat, 4pm-11pm Sun), an eatery named after the Italian town with which Sárospatak is twinned, has tables both in a cellar and, in warmer months, a back courtyard.

Vár (☎ 311 370; Árpád utca 35; mains 750-2000Ft; open noon-10pm daily), across the Bodrog from the castle, is the best restaurant in Sárospatak. Try one of its specialities like harcsapaprikás (catfish cooked with sour cream and paprika) served with pasta – better than it sounds.

Heitzmann Cukrászda (☎ 311 567; Rákóczi út 16; open 9am-6pm Tues-Sun) is an ice-cream parlour that usually has lickers lining up all day.

Entertainment
Sárospatak Cultural House (Sárospatak Művelődés Háza; ☎ 311 811; Eötvös utca 6; open 8am-8pm Mon-Fri, 9am-7pm Sat, 9am-1pm Sun) will fill you in on what's on in town. Be sure to ask about organ concerts at the **Castle Church**.

A popular place with students after dark is the hole-in-the-wall **Club Win** (☎ 311 185; Szent Erzsébet utca 22; open 11am-midnight daily).

Sárospatak is included in the free biweekly Miskolci Est magazine.

Getting There & Away
Bus Most of the southern Zemplén region is not easily accessible by bus from Sárospatak, though there is one bus daily Monday to Saturday to the pretty village of Erdőbénye from where you can connect to Baskó and Boldogkőváralja. Other destinations include Debrecen (two buses daily), Miskolc (one or two), Nyíregyháza (two), Sátoraljaújhely (at least hourly) and Tokaj (two or three). Buses to Debrecen, Nyíregyháza and Miskolc can be boarded just outside the Bodrog department store on Rákóczi út; catch the bus to Sátoraljaújhely on the other side of the street in front of Rákóczi út 40.

Train To explore the southern Zemplén you'd do better to take one of six daily trains up the Hernád Valley from Szerencs and use one of the towns along that line, such as Abaújkér, Boldogkőváralja or Korlát-Vizsoly as your base. For the northern Zemplén, take a train or bus to Sátoraljaújhely.

Up to 10 daily trains connect Sárospatak and Sátoraljaújhely with Miskolc, and a couple of those continue on to Slovenské Nové Mesto in Slovakia, from where you can board a train to Košice. If you are coming from Debrecen, Nyíregyháza or Tokaj, change trains at Mezőzombor.

Getting Around

Hourly buses link the bus and train stations and the Bodrog shopping centre on Rákóczi út with the Végardó recreational centre to the north.

You can book a taxi on ☎ 311 744.

SÁTORALJAÚJHELY

☎ 47 • postcode 3980 • pop 19,100

Sátoraljaújhely, 12km north of Sárospatak, fell into the hands of the Rákóczi family in the 17th century and, like the family's base, Sárospatak, the town played an important role in the struggle for independence from Austria. It was not the last time the city would be a battleground. In 1919 fighting took place in the nearby hills and ravines between communist partisans and Slovaks, and broke out once again in the closing days of WWII.

Today Sátoraljaújhely (roughly translated as 'tent camp new place' and pronounced shah-toor-all-ya-oy-hay) is a quiet frontier town surrounded by forests and vineyards and dominated by 514m Magas-hegy (Tall Mountain). Though perhaps not worth a visit in its own right, Sátoraljaújhely is a good base for trekking into the northern Zemplén Hills and for crossing the border into Slovakia.

Orientation & Information

The bus and train stations sit side by side a kilometre south of the city centre. From there, follow Fasor utca north past the old Jewish cemetery to Kossuth Lajos utca. This will lead you to Hősök tere and then Széchenyi tér. Two more squares follow – Kossuth tér and Táncsics Mihály tér – and then Kazinczy Ferenc utca. Slovakia comes next.

Tourinform (☎/fax 321 458; e satoral aujhely@tourinform.hu; Táncsics Mihály tér 3; open 9am-6pm Mon-Fri, 9am-5pm Sat & Sun mid-June–mid-Sept; 7.30am-4pm Mon-Thur, 7.30-1.30pm Fri mid-Sept–mid-June) shares a building with the cultural centre. Commercial travel agencies include **Ibusz** (☎ 521 230, fax 321 757; Kossuth tér 26; open 8am-4.30pm Mon-Fri, 8.30am-noon Sat). There's an **OTP bank** (Széchenyi tér 13;

open 7.45am-4pm Mon-Wed & Fri, 7.30am-5pm Thur) almost opposite the Catholic church; the **main post office** (Kazinczy Ferenc utca 10; open 8am-6pm Mon-Fri, 8am-noon Sat) is north of Tourinform.

For general information, see ⒲ www.satoral jaujhely.hu.

Things to See & Do

The decrepit neo-Gothic former **Temple of Wine** (Bortemplom), built in 1911 and decorated with seals of the Tokaj-Hegyalja towns in Zsolnay porcelain, greets you upon arrival at the bus or train station. Don't expect much from this Frankenstein's castle; it's now just used to store wine in the cellars below. Due north, at the top of Fasor utca is the **old Jewish cemetery**, where the zaddik (miracle-working rabbi) Moses Teitelbaum (1759–1841) is buried and pilgrims pay their respects on 16 July each year.

The central **Catholic church** (Széchenyi tér 10), rebuilt in the late-baroque style in 1792, has a stark interior and is not very interesting in itself, though it was here that the teachings of Martin Luther were first read aloud in public in Hungary. The same can be

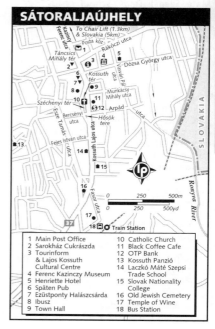

SÁTORALJAÚJHELY

1 Main Post Office
2 Sarokház Cukrászda
3 Tourinform & Lajos Kossuth Cultural Centre
4 Ferenc Kazinczy Museum
5 Henriette Hotel
6 Späten Pub
7 Ezüstponty Halászcsárda
8 Ibusz
9 Town Hall
10 Catholic Church
11 Black Coffee Cafe
12 OTP Bank
13 Kossuth Panzió
14 Laczkó Máté Szepsi Trade School
15 Slovak Nationality College
16 Old Jewish Cemetery
17 Temple of Wine
18 Bus Station

said for the **town hall** *(Kossuth tér 5)*, but it too is remembered for a momentous event. In 1830 then-lawyer Lajos Kossuth gave his first public speech from the outside balcony.

The **Ferenc Kazinczy Museum** *(☎ 322 351; Dózsa György utca 11; adult/child 200/100Ft; open 8am-4pm Mon-Sat)* covers the history of the city from the 13th to 19th centuries, with much emphasis on the illustrious Rákóczi family and the natural history of the Zemplén region. The museum is named after the 19th-century language reformer and patriot who did much of his research at the Zemplén Archives (now the town hall) from 1815 to 1831.

The **chair lift** *(libegő; ☎ 321 458, 321 140; Torzás utca; adult/senior & child 500/300Ft return; 2pm-6pm Tues, Wed & Fri, 10am-6pm Sat & Sun summer; 1.30pm-3.30pm Tues, Wed & Fri, 8.30am-3.30pm Sat & Sun winter)*, to the top of Magas-hegy, is the longest in Hungary.

Places to Stay & Eat

Accommodation is available in summer and at the weekend throughout the year at two colleges south of the centre: the 250-bed **Laczkó Máté Szepsi Trade School** *(☎ 322 244; Kossuth Lajos utca 26; beds in triples/quads 1500/1200Ft)* and the **Slovak Nationality College** *(☎ 322 568; Kossuth Lajos utca 31; beds 780Ft)*, almost opposite, with 300 beds. Tourinform has a list of **private rooms** costing from 1500Ft per person. Private rooms are also available independently round the corner at Dózsa György utca 17.

Kossuth Panzió *(☎ 321 164, fax 521 173; Török utca 1; doubles/triples 3000/4000Ft)* is a very basic 19-room tourist hostel in the upper part of town known as Váralja; it's a bit far out but cheap.

Henriette *(☎ 323 118, fax 323 497; e henriette.kft@mail.matav.hu; Vasvári Pál utca 16; singles/doubles 3500/7000Ft)* is Sátoraljaújhely's new nine-room hotel with three stars.

Ezüstponty Halászcsárda *(Silver Carp Fish Restaurant; ☎ 321 620; Kossuth tér 8; fish mains 380-700Ft; open 7am-10pm daily)* offers fish (and a few meat) dishes. **Späten** *(☎ 321 527; Kossuth tér 10; mains 440-1250Ft; open 9am-10pm Mon-Sat, 10am-10pm Sun)*, just next door, has Hungarian pub grub.

Sarokház Cukrászda *(☎ 322 742; Táncsics Mihály tér 2; open 7.30am-6pm Mon-Fri,* 7.30am-4pm Sat & Sun)* is the right place for something sweet.

Entertainment

Consult with the staff or the listings posted at the **Lajos Kossuth Cultural Centre** *(Kossuth Lajos Művelődési Központ; ☎ 321 727, fax 321 458; Táncsics Mihály tér 3)* for what's on in Sátoraljaújhely. The new **Black Coffee** *(☎ 06-30 981 3817; Széchenyi tér 2)* is a decent place for a cuppa or pint.

For more listings for Sátoraljaújhely, check out the free biweekly *Miskolci Eat* magazine.

Getting There & Away

There are frequent buses to the towns and villages of the northern Zemplén Hills, including three on weekdays (four at the weekend) to Füzér, up to nine on weekdays (10 at the weekend) to Hollóháza, one to Telkibánya and one to Hidasnémeti, from where you can pick up trains north to the Slovakian city of Košice, south to Miskolc, or to Szerencs and the towns along the western edge of the Zemplén.

Some 10 trains a day link Sátoraljaújhely with Sárospatak and Miskolc; two of them cross the border with Slovakia at Slovenské Nové Mesto, where you can catch a train to Košice. If you are approaching Sátoraljaújhely from the south or east (Debrecen, say, or Nyíregyháza or Tokaj), you must change at Mezőzombor.

AROUND SÁTORALJAÚJHELY
Füzér & Hollóháza
☎ 47 • postcodes 3996/3999
• pop 620/1200

An easy excursion into the Zemplén Hills can be made to Füzér, an idyllic little village about 25km northwest of Sátoraljaújhely, to see the remains of the dramatic hill-top **Füzér Castle**, dating from the 13th century. The medieval **Calvinist church**, in the village centre, has a 19th-century painted ceiling similar to those found in the Tiszahát and Erdőhát regions of the Northeast. The 50 panels were decorated with geometric patterns and flowers by a local artist in 1832.

To reach what's left of the castle from the village bus stop, follow the steep, marked trail and you'll soon come to the ruins sitting 370m up on a rocky crag. The castle's claim to fame is that it was chosen as a 'safe house' by Péter Perényi for the Hungarian coronation regalia from Visegrád for a year or so after the disastrous defeat at Mohács in 1526. Like most castles in the area, it was heavily damaged by the Austrians after the unsuccessful *kuruc* revolt of in the late 17th century, but parts of the chapel, a tower and the outer walls remain.

The attractive **Koronaőr** *(Crown Guardian;* ☎ *340 020, 06-20 921 2289; Dózsa György utca 2/a)* has three modern rooms in an old peasant house.

From Füzér you can return to Sátoraljaújhely or catch one of several daily buses for the 9km trip to Hollóháza, Hungary's northernmost town and in third place after Herend and Zsolnay for its porcelain. The **Porcelain Museum** *(Porcelánmúzeum;* ☎ *505 400, 505 155; Károlyi út 11; adult/ child 200/100Ft; open 9am-4.30 daily Apr-Nov)* tells the whole story. Accommodation is available at the **Éva** *(☎ 305 038; Szent László utca 4)*, a three-room pension in the centre of town.

Füzér and Hollóháza are excellent springboards for beginning a hike into the Zemplén; several well marked trails start here, including one that runs northeast to **Nagy Milic**, an 893m hill on the Slovakian border. Just make sure you're armed with drinking water and *A Zempléni-hegység – északi rész*, Cartographia's 1:40,000 map (No 22; 650Ft) of the Zemplén's northern section.

See the Sátoraljaújhely Getting There & Away section for transport information.

NORTHERN UPLANDS

Northeast

On the map, Hungary's northeast corner may appear to be a coextension of the Northern Uplands or even the Great Plain. But it is so different physically, culturally and historically from both of those regions that most consider it to be a separate area. Essentially Northeast Hungary encompasses just one administrative county (Szabolcs-Szatmár-Bereg) and is bordered by Slovakia, Ukraine and Romania.

The Northeast is neither mountainous nor flat, but a region of ridges and gentle hills formed by sand blown up from the Tisza River basin. Apart from the industries based in and around the county seat of Nyíregy-háza, the landscape is almost entirely given over to agriculture – apples are the most important crop – with occasional stands of silver poplars and birch trees.

Until the regulation of the Tisza in the 19th century, large parts of the Northeast were often flooded and cut off from other areas by swampland. This helped to protect against the devastation suffered elsewhere during the Turkish occupation. As a result, the Northeast has always been more densely populated than the Great Plain and the region's distinctive wooden churches and other traditional architecture have been saved.

Isolation has also worked against the Northeast. Szabolcs-Szatmár-Bereg was hard hit by the recession of the 1990s, and the stagnant economies of Ukraine and Romania have contributed little to overall development; Slovakia's stagnant economy had a lesser effect on the economy of the Northeast. However, recent foreign investments, notably by Germany and the USA, could change all that in the near future.

Before WWII the Northeast was home to most of the Jews in Hungary living outside Budapest, and their erstwhile presence can be seen in the region's dilapidated synagogues and untended cemeteries. Today a large percentage of the country's Roma (see the boxed text 'The Roma' later in this chapter) live here.

The Northeast's remoteness and cultural diversity make it an interesting area to visit. If you want to see real Hungarian village life – replete with dirt roads, horse-drawn carts laden with hay, thatched roofs and ancient churches – this is the place to come.

Highlights

- The Gothic Calvinist church and bell tower, and the carved wooden altars at the Minorite church in Nyírbátor

- The enormous iconostasis at the Greek Catholic cathedral in Máriapócs

- The ancient cemetery with its intriguing boat-shaped grave markers in Szatmárcseke

- The folk baroque painted wooden ceiling at Tákos' Calvinist church

- The cultural diversity and traditional village life of one of Hungary's least-explored corners

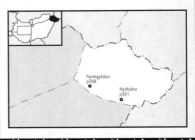

Nyírség Region

Two rivers – the Szamos and the serpentine Tisza – carve the Northeast into three distinct areas. The largest of these is the Nyírség, the 'Birch Region' of grassy steppes and hills that lies between Nyíregyháza and the historical town of Nyírbátor. Until just a century ago, the life of the people here was shaped by the Tisza floods and the swamps that remained year round. A cyanide spill in early 2000 has affected the ecology of this river, and experts believe it will not fully recover for another eight years (see the boxed text Cyanide Spill in the Facts about Hungary chapter).

NYÍREGYHÁZA
☎ 42 • postcode 4400 • pop 119,400
Nyíregyháza (roughly 'Birch Church'), the commercial and administrative centre of the Nyírség, is not a particularly historically

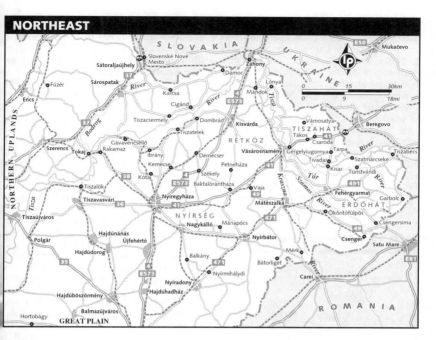

significant town. For many centuries this town was the private domain of Transylvanian princes, then, in the 18th century, it was resettled by Slovaks from Szarvas on the southern Great Plain. But with its well-tended squares and gardens and some beautifully restored buildings, Nyíregyháza is not a bad place to spend some time. The town is also an excellent springboard for visiting other Northeast towns, as well as northern Romania and Ukraine.

Orientation

Nyíregyháza's centre is made up of a handful of interconnecting squares, including Országzászló tér, Kálvin tér, Kossuth tér and Hősök tere, and is surrounded by both an inner and an outer ring road. Streets running north lead to Sóstófürdő, the city's sprawling 600-hectare recreational area consisting of woods, parkland, the little Salt Lake (Sóstó) and a large spa complex.

The **main train station** on Állomás tér is about 1.5km southwest of the centre at the end of Arany János utca. The **bus station** is on Petőfi tér, just north of the train station, at the western end of Széchenyi utca.

Information

The helpful staff at **Tourinform** (☎/fax 504 647; e szabolcs-m@tourinform.hu; Országzászló tér 6; open 9am-5pm Mon-Fri, 10am-6pm Sat June-Sept; 8am-5pm Mon-Fri Oct-May), will supply as much information as you can carry and/or absorb about the city and the region. There's also a seasonal branch in the **Water Tower** (Víztorony; ☎/fax 411 193; e sostofurdo@tourinform.hu; Sóstófürdő; open 9am-5pm daily mid-May–mid-Sept), which is 5km north of the town in the Sóstófürdő area. **Ibusz** (☎ 311 817; open 8am-5pm Mon-Fri, 8am-noon Sat) is in the same street as the main Tourinform branch.

There is a branch of the **OTP bank** (Dózsa György utca 2) near Kossuth tér; the **main post office** (Bethlen Gábor utca 4) is south of the town hall.

Things to See

There is a variety of houses of worship in the inner city, including the late baroque (1786) **Evangelist church** (Luther tér 14; admission free; open 9am-5pm Mon-Fri) and, dominating the tér, the 1904 neo-Romanesque **Catholic cathedral** (Kossuth tér 14; admission free;

open 6.30am-6pm Mon-Fri, 6.30am-10.30am Sun), which has arabesque pastel-coloured tiles inside. The **Greek Catholic church** (☎ 415 901; Bethlen Gábor utca 5; admission free; open 8am-4pm Mon-Fri), built in 1895, contains a rich **liturgical collection** of vestments and plate. The **synagogue** (Síp utca 6; open 8am-2pm Mon-Thur) still functions as a house of worship.

A lot of the architecture in the centre is worth more than a casual glance. If you can, visit the Eclectic (1892) **county hall** on Hősök tere with its splendid Ceremonial Hall (Nagy Terem); the blue-and-white Art Nouveau building, which houses a bank and offices on Országzászló tér; or the restored **Korona hotel**, which is on Dózsa György utca. **Benczúr Gyula tér** is another treasure

trove of Art Nouveau and Secessionist architecture. A modern must-see is the bizarre **Mihály Váci Cultural Centre** on Szabadság tér. Built in 1981 this wobbly-looking, bridge-like structure was inspired by 'the principles of Japanese metabolism', we're told. The graffiti on its lowest level doesn't look particularly Japanese though.

The huge **András Jósa Museum** (☎ 315 722; Benczúr Gyula tér 21; adult/child 200/100Ft; open 9am-4pm Tues-Sat, 9am-2pm Sun), just southwest of the main city centre has exhibits devoted to Nyíregyháza's history since the Middle Ages.

Nyíregyháza's most interesting sight, however, is the open-air **Sóstó Museum Village** (Sóstói Múzeumfalu; ☎ 500 552; Tölgyes utca 1; adult/child 200/100Ft; open 9am-5pm or 6pm Tues-Sun, Apr-Oct) in Sóstófürdő, 5km north of the city centre. Though not as big as the *skanzen* at Szentendre, its reconstructed three-room cottages, school, draw wells, fire station and general store offer an easy introduction to the architecture and way of life in the various regions of Szabolcs-Szatmár-Bereg. All the nationalities that make up this ethnically diverse region are represented, including the Tirpák, Slovakians who lived in isolated 'bush farms' known as *bokor tanyák*. The **zoo** (állatpark; ☎ 479 702; adult/student/child 500/400/350Ft; open 9am-7pm daily) is a short distance to the southeast.

The **fruit & vegetable market** on Búza tér is one of the more colourful in provincial Hungary, but the **Nagybani flea market** on Tokaji út, the northwest extension of Rákóczi út, is even more vibrant, attracting a motley crowd consisting of Hungarians, Romanians, Poles, Ukrainians and Roma selling the usual diamonds-to-rust mixture of goods.

Activities

The **Park Baths** (Parkfürdő; ☎ 475 736; adult/child 400/280Ft; open 9am-8pm daily mid-May–mid-Sept) in Sóstófürdő is just the place to while away a hot summer's afternoon, with a half-dozen large pools of fresh and thermal water, a sauna, solarium and so on. The **Lake Baths** (Tófürdő; ☎ 479 701; adult/child 400/280Ft) is open the same times as the Park Baths. A more central, less crowded option is the **Julia Fürdő** (☎ 315 800; Malom utca 19; adult/child 340/225Ft; open 10am-8pm Mon-Fri, 9am-8pm Sat & Sun), an indoor thermal spa with three pools

NYÍREGYHÁZA

To Nagybani Flea Market (2km)
To Ózon Hotel, Tölgyes Restaurant (2.5km), Sóstófürdő (5km), Camp Sites, György Bessenyei Teachers' Training College & 424 Irish Pub (5km)
To Bus Station (50m)
To Nyíregyháza Horse Club (5km)

0   250   500m
0   250   500yd

PLACES TO STAY
2 Senátor Pension
9 Korona Hotel; John Bull Pub; X Café
11 Európa Hotel
26 Ilona Zrínyi College

PLACES TO EAT
7 Café Piano
13 City Grill
19 Gösser Restaurant
29 Mozzarella Pizzéria

OTHER
1 Fehér Narancs
3 Fruit & Vegetable Market
4 Colorado Western Pub
5 Synagogue
6 County Hall
8 OTP Bank
10 Cultural Centre; Club Arsenal
12 Catholic Cathedral
13 Town Hall
14 Greek Catholic Church & Liturgical Collection
15 Golden Age
16 Zsigmond Móricz Theatre
17 Main Post Office
20 Art Nouveau building
21 Ibusz
22 Tourinform
23 Evangelist Church
24 András Jósa Museum
25 Julia Fürdő
27 Summer Beer Garden
28 City Open-Air Theatre

The **Sóstó Riding Club** (☎ 475 202; Tölgyes utca 1), next to the Sóstó Museum Village, hires out horses. Another excellent place for riding is the **Nyíregyháza Horse Club** (☎/fax 490 696; Bem József utca 22-23), southwest of the centre. Expect to pay around 2500Ft per hour.

Places to Stay

There are several camp sites in Sóstófürdő, the average prices for which are 400–500Ft per adult, 200–300Ft per child and an additional 480–500Ft for the tent. They also offer indoor accommodation. The following three are the best options.

Fenyves (☎ 501 360, fax 501 366; Sóstói út 72; dorm beds 700Ft) has hostel accommodation in five- to 20-bed dorms.

Paradise (☎ 402 038, fax 402 011; Sóstói út 76; doubles/triples/quads 1580/2340/2520Ft) has a tourist hotel with rooms available from mid-April to mid-October.

Igrice (☎ 479 705, Blaha Lujza sétány 8; bungalows sleeping up to four 7600Ft) also has motel rooms with doubles for 2800Ft.

Tourinform can advise on **dormitory rooms** that are available at local colleges in summer. If the agencies are closed, try going directly to the **György Bessenyei Teachers' Training College** (☎ 402 488; Sóstói út 31b; beds 1680Ft) north of the centre, or the **Ilona Zrínyi College** (☎ 318 091; Széchenyi utca 35-39; doubles 4000Ft).

Private rooms, available through Ibusz, cost 2000Ft to 3000Ft per person.

Senátor (☎/fax 311 796; Búza tér 11; rooms with washbasin/shower 3000/4500Ft), a 15-room pension opposite the lively produce market, is in desperate need of an upgrade and a clean, but the staff are friendly and the rooms are large.

Ózon (☎ 402 001, fax 402 002; Csaló köz 2; rooms 7500Ft), a former communist summer retreat with an alpine feel, near Sóstófürdő, has 26 modern doubles.

Európa (☎ 508 670, fax 508 677; Hunyadi utca 2; singles/doubles 6000/7500Ft) is a nondescript modern 60-room hotel facing the busy outer ring road. It has an attached restaurant and Internet café.

Korona (☎ 409 300, fax 409 339; Dózsa György utca 1-3; singles/doubles 9000/12,500Ft), which first opened its doors in 1895, has been lovingly restored and is the place to stay for a splurge. It has 35 rooms with all the mod cons, scattered along seemingly endless corridors.

Places to Eat

City Grill (Bethlen Gábor utca 2; burgers from 200Ft), next to the main post office, will do for a cheap, fast meal.

Gösser (Országzászló tér 10; dishes from 700Ft) is a rather cramped but central restaurant that has Hungarian dishes alongside pizzas and pasta dishes – though for the latter you're better off venturing farther south to **Mozzarella Pizzéria** (☎ 424 008; Kiss Ernő utca 10; pizzas from 300Ft).

Tölgyes (☎ 410 590; Sóstói út 40; most mains under 1000Ft), to the north near the Ózon hotel, is extremely popular for its cheap, tasty Hungarian dishes, and its lush, green surroundings.

The only thing Irish about the **424 Irish Pub** (☎ 726 222; Blaha Lujza utca 1; mains around 1000Ft) is the Guinness sign hanging out the front. But that doesn't matter; there's lots of outdoor seating near the lake and good food on offer. It's 5km out at Sóstófürdő.

Cafe Piano (Hősök tere 8; ice cream from 60Ft) is a quiet spot for ice cream, coffee and cake.

Entertainment

Check with the staff at the **Zsigmond Móricz Theatre** (☎ 311 333; Bessenyei tér 13) or the **Mihály Váci Cultural Centre** (☎ 411 822; Szabadság tér 9) for current listings. If there's a concert on at the **Evangelist church** on Luther tér, jump at the chance. The **theatre ticket office** (☎ 507 007; Országzászló tér 6; open 9am-5pm Mon-Fri) is at the Tourinform office. From June to August, Benczúr Gyula tér is the site of the **City Open-Air Theatre** (Városi Szabadtéri Színpad) and attached outdoor **beer garden**.

John Bull (Dózsa György utca 1-3), a pub-restaurant at the bottom of the Korona hotel, is a little bit of ersatz England in northeastern Hungary.

Colorado Western Pub (Búza tér 15; open until 2am Mon-Thur, until 4am Fri & Sat, until midnight Sun) is the place of the moment; expect a packed house and live music on Saturday.

Fehér Narancs (White Orange; Pacsirta utca 20; open until 2am Mon-Fri, until 4am Sat & Sun), west of Búza utca, remains a popular venue for jazz.

NORTHEAST

The most popular clubs in town are the **Golden Age** *(Bethlen Gábor utca 24)*, the **X Cafe** below the John Bull pub, and the **Club Arsenal** at the cultural centre. House music is the most popular style at all three.

Getting There & Away

Bus Generally, buses serve towns near Nyíregyháza or those not on a railway line – and there are up to four departures an hour to Nagykálló and frequent buses run to Mári-

apócs, Mátészalka and Nyírbátor. Further afield, other destinations include Debrecen (four buses daily), Eger (two), Fehérgyarmat (four to seven), Gyöngyös (one), Hajdúnánás (four), Kisvárda (up to nine), Miskolc (one) and Vásárosnamény (seven). International destinations include Užgorod in Ukraine at 2pm and 3pm daily and Satu Mare in Romania at 7.30pm on Tuesday and Saturday.

Train Up to 17 daily express trains link Nyíregyháza with Debrecen and Budapest's Nyugati or Keleti stations, and you can count on at least one normal train an hour to Debrecen and up to 14 daily to Miskolc. Up to 10 trains depart Nyíregyháza each day for Vásárosnamény and eight head for Mátészalka, stopping at Nagykálló, Máriapócs and Nyírbátor en route. The *Tisza Express* train en route to Lviv, Kyiv and Moscow also stops here every day at 7.53pm; the *Partium*, crossing the Ukrainian border to Csop, departs at 9.35am.

Getting Around

Almost everything in the city – with the exception of Sóstófürdő – can be easily reached on foot. Take bus No 7 or 8 from the train or bus stations to reach the centre of town; the latter then carries on to Sóstófürdő. For Nagybani flea market, catch bus No 1 or 1/a; the former carries on to the airport, the latter terminates at the market. You can order a taxi on ☎ 444 444.

AROUND NYÍREGYHÁZA

Nagykálló

☎ 42 • postcode 4320 • pop 9985

This dusty town, 14km southeast of Nyíregyháza, boasts some listed protected buildings on its central square (Szabadság tér) – a baroque **Calvinist church** *(admission free; open 9am-5pm Mon-Fri)*, on the south side with a free-standing Gothic bell tower originally built in the 15th century, and the splendid former **county hall** *(☎ 263 128; Szabadság tér 13; visit by appointment only)* to the northeast at No 13, which was built in the Zopf style in 1749 and later turned into a notorious asylum for the insane.

But most visitors to Nagykálló are Orthodox Jewish pilgrims who come to pay their respects at the **tomb of Isaac Taub** especially on the anniversary of his death (February/March). Known as the 'Wonder Rabbi of

The Roma

The origins of the Gypsies (Hungarian: *cigány*), who call themselves the Roma (singular Rom) and speak Romany, a language closely related to several still spoken in northern India, remain a mystery. It is generally accepted, however, that they began migrating to Persia from India sometime in the 10th century and had reached the Balkans by the 14th century. They have been in Hungary for at least 500 years, and their numbers today are estimated at being anywhere between 125,000 and 250,000.

Though traditionally a travelling people, in modern times the Roma have by and large settled down in Hungary and worked as smiths and tinkers, livestock and horse traders, and as musicians (see Music & Dance under Arts in the Facts about Hungary chapter). As a group, however, they are chronically underemployed and have been the hardest hit by economic recession. Statistically, Roma families are twice the size of *gadje*, or 'non-Roma' ones.

Unsettled people have always been persecuted in one form or another by those who stay put, and Hungarian Roma are no exception. They are widely despised and remain the scapegoats for everything that goes wrong in certain parts of the country, from the rise in petty theft and prostitution to the loss of jobs. Though their rights are inscribed in the 1989 constitution, along with other ethnic minorities, their housing ranks among the worst in the nation, police are regularly accused of harassing them and, more than any other group, they fear a revival of right-wing nationalism. You will probably be shocked at what even educated, cosmopolitan Hungarians say about Roma and their way of life.

Kálló' (a *zaddik* in Yiddish), he was an 18th-century philosopher who advocated a more humanistic approach to prayer and study. You can visit his small tomb in the old Jewish cemetery on Nagybalkányi út, less than 1km due south of Szabadság tér. To do so, request the key from the house at Bessenyei út 15 (☎ 06-30 465 1800; 8am-4pm).

The **Belvárosi Eszpresszó** on Kossuth Lajos utca, to the northeast of the square, has sandwiches or, for a fuller meal, there's **Kálló restaurant** *(mains 600-1000Ft)* on the square itself. In late June, Nagykálló hosts the popular **Téka Tábor**, a nine-day folk festival 'camp' held in a bizarre structure designed by Imre Makovecz at Harangodi-tó, some 2km north of town. You can contact the **Rákóczi Cultural Centre** (☎ 263 141; Báthory utca 1) for more information.

Up to eight daily trains linking Nyíregyháza and Mátészalka stop at Nagykálló. A bus meets each incoming train and goes as far as Szabadság tér. You can also reach Nagykálló by bus throughout the day from Nyíregyháza. Many of these carry on to Máriapócs and Nyírbátor on weekdays but only four each day at the weekend.

NYÍRBÁTOR
☎ 42 • postcode 4300 • pop 14,000
Nyírbátor, 38km southeast of Nyíregyháza in the centre of the lovely Nyírség region, is well worth a visit – however fleeting. It contains two Gothic churches built in the latter part of the 15th century by István Báthory, the ruthless Transylvanian prince whose family is synonymous with the town. As the Báthory family's economic and political influence grew from the 15th to 17th century, so did that of Nyírbátor.

Orientation & Information
Nyírbátor is compact, and everything of interest can be easily reached on foot. The train and bus stations are on Ady Endre utca which is in the northern part of town, less than a kilometre from the centre (Szabadság tér) via Kossuth Lajos utca.

There's an **OTP bank** (Zrínyi utca 1), across the road from Szabadság tér. The **main post office** is on the southwest side of Szabadság tér.

Things to See
The **Calvinist church** (☎ 281 749; adult/child 60/30Ft; open 8am-noon & 2pm-4.30pm Mon-Sat, 10am-noon & 3pm-4pm Sun) on a small hill just off Báthory István utca, is one of the most beautiful Gothic churches in Hungary. The ribbed vault of the nave is a masterpiece, and the long lancet windows flood the stark white interior with light. István Báthory's remains lie in a marble tomb at the back of the church; the family's

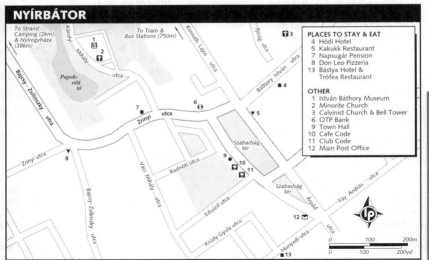

NYÍRBÁTOR

PLACES TO STAY & EAT
4 Hódi Hotel
5 Kakukk Restaurant
7 Napsugár Pension
8 Don Leo Pizzeria
13 Bástya Hotel & Trófea Restaurant

OTHER
1 István Báthory Museum
2 Minorite Church
3 Calvinist Church & Bell Tower
6 OTP Bank
9 Town Hall
10 Cafe Code
11 Club Code
12 Main Post Office

NORTHEAST

coat of arms embellished with wyverns (dragon-like creatures) is on top of the tomb. The 17th-century wooden **bell tower**, standing apart from the church (as was once required of Calvinists in this overwhelmingly Catholic country) has a Gothic roof with four little turrets. You can climb the 20m to the top 'at your own risk'. The pastor, who lives in the modern house just behind the church to the west, holds the massive medieval keys to the church and tower.

The **Minorite church** (Károlyi Mihály utca 19; admission free; open 9am-6pm Mon-Sat, 8am-6pm Sun May-Oct; 9am-11am & 4pm-5pm Mon-Sat, 8am-11am Sun Nov-Apr) is another Báthory contribution. Originally late Gothic, it was ravaged by the Turks in 1587 and rebuilt in the baroque style 130 years later. Five spectacular altars carved in Presov (now eastern Slovakia) in the mid-18th century fill the nave and chancel. The most interesting is the first on the left, the **Krucsay Altar of the Passion** (1737), with its diverse portraits of fear, longing, devotion and faith.

The **István Báthory Museum** (☎ 510 218; Károlyi Mihály utca 21; adult/child 200/100Ft; open 9am-5pm Tues-Sun Apr-Sep, 8am-4pm Mon-Fri Oct-Mar), in the 18th-century monastery next to the church has a very good ethnographic collection and some medieval pieces connected with the Báthory family and the churches they built.

Early July sees the streets of Nyríbátor come alive during the **Week of the Winged Dragon International Street Theatre Festival**; expect to see actors, puppeteers and musicians trying to out-perform each other.

Places to Stay

Strand Camping (☎ 281 494; camping per adult/child/tent 700/500/700Ft, bungalows up to four persons 5000Ft) is near the lake and swimming pools (entry to pools 350Ft) at Széna rét northwest of the town centre.

Hódi (☎ 283 556, fax 281 012; Báthory István utca 12; singles/doubles 10,700/11,700Ft) is by far the best place to stay in town. Set in a small courtyard east of Szabadság tér, it has 20 rooms with all the features of a top-class place, and there's a small indoor swimming pool, sauna, restaurant and bar.

Bástya (☎/fax 281 657; Hunyadi utca 10; singles/doubles 5376/6496Ft) is a 22-room hotel just south of the main square. All rooms have a bathroom and air-con.

Napsugár (☎ 283 878, fax 284 491; Zrínyi utca 15; singles/doubles 3800/5600Ft) is a pension with eight small but modern rooms just beyond the turn-off for the Minorite church.

Places to Eat

Don Leo Pizzeria (Bajcsy-Zsilinszky utca 62; pizzas 300-700Ft), a couple of hundred metres southwest of Napsugár pension, is a popular place for a light meal. Attached to the pizzeria is an excellent cake and ice cream shop.

Kakukk (☎ 281 050; Szabadság tér 21; mains 700-1200Ft) is the only real restaurant in the centre. Its well-prepared daily menu (around 330Ft) is very reasonable.

Trófea (☎ 281 880; Hunyadi utca; mains around 1000Ft) is the name of the csárda-style restaurant at the Bástya hotel. It serves fish and – ever popular in these parts – game.

Entertainment

Organ concerts and recitals can be heard throughout the year at the **Calvinist church**.

Cafe Code (Szabadság tér 7; open until midnight Mon-Fri, until late Sat & Sun) is a small, cosy place in the centre, and the only bar in town open late daily.

Club Code, next door to Cafe Code, has live music and DJs and is open on Saturday night only.

Getting There & Away

There are seven buses throughout the day to Nyíregyháza via Nagykálló and up to six daily buses go to Máriapócs.

There are up to eight daily trains from Nyíregyháza that call at Nyírbátor on their way to Mátészalka; as many as 14 trains heading for Mátészalka from Debrecen also stop here. You can catch one of up to seven daily trains at Mátészalka heading north for Záhony on the border of Ukraine, or three going south to Carei in Romania.

AROUND NYÍRBÁTOR
Máriapócs
☎ 42 • postcode 4326 • pop 2,300

This town, 12km northwest of Nyírbátor, has a beautiful **Greek Catholic cathedral** (☎ 385 142; Kossuth tér 25; admission free; open 6.30am-6pm daily), with an ornate gold iconostasis soaring some 15m up to the vaulted ceiling. Built in the middle of the 18th century on the site of a small wooden church, the cathedral has been an important pilgrimage site from at least 1696, when the **Black Madonna** icon, which now takes pride of place above the altar on the north side of the church, first shed tears (she wept again in 1715 and 1905). In fact, this is not the original icon but a 19th-century copy; the real one is now in St Stephen's Cathedral in Vienna.

Buses from Nagykálló, Nyírbátor and Nyíregyháza (between two and eight daily) will drop you off by the church. All the trains between Nyírbátor and Nyíregyháza stop at the Máriapócs train station, which is 4km south of the town centre. Buses make the run between the centre and the station, but they are not very reliable. Should you need to spend the night, the cathedral has a 22-room **guesthouse** (*☎*/fax 585 020; *e* zarandok haz@freemail.hu; Kossuth tér 17; beds 2300Ft).

Otherwise there's the six-room **Fekete Bárány** (*☎* 385 722; Állomás tér; singles/doubles 2500/5000Ft), an inn opposite the train station on the road linking Nyírbátor and Nagykálló.

Tiszahát & Erdőhát Regions

The most traditional parts of the county lie east and south of the Tisza River and are commonly referred to by their geographical locations: 'Behind the Tisza' (Tiszahát) and 'Behind the Woods' (Erdőhát) of Transylvania. Because of these regions' isolation, folk traditions have lived on. Some of the finest examples of Hungarian popular architecture and interior church painting are found here. It is also the site of Hungary's most unusual cemetery.

With its rolling hills, the ever-present Tisza and the soft silver-green of the poplar trees, the area is among the prettiest in Hungary. Unfortunately, it is also one of the most difficult to get around and, without your own transport, you should be prepared for long waits to connect between small towns. Distances are generally not great, though.

Things to See & Do
Vásárosnamény Vásárosnamény is today a sleepy town of just over 9000 people, but it was once an important trading post on the lucrative Salt Road, which ran from the forests of Transylvania, via the Tisza River and then across the Great Plain to Debrecen. Though it won't hold your interest for long, the **Bereg Museum** (*☎* 45-470 638; Rákóczi utca 13; adult/child 200/100Ft; open 8.30am-4.30pm Tues-Fri, 8am-4pm Sat & Sun mid-Mar–Oct; 8.30am-4.30pm Mon-Fri Nov–mid-Mar), has a small, though interesting, collection of local embroidery, weaving and painted Easter eggs – a popular local art form. Be sure to see the famous Bereg cross-stitching, a blend of many different styles.

Tákos The 18th-century wattle-and-daub **Calvinist church** (Bajcsy-Zsilinszky utca 25; adult/child 70/50Ft; open 7am-7pm daily) in this village (population 460) is 8km northeast of Vásárosnamény on route No 41. It has a spectacularly painted coffered ceiling of blue and red flowers, a floor of beaten earth and an ornately carved 'folk baroque' pulpit sitting on a large millstone. Outside the church, which villagers call the 'barefoot Notre Dame of Hungary', stands a perfectly preserved **bell tower** (1767). The keeper of the keys lives in a house just north of the church at Bajcsy-Zsilinszky utca 40.

Csaroda A beautiful **Romanesque church** (Kossuth utca 2; adult/child 70/50Ft; open 10am-6pm Mon-Fri Mar-Oct) dating from the 13th century stands in this village (population 680), which lies some 3km east of Tákos. The church is thought to have been founded by King Stephen himself, following his plan to have at least one church for every 10 villages in his domain. The church is a wonderful hybrid of a place with both Western- and Eastern-style frescoes (some from the 14th century) as well as some fairly crude folk murals dated 9 July 1647. On the short walk from the car park or bus stop, you'll pass two wooden **bell towers** of much more recent vintage. The key to the church is kept at Alkotmány utca 3.

Tarpa Some 6km further east on route No 41 will take you to the turn-off for Fehérgyarmat. Another 10km south of the turn off is Tarpa, a town of 2460 people boasting one of Hungary's last examples of a horse-driven **dry mill** (szárazmalom; *☎* 45-488 331; Árpád utca 36; admission 30Ft; appointment needed). The mill, with a distinctive conical roof, went through many incarnations – as a bar, a cinema and dance hall – before its renovation in the late 1970s and early 1980s. Nearby is a decorated **Calvinist church** (Kossuth utca 13; admission free; open 8am-noon Mon-Fri) and a small **provincial house** (tájház; ☎ 45-488 001; Kossuth utca 21; adult/child 100/50Ft; open 10am-5pm daily Mar-Sept).

Szatmárcseke To get to this village, site of a cemetery with intriguing boat-shaped **grave markers** (kopjafák; Táncsics utca), travel another 5km south to Tivadar and the Tisza River. After crossing the river, turn east and carry on another 7km northeast to Szatmárcseke. The 600 carved wooden markers in the cemetery are unique in Hungary, and the notches and grooves cut into them represent a complicated language all of their own: they detail marital status, social position, age and so on. One of the few stone markers in the cemetery is that of native son Ferenc Kölcsey (1790–1838), who wrote the words to *Himnusz*, the Hungarian national anthem. Nearby is a small **museum** (☎ 44-432 142; Kölcsey utca 44; admission 100Ft; open 10am-5pm daily) devoted to Kölcsey.

Túristvándi There is a wonderfully restored 18th-century **water mill** (vízimalom; ☎ 44-434 066; Zrínyi út 4; adult/child 100/70Ft; open 8am-6pm daily Apr-Sept, 8am-4pm daily Oct-Mar) on a small tributary of the Tisza at Túristvándi, 4km due south of Szatmárcseke.

Places to Stay
Diófa Camping (☎ 45-712 298; Gulácsi út 71; camping per person/tent 600/600Ft, bungalows 6000Ft) is across the Tisza River from Vásárosnamény in Gergelyiugornya. Bungalows sleep up to four persons.

Marianna Center (☎ 45-470 401, fax 470 434; Szabadság tér 19; singles/doubles 6000/7000Ft) is a 21-room hotel on the 2nd floor of a restaurant/pub complex in Vásárosnamény.

Szatmár (☎ 44-311 429, fax 310 428; Hősök tere 8; singles/doubles 5376/6496Ft) hotel has 20 rooms and is an option in Mátészalka.

Kúria (☎ 45-311 202; József Attila utca 70; rooms 2000-3000Ft), in Csaroda, is an old manor house functioning as an inn, and has four three-bed rooms.

Riviera (☎/fax 45-311 763; Árpád utca 24; rooms 5000Ft) is a pension in Tarpa, near the dry mill.

Katica Camping (☎ 44-363 859; Petőfi utca 11; camping per adult/child/tent 400/350/300Ft), in Tivadar near the Tisza River, opens from mid-June to August only.

Kölcsey (☎ 06-20 511 4828, fax 44-432 053; Honvéd utca 6; rooms from 3000Ft), a 14-room inn in Szatmárcseke, is a run-down old place on a quiet, leafy street. It's good value but it closes in winter. You'll see quite a few houses along the main street in Szatmárcseke with *szoba kiadó* or *Zimmer frei* (both mean 'room for rent') signs outside.

Vízimalon (☎ 44-424 075; Malom utca 3; camping per adult/child/tent 600/300/600Ft, beds per person 2200Ft), a pension in Túristvándi, is next to the old water mill and has eight rooms, plus a camp site.

Getting There & Away
The ideal way to visit this part of Hungary is by car or bicycle. If neither is an option, you can visit most of the places mentioned here by bus from Vásárosnamény, Mátészalka or Fehérgyarmat. Departures are infrequent, averaging only two or three daily. Carefully check return schedules from your destination before setting out.

From Nyíregyháza, up to 10 trains leave daily for Vásárosnamény, with eight for Mátészalka via Nagykálló, Máriapócs and Nyírbátor. You can reach Fehérgyarmat via two direct trains daily or travel to Mátészalka and change there on up to nine others.

Getting Around
For those of you not under your own steam, the best idea is to take the train or bus from Nyíregyháza or Nyírbátor to Vásárosnamény and use that town as your springboard. Or, better still, go on a tour organised by **Air-Mediterrán** (☎ 42-501 490, fax 501 494; W www.airmed.hu; Szarvas utca 5-7) in Nyíregyháza; no one knows this part of the country better than they do. See Organised Tours in the Getting Around chapter for details.

Rétköz Region

The Rétköz area northeast of Nyíregyháza lies somewhat lower than the rest of Northeast Hungary and used to be particularly prone to flooding. Agriculture was possible only on the larger of the islands in this mosquito-infested swampland, and the isolation spurred the development of strong clan ties and a wealth of folk tales and myths. That's all in the past now, and you won't see any evidence of it, other than the once-celebrated Rétköz homespun cloth. But you might get lucky...

KISVÁRDA
☎ 45 • postcode 4600 • pop 18,800

Kisvárda, 45km northeast of Nyíregyháza and the centre of the Rétköz region, was an important stronghold during the Turkish invasions, and the remains of its fortress can still be seen. It's only 23km north to Ukraine and, if you're continuing onward, it's a much nicer place to spend the night than the border town of Záhony.

Orientation & Information
Kisvárda's bus and train stations lie just over 2km southwest of Flórián tér, the town centre. Local buses await arriving trains, but it's an easy, straightforward walk north along tree-lined Bocskai utca, Rákóczi Ferenc utca and Szent László utca to town. The last stretch of Szent László utca is particularly colourful. Some buses also go as far as Flórián tér. There's a schedule posted outside the Volán office at Flórián tér 2.

You'll find an **OTP bank** (cnr Mártírok útja & Szent László utca) south of Flórián tér and the **main post office** (Somogyi Rezső utca 4) is to the west of the bank.

Things to See & Do
Flórián tér offers the usual Gothic-cum-baroque **Catholic church** (admission free; open 7.30am-6pm Mon-Sat, 8.30am-6pm Sun) painted lime green, and a late-19th-century dusky pink **Calvinist church** (admission free; open 7.30am-6pm Mon-Sat, 8.30am-6pm Sun) sitting uncomfortably close by. Far more interesting is the Zopf-style **town library** which takes pride of place on the square.

A short distance to the east of the square is the **Rétköz Museum** (☎ 405 154; Csillag utca 5; adult/child 100/50Ft; open 9am-noon, 1pm-4.30pm Tues-Sun, Apr-Oct). Housed in a disused synagogue built in 1900, the building itself is as interesting as the exhibits, with its geometric ceiling patterns, blue and yellow stained glass, and wrought-iron gates in the shape of menorahs. Lots of 'typical' Rétköz village rooms and workshops (a smithy, loom etc) are set up on the ground floor of the museum, but the 1st floor has some interesting art. Just inside the west entrance is a memorial tablet with more than 1000 names of Kisvárda Jewish citizens who died in Auschwitz.

The ruins of **Kisvárda Castle** (☎ 405 239; Várkert; admission free; appointment necessary) are about 10 minutes on foot northwest of Flórián tér at the end of the street. Though part of one wall dates from the 15th century, most of the castle has been heavily restored. The courtyard is used as an open-air theatre in summer.

The **Várfürdő** (Városmajor utca; adult/child 300/200Ft; open 9am-7pm daily May-Sept), beside the castle ruins, is a small complex of freshwater and thermal pools, with sauna and sunbathing areas.

Places to Stay
Vár (☎ 421 578, fax 405 242; Városmajor utca 43; bungalow/motel/hotel beds per person 1350/1350/1850Ft), a run-down holiday house beside the castle ruins and baths, has very basic accommodation in the form of six bungalows, nine motel rooms and 16 hotel rooms.

Bástya (☎/fax 421 100; Krucsay Márton utca 2; doubles with/without shower 4000/3700Ft) is a more central hotel in a 'turret' on the 1st floor of a modern shopping arcade. It has 18 double rooms.

Places to Eat
Szinnbad Grill (Szent László utca 2; light meals from 300Ft) is a cheap eatery serving up gyros, hamburgers and such.

Amadeus (Szent László utca 27; mains 800-1300Ft), a cellar restaurant, is a better choice for a fuller meal. It's a bit further south.

Fekete Nyolcás (Black Eight Ball; Mártírok útja 3; pizzas from 320Ft) is a basic pizzeria near the OTP bank.

The cukrászda (cake shop) with the best cakes and ice cream in town is the **Poncsák** (Mártírok útja 2), though the **Sarok** (Szent László utca 2), next to Szinnbad, is a bit more central.

Entertainment
Plays are sometimes put on at the **Castle Stage** (Várszínpad) at the castle in summer;

NORTHEAST

check with the staff at the modern **cultural centre** *(☎ 500 451; Flórián tér 20)*, which also contains the small **Castle Theatre** (Várszínház).

Belvárosi Kávézó *(Szent László utca 22)* is more a pub than a coffee shop, but a place keeping much later hours is the **Fortuna Club** *(Csillag utca; open until midnight daily)*, a bar opposite the Rétköz Museum.

Getting There & Away

Only a few destinations are accessible by bus from Kisvárda including Dombrád (up to 14 buses daily), Nyíregyháza (two) and Vásárosnamény (six).

The town is on the railway line connecting Nyíregyháza with Záhony, and you have a choice of up to 17 daily trains, five of which originate in Budapest.

L

ian (... her
minority ... tern
Siberia (with far ... ot an
Indo-European langu... that
English is actually close ... French,
Russian and Hindi in vocabulary and structure than it is to Hungarian. As a result
you'll come across very few recognisable
words – with the exception of borrowings
like *disco*, *szex* or *hello*, which is the slangy
way young Hungarians say 'goodbye'.

There are also a fair number of misleading
homophones (words with the same sound but
different meanings) in Hungarian: *test* is not a
quiz but 'body'; *fog* is 'tooth'; *comb* is 'thigh';
and *part* is 'shore'. *Ifjúság*, pronounced (very
roughly) 'if you shag', means 'youth'; *sajt*
(pronounced 'shite'), as in every visiting
Briton's favourite *sajtburger*, means 'cheese'.

For more Hungarian words and phrases
than there is space for here, get a copy of
Lonely Planet's *Eastern* or *Central Europe
phrasebook*.

Pronunciation

Hungarian isn't difficult to pronounce –
though it may look strange with all those
accents. Unlike English, it's a 'one-for-one'
language: the pronunciation of each vowel
and consonant is almost always consistent.
Stress falls on the first syllable (no exceptions), making the language sound a bit
staccato at first.

Consonants

Consonants in Hungarian are pronounced
more or less as in English, with the exceptions listed below. The double consonants
(**ll**, **tt**, **dd**) are not pronounced as one letter
as in English, but lengthened so you can
almost hear them as separate sounds. Also,
what are called consonant clusters (**cs**, **zs**,
gy and **sz**) are considered separate letters in
Hungarian and appear that way in the telephone directory and alphabetical listings.
For example, the word *cukor* (sugar) appears in the dictionary before *csak* (only).

c	as the 'ts' in 'hats'
cs	as the 'ch' in 'church'
gy	as the 'j' in 'jury' with the tongue pressed against the roof of the mouth
j	as the 'y' in 'yes'
ly	also as the 'y' in 'yes', but with a slight 'l' sound
ny	as the 'ni' in 'onion'
r	pronounced with the tip of the tongue; a slightly trilled 'r' as found in Spanish or Scottish
s	as the 'sh' in 'shop'
sz	as the 's' in 'salt'
ty	as the 'tu' in 'tube' in British English
w	as the 'v' in 'vat' (found in foreign words only)
zs	as the 's' in 'pleasure'

Vowels

Vowels are quite tricky in Hungarian, and
the difference between an **a**, **e** or **o** with and
without an accent mark is great. *Hát* means
'back' while *hat* means 'six'; *kérek* means
'I want' while *kerek* means 'round'. Try to
imagine a Briton with a standard television
accent or an American from Boston pro-
nouncing the following sounds:

a	as the 'o' in hot
á	as the 'a' in 'father' or 'shah'
e	as in 'get'
é	as the 'e' in 'they' (without the 'y' sound)
i	similar to the 'i' in 'hit'
í	as the 'i' in 'police'
o	as in 'open'
ó	a longer version of **o** above
ö	as the 'o' in 'worse' (without any 'r' sound)
ő	a longer version of **ö** above
u	as in 'pull'
ú	as the 'oo' in 'food'
ü	a tough one; similar to the 'u' in 'flute' or as in German *fünf*
ű	a longer, breathier version of **ü** above

Polite & Informal Address

As in many other Western languages, verbs
in Hungarian have polite and informal
forms in the singular and plural. The polite
address (marked as 'pol' in this section) is

LANGUAGE

used with strangers, older people, officials and service staff. The informal address (marked as 'inf') is reserved for friends, pets, children and sometimes foreigners, but is used much more frequently and sooner than its equivalent in, say, French. Almost all young people use it among themselves – even with strangers.

In the following phrases, the polite 'you' (*Ön* and *Önök*) is given except for situations where you might wish to establish a more personal relationship.

Greetings & Civilities

Hello.	*Jó napot kívánok.* (pol)
Hi.	*Szia/Szervusz.* (inf)
Goodbye.	*Viszontlátásra.* (pol)
	Szia/Szervusz. (inf)
Good day.	*Jó napot.*
Good morning.	*Jó reggelt.*
Good evening.	*Jó estét.*

Small Talk

How are you?	*Hogy van?* (pol)
	Hogy vagy? (inf)
I'm fine, thanks.	*Köszönöm, jól.*
What's your name?	*Hogy hívják?* (pol)
	Mi a neved? (inf)
My name is ...	*A nevem ...*
I'm a tourist/ student.	*Turista/diák vagyok.*
Are you married?	*Ön férjezett?* (to women)
	Ön nős? (to men)
Do you like Hungary?	*Tetszik önnek Magyarország?*
I like it very much.	*Nagyon tetszik.*
Where are you from?	*Honnan jön?*
I'm ...	*... vagyok.*
American	*amerikai*
British	*brit*
Australian	*ausztrál*
Canadian	*kanadai*
New Zealander	*új-zélandi*
How old are you?	*Hány éves vagy?* (inf)
	Hány éves? (pol)
I'm 25 years old.	*Húszonöt éves vagyok.*
Just a minute.	*Egy pillanat.*
May I?	*Lehet?* (general permission)
	Szabad? (eg, asking for a chair)
It's all right.	*Rendben van.*
No problem.	*Semmi baj.*

Signs

Bejárat	**Entrance**
Felvilágosítás	**Information**
Foglalt	**Reserved/ Occupied**
Hideg	**Cold**
Információ	**Information**
Kijárat	**Exit**
Meleg	**Hot**
Nyitva	**Open**
Tilos	**Prohibited**
Tilos Belépni	**No Entry**
Tilos a Dohányzás	**No Smoking**
Vészkijárat	**Emergency Exit**
WC/Toalett	**Toilets**
Férfiak	**Men**
Nők	**Women**
Zárva	**Closed**

Essentials

Yes.	*Igen.*
No.	*Nem.*
Maybe.	*Talán.*
Please.	*Kérem.* (when asking for something)
	Tessék. (when inviting or offering something)
Thank you (very much).	*Köszönöm (szépen).*
Thanks.	*Köszi.* (inf)
You're welcome.	*Szívesen.*
Excuse me.	*Legyen szíves.* (for attention)
	Bocsánat. (apology)
I'm sorry.	*Sajnálom/Elnézést.*

Language Difficulties

Do you speak ...?	*Beszél ...?*
English	*angolul*
French	*franciául*
German	*németül*
Italian	*olaszul*

Does anyone here speak English?
Van itt valaki, aki angolul beszél?
I understand.
Értem.
I don't understand.
Nem értem.
I don't speak Hungarian.
Nem beszélek magyarul.
How do you say ... in Hungarian?
Hogy mondják magyarul ...?
Please write it down.
Kérem, írja le.

Would you please show me (on the map)?
Meg tudná nekem mutatni (a térképen)?

Getting Around
What time does ... *Mikor indul/érkezik ...?*
leave/arrive?
the boat	*a hajó*
the bus	*az autóbusz*
the ferry	*a komp*
the train	*a vonat*
the tram	*a villamos*
the plane	*a repülőgép*

The train is ...	*A vonat ...*
delayed	*késik*
on time	*pontosan érkezik*
early	*korábban érkezik*
cancelled	*nem jár*

I want to go to ...	*... akarok menni.*
Esztergom	*Esztergomba*
Debrecen	*Debrecenbe*
Pécs	*Pécsre*

I want to book a seat to Prague.
Szeretnék helyet foglalni Prágába.
How long does the trip take?
Mennyi ideig tart az út?
Do I need to change trains?
Át kell szállnom?
You must change trains.
Át kell szállni.
You must change platforms.
Másik vágányhoz kell menni.

train station	*vasútállomás/ pályaudvar*
bus station	*autóbuszállomás*
platform	*vágány*
ticket	*jegy*
one-way ticket	*egy útra/csak oda*
return ticket	*oda-vissza/retúrjegy*
ticket office	*jegyiroda/pénztár*
timetable	*menetrend*
left-luggage	*csomagmegőrző*

The following may appear in bus and train timetables: *naponta* (daily), *hétköznap* (weekdays), *munkanap* (workdays), *szabadnap* (Saturday), *szabad és munkaszünetes nap* (Saturday and holidays), *munkaszünetes nap* (holidays), *iskolai nap* (school days), *szabadnap kivételével naponta* (daily except Saturday), *munkaszünetes nap kivételével naponta* (daily except holidays).

I'd like to hire a ...	*... szeretnék kölcsönözni.*
bicycle	*kerékpárt*
motorcycle	*motorkerékpárt*
horse	*lovat*

I'd like to hire a car.
Autót szeretnék bérelni.
I'd like to hire a guide.
Szeretnék kérni egy idegenvezetőt.
I have a visa/permit.
Nekem van vízum/engedélyem.

Directions
How do I get to ...?	*Hogy jutok ...?*
Where is ...?	*Hol van ...?*
Is it near/far?	*Közel/messze van?*

What ... is this?	*Ez melyik ...?*
street/road	*utca/út*
street number	*házszám*
city district	*kerület*
town/city	*város*
village	*falu/község*
(Go) straight ahead.	*(Menyen) egyenesen előre.*
(Turn) left.	*(Forduljon) balra.*
(Turn) right.	*(Forduljon) jobbra.*
at the next traffic lights	*a közlekedési lámpánál*
next/second/third corner	*következő/második/ harmadik saroknál*
up/down	*fent/lent*
behind/in front	*mögött/előtt*
opposite	*szemben*
here/there	*itt/ott*
everywhere	*mindenhol*
north	*észak*
south	*dél*
east	*kelet*
west	*nyugat*

Around Town
Where is ...?	*Hol van ...?*
a bank	*bank*
an exchange office	*pénzváltó*
the city centre	*a város központ/ a centrum*
the ... embassy	*a ... nagykövetség*
the hospital	*a kórház*
the market	*a piac*
the police station	*a rendőrkapitányság*
the post office	*a posta*
a public toilet	*nyilvános WC*
a restaurant	*étterem*
tourist office	*idegenforgalmi iroda*

bridge	*híd*
beach	*strand*
castle	*vár*
cathedral	*székesegyház*
church	*templom*
island	*sziget*
lake	*tó*
(main) square	*(fő) tér*
market	*piac*
palace	*palota*
mansion	*kastély*
ruins	*rom/romok*
synagogue	*zsinagóga*
tower	*torony*

Accommodation

I'm looking for ...	*... keresem.*
a camping ground	*campinget/ kempinget*
a guesthouse	*fogadót*
the youth hostel	*az ifjúsági szállót*
a hotel	*szállodát*
the manager	*a főnököt*
the owner	*a tulajdonost*
rooms available	*szoba kiadó*

Do you have a ... available?	*Van szabad ...?*
bed	*ágyuk*
cheap room	*olcsó szobájuk*
single room	*egyágyas szobájuk*
double room	*kétágyas szobájuk*

What is the address?
Mi a cím?
How much is it per person/night?
Mennyibe kerül személyenként/ éjszakánként?
for one/two nights
egy/két éjszakára
Is service included?
A kiszolgálás benne van?
May I see the room?
Megnézhetem a szobát?
Where is the toilet/bathroom?
Hol van a WC/fürdőszoba?
It is very dirty/noisy/expensive.
Ez nagyon piskos/zajos/drága.
I'm/We're leaving.
El megyek/megyünk.

Do you have ...?	*Van ...?*
a clean sheet	*tiszta lepedő*
hot water	*meleg víz*
a key	*kulcs*
a shower	*zuhany*

Emergencies

Help!	*Segítség!*
It's an emergency!	*Sűrgős!*
There's been an accident!	*Baleset történt!*
Call a doctor!	*Hívjon egy orvost!*
Call an ambulance!	*Hívja a mentőket!*
Call the police!	*Hívja a rendőrséget!*
I've been raped.	*Megerőszakoltak.*
I've been robbed.	*Kiraboltak.*
I'm lost.	*Eltévedtem.*
Go away!	*Menjen el!*
Where are the toilets?	*Hol van a WC?*

Shopping

I'm looking for ...	*Keresem ...*
the chemist/ pharmacy	*a patikát*
clothing	*ruhát*
souvenirs	*emléktárgyat*

I'd like to buy this.	*Szeretném megvenni ezt.*
How much is it?	*Mennyibe kerül?*
It's too expensive.	*Ez túl drága.*
Can I look at it?	*Megnézhetem?*
I'm just looking.	*Csak nézegetek.*

Time & Dates

When?	*Mikor?*
At what time?	*Hány órakor?*
What time is it?	*Hány óra?*

It's ... o'clock.	*... óra van.*
1.15	*negyed kettő*
1.30	*fél kettő*
1.45	*háromnegyed kettő*

in the morning	*reggel*
in the evening	*este*
today	*ma*
tonight	*ma este*
tomorrow	*holnap*
day after tomorrow	*holnaputén*
yesterday	*tegnap*
all day	*egész nap*
every day	*minden nap*

Monday	*hétfő*
Tuesday	*kedd*
Wednesday	*szerda*

Thursday	csütörtök
Friday	péntek
Saturday	szombat
Sunday	vasárnap

January	január
February	február
March	március
April	április
May	május
June	június
July	július
August	augusztus
September	szeptember
October	október
November	november
December	december

Numbers

0	nulla
1	egy
2	kettő (két before nouns)
3	három
4	négy
5	öt
6	hat
7	hét
8	nyolc
9	kilenc
10	tíz
11	tizenegy
12	tizenkettő
13	tizenhárom
14	tizennégy
15	tizenöt
16	tizenhat
17	tizenhét
18	tizennyolc
19	tizenkilenc
20	húsz
21	huszonegy
22	huszonkettő
30	harminc
40	negyven
50	ötven
60	hatvan
70	hetven
80	nyolcvan
90	kilencven
100	száz
101	százegy
110	száztíz
1000	ezer

one million	egy millió

Health

I'm ...	... vagyok.
diabetic	cukorbeteg
epileptic	epilepsziás
asthmatic	asztmás
I'm allergic to ...	... allergiás vagyok.
penicillin	penicillinre
antibiotics	antibiotikumra

I've got diarrhoea.	Hasmenésem van.
I feel nauseous.	Hányingerem van.
antiseptic	fertőzésgátló
aspirin	aszpirin
condoms	óvszer/gumi
contraceptive	fogamzásgátló
insect repellent	rovarírtó
medicine	orvosság
suntan lotion	napozókrém
sunblock cream	fényvédőkrém
tampons	tampon

FOOD

restaurant	étterem/vendéglő
food stall	Laci konyha or pecsenyesütő
grocery store	élelmiszer
delicatessen	csemege
market	piac

breakfast	reggeli
lunch	ebéd
dinner/supper	vacsora
the menu	az étlap
set/daily menu	napi menü

At the Restaurant

I'm hungry.	Éhes vagyok.
I'm thirsty.	Szomjas vagyok.
The menu, please.	Az étlapot, kérem.
I'd like today's set menu, please.	Mai menüt, kérnék.
Is service included in the bill?	Az ár tartalmazza a kiszolgálást?
I'm a vegetarian.	Vegetáriánus vagyok.
I'd like some ...	Kérnék ...
Another ... please.	Még (egy) ..., kérek.
The bill, please.	A számlát, kérem/ Fizetek.

bread	kenyér
chicken	csirke
eggs	tojás
fish	hal
food	étel
fruit	gyümölcs

LANGUAGE

meat	hús
pepper	bors
pork	disznóhús
salt	só
soup	leves
sugar	cukor
vegetables	zöldség

hot/cold	meleg/hideg
with/without ice	jéggel/jég nélkül
with/without sugar	cukorral/cukor nélkül

DRINKS

water	víz
mineral water	ásvány víz
milk	tej
fruit juice	gyümölcslé
apple juice	almalé
orange juice	narancslé
lemondade	limonádé
tea	tea

coffee	kávé
cappuccino	tejes kávé

bottle	üveg
drinks list	itallap
lager	világos sör
draught beer	csapolt sör
glass of beer (.3L)	pohár sör
mug of beer (.5L)	korsó sör
wine	bor
red wine	vörös bor
sweet wine	édes bor
white wine	fehér bor
glass of wine	pohár bor
champagne/ sparkling wine	pezsgő
spritzer	fröccs
apricot brandy	barackpálinka
pear brandy	körtepálinka
plum brandy	szilvapálinka

Cheers!	Egészségére!

Glossary

If you can't find the word you're looking for in the Glossary, try the previous Language section.

ÁEV – Állami Erdei Vasutak; United Forest Railways
ÁFA – value-added tax (VAT)
Alföld – same as *Nagyalföld* and *puszta*
aszú – key ingredient in the preparation of Tokaj sweet wine
Ausgleich – German for 'reconciliation'; the Compromise of 1867
autóbusz – bus
autóbuszállomás – bus station
Avars – a people of the Caucasus who invaded Europe in the 6th century
ÁVO – Rákosi's hated secret police in the early years of communism; later renamed ÁVH

bal – left
bejárat – entrance
bélyeg – stamps
benzin – petrol
BKV – Budapest Közlekedési Vallálat; Budapest Transport Company
bokor tanyák – bush farms
bolhapiac – flea market
borozó – wine bar; any place serving wine
Bp – abbreviation for Budapest
búcsú – farewell; also, a church patronal festival
büfé – snack bar

centrum – town or city centre
čevapčiči – (spicy Balkan meatballs)
Compromise of 1867 – agreement which created the dual monarchy of Austria-Hungary
Copf – a transitional architectural style between late baroque and neoclassicism (same as *Zopf*)
csárda – a Hungarian-style inn or restaurant
csatorna – canal
csikós – cowboy from the puszta
csomagmegőrző – left-luggage office
cukrászda – cake shop or patisserie

D – map/compass abbreviation for *dél*
Dacia – Latin name for Romania and lands east of the Tisza River
db or **drb** – piece (measurement used in markets)
de – am; in the morning
dél – south
du – pm; in the afternoon/evening

É – map/compass abbreviation for *észak* (north)
Eclectic – an art and architectural styles popular in Hungary in the Romantic period, drawing from sources both indigenous and foreign
élelmiszer – grocery shop; convenience store

előszoba – vestibule or anteroom; one of three rooms in a traditional Hungarian cottage
em – abbreviation for *emelet* (floor or storey)
emelet – floor or storey
erdő – forest
érkezés – arrivals
észak – north
eszpresszó – coffee shop, often also selling alcoholic drinks and snacks; strong, black coffee; same as *presszó*
étkezde – canteens that serve simple dishes
étterem – restaurant

falu – village
fasor – boulevard, avenue
felvilágosítás – information
fogas – pike-perch fish indigenous to Lake Balaton
földszint – ground floor
folyó – river
forint – Hungary's monetary unit
főkapitányság – main police station
főváros – main city or capital
főzelék – a traditional way of preparing vegetables, where they're fried or boiled and then mixed into a roux with cream
fsz – abbreviation for *földszint*
Ft – forint, see also *HUF*

gázolaj – diesel fuel
gulyás or **gulyásleves** – a thick beef soup cooked with onions and potatoes and usually eaten as a main course.
gyógyfürdő – bath or spa
gyógyvíz – medicinal drinking water
gyorsvonat – fast trains
gyűjtemény – collection
gyula – chief military commander of the early Magyar

hajdúk – Hungarian for *Heyducks*
hajó – boat
hajóállomás – ferry pier or landing
ház – house
hegy – hill, mountain
hegyalja – hill country
helyi autóbusz pályaudvar – local bus station
HÉV – helyiérdekű vasút; suburban commuter train in Budapest
Heyducks – drovers and outlaws from the puszta who fought as mercenaries against the Habsburgs
híd – bridge
HNTO – Hungarian National Tourism Office
hőforrás – thermal spring
honfoglalás – conquest of the Carpathian Basin by the Magyars in the late 9th century

HUF – international currency code for the Hungarian forint
Huns – a Mongol tribe that swept across Europe under Attila in the 5th century AD

Ibusz – Hungarian national network of travel agencies
ifjúsági szálló – youth hostel
illeték – duty or tax
indulás – departures

jobb – right

K – abbreviation for *kelet*
Karma – workshop or shed; one of three rooms in a traditional Hungarian cottage
kastély – manor house or mansion (see *vár*)
kb – abbreviation for *körülbelül*
kékfestő – cotton fabric dyed a rich indigo blue
kelet – east
kemping – camping ground
képtár – picture gallery
kerület – city district
khas – towns of the Ottoman period under direct rule of the sultan
kijárat – exit
kincstár – treasury
kirándulás – outing
Kiskörút – 'Little Ring Road' in Budapest
kocsma – pub or saloon
kolostor – monastery or cloister
komp – ferry
könyvesbolt – bookshop
könyvtár – library
konzumlányok – 'consume girls': attractive young women who work in collusion with bars and clubs to rip off unsuspecting male tourists
kórház – hospital
korhely halászlé – drunkard's fish soup
körülbelül – approximately
körút – ring road
korzó – embankment or promenade
köz – alley, mews, lane
központ – centre
krt – abbreviation for *körút*
kúria – mansion or manor
kuruc – Hungarian mercenaries, partisans or insurrectionists who resisted the expansion of Habsburg rule in Hungary after the withdrawal of the Turks (late 17th/early 18th centuries)

lángos – deep-fried dough with toppings
lekvár – fruit jam
lépcső – stairs, steps
liget – park

Magyarország autóatlasza – road atlas of Hungary
Mahart – Hungarian passenger ferry company
Malév – Hungary's national airline
MÁV – Magyar Államvasutak; Hungarian State Railways

megye – county
menetrend – timetable
mihrab – Mecca-oriented prayer niche
MNB – Magyar Nemzeti Bank; National Bank of Hungary
Moorish Romantic – an art style popular in the decoration of 19th-century Hungarian synagogues
mozi – cinema
műemlék – memorial, monument
munkavállalási engedély – work permit

Nagyalföld – the Great Plain (same as the *Alföld* and *puszta*)
Nagykörút – 'Big Ring Road' in Budapest
népművészeti bolt – folk-art shop
Nonius – Hungarian breed of horse
nosztalgiavonat – vintage steam train
Ny – abbreviation for *nyugat* (west)
nyitva – open
nyugat – west

ó – abbreviation for *óra*
önkiszolgáló – self-service
óra – hour, o'clock
orvosi rendelő – doctor's surgery
osztály – department
OTP – Országos Takarékpénztár; National Savings Bank
Ottoman Empire – the Turkish empire that took over from the Byzantine Empire when it captured Constantinople (Istanbul) in 1453, and expanded into southeastern Europe

pálinka – Hungarian fruit brandy
palota – palace
pályaudvar – train or railway station
Pannonia – Roman name for the lands south and west of the Danube River
panzió – pension, guesthouse
part – embankment
patika – pharmacy
patyolat – laundry
pénztár – cashier
pénzváltó – exchange office
piac – market
pince – wine cellar
plébánia – rectory, parish house
polgármester – mayor
pörkölt – (stew)
porta – type of farmhouse in Transdanubia
presszó – same as *eszpresszó*
pu – abbreviation for **pályaudvar**
puli – Hungarian breed of sheepdog with shaggy coat
puszta – literally 'deserted'; other name for the Great Plain (see *Alföld* and *Nagyalföld*)
puttony – the number of 'butts' of sweet *aszú* essence added to other base wines in making Tokaj wine

racka – sheep on the Great Plain with distinctive corkscrew horns

rakpart – quay, embankment
rendőrkapitányság – police station
repülőtér – airport
Romany – the language and culture of the Roma (Gypsy) people

sebesvonat – swift trains
Secessionism – art and architectural style similar to Art Nouveau
sedile (pl sedilia) – medieval stone niche with seats
sétány – walkway, promenade
shahoof – distinctive sweep-pole well found only on the Great Plain (Hungarian: *gémeskút*)
skanzen – open-air museum displaying village architecture
söröző – beer bar or pub
spahi – name given to a member of the Turkish irregular cavalry. The officers of the spahis were granted fiefs by the Sultan, and were entitled to all income from the fief in return for military service to the Sultan
stb – abbreviation of *s a többi* (and so on) equivalent to English 'etc'
strand – grassy 'beach' near a river or lake
sugárút – avenue
szálló – hotel
szálloda – same as *szálló*
székesegyház – cathedral
Személyvonat – passenger trains that stop at every city, town, village and hamlet along the way
sziget – island
színház – theatre
szoba kiadó – room for rent
szűr – long embroidered felt cloak or cape traditionally worn by Hungarian shepherds

Tanácsköztársaság – the 1919 Communist Republic of Councils under Béla Kun
táncház – folk music and dance workshop
tanya – homestead or ranch
tartózkodási engedély – residence permit
távolsági autóbusz pályaudvar – long-distance bus station
templom – church
tér – town or market square
tere – genitive form of *tér* as in Hősök tere (Square of the Heroes)

tilos – prohibited, forbidden
tista szoba – parlour; one of three rooms in a traditional Hungarian cottage
tó – lake
toalett – toilet
Trianon Treaty – 1920 treaty imposed on Hungary by the victorious Allies, which reduced the country to one-third of its former size
Triple Alliance – 1882–1914 alliance between Germany, Austria-Hungary and Italy – not to be confused with the WWI Allies (members of the *Triple Entente* and their supporters)
Triple Entente – agreement among Britain, France and Russia, intended as a counterbalance to the *Triple Alliance*, lasting until the Russian Revolution of 1917
turul – eagle-like totem of the ancient Magyars and now a national sysmbol

u – abbreviation for *utca*
udvar – court
ünnep – public holiday
úszoda – swimming pool
út – road
utca – street
utcája – genitive form of *utca* as in Ferencesek utcája (Street of the Franciscans)
útja – genitive form of *út* as in Mártírocká útja (Street of the Martyrs)
üzlet – shop

va – abbreviations for *vasútállomás*
vágány – platform
vár – castle
város – city
városház, városháza – town hall
vasútállomás – train or railway station
vendéglő – a type of restaurant
vm – abbreviations for *vasútállomás*
Volán – Hungarian bus company
vonat – train

WC – toilet (see *toalett*)

zárva – closed
Zimmer frei – German for 'room for rent'
Zopf – German and more commonly used word for *Copf*

Alternative Place Names

On many (though not all) bus and train timetables, Hungarian names are used for cities and towns in neighbouring countries. Many of these are in what once was Hungarian territory and the names are used by the Hungarian-speaking minorities who live there. You should at least be familiar with the more important ones (eg, Pozsony for Bratislava, Kolozsvár for Club-Napoca, Bécs for Vienna) to help decipher bus and some train timetables.

The following abbreviations are used:

(A) Austrian
(C) Croatian
(E) English
(G) German
(H) Hungarian
(R) Romanian
(S) Serbian
(Slk) Slovak
(Slo) Slovene
(U) Ukrainian

Alba Iulia (R) – Gyula Fehérvár (H), Karlsburg/
   Weissenburg (G)

Baia Mare (R) – Nagybánya (H)
Balaton (H) – Plattensee (G)
Belgrade (E) – Beograd (S), Nándorfehérvár (H)
Beregovo (U) – Beregszász (H)
Braşov (R) – Brassó (H), Kronstadt (G)
Bratislava (Slk) – Pozsony (H), Pressburg (G)

Carei (R) – Nagykároly (H)
Cluj-Napoca (R) – Kolozsvár (H),
   Klausenburg (G)

Danube (E) – Duna (H), Donau (G)
Danube Bend (E) – Dunakanyar (H),
   Donauknie (G)
Debrecen (H) – Debrezin (G)

Eger (H) – Erlau (G)
Eisenstadt (G) – Kismárton (H)
Esztergom (H) – Gran (G)

Fertő-Hanság (H) – Neusiedlersee (A)

Great Plain (E) – Nagyalföld, Alföld, Puszta (H)
Győr (H) – Raab (G)

Hungary (E) – Magyarország (H), Ungarn (G)

Kisalföld (H) – Little Plain (E)
Komárom (H) – Komárno (Slk)
Košice (Slk) – Kassa (H), Kaschau (G)
Kőszeg (H) – Güns (G)

Lendava (Slo) – Lendva (H)
Lučenec (Slk) – Losonc (H)

Mattersburg (G) – Nagymárton (H)
Mukačevo (U) – Munkács (H)
Murska Sobota (Slo) – Muraszombat (H)

Northern Uplands (E) – Északi Felföld (H)

Oradea (R) – Nagyvárad (H),
   Grosswardein (G)
Osijek (C) – Eszék (H)

Pécs (H) – Fünfkirchen (G)

Rožnava (Slk) – Rozsnyó (H)

Satu Mare (R) – Szatmárnémeti (H)
Senta (S) – Zenta (H)
Sibiu (R) – Nagyszében (H), Hermannstadt (G)
Sic (R) – Szék (H)
Sighişoara (R) – Szegesvár (H), Schässburg (G)
Sopron (H) – Ödenburg (G)
Štúrovo (Slk) – Párkány (H)
Subotica (S) – Szabadka (H)
Szeged (H) – Segedin (G)
Székesfehérvár (H) – Stuhlweissenburg (G)
Szombathely (H) – Steinamanger (G)

Tata (H) – Totis (G)
Timişoara (R) – Temesvár (H)
Tirgu Mureş (R) – Marosvásárhely (H)
Transdanubia (E) – Dunántúl (H)
Transylvania (R) – Erdély (H),
   Siebenbürgen (G)
Trnava (Slk) – Nagyszombat (H)

Užgorod (U) – Ungvár (H)

Vác (H) – Wartzen (G)
Vienna (E) – Wien (G), Bécs (H)
Villány (H) – Wieland (G)
Villánykövesd (H) – Growisch (G)

Wiener Neustadt (G) – Bécsújhely (H)

Thanks

Many thanks to the travellers who used the last edition and wrote to us with helpful hints, useful advice and interesting anecdotes:

Ofer Aderet, Nick Adlam, Saara Arvo, Brian & Mary Ashmore, Tim Atchison, Neil Audley, Kyle Austen, J Ayres, Monika Bailey, Steve Barnett, Rita Baskin, Thomas Baumeister, Pierre Bayenet, Szirti Bea, Laurent Bianchi, Brenda Bierman, Gerry Bierman, Esther Blodau-Konick, Chris Bolger, Vincent Borlaug, Bela Borsos, Angela Brady, Frédéric Brahim, Helen Bray, Carol & Gail Brown, Dylan Browne, Rod George Bryant, Guillem Castella, Andrea Cervenka, Anthi Charalambous, Catalin Coroama, Jessika Croizat, Sigal Dabach, Mike Dean, Andy Dennis, Kathleen Diamond, Martin d'Idler, Sarah Dillon, Graham & Paula Doro, David Doughan, Loretta Dupuis, Moray Easdale, Jariko Eastvold, Jill Eskdale, Robert Essenyi, Mario Falzon, Anne Fenerty, Rob Ferrara, Stephen Fiedorczukg, Anita Forster, Karen Forster, Emma French, Nancy Frishberg, Charlotte Froomberg, Ricardo Gama, Agnes Garnai, Cervetti Giancarlo, Janos Ginstler, Sandra Gordon, Tyler Gore, Jerry Gwee, Nagy Atilla Gyorgy, Brian Haigh, David Hart, Vanessa Haye, Catherine Hegyi, Mark Henderson, Kane Hillman, Kevin B Hubbard, David Hunt, Bob & Jo Hunter, Becky Ip, Victor & Agnes Isaacs, Rok Jarc, Oliver Johnston, Thomas Neumark Jones, Helene J Josovitz, Maritta Jumppanen, Sugano Jun, J Kalina, David Katz, Gerald Kellett, Kerry King, Rob Kingston, Warren Knock, Mihaly Kovacs, Maja Krause, Ben Kurrein, Anne-Mari Laiho, San Lauw, Hana Leed, Juliet Lehair, Juha Levo, Ralf Liebau, Nick Lux, Pauline Mahalski, Stephane Makk, William Malone, Daz Marks, Olivier Mauron, Florence & Michael McBride, Matiss Melecis, Robin Meyerhoff, Melissa Michels, Elina Mielityinen, Greg Mills, David Minkin, Lee Gerard Molloy, Thomas Morgan, Tim Morgan, Miranda Morton, Mary Nagy, Susan Nagy, Beryl Nicholson, Marjan Nieuwland, Anna Nordmark, L E Nowosielska, Amy Paden, Eleni Paliouras, Rich Palm, Rolf Palmberg, Robyn Park, Justin Peach, Michael Phillips, Jean Pinto, Kris M Piorowski, Louisa Prest, Rahmin Rabenou, Ron Regan, Werner Reindorf, J Reusch, Diane C Reynolds, Tony Richmond, Nick Robinson, Jay Russian, Andrew Ruttkay, Kym Ryan, Adam Schreck, Michael L Sensor, Paul Shenton, Alex Shore, Nolan Shulak, Eszter Simonfi, Mary Smith, Joanna Stefanska, Julie Stenberg, B Stoney, Samo Stritof, Aldo Strydom, John & Lynn Sullivan, G Swafford, Clare Szilagyi, Bea Szirti, Janice Tausig, Robin & Janice Tausig, Dan Tebbutt, Valer Tosa, Wim Van De Water, Corne van Dyk, Joost van Ebbenhorst-Tengbergen, Marc van Gend, Mathieu Vandermissen, Knut Vold, Alexander Waanders, Karen Walker, Astrid Walstra, Michelle Warburton, Henrik Weston, Luke Wilkinson, David Williams, Ernst Williams, Kormelia Zabo, Z K Zadar, Ivanka Zemanova, Eric Zimmerman, Paul Zoglin, Attila Zsunyi

Index

Text

Bold indicates maps.

Boxed Text

Bold indicates maps.

MAP LEGEND

CITY ROUTES

Freeway .... Freeway	⊐ ⊐ ⊐ ⊐ ...... Unsealed Road
Highway .... Primary Road	⟶ .... One Way Street
Road .... Secondary Road	.... Pedestrian Street
Street .... Street	⊓⊓⊓⊓⊓⊓⊓ .... Stepped Street
Lane .... Lane	⟩= = = ... Tunnel
.... On/Off Ramp	.... Footbridge

HYDROGRAPHY

.... River, Creek	Dry Lake; Salt Lake
.... Canal	Spring; Rapids
Lake	Waterfalls

REGIONAL ROUTES

.... Tollway, Freeway
.... Primary Road
.... Secondary Road
.... Minor Road

TRANSPORT ROUTES & STATIONS

⟶O⟶ .... Train	⊟ .... Ferry
.... Underground Train	.... Walking Trail
⟶M⟶ .... Metro	.... Walking Tour
.... Tramway	.... Path
Cable Car, Chairlift	.... Pier or Jetty

BOUNDARIES

.... International
.... State
— — — .... Disputed
.... Fortified Wall

AREA FEATURES

.... Building	.... Market	Beach	.... Forest
⊛ .... Park, Gardens	...... Sports Ground	+ + + ... Cemetery	.... Plaza

POPULATION SYMBOLS

◎ **CAPITAL** ...... National Capital	● **CITY** .... City	● Village .... Village
◉ **CAPITAL** ...... State Capital	● **Town** .... Town	.... Urban Area

MAP SYMBOLS

■ .... Place to Stay	▼ .... Place to Eat	● .... Point of Interest	
✈ .... Airport	⊞ .... Cinema	⊞ .... Museum	⊠ ..... Swimming Pool
⊖ .... Bank	⊡ .. Embassy, Consulate	⊞ ...... Police Station	⊡ .... Synagogue
⊛ .... Border Crossing	♈ .... Fountain	⊟ ...... Post Office	⊟ .... Theatre
⊟ .... Bus Station	⊕ .... Hospital	⊟ .... Pub or Bar	▣ .... Tomb
⊞ .. Castle, Chateau	⊡ ..... Internet Cafe	⊠ .... Ruins	⊕ . Tourist Information
⊞ .. Cathedral, Church	⚲ .... Monument	⊗ .. Shopping Centre	⊞ .... Winery
⌂ .... Cave	⊙ .... Mosque	⋔ ..... Stately Home	⊡ .... Zoo

Note: not all symbols displayed above appear in this book

LONELY PLANET OFFICES

Australia
Locked Bag 1, Footscray, Victoria 3011
☎ 03 8379 8000 fax 03 8379 8111
email: talk2us@lonelyplanet.com.au

USA
150 Linden St, Oakland, CA 94607
☎ 510 893 8555 TOLL FREE: 800 275 8555
fax 510 893 8572
email: info@lonelyplanet.com

UK
10a Spring Place, London NW5 3BH
☎ 020 7428 4800 fax 020 7428 4828
email: go@lonelyplanet.co.uk

France
1 rue du Dahomey, 75011 Paris
☎ 01 55 25 33 00 fax 01 55 25 33 01
email: bip@lonelyplanet.fr
www.lonelyplanet.fr

**World Wide Web: www.lonelyplanet.com *or* AOL keyword: lp
Lonely Planet Images: www.lonelyplanetimages.com**